Introduction:
How to Use This Book

For decades, Latin American independent/national filmmakers and video makers have been producing historically important works that reflect their communities from their own points of view. Yet, because the established flow of information moves primarily from north to south, there are few opportunities for U.S. audiences to be exposed to these works. To address this imbalance, the International Media Resource Exchange (IMRE) has organized the Latin American Video Archive (LAVA) and Database, a project in which filmmakers and video makers, distributors, educators, media curators, and exhibitors have collaborated to bring many previously inaccessible works to the United States. In this process, IMRE computerized information about more than four thousand Latin American, Caribbean, and Latino film and video titles; created a video archive; and developed a reference and distribution service to assist potential users in locating and obtaining these materials. It is clear from the overwhelming response we received for this project that there is a growing consciousness and enthusiasm on the part of U.S. educators and arts programmers for using indigenously produced materials in their classes and exhibitions. The problem has been the lack of a centralized resource to learn which media materials exist and how to gain access to them. The LAVA project now facilitates this communication.

This book is the result of the collective effort of hundreds of educators, communications professionals, and arts programmers from throughout the United States who volunteered to evaluate materials from IMRE's computerized list. Evaluators chose works that related to their areas of interest and expertise. We aimed to have each title reviewed by at least three academic professionals. Our questionnaire asked evaluators to describe the film or video as they understood it, reflecting a U.S. user's point of view; discuss areas where U.S. audiences might need additional information; share ideas for how to incorporate the works into diverse courses and disciplines; and suggest complementary reading materials. The 445 titles included in this directory represent a subjective selection and evaluation of the Latin American/Caribbean/Latino-produced works that are available for distribution in the United States. The edited entry for each title incorporates many voices, as the evaluators' backgrounds varied considerably (including anthropology, Latin American history, cinema studies,

communications, and Spanish and Portuguese language and literature). In combining their diverse views, we attempted to reflect each of the evaluator's opinions about the works and their usefulness in U.S. education, as well as to include any additional pertinent information about the programs. Clearly, the evaluators' and editors' own cultural perspectives about these works and their use with U.S. audiences are reflected in the descriptions that appear in this book.

Throughout, evaluators identified questions that are raised but left unanswered by the films and tapes. As many of these works were not originally made for U.S. audiences, they often assume a historical and cultural background that U.S. viewers may lack. In cases where the evaluators or editors were unable to provide the background needed to answer these questions, we left them as guidelines for instructors when preparing for screenings and discussions of these materials. In general, U.S. audiences would benefit from background knowledge of the national and international historical context of the productions, as well as specific information regarding the culture, setting, and events of the time period reflected. As basic tenets and modes often found in modern art are reflected in many of the fictional and experimental works, a basic understanding of twentieth-century art and literature would be very helpful. As works of visual art, the films very often employ formal strategies that can also have political motivations. Leaving a work open-ended, ambiguous, or abstract, for example, might be to work against realism and its conventions (and ideology). Unresolved questions demand work from the viewer, requiring an active, rather than passive, relation to the work. It is our hope that the extensive bibliography, based on evaluators' suggested readings, will help media users fill in the gaps and be an inspiration to explore further the diverse issues raised by both the form and content of the programs.

This guide is intended as a directory to help U.S. viewers become familiar with the quality and quantity of work produced in Latin America, the Caribbean, and the Latino diaspora to facilitate learning from and about their diverse cultures and communities. Far from offering final words on each program, these descriptions are meant to open up the dialogue about the multiple interpretations and usefulness of these works across disciplines and settings.

A FINAL NOTE

While this book functions as a reference manual, the LAVA project continues to be a live and interactive project. The database is regularly updated and will soon be available via the Internet, making it possible for individuals to search for materials on line as well as add information about titles. **If you are interested in participating in this project, you can!** Let us know if you have information about materials not listed in this directory. If you travel, bring back examples of work not yet represented here. IMRE can also arrange exchanges in which people who offer their services to translate or subtitle tapes can receive a free copy of the work. Our goal is to facilitate the use of these materials in ways that will be useful for U.S. audiences while assisting the video and filmmakers to disseminate their works abroad. We welcome your participation in making this resource grow.

The LAVA Project
International Media Resource Exchange
124 Washington Place
New York, N.Y. 10014
Telephone: (212) 463-0108
Fax: (212) 243-2007
Email: imre@igc.apc.org
Web: http://www.lavavideo.org

HOW TO USE THIS BOOK

The format for each entry is as follows:

ORIGINAL TITLE (English Title)
Genre.   *Language.   Running time.   Year
(*If available in English or with subtitles at the time of publication [check with IMRE for updates].)
Directed by:
Produced by: (Contact information, when available.)
Distributed by: (If different from director/producer.)
Evaluators: (Names of those who reviewed the tape.)
Description:

Strengths and Weaknesses:
Introducing the Tape: (Areas where questions may be raised or contextual information may be needed for U.S. audiences.)
How to Use: (Suggestions for ways to incorporate programs into particular courses. Classes or subject areas are highlighted in italics.)
Suggested Readings: (See bibliography for full citations and additional readings on the program's country/subject.)
Complementary Films/Videos: (Titles in this directory are found in their country chapters. For titles not in the directory, a distributor is noted when possible.)
Level: (Suggested academic level for audiences.)

The titles are separated into categories by country. Within each country section, they are alphabetized by their original-language title.

The bibliography took the suggested readings section of the evaluations as a starting point, providing reference information for the books, journals, and articles to accompany particular programs. However, it also includes many important additional references on diverse subjects, and many of the readings suggested for a particular program would be useful to accompany other productions. Please browse the country sections as well as the two additional categories, Latin America and Cinema/Media/Cultural Studies, for useful readings. In a few cases, references from the readings section are not fully cited in the bibliography. Rather than eliminate these incomplete references, we have chosen to include whatever information we were able to locate.

Film/video titles are indexed by various subjects, listed alphabetically. The distributor index primarily lists the U.S. source(s) for the videos (or films on videotape). Check with distributors for additional tapes in their collections since the publication of this book. Tapes listed with IMRE Archive as the distribution contact have no official U.S. representative. However, they are available for preview through IMRE's Latin American Video Archive. IMRE can help contact the foreign representative of these films/tapes.

The title index is in two parts. The first part lists the titles as they appear in the book (by original language title in country category). If the original title is Spanish or Portuguese, the English title appears next to it. The second part is alphabetized by English title, with the Spanish or Portuguese equivalent appearing beside it.

Contributing Evaluators

Abelman, Aleta Ulibarri, Richel Middle School
Acevedo, Angelique M., Jefferson Public Schools
Aching, Gerard, Rutgers University
Acosta, María Consuelo, University of Pittsburgh
Adam, Walter R.
Adams, Anna R., Muhlenburg College
Adams, Marilyn & Walter R., Kansas State University
Addelston, Susan, High School of Art & Design
Adelman, Jeremy, Princeton University
Ainsworth, Stephen K., University of Texas/San Antonio
Albro, Ward S., III, Texas A&I University
Alchon, Susan Austin, University of Delaware
Altgelt, Susan, Telecomm. Reg. 20 ESC
Alvarez, Robert, Arizona State University
Andersen, Robin, Fordham University
Anderson, Danny J., University of Kansas
Anderson, Reed, Miami University
Andrews, Reid, University of Pittsburgh
Arreaza-Camero, Emperatriz, University of Iowa
Arrington, Melvin S., Jr., University of Mississippi
Arrom, Silvia, Brandeis University
Auchter, Craig, Butler University
Aufderheide, Patricia, American University
Autry, William O., Goshen College/University of Chicago
Ayala, César, Lehman College
Babb, Florence, University of Iowa
Bakewell, Peter, Emory University
Baumann, Friederike, University of California at Davis
Becker, Carol, Chicago Art Institute
Beelen, George D., Youngstown State University
Beethlen, Francis R., SUNY Plattsburg
Beltrán, Clara López, Smith College
Benjamin, Jules, Ithaca College
Bente, Thomas O., Temple University
Bergeman, Rich, Linn Benton Community College
Bergquist, Charles, University of Washington
Besse, Susan, City College of New York
Bethlen, Francis R., SUNY of Plattsburgh
Birmingham-Pokorny, Elba D., Southern Arkansas University
Blanas, Kate, Horizon High School
Blum, Ann S., University of California at Berkely

Blum, Leonor, College of Notre Dame
Bolános, Alvaro Félix, Tulane University
Boly, Richard C., Inter-American Foundation
Borinsky, Alicia, Boston University
Boschetto-Sandoval, Sandra M., Michigan Tech. University
Boyle, Dierdre, New School for Social Research
Brana-Shute, Rosemary, College of Charleston
Brockett, Charles, University of the South
Brown, Kendall W., Brigham Young University
Browne, George P., Seton Hall University
Brungardt, Maurice P., Loyola University
Burger, Carolyn, Rutgers College
Bushby, Alfredo, University of Texas at Austin
Bushnell, David, University of Florida
Cade, Sandra L., Oregon Episcopal School
Calvo-Roth, Fortuna, ANACITEC
Carlos, Alberto J., SUNY Albany
Carpignano, Paolo, Fordham University
Carreño, Angela, New York University Bobst Library
Castex, Graciela M., Lehman College
Castillo-Crimm, Ana Caroline, Sam Houston State University
Castro, Donald S., California State Polytechnic University
Castro-Mitchell, Amanda, Westminster College
Chambers, Sarah, University of North Carolina
Chapa-Guzmán, Hugo, University of Texas
Chasteen, John, University of North Carolina
Chávez, Carmen, Wofford College
Chernick, Marc, Columbia University
Chinchón, Osvaldo, SUNY College at Fredonia
Church, Nancy J., SUNY Plattsburgh
Claxton, Robert, West Georgia College
Collins, Judith M., P.S. 217
Conde, Susana, Boise State University
Cooney, Jerry W., University of Louisville
Cooper, James W., Parkway South High School
Cordero, Wilma, IS 70 - Manhattan
Cotto, Marguerite, Northwestern Michigan College
Coughlin, Ann K., Hoover High School
Cournia, Audrey, Reed High School
Craver, Mary Jane, Adult Education Center
Cronshaw, Francine, University of New Mexico

Culver, Carmen Madariaga, Plattsburgh University
Davey, Donald W., Ohio Northern University
Davis, Darién J., Middlebury College
Davis, Roger P., University of Nebraska at Kearney
de la Vega Hurtado, Margarita, University of Michigan
Dean, Marcia, Lowville Academy
Dean, Warren J., New York University
Deeds, Susan M., Northern Arizona University
Delgado, Carlos R., University of California at Berkeley
Desmangles, Leslie, Trinty College
DiAntonio, Robert, Kirkwood High School
D'Lugo, Marvin, Clark University
Doll, Kristine, SUNY College at Old Westbury
Douglass, Susan, Tottenville High School
Dudley, Mary Jo, Cornell University
Eakin, Marshall, Vanderbilt University
Edelstein, Joel C.
Egan, Catherine, New York University
Elbow, Gary S., Texas Tech.
Elkin, Judith, University of Michigan
Engstrand, Iris, University Of San Diego
Espadas, Juan, Ursinus College
Espinal, Rosario, Temple University
Espinosa, Francia, Broome Community College
Fejes, Fred, Florida Atlantic University
Ferguson, Linda W.
Férnandez, Lourdes, University of Chicago
Fernández, María Elisa, Carnegie Mellon University
Fett, John, University of Wisconsin
Flores, Oscar
Flowers, Nancy, Hunter College
Fogarty, Mary Margaret, Dunkirk High School
Fontez, Carlos, University of Massachusetts
Foster, David William, Arizona State University
Franco, Jean, Columbia University
Frechione, John, University of Pittsburgh
Fried, Mark, NACLA
Funez, Henry, Phillip Randolph High School
Gagliano, Joseph A., Loyola University Chicago
Garatea, Victor, East High School
Garner, Lydia M., S.W. Texas University
Gass, Lavina Tilson, Yonkers Public Schools
Glover, William
Goldfarb, Brian, University of Rochester
Gonzáles, René Abelardo, University of Pennsylvania
Gottlieb, Marlene, Lehman College
Greenfield, Sidney M., University of Wisconsin
Griswold, Susan, Wofford College
Guardado, Sandra J., University of Texas at Austin
Halleck, Dee Dee, San Diego State University
Harclerode, Rebeca, Julia Richman High School
Haskett, Robert, University of Oregon
Hays, John, Tyler Junior College
Helg, Aline, University of Texas at Austin
Helguera, J. Leon, Vanderbuilt University

Hering, Tânia M., University of Georgia
Herzog, William, Northwestern College
Hess, John, Ithaca College
Higgens, John, Ohio State University
Holmlund, Christine, University of Tennessee
Huarcaya, Miguel, TVCA Cable Access
Huesca, Rob, Ohio State University
Hunt, Daniel P., Idaho State University
Huarcaya, Miguel, TVCA Cable Access
Hyre, Silvia, Youngstown State University
Iacovelli, Vincent D., Isaac E. Young Junior High School
Jeffrey, Liss, Trent University
Jímenez, Marilyn, Holbart & William Smith College
Jonakin, Jon, University of Tennessee, Knoxville
Karl, Terry, Stanford University
Kist, Glenn J., Rochester Institute of Technology
Knight, Franklin W., Johns Hopkins University
Kowalczyk, Kim, University of San Diego
Kregar, Shirley A., Universityof Pittsburgh
Landau, Saul, Institute for Policy Studies
Langhorst, Rick, Spelman College, Spanish Dept.
Langley, Lester D., University of Georgia
Laraque, Frank, City University of New York
LaReau, Paul J., Munster High School
Lazarini, María A., Brooklyn New School at P.S. 146
Leavitt, Grace, Greely High School
Lesage, Julia, University of Oregon at Eugene
Lesser, Jeff, Connecticut College
Levine, Robert, University of Miami
Levy-Konesky, Nancy, Brandeis University
Lewis, James A., Western Carolina University
Leyba, Raúl, Arizona State University
List, Christine, Chicago State University
Littmann, Mark, University of Tennessee
López, Hilda Mundo, Hostos Community College
Lozada, Susan, P.S. 145
Mabry, Donald J., Mississippi State University
Maciel, David, University of New Mexico, History
Madariaga-Culver, Carmen, SUNY Plattsburg
Madden, Lori, Shippensburg University
Mahan, Elizabeth, University of Conneticuit at Storrs
Maram, Sheldon, California State University
March, Kathleen, University of Maine
Marchant, Elizabeth, Brandeis University
Marcone, Jorge, Rutgers University
Martínez-Fernández, Luis, Colgate University
Martínez-Vergne, Teresita, Macalester College
Marting, Diane, Columbia University
Matthews, Irene, Northern Arizona University
Mazzoli, Estela Moreno, Oakland University
McCreery, David, Georgia State University
McGinnis, Joan A., Sunny Hills High School
Mejias, Ulises, Ithaca University
Melville, Elinor G. K., York University
Mendelson-Forman, Johanna, American University

Merena, Elizabeth, New York State Council on the Arts
Meskill, Carla, SUNY at Albany
Meson, Danusia L., American University
Metcalf, Alida, Trinity University
Michelotti-Cristóbal, Graciela, Haverford College
Monteón, Michael, University of California
Morris, Barbara, Fordham University
Morris, Robert J., Lander College
Mueller, Claus, Hunter College
Navarro, José-Manuel, Seton Hall University
Nesman, Edgar G., University of South Florida
Norden, Janet B., Baylor University
Noriega, Chon, University of New Mexico
Nunn, Frederick M., Portland State University
Oboler, Suzanne, Brown University
Ocasio, Rafael, Agnes Scott College
O'Neill, Stephen P., Bronx Community College
Ortiz, Christopher, University of New Mexico
Osborn, Wayne S., Iowa State University
Pacini-Hernandez, Deborah, University of Florida
Page-Reeves, Janet, School of Visual Arts
Parker, Nichole, University of Pittsburgh
Pato, Hilda, Ph.D., SUNY Geneseo
Paz, Gustavo L., Emory University
Pérez, Carlos, Wayne State
Pérez, Carlos A., Clark University
Pérez, Laura Elisa, California State University, Long Beach
Picó, Eliseo, Embassy of Spain
Piña, Gerardo, Lehman College, CUNY
Pont, Margarita, Churchill School
Poor, Allen, University of Chicago
Porras, Jorge, Sonoma State University
Price, Marie, George Washington University
Prieto, Yolanda, Ramapo College
Radding, Cynthia, University of Missouri
Raggio, Eliana Moya, University of Michigan
Ramírez, María, P.S. 151
Ramírez, Susan, De Paul University
Ramos, Alicia, Barnard College
Reber, Vera Blinn, Shippensburg University
Rees, Martha, Anges Scott College
Renique, José Luis, Lehman College
Reyes, Debbie, Bilingual/Bicultural Mini-School
Rívera, J. Julian, Adelphi University
Robinson, David J., Syracuse University
Rodríguez, Enríque R., Teen-Aid High School
Rodríguez-Florido, Jorge J., Chicago State University
Romero-Downing, Gloria, Creighton University
Roos, Barbara, Grand Valley State University
Ross, Jesikah María, Davis Community TV
Ross, Kathleen, Fairport Central Schools

Roth, Marc S., Curtis High School
Russo, Catherine, Independent Producer
Ryan, Susan, Ryan/Stone Productions
Sánchez-Berroa, Roger A., Wesleyan University
Schuster, Engracia A., Syracuse University
Scroggins, Daniel C., University of Missouri/Columbia
Segura, Margot M.
Shane, Michael, Colombia Presbyterian Medical Center
Shapiro, Carolyn, U 32 High School
Shen, Virginia, Chicago State University
Shirey, Lynn M., Harvard Law School Library
Sieber, Sharon, Idaho State University
Silcox, S. Travis, University of California
Simões, Antônio R. M., University of Kansas
Small, Michele Geslin, Northland College
Smith, Naomi, Latin American Studies for Teachers
Smith, Patricia Thomas, Braintree High School
Smorkaloff, Pamela M., New York University
Stahler-Sholk, Richard, Pitzer College
Stern, Irwin, Columbia University
Sternbach, Nancy Saporta, Smith College
Stock, Ann Marie, College of William & Mary
Stone, Cynthia L., Holy Cross College
Stoney, George, New York University
Suárez, Susy, Ramapo College
Tambs, Lewis A., Arizona State University
Taylor, Jennifer M., Cine Acción
Thompson, Currie Kerr, Gettysburg College
Torres, Elaine, East Village Exchange
Torres-Rivera, Rebecca, Central Michigan University
Valdivia, Angharad N., Penn State University
Vieira King, Rosangela, Howard University
Vinck, Aaron, Davis Community TV
Voekel, Pamela, University of Texas
Weatherford, Elizabeth, Museum of the American Indian
Webre, Stephen, Louisiana Tech University
Welch, Cliff, Grand Valley State University
Wells, Allen, Bowdoin College
Werlich, David P., Southern Illinois University
West, Dennis, University of Idaho
Whichard, Mitchell L., University of North Carolina
Whigham, Thomas, University of Georgia
Whiteford, Linda, University of South Florida
Williams, Dessima, Brandeis University
Williams, Gayle, University of Georgia Library
Williamson, Robert C., Lehigh University
Wood, Susan
Woods, Richard D., Trinity University
Young, Lynn, University of Pittsburgh
Zevallos, José, University of Pittsburgh

Acknowledgments

I would like to thank my husband and friend, **Michael Ratner,** for his unyielding support, guidance, and encouragement.   (Karen Ranucci)

We would particularly like to thank **the 356 evaluators (see list)** — the writers of this guide — whose commitment to making these works accessible in the United States meant hours of screening and writing reviews, and whose continued enthusiasm for these materials brings them to greater and greater numbers of U.S. viewers. Very special thanks to:

Catherine Benamou (City University of New York — College of Staten Island, Museum of the American Indian), for always keeping us in mind and being our bridge to Brazil.

Angela Carreño (New York University/Bobst Library), for sharing her expertise, lending her time, and putting up with our "daily punctuation" calls.

Anne Checler, for her research and contributions to the bibliography and subject index and patient attention to the numerous details of the Latin American Video Archive project.

Ellen Davidson, for sharing her computer, proofreading, and bibliography expertise and spending many sleepless nights working on this book.

Robin Ginsburg, for her artistic contributions to the cover design.

Karen Schwartzman (New York University/Cinema Studies Ph.D. Program, Independent Feature Project), without whose invaluable editing skills, wealth of knowledge, dedication, and willingness to share this book would not have a Venezuela chapter.

and to all our funders: **The John D. and Catherine T. MacArthur Foundation, National Video Resources, the National Endowment for the Arts, the New York State Council for the Arts,** and **the National Alliance for Media Arts Centers,** whose generous support enabled the research and publication of this directory.

Special thanks to:
Rafael Andreu, Ramm Productions
Patricia Aufderheide, American University
Paul Bardwell, Centro Colombo Americano

Bob Beck, Electronic Arts Intermix
Tania Blanich, National Video Resources
Patricia Boero, MacArthur Foundation
Conchita Bolenange, Forest City Ratner Cos.
Richard C. Boly, Inter-American Foundation
Julianne Burton, Merril College
Jonathan Buxbaum, Rutgers University
Jerry Carlson, City University of New York
Eline Charnov, Margaret Mead Film Festival
Margaret Cooper, Independent Consultant
Gary Crowdus, The Cinema Guild
John DiGiacomo, Direct Marketing Consultant for NVR
Michael Donnally, University of California at Los Angeles
Esther Duran, Macario Films
Debra Evanson, Rabinowitz, Boudin, Standard, Krinsky, Lieberman
Peggy Gilpen, independent producer
Joan Giummo, NYC Office of Adult and Continuing Education
Tim Gunn, NVR
Dee Dee Halleck, University of California at San Diego
Lillian Haugen, Tiempo y Tono/Mexican Biennial
Leonard Henny, Center for International Media Research
Linnet Henry, Forest City Ratner Company
Kate Horsfeld, Video Data Bank
Diana Jaramillo, Centro Colombo Americano
Pat Keeton, Ramapo College
Michael Krinsky, Rabinowitz, Boudin, Standard, Krinsky, Lieberman
Marisa Leal, National Latino Communications Center
James Lee, Icarus Films
Francisco Leon, ICAIC
Ruby Lerner, Foundation of Independent Video and Filmmakers
Sandra Levinson, Center for Cuban Studies
Lillian Liberman, independent producer
Ana Lopez, Tulane University
Cynthia Lopez, Deep Dish TV
Juliet Lowe, New York University
Sam McElfresh, Museo del Barrio
Monica Melamid, Ramm Productions

Ileana Montalvo, Latino Collaborative
Margarite Montez
Coaracy Nuñez, Media Flux
Diana Papademas, SUNY at Old Westbury
Margaret Ratner, Center for Constitutional Rights
B. Ruby Rich, film critic
Peter Rist, Concordia University
Jorge Ruffinelli, Stanford University
Lawrence Sapadin, independent consultant
Bill Schaap, Van Leirop, Burns, Schaap
Franklin Seigel, Center for Constitutional Rights
Margarita Sierra, University of Guadalajara
Debra Silverfine, New York State Council for the Arts
Ana Sokoloff, The Permanent Mission of Colombia

Robert Stam, New York University
Marina Stavenhagen, Centro de Capaticiómatografico
Milos Stehlik, Facets Multimedia
George Stoney, New York University
Jennifer Taylor, Cine Acción
Teresa Toledo, Cuban Cinemateca
Patricia Torres, University of Guadalajara
Pepe Vargas, Chicago Latino Film Festival
Daniel Varela, University of Guadalajara
Beatriz Vieira, video/film programmer
Elizabeth Weatherford, Museum of the American Indian
Woodward Wicham, MacArthur Foundation
Debra Zimmerman, Women Make Movies

Titles

ARGENTINA

ALGUNAS MUJERES (Some Women)
Documentary. In English. 13 min. 1992
Directed by: Sabrina Farji
Produced by: El Ojo Avisor (Gelly Oboes 2207 2B, Buenos Aires; tel: [541] 803-5320)
Distributed by: IMRE
Evaluators: Jeremy Adelman, Lori Madden
Description: This short film is a dramatic reading of the testimony of a daughter whose mother "disappeared" during the dictatorship in Argentina. The focus is on the experience of restitution (return to the "natural" family) and the recovery of identity.
Strengths and Weaknesses: The taped testimony presents a powerful message about a pressing human rights violation. One evaluator felt that the superimposition of consecutive images of women dressed alike drove home the universal element of the dramatic reading. Others felt that this device was visually repetitive. Without an introduction, a U.S. audience might find the tape vague.
Introducing the Tape: Viewers should be aware of the histories of the "disappeared" in various Latin American countries and the illegal practice of adopting the children of disappeared women.
How to Use: I would use the video to convey the idea that despite the fall of military governments, human rights violations continue. (Adelman)

In a *Latin American Culture* (*Politics*/*Feminism*) class the video could be used to discuss issues surrounding the disappeared. (Madden)

In an *English Composition* or *Creative Writing* class the students could write essays from each perspective: the point of view of the child, the estranged family, the members of the military who adopted the children, etc.
Suggested Readings: Comisión Nacional sobre la Desaparición de Personas. *Nunca Más: The Report of the Argentina National Commission on the Disappeared.*

Simpson, John, and Jana Bennett. *The Disappeared and the Mothers of the Plaza: The Story of the 11,000 Argentinians Who Vanished.*
Complementary Films/Videos: *La historia oficial (The Official Story)* (Argentina); *Las Madres de la Plaza de Mayo (The Mothers of the Plaza de Mayo)* (Argentina); *Niños desaparecidos (Disappeared Children)* (Argentina); *La voz de los pañuelos (The Voice of the Shawls)* (Argentina)
Level: University

ALLA LEJOS Y HACE TIEMPO (Far Away and Long Ago)
Feature. With Subtitles. 91 min. 1974
Directed by: Manuel Antín
Produced by: Profilme SRL
Distributed by: IMRE
Evaluators: Jeremy Adelman, Melvin S. Arrington Jr., Warren J. Dean, María Fernández
Description: In this film, Anglo-Argentine novelist and naturalist William Henry Hudson (born Argentina 1841, died England 1922) reflects on his childhood in rural Argentina. The film offers a poetic evocation of lost youth, as the elderly Hudson revisits key moments in his early life. Hudson's melancholic demeanor as he observes and comments on the various scenes contrasts markedly with the magical view of life seen through the eyes of the young Hudson. A central issue throughout the film is how Hudson came to love nature. The story is enriched by depictions of the pampas, gaucho culture, folklore, and witchcraft.
Strengths and Weaknesses: Evaluators' reactions to this film varied. A few appreciated the cinematography of the pampas, the beautiful nature scenes, and numerous folkloric elements, calling the tape a wonderful portrait of mid-nineteenth-century rural Argentina. Others, however, found the tape too sentimental, slow moving, and primitive in technique, distancing the viewer from the pampas and Argentine nature. The film has good sound quality and large, easy-to-read subtitles.
Introducing the Tape: Viewers need some background on Hudson and nineteenth-century Argentina.
How to Use: The tape would work well in a *Culture* unit on the pampas and the figure of the gaucho. Students can see reconstructed scenes that have been immortalized in gaucho literature (taming wild horses, a knife fight, etc.). The video can also be used to illustrate the distinctive characteristics of Argentine Spanish. (Arrington)

Suggested Readings: Guiraldes, Ricardo. *Don Segundo Sombra.*

Hudson, William Henry. *Far Away and Long Ago: A History of My Early Life.*

Lynch, John. *Argentine Dictator: Juan Manuel de Rosas, 1829–1852.*

Rock, David. *Argentina 1516–1982: From Spanish Colonization to the Falklands War.*

Scobie, James R. *Argentina: A City and a Nation.*

Slatta, Richard W. *Gauchos and the Vanishing Frontier.*

Level: University

CAMILA (Camila)

Feature.   With Subtitles.   102 min.   1984
Directed by: María Luisa Bemberg
Produced by: GEA Cinematográfica (Ricardo Levene 980, Buenos Aires, 1425; tel: [541] 803-5185; fax: [541] 805-5894)
Distributed by: IMRE, Meridien
Evaluators: Joan A. McGinnis, Gustavo L. Paz, Susan Ramírez
Description: Set in the nineteenth century, this is a hauntingly beautiful story of forbidden love between a young upper-class woman and her parish priest. Camila rebels against her family's authority, and the two elope. The lovers are eventually caught and executed. The film also explores themes of the church and state and the role of Jesuit women.
Strengths and Weaknesses: This is a good reconstruction of nineteenth-century society and daily life in Argentina. While portraying a sensitive love story, the film shows family life, rural customs, the role of women, and the importance and strength of religious values in society. The subtitles are excellent.
Introducing the Tape: Viewers could use some historical context for the film, particularly in reference to Juan Manuel de Rosas, the dictator from 1829 to 1852.
How to Use: I would give a background of the epoch, with a question guide and vocabulary, and break the film into thirds with a pre-discussion as well as post-discussion. A composition after the film and discussion could include suppositions as to what might happen today. (McGinnis) The tape would be useful as an introduction to a lecture on Latin American women, family, and patriarchal society in the nineteenth century. (Paz)

I would use the tape to illustrate life in mid-nineteenth-century Latin America and life under the dictatorship of Juan Manuel de Rosas. (Ramírez)
Suggested Readings: Mármol, José. *Amalia; Novela historica americana.*

Lavrín, Asunción. *Latin American Women.*

Lynch, John. *Argentine Dictator: Juan Manuel de Rosas 1829–1852.*
Level: University

LA CRUZ INVERTIDA (Shattered Cross)

Feature.   With Subtitles.   103 min.   1985
Directed by: Mario David
Produced by: NAMA Producciones
Distributed by: IMRE
Evaluators: Osvaldo Chinchón, David William Foster, Diane Marting, José Luis Rénique, Patricia Thomas Smith
Description: This film is based on the award-winning fictionalized biography *La cruz invertida,* by Argentine writer Marcos Aguinis. It is the story of a young priest, Father Carlos Samuel (Camilo) Torres, whose parishioners are impoverished people living in one of the *villa miserias* (slums) of Buenos Aires. Father Torres finds himself caught between the traditional conservative role of the church and his moral responsibility as a community leader to aid the victims of military oppression. The story focuses on Torres's progressive radicalization during the rise of his nemesis, a violent police commissioner who had been a childhood schoolmate. Father Torres sides with the oppressed, supports the workers on strike against abusive managers, and gives aid and comfort to Magdalena, a young prostitute who lost both her parents and cares for her retarded brother. Father Torres is accused of being a communist and is eventually excommunicated. His sworn enemy, the police chief, is now in charge of a military junta that tries to purify society by eliminating "subversive" elements. Father Torres is his favorite target.
Strengths and Weaknesses: The film is valuable for its portrayal of the conflict in many Latin American countries between the traditionally well-to-do Right and the underprivileged Left and clearly presents the psychological, political, and physical elements of such a conflict. It illustrates the role of the army, the police, and the church in political life and shows how the forces of law and order classify as subversives those who protest the repression and persecute them. The film also powerfully portrays the dilemma of socially active Catholic priests in many Latin American countries. It is rich in symbolism and makes human the "mythical" figure of Camilo Torres. There are excellent dialogues for advanced language practice.

Some reviewers felt that the film had a rather simplistic good-versus-evil story line based on stereotypes. A few characters are not developed enough, and the film can seem slow paced.
Introducing the Tape: If the audience is not aware of the nature of Latin American military dictatorships, the film might reinforce the stereotype that Latin American culture is inherently inclined to violence. Some background on class struggle in Latin America may be necessary, as well as information about the role of the Catholic Church and liberation theology in the area. It should be pointed out that although the film was made in 1985 about a specific priest, there are many other instances of clergy members being killed for helping the poor, such as the 1989 murders of six Jesuit priests in El Salvador.

How to Use: I would use this film in a *Spanish Conversation* class to promote discussion of different points presented through the interaction of the various characters. It could also be used to promote discussion of human rights violations. (Chinchón)

This film seems to complement the situations presented in the film *The Official Story*. While *La cruz invertida* may provide a view of the scenario and the main protagonists, *The Official Story* could give a sense of how complex human situations could be created in this environment of terror and "dirty war." (Renique)

I would use this in an advanced *Spanish Language* class to give students practice in listening comprehension. (Smith)

Suggested Readings: Aguinis, Marcos. *La cruz invertida.*

Readings on liberation theology.

Level: University

CUARTELES DE INVIERNO (Winter Barracks)

Feature.   With Subtitles.   116 min.   1984
Directed by: Lautaro Murua
Produced by: Guillermo Smith Producciones
Distributed by: IMRE
Evaluators: Alicia Borinsky, Robert DiAntonio, Allen Wells
Description: Based on a story by Osvaldo Soriano, this film chronicles the growing friendship between a crude yet lovable over-the-hill boxer and an elderly, refined tango singer. This odd couple teams up to oppose the local authorities in a provincial port town in Argentina at the height of that country's political repression. The film shows how the ultrafascist ideas of the dictatorship have an impact on even the simplest of lives.
Strengths and Weaknesses: This is a wonderful adaptation of Osvaldo Soriano's novel, well shot and acted, with excellent music. It captures the spirit of the Argentine culture and vividly captures the workings of the military dictatorship. The film portrays people from diverse social classes and effectively shows how political repression reached small towns far beyond Buenos Aires. Viewers can sense the people's fear from the first scene, when the main characters are detained by the military at a train station. By the end of the film, we really care about the two protagonists.

One reviewer felt that the presentations of the military and the local authorities were one-dimensional. Some of the characters' speech in Argentine Spanish is too fast for use in Spanish language instruction.
Introducing the Tape: An introduction should include background on Argentina since Perón, with special attention to the "dirty war." Students should be told that the Ford Falcon is notorious for being the model used by the secret police. They should also be introduced to the role of, and reverence for, the tango in Argentine culture.
How to Use: The film effectively portrays Argentine life, history, language, and culture and can be applied toward teaching *History* and *Language*. (DiAntonio)

I would use this in my *Modern Latin American History* survey. Because of the film's length, I would have to assign it out of class or at a special evening showing, but it would be worth it. I would use it in conjunction with some short stories by Luisa Valenzuela and a showing of the film *The Official Story*. (Wells)
Suggested Readings: Valenzuela, Luisa. *Other Weapons.*
Complementary Films/Videos: *La historia oficial (The Official Story)* (Argentina)
Level: University

LA DEUDA INTERNA (Verónico Cruz)

Feature.   With Subtitles.   80 min.   1989
Directed by: Miguel Pereira
Produced by: Acoraite Film LTDA & Mainframe Films
Distributed by: IMRE
Evaluators: Carmen Chávez, Robert DiAntonio, Susan Griswold, Vincent D. Iacovelli, Joan A. McGinnis, José Luis Renique, Susy Suárez
Description: This beautiful film is based on the short story "Verónico Cruz" by Fortunato Ramos. It is a portrait of Verónico, an orphaned indigenous boy whose life as a solitary and impoverished shepherd is enriched by a schoolteacher who comes to work in his remote village in Jujuy in northwest Argentina. The touching relationship grows as the teacher brings the boy out of his shell. Excellent cinematography depicts the tranquility of Jujuy and illustrates the consequences of the Malvinas (Falklands) War for Verónico's village. The boy, who has always wanted to see the ocean, is finally killed on board a ship in the war.
Strengths and Weaknesses: This is a moving film with fine acting, an absorbing story, and magnificent visual scenery of the stark Jujuy landscape. The characters are very appealing and the film is filled with the joy of seeing relationships develop. It provides an excellent depiction of the northwest region of Argentina and a sensitive view of the life and traditions in an isolated village. It was awarded four Silver Condors by the Argentine Society of Film Critics.

One reviewer felt that the film would have been stronger if more Indian culture were presented, including religion and traditional costumes. There is little dialogue, especially in the first part of the film. The pace is slow by Hollywood standards, and in some places the subtitles are unclear.
Introducing the Tape: The film illustrates the *dictadura* in simple and personal terms. Its references to the military dictatorship and the war, while central to the meaning of the film, are quite subtle. An introduction to recent Argentine history would be essential, including a brief description of the Malvinas War, the Monroe Doctrine, and the immigrant population in Argentina. Students need to be told that Jujuy is an Andean region in the north of Argentina. It would be useful to describe the isolation of indigenous cultures in Latin America and the particular situation of indigenous

peoples in Argentina. An understanding of Indian culture would enhance the appreciation of the film.

How to Use: This tape could be used by historians to show another point of view on the Malvinas War.

I used this video in my *Latin American Culture* course to show the theme of Sarmiento's *Facundo: Civilización y barbarie* (1845). I have also used this tape after having the students read the short story "Verónico Cruz." (Chávez)

I would use the film in *Spanish 5* to show that there are indigenous people in Argentina living as they have for centuries. It is a moving story that would interest students. (DiAntonio)

In *Education* classes the film could also be used to illustrate the need for an educational system in a small town and how a new teacher must cope with the mistrust of the villagers. (Iacovelli)

For *High School Spanish* I would give a historical sketch of the Falklands and Argentina and develop a vocabulary list, study guide, and discussion questions. For homework, I would ask students to write an essay from various points of view: (1) the boy, (2) the teacher,(3) Juanita (the girlfriend), and (4) the commissioner of Don Domingo. (McGinnis)

I would use this film to complement artwork that was created during and after the "dirty war," including protest music and poetry. It could also be used as part of a film festival for Latino heritage month. (Suárez)

Suggested Readings: Comisión Nacional sobre la Desaparición de Personas, *Nunca Más: The Report of the Argentine National Commission on the Disappeared.*

Hodges, Donald. *Argentina's "Dirty War," an Intellectual Biography.*

Ramos, Fortunato. "Verónico Cruz."

Sarmiento, Domingo Faustino. *Facundo: Civilización y barbarie,* originally published in 1845.

Level: University

FATAL, FATAL MIRADA (Fatal, Fatal Look)
Documentary.   With Subtitles.   18 min.   1990
Directed by: Sara Fried
Produced by: Del Bronx Producciones (Coronel Díaz 1714 9 piso, (1425) Buenos Aires; tel: [541] 822-2644; fax: [541] 826-3896)
Distributed by: IMRE
Evaluators: Jeremy Adelman, Susana Conde, Catherine Russo
Description: This documentary was shot at the "Woman and the Movies" festival that took place in Mar del Plata, Argentina, in the summer of 1990. Its theme was developed around the question of the woman's view in films. Is it different from the man's? How does the feminine view and the feminist view differ? Is there such a thing as a woman's cinema? The video opens with scenes of women being shaken, slapped, kicked, and thrown down stairs. The two main pieces of background music are "My Baby Don't Care" and "Mira, que eres linda," which promote the stereotype of the

female as an adoring companion or ornament. To answer its questions, the documentary then presents interviews with women cinematographers, poets, artists, and others. There is no consensus: Some say that the woman's perspective is different from the man's and ought to be taken into account in making films, and others feel that the creative work is what matters, not the gender of the artist. A few believe that men do everything better than women and that females are insignificant. The tape is somewhat tongue-in-cheek, but it presents a picture of some of the discussion within the Argentine feminist movement.

Strengths and Weaknesses: The tape provides a good sense of the problems facing Argentine feminists and is also humorous. The content, shooting, and editing are strong. It has plenty of action, and there are good images.

Although the debate about the woman's view is acknowledged, the inconclusiveness of the collective answers can leave the spectator confused about the point of the project. There is no sense of what kind of films are being produced by women in Argentina or of the general difficulties confronting independent filmmakers. One reviewer pointed out that all of the crew was male, except for the director, and saw this as a weakness that could be sensed throughout the film.

Introducing the Tape: An introduction about the work of women filmmakers in Latin America, and in Argentina in particular, would be helpful, as would some background on current film theory and contemporary feminist film theory.

How to Use: I would use this tape in a section of a course on *Women and Representation in Contemporary Argentina or Latin America*. (Adelman)

This short videotape could be used effectively by students of film theory and the representation of women in film. (Conde)

Instructors could show clips of the depiction of women in U.S. films and have students discuss the issues covered in the tape, relating them to Hollywood films.

Suggested Readings: Bergmann, Emilie, et al. *Women, Culture, and Politics in Latin America.* Seminar on Feminism and Culture in Latin America.

Burgin, Victor, James Donald, and Cora Kaplan, eds. *Formations of Fantasy.*

Carlson, Marifran. *Feminismo: The Women's Movement in Argentina from Its Beginnings to Eva Perón.*

Castro-Klaren, Sara, Sylvia Molloy, and Beatriz Sarlo, eds. *Women's Writing in Latin America: An Anthology,* particularly part 3, "Women, History, and Ideology."

Erens, Patricia, ed. *Issues in Feminist Film Criticism.*

Flitterman-Lewis, Sandy. *To Desire Differently: Feminism and the French Cinema.*

Guy, Donna. *Sex and Danger in Buenos Aires.*

Heath, Stephen. *Questions of Cinema.*

Kuhn, Annette, with Susannah Radstone. *Women in Film: An International Guide.*

Level: University

GERÓNIMA (Gerónima)

Feature.   With Subtitles.   93 min.   1985

Directed by: Raul A. Tosso

Produced by: Inst. Arte Cine de Avellaneda (Avenida Mitre 1512 primero C, Avellaneda 1870, Buenos Aires; tel: [541] 203-0264)

Distributed by: CIMR, IMRE Archive (available for viewing only)

Evaluators: David William Foster, Julia Lesage

Description: Based on a historical figure, this is a neorealist depiction of a Patagonian indigenous woman (Gerónima) who lives in extreme poverty in the pampas. She is taken to a hospital by local authorities for a psychiatric evaluation and separated from her children. The film powerfully portrays the animal-like treatment and prodding to which Gerónima is subjected to by well-meaning social workers. Because of her cultural differences, Gerónima is viewed as a misfit and an outcast and is slowly driven mad by her captivity in the hospital. Feeling that her children have been taken from her forever, Gerónima breaks into the ward where they are being kept and tries to kill her baby. Bit by bit, her spirit is worn away, and finally, when she is near death, an ambulance deposits her back in her shack. The film combines dramatic portrayals by a professional actress who is an indigenous Patagonian with documentary footage and audiotapes of the woman who was actually in hospital custody.

Strengths and Weaknesses: The real-life setting and cinema vérité style create a powerful and sensitive image of the alienation of Argentina's Patagonian indigenous population.

While the film may be slow paced for general U.S. audiences, its timing authentically reflects the rhythm of the culture.

Introducing the Tape: A lead-in discussion of the origins of the film would be useful, explaining that the lead actress comes from the same culture as the historical protagonist and discussing what this means in terms of cultural authentification.

How to Use: I have used this film in a course on ideological conflict to discuss the problematics of its view of indigenous women, both its accurate image of the destructiveness of cultural/social/medical interventionism and the difficulties of maintaining the documentary register. (Foster)

Suggested Readings: Foster, David William. *Contemporary Argentine Cinema.*

Level: University

LA HISTORIA OFICIAL (The Official Story)

Feature.   With Subtitles.   112 min.   1985

Directed by: Luis Penzo

Distributed by: IMRE

Evaluators: Patricia Aufderheide (excerpted from *Cross Cultural Film Guide*), Carmen Chávez, Donald W. Davey, Susan Griswold, Daniel P. Hunt, Joan A. McGinnis, Enríque R. Rodríguez

Description: Famed Argentine actress Norma Alejandro plays Alicia, a bourgeois history teacher married to a military man, who suspects that her adopted daughter is a child of a *desaparecida* (a disappeared person). A victim of her country's past injustices, Alicia at first refuses to think that she is part of the problem, then gradually she comes to grips with her complicity. Upon learning that her husband was instrumental in kidnapping the baby from victims of the genocide following the 1976 Videla coup, Alicia tries to find the baby's real family. She seeks out a group formed by mothers of the "disappeared." In searching for the truth, Alicia risks tearing her family apart. The film's tension lies between her need to know and her desire not to know. When Alicia finally meets the child's grandmother, her eyes are opened to the realities of the military dictatorship. She learns that the child's mother had been arrested and raped while in custody. After giving birth, she was killed and buried in a mass grave. Alicia's husband, whose power clique is beginning to crumble, attempts to beat her into submission when she questions him. Through her character, viewers learn about the subtle villainy of those who avoid asking disturbing questions.

Strengths and Weaknesses: The film was a blockbuster in Argentina. It won an Academy Award in 1986 for Best Foreign Film, and Norma Alejandro was chosen as best actress in the 1985 Cannes Film Festival. It has also had a successful commercial release in the United States. The film is artfully structured, with strong characterization, story development, and cinematic production, and mesmerizing acting. The focus on a middle-class couple makes it accessible for general U.S. audiences.

Introducing the Tape: A screening could be preceded by a brief introduction to Argentina's history, particularly the events leading to the coup that ousted Isabel Perón in 1976. Some background on life under the military dictatorship and the *desaparecidos* in Argentina (and in Chile) would help viewers understand the central theme of complicity by default. The film makes references to the "dirty war" waged against the population by the new government and the failed war in the Falklands. Even for those with no prior study, however, the film explains itself quite nicely.

How to Use: The film works well in *Latin American Culture* courses because it shows the effects of the "dirty war" under the military dictatorship. Discussion could focus on how Alicia is a victim of the atrocities committed by her government and whether her silence at the adoption makes her an accomplice. (Chávez)

When we study the "missing" in Argentina and Chile, I present three segments of the film on three separate days: (1) when Ana, the middle-class woman who chose to denounce the violence, appears at a luncheon with her former "girlfriends," followed by her narration of what happened to her when she was captured; (2) the family dinner when the son who has taken advantage of the military regime to enrich himself is confronted by his family; and (3) the scene when the child's real grandmother is introduced to Alicia's husband. (Davey)

I have used it in intermediate *Spanish* classes, providing a script to facilitate aural comprehension and concentrating on the linguistic and cultural content. Students watched the film repeatedly, and it inspired much debate. (Griswold)

In *Language* courses I simply have the students watch the film and listen for dialect peculiarities in Argentine Spanish—the use of *vosotros,* pronunciation differences, etc. Depending on the level of the course in question, we may either discuss the film in Spanish or write personal opinion reviews. In a recent *Conversation and Composition* course, the students broadened the question of who writes official histories into a consideration of history writing and the mass media in the United States. (Hunt)

This film could be used to show the effects of military dictatorship (murder and torture) on women and society in general.

Suggested Readings: Aufderheide, Patricia. "The Official Story." In *Cross-Cultural Film Guide.*

Aufderheide, Patricia. "Awake, Argentina." *Film Comment,* 51–55.

Aufderheide, Patricia. "Latin American Cinema and the Rhetoric of Cultural Nationalism: Controversies at Havana in 1987 and 1989." *Quarterly Review,* 64–78.

Barnard, Tim, ed. *Argentine Cinema.*

King, John. *Magical Reels: A History of Cinemas in Latin America.*

Skidmore, Thomas E., and Peter H. Smith. *Modern Latin America.*

Timerman, Jacobo. *Prisoner without a Name, Cell without a Number.*

Valenzuela, Luisa. *Strange Things Happen Here: Twenty Short Stories and a Novel.*

Complementary Films/Videos: *La cruz invertida (The Shattered Cross)* (Argentina); *Las Madres de la Plaza de Mayo (The Mothers of the Plaza de Mayo)* (Argentina); *Que bom te ver viva (How Nice to See You Alive)* (Brazil); *Niños desaparecidos (Missing Children); Chile: Sueños prohibidos (Chile's Forbidden Dreams)* (Chile); *Retornando a Chile (Returning to Chile); Algo de tí (Something of You)* (Panama)
Level: High School—University

HOMBRE MIRANDO AL SURESTE (Man Facing Southeast)

Feature.   With Subtitles.   105 min.   1986
Directed by: Eliseo Subiela
Produced by: Cinequanon
Distributed by: IMRE
Evaluators: Jeremy Adelman, Lori Madden, Sharon Sieber, Patricia Thomas Smith
Description: This film explores the relationship between a psychiatrist working in a psychiatric hospital in Buenos Aires and one of his patients, who claims (perhaps plausibly) to be from another planet. Ironically, the patient is the only sane and authentic voice in the film. In the crazy world outside the asylum, the doctor must pay lip service to conven-

tional expectations about thought and behavior, to the detriment of his patient. The patient dies after being sedated, which cuts off communication with his alien spacecraft, or, symbolically, with his deeper self. The film's central theme is the gray zone between sanity and insanity, justice and injustice, and the limits of human tolerance.

Strengths and Weaknesses: This is a beautiful and sensitive treatment of insanity, both of the patient and of the system. The penetrating story questions modern society's concepts of science, mental health, and good and evil. The film is well acted, finely crafted, and stirring.

Introducing the Tape: U.S. viewers would need an introduction orienting them to what to expect, but it should not be a plot summary.

How to Use: In my own survey courses on *Latin American History,* this would be a good example of many of the moral problems facing Latin American countries that made the "democratic turn" in the 1980s and how issues of social justice remain equally pressing. It would also be useful in a course on *Public Health in Latin America.* (Adelman)

The film can be used as entertainment in a *Spanish Language* course for the language club or for an international film series. (Madden)

I would use this film in a *Literature* class for students to analyze just as they would a novel or play. In an upper-level *Spanish Language* course I would use it to expose students to a riveting and well-executed plot that would hold students' attention and motivate them to learn Spanish. With a film like this one, students begin to listen spontaneously and understand as they relax and immerse themselves in the world of the story. This wonderfully modern film could be shown in juxtaposition to other postmodernist works, such as Robbe-Grillet, Beckett, and Carlos Fuentes, or the Theater of the Absurd, such as Ionesco. The fragmented story line and creation of its own world place it firmly in the tradition of the Moderns. (Sieber)

This tape could be used as a conversation tool and for increasing class awareness of different themes and styles of writing and acting. It could be shown in an advanced high school *Spanish Language* class with mature students, but instructors should preview it first. The end is depressing, and some parts are difficult to interpret. There seem to be some parallels drawn between the lead character and Christ. (Smith)

Suggested Readings: Barnard, Tim. *A History of Argentine Film.*

Works by Beckett, Carlos Fuentes, Ionesco, and Robbe-Grillet.

Level: High School—University

LAS MADRES DE LA PLAZA DE MAYO (The Mothers of the Plaza de Mayo)

Documentary.   With Subtitles.   64 min.   1985
Produced and Directed by: Lourdes Portillo and Susana Muñoz (981 Esmeralda St., San Francisco, CA 94110)

Distributed by: Women Make Movies
Evaluators: Silvia Arrom, Angela Carreño, Miguel Huarcaya, Grace Leavitt, Carla Meskill, Chon Noriega, José Luis Rénique, Enríque R. Rodríguez
Description: Four mothers whose children disappeared during the military government in Argentina relate the events surrounding the children's disappearance, the sense of terror and helplessness they felt, and the strength they derived from organizing and joining a protest movement. The film chronologically shows the development of *Las Madres de la Plaza de Mayo* (the Mothers of the Disappeared) intercut with a history of the military regime. It includes interviews with government officials and victims of imprisonment and torture. The tape explains that the main purpose of the mothers' movement was to demand information about their "disappeared" children. With time, the group took on other responsibilities, such as providing financial assistance to grandmothers for the care of their grandchildren and seeking international support through foreign press coverage. Their brave activism was crucial in exposing the atrocities of the military regime, and their organized protests helped bring down the dictatorship.
Strengths and Weaknesses: This is an extremely powerful tool for bringing students closer to the atrocities committed by the Argentine dictatorship. It is moving and informative, with impressive footage, and the variety of interviews from different perspectives is emotionally effective. The pacing is generally good, and the powerful testimonials open up broader historical events. The narration, well written and in the right place, clarifies the situation. Other strong points are the tape's organization and structure. It provides a historical context, discussing the return of Juan Perón, the administration of Isabel Perón, the 1976 military coup, and the subsequent suspension of civil rights. It conveys the horror and senselessness of the military suppression of Argentine youth, using interviews and newsreel footage. Closing scenes that show similar situations in other areas in the world make a subtle but powerful statement. The interviews with subtitles provide excellent material for language practice, but at times the subtitles are difficult to read.

The film does not emphasize how an atmosphere of terror was created by the random violence of guerrilla groups. Some of the interviews about individual children can be a bit slow for U.S. audiences.
Introducing the Tape: Some historical background on Argentina during the 1970s and information regarding the fascistlike political project upheld by Videla's military junta would be extremely helpful to put the tape into context. Also, the tape's loose-ended coverage of the trial of the military in the 1980s may be confusing for students and should be clarified.
How to Use: Teachers can lecture on the issue of the "disappearance" of people—how, why, etc.—then introduce the screening and hand out questionnaires relating to the film. Discussion would then follow. (Rodríguez)

In *Political Science* or *Women's Studies* courses the tape could be used to explore the intersection of gender and politics. How the role of "mother" motivated, empowered, and facilitated these women's protests and the importance of women's organizing in bringing world attention to the human rights abuses in Argentina should be discussed.
Suggested Readings: Comisión Nacional sobre la Desaparición de Personas. *Nunca Más: The Report of the Argentine National Commission on the Disappeared.*

Hodges, Donald. *Argentina's "Dirty War": An Intellectual Biography.*

Navarro, Marysa. "The Mothers of the Plaza de Mayo." In *Power and Popular Protest in Latin America,* ed. Susan Eckstein.
Level: High School—University

NIÑOS DESAPARECIDOS (Missing Children)
Documentary.   With Subtitles.   24 min.   1985
Directed by: Estela Bravo
Produced by: Producciones America Latina
Distributed by: The Cinema Guild
Evaluators: Jeremy Adelman, Kendall W. Brown, Ann K. Coughlin
Description: This is a moving documentary about children kidnaped from mothers or born to pregnant women who were "disappeared" by Argentine security forces during the "dirty war" of the 1970s. The tape explores the technical, legal, forensic, and medical aspects of the problem. There are some stirring interviews with grandmothers who are searching for the children, as well as with some of the few children who were found by the time the film was made. Only twenty-four of two hundred children had been recovered by the grandparents. Some were found living with families of security forces.
Strengths and Weaknesses: The tape is a short, emotional, and well-put-together portrayal of the human rights problems in Argentina. Viewers can feel the rage, frustration, and sorrow expressed by the mothers.
Introducing the Tape: The tape is straightforward and can stand on its own, but some background on the dictatorship (1976–1983) would be helpful. To update the tape, audiences need to know about the controversy that arose after democracy was restored in the mid-1980s about punishing military personnel who perpetrated the atrocities. The "democratic" government temporarily detained or jailed those who were found guilty, and then pardoned them.
How to Use: I would use this tape for any course on recent *Latin American Politics* or *Human Rights* worldwide to show the human tragedy suffered at the hands of repressive governments. (Adelman)

I would use the film in *Modern Latin American History* to illustrate the consequences of Argentina's fascination with Peronism and the resulting "dirty war." Discussion would include questions about the video's assertion that these atrocities were orchestrated by the Pentagon. (Brown)

I would use this video in connection with the showing of the film *The Official Story* and have students read *Amalia* by Mármol. The students can compare and contrast military dictatorships of the nineteenth and twentieth centuries, particularly *la novela de tesis* and *la película de tesis*. This video would be an excellent addition to this unit of study. (Coughlin)

Suggested Readings: Andersen, Martin Edwin. *Dossier Secreto: Argentina's Desaparecidos and the Myth of the Dirty War.*

Comisión Nacional sobre la Desaparición de Personas. *Nunca Más: The Report of the Argentine National Commission on the Disappeared.*

Guest, Iain. *Behind the Disappearances: Argentina's Dirty War against Human Rights and the United Nations.*

Mármol, José. *Amalia; novela historica americana.*

Simpson, John and Jana Bennett. *The Disappeared and the Mothers of the Plaza: The Story of the 11,000 Argentinians Who Vanished.*

Complementary Films/Videos: *La historia oficial (The Official Story)* (Argentina); *La voz de los pañuelos (The Voice of the Shawls)* (Argentina); *Las Madres de la Plaza de Mayo (The Mothers of the Plaza de Mayo)* (Argentina)

Level: High School—University

NO HABRA MAS PENAS NI OLVIDO (Funny Dirty Little War)

Feature.   With Subtitles.   80 min.   1983
Directed by: Hector Olivera
Produced by: Aries Cinematografica Argentina
Distributed by: IMRE
Evaluators: Roger P. Davis, Joséph A. Gagliano
Description: A faithful adaptation of Osvaldo Sorian's novel, this film dramatizes the extreme factionalism among the Peronistas following the 1974 return to power of Juan Perón in Argentina. It portrays a right-wing Peronista leader with strong ties to labor and the commercial sector who has ambitions of replacing the administrator of a small provincial town. He accuses the administrator of being a tool of local communists who are trying to manipulate the town's Perón youth group. With the support of the police chief and the regional mayor, the right-wing Peronistas demand that the administrator relinquish his position. The administrator, refusing to resign, gains the backing of several bizarre characters and Perón youth group members. Things quickly get out of hand, and the tragicomedy moves from farce to horror. A battle ensues between the right- and left-wing Peronistas for control of the town. The violence escalates, and all parties proclaim their authentic Peronist loyalty as they shoot each other. Using scatological and gallows humor, the film depicts the struggle with a comic, as well as a somber and violent, tone. The townspeople's confusion during the battle reflects that of the Argentine nation during the troubled 1970s. The people speculate that military intervention will be necessary to restore peace and order. Demonstrating the widespread cynicism of the period, characters indicate at the end of the film that army leaders will use the conflict to strengthen their role in national politics.

Strengths and Weaknesses: This excellent film, adapted from a great novel, successfully depicts the confusion and cynicism evident in Argentine politics during the 1970s. It highlights the divisions in Peronism between the Right and the Left and the tragedy they will jointly bring to Argentina. The acting is outstanding.

One reviewer felt that the film's weak points included stereotyped characters and excessive violence in several scenes. An introduction would be necessary to provide context for U.S. audiences.

Introducing the Tape: U.S. viewers need background on Argentine politics and history, particularly during the Peronista era. There are several deliberately confusing aspects to this film that seem to be intended to reflect the political befuddlement of the Argentine population during the 1970s; these would need to be pointed out to students.

How to Use: I would use this tape in my *Latin American History* classes to demonstrate some of the dynamics of the political and social culture of Latin America. While the film is specific to Argentina and the Peronista experience and is a good tool for teaching those themes, it also works as a broader discussion of the public life in Latin American culture. Students would discuss characters, the degree to which things get out of control, the question of ideology and its power, and comparisons with similar scenarios in the United States, such as McCarthyism. (Davis)

Suggested Readings: Crasswaller, Ronald. *Perón and the Enigma of Argentina.*

Hodges, D. C. *Argentina 1943–1976: The National Revolution and Resistance.*

Page, Joséph. *Perón, a Biography.*

Peralta-Ramos, M., and C. H. Waisman. *From Military Rule to Liberal Democracy in Argentina.*

Rock, David. *Argentina 1516–1982: From Spanish Colonization to the Falklands War.*

Rock, David. *Authoritarian Argentina: The Nationalist Movement, Its History and Its Impact.*

Smith, Peter H. *Argentina and the Failure of Democracy.*

Thornton, Lawrence. *Imagining Argentina.*

Level: University

PUBIS ANGELICAL (Pubis Angélical)

Feature.   With Subtitles.   117 min.   1983
Directed by: Raul de la Torre
Produced by: Artediez S.A.
Distributed by: IMRE
Evaluators: Marlene Gottlieb, Ann Marie Stock, Allen Wells
Description: Adapted from the novel by Manuel Puig, this film presents the psychological portrait of a woman struggling to come to grips with her own life and place in Argentine society during the chaotic 1970s. Ana finds herself un-

happily married to a right-wing patrón and in love with a human rights activist who works with the guerrillas. She is forced to flee to Mexico, where she deals with her own deteriorating health and her perceptions of Argentina during and after the Perón regime. Ana takes stock of her life as she is dying of cancer and is confined to a hospital bed in Mexico. She represents the conflicts of the Argentine intellectual as she confronts her identity as a woman, a citizen, and a human being.

Strengths and Weaknesses: This is an exceptionally well-done film with excellent acting and subtitles. It provides students with a great deal of information about how and why Argentine society was so divided during the 1970s. Although the uninitiated would need additional context, the film gives a fascinating critique of how Argentina could have reached this nadir. There is one scene in the hospital where a human rights activist explains his political evolution and places Argentina's political history in context. That scene alone would be very useful for a history class. Also, there is telling commentary about sexism and the role of women. The film incorporates magical realism, constantly shifting between Ana's dreams and her reality.

The innovative narrative structure, with shifts in time and place, can be confusing. There is also a good deal of gratuitous sex that some may find objectionable. One reviewer felt that the film was a bit too long.

Introducing the Tape: The film can be viewed and understood without prior knowledge of Argentine history, but it would be less confusing and more meaningful to a viewer who has some knowledge of Peronism.

How to Use: *History* students would find the scenes taken from the Peronist era illuminating. The film could also be used in a course on female identity in a *Women's Studies* program. Since I teach *Literature,* I would probably have my students read the novel and then view the film for purposes of comparison. A further reading of Puig's novels could lead into a discussion of his characterization of women, his intertwining political and personal conflicts, and his use of dialogue and film. (Gottlieb)

Suggested Readings: Foster, David William. *Contemporary Argentine Cinema,* a useful general frame of reference, although it doesn't mention this particular film.

Puig, Manuel. *Pubis Angélical.* See bibliography for other works by this author.

Complementary Films/Videos: *No habra mas penas ni olvido (A Funny Dirty Little War)* (Argentina)

Level: University

TANGO BAR

Feature.   With Subtitles.   90 min.   1988
Directed by: Juan Carlos Codazzi and Marcos Zurinaga
Produced by: Castle Hill Productions
Distributed by: IMRE
Evaluators: Jeremy Adelman, Elizabeth Mahan, Margarita Pont

Description: This is the story of tango. Its evolution as a dance and the narratives of the songs' lyrics are told through the complicated relationships and nightclub act of three aficionados. The backdrop is Buenos Aires under the military dictatorship of the late 1970s. Two musicians who run a well-frequented tango bar in Buenos Aires are in love with the same woman, the wife of the bandleader, who also, on occasion, sings with the pair. Sometime around 1976, the bandleader leaves for exile in the United States. The film culminates with his return to Buenos Aires and an anxiously awaited musical reunion.

Strengths and Weaknesses: This is an excellent film with a visually glorious illustration of the various incarnations of tango. Viewers will learn much about the tango, as there is plenty of good music and dance. The theme, as it is portrayed, is sentimental and romanticizes the tango.

The increasing levels of repression in Argentine society are subtly conveyed and might be confusing to a viewer unfamiliar with the "dirty war." In addition, without prior knowledge of how tango worked as a song, the story of the three protagonists as an illustration of another form of tango might be lost. One evaluator felt that sections of the tape were not appropriate for high school audiences.

Introducing the Tape: Some background on Argentine politics in the 1970s and 1980s, as well as on tango as dance and song, would be helpful.

How to Use: In my general survey of *Latin American History,* I would use this to convey the problems artists faced with the spread of dictatorships in the 1970s. It is also a useful portrayal of some romantic ideas of Argentine sexuality. (Adelman)

I would use this film in my course on *Latin American Popular Culture* to illustrate the development of tango. (Mahan)

The tape can be presented to show how the tango started and became popular not only in Argentina but in the world. (Pont)

Suggested Readings: Castro, Donald. "Popular Culture as a Source for the Historian: The Tango in Its Era of Guardia Vieja."

Castro, Donald. "Popular Culture as a Source for the Historian: Why Carlos Gardel?"

Collier, Simon. *The Life, Music, and Times of Carlos Gardel.*

Rock, David. *Argentina 1516–1982: From Spanish Colonization to the Falklands War.*

Vila, Pablo. "Tango to Folk: Hegemony, Construction, and Popular Identities in Argentina."

Level: University

LA VOZ DE LOS PAÑUELOS (The Voice of the Shawls)

Documentary.   With Subtitles.   45 min.   1992
Directed by: Carmen Guarini and Marcelo Cespedes
Produced by: Cine-Ojo (Casilla de Correo 1752, Correo Centro 1000, Buenos Aires; tel/fax: [541] 375-4061)
Distributed by: IMRE

Evaluators: Carlos R. Delgado, Joseph A. Gagliano

Description: This moving documentary traces the activities of the Mothers of the Plaza de Mayo from the period of Argentina's "dirty war" during the 1970s and early 1980s to the presidency of Carlos Menem in the 1990s. This movement started after the 1976 coup headed by General Jorge Rafael Videla and the installation of what has been called the clandestine phase of the terrorist state. The Mothers' demonstrations were initially concerned with calling national and world attention to the thousands of young people who were "disappeared" by Argentine military and death squads. Since the return of representative government in 1983, the Mothers' efforts have focused on bringing to justice those responsible for the human rights violations. The film uses black-and-white newsreel clips from local and French media to show many of the early protests and testimony of victims of violence against the military. The story focuses primarily on a single group of women who organized protest activities while taking care of their normal household routines. In often poignant scenes, they come together in private homes to plan social events, as well as demonstrations against government inaction. The women develop a particularly strong sense of camaraderie as they work to denounce the military's involvement in these acts of terror. The film ends by showing the women's frustration and anger because cautious civilian presidents since 1983 have been reluctant to punish prominent military leaders for their excesses during the "dirty war."

Strengths and Weaknesses: The film strongly depicts human solidarity and the strength of working together to achieve a common goal. It demonstrates how pain can be transformed into political and social action and shows how the determined Mothers turned Argentine and world opinion against the military regime. The scenes showing their organizational activities are especially informative.

Those unfamiliar with Argentine Spanish and colloquialisms will have difficulty keeping up with the rapidly moving and sometimes poorly synchronized subtitles. The color quality of some scenes is poor, and many of the interspersed newsreel clips are not adequately explained.

Introducing the Tape: An introduction to the history of the period and an explanation of why these women are significant in the democratization of Argentine politics would be useful. There should also be additional information about the importance of the Falklands War in ending the Argentine military regime. Also, a general study of the use of terror as a tool of political control could serve as a framework for better understanding.

How to Use: This tape is particularly useful for showing the development of grassroots movements, especially in the context of repressive governments. It is also useful for illustrating *Women's Issues* and the power of women in organizing for social change. (Delgado)

The tape could be used in the *Twentieth-Century Latin America* course to inform students of contemporary issues and human rights abuses in Argentina. It could be used as the basis for extensive class discussions. It would be appropriate for a *Dictatorships in Latin America* course. After its viewing, students could consider the role of contemporary grassroots movements in democratizing Latin America and how effectively they resist authoritarian rule. (Gagliano)

Suggested Readings: Calvert, Susan. *Argentina: Political Culture and Instability.*

Hodges, Donald Clark. *Argentina's "Dirty War": An Intellectual Biography.*

Erro, David G. *Resolving the Argentine Paradox.*

Peralta-Ramos, M., and C. H. Waisman, eds. *From Military Rule to Liberal Democracy in Argentina.*

Rock, David. *Authoritarian Argentina: The Nationalist Movement, Its History and Its Impact.*

Simpson, John, and Jana Bennett. *The Disappeared and the Mothers of the Plaza: The Story of the 11,000 Argentinians Who Vanished.*

Level: University

YO NO SOY UNA CUALQUIERA (I Am Not a Common Woman)

Experimental.   With Subtitles.   20 min.   1989

Directed by: María Cristina Civale

Distributed by: Women Make Movies

Evaluators: Rick Langhorst, Paul J. LaReau, Janet Page-Reeves, Daniel C. Scroggins

Description: This experimental video juxtaposes *machista* and male stereotyped perspectives with five women's struggle against these attitudes. It opens with five men sitting naked on a bench making insulting and sexist comments about women. The video then cuts to interviews with five women who are considered "just anybody": a prostitute, an old woman, a nun who is a radio broadcaster, a birthing instructor, and a mother of a *desaparecido* (disappeared person). These strong and dedicated women are engaged in things traditionally "female," but they break out of stereotyped molds. The male actors make choreographed responses to the statements contained in the women's interviews, all of which deal with two questions: (1) Was Eve's disobedience in the Garden of Eden the origin of human suffering? and (2) Are you a *cualquiera*? (In Spanish, *cualquiera,* which translates literally as "whatever," can mean "tramp," "trash," or "person of no importance.") At the tape's end, each woman states powerfully that she is not a *cualquiera*.

Strengths and Weaknesses: The tape presents valuable insights about women in Latin American society and a unique treatment of machismo. The experimental presentation of the men's perspective effectively demonstrates the absurdity of *machista* views of women. The video presents an interesting take on feminism, and is avant-garde in that there are many images of male genitalia and none of female (quite a change from the usual practice). The tape contains clear, direct language that is accessible to students with third-year-college language skills. While the extreme close-up shots of the speakers' lips and teeth are one of the experimental strategies, they are also extremely useful to language students, who can gain valuable clues by paying close attention to the articulation of native speakers.

One evaluator found the tape incoherent and disconnected. Another felt that the nondocumentary portions of the film constituted a controversial editorial on Latin American males' perceptions of women. At times it is unclear who is being interviewed. The subtitles are small and hard to read, and some scenes may not be suitable for high school students.

Introducing the Tape: While sexism and stereotypes of women exist in all cultures, background about the meaning of machismo in Latin America would be useful in introducing the tape. Language students may need help understanding the old woman interviewed, and U.S. viewers may require some background for the last and most important interview with one of the *Madres de la Plaza de Mayo* (Mothers of the Plaza de Mayo). U.S. audiences would need an explanation of the phenomenon of the *desaparecidos* (disappeared persons), the *guerra sucia* (dirty war), and the protests of the *Madres de la Plaza de Mayo*.

How to Use: This video would be helpful in presenting the struggle of women against the *machista* views of women in Latin America. (LaReau)

I would use this tape in conjunction with readings of novels and short stories by Luisa Valenzuela in an *Argentine Literature* course. Students would see parallels between the nontraditional figures in the tape and fictional characters in the novels and short stories. In a *Latin American Civilization* course I would also like to use the tape for contrast with readings that provide a traditional male view, such as *Laberinto de la soledad* by Octavio Paz. (Scroggins)

Suggested Readings: Paz, Octavio. *Laberinto de la soledad.*

Valenzuela, Luisa. *Other Weapons.*

Valenzuela, Luisa. *Strange Things Happen Here: Twenty Short Stories and a Novel.*

Level: University

BOLIVIA

BOLIVIA DESCONOCIDA: LAGO TITICACA
Documentary. Without Subtitles. 15 min. 1990
Directed by: Ariel Pérez, Francisco Ormachea
Produced by: Portafolio SRL (Casilla Postal 688, La Paz; tel: [5912] 797-378; fax: [5912] 328-318)
Distributed by: IMRE
Evaluators: Lavina Tilson Gass, Paul J. LaReau, Roger A. Sánchez-Berroa, Carolyn Shapiro, Naomi Smith
Description: This is a detailed history of Lake Titicaca from prehistory to modern times. Using several historic and new, electronically generated maps, the documentary explores the geologic history—from rocks, fossils, and glacial movement to the lake's contemporary effect on weather, seasons, etc. The focus is almost solely on the lake and the geology and meteorology of the area; there is no material on wildlife, plants, or cultures.

Strengths and Weaknesses: This tape has excellent photography and images and is full of informative details. However, it is a rather dry presentation with a great deal of data to assimilate. One evaluator appreciated the good scientific exploration of the lake but would have liked to see more about the grasses and wildlife and the lake's importance to the cultures situated around it.

Introducing the Tape: No introduction is necessary; the tape is self-explanatory.

How to Use: I would tell students what to expect and give them five to ten questions in advance, which we would discuss afterward. A comparison with lakes in the United States could be useful. (Tilson Gass)

In *Spanish* courses I would present a little background on the area, explain class objectives (whatever they might be—language, vocabulary, information), let students view and listen a couple of times, and follow with discussion and maybe a little quiz. (Sánchez-Berroa)

This would be a good example of how scientists look at natural phenomena to learn more about the earth's history. (Shapiro)

I used *Titicaca* (in part only) to establish what the area of the Altiplano is like; when we talked about *Ecology,* I used the "raised field" section. (Smith)

Suggested Readings: Albo, Xavier, José M. Barnadas, and Arturo Sist. *La cara campesina de nuestra historia,* chapter 1, 15–33.

Barrionuevo, Alfonsina. *Los dioses de la lluvia,* 7–13, 16–20, 22–28, 33–37, 69–72, 88–92, 127–35.

Isbell, Billie Jean. "From Unripe to Petrified: The Feminine Symbolic in Andean Gender Schema."

Klein, Herbert S. *Historia general de Bolivia,* chapter 1, 1–46.

Mantilla, Roberto. "Arquitectura Rupestre en Copacabana."

Moseley, M. *The Incas and Their Ancestors: The Archaelogy of Peru.*

Pereira, David H. "Incallacta."

Salomon, Frank, and George L. Urioste. *The Huarochiri Manuscript: A Testament of Ancient and Colonial Andean Religion,* introduction, 1–38, and chapter 31, 440–87.

Spalding, Karen. *Huarochiri: An Andean Society under Inca and Spanish Rule,* chapter 2, 42–71.

Zuidema, R. T. *Inca Civilization of Cuzco,* chapter 1, 1–13; chapter 3, 34–50; chapter 5, 67–78.
Level: High School—University

BOLIVIA DESCONOCIDA: TIWANAKÚ
Documentary. Without Subtitles. 14 min. 1989
Directed by: Ariel Pérez, Francisco Ormachea

Produced by: Portafolio SRL (Casilla Postal 688, La Paz; tel: [5912] 797-378; fax: [5912] 328-318)
Distributed by: IMRE
Evaluators: Gary S. Elbow, Lavina Tilson Gass, Paul J. LaReau, Roger A. Sánchez-Berroa, Carolyn Shapiro
Description: This video is an information-rich study of the archaelogical site Tiwanakú and the tribe that inhabited the region. Tiwanakú is located a few kilometers south of Lake Titicaca in the Bolivian Altiplano. It was the center of the first truly imperial culture in South America. The film opens with scenes of the Altiplano and Lake Titicaca. It then surveys the ruins and moves to the museum, where it presents Tiwanakan culture through the pottery, tools, weaving, agricultural, and skeletal remains. It discusses the symbolism of the artifacts, rituals, and medical practices, including skull deformation and trepanning. It makes some connections to contemporary indigenous culture through music, dance, and agricultural practices.
Strengths and Weaknesses: The video contains outstanding, captivating photography, excellent writing and pacing, and clear, well-articulated Spanish language. It treats the topic completely and is a good introduction to the archaeological findings at a little-known but important site. The indigenous background music is well done.

The tape's traditional documentary format includes a rather dry narration. It also contains too many facts for most students to assimilate in one viewing. The language is a little poetic and contains many Indian words as well as sophisticated technical terminology from archaeology. One reviewer felt that the film fails to place Tiwanakú in a cultural context within South American prehistory, which may cause problems for the nonprofessional viewer.
Introducing the Tape: The tape is self-explanatory; however, for viewers unfamiliar with South American cultural history, a preliminary explanation of Tiwanakú's place in time and geography (maybe a map) and its importance in the development of Andean civilization would be helpful. The film refers to different phases of cultural development but fails to place them in time. Some sort of chronology is needed.
How to Use: As a cultural geographer, I would focus on the setting (beautiful photography of the Altiplano) and on subsistence activities, of which the film has a bit. The focus is on raised-field technology (*terreplenes*), which allowed farmers to use the shallow lake edges for food production. Beyond this, the film is of relatively little use for *Geography*. (Elbow)

For my *Spanish* (kindergarten through third-grade) students, the tape would have to be shown with the current narration turned off. It is really superb for advanced classes. It makes me yearn to visit the place. The Spanish is beautiful and informative. (Tilson Gass)

The Spanish in the video is suitable for high-intermediate or advanced *Language* classes. In any case, I would need to prepare an advance organizer, since students at this level have a difficult time filtering out major themes from less important details. (LaReau)

I would assign this as a project for oral presentations in *Spanish* class or for general discussion. (Sánchez-Berroa)

In studying *Contemporary Indigenous Cultures,* I would use this tape to show the complex and sophisticated techniques used in agriculture and textiles that reflect a great understanding of the environment and how to adapt to it. (Shapiro)

This video complements the unit I teach on the *Pre-Columbian Cultures of the Andes.*
Suggested Readings: Browman, David L. "Toward the Development of the Tiahuanaco (Tiwanakú) State," in *Advances in Andean Archaelogy.*

Weatherford, Jack. *Indian Givers: How the Indians of the Americas Transformed the World.*

Cultural Survival Quarterly (Summer 1991, 1986).

National Geographic (February 1966, December 1973, May 1982, and May 1988).
Level: High School—University

CAMINO DE LAS ALMAS (Path of the Souls)
Docudrama.   With Subtitles.   25 min.   1989
Directed by: Eduardo López and Cristina Bubba Z. (Casilla 14066, La Paz; tel: [5912] 355-666)
Produced by: Hisbol
Distributed by: CIMR, IMRE
Evaluators: Angela Carreño, John Higgens, Vincent D. Iacovelli, Janet Page-Reeves, University of Pittsburgh Group (María Consuelo Acosta, John Frechione, Shirley A. Kregar, Nichole Parker, Lynn Young, José Zevallos)
Description: For more than five hundred years, the Aymara Indian residents of Coroma, Bolivia, have worshiped the woven garments worn by their founding grandmothers and grandfathers. These sacred textiles are believed to embody the souls of their ancestors. The weavings, kept in bundles called *q'epis,* are prayed to in rituals and consulted in times of trouble and are a favored prize of international traffickers in Andean weavings. *Camino de las almas* is a videotape written and acted by the Coroman villagers in collaboration with professional Bolivian video producers and anthropologists. In their docudrama, the Coromans tell the tale of their *q'epis.* The story begins as the townsfolk fall victim to a series of calamities. They perform various rituals asking the *q'epis* why they are suffering. The answer is returned: the *q'epis* say they are lonely. Searching for the meaning of the *q'epis'* response, the Indians discover that many of the textiles have been stolen and replaced with other weavings. Continuing their investigation, they learn that a North American art dealer paid intermediaries to substitute less valuable textiles and give him the originals. And so begins the Indians' quest to find the souls of their ancestors and have their sacred, ancient patrimony returned to Coroma.

Strengths and Weaknesses: This is a moving outcry against Western desecration of Indian belief and ritual. It provides an excellent example of an indigenous perspective and the issues of the consumption of textiles, sacred art, and artifacts in the United States. The tape has no intermediary. The residents perform and tell their own story, making the community's pain and sorrow palpable. Coroma is an isolated Andean village. The participation of the Coroman residents in relating their own tale makes this an incredibly powerful and genuine tape. Their video also provides an excellent portrayal of everyday life in the Altiplano of the Bolivian Andes: depicting how the people live, their motivations, aspirations, rituals, and the Aymara language.

The tape is a bit slow paced, but this allows the culture to be effectively communicated.

Introducing the Tape: Viewers should be told that this tape is an example of advocacy video at its best. The residents of Coroma had never before seen a film or television. They made this tape to share their experiences with others, both to prevent this type of theft from occurring in other Andean villages and to seek international assistance in repatriating their sacred textiles. It worked! After a group of U.S. lawyers saw this moving video, they offered to take the Coroman residents' case *pro bono*. The lawyers brought the United States art dealer to court and succeeded in getting a number of the textiles returned to their rightful home.

This tape takes on additional significance if students are introduced to the history of Incan resistance to Christian conversion, despite the destruction and theft of their sacred religious items. Background and follow-up discussion on the textiles and rituals presented in the tape (reading coca leaves, consulting the heart of the sacrificed llama), as well as on the women's role in the community, would be useful. The mixture of Spanish and Aymara languages should also be discussed. *Camino de las almas* could be presented in conjunction with *Los jallq'a: identidad y tejido* (a documentary detailing the significance of the designs in the textiles of this region).

How to Use: I would use the tape to start a discussion of culture, art, and imperialism. In *Video Production* courses it would be useful to show examples of social activism using video. (Higgens)

In courses on *Visual Anthropology* the tape could be an example of how anthropologists can work with communities to help them tell their own stories. In my *Anthropology* class we would use the tape to discuss issues of cultural patrimony and repatriation. (Page-Reeves)

Camino de las almas serves as an excellent introduction to life in the Altiplano of the Bolivian Andes. I would follow the film with a discussion of the use of coca in ceremonies, the role of women in the community, and the mix of the Spanish and Aymara languages. (University of Pittsburgh Group)

Suggested Readings: Anner, John. "Aymara: With Help from Indian People in the United States, Aymara Indians from Bolivia Recover Their Sacred Weavings."

Anner, John. *Study Guide: Native Peoples: The Arts and Lifeways.*

Bomberry, Victoria. "Text and Context: Organizing the Return of the Sacred Textiles to the Community of Coroma, Bolivia."

Lobo, Susan. "The Fabric of Life."

Level: University

EL CORAGE DEL PUEBLO (The Courage of the People)

Docudrama.   With Subtitles.   90 min.   1971
Directed by: Jorge Sanjinés
Produced by: Grupo Ukamau (Casilla 1073, Miraflores, La Paz)
Distributed by: The Cinema Guild
Evaluators: John Higgens, Marilyn Jímenez, Joan A. McGinnis, Carlos A. Pérez, Susy Suárez
Description: This film reenacts a miners' strike in the company town of Siglo XX, using many of the original strikers and their families. It begins with footage of a protest march and its confrontation with the army, which massacred a large number of the protesters. This scene is repeated at the conclusion of the film, but with an open ending, suggesting the people's continuing struggles. Throughout the film are scenes depicting the miners' grievances and montages of the politicians and military officials responsible for the repression of various people's movements in contemporary Bolivian history. The narrative refers to previous strikes and uprisings in an attempt to develop a dialectical notion of the history of the period between 1942 and 1965. Women's voices are included: Members of an organization of miners' wives recount the events that led to the massacre depicted. The film is explicit about its leftist politics and is highly critical of U.S. imperialism.

Strengths and Weaknesses: This superb and moving film is rich in drama and testimony. It effectively incorporates point-of-view shots to position the viewer in various ideological perspectives. Student viewers reacted most favorably to the sense that the people who played the roles were not actors but actual participants; they spoke of the greater impact of realism that this gave to the film.

The film lacks context and background needed for U.S. audiences. It is a difficult and long film for people accustomed to Hollywood techniques and with little experience viewing alternative kinds of films. However, the experience of watching such a lengthy exposition is part of the film's effect. Unlike the frenetic rhythms of Hollywood films, the film incorporates an Amerindian sense of time by lingering on a scene to describe a temporal dimension.

Introducing the Tape: U.S. viewers would need a statement introducing the miners as the most important and radical force of the working-class movement in Bolivia, and perhaps the most radical workers in Latin America, and a discussion about why the state has frequently chastised them. The presidents and generals listed at the beginning of the film should also be identified. The film does not explain the threat (real or not) that the guerrilla movement led by Che Guevara represented to the government at that time, nor the political power that miners have had for most of this century. Also, viewers should be updated on the current history of the miners. In 1986 they were "retired" from the mines as the state enterprise closed down in preparation for privatization. It may be helpful to provide a map and general information about how peasant cultures have been transformed into a proletariat.

Audiences could also be instructed on how to view non-Hollywood-type films, particularly in the use of a collective rather than an individual main character.

How to Use: A shortened version might help illustrate the living conditions of Bolivian peasants and the concept of resistance to government authority. (Higgens)

I have used this film in a *Latin American Cinema* class as the first film that students watch. It represents a style of filmmaking that is the opposite of Hollywood films. Students learn to identify with a collective protagonist and are exposed to a non-Western culture. The film states its ideological position in a "dogmatic" way that students tend to see as propaganda and thus dismiss. I found it useful to discuss the difference between propaganda and an ideologically committed film that presents the point of view of those being oppressed. (Jiménez)

In *High School Spanish* classes I would present a brief historical background of the period (1942–1965) and a vocabulary list. The students would have a study guide with questions to be considered while viewing and discussion questions for after viewing. Essay topics might be to relate this story from the point of view of a parent (miner), a representative of the Siglo XX mine, a child, or a governmental official. (McGinnis)

I would use the film in a *Latin American History* or *Women's Studies* course emphasizing the political role of housewives and having students read Domitila Chungara's book, *Let Me Speak,* the biography of a Bolivian married to a miner. Chungara (depicted in the film) and other women organized the hunger strike that allowed miners to take a more militant position regarding the state. The film could also be used in a comparative course on the labor movement in the United States and Latin America. (Pérez)

This tape would be excellent to illustrate the mining industry in *Latin American Studies* courses. (Suárez)

Suggested Readings: Chungara, Domitila. *Let Me Speak.*

Sanjines, Jorge. "Language and Popular Culture."

Sanjines, Jorge. "The Courage of the People: An Interview with Jorge Sanjines."

Level: University

GRAN PODER

Documentary.   Without Subtitles.   15 min.   1988

Directed by: Alfredo Ovando

Produced by: Movimiento Boliviano de Video (Av. Saavedra #1036 Miraflores, La Paz; tel: [5912] 376-962; fax: [5912] 340-604)

Distributed by: IMRE

Evaluators: Marc Chernick, Mary Jo Dudley, Janet B. Norden, Janet Page-Reeves, Marc S. Roth, Catherine Russo

Description: This documentary captures a series of events that take place as part of the traditional indigenous *Gran poder* celebration in La Paz, Bolivia. This festival is celebrated with a parade. The participants don brilliant, elaborate costumes, including the masks of Oruro, a town in the Bolivian Andes. Indigenous customs are blended with Christianity. The festivities incorporate mythology and popular religiosity through music and colorful choreography. The tape shows the festival preparation activities (building the grandstands, finishing the costumes) and then focuses on a variety of participating musical groups. It includes scenes with musicians from La Paz, Tarabuco, Potosí, Oruro, and several other areas of Bolivia. There is little narration, mostly scenes of the actual parade.

Strengths and Weaknesses: This is a visually stunning and extremely interesting tape that conveys the brilliant colors of the Bolivian Indian culture and captures the feeling of the real festival. A strength is its emphasis on the high artistic value of the masks. Spanish classes would be able to learn much about the Bolivian Indian culture from this portrayal.

The Indian narrator gives a sense of the excitement that accompanies the celebration of *Gran poder.* However, he does not offer a great deal of information about the history and significance of the celebration. All reviewers felt that the tape's biggest weakness was this lack of discussion of symbolic significance.

Introducing the Tape: It would be extremely helpful to have some background or additional materials that explain the significance of the masks and the characters (*diablos, osos, chinas*) that constitute part of the celebration.

How to Use: I could use segments of the tape in an *Anthropology* course dealing with contemporary topics in Latin America. With some editing, it could also be used with explanation in elementary school classes. (Dudley)

I would show this tape to enable the students to understand how the Bolivian Indians have blended their own beliefs with Christianity, how religious they are, and their zeal in celebrating religious holidays. I would explain how important vibrant colors are to the Indians and how artistic the people are. The students would see how Indian inhabitants of La Paz celebrate this important event. (Roth)

Level: Elementary School—University

LOS JALLQ'A: IDENTIDAD Y TEJIDO (The Jallq'a: Identity and Textiles)

Documentary.   With Subtitles.   20 min.   1987

Directed by: Francisco Cajias

Produced by: ANTARA (Casilla Postal 688, La Paz; tel: [5912] 797-378; fax: [5912] 328-318 or 2-365-848)

Distributed by: IMRE
Evaluators: Susan Altgelt, Mary Jo Dudley, Clara López-Beltrán, Wayne S. Osborn, Janet Page-Reeves, Enríque R. Rodríguez
Description: This tape details the creation of a textile workshop among the Jallq'a Indians of Iru Pampa, in the Bolivian highlands. The Jallq'a believe themselves to be one of the oldest peoples on earth and are noted for their beautiful weavings. The weavings are produced on a back-strap loom and contain intricate animal designs specific to different neighboring communities. The ethnic identity and beliefs of the Jallq'a people are greatly connected to the textiles. When the art form was in danger of disappearing owing to the people's increased poverty, a group of anthropologists helped set up the textile workshop to preserve traditional culture and develop an economic resource for the community. The workshop's success has led to better educational opportunities for the Jallq'a. The women were retrained in ancient design and weaving techniques, and the group managed to reproduce models copied from photographs of old textiles. A production cooperative was established to sell the textiles and rugs locally and internationally. The film demonstrates the production, use, and symbolic meanings of the textiles.
Strengths and Weaknesses: This is a beautiful and informative film that offers a rare documentation of the Iru Pampa. It shows how the rescue of knowledge leads to the rediscovery of ethnic identity and demonstrates how the project was successful in creating a positive message for the future. The tape uses images of textiles preserved in museums to supplement the presentation of weaving concepts that was offered to workshop participants. There is also good background music.

The video is slow paced, like many anthropological films. It does not give much space to the techniques of weaving or the explanation of the designs' significance.
Introducing the Tape: The video could be introduced as a visual representation of the culture of the Jallq'a, an indigenous community in Bolivia.
How to Use: The tape could be a useful enrichment at the high school or college level. Several years of Spanish are required to understand the narration. (Altgelt)

The tape can be used to illustrate the positive creation of a development project that is able to stimulate the creativity and productivity of a group using its own culture, without imposing modernizing models. It can also be used to show the richness of pre-Hispanic textile art. (López-Beltrán)

Segments of the video can be used during a discussion of the history of Bolivia for a glimpse of the continuity of culture in this region of Latin America. (Osborn)

The film introduces students to ancient patterns, their meanings, and what they represent to present-day and past peoples. (Rodríguez)

The tape allows the opportunity to compare various indigenous peoples and demonstrate how they use similar processes in solving problems, such as reproducing ancient patterns.
Level: University

EL LLAMERO Y EL SAL

Documentary.   Without Subtitles.   35 min.
Directed by: Alfredo Ovando and Jose A. Miranda
Produced by: Producciones Nicobis (Av. Saavedra #1036 Miraflores, La Paz; tel: [5912] 376-962; fax: [5912] 340-604)
Distributed by: IMRE
Evaluators: Marcia Dean, Mary Jo Dudley, Michael Huarcaya, Rick Langhorst, Clara López-Beltrán, Janet B. Norden, Marc S. Roth
Description: Each year, during the agricultural recess between the planting and the harvest seasons, the Aymara people of Pampa Aullagas travel with a caravan of llamas to obtain blocks of salt from high-elevation lake beds. The people make an arduous three-month journey from their remote village high in the Bolivian Andes down to the valley and then home again. The trek is both a means of sustaining life and a commercial and informational link between remote communities not connected by a highway system. On the return trip the Aymara trade the salt in isolated communities in the valley for basic foodstuffs, such as corn, coca, and wheat. In this way, the villagers living at lower altitudes can obtain products grown at higher altitudes and vice-versa. The camera follows the Aymara herdsmen on their journey through the Altiplano. The tape makes some references to history and shows glimpses of everyday life. The long-standing tradition and ritual of this process are evident, particularly when the Aymara reach the established stopping areas along their route.
Strengths and Weaknesses: This excellent tape allows students to view the unique culture of the Aymara Indians and the hardships of life in the high plains. It vividly illustrates an ancient tradition that enables this ethnic group to survive in an inhospitable region. The tape has a good historical and geographic introduction and shows the diversity of the climate in the two zones where the journey takes place. The images of the Andes are beautiful, and the diagrams of the region are very clear. The opening scene provides viewers with a visual experience and an opportunity to hear the native Aymara language. This part, however, is not subtitled. The Spanish in the rest of the tape is quite clear.

The tape may seem too long for U.S. audiences, but if shortened, it would lose much of the beautiful scenery, a sense of distances traveled, and the lives of the Aymara.
Introducing the Tape: Viewers should be told that the Spanish subtitles begin a few minutes into the tape. A brief overview of the tape could include the following information: In the mountainous country of Bolivia, indigenous peoples live at varying altitudes. The lower altitudes have more fertile earth, which can grow certain crops that cannot survive in the cold, harsh conditions at higher altitudes. For

centuries, the Indians living at high altitudes have had to travel to lower altitudes to trade salt for food items. Preparing for the trip, they load their supplies onto the backs of llamas, animals they depend upon for their livelihood and survival. The journey requires physical strength and can last as long as three months. Before the Indians make the yearly trek, they have a religious ceremony and pray for good fortune.

How to Use: I would use this video to show how the people of the Andes eke out a living and the lifestyle of the mountain communities. (Dean)

I would use this film to show some of the issues involved in marketing goods in a country that doesn't have an evenly sophisticated marketing infrastructure. (Dudley)

In an intermediate *Spanish* class I would choose small sections of the film to show several aspects of Andean society, such as agriculture, use of the llama, ceremonial use of coca, trade, and Andean geography. (Langhorst)

This is an extraordinarily clear example of the complementariness of the ecological "floor," widely used by the Andean villages since prehistoric times. It also illustrates the *desestructuración* that these villages have suffered as a result of the imposition of the colonial Spanish system in Latin America. (López-Beltrán)

Level: University

MARCHA POR LA VIDA

Documentary.   Without Subtitles.   24 min.   1988
Directed by: Alfredo Ovando
Produced by: Movimiento de Video Popular (Av. Saavedra #1036 Miraflores, La Paz; tel: [5912] 376-962; fax: [5912] 340-604)
Distributed by: IMRE
Evaluators: Marc Chernick, Marcia Dean, Mary Jo Dudley, Vincent D. Iacovelli, Janet B. Norden
Description: This video presents a history of the protests against the closing of tin mines in Bolivia and the miners' opposition to the government's policies that have caused economic hardship. These policies include debt payment, institution of International Monetary Fund austerity measures, and U.S. economic intervention. Bolivian workers have a tradition of going to the center of power to call for changes in policy. In this film the protesters march from the tin mines of Potosí to mines in Oruro and finally on to La Paz. Huge numbers of people participate and confront the members of the military who try to block the way.
Strengths and Weaknesses: The tape poignantly captures the hardship and struggles of the miners and their attempts to pressure the government. There is a moving and effective use of personal stories, along with beautiful shots of the multitude of marchers on the road to La Paz. Voices from many different backgrounds and social levels are included.

At times the spoken Spanish is fairly clear; at other times the accents are difficult to understand. The tape is a bit long. One reviewer felt that there was no climactic point and found the end confusing. Excerpts might make a more forceful presentation.

Introducing the Tape: The tape requires some background on the use of protest marches to influence economic policy. Information on the tin mines, the exploitation of miners, and the reasons for closing the mines should be presented.
How to Use: I would use this tape to show the role of protest marches in changing national economic policies in Bolivia. (Dudley)

It provides a good lesson about U.S. intervention in foreign affairs. (Norden)

Suggested Readings: Albo, Xavier, José M. Barnadas, and Arturo Sist. *La cara campesina de nuestra historia,*
    Klein, Herbert S. *Historia general de Bolivia.*
Level: University

PINTAMOS EL MUNDO DE COLORES (We Will Paint the World with Colors)

Animation.   No Dialogue.   12 min.   1991
Directed by: Alfredo Ovando
Produced by: Producciones Nicobis (Av. Saavedra #1036, Miraflores, La Paz; tel: [5912] 376-962; fax: [5912] 340-604)
Distributed by: IMRE
Evaluators: Susan Altgelt, Craig Auchter, Lavina Tilson Gass, James Lewis, Elinor Melville, Yolanda Prieto
Description: A charming animated video showing idyllic life in the tropical rain forest until wildlife is destroyed by deforestation and pollution. We see animals living happily in a beautifully colored world, full of flowers and trees surrounding a river. Suddenly there is an oil spill, and the animals are trapped in oil and fumes. Trees are cut down by local people and foreign companies. Everything is painted in dark colors. A couple of animals go to a nearby town where they are overwhelmed by the noise and garbage on the streets. They befriend a boy, absorbed in playing pinball, and convince him to come with them to help clean up the environment. Together they revive the forest. The piece ends when they build a national solar energy plant that says "Hecho en Bolivia" (Made in Bolivia).
Strengths and Weaknesses: This superb, colorful piece has delightful pictures and music. It is a charming story of ecological links between people, animals, plants, and technology, and there is clever juxtaposition of the video game and the destruction of the forest. The topic is timely, and students will probably be familiar with deforestation. Because there are no spoken words, the tape could be used in courses taught in any language.

One reviewer felt that the tape would have limited appeal to college audiences and might work better with younger audiences.

Introducing the Tape: No introduction is necessary. The tape would nicely complement other materials about the destruction of the rain forest and environment.
How to Use: Students could be asked to narrate orally or to

write a script. I showed the film to a group of kindergartners in an extended-day program at school, just to gauge their reaction. They were absolutely fascinated and did not lose interest for a minute. They also were eager to discuss the message. In my classes I would use it for simple description, for reinforcement of language, and also for discussion on ecology. (Tilson Gass)

I would use this to present my U.S. students with a study of point of view. This clearly presents a distinct anti-U.S. point of view with which it is useful to acquaint U.S. students. For example, when the forest is being destroyed, all words are written in English, and when it is being replanted, all the words are in Spanish. (Lewis)

This would be an excellent tape for primary or early secondary schools. (Melville)
Level: Kindergarten—University

SIEMPRE VIVA

Documentary.   Without Subtitles.   28 min.   1988
Directed by: Liliana de la Quintana
Produced by: Producciones Nicobis (Av. Saavedra #1036 Miraflores, La Paz; tel: [5912] 376-962; fax: [5912] 340-604)
Distributed by: IMRE
Evaluators: Anna R. Adams, Carlos R. Delgado, Michael Monteón, Allen Poor
Description: Set in the 1930s in La Paz, Bolivia, this docudrama is based on the life of labor organizer Catalina Mendoze, founder of the Unión Sindical Femenina de Floristas (The Union of Women Flower Vendors.) The film both recreates scenes and contains documentary interviews with union members who knew Mendoze. It depicts the process undertaken by a group of indigenous women flower sellers to organize to improve working conditions with the help of the Federación Obrera Local (Local Labor Federation), an offshoot of the Unión Gráfica Nacional (National Graphics Union) founded in 1905. The organizing process unfolds before the viewer. It begins with group meetings in which the women become aware of their common problems and the strength of their numbers, and it concludes with conflicts with government authorities and the eventual fulfillment of the women's dreams with the inauguration of a new flower market on March 19, 1939. The union declines after its leader is accused of being a communist.
Strengths and Weaknesses: The film clearly depicts the process of labor organization and shows how a group of indigenous women came together to demand more equitable working conditions. There are nice shots of women making wreaths and interesting interviews.

Reviewers felt that the dramatization was somewhat stiff and not professionally acted. The tape does not provide context, and its progression can be confusing. One reviewer felt that there could have been more time dedicated to exploring how the international labor organizations affected Mendoze's standing in local labor organizations.

Introducing the Tape: Instructors should inform viewers that this tape takes place in Bolivia, provide an outline of the particular struggle, and identify some of the major labor figures represented. An introduction to the political situation in Bolivia in the early part of this century would also be helpful. This should include a discussion of the place of women and indigenous populations in the more general framework of Latin American society.
How to Use: I would use this tape as a case study, to highlight the growing awareness of Latin American indigenous groups and women to the importance or organizing themselves to defend their rights. (Delgado)

In a *Labor Studies* course the tape could be used as an example of successful organizing. In *Cross-Cultural Studies* the parallels and differences between labor organizing in the United States during this same historical period and today can be examined.
Suggested Readings: Arteaga, Vivian. *La mujer pobre en la crisis económica: las vendedoras ambulantes de La Paz.*
Level: University

BRAZIL

ALAFIN OYO

Music Video.   English Voice-over.   7 min.   1989
Directed & Produced by: TV Viva-Centro Luiz Freire (Rua São Bento 344, Ribeira, 53110, Olinda PE; tel: [5581] 429-4109; fax: [5581] 429-4881)
Distributed by: IMRE
Evaluators: Mary Jane Craver, Tânia M. Hering, Vincent D. Iacovelli, Irwin Stern
Description: This lively music video focuses on how Afro-Brazilian ethnic heritage is maintained through Afoxé, a type of African religious/cultural dance. The Afoxé musical group featured in the tape explains that it seeks to create a "black" space for this popular Afro-Brazilian music tradition in Brazilian music. The tape mixes scenes of the group's performance in Olinda, Pernambuco, and interviews with group members about the movement. The socioeconomic and religious aspects of the music and dance are described. The song is a tribute to Alafin, who was the king of Oyo, in Africa.
Strengths and Weaknesses: This tape contains an excellent description of the music and dance, with good shots of Afoxé in development. The music is great.

One reviewer felt that the tape could use more detail.
Introducing the Tape: Some background regarding Brazil's non-Western religions, derived from Africa, should be explained. Also, Alafin's role in relation to Afro-Brazilians should be clarified. Was he a mythical or an authentic ancestor?
How to Use: In *Portuguese Language* class I would give some background on African-Brazilian religions (*Condomble, Umbanda, Macumba*) or have the students research the topics. They could be compared and contrasted to off-

shoots of African religion of the slave era in the Caribbean and the United States. Students would love the music. (Craver)

I would use this tape in conjunction with course materials to help students understand Afro-Brazilian people's background and their folklore. (Hering)

The video would be useful as part of a section on *Afro-Brazilian Traditions* in Brazil. (Stern)

Suggested Readings: Simpson, George E. *Black Religions in the New World.*

Level: Junior High School—University

ALEM DE TRABALHADOR, NEGRO

Documentary.   Without Subtitles.   35 min.   1989
Directed by: Daniel Brazil
Produced by: Ely Azevedo, Arnaldo Pereira dos Santos, Daniel Brazil
Distributed by: ABVP, IMRE Archive (available for viewing only)
Evaluators: Reid Andrews, George P. Browne, Cliff Welch
Description: This film surveys the participation of Afro-Brazilians in the labor force and the labor movement in São Paulo, Brazil. The first half is historical, covering the period from emancipation in 1888 through the 1960s. It intercuts period photos with interviews describing the development of black organizations and consciousness in the working class. It starts with the growth of the anarchist movement at the beginning of the century, which was dominated by immigrant workers and black unskilled laborers. The film digresses to describe the sponsorship of labor by the Vargas regime and the repression of the whole labor movement under the military dictatorship. The second half focuses on the modern black labor movement. It finds the growing race consciousness in the international scene of the 1960s and 1970s echoed in Brazil and looks at the relationship of the black consciousness movement to São Paulo's labor movement and left-wing political parties.
Strengths and Weaknesses: The tape provides a good survey of this topic and gives a strong and accurate sense both of the political economy of race relations in Brazil's most economically developed state and of the dilemmas facing the present-day black movement. It provides varied viewpoints of black spokespersons, and historical vision and interpretation. One reviewer felt that the tape was especially strong in taking on the Brazilian Left for subsuming race issues into class issues.

All the reviewers felt that the visual format of the tape was its weakest point. The "talking head" interviews and lack of variety make it a bit sterile. Also some of the speakers are not identified until the end credits.
Introducing the Tape: No introduction is necessary. The tape provides significant contextual information, much of it in rare photographs of the nineteenth-century black experience in São Paulo.
How to Use: I would show the film after students had read

about the present-day Brazilian black movement and use it to raise questions about the historical background of that movement and the issues it currently faces. (Andrews)

The major lesson I can find in this program is the poverty of racial self-consciousness, or evidence thereof, which exists in the Brazilian records. (Browne)

I usually discuss race relationships and black experience as a separate unit in my *Latin American* and *Brazilian History* courses. This video would be useful to discuss these issues and some of the debates regarding solutions to the problems racism causes in Brazil. One could use the tape instead of a book and have students review it in written form. (Welch)
Suggested Readings: Andrews, George Reid. *Blacks and Whites in São Paulo, Brazil, 1888–1988.*

Hanchard, Michael. *Orpheus and Power: The movimiento negro of Rio de Janeiro and São Paulo, Brazil, 1945–1988.*
Level: University

ALINHAVANDO UMA VIDA MELHOR

Documentary.   Without Subtitles.   11 min.
Directed by: TV Maxambomba
Produced by: CECIP—Centro de Criação de Imagem Popular (Rua Senador Dantas 80, 20031 Rio de Janiero, RJ; tel: [5521] 533-0772)
Distributed by: IMRE Archive (available for viewing only)
Evaluator: Rosangela Vieira King
Description: This tape describes an initiative taken by a group of poor women to generate jobs for themselves, while caring and providing for their children. The women organize a cooperative and start to work together in a common cause. Creating their own job market, they train themselves and involve the community (other women) in this same process. The women produce their own marketable resources (manufacturing clothes) and sell them for a profit. At the same time they help each other in a variety of ways, including babysitting the children of the working mothers. The workplace is viewed as an extension of the home.
Strengths and Weaknesses: This tape illustrates the women's resolve to take control of their lives, become financially independent, and therefore conquer a space for themselves that has been historically denied in a patriarchal society such as Brazil. They decided to take their destiny into their own hands, not waiting for the action of a government historically known to neglect the poor masses and particularly women, who are frequently considered second-class citizens. The tape shows how the women's self-esteem and hopes for the future greatly improved as a result of the project.

The tape does not offer a specific model for how women in other poor societies could implement a similar project. At times, the narration is not clear, and the progression is confusing.
Introducing the Tape: Readings or discussion before the video should inform audiences about the economic realities

of Brazil, the uneven distribution of wealth, and the status of women in Brazilian society.

How to Use: I would introduce the tape as a problem-solving technique in the struggle of Latin American women caught in a historically unfair system. I would suggest that the students viewing this video also devise a similar plan of action that could work for the peoples of Brazil, or for the poor masses in general, going beyond gender issues. (Vieira King)

Level: High School—University

ALÔ SAO PAULO

Documentary. Without Subtitles. 23 min. 1990
Directed by: Paulo Baroukh
Produced by: VTV Video (Rua Itapeva, 187 CEP 01332-000, São Paulo; tel: [5511] 251-1313; fax: [5511] 251-3740)
Distributed by: IMRE
Evaluators: George P. Browne, Warren J. Dean, Catherine Egan, Tânia M. Hering, David McCreery
Description: This public service spot integrates dramatized scenes produced by the city government planning office for São Paulo TV in 1990, when the city was run by the Workers Party (PT). Using radio as a narrative device, it is a call to the citizens to actively participate in the *Plano Directo* (Master Plan), a campaign being developed for city services, zoning, etc. Issues identified and well illustrated include the existence of *favelas* (slums) and the problems of slum dwellers; the pollution of the water system, transportation, and zoning problems; and urban sprawl and public housing. In dramatized segments, rural people go about their lives while a radio program, ever present in the background, implores them to become involved. The tape includes interviews with citizens of various sectors of the city and concludes with an appearance of the then-mayor of São Paulo, Luisa Erundina, who proposes a public debate on the plan.

Strengths and Weaknesses: With excellent camera work and editing, this tape has a slick imaginative format that avoids preaching. The viewer is exposed to much footage of the city and gains an idea of how the PT tried to construct political consensus. The video is a clear but not exhaustive treatment of a range of problems, with varied approaches to different segments. It also avoids simplification or easy solutions to problems.

The tape is very long, and because of its specificity, it functions best as a historical document. It is clearly a public relations document that reflects a particular administration's viewpoint. The Brazilian slang will be difficult for nonnative speakers.

Introducing the Tape: The tape could use some background on the Workers Party (PT), its political program, and theories about how to run a city administration. Viewers should be told that the city's master plan was completed and published, and when the Workers Party was voted out of office, the plan was put through the shredder. Also, Portuguese-language students may need some preparation for Brazilian slang words.

How to Use: In *Latin American Political Institutions* classes I could use this film for its description of typical urbanization problems; it provides vivid illustrations of the existence and consequences of the issues it addresses. It also provides an example of how media campaigns can be used to develop political viewpoints. Because this film represents the perspective of a left-wing administration that held power in São Paulo for only one term, it could also serve as a trigger for discussion of continuity/discontinuity in politics. Finally, in its cry for public participation in urban planning, it raises questions about the viability and utility of public debate. (Browne)

I could imagine using the tape in my *Modern Latin American History* course or in one of the *Latin American Culture* courses taught in the Foreign Languages Department. (McCreery)

In *Communications* classes it can be used as an example of innovative ways to make public service media.

Suggested Readings: Keck, Margaret. *PT: a lógica da diferença: o Partido do Trabalhadores na construção da democracia brasileira.*

Local Brazilian publications: *A folha de São Paulo; Veja.*
Level: University

ALTO A LOS INCENDIOS FORESTALES (Halting the Fires)

Documentary. With Subtitles. 52 min. 1990
Directed by: Octavio Bezerra (Ladeira do Ascurra 143, Rio de Janeiro 22241; tel: [5521] 285-2386)
Produced by: Channel Four TV
Distributed by: Filmmakers Library
Evaluators: Osvaldo Chinchón, Carlos A. Pérez, Carolyn Shapiro
Description: This is one of the most informative and complete accounts of the tragic deforestation of the Amazon, where 20 million hectares of virgin forest are burned each year. The tape shows the growing number of religious and intellectual leaders who are raising their voices to protest this ecological disaster. It also shows how Indian leaders, such as the Yanomami, resent the presence of white men, who have come to "bring progress" and to clear the Amazonian jungle for their selfish pursuits: to build dams, construct highways, create huge cattle ranches, and exploit and corrupt the Indians. The relationship between cattle ranching and deforestation is explained. Cattle ranching is inefficient and is economically viable only because of large state subsidies; thus it is tied to urban bureaucracy, land speculation, and government-sponsored greed. Arguments from all sides are presented in interviews with the ranchers, union leaders, rubber tappers, indigenous leaders, priests, and government representatives. The tape also shows that the Brazilian government has finally come to realize that after more than twenty years of destruction of the virgin forest, the moment has

come to halt the devastation, not only for national concerns but also because of the global impact of such destruction. The video explores both the obstacles to halting the burning of the Brazilian rain forest and the possible solutions, such as extractive reserves.

Strengths and Weaknesses: This excellent tape is concise, complete, and consistently strong. It powerfully points out the greed of ranchers and big landowners who violently oppose the arrival of settlers wanting to escape the impoverished, miserable conditions in the urban centers of eastern Brazil.

Introducing the Tape: No introduction is necessary.

How to Use: I would use the tape as an example of the complex web of interactions between town and city, modern sectors and traditional ones, politics and ecology. I would also emphasize that local-level solutions to ecological and development problems are good but insufficient. Since causes and effects are distributed throughout a region and a nation, actions are always potentially structural. (Pérez)

There are numerous areas for discussion around issues of foreign debt, corporate controls, economic development, and human rights. I would have students take roles (an indigenous person, priest, squatter, government official, logger, or rancher) to develop views on the issue and in the role-playing ask students to develop possible solutions. Students could also look up information and report on the life of Chico Mendes and on any of the indigenous groups. (Shapiro)

Suggested Readings: See *Cultural Survival*'s list of papers, books, and magazines.

Level: High School—University

AMAZONIA: VOZES DA FLORESTA (Amazônia: Voices from the Rain Forest)

Documentary.   With Subtitles and English Narration.   70 min.   1991

Directed by: Monti Aguirre and Glen Switkes

Produced by: Amazônia Film Project/FX Cinema (P.O. Box 77438, San Francisco, CA 94107; tel: [510] 243-4146; fax: [510] 655-9115)

Distributed by: The Video Project

Evaluators: Carol Becker, Marc Chernick, María A. Lazarini, Marie Price, Jesikah María Ross, University of Pittsburgh Group (María Consuelo Acosta, John Frechione, Shirley A. Kregar, Nichole Parker, Lynn Young, José Zevallos)

Description: Through a creative blend of indigenous mythology, animation, interviews, and a plethora of scenic images, *Amazônia* gives voice to the different peoples who inhabit and work in this resource-rich region of northern Brazil. The film depicts the history and current living conditions of its inhabitants—the indigenous people, river dwellers, and landless and landed peasants. It explores the cross-pressures found among the native inhabitants and the settlers of the Brazilian rain forest. Examining the historical and present-day relationship between the indigenous people

and the "whites," the documentary stresses the impact of disease, loss of land, attempts at cultural integration, and mutual violence. The tape first portrays the indigenous viewpoint in contrast to the commercial exploitation represented by the rubber industry and the organized unions of rubber tappers. Then it moves beyond the traditional antinomies to show Indians' and rubber tappers' common interest in preventing large landowners from destroying the forests for cattle raising. The underlying theme of the film is how the destructive actions and policies towards Amazônia affect these people, the region, and the world.

Strengths and Weaknesses: *Amazônia* creatively tackles a broad subject with its innovative use of the traditional tools of documentary film. The program contains beautiful camera work with wonderful visual images of indigenous people using video cameras to document their own plight, gorgeous footage of the scenic environment, and historical clips of the rubber bean, and the growth of Manaus. The cinematography, combined with marvelous music, interviews, animation, and mythology, creates a video meant not to be comprehensive or linear, but rather evocative. The tape gives the viewer a well-rounded, balanced picture of the situation in Amazônia by revealing multiple points of view from distinct groups of people (indigenous, river dwellers, peasants, farmers, military, economists, etc.). It shows the indigenous people's deep sense of being one with nature and demonstrates the misunderstandings among different cultures and peoples and the problems of diverse languages. The tape takes a complex set of politics and moves beyond the usual clichés of "good indigenous culture/bad Western-Latin American capitalist culture." It educates viewers without drowning them in unfamiliar detail.

There is not, however, enough information on the conflicts between gold miners and Indians that have become so pronounced in the past few years. Gold mining is also causing severe ecological destruction. The tape also lacks sufficient geographical orientation. One reviewer thought that the tape was too much of a traditional narrative and not experimental enough. Another felt that it was a bit too long. At times, the voice-over can be difficult to understand because it is given by a nonnative English speaker. However, the use of a Brazilian (and a woman) lends the piece greater credibility and creativity, even though audiences may have to work harder to understand the words.

Introducing the Tape: No real introduction is necessary. Most Americans know enough about the subject, and the presentation is excellent and clear. However, the part with Chico Mendes should be updated with a footnote about his death.

How to Use: I am presently conducting a rain forest curriculum for which this tape would be ideal. It serves as a good example of how native populations can work together to fight the "big guys." The tape could illustrate to children who Chico Mendes was and what some of his ideas are and show actual images of deforestation and burning of forests to give them ideas about what they could do to help. (Lazarini)

For a course on *Amazônia* the video could be used in the first class as a general visual introduction to the region that illustrates the complexity of the situation. The course could then build on themes introduced by the tape. The tape could be shown again towards the end of the course and used for a wrap-up discussion. (University of Pittsburgh Group)

In *Environmental Studies* or *Development* courses the tape can be used in conjunction with other videos listed below to show different aspects of environmental and cultural disintegration in the Amazon.

Suggested Readings: Hecht, Susana, and Alexander Cockburn. *The Fate of the Forest: Developers, Destroyers, and Defenders of the Amazon.*

Schmink, Maríanne, and Charles H. Wood. *Contested Frontiers in Amazônia.*

Zak, Monica. *Salven mi selva.*

Complementary Films/Videos: *Alto a los encendios forestales (Halting the Fires)* (Brazil); *Balbina o marco da destruição (Balbina: Mark of Destruction)* (Brazil); *Crisis in Brazil: A Conversation with Nilson Araujo* (Brazil); *O espiritu da televisao (The Spirit of TV)* (Brazil); *O povo do veneno (The Poison People)* (Brazil); *Para onde? (Where to Now?)* (Brazil)

Level: Junior High School—University

ANTONIO DAS MORTES (Antonio das Mortes)

Feature.   With Subtitles.   100 min.   1968
Directed by: Glauber Rocha
Distributed by: Festival Films, IMRE Archive (available for viewing only)
Evaluators: Walter R. Adam, Patricia Aufderheide (excerpted from *Cross Cultural Film Guide*), Sidney M. Greenfield, Diane Marting, Michael Monteón
Description: This experimental feature film by Glauber Rocha is set in the poverty-stricken Brazilian northeast, in modern times. It refers to the power of landowners, bandits, and modern illusion in shaping the region. The action takes place in the *sertão,* the desertified northeast backlands, traditionally beyond the rule of law, and the site of some of Brazil's most enduring folklore. In the early years of the twentieth century, rebel leaders like Padre Cicero, Lampião, and Antonio Conselheiro fought the landowners and the political establishment on behalf of the poor and oppressed. In the tradition of Robin Hood, they robbed from the rich and gave to the poor. The landowners hired *jagunços* (paid killers) to stop the *cangaceiros* (bandits who became followers of the rebel leaders). This is a highly symbolic story of one paid killer, Antonio das Mortes. Das Mortes is a character from Rocha's earlier film *Black God, White Devil,* and the opening sequence reprises his earlier role. Das Mortes was called by a landowner to kill Coirana, the self-proclaimed successor of the celebrated bandit Lampião. When Coirana meets das Mortes, they have a long, choreographed fight, during which Coirana explains how he came to be a bandit. Coirana dies, transferring his mantle to das Mortes, who then meets a band of rebels he had wronged earlier and takes their side.

Strengths and Weaknesses: With vivid, poignant images, the film powerfully portrays the struggle between the landless and the landowners in the *sertão*. The directing is fascinating, and the story, folk music, costumes, and acting are excellent. The film has won numerous awards at international festivals.

One reviewer felt that the tape was too long and elliptical for most U.S. students and thus would have limited appeal without a thorough introduction. The subtitles and song lyrics are difficult to follow.

Introducing the Tape: An introduction to Rocha's rhetorical directing style and to the history of the *cangaceiros* is necessary. It is important to discuss the relationship between the *cangaceiros* and the *beatas* (religious fanatics); the complex symbolism of Rocha (the blind landowners, bandits, saints used in the film), and the history and socioeconomic realities of the region.

Viewers should be told that this experimental feature film by Glauber Rocha (a genius of Brazil's *Cinema Novo*) reflects Rocha's political and aesthetic goals to create a cinematic expression of what he saw as the central dilemma of Brazilian culture: to find its identity, given the contradictions of a colonialist heritage and the realities of underdevelopment. (Aufderheide)

How to Use: I would use this film with readings on Lampião or in combination with some of the excellent short documentaries on the *cangaceiros* that are available. I would treat it as historical fiction. (Marting)

In a *Twentieth-Century Latin America* class the film could be used as an example of the region's modernity. This is an artsy film and it cannot be used as an example of actual life in Brazil. (Monteón)

Suggested Readings: Aufderheide, Patricia. *Cross Cultural Film Guide.*

Cunha, Euclides da. *Rebellion in the Backlands.*

Freyre, Gilberto. *Order and Progress: Brazil from Monarchy to Republic.*

Any standard history or description of the Brazilian northeast.

Complementary Films/Videos: *Deus e o diabo na terra do sol (Black God, White Devil)* (Brazil)
Level: University

ARAPUÃ: AZUCRINANDO NAS ESCOLAS

Documentary.   Without Subtitles.   16 min.   1992
Directed & Produced by: TV Viva-Centro Luiz Freire (Rua São Bento 344, Ribeira 53110, Olinda PE; tel: [5581] 429-4109; fax: [5581] 429-4881)
Distributed by: IMRE Archive (available for viewing only)
Evaluators: David William Foster, Brian Goldfarb, Tânia M. Hering, Enríque R. Rodríguez, Irwin Stern
Description: This documentary examines the lamentable state of public education in Brazil and highlights the student

and teacher protests against the Collar government's proposal to privatize segments of the educational system. *Arapuã* is an organized movement with the purpose of improving schools in every way possible: curriculum, facilities, faculty, attendance, and organization. The tape contrasts traditional public schools with the more conducive environments and creative pedagogical approach used in an alternative community-based school. Much like the alternative school it presents, the video's pedagogical approach is hybrid; it incorporates music, dance, and a variety of documentary strategies to get its point across. It is an excellent example of Paolo Freire's "pedagogy of the oppressed."

Strengths and Weaknesses: This informative and enjoyable tape contains powerful visuals of bad conditions in the school, such as overcrowded classrooms and bathrooms in disrepair. It presents alternative pedagogical methods and philosophy combined with documentation of student demonstrations that provide positive models for affecting change. The tape is an appropriate length, conducive to classroom use, and includes good music with lyrics that talk about problems.

Introducing the Tape: It would be helpful to have background on the politics of education in Brazil, including the Arapuã movement to improve the schools and the areas in which it operates. Instructors could explain that TV Viva is a community-based production group that makes short documentary reports on local social issues and culture. Its tapes are not broadcast on television but are shown weekly on a large screen set up in the town plaza. Local residents watch the tapes and discuss the isssues raised. TV Viva's videos are used to stimulate residents to take direct action to deal with the common problems they face.

How to Use: The program could be used in a *Portuguese Language* course where the study of colloquial speech could have some language practice value. (Foster)

I would screen this tape along with other tapes that document related interventions in U.S. school systems (e.g., Frederik Wiseman's *High School-2,* a tape about Principal Debbie Meyer's Central Park East school in New York City) and follow up with discussion comparing and contrasting school reform movements in differing cultural, institutional, and political contexts. (Goldfarb)

In *Communication* courses it could be used to demonstrate how video can be used as a tool to organize communities to work to solve problems in their society. It can also be used thematically when comparing issues that concern people universally. (Rodríguez)

This is an excellent example of how a video can serve as an organizing tool for teachers' and parents' groups and can also be used in *Teacher Education* classes.

In *Education* class it would stimulate discussion of various approaches to pedagogy, as well as how communities can affect the quality of the education offered.

Suggested Readings: Agosta, Diana. "Mo' Better News: A Discussion on Media Education."

Brookfield, Stephen. "Media Power and Literacy."

Elsworth, Elizabeth and Marianne Whatley, eds. *The Ideology of Images in Educational Media: Hidden Curriculums in the Classroom.*

Fine, Michelle. *Framing Dropouts: Notes on the Politics of an Urban Public High School.*

Freire, Paulo. *Pedagogy of the Oppressed.*

Goldfarb, Brian. "Video Activism and Critical Pedagogy: Sexuality at the End of the Rainbow."

Gordan, Beverly M. "The Necessity of African American Epistemology for Educational Theory and Practice."

Mattelart, Michele, and Armand Mattelart. *The Carnival of Images: Brazilian Television Fiction.*

Schwoch, James, Mimi White, and Susan Reilly. *Media Knowledge: Readings in Popular Culture, Pedagogy, and Critical Citizenship.*

Complementary Films/Videos: Frederik Wiseman's *High School-2.*

Level: High School—University

AXE DE FALA (Talking Strong Vibes)

Music Video.   English Voice-over.   3 min.   1991

Directed & Produced by: TV Viva-Centro Luiz Freire (Rua São Bento 344, Ribeira 53110, Olinda PE; tel: [5581] 429-4109; fax: [5581] 429-4881)

Distributed by: IMRE

Evaluators: Mary Jane Craver, Victor Garatea, Tânia M. Hering, Irwin Stern

Description: Musician Waldir Afonxa presents a music video of his new song "Axé de fala," attempting to place it within Afro-Brazilian contexts and Pernambucan culture. With simple yet extremely well-done video techniques, the music video is a stunning visualization of the culture and the song. Interspersed throughout are scenes of Afro-Brazilian cultural rituals: *capoeira, berimbau,* and *afoxé.* Afonxa discusses *afoxé* not only as a religious movement but also as a contemporary Afro-Brazilian way of thinking.

Strengths and Weaknesses: The video presents Afro-Brazilian folklore, music, and dance. The music and technical quality are excellent. One evaluator felt that a few scenes moved too quickly.

Introducing the Tape: The video includes an introduction, but some more background on Afro-Brazilian culture and religion would be helpful.

How to Use: In *Portuguese Language* classes I would have my students learn the words to the music, and we would sing it together. In *Adult Education,* as part of a *Social Studies* course we would watch and discuss students' feelings about their African heritage and hopefully inspire some to want to visit Africa, Brazil, and other parts of the world. (Craver)

I would use the tape in addition to course work, as an audiovisual experience where students would learn about Brazilian culture and some aspects of its folklore. (Hering)

This music video would work well in a section on *Afro-Brazilian Culture.* It brings together many of the character-

istics of the culture that are essential: dance, religion, and how they are popularized to be maintained. (Stern)
Suggested Readings: Simpson, George E. *Black Religions in the New World.*
Level: Junior High School—University

BAIRRO DO RECIFE A DANÇA DA VIDA

Documentary.   Without Subtitles.   26 min.   1989
Directed & Produced by: TV Viva-Centro Luiz Freire (Rua São Bento 344, Ribeira 53110, Olinda PE; tel: [5581] 429-4109; fax: [5581] 429-4881)
Distributed by: IMRE Archive (available for viewing only)
Evaluators: John Chasteen, Mary Jane Craver, William Herzog
Description: The growth and demise of Old Town in Recife (the capital of the state of Pernambuco) is chronicled through interviews with present-day inhabitants of the quarter and visitors to the area. Workers, housewives, bartenders, academicians, and prostitutes discuss the economic woes, cultural shifts, history, and past glories of Recife and its need for "revitalization." The tape includes a recorded session of the Preservation Committee working for urban renewal. There are also shots of the district from the air and the water, including many crumbling historic buildings.
Strengths and Weaknesses: The tape features great video footage and music and is most notable for its motley cast of colorful characters.

Not much historical information is provided, and contrastic photos are wanting. One reviewer felt that the presentation was not clear enough; there was too much attention given to the role of prostitution in the district, too little to institutions such as theaters or shops, and too much footage depicting the city as depressed, although it is still an exciting area. Another felt that some of the interviews were a bit tedious.
Introducing the Tape: Some background, including the historical event of the *Guerra dos Mascates,* should be explained to U.S. audiences, as the film refers to it in places. Viewers could be told that in 1711 this was a Brazilian independence movement in the Pernambuco state, in the northeast of the country, against the Portuguese. The Mascates were businessmen who opposed paying taxes.
How to Use: The tape could provide an interesting perspective on urban problems in the Third World. The decay of central cities is not usually cited as one of those problems. In addition, this program might be useful as a view of contemporary Brazil, although the matters it addresses are not staple items in courses on Brazil. In my *History of Brazil* course I might use it to give students a few images of Recife, a historically important city that rarely appears on film. Because the *Guerra dos Mascates* is mentioned, I might have my students read the chapter of that event in Charles Boxer's book. (Chasteen)

I could use this in an adult beginning *Portuguese* class provided I disclaimed the gloominess beforehand. (Craver)

Suggested Readings: Boxer, Charles. *The Golden Age of Brazil: 1695–1750 Growing Pains of a Colonial Society,* about the *Guerra dos Mascates.*
Level: University

BALBINA: O MARCO DA DESTRUIÇÃO (Balbina: Mark of Destruction)

Documentary.   English Voice-Over.   26 min.   1990
Directed by: Luis Fernando Santoro
Produced by: TV dos Trabalhadores (Rua Ouvidor Peleja 112, Saúde São Paulo, SP, CEP 04128-000; tel: [5511] 5589-2208; fax: [5511] 275-6318)
Distributed by: IMRE
Evaluators: Kendall W. Brown, Paolo Carpignano, Warren J. Dean, Miguel Huarcaya, Vincent D. Iacovelli
Description: This documentary describes the environmental destruction caused by the building of a large-scale hydroelectric power dam near Manaus, in the Amazon region of Brazil. Manaus lured many businesses to the area with tax incentives. The capital-intensive, rather than labor-intensive, industries required large amounts of electricity, so the government decided to build the disastrous Balbina dam. Not only is the electricity produced by the dam not economical (the project cost many millions of dollars, far more than planned, and suffered numerous delays due to poor construction and corruption), but the dam's output is insufficient to meet the needs of the industries (mostly multinationals). From a social and ecological point of view, the project has been a complete disaster. The submersion of thousands of acres of forest resulted in the production of toxic substances that are destroying the rivers and the livelihood of the local inhabitants, dislocating the indigenous populations, and transforming the ecological balance of the region.
Strengths and Weaknesses: This excellent, well-documented, and straightforward analysis presents opinions from both sides of the conflict and clearly illustrates the present situation of the Indians. The camera work is good, and images complement the narration. The tape's relatively short length allows for introductory remarks and postviewing discussion.

Some reviewers felt that the editing and choice of music could have been better.
Introducing the Tape: Viewers should be told that the tape was made by the Workers Party television unit, made up of volunteer independent filmmakers and videomakers. The tape brings together material shot by many different local crews. It provides its own clear introduction, but some discussion of the economic consequences of development projects in Latin America in general could be presented to U.S. viewers. Students would benefit from more information about the state of the environment before the dam was built and the struggles of the Brazilian environmental movement.
How to Use: In *History of Modern Latin America* I spend considerable time on development issues. This video would be useful when we talk about post-World War II attempts

at modernization. I would also have a discussion after the video, dealing with the ideological perspective of the film. (Brown)

The tape could be used in courses on *Brazil's History* to illustrate the subject of environmental disasters. (Dean)

I would use this film to show the class, social, cultural, and economic problems associated with the building of a new hydroelectric plant. (Iacovelli)
Level: University

BEJO NA BOCA (A Kiss on the Mouth)
Documentary.   With Subtitles.   30 min.   1987
Directed by: Jacira Melo
Distributed by: Women Make Movies
Evaluators: Sarah Chambers, Robert DiAntonio, Tânia M. Hering, Christine List
Description: In informative interviews, prostitutes on the streets of São Paulo discuss several issues: how they got into prostitution, their families, health, AIDS, sex, drugs, crime, and their experiences with the police. Interspersed are scenes of the red-light districts of São Paulo and popular music about "the life." The tape does not glamorize the subject but gives the women an opportunity to speak about their own lives.
Strengths and Weaknesses: The women's interviews are very interesting and reflect a variety of perspectives and personalities. Most seem independent and speak about their work matter-of-factly. The tape does not make moral judgments or take a superior attitude toward the women. The Portuguese is well translated into English.

A few reviewers felt that the tape did not provide an insightful look at prostitution. The sad content lacks depth and story vision and moves quickly from one topic to the next.
Introducing the Tape: The tape needs to be put into the context of the social situation in Brazil. Teachers may want to mention that the tape approaches a serious topic in an apparently lighthearted fashion. Only toward the end do the women mention the hardships of being a prostitute.
How to Use: I would use the tape as part of a discussion of contemporary urban women and the choices they make about their lives. (Chambers)

I would use this in a *Feminist Film* course and compare it with other films on prostitution such as *Working Girls* (distributed by Facets). In a *Latin American Media* course it could be used as an example of testimonial documentary filmmaking. (List)
Suggested Readings: Martinez, Oscar J. "Soledad fuente," in *The Human Tradition in Latin America: The Twentieth Century,* eds. William H. Beezley and Judith Ewell, 195–206, testimony of a Mexican prostitute.

Patai, Daphne. *Brazilian Women Speak: Contemporary Life Stories.*

Local Brazilian publications: *Jornal do Brasil; Manchete; O Globo; Veja.*

Complementary Films/Videos: Working Girls
Level: High School—University

BENEDITA DA SILVA (Benedita da Silva)
Documentary.   With Subtitles.   30 min.   1991
Directed by: Eunice Gutman
Produced by: Cinequanon, Ltda. & Iser Video (Rua Prf Ant. María Teixeira 120, Leblon, Rio de Janeiro; tel: [5521] 259-1114)
Distributed by: The Cinema Guild
Evaluators: Reid Andrews, Susana Conde, Darién J. Davis, Robert Haskett, Tânia M. Hering, Rosangela Vieira King
Description: This documentary describes the life and struggles of Benedita da Silva, a black, female resident of the shantytown Chapeu Mangueira, who was reelected in the fall of 1990 as federal deputy to represent Rio de Janeiro in Brasilia. Benedita (Bene) defends the rights of black people in Brazil, speaks against racism, and fights for improved living quarters and more job opportunities for residents of Rio's *favelas* (slums). Bene and an old black *favela* dweller who has known her since childhood narrate the story. We learn Bene was mischievous but bright and worked hard to buy herself a house, a telephone, and an old car. She now divides her life between Brasilia and Rio and devotes herself first to the plight of the women slum dwellers and, second, to all the other concerns of the workers of her area. The old woman, a daughter and granddaughter of slaves, tells us that slavery has not ended but has taken a new shape: while there are no whips, the rights of blacks to schooling, work, and good living conditions are deferred or denied. For Benedita there is no difference between her religious and political fervor; and the people of her district feel that Bene is, indeed, a blessing. While the film centers around Benedita's reelection campaign in 1990 (which she ultimately won), it goes far beyond this, providing a vivid look at life in the *favela,* street children, and racism in Brazil.
Strengths and Weaknesses: The documentary does a good job of portraying the grassroots movement that Benedita started and shows that her people and those closely associated with her are truly engaged. The tape creatively intermingles popular and political culture; the camera work is beautiful, and the songs are particularly impressive. The interviews with Benedita and other *favela* dwellers, intercut with compelling footage, help dispel many "myths" about such urban slums; it is clear that, though many outsiders view these impoverished people as unemployed, lazy "bandits," most of them (99 percent according to this film) are workers. Also significant is the hard-hitting look at racism in Brazil, which is linked to the institution of slavery. Important issues such as the traditional lack of government sensitivity to the poor are also covered. Benedita, a Pentecostal, puts a much more positive spin than one usually gets on the ways in which this sect is attempting to help the poor help themselves. Finally, the tape sends a powerful message about the ways in

which political awareness and activism can empower people like Benedita, her supporters, and her neighbors.

The tape, however, only whets the appetite of the viewer who wants to see what progress has been made in the fight for the rights of blacks in Brazil and which methods might be more effective in achieving those goals. Besides the degree of awareness of the problems confronted, there is no indication of more concrete fruits of Benedita's struggle. Therefore, the viewer remains in doubt as to whether things have truly improved in Brazil in the areas of racism and the historical lack of representation for the black population (51 percent). Also, one does not get a sense of how Benedita is accepted or regarded within the political system; the film focuses only on the positive. One evaluator felt that the narration was a bit confusing at times.

Introducing the Tape: Viewers should be provided with some information about the history of Brazil and the cultural heritage of the population, with emphasis on class struggles and on the condition of black women in Brazilian society. An introduction to the conservative nature of Brazilian politics would be useful, as would information about the Workers Party to which Benedita belongs and the process of redemocratization in which she is taking part. Audiences who have not been exposed to issues of urban poverty and racism in Brazil might benefit from some brief background explaining what *favelas* are, where they are located, etc. Issues of racism and slavery are probably self-evident, but it might be good to remind the audience that slavery persisted in Brazil until the end of the nineteenth century. It might be wise to note that there is a general perception in this country that racism is relatively weak in Brazil, since the film presents a different reality.

How to Use: I would use this film in my course on *Afro-Latin America* in the segment on race relations in modern Brazil. (Andrews)

I teach *History* and would use this in the context of urban culture and grass roots to show how collective action can lead to positive results for a community. Despite the conservative, elite white political culture, grass roots progressive politicians such as Benedita can overcome barriers of race, class, and gender. (Davis)

I would use this film in the twentieth-century section of the *Latin American Survey.* I already cover the problem of urban poverty and squatter settlements in this course, using the *favelas* of Brazil as an extended example. This film would be an excellent complement to readings, lectures, and a writing assignment I often present. In them, I highlight the myth of the "lazy bandit" slum dweller, and stress such issues as racism, women's activism, and the like. (Haskett)

I would use this tape to generate discussion and illustrate issues pertaining to racial relations in Brazilian society, or to discuss the condition of poor women in a Third World society. Readings should be assigned on this topic (the realities of racism in Latin America and Brazil) before showing the tape, and then the topics covered should be opened for wide discussion. (Vieira King)

Suggested Readings: Alvarez, Sonia E. *Engendering Democracy in Brazil: Women's Movements in Transition Politics.*

Andrews, George Reid. *Blacks and Whites in São Paulo, Brazil, 1888–1988.*

Bacha, Edmar L., and Herbert S. Klein, eds. *Social Change in Brazil, 1945–85; The Incomplete Transition.*

Black, Jan Knippers, ed. *Latin America. Its Problems and Its Promise.*

Carneiro, Sueli, and Thereza Santos. *Mulher negra: politica governamental e a mulher.*

Fernandes, Florestan. *The Negro in Brazilian Society.*

Galeano, Eduardo. *Open Veins of Latin America. Five Centuries of the Pillage of a Continent.*

Green, Duncan. *Faces of Latin America.*

Hahner, June E. *Emancipating the Female Sex: The Struggle for Women's Rights in Brazil, 1850–1940.*

Hahner, June E. *Poverty and Politics: The Urban Poor in Brazil, 1870–1920.*

Hasenbalg, Carlos Alfredo, *Race Relations in Post-Abolition Brazil: The Smooth Preservation of Racial Inequalities.*

Humphrey, John. *Gender and Work in the Third World: Sexual Divisions in Brazilian Industry.*

Ireland, Rowan. *Kingdoms Come: Religion and Politics in Brazil.*

Jesus, Carolina María de. *Child of the Dark: The Diary of Carolina María de Jesus,* for another perspective on race, class, and gender in Brazil.

Landes, Ruth. *The City of Women.*

Moraes, María Quartim de. *Mulheres em movimento: o balanco da década da mulher do ponto de vista do feminismo, das religiões e da política.*

O'Gorman, Frances. *Morro mulher.*

Patai, Daphne. *Brazilian Women Speak: Contemporary Life Stories.*

Perlman, Janice E. *The Myth of Marginality: Urban Poverty and Politics in Rio de Janeiro.*

Perlman, Janice E. *Portrait of the People: Migrants to Rio de Janeiro.*

Skidmore, Thomas. *Black Into White: Race and Nationality in Brazilian Thought.*

Skidmore, Thomas E., and Peter H. Smith. *Modern Latin America.*

Toplin, Robert Brent. *Freedom and Prejudice: The Legacy of Slavery in the United States and Brazil.*

Local Brazilian publications: *Isto É, Jornal do Brasil, Veja.*
Level: High School—University

BOLA NA TRAVE

News Report.　Without Subtitles.　17 min.　1990
Directed & Produced by: TV Viva-Centro Luiz Freire (Rua São Bento 344, Ribeira 53110, Olinda PE; tel: [5581] 429-4109; fax: [5581] 429-4881)
Distributed by: IMRE Archive (available for viewing only)

Evaluators: Mary Jane Craver

Description: Does Brazilian soccer par excellence have a future? The vacant areas or neighborhood lots where Brazilians have naturally developed their prowess in the past are disappearing, as they are closed off and used for other purposes. Much Brazilian talent will go untapped as the soccer fields vanish, and only those who can afford to go to soccer training clubs will be able to develop their skills for recruitment.

Strengths and Weaknesses: This tape's strength is the interviews with diverse nationally known soccer players who started out playing this way.

The tape assumes background knowledge about Brazil.

Introducing the Tape: U.S. viewers need context about different geographical locations in Brazil, the Brazilian lifestyle, and the distinction between rich and poor in the country. Introductory comments should also include the importance and popularity of the sport in the country and the encroachment of economic development on the people's space. This could be related to similar growth in the United States and its negative impact on the quality of U.S. life.

How to Use: I would explain the migration of the rural poor to the city and the space taken by their new abodes, along with the razing of the areas for so-called urban development. Soccer is a healthful form of recreation for the urban poor, but even that is being taken away from them, along with the opportunity to "make it big" for some kids who could grow naturally in the sport. I would also use this film to expose the students to different players' accents, as those interviewed did not all come from the same regions of Brazil. (Craver)

Level: Junior High School—University

BYE BYE BRAZIL

Feature.   With Subtitles.   110 min.   1980

Directed by: Carlos Diegues

Produced by: Carnaval Film

Distributed by: IMRE

Evaluators: Robert Alvarez, Thomas O. Bente, Susana Conde, Roger P. Davis, Robert DiAntonio

Description: Set in the 1970s, this film follows a small-time carnival and its chief performers, Solome and Rolidei, as they travel across the northeast and interior of Brazil. A young man and his pregnant wife join the troupe and experience a series of picaresque adventures. The troupe falls on hard times, as television replaces live entertainment, and they set off for Altamira, seeking the gold-mining town located deep in the interior. Altamira turns out to be fully commercialized, complete with television. Rolidei loses the carnival in a gambling match there. The young man is briefly tempted to allow his wife to enter into prostitution, but he eventually goes with her to Brasilia, where they settle and raise a family. Years later, Rolidei, Solome, and the carnival return and beckon the man to rejoin and head to Rondonia. He and his wife reject the offer, choosing to stay with responsibility and family.

Strengths and Weaknesses: This film presents a provocative look at a country in transition and the changing of material culture. The circus, symbolically displaced by television, and the Indian family, whose obsession is to ride on an airplane, speak to the dissonance in modernization and rapid change. As an allegory the film stresses the carnivalesque in Brazilian (or any) society, as the inevitable perversion of traditional values plays against the stability, however fragile, of conventional institutions. The utopian promise of the interior and the corruption or salvation of Brasilia are central Brazilian themes. The film allow viewers to experience the social conditions of the region by showing the destruction of the rain forest, the displacement of the indigenous people, poverty, and the lack of education. One reviewer felt that *Bye Bye Brazil* was one of the best films to come from Brazil. It has clear subtitles and spoken language.

One reviewer saw little explicit social commentary in the film, feeling that it was primarily a sexual, farcical romp. Another evaluator felt that the film was long and the story line and characters were abstract. The film contains scenes with sexual activity, making it inappropriate for use in high school classes.

Introducing the Tape: One evaluator felt that the film existed on many levels and needed no contextual introduction. Another felt that the story line should be outlined. Some information about the history of the region and the cultural heritage of the population, the plight of the Indian in Brazil, the *sertão,* Altamira, Rondonia, the significance of Brasilia, and the frontier theme in Brazilian history, as well as the role of U.S. interests in the Amazon, would benefit viewers. Also a brief introduction to *Cinema Novo* should be part of the preparation for the screening. College students need to be advised that the film contains much explicit sex.

How to Use: I would use the film to illustrate the general dissonance caused by the advent of development and the introduction of technology. The characters display stereotypic gender roles set in a Latin American context. (Alvarez)

The film is good as an enhancement for an advanced *Portuguese Language* course. It is full of Brazilian slang and vulgarities. (Bente)

In teaching the reconfigurations of family and nation through the study of *Latin American Film,* I would focus first on the history of Brazil, paying particular attention to the role of Europeans and blacks, and what influence they had on the lives of the native Brazilians. U.S. interests in Brazil would constitute an interesting focus of class discussions. Questions involving the history of Brazilian cinema, particularly the period of *Cinema Novo* and subsequent developments, would be explored. (Conde)

As the film is long for classroom use, I would use it as a special presentation for extra credit. Students would view the film toward the end of a class on *Brazil* or *Latin American Studies* and write an essay attempting to draw the themes of history and culture from the film. (Davis)

Suggested Readings: Black, Jan Knippers, ed. *Latin America. Its Problems and Its Promise.*

Burns, E. Bradford. *A History of Brazil.*

Cunha, Euclides da. *Rebellion in the Backlands.*

Freyre, Gilberto. *Order and Progress: Brazil From Monarchy to Republic.*

Galeano, Eduardo. *Open Veins of Latin America. Five Centuries of the Pillage of a Continent.*

Green, Duncan. *Faces of Latin America.*

Johnson, Randal. "Film, Television and Traditional Folk Culture in *Bye Bye Brazil.*"

King, John. *Magical Reels: A History of Cinemas in Latin America.*

Poppino, Rollie. *Brazil: The Land and the People.*

Skidmore, Thomas E., and Peter H. Smith. *Modern Latin America.*

Stam, Robert. *Subversive Pleasures. Bakhtin, Cultural Criticism, and Film.*

Worcester, Donald. *Brazil: Colony to World Power.*

Level: University

UM CABRA MARCADO PARA MORRER (Twenty Years Later)

Documentary.   With Subtitles.   119 min.   1984
Directed by: Eduardo Coutinho
Produced by: CECIP—Centro de Criação de Imagem Popular (Rua Sanador Dantas 80–201, Rio de Janeiro; tel: [5521] 533-0772)
Distributed by: The Cinema Guild
Evaluators: Ana Carolina Castillo-Crimm, John Hess, Sheldon Maram, Cliff Welch

Description: This is an intriguing look back at the peasant movement and its student supporters before Brazil's military coup d'état of 1964. Director Eduardo Coutinho, at that time a radical student filmmaker, set out to make a docudrama about the murder of a famous peasant leader, João Pedro, in the impoverished northeast. He worked with João Pedro's colleagues, friends, and widow, Elizabeth Teixeira. Shortly after they began filming, however, the military took power and forced the filmmakers to leave the countryside. Elizabeth Teixeira went into hiding, and her many children were scattered about, left with relatives and friends. Almost twenty years later, as the power of the dictatorship was waning, Coutinho returned to look for Elizabeth, her family, and the people with whom he originally worked.

In *Um cabra marcado para morrer* Coutinho juxtaposes footage from his original film, documentary images from the peasant struggles in the northeast; and contemporary footage of many of the same people recounting what happened to them in the last two decades. But neither Elizabeth nor the children can be found. Coutinho documents his search for the family as one person leads him to another, and, piece by piece, the puzzle comes together. He eventually finds Elizabeth, who retains her vibrancy, passion, and ideals, though she has been ravaged by nearly twenty years of poverty and life underground. To protect her children, Elizabeth has had no contact with them. As Coutinho finds each of the now-grown children, he documents the family's reencounter. His film provides a powerful statement about the devastating effects of repressive governments on society, families, and individuals and how ideals can survive in spite of horrendous repression.

Strengths and Weaknesses: This is one of the great Latin American documentaries of the last few decades. The juxtaposition of fiction and documentary, of black-and-white historical footage and modern-day interviews in color, gives the filmmaker a powerful means of relating the past to the present. The tape tells an important and well-contextualized story about the human toll of Latin America's ongoing class struggle. It is very much about survival and the ideals that inspire people to keep going in spite of the odds against them. The interaction of the filmmaker with this story and his dedication in following it for twenty years are fascinating.

Evaluators felt that the film was a bit too long and included some repetitive interviews. One commented that the story of Teixeira was excellent and carefully woven into the script but that the detailed search to reunite the family was time-consuming and could cause confusion. Also, the framework of the story is difficult to understand; the film could use more detail about the peasant movement and the politics of its participants. The white-on-white subtitles are sometimes difficult to read.

Introducing the Tape: U.S. audiences could use information about pre- and post-1964 Brazil, including the rural labor movement, the student movement, and *Cinema Novo.*

How to Use: This is an interesting sociological study of a family in crisis and a view of the repression of labor movements. (Castillo-Crimm)

This work can be presented as a wonderful example of the *Brazilian Cinema* and as an experimental documentary. It is a terrific film. (Hess)

I would use the tape in a *Modern Brazilian History* class or a graduate seminar on *Rural Social Movements* to depict the enthusiasm of participants in the movements, the importance of urban supporters, the effects of military takeover on popular movements, and the importance of politics to Brazilian filmmakers. (Welch)

Suggested Readings: Burton, Julianne. *The Social Documentary in Latin America.*

Horowitz, Irving Louis. *Revolution in Brazil: Politics and Society in a Developing Nation.*

King, John. *Magical Reels: A History of Cinemas in Latin America,* has a section on Brazil, but does not mention this film.

Moraes, Clodomir. "Peasant Leagues of Brazil," in *Rural Social Moments in Latin America,* ed. Stavenhagen, R.

Skidmore, Thomas. *Politics in Brazil 1930–1964: An Experiment in Democracy.*

CAMISINHA (The Condom)

Documentary.   English Voice-over.   6 min.   1986
Directed by: Angela Freitas

Produced by: SOS Corpo (Rua Major Codeceira, 37 St. Amaro, 50100-070 Recife, PE; tel: [5581] 221-3018; fax: [5581] 221-3947)
Distributed by: IMRE
Evaluators: Brian Goldfarb, Tânia M. Hering
Description: This is an informative and humorous tape about condoms. Through a parody of conventional documentary and newscast genres, the tape presents an unbiased report on the condom. On-the-street interviews provide a variety of opinions and experiential accounts of condom use. Additionally, the tape presents practical information on condoms: where to buy them, how and why to use them, and more.
Strengths and Weaknesses: This is a community-based educational film that provides important information in an accessible and memorable way. Through its understated parody and personal testimony, the tape avoids dry and didactic approaches common to much educational health-care work. Importantly, condom use is presented as a social rather than medical or mechanical issue. The tape is a good length, and its format presents many opportunities for pausing to engage class or group discussion.

One reviewer felt that there were too many interviews.
Introducing the Tape: The tape is self-explanatory.
How to Use: I would use the film to discuss how alternative video groups in Brazil are appropriating and transforming mainstream genres for community education and advocacy. Viewing of this tape could be productively combined with other tapes on safer sex from Brazil, elsewhere in Latin America, and the United States (see Complementary Films/Videos). (Goldfarb)

In a *Health* class the tape could be used effectively with teenagers to discuss the issues of condom use and safe sex.
Suggested Readings: Boyle, Deirdre. "A Brief History of American Documentary Video," in *Illuminating Video: An Essential Guide to Video Art,* ed. Doug Hall and Sally Jo Fifer, 51–70.

Burton, Julianne. *Cinema and Social Change in Latin America: Conversations with Filmmakers.*

Burton, Julianne, ed. *The Social Documentary in Latin America.*

Machado, Arlindo. "Inside Out and Upside Down: Brazilian Video Groups TVDO and Olhar Electronic."

Pines, Jim, and Paul Wileman. *Questions of Third Cinema.*

Roncagliolo, Rafael. "The Growth of the Audio Visual Imagescape," in *Video the Changing World,* eds. Alain Ambrosi and Nancy Thede.

Saalfield, Catherine. "Pregnant with Dreams: Julia Barco's Visions from Latin America."

Santoro, Luiz Fernando. *A imagem nas mãos: o video popular no Brasil.*

Sarti, Ingrid. "Between Memory and Illusion: Independent Video in Brazil," in *Media and Politics in Latin America: The Struggle for Democracy,* ed. Elizabeth Fox, 157–63.

Complementary Films/Videos: *Safer Sex Shorts* (distributed by Gay Men's Health Crisis); Alex Juhasz and Juanita Mohammed's *We Care: A Video for Care Providers of People Affected by AIDS.*
Level: High School—University

A CLASSE QUE SOBRA

Documentary.   Without Subtitles.   34 min.   1985
Directed by: Peter Overbeck
Distributed by: CDI, IMRE Archive (available for viewing only)
Evaluators: Reid Andrews, George P. Browne, John Hays, David McCreery
Description: With extensive interviews, this documentary examines the lives of *bóias frias* (day-wage workers) in the sugarcane fields of northern São Paulo State, focusing especially on the situation of women. The tape discusses the growth of the *usina* (sugar factory system from the sugar plantations of the nineteenth century) and shows how expansion of cane production for alcohol has destroyed alternative forms of agriculture in the area. The tape begins by showing conditions in which the cane workers live and work and the problems they face: poverty, malnutrition, miserable housing, and lack of education due to the need for children to work. It then follows the efforts of workers from Guariba, São Paulo, to obtain basic urban services for their neighborhood (water, electricity, schools, better housing) and improved working conditions on the plantations and in the local sugar mill. It documents an apparently successful strike of the *bóias frias* against the sugar mills. The employers threaten to blacklist workers and replace them with mechanization and migrant workers from other states. The tape's unsentimental conclusion is that workers must continue to organize and seek agrarian reform that will give *caboclo* (rural people) access to land for farming.
Strengths and Weaknesses: This is a convincing and effective film with a good mix of dialogue, commentary, music, and footage of the daily life of a social class of workers. The cane cutters themselves tell their story in simple, matter-of-fact tones. The contrast between workers and political organizers is evident in their language and appearance. In addition to depicting the conditions agricultural workers face, the film also shows them organizing and mobilizing to change those conditions. They are portrayed as active agents rather than passive victims.

Knowledge of Third World poverty systems and familiarity with the events reported are assumed; there are no explanations about the strike, the worker rebellion and its repression, or the political conditions within which the events took place. The tape's language and assumptions are of class struggle, without room for accommodation or compromise. The film prettifies participants and scenery somewhat, and abbreviates the politicization process among the workers. The Portuguese language is sometimes unclear, even to native speakers.

Introducing the Tape: Viewers need a brief outline of the geography and events, and a discussion of the language of political organization and confrontation. They should be told that a moderate version of agrarian reform was passed by the Brazilian Congress in 1985, but has been largely unimplemented.

How to Use: I would focus class discussion on: (1) the problems these workers face; (2) how those problems are connected to Brazil's history and current situation of plantation agriculture; and (3) what workers are doing to change those conditions. (Andrews)

The program would be useful in *Latin American Political Institutions* class to illustrate the problems of rural and migrant labor, illiteracy, and the persistence of poverty. It can also be used for the study of the language of political attitudes, dialogue, and confrontation, and to reinforce appreciation of the complexity of contemporary development problems. (Browne)

I would use this as an example that the poor of the world will organize vis-à-vis governments unwilling to listen. (Hays)

I would introduce this tape into the discussion about women in agricultural labor in my *Modern Latin American History* course. (McCreery)

Suggested Readings: Scheper-Hughes, Nancy. *Death without Weeping: The Violence of Everyday Life in Brazil.*

Stolcke, Verena. *Coffee Plantations, Workers and Wives: Class Conflict and Gender Relations on São Paulo Plantations, 1850–1980.*

Level: University

CLIPS OF LULA'S PRESIDENTIAL CAMPAIGN

Documentary. English Voice-Over. 5 min. 1989

Directed by: Luiz Fernando Santoro

Produced by: TV dos Trabalhadores (Rua Ouvidor Peleja 112, Saude-Sao Paulo, SP, CEP 04128-000; tel: [5511] 5589-2208; fax: [5511] 275-6318)

Distributed by: IMRE

Evaluators: Paolo Carpignano, Catherine Egan, David William Foster, Liss Jeffrey, Elizabeth Mahan

Description: A selection of clips from the television campaign of the Workers Party's presidential candidate, Luis Ignacio da Silva (Lula), in the 1989 election against Fernando Collor de Melo. This is an adulatory portrait of Lula, alternated with satirical skits and social commentary. There are excerpts of speeches, demonstrations, U.S.-style commercials, and musical endorsements.

Strengths and Weaknesses: The material is quite good and is seemingly effective campaign propaganda, including a wide range of strategies used by the Lula campaign to reach voters. The tape has historical significance and contains strong material for comparison with U.S. political ad campaigns. In retrospect, given the events that led to Collor's impeachment, the tape achieves an irony and poignancy.

The tape offers no context for U.S. viewers. Segments are reproduced without identifying the political figures or celebrity supporters featured in the advertisements. The clips of the various ads and speeches are separated by short blank spaces and at times there is a voice-over in English that explains what the ad is addressing. More often the pictures are left to speak for themselves. The video would be more effective if shown together with material from the Collor campaign.

Introducing the Tape: The tape needs much introduction and explanation for U.S. students about the candidate, the campaign, and the context of Brazilian politics. Viewers should be given information about the format of Brazilian political campaigns and told that public air time is allotted by law to each party. They should be informed that unlike Collor's campaign, which received large contributions from businesses, the Workers Party campaign had little money and relied on the volunteer labor of Brazil's independent video makers for the television campaign. This explains the "unorthodox" look of Lula's spots. The importance of music and musicians in Brazilian society should also be pointed out, for instance, the campaign theme song should be compared with the theme song of the *Escola de Samba* during Carnival.

Explanation of some of the content is also necessary. The many shots of Brazilian celebrities singing Lula's campaign song won't mean much to a non-Brazilian audience unfamiliar with Chico Buarque and the large number of soap opera actors. In addition, a number of acronyms for political organizations are dropped into the English voice-over, many of which are not explained. For example, the negative commercial against Collor cannot be understood without knowing who Sarney is and why he is depicted as the heir of the military regime.

Viewers should be updated and told that Lula ran again for the presidency in 1994, but was defeated.

How to Use: The tape could be used in comparative analysis in *Advertising* classes or *Political Science* courses that deal with political campaigns. (Carpignano)

I would discuss a unit on *Political Communication* in terms of the mass media and political system. I would intersperse political commercials of U.S. candidates and discuss the role of the television commercial, raise questions about the nature of political speech embodied in a commercial, and use the video to indicate similarities and differences in Latin America and in Brazil (with its own television tradition), and to encourage critical thinking. (Jeffrey)

In a *Video Production* class these clips could be shown with clips from U.S. campaigns to critically analyze the approach and impact on audiences. Students could then make short political clips of their own.

In a *Brazilian Political History* class these clips could be shown, pausing the tape at appropriate points to discuss the roles played by the various politicians mentioned.

Suggested Readings: Kottak, Conrad Phillip. *Prime-Time Society: An Anthropological Analysis of Television and*

Culture, 1990; students should do a critical reading of Kottak as well.

New York Times. "How Lula's TV Campaign Affected Rise in His Popularity."
Level: University

CONSTRUÇÃO DA ESCRITA

Documentary.   Without Subtitles.   41 min.
Directed by: Taunay M. Daniel
Produced by: Fundação Pan Desenvolvimiento (M. Salles, Gerente de Doc., Rua Rodolfo Miranda, 636-Bom, Retiro 01121, São Paulo; tel: [5511] 228-9493; fax: [5511] 228-1922)
Distributed by: IMRE Archive (available for viewing only)
Evaluators: Mary Jane Craver, Michael Shane, Antônio R. M. Simões
Description: This documentary deals with the process of children's literacy in Brazil, drawing on the work of Emilia Ferreiro (an Argentinian student of Piaget) and Ana Teberosky. The film observes five- to six-year-old children as they learn to write basic Portuguese. Several children are asked to write a series of words and then to read words that caption a picture. They all show the development of syllabic writing, which leads later to alphabetic writing. The theory presented in the tape reverses the traditional view of the literacy process. An early interpretation of missing letters in children's writing was that children were leaving out, or "swallowing," letters. The tape, based on the study of error patterns, asserts that children do not omit letters but actually add letters. Children represent syllables with one letter and gradually add more letters attempting to represent each phoneme (every consonant and vowel) in a word. The documentary invites teachers to allow children to make mistakes, have their own explanation of how letters represent words, and reason about the writing process. In Piaget's view, errors are necessary in the learning process. The tape contains entertaining and illuminating explanations from children themselves about how letters represent words.
Strengths and Weaknesses: The presentation is clear about its purpose; it is an attempt to explain how children understand written language as a representation of spoken language. The conception of how these children think and acquire the alphabet is pedagogically and linguistically interesting and valuable to educators. Whether or not one agrees with its view of how children understand the mechanics of writing, the presentation and interpretation of the facts are quite clear and accessible, even to nonspecialists.

One evaluator felt that the tape would have been more interesting if it had a better balance between longitudinal and cross-sectional cases. The facts are presented mostly in a cross-sectional approach, although one case is studied longitudinally over a period of a year. Another reviewer felt that the tape would have been more engaging if the format were more varied.
Introducing the Tape: To avoid confusion, audiences should be told that the children in the tape were enrolled in an experimental group as part of a special project by the Department of Education of São Paulo and had never before received formal training. This information is not given until the end of the tape. Also, it would be useful to give viewers a brief introduction to the work of Emilia Ferreiro, Ana Teberosky, and Jean Piaget.
How to Use: This would be an excellent tape for demonstration in a *Linguistics* or *Reading Education* course at college. It could also be shown to a beginning *Portuguese* class to hear the sounds pronounced by native speakers. (Craver)

The tape could be used as a first-day exercise in *Portuguese* conversation. The repetition and phonetics would be great training material. (Shane)

I would present the works of Emilia Ferreiro, Ana Teberosky, and Jean Piaget to the class, as well as another different view that studies the discursive aspect of child development. The documentary shows a study of isolated words, except for a few sentences at the end, in contrast to studies of children's discourse. Next, the audiences would see the film, preferably outside of class, and then discuss the topic in class. The discussion may have preliminary conversation in pairs, and then include the whole class. Once the topic is well understood, it would be interesting to ask the class to attempt their own investigation of the writing process. Some students in groups, pairs, or individually could study children of different ages and gather their data for a follow-up discussion in class. If the documentary is correct, the researchers should see a progression from syllabic to letter representation. The class, however, may independently find other results not discussed in the film. (Simões)
Suggested Readings: Ferreiro, Emilia. *Nuevas perspectivas sobre los procesos de lectura y escritura.*

Ferreiro, Emilia. *Proceso de alfabetización en proceso.*

Ferreiro, Emilia. *Les relations temporelles dans le langage de l'enfant.*

Ferreiro, Emilia, and Ana Teberosky. *Literacy before Schooling/Sistemas de escritura en el desarrollo del niño.*

Piaget, Jean. *Biology and Knowledge: An Essay on the Relations between Organic Regulations and Cognitive Processes.*

Piaget, Jean. *The Construction of Reality in the Child.*

Piaget, Jean. *The Early Growth of Logic in the Child: Classification and Seriation.*

Piaget, Jean. *The Essential Piaget.*

Piaget, Jean. *The Science of Education and the Psychology of the Child.*
Level: University

CONTRÁRIO AO AMOR

Documentary.   Without Subtitles.   13 min.   1986
Directed by: Jacira Melo
Produced by: Silvana Afram
Distributed by: IMRE Archive (available for viewing only)
Evaluators: Irene Matthews

Description: This short documentary is based on interviews with women involved with clients of the local organization for defense and support for battered women in São Paulo. Each interviewee is presented in extreme closeup, and the conversations cut around themes such as, "What is it like to sleep beside someone who beats you?" Interspersed are street shots of women going about their daily tasks who are also interviewed about men's/women's roles in marriage.

Strengths and Weaknesses: The tape presents a variety of opinions, including some quite conservative viewpoints and some strong clear opinions on both men's and women's rights. Some minimal statistics are provided.

The tape does not present a larger context for the situation of women in Brazil, nor any detail of local context.

Introducing the Tape: An introduction should provide both more general and local information, for example, some statistics on overall instances of domestic violence in Brazil, legal attitudes, etc.

How to Use: I would only use this tape as an example of a women's documentary with poignant and contrastive opinion. (Matthews)

Suggested Readings: Any general histories of women in Latin America or in Brazil.

Complementary Films/Videos: *Update Brazil* (Brazil)

Level: University

A COR DO SEXO

Documentary.   Without Subtitles.   50 min.   1989

Directed by: Sergio Melgaco

Distributed by: ABVP, IMRE Archive (available for viewing only)

Evaluators: Amanda Castro-Mitchell, Tânia M. Hering, Elizabeth Marchant, José-Manuel Navarro

Description: This documentary about race issues and sexuality in Brazil features a series of interviews with Brazilians of diverse social class, age, and gender. The tape reviews the status of race relations in the 1980s, looking at images of blacks in media, and preferences in sexual partners by blacks, mulattos, and whites in both marriage and prostitution. The documentary questions the myth of racial harmony in Brazil, showing that racial discrimination remains in Brazilian society. When asked, "Would you would have sex with a black person?" most black men said that they prefered white women; white women preferred white men; and white men preferred white women as wives and mulattas as lovers. The tape addresses social stereotypes about sexuality and race. It shows that mulattas are still seen by white males as exotic objects of pleasure and blacks are still very much discriminated against.

Strengths and Weaknesses: The video provides a thorough and honest examination of racial attitudes, especially in relation to sex and sexuality—a topic that many Brazilians skip over and courses on *Latin American Studies* rarely cover. It portrays some of the social conventions and stereotypes held by Brazilians about race and sexuality, and there is vivid and frank first-person commentary by a wide variety of people. The video includes people who are often left out, such as homosexuals, and shows how issues of race affect them.

Introducing the Tape: The tape requires an introduction to the present status of Brazilian black-white relations and the situation of Afro-Brazilians in Brazil's economy and society today. The introduction should also include a discussion of contemporary racism in Brazil.

How to Use: After presenting an introduction (as above) and assigning readings on the topic, I would ask students to write a response paper to the issues discussed in the film. They could relate the situation in Brazil to that in the United States. (Navarro)

Students could conduct a survey to see if attitudes in the United States are similar or different.

Suggested Readings: Barroso, Carmen, and Cristina Bruschini. "Building Politics from Personal Lives: Discussions on Sexuality among Poor Women in Brazil," in *Third World Women and the Politics of Feminism,* ed. Chandra Mohanty et al.

Degler, Carl N. *Neither Black nor White: Slavery and Race Relations in Brazil and the United States.*

Parker, Andrew, ed. *Nationalisms and Sexualities.*

Works by Jorge Amado, because of the treatment of the *mulatta* (see bibliography for selection).

The *Lusophone* literature (Brazilian) section of the Afro-American bibliography *Callaloo* published by Johns Hopkins University.

Level: High School—University

CORDEL (Cordel)

Animation.   No Dialogue.   6 min.   1983

Directed by: Daniel Alves

Produced by: Milton Zini Jr.

Distributed by: IMRE Archive (available for viewing only)

Evaluators: Mary Jane Craver, Tânia M. Hering, Jeff Lesser, Antônio R. M. Simões

Description: This is an animated film with music and no words that depicts the religious mysticism in the *sertão* (backlands) of Brazil, culminating in a June festival. It portrays the *cordel,* a popular rural printed story from northeast Brazil that mixes fact and fantasy and often messianic/religious overtones. The film presents the usual elements in *cordel:* stories and news, usually printed on inexpensive materials and hung along a rope for sale; the *cangaceiro* (the northeastern cowboy, bandit, or hero, often the equivalent of the southern gaucho); the figure and story of São Jorge (Saint George) in the moon killing the dragon; the *festas do Arraial* or *quadrilhas* (countryside celebrations during June); the *onca* (kind of jaguar or puma); and the *bumba-meu-boi* (literally, "beat my bull"), a popular dance led by a figure of a bull followed by a group parading and performing comic-dramatic stories.

Strengths and Weaknesses: The beautiful background music from the Brazilian northeast and the selection of representative elements and types from *cordel* are particularly strong and faithful to *cordel* style. Several aspects of folklore are presented in a short period of time. The presentation of the June festivals is very comprehensive.

Introducing the Tape: Without sufficient background, U.S. audiences might view the film as a cartoon. They should be presented with context about *cordel* and its role in Brazilian culture. An introduction to northeastern Brazil's history and how the people relate to God as a result of their environment and ethnic history would also be useful.

How to Use: In a *Portuguese Language* class we would read some *cordel* literature. Pictures of *sertão* events at which some *cordel* is spontaneously created would be shown. Brazilian history would be covered beforehand. Brazilian natives would be invited to explain symbols. (Craver)

Combined with a written explanation of Brazilian's folklore, I would show this tape to my students during language lab. (Hering)

Instructors could give a short lecture on rural life and show it in an advanced *Language* class. (Lesser)

In *Language* classes the students could create a *cordel*-style *feira* (fair) inside the classroom. Students would bring sweets, drinks, etc., for sale and make believe they buy things from each other. They can write page-long stories about any topic (the president, a teacher, a crime, an accident scene), draw illustrations, and, once their leaflets are prepared, hang them on a string for sale. (Simões)

Suggested Readings: Curran, Mark J. "A literatura de cordel antes e agura."

A literatura de cordel (also available in a bilingual Spanish-Portuguese anthology, *La literatura de cordel Brasileña*).

Maxado, Franklin. *O que é a literatura de cordel.*

Slater, Candace. "Literatura de Cordel and the Mass Media in Today's Brazil."

Slater, Candace. *Stories on a String: The Brazilian Literatura de Cordel.*

Level: High School—University

CRISIS IN BRAZIL: A CONVERSATION WITH ANDREA TONACCI

Documentary.   In English with Portuguese Portions Subtitled.   29 min.   1992
Directed by: Don Lynn and Catherine Benamou
Produced by: Don Lynn Productions
Distributed by: IMRE
Evaluators: Tânia M. Hering, Stephen P. O'Neill, Carlos A. Pérez, Carolyn Shapiro, University of Pittsburgh Group (María Consuelo Acosta, John Frechione, Shirley A. Kregar, Nichole Parker, Lynn Young, José Zevallos)
Description: Part of the *Crisis in Brazil* series, this half-hour segment is a conversation with Brazilian filmmaker Andrea Tonacci, who in the late 1970s started a series of films on the indigenous peoples of the Amazon. Tonacci talks about his contacts with indigenous peoples and reflects on film and

filmmaking as tools for empowering people whose voices don't usually carry outside of their own communities. Through Tonacci's film *Conversations in Maranhão*, the Canela Indians were able to send protest messages about land demarcations to the Brazilian president and authorities. Tonacci also shows the video recording of the first contact between white people and the Arura tribe of Brazil in 1981. In the tape, the Arura are introduced to Western utensils, clothing, jewelry, food, tape recorders, video cameras, and illness. Their fascination with radios, cameras, mirrors, and clothes reflects their isolation. The theme of invasion is also evident in powerful clips of bulldozers knocking down trees and, subsequently, the homes of these indigenous peoples.

Strengths and Weaknesses: This is an interesting view of the strategies scientists used in approaching a native Brazilian tribe that had had little amicable contact with modern cultures and in luring its members out of the rain forests. The tape has amazing images of Indians during their first open contact with the Western world. The depiction of the agency that deals with indigenous people, Fundação Nacional do Indio (FUNAI), and its treatment of Indians is disturbing but realistic.

One reviewer felt that the tape had a limited range of information, relying mostly on visual impression without background or a map. Others wondered if some of Tonacci's work was propaganda for FUNAI. It takes a while to understand that the film is not about Indians but about Tonacci's approach to filmmaking.

Introducing the Tape: Viewers should be told that the video is about Tonacci's work. They should be provided with background about FUNAI to place it in historical context.

How to Use: In a course on *Visual Anthropology* I would primarily use the tape to discuss the consequences (and unsolved dilemmas) of the contact between Western and non-Western societies. Also, I would show this film along with films that portray the Kayapo Indians of Brazil, who now bear their own video cameras and send messages to the president of Brazil, and emphasize the difference in treatment of the subject of culture contact (deculturation) from the perspective of journalism and anthropology. (Pérez)

The tape could stimulate discussion with the class about the concept of making a first contact between cultures. What is the value of the contact? How will each be changed? (Shapiro)
Suggested Readings: Hemming, John. *Red Gold: The Conquest of Brazilian Indians.*
Level: University

CRISIS IN BRAZIL: A CONVERSATION WITH NILSON ARAUJO

Documentary.   In English with Portuguese Portions Subtitled.   29 min.   1992
Directed by: Don Lynn, Catherine Benamou
Produced by: Don Lynn Productions
Distributed by: IMRE
Evaluators: Mary Jane Craver, Tânia M. Hering, Vincent D.

Iacovelli, Stephen P. O'Neill, Carlos A. Pérez, Enríque R. Rodríguez, Irwin Stern

Description: Brasilia-based independent video maker Nilson de Araujo and his group, Seculo Video, use an approach that develops alternative communications to raise the public's political awareness on issues that the major media ignore or censor. De Araujo and Seculo Video's independent style of reporting is considered nontraditional in Brazil, where journalism is often manipulated by the government and controlled by powerful business interests. He discusses the limited opportunities for independent artists to get their work shown on Brazilian television, as well as grassroots exhibition strategies.

De Araujo's interview includes samples of work on issues ranging from racism and the democratization process in post-military Brazil to environmental preservation. Shocking and courageous excerpts include commentary on the government's use of false promises to secure votes; police brutality in quelling street demonstrations (including images of police discouraging the filming of the various incidents); and interviews with many black Brazilians about discrimination.

Strengths and Weaknesses: This is an excellent and educational tape. While Brazilian television is very influential in the creation of popular cultures, this tape presents a much less well-known media production that challenges the generally acritical mainstream. Nilson de Araujo is highly articulate and understands the subject matter he films. The tape is well organized and technically strong, and the translation is great.

One reviewer felt that the tape was a bit long. For language classes there is not much emphasis on Portuguese dialogue.

Introducing the Tape: The tape is self-explanatory, but U.S. viewers would find it useful to have information on the power of television in Brazil and the role of alternative media in this context. Some understanding of Brazilian history would also be helpful.

How to Use: I would show the film in *Portuguese* and *Adult Education* classes, then discuss and use sections of it again, according to the topic. Also we would learn the sugarcane mill song in both classes. (Craver)

In a course on *Urban Development* or *Urban Issues* the tape could illustrate several issues. For instance, it presents one of the most shocking documentations of police brutality. It also shows that ecological concerns should not be limited to the deforesting of Amazônia, by showing environmental deterioration in other zones of Brazil. Finally, the video could be used as an example of the options that some intellectuals take when they want to be close to the people. (Pérez)

Suggested Readings: Alfaro Moreno, R. "Democracia y comunicación en la organización popular."

Ambrosi, Alain, and Nancy Thede, eds. *Video the Changing World.*

Criticos, S., and T. Quinlan. "Community Video: Power and Process," 39–52.

Escobar, Arturo, and Sonia Alvarez, eds., "Introduction: Theory and Protest in Latin America Today," in *The Making of Social Movements in Latin America,*

Festa, Regina. "Movimentos sociais, comunicação alternativa e popular," in *Comunicaçäo popular e alternativa no Brasil,* ed. Regina Festa and C. E. Lins da Silva.

Fontez, Carlos. *Defining Popular Video: Emerging Strategies in Latin America and the United States*

Mejia, A. L. "Um novo conceito de comunicação: o destinatário e o sujeito."

Protz, M. *Seeing and Showing Ourselves.*

Ruby, J. *Speaking for, Speaking about, Speaking with, or Speaking alongside: An Anthropological and Documentary Dilemma.*

Sector Audiovisual Fase. "Percepção, reflexao, e expressão: uma discussao metodológica."

Tomáselli, K. "Transferring Video Skills to the Community: The Problem of Power."

Turner, Terence. "Visual Media, Cultural Politics, and Anthropological Practice: Recent Uses of Film and Video among the Kayapo of Brazil."

Valdeavellano, P., ed. *El Video en la educación popular.*

Wasco, Janet, and Vincent Mosco. *Democratic Communication in the Information Age.*

Level: High School — University

DEUS E O DIABO NA TERRA DO SOL (Black God, White Devil)

Feature.   With Subtitles.   102 min.   1964

Directed by: Glauber Rocha

Distributed by: Festival Films, IMRE Archive (available for viewing only)

Evaluators: Sidney M. Greenfield, John Hess, David McCreery, David J. Robinson, Cliff Welch

Description: This is a story of the social movement growing out of the poverty and misery of the dry backlands in northeast Brazil. It is a dark and allegorical sketch of the human condition in the drought- and tradition-ravaged region. When a landowner, Colonel Moraes, beats cowboy Manoel for refusing to take the blame for losing four head of cattle, Manoel turns on the colonel and kills him. On the run, Manoel and his wife, Rosa, join a band of followers of Sebastião, a black messiah who wanders through the backlands (*sertão*) claiming that only those loyal to him will be spared on Judgment Day. In the meantime, area powerbrokers (including a priest and a landlord) hire an assassin, Antonio das Mortes, to kill the heretic Sebastião and his fanatical followers. Manoel and Rosa manage to survive the massacre to tell the tale and join a band of outlaws led by Corisco, a survivor of a famed group of bandits once led by Lampião. Antonio das Mortes is then hired to kill Coirana and his gang. He carries out his orders but lets Manoel and Rosa escape once again. The film ends with a sweeping shot of the couple running toward the ocean. Rosa falls, but Manoel makes it to the shore where, as the soundtrack narrates, "sea and *sertão* are one and the same; because earth belongs to man and not to God and the Devil."

Mixing European and African folklore and religion, the film reveals much about the culture of the northeast. Nature, in the form of earth, sun, and sky, is an ever present force. The stark class relations of the region are laid bare in the conflict between Manoel and various authorities. The film poses many questions related to moral and religious value systems, the antagonism of state agencies toward nonconformity, and the eternal hope of utopia. Gender relations are also revealed in the tense relationship between Rosa and Manoel: she follows him on his mad journey, but not uncritically. Director Rocha added a unique twist to the film, one typical of the times and yet so revolutionary that he was later exiled by the military regime in the 1960s. Rather than depicting Manoel as a helpless victim, the film shows him becoming gradually empowered, taking responsibility for his actions and, ultimately, arguing that each person must carry his own burden. Manoel stops searching for saviors and starts relying on himself.

Strengths and Weaknesses: This film has great significance both as one of the foundational films of Brazilian *Cinema Novo* and as one of the most notable of Glauber Rocha's works. It is a complex and unusual film that overturns any conventional realist representation of events. This antirealism is both a part of its strength and importance and a weak point, particularly for audiences not familiar with Rocha's work. The film examines in an original way questions of great concern to the northeast and to the poor in general. For Brazilians and Brazilianists, it is an unusually provocative and visually stunning film.

Overall, this is not an easy film. It would definitely need an introduction for U.S. audiences. For nonspecialists, the film can be confusing and boring. There are sequences of songs that are not translated and there is very little dialogue generally; thus viewers must work hard to understand the narrative and message. The tape includes many references that would be meaningless to most U.S. viewers. The subtitles are poor.

Introducing the Tape: It should be pointed out that this black-and-white film made in 1964 is considered to be director Glauber Rocha's masterpiece and a key work in the development of Brazil's *Cinema Novo*. As its presentation is experimental, a U.S. audience would need considerable information about the film's place in Brazilian film history and its form. Many of the references to legend, myth, history, and culture are invented by Rocha in imitation of folk-cultural forms and would need to be explained. An introduction to life in the arid northeast, utopianism, messianism, and Canudos (on which the film is modeled) is necessary.

How to Use: I would use the film as an example of *Brazilian Cinema Novo* and of Glauber Rocha's work. (Hess)

For the *History* courses I teach, there are a number of more useful films, but Glauber Rocha is perhaps Brazil's most famous director of the *Onda Nova* period, making this film important as a cultural artifact. (McCreery)

This film could be used in at least three ways: (1) to portray life in the northeast from about 1890 to 1970; (2) to portray the role of messianic movements and outlaws (*cangaceiros*) in the folk life of Brazil; and (3) to serve as an example of *Cinema Novo* and its role in empowering common people and challenging authority during the 1960s. (Welch)

Suggested Readings: Chandler, Billy J. *The Bandit King. (Lampião of Brazil).*

Cunha, Euclides da. *Rebellion in the Backlands.*

Diacon, Todd A. *Millenarian Vision, Capitalist Reality: Brazil's Contestado Rebellion.*

Johnson, Randal, and Robert Stam. *Cinema Novo X 5: Masters of Contemporary Brazilian Film.*

Johnson, Randal, and Robert Stam, eds. *Brazilian Cinema.*

Levine, Robert. *Vale of Tears: Revisiting the Canudos Massacre in Northeastern Brazil 1893–1897.*

Lewin, Linda. *Politics and Parentela in Paraiba: A Case Study of Family-Based Oligarchy in Brazil.*

Vargas Llosa, Mario. *The War of the End of the World.*

Complementary Films/Videos: *Antonio das Mortes* (Brazil)

Level: University

O DIA EM QUE DORIVAL ENCAROU A GUARDA
Fiction.   Without Subtitles.   14 min.   1986
Directed by: José Pedro Goulart and Jorge Furtado
Produced by: Gisele Leite and Henrique Lima
Distributed by: CDI, IMRE Archive (available for viewing only)
Evaluators: Warren J. Dean, Tânia M. Hering, Antônio R.M. Simões

Description: A black man in prison attempts to obtain permission to take a shower after not bathing for ten days. He asks each prison guard, going up the military hierarchy from the lowest-ranking soldier to the lieutenant. One by one, the soldier, the corporal, the sergeant, and the lieutenant come to his cell and deny him the shower. The prisoner insults each one furiously and finally spits in the face of the lieutenant, who then calls for reinforcements. They all enter the cell and beat the black prisoner until he falls apart. One of the guards is also black and shows some pity and comradeship for the prisoner. Ironically, after being badly beaten, the prisoner is ordered to the shower to wash all evidence of blood from his body. Lying on the ground beneath the shower, the prisoner smiles at his "achievement." The black guard lights two cigarettes and offers him one, but the prisoner refuses. Interspersed in the film are scenes from classic movies to illustrate some of the characters' fantasies.

Strengths and Weaknesses: This well-paced film delivers a powerful message about authority and military repression and how each military person just follows orders without caring whether they make sense or not. The film also depicts race relations in Brazil, to some extent.

Evaluators had mixed reactions to the performances. One

reviewer found the story somewhat predictable. The language used is difficult for nonnative speakers because of jargon and regionalisms.

Introducing the Tape: Students may need to be introduced to the film's ironic style in its portrayal of military hierarchy and power. Also, instructors could note the news reports mentioned in the film of the police massacre in São Paulo Prison in October 1992, which left 110 people dead. There is some violence in the tape, for which audiences should be prepared.

How to Use: In *Portuguese Language* class the teacher could have students rewrite or copy some of the dialogue and perform a play in class at the end of the semester, after having discussed and understood it. Second-year language students can observe how the orders are given and list some of the commands in dialogues for grammar practice. (Simões)

Suggested Readings: Every year *Callaloo* bibliography provides readers with a list of newly published material on racial discrimination in Brazil. Check the *Lusophone* (Brazilian) literature section for this subject and much more.

Level: University

O ESPIRITO DA TELEVISÃO (The Spirit of TV)

Documentary.   With Subtitles.   18 min.   1990
Directed by: Vincent Carelli
Produced by: Centro de Trabalho Indigenista (Rua Fidalgo 548- Sala 13, São Paulo 05432, SP; tel: [5511] 813-3450; fax: [5511] 212-3692)
Distributed by: IMRE, Video Data Bank, Videographe
Evaluators: Rich Bergeman, Fred Fejes, Carlos Fontez, Victor Garatea, Sidney M. Greenfield, Carolyn Shapiro
Description: *The Spirit of TV* documents the Waiapi Indians' first contact with the technology of video and television. The tape explores how the Waiapi conceptualize the images of video and the possible uses of television. While they watch programs of other indigenous groups, they express diverse views on the benefits and drawbacks of television. The Indians discuss how video can unite their people by preserving their stories, beliefs, and rituals; facilitating connections with other tribes; and communicating their message of protest to the government. Imagining the possible uses of video, one of the Indians urges the cameraman to make a wide-angle shot including as many Indians as possible, saying, "With these pictures, they will see that we have many in our villages. It is not good to show that there are few of us." In another scene, feeling that video can help scare cattle ranchers and gold miners away, an Indian graphically describes to the camera how he will kill an invader, saying, "I will eat his liver, it will be more delicious than a tapir." The Indians also discuss the possible detrimental effects of video capturing the spirits of the people. Indigenous music and language and scenes of life in the village provide the context for the tape.

Strengths and Weaknesses: The strength of this video lies in its honest exploration of the Waiapis' views on the differing effects of television. It is also an important document on the use of video to empower indigenous people and help them forge connections among different tribes. In an engaging way, the tape reveals television's novelty and appeal and is effective in showing how even those unfamiliar with television quickly become aware of its power, influence, and potential. The Waiapis' reactions to the content and the function of television enable viewers to distance themselves from the medium and approach it with a fresher perspective. This can be an excellent introduction to a discussion of the importance of seeing images of one's own community on television and to questions of self-reflexivity in television watching. The tape is extremely useful for exploring the issues of intracultural contact and some of its unanticipated consequences. While images of village life provide a somewhat superficial exploration of the Waiapi culture, the tape powerfully expresses the people's anger at the white man and provides excellent material for discussing the causes of this anger.

The tape's impressionistic nature makes it difficult to distinguish between the recordings being shown to the Waiapi and the documentary footage shot with them, leaving viewers somewhat confused about how scenes relate in terms of time and space.

Introducing the Tape: To avoid confusion, viewers should be told that this documentary contains fast cuts between tapes shown to the villagers on television and shots of the people's reactions to the tapes. The recordings being shown to the people can be identified by their visible scan lines (horizontal lines that run across the television screen). Audiences should be told that the Waiapi Indians of the state of Amapá were first contacted in 1973 during the construction of the Perimitral Norte highway through the Brazilian Amazon. Soon the Indians were decimated by the illnesses introduced by the Brazilian construction workers and the gold miners who followed them.

A brief description of the work of the Centro de Trabalho Indigenista (CTI) and a synopsis of the history of the use of video among native Brazilians would be necessary for those who have not been previously exposed to this theme. CTI has trained indigenous groups throughout the Brazilian Amazon to use video as a tool of cultural preservation and political resistance. The indigenous people have created a huge archive of tapes that they use to communicate among groups and to bring their message to the government. This tape could be seen in conjunction with the tape *Vídeo nas aldeias (Video in the Villages)*, which explains the work of the CTI with various native tribes of Brazil.

How to Use: I would show the tape to initiate a discussion on how television impacts culture; how television captivates audiences; and the manner in which television's power is so obvious, yet so easy to ignore or deny. (Bergeman)

The program is most useful in illustrating the conflict between the government and the Indians. (Fejes)

For *Introduction to Mass Communication* the tape has a scene in which the Waiapi see a news report about the tribe

Gaviao on the verge of war. This is followed by scenes of the Waiapi threatening to kill whites, especially gold miners. This sequence is a good starting point for a discussion about the dynamics of audience reception of television and of the different factors that influence the way in which a particular audience may understand and use a program. The teacher can start by eliciting students' reactions to the news report and then contrast these to the reactions of the Waiapi. This exercise could be used as a clear example of the role of culture, ethnicity, and other factors in audience reception. In *Advanced Video Production* this tape could be used as an example of the range of video genres and uses of video beyond those seen in mass television. The discussion could lead students to identify the major elements of alternative video. For *Alternative Media and Society* this tape illustrates key themes of the role of alternative media in society and could be used as the leitmotif for a discussion of the use of media in processes of organization and education, the role of community media, the relationship between alternative and mass media, reflexivity and the role of media activists, etc. (Fontez)

The tape could be used to explore how cultures can clash or be rapidly assimilated. (Garatea)

The video provides excellent discussion material for U.S. students. Students could take roles, some representing those coming in to film the Indians, analyzing their motivations and possible uses for video. Others could take the indigenous perspectives, to explore questions of the value of television as a tool to record and unite, as well as its possible detrimental effects. We would also talk about the anger toward "white men," looking into the issues generating their anger. (Shapiro)

Suggested Readings: Readings from *Cultural Survival*'s papers, books, and quarterly journal.

Reading materials on using video as an organizing tool with indigenous people.

Complementary Films/Videos: *Video nas aldeias (Video in the Villages)* (Brazil); *Meeting Ancestors* (distributed by IMRE).

Level: Junior High School—University

ESQUINAS DA VIDA (Corners of Life)

Documentary.   With Subtitles.   18 min.   1991
Produced by: TV Viva-Centro Luiz Freire (Rua São Bento 344, Ribeira, 53110, Olinda PE; tel: [5581] 429-4109; fax: [5581] 429-4881)
Distributed by: IMRE
Evaluators: Robert Alvarez, Mary Jane Craver, Elizabeth Marchant, Irwin Stern
Description: This short documentary consists of interviews with prostitutes and their customers in northeastern Brazil. It raises issues of health awareness, poverty, and unionization of prostitutes.
Strengths and Weaknesses: This is a well made, vivid portrait of the economic circumstances of women working as

prostitutes in an urban setting. It is specific in that individuals tell of their plight and profession. By allowing the prostitutes to speak for themselves, the tape provides viewers an authentic viewpoint on some of their reasons for becoming prostitutes. Men are also interviewed about why they go to prostitutes. Many perspectives and opinions are presented, and the video gives a good, albeit brief, picture of urban life in Brazil.

The older generation is interviewed more than the younger, and the AIDS question is only alluded to. The tape is not suitable for minors; there is graphic dancing that may need to be edited, even for adult viewers.
Introducing the Tape: Audiences should be aware of the abject poverty and hopelessness that many poor people feel in both developing and developed countries.
How to Use: I would use this tape as an example of the role of women and the political economy of urban blight. (Alvarez)

The tape would be good for an intermediate level of *Portuguese* for the adult learner. In my *Adult Basic Education* class we could do cross-cultural essays comparing and contrasting the Brazilian prostitute situation to the local one. Values, morals, religious beliefs, and economic comparisons could be made. (Craver)

The tape could be used in conjunction with readings from Daphne Patai's *Brazilian Women Speak* in a *Literature* or *Culture* class. I might also use it in an advanced *Portuguese* class as a supplement. (Marchant)
Suggested Readings: Herbert, Daniel. *Sexuality, Politics, and AIDS in Brazil.*

Mohanty, Chandra, et al., eds. *Third World Women and the Politics of Feminism.*

Patai, Daphne. *Brazilian Women Speak: Contemporary Life Stories.*

Schuler, Margaret, ed. *Freedom from Violence: Women's Strategies from Around the World.*
Level: University

FABULA DE LA BELLA PALOMERA (Fable of the Beautiful Pigeon Fancier)

Feature.   With Subtitles.   73 min.   1988
Directed by: Ruy Guerra
Produced by: RTVE
Distributed by: IMRE
Evaluators: Elba D. Birmingham-Pokorny, Lourdes Fernández, Joan A. McGinnis
Description: Based on the tormented love story by Gabriel García Márquez, this film deals with the obsessive sexual desires of a wealthy sugarcane aristocrat who finally meets the woman of his dreams, a beautiful mulatta. It is an excellent portrayal of the vain, self-centered man searching for true love. The young woman, married to a musician and mother of a one-year-old boy, raises pigeons in her house. One of the birds eventually becomes a love messenger, and she and the aristocrat finally meet for an amorous, passionate evening.

When the woman's husband finds out, he violently slits her throat, leaving the aristocrat adrift in a life without meaning. **Strengths and Weaknesses:** Lyrically filmed and well acted, this film has a compelling story line with a slight surrealistic flavor. It brilliantly combines myths, dreams, and legends to give expression to the inner tensions and struggles between the upper and lower classes and the male and female subjects. The film captures the delicate subjects of sexual taboos, homosexual love, incest, and adultery. The background music and imagery are impressive.

The scenes containing nudity make this tape inappropriate for viewing in high school classes.
Introducing the Tape: Viewers should be provided with some background on Gabriel García Márquez and surrealism.
How to Use: This film can be used to introduce students to the importance of myths and legends as a literary device. I would use it to introduce students to spoken *Spanish* as well as to the works of Gabriel García Márquez. (Birmingham-Pokorny)

Students can first read the story and then watch the film. This would lead to a good discussion about machismo and the male code of honor in Latin America. (Fernández)
Suggested Readings: García Márquez, Gabriel. *Amores dificiles* (see bibliography for selection of Márquez's works).
Level: University

FAVELAS (Slums)
Documentary.   With Subtitles.   50 min.   1989
Directed by: Chico Teixeira
Distributed by: The Cinema Guild
Evaluators: Paolo Carpignano, Iris Engstrand, Elizabeth Merena, Virginia Shen
Description: This documentary describes the migration of people from the countryside to the *favelas* (slums) of São Paulo and the living conditions they encounter. It discusses the economic gap and class struggles in Brazil, focusing primarily on the emotional and physical difficulties of living in substandard conditions that breed disease, malnutrition, death, social "invisibility," crime, and lack of human rights and education. Included in the tape are archival photographs, stories from current residents, and interviews with "experts" (philosophers, educators, social workers, and sanitation planners). Among the voices are notable Brazilian intellectuals such as educator Paolo Freire and musician Gilberto Gil. Interwoven with these opinions and testimonies is an anonymous, somewhat poetic, female voice that thematically links some of the material.
Strengths and Weaknesses: The film provides findings about the existing problems from diverse points of view. It could be a wonderful reminder of the Brazilian government's ignorance of the marginal areas and the failure of social welfare projects.

A few evaluators noted that the tape does not provide adequate social and political context.

Introducing the Tape: A U.S. audience would need an introduction with historical background and economic data.
How to Use: The tape could be used to show slum conditions in Brazil (such as São Paulo)and discuss problems that arise when social services break down. (Engstrand)

It could be used in an *Urban Planning* class to increase student awareness of the problems of the poor in Brazil. Students could write essays on possible solutions.
Level: University

A FESTA DA MOÇA (The Girl's Party)
Documentary.   With Subtitles.   18 min.   1987
Directed by: Vincent Carrelli
Produced by: Centro de Trabalho Indigenista (Rua Fidalga 548, Sala 13, São Paulo 05432-000; tel: [5511] 813-3450; fax: [5511] 813-0747)
Distributed by: IMRE, Video Data Bank, Videographe
Evaluators: Amanda Castro-Mitchell, José-Manuel Navarro, Enríque R. Rodríguez
Description: This tape is part of a series of programs made by the Centro de Trabalho Indigenista (CTI), which provides Amazonian Indian groups with video training and equipment. The tape focuses on the Nambiquara people who live in the Amazon Basin in Bolivia, near Brazil. Their pre-twentieth-century population was over ten thousand; today there are only about six hundred people. The villagers explain and perform various important rituals. One is the exchange of women; another is the rite of passage for young girls, beginning with the onset of menstruation. Finally, there is a strong scene in which, as a way of recovering their identity, the males ceremonially pierce their noses and lips, without anesthesia, using wooden sticks. The tape exemplifies the value of video as a tool in cultural preservation. The Nambiquara tape their dance patterns and compare them to the way other clans perform the same dance. A facilitator from CTI replays a tape shot with the tribe. Upon seeing their own images on tape, the members of the tribe realize that they appear occidental and feel that they are losing their own identity. So they decide to retape the same dance wearing traditional clothing.

There is some nudity in the tape.
Strengths and Weaknesses: The tape captures how the Indians love to watch themselves on TV and enjoy making their own television program. This portrait of the Nambiquara is extremely valuable, as the tribe is in danger of disappearing. The visual representations in the tape allow students to view and compare different indigenous peoples.
Introducing the Tape: A map of the region and some background materials about this specific group would be useful for viewers before watching the tape, as would general background on indigenous groups in Brazil and on the work of CTI.
How to Use: I would show this film in my *Latin American Civilization and Culture* course to illustrate that there are still many Indian groups in Latin America; to talk about the problems of land ownership that they all face; to explore different

customs and rituals; and especially to analyze the loss of identity and how, in this case, technology helps the Indians regain their cultural identity. (Castro-Mitchell)

It is important for students to be exposed to the Nambiquara and to know why they are in decline. This video documents important rites and rituals of the group. It will assist in comparing those rites and rituals with other clans in the Americas and abroad. (Rodríguez)
Level: High School—University

THE FORBIDDEN LAND
Documentary.   English Narration with Spanish Portions Subtitled.   58 min.   1990
Directed by: Helena Solberg Ladd
Produced by: International Cinema Inc. (200 West 90th Street, Suite 6H, New York, N.Y. 10024; tel: [212] 877-2972; fax: [212] 877-3462)
Distributed by: International Cinema, Jane Balfour Films
Evaluators: Thomas O. Bente, Mary Jane Craver, Yolanda Prieto
Description: The tape presents a case study of the role of progressive sectors of the Catholic Church in Brazil in the land-reform movement. While concentrating on a particular example, the documentary gives background on the emergence of liberation theology in Latin America and the functioning of Christian base communities. The struggle of the conservative institutional church (although there have been many progressive bishops within the institutional structures, especially in Brazil) against the progressive or "popular" church is documented. The progressive church is seen by the institution as creating conflict and divisions within Catholicism. There is a clear line determined by social class in this struggle. Some Catholics have sided with the rich and others with the oppressed—adhering, as they see it, to Christ's own "preferential option for the poor."
Strengths and Weaknesses: This is an engrossing, balanced, and worthwhile documentary. It presents a wealth of information about an important topic. The schism between the Catholic Church of the landowners and that of the poor is described well. A central issue is: Should politics enter into church doctrine or into religious services? A secondary issue is: Do poor people in Brazil have any rights to land, and how can agrarian reform be accomplished? Both sides present strong arguments, and the documentary's ending is particularly powerful. One reviewer felt that the tape was a bit long for U.S. viewers.
Introducing the Tape: Instructors need to update the film and explain how liberation theology has been repressed in Latin America. Although this is documented in the film, the tape's introduction makes it seem as if this were still a powerful movement. The movement may not be dead, but it has been seriously undermined by political trends in the region and, most of all, by Rome. U.S. audiences could also benefit from commentary on the history of land acquisition in Brazil.
How to Use: I would use the tape either in a *Culture/Civi-*

lization course or in a *Portuguese Language* course as cultural background on Brazil. (Bente)

Students could take sides and debate topics: Should the church have a political role? Should landowners or the workers/squatters have rights? If compromise is inevitable, what concessions could be made? Should the government get involved to solve the problem? Should a revolution occur? (Craver)

I would use the tape to document changes in religion, society, and politics, to be followed by readings. (Prieto)
Suggested Readings: Gutierrez, Gustavo. *The Future of Liberation Theology: Essays in Honor of Gustavo Gutierrez* (Peruvian theologian and the original author on this subject).

Lernoux, Penny. *Cry of the People.*

The Centro Valdivieso in Managua, Nicaragua, may have good reference material on what is going on now.
Level: High School—University

FRUTO DA ALIANÇA DOS POVOS DA FLORESTA
Documentary.   Without Subtitles.   25 min.   1990
Directed by: Sia Runikuê
Produced by: ASKARJ (Rua João de Paiva 665, Bairro Senador Pompeu, Tarauacá/AC, CEP 69970-000; tel: [5568] 462-1195)
Distributed by: IMRE Archive (available for viewing only)
Evaluators: Susan M. Deeds, John Fett, Carlos Fontez, Martha Rees, Carolyn Shapiro
Description: This tape documents the struggle of indigenous people and white rubber tappers in the state of Acre to organize to protect the Amazonian jungle from further encroachment and degradation by cattle-raising landowners and other developers. Through cooperatives, Indian communities and rubber tappers are pooling their resources to pressure the government to promote environmental conservation and social justice in the region. The tape features the various Karixanua indigenous communities along the rivers Puru, Jurua, Envira, Jordão, and Curanja and their efforts to establish an indigenous reservation in an area occupied by big rubber bosses. It incorporates scenes of communal celebrations and meetings to present the views of indigenous peoples themselves (speaking in their own languages with Portuguese subtitles), as well as those of rubber tappers and labor organizers. The tape includes the founding meeting of the National Council of Rubber Tappers, as well as an interview with Chico Mendes intercut with scenes from his funeral (where a speaker says, "They killed Chico Mendes, but they created a thousand more Chico Mendeses").
Strengths and Weaknesses: This powerful tape is a unique document of the organization and alliance of indigenous people and white people who live from the extraction of rubber; for this reason, it would be of value to students in a variety of fields. The tape presents effectively the indigenous points of views about native relationships with the rain forest and the arguments for environmental preservation. The inclusion of Chico Mendes and footage

of funerals of those killed by large landowner interests makes the video very dramatic.

Evaluators felt that the tape lacked context and suffered from a disjointed narrative line. Viewers get the sense that there were different events and groups of people involved in the struggle, but the story line of the struggle as a whole is not clear. The tape assumes considerable knowledge of the region and its geography. For example, the names of different rivers appear on the screen, but the viewer is not provided with a map showing the rivers' relative location.

Introducing the Tape: U.S. viewers will need background about land struggles in Brazil, as well as contextualization about the geography, politics, and economics of the region. More information is needed about how the power structure at the national and state levels has supported the landowners and developers. A map and specific geographical information about where the tape was shot, the situation of indigenous people in the Amazon, and key issues in the recent struggle of the rubber tappers would also be helpful. It would also be interesting to know how the footage was used during the struggle and about the progress of the struggle since 1990.

How to Use: I would use this to illustrate how native peoples of Latin America/Brazil are still struggling to conserve their culture and environment. (Deeds)

Provided I would have information about the ways in which this footage was used during the process of struggle, I would use this tape as an example of how video can be used as an organizing tool. In its present form, the tape can be shown as an unsuccessful example of the transition from video process to video product. (Fontez)

This is good material for discussing people's rights to land, comparing it to the situation of Native Americans here in the United States. (Shapiro)

Suggested Readings: Davis, Shelton. *Victims of the Miracle: Development and the Indians of Brazil.*

Dean, Warren. *Brazil and the Struggle for Rubber: A Study in Environmental History.*

Murphy, Yolanda, and Robert E. Murphy. *Women of the Forest.*

Any readings on the life and efforts of Chico Mendes would be helpful.

Readings from *Cultural Survival*'s catalog of papers, books, and quarterly journals.

Level: University

A FUNDAÇÁO DO BRASIL (The Founding of Brazil)
Animation.   No Dialogue.   8 min.   1980
Directed by: Mo Toledo
Produced by: Gira Films
Distributed by: CDI, IMRE Archive (available for viewing only)
Evaluators: Amanda Castro-Mitchell, Warren J. Dean, Tânia M. Hering, Jeff Lesser, Cliff Welch, Gayle Williams
Description: This is a conceptual, stylized view of the found-

ing of Brazil, the development of a class/race-based hierarchical society, and modernization and its consequences. The animated film presents the arrival of the Portuguese in the 1500s, their encounter with the native people, the introduction of African slaves, and the mixture of the three different peoples, resulting in the Brazilian nation. The combination of old and new elements suggests that the Afro-Brazilian population is still exploited and that the Indians are still resisting colonization. The Portuguese (or whites) are portrayed as greedy usurpers into the present day. At the tape's end the white race becomes the race consumed. The video includes elements of environmental concerns and international intervention with the presence of Uncle Sam. It is quite abstract, with background sound and music from contemporary sources that reinforce the subtle messages of the screen.

Strengths and Weaknesses: This creative, clever tape presents a more recent view of discovery and colonization, not the one taught in history books. It presents an interesting vision of Brazil and modernity and the price that the poor, lower classes, and blacks have had to pay in order for Brazil to become an industrialized country. The video makes brilliant use of color, figures, and juxtaposition of musical themes. The soundtrack's mix of Brazilian popular music and sound effects (without dialogue) contributes to the rhythm of the images. A major strength of the work is its portrayal of the tripartite cultural origins of Brazilians.

A couple of evaluators felt that the tape may be too abstract for the classroom; there is little explanation, and at times, the experimental format leaves viewers confused about what is taking place. Because of this abstract treatment of historical references, the tape would be most useful to people specializing in *Brazilian Studies*. There is mild nudity in the tape.

Introducing the Tape: The animation would benefit from some background on Brazil's history, including context regarding the role of miscegenation in the founding and development of Brazil. Audiences could be told that the Afro-Brazilian population is the second largest community of African descendants outside of Africa. A translation of the song used in the film would be of great assistance in conveying the point, although the images alone effectively address the message.

How to Use: The tape could be used to start a debate about the social consequences of industrialization, issues of race, class, and slavery. Its uses no dialogue, so students must interpret the symbolism of the images. (Castro-Mitchell)

It is useful for showing how relatively sophisticated Brazilian artists portray the origins of their country's racial stratification, slavery, and destruction of Indians. (Dean)

Although the Portuguese language is not used in this program, I would use it in my *Portuguese Language* course combined with some information about the events shown in the film. (Hering)

The tape could be used in a *Seminar on Brazil* to have students evaluate the images. (Lesser)

The tape would be useful as an introduction to the problems of conquest and miscegenation. (Welch)

In a *History* course I would have students view the tape and identify important points of Brazilian culture and history represented. In a *Civilization* course the tape would be used to ask about the differences in local culture and global influences. We would also discuss the tape's use of stereotypes: Does it offend or provide a new interpretation? (Williams)

Suggested Readings: Burns, E. Bradford. *A History of Brazil.*

Costa, Viotti da. *The Brazilian Empire: Myths and Histories.*

Freyre, Gilbert. *The Masters and the Slaves (Casa grande & senzala): A Study in the Development of Brazilian Civilization.*
Level: University

GAROTOS DO FUTURO (Kids of the Future)
Documentary.   With Subtitles.   18 min.   1988
Directed & Produced by: TV Viva-Centro Luiz Freire (Rua São Bento 344, Ribeira 53110, Olinda PE; tel: [5581] 429-4109; fax: [5581] 429-4881)
Distributed by: IMRE
Evaluators: Susan Lozada, Alida Metcalf, Stephen P. O'Neill, Rosangela Vieira King
Description: Through interviews this video illustrates one of the most devastating aspects of Brazilian society: its lack of concern for the poor masses and the children of this sector. The tape shows how many of these children live on the streets and, from as early as three to five years old, become involved in crime, drug use, and prostitution. Young people who have been jailed talk about the lack of a home life and their lives on the streets, robbing and sniffing glue. The tape shows how the public views and treats these children, how organized crime uses them to carry out its activities, and the brutal actions of the police to rid neighborhoods of these unwanted elements. The system deals with these children by imprisoning them as regular criminals, many times ordering their genocide in remote areas of the country. The tape introduces a program for juvenile delinquents aimed at leading these children away from drugs, crime, poverty, and jail and on to more constructive, educated, socially acceptable lives.
Strengths and Weaknesses: The use of personal testimony by children and parents is very strong. The video provides an overview of the reasons such a problem exists. It shows that when individuals are primarily concerned with their own well-being, the resulting lack of social cohesiveness perpetuates the status quo.

One reviewer felt that the tape was too long and not technically strong.
Introducing the Tape: Reading assignments and lectures should be given on the social, political, and economic structures of Brazilian society.
How to Use: This is a good illustration of Brazil's underclass. (Metcalf)

The tape can be used to show some of social problems in Brazil and the role of rehabilitation efforts in combatting the situation. (O'Neill)

I would use the video to generate further discussion on the issue of poverty, the treatment of children, and the fate of the poor masses of Brazil. I would also suggest that after a historical analysis of the characteristics of Brazilian society, the students discuss the prospects for improving the lives of these people. (Vieira King)
Suggested Readings: Jesus, Carolina María de. *Child of the Dark: The Diary of Carolina María de Jesus.*
Level: High School—University

HAIL UMBANDA (Hail Umbanda)
Documentary.   With Subtitles.   46 min.   1985
Directed by: José Araujo
Distributed by: University of California-Berkeley
Evaluators: Leonor Blum, Lori Madden, Lynn M. Shirey
Description: *Umbanda,* the animistic religion of a large and growing portion of Brazil's population, is a syncretism of Christianity with African and indigenous religions. Begun in Brazil in 1908 among African slaves, native Indians, and Portuguese, the religion has grown in popularity with the urban poor and oppressed groups. This tape contains profiles of a spiritual leader and a converted believer. The camera captures a range of authentic religious activities (costumes, rituals, purifications, consultations, offerings, and possessions) and interviews the *pai de santo* (spiritual medium). It is apparent that *Umbanda* is popular with all races in Brazil. The narrator points out the correspondence between Catholic saints and *orixás* (the spirits summoned from Africa that enter the bodies of the believers).
Strengths and Weaknesses: This informative film covers an interesting topic with a wide range of images, scenes, and activities. The tape presents a slice of real life as the camera follows the religious leader.

The scenes taped at night are not very clear. The introduction is in small print and difficult to read. One evaluator felt that the tape became tediously repetitive.
Introducing the Tape: Students need a basic understanding of *Umbanda, Candomble,* and *Macumba.* A discussion of syncretism should explain which aspects of religion tend to fuse, and why. It is important to mention the appeal of spiritist religions in today's Brazil.
Suggested Readings: Brumana, Fernando Giobellina. *Spirits from the Margin: Umbanda in São Paulo: A Study in Popular Religion and Social Experience.*

Fernandes, Florestan. *The Negro in Brazilian Society.*

Langguth, A. J. *Macumba: White and Black Magic in Brazil.*

McGregor, Pedro. *The Moon and Two Mountains: The Myths, Ritual, and Magic of Brazilian Spiritism.*

Ortiz, Renato. "Ogum and the Umbandista Religion," in *Africa's Ogun: Old World and New,* ed. Sandra T. Barnes.

Works by Nina Rodríguez and Gilberto Freyre (see bibliography for selected works).
Level: University

HAY LUGAR (There's Room)

Documentary. With Subtitles. 23 min. 1987
Directed by: Julio Wainer and Juraci de Souza
Produced by: VTV Video (Rua Itapeva, 187 CEP 01332-000, São Paulo; tel: [5511] 210-7088)
Distributed by: IMRE
Evaluators: Catherine Egan, Stephen P. O'Neill, Rosangela Vieira King
Description: This video describes the struggle of the poor masses of Brazil to find housing. High rents have driven many people to demonstrate against the conditions and/or to seek their own piece of land as squatters. The tape shows a group of poor people appropriating an area that had been vacant. When the people showed an interest in the land, and even hired a person to negotiate and make an offer to the landowners, the proprietors had armed authorities disperse them and destroy their initial constructions. The tape discusses the difficulty of acquiring housing and paying rent in a society that has no controls or policies regarding these issues. The result is that the majority of families in the lower-middle class or at poverty level can live only in the streets, or, if they're lucky, they may be able to afford rent in a shantytown area of the Brazilian cities. The tape includes interviews with impoverished people and government officials. A spokesman for the church emphasizes the injustice of the system; others, including community organizers and architects, advocate self-help and cooperative efforts within the communities. The people's groups are not satisfied with the government's efforts but point to small victories.
Strengths and Weaknesses: The video's use of people speaking for themselves, *cordel* (popular rural stories), and music gives it an immediacy, urgency, and power that is very convincing. The presentation of religious and community leaders' criticism of the government is also very effective. The tape calls for an understanding of the land as a natural resource from God for the people and the need for agrarian reform to accommodate the needs of the poor. This is a clear and accessible presentation that generates curiosity and discussion.

One reviewer felt that the tape might be too long.
Introducing the Tape: Lectures or readings should be given on agrarian reforms in Latin America (and in Brazil in particular). Other topics to be considered are urbanization in an overwhelmingly poor country and how to meet the social needs of the poorer groups.
How to Use: For *English as a Second Language* classes the tape offers many topics for conversation and writing: fact and opinion, comparison of the people's native housing and present housing, and the role of the police in different societies. For *Sociology* classes issues for discussion and writing could include identification of common global problems, poverty, housing, the role of the government, and the role of the police. (O'Neill)

I would use this tape to illustrate a lecture series on this topic and would ask the students to present other ideas on how to solve the housing problems of poor masses in Third World countries. (Vieira King)
Level: University

A HORA DA ESTRELA (The Hour of the Star)

Feature. With Subtitles. 85 min. 1985
Directed by: Suzana Amaral
Distributed by: IMRE
Evaluators: Patricia Aufderheide (excerpted from *Cross Cultural Film Guide*), David William Foster, Carmen Madariaga Culver, Michael Shane
Description: This award-winning feature film, based on a short story by Clarice Lispector, is the story of a young woman from the provinces attempting to make her way as a secretary in São Paulo. She is spiritually crushed by the harsh realities of big-city survival and the gap between her romantic notions and those realities. The film is a poetic rendering of the alienation of industrial society for the poor.

We meet young, homely office worker Macabea as she dismally confronts an aged typewriter, smudging the copy with greasy fingerprints. Her roommates and her office mate (the sexpot secretary, Gloria) can barely stand her stench, but she scarcely registers their complaints.

Macabea is a loser, and her humility in the face of it is as exasperating as the fact itself. But that doesn't mean she doesn't have her moments of illumination and joy. They occur in moments that highlight the pathetic quality of her life: for instance, dancing alone on a stolen day off from work while she listens to the radio in the room she shares with several working girls.

Macabea haplessly struggles to emerge from her darkness. She solemnly memorizes informational nuggets from the news, treating them like mysterious treasures rescued from the dark of unknowing. The radio and the movies are Macabea's link with a world beyond her dank urban hole. There, unbeknownst to the throngs on the street or her roommates or her boss, she's a star.

When Macabea meets Olimpico, a stubborn hustler with his own dreams and expectations, she clutches at the unmentionable possibility of love. His cruelty is encouraged by Gloria, who moves in to poach on the affair. Gloria, feeling some guilt, tries to make it up to Macabea by introducing her to a fortune-teller who might bring her luck. What happens next is both tragic and transcendent. (Aufderheide)
Strengths and Weaknesses: Reviewers felt that this film was an outstanding adaptation of Lispector's writing, with excellent performances. It reflects contemporary Brazilian society, culture, and language and is a realistic film about a member of the underclass with all her virtues and faults. The filmmaker's intimate style carries the shock of confrontation—the simultaneous quality of invasion and empathy that the interventions of Lispector accomplished in print.

One reviewer felt that a shortcoming of the film was the

perpetuation of the image of a weak woman unable to control her own destiny—a victim rather than an agent.

Introducing the Tape: Some information on Lispector's writing would be useful.

How to Use: I would use this film to illustrate the dense, rich genre of women's writing exemplified by Clarice Lispector and then move on to conflicting images of women in Latin America, in terms of the victim-agent dichotomy. Lispector represents sort of a second-generation feminism that has been superseded by a consciousness that has evolved since her death in the 1970s (this would need to be taken into account). Finally, the film is a superb example of the Brazilian _Cinema Novo_ (New Latin American Cinema) in virtually every aspect of its cinematographic structure. (Foster)

I would use this tape as entertainment, in conjunction with a reading of the novel. Students would be encouraged to write their own reviews, compare the film with the novel, and comment on the reflection of Brazilian society as well as the depiction of Brazilian women. (Shane)

Suggested Readings: Aufderheide, Patricia. _Cross Cultural Film Guide._

Fitz, Earl. _Clarice Lispector._

Johnson, Randal, and Robert Stam, eds. _Brazilian Cinema._

Lispector, Clarice. _Hour of the Star and Other Stories._

Level: High School—University

IRACEMA (Iracema)

Documentary/Fiction.   With Subtitles.   90 min.   1975

Directed by: Jorge Bodansky

Distributed by: The Cinema Guild

Evaluators: Patricia Aufderheide (excerpted from _Cross Cultural Film Guide_), Alvaro Félix Bolános, Cliff Welch

Description: This is a film about individual and collective false dreams in a nation under the pressure of economic development. It is structured as a "road movie," in which the journeys of two central characters intersect—Iracema, an innocent young Amazon Indian woman, and Tião, an opportunistic trans-Amazonian truck driver. Iracema leaves the forest to explore life in the city (Belém); Tião encounters her during a religious procession and offers to take her with him. The fare is Iracema's body. When Tião tires of Iracema, he pushes her out of the truck, and she drifts from one job to another, working mainly as a prostitute. Her experiences expose viewers to the seamier side of the first years of Amazonian development in the late 1970s and early 1980s. At the story's end, Tião reencounters Iracema at a desolate roadside _puteiro_ (whorehouse). She demands his recognition and asks him if she's changed for the better or worse. Iracema tries to hold Tião accountable for her destruction, but he accepts no responsibility and flees down the dusty highway in his new cattle truck.

The film contains some nudity and profanity.

Strengths and Weaknesses: The strength of this film is its moral ambiguity. Neither Iracema nor Tião attracts the viewer's sympathy. Of equal value is the allegory of Amazonian destruction. The film introduces many culprits, yet it is difficult to blame them for acting in their own self-interest. Thus, the film works well as an introduction to the social dimensions of the Amazonian frontier; the general coarseness of frontier society is vividly portrayed. As is traditional in Brazilian film, many actors are obviously authentic frontiersmen and -women (there is only one professional actor; the other characters play themselves), and there is much improvised dialogue. The characters look directly into the camera, confronting the viewer. The film is important not only for its current theme but also because its gritty style implicitly comments on the resources of developing countries and puts the grassroots participants at the center of the narrative and frame.

The film's weaknesses are comparatively minor. The narrative flow is not always apparent owing to some surprising plot leaps and sudden transitions. These may be problems for viewers schooled on Hollywood films, but most can be educated to either ignore or appreciate these features. Also, the film reveals the complex social reality without offering a single direct comment on the context.

Introducing the Tape: For audiences unfamiliar with the subject, the tape should be placed in the context of the history of rain forest development and its consequences. U.S. audiences will need to know about the foreign debt pressures on Brazil that encourage rain forest destruction; the foreign loans made to exploit the rain forest's resources; the urban poverty that drove all kinds of people to migrate to the region; the Indian communities that have been confronted by these migrants; the function of roads and trucks in facilitating development; and the clash of traditional and modern cultures that accompanies capitalist expansion. The strength of the film is that it puts faces on these abstractions.

The film could also be put in the context of _Cinema History._ Viewers could be told that the film builds on the traditions of Brazilian _Cinema Novo,_ which began in the late 1950s and was influenced by the Italian neorealists, the New Wave, and the political movements of the 1960s. Brazilian filmmakers participating in the _Cinema Novo_ movement struggled to find a film vocabulary for an authentic Brazilian experience. After 1968, when a coup brought fierce repression to the arts, it was difficult for filmmakers with a social mandate to produce. The Brazilian film agency Embrafilme was launched by filmmakers themselves, but it often fell hostage to governmental politics and had a roller-coaster history ending with its abolition in 1990 by the Collor administration. _Iracema_'s director, Bodanzky, worked in documentary style and in 16 mm—well outside the normal sphere of the government's vigilance, since his work could not be screened in major cinemas. His work was partially funded by Embrafilme, but he did not succeed in showing it in Brazil for five years. When the tape was finally allowed to be released in Brazil in 1980, it won major Brazilian awards and circulated internationally on the festival circuit. (Aufderheide)

Suggested Readings: Aufderheide, Patricia. "Brazil," in *World Cinema since 1945,* ed. William Luhr.

Aufderheide, Patricia. *Cross Cultural Film Guide.*

Cowell, Adrian. *The Decade of Destruction: The Crusade to Save the Amazon Rain Forest.*

Cowell, Adrian, and Alexander Cockburn. *The Fate of the Forest: Developers, Destroyers, and Defenders of the Amazon.*

Johnson, Randal. *The Film Industry in Brazil: Culture and the State.*

Mendes, Chico. *Fight for the Forest: Chico Mendes in His Own Words.*

Place, Susan, ed. *Tropical Forests: Latin American Nature and Society in Transition.*

Revkin, Andrew. *The Burning Season: The Murder of Chico Mendes and the Fight for the Amazon Rain Forest.*

Wagley, Charles. *Amazon Town: A Study of Man in the Tropics.*

Level: University

ISLA DAS FLORES (Isle of Flowers)

Documentary.   English Narration with Portuguese Portions Subtitled.   15 min.   1990
Directed by: Jorge Furtado
Distributed by: First Run/Icarus Films
Evaluators: Robin Andersen, Gary S. Elbow, S. Travis Silcox

Description: An extraordinary and devastating film that succeeds, through a unique rhetorical style, in connecting recognizable everyday life experiences with broader economic, social, and philosophical issues. The story is about "human beings, who have highly developed encephalons and opposable thumbs," and have therefore been able to "make many improvements on their planet." Humorous irony is achieved through a Monty Python montage-graphic style, juxtaposing images of the pyramids with mushroom clouds. The film uses the life history of a tomato (from production to disposal) as a way of pointing out inequities in the capitalist system. At the tomato's ultimate destination, the Island of Flowers, there are no flowers, only great mountains of garbage. At the garbage dump, we find pigs and human beings competing for organic material. Even though women and children have highly developed enchephalons and opposable thumbs, they have no money. But, we also learn, they are "free." Viewers are left with this contradiction.

Strengths and Weaknesses: With an interesting concept, strong visuals, and brilliant editing, the film's message is presented indirectly but unequivocally. The narrative style of "This Is the House That Jack Built" shows the layers upon layers of complexity that build an economy. The repetition of simple but penetrating definitions reveals modern contradictions (normally taken for granted) and, most devastatingly, the hypocrisy of an economic system that defines people as free but gives them fewer rights than pigs. The brevity of the film would provide plenty of time for discussion during a class period. Audiences will want to see it twice, as it moves at quite a fast pace. A multitude of side issues are presented that will stimulate as much discussion as the basic theme. This film would be especially useful in courses that focus on issues such as resource allocation, human equality, etc. Despite the seriousness of the subject matter and final messages, the film also contains much humor.

The film's presentation of Jews is its weak point. Images of Auschwitz are gratuitously inserted into the narrative. Also, some of the film's verbal and visual irony may be lost on some (especially younger) viewers.

Introducing the Tape: With conservative audiences, this film is guaranteed to offend some viewers. Thus, some kind of advance notice about the content and satirical style would be useful.

How to Use: The video would be useful for a number of *Liberal Arts* courses because it so effectively connects everyday, taken-for-granted experiences with larger socioeconomic and environmental processes. Increasingly, it seems that the U.S. media are highly invested in denying the negative consequences of a market-driven society, especially for the poor. (Andersen)

I would use this piece to get audiences to consider the status of the poor and to think about the implications of being poor. There is a great deal of ancillary information imparted in the film that could be discussed as well. All of it relates in one way or another to human welfare (or the lack thereof). Another possibility would be to have students write a commentary after having seen the film and then discuss the subject matter as a group. That way, students would have an opportunity to compare their own reactions with those of other members of the class (or group). (Elbow)

I would use this film to interrogate traditional documentary techniques. The film is an example of the innovation and creative process that transcends any particular genre. (Silcox)

Suggested Readings: Jesus, Carolina María de. *Child of the Dark: The Diary of Carolina María de Jesus.*

Level: High School — University

JOAO DO PIFI

Documentary.   Without Subtitles.   7 min.   1989
Directed & Produced by: TV Viva-Centro Luiz Freire (Rua São Bento 344, Ribeira 53110, Olinda PE; tel: [5581] 429-4109; fax: [5581] 429-4881)
Distributed by: IMRE Archive (available for viewing only)
Evaluators: Mary Jane Craver, John Fett
Description: A northeastern Brazilian master flute maker demonstrates how to make and play the folkloric flute of Pernambuco. He crafts the flutes by hand, explaining how this skill was passed on to him from his father, who learned from past generations. The tape follows the flute master as he takes the instruments to the open market to sell. It contains many shots of him playing the flute and includes folk music and dancing.

Strengths and Weaknesses: This is an engaging film of authentic folklore, showing the simple pleasures gained from making and playing the flute. The instrument is both this man's livelihood and source of enjoyment.

One evaluator felt that the tape was too short and could have contained more detail.

Introducing the Tape: An introduction situating the tape and its relation to the people and culture of northeastern Brazil (probably the poorest region of the country) is necessary for U.S. viewers.

How to Use: For a beginning *Portuguese* class I would summarize the film then let the students ask questions, pausing the tape as we went along. We would play it at least once without any interruption. (Craver)

Level: Junior High School—University

O JOGO DA DIVIDA: QUEM DEVE A QUEM? (The Debt Game: Who Owes Whom?)

Documentary.   In English.   58 min.   1991
Directed by: Eduardo Coutinho
Produced by: CECIP—Centro de Criação de Imagem Popular (Rua Sanador Dantas 80–201, Rio de Janeiro; tel: [5521] 533-0772)
Distributed by: IMRE
Evaluators: Nancy J. Church, Sidney M. Greenfield, Jon Jonakin, Michele Geslin Small
Description: *The Debt Game* examines the problem of the external debt of many Latin American countries, from the point of view of the Third World. It offers a historical treatment of the emergence and persistence of Latin America's chronic indebtedness to the First World. A common theme runs throughout: From the primitive accumulation following the Spanish conquest to the postcolonial British loans to the International Monetary Fund austerity conditions, oil price shocks, and floating interest rates of the 1970s and 1980s, Latin America has been a net loser in the game of international trade and finance. The tape, sectioned loosely into several parts and focusing mostly on Brazil, deals with the historical origins of the debt, its explosion in the 1980s, the human consequences of the IMF's policies, and a reflection on "what is to be done."

Strengths and Weaknesses: This video uses a unique and creative blend of historical footage, interviews with experts, political cartoons, animation, and theatrical skits to convey its message. The tape is best when it relies on the testimony of regional political scientists, economists, and religious workers to bolster the case made by the voice-over narration. The animated segments are useful in highlighting particular issues—for instance, quantifying the costs of servicing the debt in terms of the number of bags of coffee or sugar, per capita, etc. Particularly forceful and effective is the tape's portrayal of the role of the debt in constraining and redirecting national political initiative and in reducing living standards.

The tape is overly ambitious in its attempt to cover five

hundred years of financial history in one hour. One reviewer felt that tape was repetitive and propagandistic. First World perspectives via interviews with IMF economists or bankers are not included. Others pointed out that the tape offers a clearly Third World/debtor perspective that is rarely available to U.S. viewers.

Introducing the Tape: Because of the brevity with which complex events are treated, issues such as the relation between the Vietnam War, growing U.S. balance of payments deficits, excess money supply, the collapse of the Bretton Woods agreements under Nixon, and the Brady Plan need to be discussed in greater detail. The video's basic recommendatson that Latin American nations simply declare a moratorium on debt payments is, despite its intuitive appeal, too simplistic. This point needs to be put into context by explaining that in the 1980s a number of countries that were facing economic collapse responded to the call to boycott their debt payments to First World banks. In fact, many countries did default on their loans because they were literally unpayable. However, these loans have since been renegotiated, and the boycott movement failed owing to the pressures exerted on the debtor countries by international capital.

How to Use: Students could be shown the tape to motivate their attempt to investigate solutions to the debt problem. They could then debate the issue of lending and repaying loans. (Church)

This is one of the best documentaries I have seen. I would use it to present a general picture of the major reasons for social injustice (the lack of distributive justice) in Latin America. It is self-contained and really doesn't need anything in the way of background. (Greenfield)

The tape would be useful in a course on *Development Economics* or *Political Economy* to highlight issues of finance and international relations. A quick summary of what to expect would be helpful. Depending on the audience, a mention of what import substitution industrialization meant historically, as well as a brief focus on the importance of the "debt mechanisms"—changes in the debt portfolio, the differential effects of the two oil price shocks, and the changes in the terms of trade—would better prepare the viewers. (Jonakin)

Suggested Readings: Galeano, Eduardo H. *Open Veins of Latin America: Five Centuries of the Pillage of a Continent.*

Todaro, Michael. *Economic Development in the Third World: An Introduction to Problems and Policies in a Global Perspective,* an undergraduate text that has a useful treatment of trade and Third World debt; chapters 12, 13, and 14 provide corroboration for much of what is presented in the video and discuss IMF requirements for granting loans and repayment.

Level: University

JOGOS SEXUAIS INFANTIS

Documentary.   Without Subtitles.   5 min.   1986
Directed by: Angela Freitas
Produced by: SOS Corpo (Rua Major Codeceira 37, St.

Amaro, 50100-070 Recife, Pernambuco; tel: [5581] 221-3018; fax: [5581] 221-3947)
Distributed by: IMRE Archive (available for viewing only)
Evaluators: Brian Goldfarb
Description: This documentary explores adult views on the sexuality of children. Interviews with parents, psychologists, and teachers begin to confront social taboos concerning the sexual and sensual lives of children. The tape suggests that children should be allowed and encouraged to experiment with intimacy and sensual contact and that parental repression impedes children from learning about their own bodies and respecting others.
Strengths and Weaknesses: The tape combines interviews, role-playing, and music in a creative and thoughtful manner. It covers its topic from a range of viewpoints, doing justice to a complex subject within a short format. The video is conducive to classroom discussion and would be excellent for use in various courses and levels.
Introducing the Tape: It would be helpful to have background on low-budget production, access to equipment and distribution in Brazil, and how groups like SOS Corpo and TV Viva are organized, funded, structured, etc.
How to Use: I would use this tape to focus discussion on the use of video as a pedagogical tool, raising questions about how authority is framed and conferred on subjects in the video. Students would consider strategies with documentary practice that effectively draws upon popular forms of knowledge to engage everyday concerns in a critical manner. (Goldfarb)
Suggested Readings: Agosta, Diana. "Mo' Better News: A Discussion on Media Education."

Castaño, Eleonora Ferrieira, and João Paulo Castaño. *Making Sense of the Media: A Handbook of Popular Education Techniques.*

Elsworth, Elizabeth, and Marianne Whatley, eds. *The Ideology of Images in Educational Media: Hidden Curriculums in the Classroom.*

Fine, Michelle. "Sexuality, Schooling, and Adolescent Females: The Missing Discourse of Desire," in *Beyond Silenced Voices,* ed. Lois Weis and Michelle Fine.

Goldfarb, Brian. "Video Activism and Critical Pedagogy: Sexuality at the End of the Rainbow."

Johnson, Randal, and Robert Stam, eds. *Brazilian Cinema.*

Schwoch, James, Mimi White, and Susan Reilly. *Media Knowledge: Readings in Popular Culture, Pedagogy, and Critical Citizenship.*

Sedgwick, Eve Kosofsky. "How to Bring Your Kids Up Gay."
Level: High School—University

LIGHT MEMORIES OF RIO
Documentary.   With Subtitles.   33 min.   1987
Directed by: José Inacio Parente
Produced by: Interior Producoes Ltda. (Rua Barao de Jaguaribe 243, Rio de Janeiro 22421; tel: [5521] 521-5700)

Distributed by: The Cinema Guild
Evaluators: Ann S. Blum, Warren J. Dean, John Fett, Tânia M. Hering
Description: This documentary presents the history of photography in Rio de Janeiro, illustrating a wide variety of city scenes from 1840 to 1920, from daguerreotypes through motion pictures. The tape integrates technical and artistic history with social history. It depicts the development of urban Rio from its small-town origins to the cosmopolitan metropolis of the early twentieth century, including mention of the slave trade, the large influx of immigrants from Europe, difficult working conditions, and unionism. Paralleling the history of Rio with that of its photography, the film shows how photography made possible the memories of historical periods. The film's conclusion puts more emphasis on the discovery of photography than on the history of Rio.
Strengths and Weaknesses: The photo documentation is very strong and portrays a substantial amount of the history of Rio in pictures. There is excellent coordination of photos with poetic and intelligent narration. The images selected would overturn students' stereotypes of nineteenth-century Latin America. Images include slavery, European immigration, urban leisure activities, working-class neighborhoods, fancy shopping districts, city redesign and rebuilding, industrialization, and the introduction of the automobile. Different periods of Rio's evolution are covered.

One evaluator felt that the tape did not present enough information about social issues.
Introducing the Tape: This film is not intended as a history of Brazil, but it would benefit from being shown in a context of political, economic, and social history, especially that of slavery and abolition, immigration, and the transition to European immigrant labor. An instructor may wish to include history readings on immigration, urbanization, and distribution of wealth. This would help students understand the fascinating images and narrative line. One reviewer felt that the piece was very evocative by itself and didn't need overexplanation.
How to Use: I would use this tape in a class on the *Social History of Brazil and/or Latin America.* Urban history is one of the growth fields in the social history of Latin America, and the literature on urban Brazil is particularly strong. This tape illustrates the complexity of late-nineteenth-century urban life; the growth of an urban working class of national and European immigrant origins; a Europe-oriented urban elite; and, to a limited extent, the rural-urban connections between the coffee-export cycle and urbanization/modernization. It would work extremely well in conjunction with the titles listed below, which I use in my *Social History* courses. (Blum)

I would use this tape in *Brazilian History* class, showing the first half in a discussion of nineteenth-century slave plantations. The second half could be used to discuss the Republic and modernization of cities. (Dean)

The tape could be used for a *Documentary Film* course or any course that would like to depict life in early Rio. (Fett)

I would use this tape as a means to bring knowledge of one of Brazil's most beautiful cities to my students. (Hering)

Suggested Readings: Bastide, Roger. *African Civilisations in the New World.*

Bastide, Roger. *The African Religions of Brazil: Toward a Sociology of the Interpenetration of Civilizations.*

Bastide, Roger, and Florestan Fernandes. *Brancos e negros em São Paulo.*

Degler, Carl N. *Neither Black nor White: Slavery and Race Relations in Brazil and the United States.*

Francisco, Alencar, et al. *História da sociedade brasileira.*

Karasch, Mary. *Slave Life in Rio de Janeiro, 1808–1850.*

Lauderdale-Graham, Sandra. *House and Street: The Domestic World of Servants and Masters in Nineteenth-Century Rio de Janeiro.*

Moura, Clóvis. *Brasil: as raízes do protesto negro.*

Nascimento, Abdias do. *Brazil. Mixture or Massacre?: Essays in the Genocide of a Black People.*

Nascimento, Abdias do. *Dois negros libertários.*

Needell, Jeffrey D. *A Tropical Belle-Epoque: Elite Culture and Society in Turn-of-the-Century Rio de Janeiro.*

Pereira, João Batista Borges. *Negro e cultura negra no Brasil atual.*

Pinto, Regina Pahim. "O movimento negro e etnicidade."

Silva, Nelson do Valle. *Relações raciais no Brasil contemporâneo.*

Skidmore, Thomas E. *Black into White: Race and Nationality in Brazilian Thought.*

Skidmore, Thomas E. *Fact and Myth: Discovering a Racial Problem in Brazil.*

Turner, Michael. "Brown into Black: Changing Racial Attitudes of Afro-Brazilian University Students."

Winant, Howard. *Racial Conditions: Politics, Theory, Comparison.*

Local Brazilian publications such as:

Afinal. "Cem anos depois: a espera da ablição." 190 (19 April 1988), 36–43.

Calalloo.

IBASE (Instituto Brasileiro de análises sociais e econômicas). "A situação do negro no Brasil: discriminação, trabalho, história." Rio de Janeiro, 1986.

Isto É. "Cem anos de abolição: a liberdade passada a limpo," 59 (20 April 1988), 30–45.

Manchete.

O Globo.

Veja. "Negros," (11 May 1988); "Operação desastrada," (26 October 1988).

Level: High School—University

MAE TERRA

Documentary.   Without Subtitles.   18 min.   1987

Produced by: TV Viva-Centro Luiz Freire (Rua São Bento 344, Ribeira 53110, Olinda PE; tel: [5581] 429-4109; fax: [5581] 429-4881)

Distributed by: IMRE Archive (available for viewing only)

Evaluators: Lydia M. Garner, David McCreery

Description: This tape examines the problems caused by lack of agrarian reform, focusing on the conditions and women peasants' struggles to gain access and rights to land. It looks at the problems of hunger and malnutrition, women's "double day" (working at home and at a day job), the different kinds of work women do, and their efforts to obtain rights both from the law and within popular organizations.

Strengths and Weaknesses: In general, reviewers felt this was a good, effective film. One evaluator commented, however, that the tape is weakened by portraying all women as paragons of virtue and ignoring their relations with men, both in the family and in the organizations in which they participate. The transitions between segments could also be smoother.

Introducing the Tape: It would be helpful to know that the film takes place in Brazil and to know more about the nature of the land conflict at the center of much of the action in the film.

How to Use: I would introduce this tape into the discussion about women in agricultural life in my *Modern Latin American History* course. (McCreery)

Level: University

MARLY NORMAL (Marly Normal)

Experimental.   No Dialogue.   5 min.   1985

Directed by: Marcelo Machado and Fernando Meirelles

Produced by: Olhar Eletronico

Distributed by: IMRE

Evaluators: Sarah Chambers, Catherine Egan, Oscar Flores, Alida Metcalf, Yolanda Prieto

Description: This is an experimental piece that compresses one day in the life of an urban, middle-class, single, working woman into five minutes. Quick cuts show her waking, going to work, eating lunch at a fast-food restaurant, and returning home to an evening in front of the television, where her day is replayed on a television screen-within-a-screen. Themes conveyed are monotony, loneliness, and the fast-paced, inhuman nature of industrial urban life. A rapidly edited montage of faces in the subway shows people looking tired, unhappy, and distrustful. Human isolation is strongly conveyed. The tape has no dialogue, but sounds of daily routine are emphasized.

Strengths and Weaknesses: The tape is creative and skillfully edited. The images and effects accomplish its idea; it is an artistic statement on the banality of daily routine.

Introducing the Tape: One reviewer suggested explaining that the woman depicted is typical of a certain class but not of the population as a whole.

How to Use: In *Spanish* class the video would help illustrate the difference in an average citizen's daily routine within Brazil and the United States. (Flores)

I would use this tape to explain the effect on people of industrialization and what is called "development." The tape would be a good illustration of lectures on such topics as industrial, urban life. (Prieto)

The tape could be played without introduction and students could be asked to discuss what they think it conveys. Comparisons could be made to the lives of working-class people in the United States.

Suggested Readings: Cooley, Mike. *Architect or Bee: The Human Technology Relationship.*

Garson, Barbara. *All the Lifelong Day: The Meaning and Demeaning of Routine Work.*

Terkel, Studs. *Working.*

Level: Junior High School—University

MEMORIA DE MULHERES

Documentary. Without Subtitles. 37 min. 1991
Directed by: María A. Lemos and Marcia Meireles
Produced by: Comulher-Comunicação Mulher (Rua Rocha, 119–504, São Paulo 01330; tel: [5511] 251-5626; fax: [5511] 660-477)
Distributed by: IMRE Archive (available for viewing only)
Evaluators: Hugo Chapa-Guzmán, Teresita Martínez-Vergne
Description: Thirty Brazilian women describe their experiences of "liberation." They come from diverse socioeconomic backgrounds and varied ethnic and racial origins and understand their position in the *movimento feminista* (women's movement) in very different terms. The tape includes brief historical sketches with documentary footage of feminist movements in Brazil and contemporary feminists offering their historical perspective. Among the women interviewed are Dulce Accioly, Santinha, Lenise Borges, Eleonora Menecucci, and María de Oliveira.
Strengths and Weaknesses: The tape's "talking heads" format is effective in highlighting the variety of experiences for women. The film, however, is edited in such a way that the women's movement appears to have undergone a linear progression—voting rights, economic parity with men, political involvement in redemocratization efforts, rising consciousness regarding domestic violence, health issues, the environment. One evaluator pointed out that racial and class divisions within the women's movement are almost ignored.
Introducing the Tape: It should be pointed out that not all women in Brazil have had their lives transformed by the feminist movement.
How to Use: I would simply present the tape to an audience and ask for comments, or let the class borrow it from the library. (Chapa-Guzmán)

I would use excerpts from the piece, selecting particularly articulate speakers to make certain, very specific points. (Martínez-Vergne)

The tape can be used in a *Sociology* class to discuss the role of men in relation to the feminist movement.

In *Comparative Culture* and *Women's Studies* courses the feminist movement in Brazil can be compared and contrasted to its counterpart in the United States.
Suggested Readings: Albornoz, Suzana, et al. *Na condição de mulher.*

Augusta, Nisia Floresta Brasileira. *Opúsculo humanitário.*

Avila Neto, María Inacia d'. *O autoritarismo e a mulher: o jogo da dominação macho-fêmea no Brasil.*

Bizzotto, Margarida. *Mulher em suas evidências.*

Burmeister, Tereza. *Década da mulher, 1976–1985: avaliação.*

Colasanti, Marina. *Aqui entre nós.*

Creusa de Goes Monteiro Negreiros, Teresa. *Emancipação da mulher: uma luta.*

D'Ans Hughes, José Oscar Beozzo. *Mulher: da escravidão a libertação.*

Hahner, June Edith. *Emancipating the Female Sex: The Struggle for Women's Rights in Brazil, 1850–1940.*

Hahner, June Edith. *Women in Brazil: Problems and Perspectives.*

Lage de Gama Lima, Lana, et al. *Mulheres, adúlteros e padres: histórica e moral na sociedade Brasileira.*

Leite, Miriam Moreira. *Outra face do feminism.*

Medeiros da Fonseca, Romy. *A condição feminina.*

Morgado, Belkis. *A marca do gado: rótulo da mulher.*

Mulheres trabalhadoras rurais: participação e luta sindical/Escher, Adelmo, et al. *Mutirão de Educação Popular: Mulher Trabalhadora Rural.*

Muraro, Rose Marie. *Sexualidade da mulher Brasileira: corpo e classe social no Brasil.*

Patai, Daphne. *Brazilian Women Speak: Contemporary LIfe Stories.*

Oliveira Costa, Albertina de and Cristina Bruschini. *Rebeldia e submissão: estudos sobre condição feminina.*

Saffioti, Heleieth Iara Bongiovani. *Mulher Brasileira: opressão e exploração*

Souza, Barbara M. de, et al. *Meu nome é mulher: temas para debate.*

Level: University

MENTIRAS & HUMILHAÇÕES (Lies & Humiliations)

Experimental. With Subtitles. 3 min. 1988
Directed and Produced by: Eder Santos
Distributed by: Electronic Arts Intermix
Evaluators: María Fernández, María A. Lazarini
Description: A haunting and lyrical work that merges poetic language and Super-8 images to invoke memory and its ghosts. Infused with an almost ethereal light, images of a house evoke its past. A voice-over of a Carlos Drumond de Andrade poem, "Poema Liquidação" (Special Sale), emphasizes the past's inablility to cope with the future.
Strengths and Weaknesses: The lack of narrative coherence in some of the piece offers a refreshing and interesting alternative to traditional formats. The tape experiments with illumination, forms, movement, and flowing figures. Descriptive poetry and prose are mixed with dance and art work. The intervention of personal imagination in the process of image-making is also explored.

Viewers with no background in the arts may find this work confusing.

Introducing the Tape: For most U.S. audiences a longer introduction to the artist's work would be required.

How to Use: The tape is good for *Junior High School, High School,* or *College Video Production.* (Lazarini)

I would use this tape in my *Latin American Art* classes as part of a section on electronic technologies and Latin American art. (Fernández)

Suggested Readings: Drumond de Andrade, Carlos. "Poema Liquidação."

Hall, Stuart. "The Local and the Global," in *Culture, Globalization, and the World-System,* ed. Anthony D. King.

Works by modern artists such as Frida Kahlo and Pepon Osorio.

Level: Junior High School—University

MULHER INDIA
Documentary.   Without Subtitles.   30 min.   1985
Directed by: Elaine Bandeira
Produced by: Montevideo
Distributed by: CDI, IMRE Archive (available for viewing only)
Evaluators: Susan M. Deeds, Irene Matthews
Description: This short ethno-documentary focuses on the lives of Guaraní Indian women in three villages of São Paulo. It opens with a visual representation of the literary image of "primitive, noble, innocent" natives then documents the roles and life cycle of Indian women who live in considerable poverty. The tape offers views of Guaraní women at all stages of life, in villages and selling goods on the city streets. In interviews, many of the women speak of survival. The women are shown as the key factor in preserving indigenous worldviews and in helping the community eke out a subsistence from farming and small-craft production and sale.
Strengths and Weaknesses: The video portrays graphic, realistic scenes of the struggles of daily life. Through the interviews, women, men, and children present their views (speaking in Portuguese and in their own dialect). These perspectives are juxtaposed with those of elementary school children learning about Indians and with reactions from the dominant culture. This juxtaposition of "indigenous" and "civilized" images is done with a strong sense of ethnographic irony (interesting from the point of view of conscious feminist ethnographic subject). The photography is attractively done, offering a variety of lifestyles and types of homes, plus an almost idyllic (but dangerous) background of the jungle and village life.

Some of the spoken Portuguese will be difficult for language students to understand.
Introducing the Tape: The tape needs to be placed within the larger context of Indian history in Brazil. Also, the somewhat ironic, contrastive presentation needs to be discussed carefully in a U.S. classroom setting.
How to Use: The video could be used to illustrate the conditions of indigenous people in Brazil today, as well as the contributions of indigenous women to the maintenance of cultural integrity and economic subsistence. (Deeds)

I might use this as a supplement in a course I teach on *Culture in Latin America* to show the contemporary version of *Iracema,* for example. I would also use it as a successful example of a certain type of documentary (subjective but not intrusive). (Matthews)

Suggested Readings: Nash, June, and Helen Safa. *Women and Change in Latin America.*

Patai, Daphne. *Brazilian Women Speak: Contemporary Life Stories.*

Any of many studies on ethnic groups in modern Brazil, or on women in society in Latin America or aspects of contemporary society in Latin America/Brazil.
Complementary Films/Videos: *Iracema* (Brazil)
Level: University

MULHERES NEGRAS (Black Women of Brazil)
Documentary.   With Subtitles.   25 min.   1986
Directed and Produced by: Silvana Afran
Distributed by: Women Make Movies
Evaluators: Lourdes Fernández, Michele Geslin Small, Angharad N. Valdivia
Description: This tape explores the meaning of "being black" and how it has affected the everyday lives of several black Brazilian women of different ages and walks of life. The women speak about the treatment of women of color—they are discriminated against first as women then as blacks. They share their pains, frustrations, and anger at the constant oppression that they have to endure. At the same time, the women reveal their impressive strength and dignity and their artistic and spiritual aspirations.
Strengths and Weaknesses: This is an incredibly strong video about the intersecting oppressions of gender and race.
Introducing the Tape: The tape could use an introduction describing its reason, circumstances, and purpose. Students may need to be told that Brazil was a Portuguese colony, not a Spanish colony. Also, it should be mentioned that Brazil, like the United States, imported slaves from Africa.
How to Use: I would compare and contrast Brazilian race and sexual relations with those in the United States. Then, I would look in detail at the women's testimonies. (Fernández)

I could use this tape as an example of the condition of women of color in my *Women of the Third World* course. (Small)
Level: University

MULHERES NO CANAVIAL
Documentary.   Without Subtitles.   33 min.   1986
Directed by: Jacira Melo, Silvana Afram, Marcia Meirelles
Produced by: Conselho Estadual Feminina
Distributed by: IMRE Archive (available for viewing only)
Evaluators: Reid Andrews, Cliff Welch
Description: This documentary, set in rural São Paulo state, follows a group of female sugarcane workers as they go

about their work from sunup to sundown. It begins with their predawn commute, crammed into the backs of trucks, to the fields where they will hack down miles of cane stalks. Every stage of their daily ordeal is explored, even how they deal with menstruation when there are no toilets or outhouses. The tape consists of interviews with several diverse women, interspersed with shots of them working. Their resilience and good spirits are striking. Topics covered include work conditions, the length of the work day, child care, relations with their spouses, lunch, strikes, land reform, and some of the women's aspirations to own their own land. The sections on child care and land reform include a discussion of the role of the state government. The musical score adds depth for those who understand the Portuguese lyrics.

Strengths and Weaknesses: This is an excellent film, which shows a great deal of respect for the women, treating them as individuals rather than types. It clearly presents the difficult conditions under which the women work, emphasizing the special problems they face as women, the double burden of doing housework, cooking, taking care of children, etc., in the hours before and after work in the fields. A number of shots of the fields and the work are quite striking. The narrative, using the structure of the workday, progresses in a clear and direct fashion.

One evaluator felt that more could have been said about politics, unions, and other contextual matters, mentioning that it would have been interesting to hear from the union official or boss. Another reviewer found the tape monotonous in both content and visual format.

Introducing the Tape: Instructors should try to tie the situation of these women to the history of plantation agriculture in Brazil and the transition over the last hundred years from African slavery to modern wage labor. Teachers might want to provide student viewers with figures for the number of women currently engaged in this kind of labor. Introductory comments could specifically mention that women became the typical cane harvesters only in the 1970s; men had previously done the work. Increasingly, as resident laborers were expelled from the sugar plantations, they migrated to the cities and created suburbs. Men eventually took industrial or other town jobs while women and children commuted to the fields. Employers may have preferred women for harvesting, considering them to be less troublesome. However, women have participated actively in the labor movement, as this film briefly discusses.

How to Use: Class discussion would be centered on having the students articulate, in their own words, the specific problems these women face. (Andrews)

I would use this tape in my *Modern Latin American History* course to counter some of the romantic images of passive and/or hot-blooded Latin American women, to show their role in the economy, and to demonstrate their strength. The issues they worry about, such as income and child care, could help U.S. students identify with them. The tape is also useful in talking about why so much sugarcane is grown in Brazil (to avoid importing more oil, and thus keep the debt down) and the rest of Latin America (exports to U.S. consumers). (Welch)

Their issues can be compared to working conditions in the United States.

Suggested Readings: Mintz, Sidney. *Workers in the Cane.*

Scheper-Hughes, Nancy. *Death without Weeping: The Violence of Everyday Life in Brazil.*

Stolcke, Verena. *Coffee Planters, Workers, and Wives: Class Conflict and Gender Relations on São Paulo Plantations, 1850–1980,* also includes chapters on contemporary female cane harvesters.

Level: University

NASCIMENTO DO PASSO
Documentary.   Without Subtitles.   11 min.   1987
Directed & Produced by: TV Viva-Centro Luiz Freire (Rua São Bento 344, Ribeira 53110, Olinda PE; tel: [5581] 429-4109; fax: [5581] 429-4881)
Distributed by: IMRE Archive (available for viewing only)
Evaluators: John Chasteen, Tânia M. Hering
Description: This tape features an interview with Nascimento do Passo, a dancer of *frevo,* the Carnival music of Recife in the Brazilian northeast. Passo received this name in 1958 in a contest he won. He speaks about his struggles as an artist and a dancer trying to preserve this traditional folk form. The interview is intercut with scenes of his dancing.

Strengths and Weaknesses: This is an educational portrait of a well-informed subject. Passo provides unstructured testimony about the general decline of everything and especially about the money-grubbing politicians in charge of cultural policies.

The tape is a snapshot and provides little in the way of an interpretive framework.

Introducing the Tape: To make sense of this video, U.S. students would need basic familiarity with the practice of Brazilian Carnival.

How to Use: *Frevo* is very different from *samba,* both in its instrumentation and in the way it is danced. Thus, the tape could be used in combination with other tapes to illustrate the varieties of African dance traditions in the diaspora. A class on Carnival could make use of Alma Guillermoprieto's *Samba,* an entertaining first-person account of Carnival preparations among the poor of Rio de Janiero during the 1980s. (Chasteen)

I would use this tape in my *Portuguese Language* course to help students learn about Brazilian music, dance, and art. (Hering)

Suggested Readings: Guillermoprieto, Alma. *Samba.*
Level: Junior High School—University

ORFEU NEGRO (Black Orpheus)
Feature.   With Subtitles.   103 min.   1959
Directed by: Marcel Camus
Distributed by: IMRE

Evaluators: Melvin S. Arrington Jr., David William Foster, William Herzog

Description: Based on a major work of Brazilian literature, *Orfeu da conceição* by Vinicius de Morales, this film is a classic of Brazilian cinema in the 1950s and an example of internationalist interest in Brazil. French director Marcel Camus reworks the Greek myth of Orpheus and Eurydice, setting it in mid-twentieth-century Rio de Janeiro during Carnival. The story concerns the ill-fated love of a streetcar conductor (Orfeu) for a young woman from the countryside (Eurydice) who flees to the city hoping to elude a masked pursuer (Death). The film features visually stunning scenes of Rio and Carnival, along with the music of Antonio Carlos Jobim and Luis Bonfa. The most powerful sequence occurs during Orfeu's visit to a spiritualist church service. Here viewers witness a practitioner possessed by a spirit and Orfeu's desperate attempts to communicate with his dead lover, Eurydice.

Strengths and Weaknesses: This is a novel presentation of a classic story. The superb photography and music are definite strengths. The nonstop *samba* (music and dance) keeps the pace lively, and viewers get a good look at the extravagant costumes and floats of Carnival, as well as the mesmerizing intensity of a *Macumba* ritual. The film also provides a view of life in Brazilian *favelas* (slums), albeit jazzed up for Carnival and the film. The spoken Portuguese is not too idiomatic for class use.

Evaluators pointed out the film's sentimentalization of Brazilian culture, especially its condescending primitivist view of black culture. Some of the characters are stereotypes. One evaluator felt that the story development and acting were weak and the Carnival footage overdone.

Introducing the Tape: Viewers could use a brief explanation of the psychological and social significance of Carnival and the role of syncretism in religious ritual.

How to Use: I would use *Black Orpheus* to illustrate the numerous contributions of blacks to the formation of Brazilian culture. (Arrington)

I have used the film in courses giving a historical overview of Latin American filmmaking. I stressed the accommodation of the classical myth of Orpheus, the semiotic use of music, the romantic sentimentalization of black culture, and the reciprocal relationship between foreign images of Brazil and Brazilian self-images inspired by the tourist imperative. (Foster)

Suggested Readings: Johnson, Randal. Several monographs on Brazilian filmmaking (see bibliography for listing).

Moraes, Vinicius de. *Orfeu da conceição: tragédia Carioca; desenhos de Carlos Scliar.*

Wagley, Charles. *An Introduction to Brazil.*

Level: Junior High School—University

OSWALD: UM HOMEM SEM PROFISSÁO
Documentary. Without Subtitles. 26 min. 1990
Directed by: Marcia Meireles

Produced by: Lilas Producoes (Rua Rocha 119–504, São Paulo 01330; tel: [5511] 883-2165)

Distributed by: IMRE Archive (available for viewing only)

Evaluators: Mary Jane Craver, Warren J. Dean, Antônio R. M. Simões

Description: This is a docudrama about Brazilian author Oswald de Andrade that uses re-creation and oral description of his personal, political, social, and artistic life. The epoch in which de Andrade lived is presented through interpretive reading of his own texts and those of other authors, such as Patricia Galvao ("Paug") and Tarsila do Amaral. Interviews with literary and historical specialists, as well as Andrade's daughter Marilia and son Ruda, make the film rich in literary, personal, and historical content. Also included are viewpoints by Andrade's two most significant loves, Tarsila do Amaral and Anita Malfatti, regarding their experiences with Oswald. The tape includes actors interpreting Oswald, Tarsila, and Paug's passages from the staging of *O rei da vela,* directed by Zé Celso Martínez.

Strengths and Weaknesses: In general, the tape is well done and informative. It has good pacing and is quite objective, while poetic language is used throughout. The tape includes participation of important personalities in Brazilian literature and theater. The interviews inside the Téatro Municipal and those with Andrade's daughter and son are extremely strong. The irony, humor, and aggression of some of the texts make this documentary not only a powerful classroom tool but also a source for research and literary criticism for the period during and after the 1922 *Semana da Arte Modern* (Week of Modern Art) at the Téatro Municipal in São Paulo.

One reviewer commented that some scenes flashed by too quickly as a moving collage, which, while it may be a glimpse into Andrade's modernistic writing, is distracting.

Introducing the Tape: An introduction is definitely necessary to explain who the author was and what he wrote. Instructors could say that Oswald de Andrade led the Futuristic literary movement in Brazil; he was a rebel in his thinking, hence his works were always creative and a step ahead. Students also should be given background on the 1922 Week of Modern Art in Brazil. The instructor should identify the celebrities who appear in the tape as well as in some of the photos.

How to Use: The video could be used in graduate and upper-level *Comparative Literature, Brazilian Literature,* and *Modern Art* classes, as Tarsila's art definitely influenced Brazilian art forms. (Craver)

In a *Portuguese Language and Literature* class students could read and discuss passages from his book before or after viewing the film. I would ask students to see the film outside the class period and write essays on different points seen in the film. For instance, students may decide to discuss spatial difficulties, as well as other obstacles, in staging Oswald de Andrade's plays (cf. Sabato Magaldi's opinion that Oswald de Andrade's theater was not meant to be staged); some students may be interested in developing the view that

Brasilia's architecture is a result of Oswald de Andrade's work, and so on. Furthermore, the teacher may ask students to organize themselves in work groups and identify the sources of text passages read in the film. (Simões)

Suggested Readings: Andrade, Oswald de. *Serafim ponte grande.*

Andrade, Oswald de. *Um homem sem profissão: Memórias e confissães.*

Ataide, Vincente. *Introdução à literatura Brasileira contemporânea.*

Fonseca, María Augusta. *Oswald de Andrade: Uma biografía.*

Martin, Wilson. *The Modernist Idea: A Critical Survey of Brazilian Writing in the Twentieth Century.*

Moises, Massand. *A Literatura Brasileira através dos textos.*

Level: University

P'TAMUNA (P'Tamuna, Son of the Earth)

Documentary.   With Subtitles.   14 min.   1990
Directed by: Paulo Baroukh
Produced by: VTV Video (Rua Itapeva, 187 CEP 01332-000, São Paulo; tel: [5511] 251-1313; fax: [5511] 251-3740)
Distributed by: IMRE
Evaluators: Craig Auchter, Susan Douglass, Catherine Egan, Mark Littman
Description: This short documentary provides an opportunity to meet the Macuxi Indians in Brazil. The Indians speak candidly to the camera, understanding that video represents a vehicle to carry their words and images beyond their own community. They speak of their relationships to "whites" and demand more respect from the white government and the right to preserve and control their land, religion, traditions, and language. Their pride in their Indian roots is evident. We hear chants of haunting beauty and see scenes of daily life, native dancing, food preparation, and religious ceremonies narrated by the Indians.
Strengths and Weaknesses: In general, evaluators felt positive about the tape. A great strength of the work is that the subjects are allowed to speak for themselves. Produced in association with the Macuxi, this is not a tape about "the Other."

One evaluator commented that the tape presented a somewhat superficial view of these Indians' lives but felt that the brief scene of the chanter sitting on a rock singing his ancient story was worth the whole film.
Introducing the Tape: The tape needs an introduction to indigenous/dominant culture relations and the policy of the Brazilian government, as well as some background on environmental discourse and the role of indigenous communities in Brazil.
How to Use: This tape would allow students to see and hear Macuxis speaking for themselves. It clearly shows how they value their own culture. (Auchter)

This film gives an excellent picture of tribal life in twentieth-century Brazil. I would use it in a ninth-grade *Global Studies* course and have students compare it to *The Emerald Forest.* (Douglass)

The segment of the chanter might be used to impress on *Writing* students the importance and beauty of telling a story. (Littman)
Complementary Films/Videos: *The Emerald Forest* (distributed by Facets)
Level: High School—University

PARA ONDE? (Where to Now?)

Music Video.   No Dialogue.   8 min.   1991
Directed by: Alfredo Alves
Produced by: IBASE Video (Rua Vicente de Souza No. 29, Rio de Janeiro, RJ 2251; tel: [5521] 226-5412; fax: [5521] 285-0541)
Distributed by: IMRE
Evaluators: Francis R. Beethlen, Mary Jane Craver, Victor Garatea, Carlos A. Pérez, Carolyn Shapiro
Description: A beautiful collage of images set to music illustrates the development of the Amazon region and the tragedies that development has created for the indigenous people, the colonizers, and the environment. The images are strong, moving from the more natural setting of indigenous life to the quick, complex, machine-laden view of the invasion of modern technologies.
Strengths and Weaknesses: This is an artistic assembly of strong, provocative visuals that demonstrate the clash of cultures. There is no text and no development of a story line, yet the video provides a perfect introduction to a study of the Amazon.

The music is a bit disconcerting. One evaluator found the tape somewhat unclear.
Introducing the Tape: Viewers need only basic familiarity with the issues of rain forest destruction to appreciate the film.
How to Use: The tape could be used to illustrate the effects of modern man's advancement and its effect on indigenous groups. (Garatea)

The film is great to demonstrate the complexities of Amazonian development, what the intended and unintended consequences of development are, and what should be considered prior to development. It shows that radical changes in the environment are needed. (Pérez)

I would have students watch this video several times and then write their reactions. I would also stop the video with certain scenes and have a discussion about what the students think is happening. (Shapiro)
Suggested Readings: *Cultural Survival*'s catalog of papers, books, and quarterly journals.
Level: Junior High School—University

PEMP (Pemp)

Documentary.   With Subtitles.   27 min.   1988
Directed by: Vincent Carelli

Produced by: Centro de Trabalho Indigenista (Rua Fidalga 548, Vila Madalena, São Paulo; tel: [5511] 813-3450; fax: [5511] 212-3692)

Distributed by: IMRE, Video Data Bank, Videographe

Evaluators: José-Manuel Navarro, Carolyn Shapiro

Description: This film presents the story of the Garrião Indians of the Paraketje community and their successful negotiations with industrialists and the Brazilian central government to preserve their culture and land amidst the influx into the Amazon Basin of settlers, roads, trains, and commerce. The Indians have been able to obtain financial security through their highly astute negotiations. Included in the tape are the community's rites of passage for a young man entering adulthood.

Strengths and Weaknesses: The film is a case study in successful community organizing of native groups. It presents native Brazilian Indian leadership in a positive light. The Garrião people come through as successful negotiators in a world not of their making. They are so successful, in fact, that they joined with three other groups and now have financial security. The tape contains strong visual images of the land and the people.

The video does not present much background about the indigenous culture in setting the historic scene for cultural conflict. Also, some of the subtitles are difficult to read and a few of the translations are inaccurate.

Introducing the Tape: U.S. viewers will need background about the indigenous culture and the geography of the area and some history about why there is an influx of settlers into the indigenous area. Critical discussion of the white Brazilians' dealings with native peoples since the 1960s would add greatly to the appreciation of the film and the lessons that can be learned from it.

How to Use: After the introduction and screening I would discuss how the film ties into, or departs from, that history. Students would write two essays critiquing the film, one immediately after viewing and another comparing the views they hold after the discussion. Students could also read Carl Degler's book (which discusses the interaction between black and white Brazilians), develop a model of cross-racial interaction in Brazil, and apply it to the Garrião Indians in this film. (Shapiro)

Suggested Readings: Degler, Carl. *Neither Black nor White: Slavery and Race Relations in Brazil and the United States.*

Level: High School — University

PIVETE (Pivete)

Documentary. No Dialogue. 6 min.

Directed by: Lucila Mirelles

Produced by: Lucila and Julia Mirelles

Distributed by: IMRE Archive (available for viewing only)

Evaluators: Enríque R. Rodríguez, Antônio R. M. Simões

Description: The tape contains visuals of Brazil's abandoned children in prisons and on the streets of Rio de Janeiro.

The camera captures different emotions and voices of children of both sexes and different colors. Some seem to be at ease and joke about their own misery; others look desperate, silently sad; some children look like adults; others show no fear or remorse for crimes they have committed. The camera is the narrator. The film renders images of the children without wordy involvement from a presenter. No violence is shown, but viewers can feel it latent in every scene. The death squad activities are evident.

Strengths and Weaknesses: The tape presents a clear picture of the lives of poor urban children in Brazil. It creates impressions without direct participation of a narrator, capturing the children's different emotions through their eyes, gestures, and expressions. The scenes with children talking, laughing, and grimacing speak powerfully for themselves.

Lack of narration limits the film to an artistic presentation. No context is provided and thus it is often not clear where the children are: in a prison? in an orphanage? on the streets?

Introducing the Tape: An introduction should emphasize the social stratification of Brazil, the development of the *favelas* (slums) that surround Rio, and the establishment of death squads that have been murdering street children since the 1960s.

How to Use: I would use this film to help the United States public further understand the struggle of the poor in Brazil and the abuse and lack of human rights for the people of the *favelas*. I would develop a questionnaire that would lead to a discussion on the issues presented by the video. (Rodríguez)

The tape could be used in *Portuguese Language* courses at all levels to discuss social issues in Brazil and bring to foreigners a social awareness of these facts. It could also be suitable for classes in *Developmental Psychology*. Because it is short, the tape could be presented during a class period and discussed directly afterward. More advanced *Language* classes may use the highly descriptive scenes to work on descriptions of emotions and the places mentioned in the tape. Naturally the most appropriate verb tenses and aspects to be practiced are the present indicative in contrast with preterit/imperfect of indicative. (Simões)

Level: University

O POVO DO VENENO (The Poison People)

Documentary. English Narration and Subtitles. 28 min. 1991

Directed by: Julio Azcarate

Produced by: IBASE—Video (Rua Vicente de Souza No. 29, Rio de Janeiro, RJ 22251; tel: [5521] 226-5412; fax: [5521] 285-0541)

Distributed by: IMRE

Evaluators: Victor Garatea, Carlos A. Pérez, Carolyn Shapiro

Description: This beautiful film describes what happened to an indigenous group in the Amazon when colonizers moved into their ancestral lands and forced them to abandon some of their traditions. It documents the plight of members of the Zuruaha tribe, who live in the Brazilian Amazon. Viewers are introduced to the Zuruahas' beliefs about the spirit world and its integration with plants, animals, and humans. When the Zuruaha tribe encountered Portuguese conquistadors in the early 1500s, they suffered a number of attacks and all their tribal leaders and medicine men were killed. Malaria, smallpox, and other diseases brought by the Europeans decimated the tribe. The survivors retreated deep into the Amazon and had no contact with the "developed" world for centuries. In 1978, the destruction of the rain forest resulting from the construction of the Transamazonia Highway forced the Zuruaha out of the rain forest. Since then, the people have been relocated to a small preserve, and the remaining 138 villagers have become known as the "poison people." Rather than witness the slow death of their tribe, many commit suicide with the poison they manufactured for their hunting arrows.

Strengths and Weaknesses: This beautiful tape is rich in detail on the ecology of the Amazon. The visual images are wonderful, and there is a fresh, natural feeling in the portrayal of the village. The treatment of issues pertaining to the indigenous group is culturally sensitive and respectful. The video highlights the relationship between ideology and ecology.

One reviewer felt that the background music was disconcerting, setting the stage for a more "Western" emotional reaction to the concept of suicide, and would have preferred indigenous songs. The film does not identify many of the daily activities shown.

Introducing the Tape: The tape can be understood as it is, but would be greatly enhanced if the context of Amazonian development is discussed beforehand. Some history of the entry of nonindigenous peoples (rubber tappers, cattle farmers, and gold miners) into the Amazon would be helpful.

How to Use: I would use this work as an illustration of *Amazonian Ecologies* (tropical ecologies in general) and in *Adaptation* and *Symbolism* courses. (Pérez)

I would use this video to teach how people respond differently to their environment—citing examples of how the Zuruaha live with respect for the natural world through their hunting and building rituals, their use of plants in making containers, food, dwellings, and their equating the felling of a tree to a person's death. Then I would talk about our connection to our environment as something we consume, manipulate, and dominate. The film also introduces a discussion on the different concepts of death and suicide. (Shapiro)

Suggested Readings: *Cultural Survival*'s catalog of papers, books, and quarterly journals.

Complementary Films/Videos: *Para onde? (Where to Now?)* (Brazil); *Amazônia: Voices from the Rain Forest* (Brazil); *Alto a los encendios forestales (Halting the Fires)* (Brazil) to present a more complete picture of the cultural and environmental destruction in the Amazon.

Level: High School—University

QUANDO O CRIOULO DANÇA (When Blacks Dance)
Docudrama.   With Subtitles.   35 min.   1989
Directed by: Dilma Loes
Produced by: Loes Producoes Artisticas (Brazil), DL Trading (U.S.) (16919 North Bay Road, #406, Miami, FL 33160; tel: [305] 944-3601; fax: [305] 944-3672)
Distributed by: IMRE
Evaluators: Darién J. Davis, Tânia M. Hering, Elizabeth Marchant

Description: Posing the question "When does the black man dance?" this documentary explores contemporary race relations in Brazil. Dance is used as a metaphor for protest, escapism, and pure celebration of culture. On-the-street interviews with both white and black Brazilians and commentary by Afro-Brazilian activists and academics explore the relationship between individuals' prejudice and racism as a societal manifestation. At times with humor, the film exposes the harassment and stereotypes that oppress blacks in Brazil. It also includes footage of civil rights demonstrations and some aspects of Afro-Brazilian culture, such as the religious tradition *Exú*.

Strengths and Weaknesses: This powerful tape is creatively shot and wonderfully edited. The interviews are well done and present many points of view on the issues.

One reviewer felt that the dance sequences could have been tied to the interviews more effectively.

Introducing the Tape: U.S. audiences would need an explanation of the title of this work and Afro-Brazilians' use of dance for protest and/or liberation. Background on some of the people interviewed would also be helpful, particularly those involved in the black movement.

How to Use: I would use this tape in my *Latin American History* class when we discuss either race relations in Brazil or popular culture. I would provide students with a background on slavery and the historical position of blacks in Brazilian society, emphasizing their limited opportunity and that dance for black people symbolizes a quest for freedom as well as a celebration of cultural roots. When focusing on popular culture or class, the tape could show how art, in general, can serve both as defiance and celebration. (Davis)

In my *Portuguese Language* courses the beautiful use of the language would help students learn the language from native Brazilians in real circumstances. (Hering)

Suggested Readings: Alencar, Francisco, et al. *História da sociedade Brasileira*.

Bastide, Roger. *African Civilizations in the New World*.

Bastide, Roger. *The African Religions of Brazil: Toward a Sociology of the Interpenetration of Civilizations*.

Bastide, Roger, and Florestan Fernandes. *Brancos e negros em São Paulo*.

Degler, Carl N. *Neither Black nor White: Slavery and Race Relations in Brazil and the United States*.

IBASE (Instituto Brasileiro de Análises Sociais e Econômicas). "A situação do negro no Brasil: discriminação, trabalho, história."

Moura, Clóvis. *Brasil: as raizes do protesto negro.*

Nascimento, Abdias do. *Brazil: Mixture or Massacre? Essays in the Genocide of a Black People.*

Nascimento, Abdias do. *Dois negros libertários.*

Pereira, João Batista. *Negra e cultura negra no Brasil atual.*

Pinto, Regina Pahim. "O movimento negro e etnicidade."

Silva, Nelson do Valle. *Relações raciais no Brasil contemporâneo.*

Skidmore, Thomas E. *Black Into White: Race and Nationality in Brazilian Thought.*

Skidmore, Thomas E. *Fact and Myth: Discovering a Racial Problem in Brazil.*

Turner, Michael. "Brown into Black: Changing Racial Attitudes of Afro-Brazilian University Students."

Winant, Howard. *Racial Conditions: Politics, Theory, Comparison.*

The Journal of Afro-Latin American Studies and Literatures.

Local Brazilian publications:

Afinal. "Cem anos depois: a espera da abolição." 190 (19 April 1988), 36–43.

Calalloo.

Isto É. "Cem anos de abolição: a liberdade passada a limpo." 59 (20 April 1988), 30–45.

Veja. "Negros" (11 May 1988). "Operação desastrada" (26 October 1988).
Level: University

QUE BON TE VER VIVA (How Nice to See You Alive)
Documentary. With Subtitles. 100 min. 1989
Directed by: Lucia Murat
Distributed by: Women Make Movies
Evaluators: Paul LaReau, Sheldon Maram, S. Travis Silcox, Angharad N. Valdivia, Susan Wood
Description: This film features interviews with eight women who survived government torture during the late 1960s and early 1970s in Brazil. The former political prisoners relate how they survived and went on with life after their release. They explain how their ordeals never leave them, and that, although they have learned to cope, they are not really free of their past. The women discuss how society, including their families, does not want to hear about their experiences. Shots of newspaper headlines and photos from the period, as well as images of the women in their present lives, help provide a context. The historical events of Brazil's coup in 1964, the "coup within a coup" of 1968 that suspended civil liberties, and the widespread torture that followed are clearly explained. Issues of amnesty and denunciations of the torturers are also covered. Intertwined with the interviews is a dramatic monologue performed by actress Irene Ravache, who makes prodding and accusatory comments to the viewers demanding to know why they are watching the tape and what they did during the dictatorship.
Strengths and Weaknesses: Emotionally moving and gripping, the film is strong and inspiring. The concept and interviews are powerful, with a surprising lack of graphic detail. The film makes clear that torture, like rape, can never be erased from the memories and actions of the victims, and the tape forcefully conveys that silence in all forms is complicity. The mixture of interviews, historical footage, and dramatized dialogue is very effective.

Because its subject matter is torture, this is a difficult film to watch. A couple of reviewers felt that the tape would benefit from tighter editing. One thought it could use more historical context. The subtitles are somewhat difficult to read.
Introducing the Tape: The film gives a brief history of events in Brazil in 1964 and 1968, but more could be done to contextualize this film for U.S. audiences. An identification of some of the jargon of the era, as well as organizations (such as the guerrilla group, MR-8) would be helpful. Students should be told that the film contains powerful material regarding torture. Also, the role of the dramatic monologue can be confusing, so an introduction to the tape should include an explanation that the actress is portraying the filmmaker's own experiences.
How to Use: In a *Women's Studies* course I could use this film to talk about the specific risks and experiences that women face in political insurgency movements. In interviews many of the women survivors talk about the role that motherhood played in their healing. In a *Film Studies* course I would use this film as an example of the creative use of interviews to blend documentary and dramatic styles. I would use Amnesty International or Americas Watch reports from this period to help document what these women report and give a sense of the magnitude of the torture. Regardless of the class, I would want to be aware of how the subject matter of torture and sexual torture could affect students viewing it, especially students who may come to the film with a history of abuse or rape. (Silcox)

The film is a bit too specialized to fit easily within the confines of a traditional *Latin American History* course. It may be more appropriate for *Psychology* and *Sociology* courses to look at the legacy of dictatorship and how people cope with this experience. It would also be interesting in a course on *Women in Latin America,* as it raises interesting questions about how women respond to such violence and cruelty. (Wood)
Level: High School—University

QUILOMBO (Quilombo)
Feature. With Subtitles. 114 min. 1984
Directed by: Carlos Diegues
Distributed by: IMRE
Evaluators: David William Foster, Robert Haskett, Diane Marting, José-Manuel Navarro
Description: Based on real events and places, this film chronicles the growth and eventual physical destruction of Palmares—a *quilombo* (a runaway slave settlement during the late seventeenth century). Palmares was the largest and

most successful of the *quilombos,* led by a king and organized in a quasi-African tribal society fashion. It withstood repeated attacks by the Dutch and Portuguese until 1694, when the capital finally fell to a large, well-equipped Portuguese military force. Yet despite Palmares's physical destruction, resistance persisted into the late eighteenth century. The film forcefully conveys the way the spirit of resistance and African pride bound up in the history of Palmares has never died. It is a typical ideological analysis of the circumstances of the revolt (a slave is tortured to death in the opening scene), the cultural coordinates of the society, and the details of reconquest by the colonial authorities. The historical events are treated in a combination of styles deriving from African theater, poetic drama, epic poetry, modern Brazilian *samba* schools, and other art forms.

Strengths and Weaknesses: This film is an excellent example of director Diegues's sociohistoric interpretations, with the compelling presence of Zezé Motta, most well known for her role in Diegues's *Xica da Silva.* It is a visually stunning and evocative presentation of colonial Brazil, with especially strong images in its unflinching portrayal of violence against the human body in the context of slavery and oppression. The film is unusual in that it emphasizes the African slave perspective and features Africans, rather than sympathetic whites, as the main characters. There is some presentation of the importance of women in *quilombo* economic and political life, although there could be much more in this area. The interweaving of realism, spirituality, and magic is often quite effective. All of this gives the viewer a greater understanding of what it was like to be a slave in Brazil at that time and what it meant to resist slavery. This can be compared to other slave experiences and the situation of slaves' descendants in the modern world. The film shows that the myth of Brazil's amicable race relations has obscured the history of African-Brazilian resistance to white oppression and colonial veniality.

The film presumes a knowledge of Brazilian history and is weak in some aspects of continuity: The early part is episodic and disjointed and might confuse some viewers. From a purely historical standpoint, much of the contemporary-sounding music and dance used during Palmares festivals seems anachronistic, as if it were Carnival time in Palmares. One reviewer found the film too long and slow, with occasional poor acting and dialogue.

Introducing the Tape: An introduction to Brazilian history from 1650 to 1800, including information on slavery and colonization in Brazil, the history of the *quilombo* of Palmares, and the significance of maroon societies in Brazil, is important for U.S. viewers. There are some continuity problems with the film's historical record. Viewers need to know early on that the work will trace several generations. For best use, instructors would need to know which sources the director used for his screenplay or, at the very least, some references for further reading (see below) and a chronology of the historical events. Some discussion of ideas like poetic theater

and magic realism would be useful for those in the *Social Sciences.*

How to Use: I would use this work in a *Film* course as an example of the historical record. I would underscore the internal contradictions of setting up an ethnist community such as Palmares and the degree to which director Diegues is able to deal with them. (Foster)

I could use this film in the colonial segment of my *Latin American Survey* class to illustrate slave resistance. In this course I already emphasize African slavery and use Brazil as an extended example. The human face given to the people of Palmares and their leader, as well as the African-slave-centered perspective of the film, would serve both to illustrate many points I try to make in the course and to provide a compelling point of departure for discussion. I would use the film in a similar fashion in an upper-division course on *Slavery in Latin America* and/or a *Latin American History Through Film* course. (Haskett)

Since I only teach *Spanish American Literature* classes and not *Brazilian Literature,* I would use this in combination with a unit on *Afro-Cuban Literature* or *Afro-Caribbean Writers.* The comparisons are many, even down to the African gods worshipped. I would emphasize the transference of poetic images in verse to the visual image. I would not study the historical basis but give students a handout with chronology, terminology, and bibliography to supplement the readings in Spanish. (Marting)

In *Latin American History,* I would present an introductory lecture on Palmares and maroon societies in Brazil, show the film, and discuss it afterwards. Discussion would include the film's treatment of the contrast between Christianity and African religions; the social organization of a *quilombo;* war strategies used by both sides; the importance of slavery in Brazilian life; and the film's portrayal of blacks and whites. These discussions would be equally applicable to my courses on *Literature, Africans in Latin American History,* and as a comparison of *Africans in Latin American and U.S. History.* The film is a quarry for discussions on many topics, limited only by the imagination of the professor. (Navarro)

Suggested Readings: Bastide, Roger. *The African Religions of Brazil: Toward a Sociology of the Interpenetration of Civilizations.*

Bethell, Leslie, ed. *Colonial Brazil.*

Boxer, C. R. *The Golden Age of Brazil 1695–1750: Growing Pains of a Colonial Society.*

Cardoso, Gerald. *Negro Slavery in the Sugar Plantations of Veracruz and Pernambuco, 1550–1680: A Comparative Study.*

Conrad, Robert E. *Children of God's Fire: A Documentary History of Black Slavery in Brazil.*

Degler, Carl N. *Neither Black nor White: Slavery and Race Relations in Brazil and the United States.*

Freitas, Decio. *Palmares, a guerra dos escravos.*

Freyre, Gilberto. *The Masters and the Slaves (Casa*

grande and senzala): A Study in the Development of Brazilian Civilization.

Karasch, Mary C. *Slave Life in Rio de Janeiro, 1808–1850.*

Queiros Mattoso, Katia M., de. *To Be a Slave in Brazil, 1550–1888.*

Ramos, Arturo. *The Negro in Brazil.*

Russell-Wood, A. J. R. *The Black Man in Slavery and Freedom in Colonial Brazil.*

Schwartz, Stuart B. *Slaves, Peasants, and Rebels: Reconsidering Brazilian Slavery.*

Schwartz, Stuart B. *Sugar Plantations in the Formation of Brazilian Society: Bahia, 1550–1835.*

Stein, Stanley J. *Vassouras, A Brazilian Coffee Country, 1850–1900: The Roles of Planter and Slave in a Plantation Society.*

The poetry of Guillén (see bibliography), the painting of Wilfredo Lam, the *Negrista* movement.

Level: University

REPORTAGEM SOBRE TV VIVA (Report About TV Viva)

News Report.   English Voice-Over.   15 min.   1990

Directed & Produced by: TV Viva-Centro Luiz Freire (Rua São Bento 344, Ribeira 53110, Olinda PE; tel: [5581] 429-4109; fax: [5581] 429-4881)

Distributed by: IMRE

Evaluators: John Fett, Carlos Fontes, Brian Goldfarb

Description: This is a closeup look at TV Viva, a grassroots community television effort based in Recife. Active since 1984, TV Viva works with various social movements and neighborhood organizations. Interviews with producers and clips of their work introduce us to the philosophy and objectives of TV Viva as well as the producers' role in the community. The group provides an alternative to commercial television. People contact the station about social issues they want covered. The completed programs are then shown on a large screen in town squares to enable crowds to discuss the issues after viewing. TV Viva aims for high production quality because viewers are used to commercial television's technical quality. Occasionally the soap opera genre is used to present social issues, as such shows are extremely popular in Brazil. TV Viva members explain that independent producers are having an influence on the large, commercial stations, which are copying some of the techniques TV Viva members employ. They feel that, unlike TV Viva's work, commercial stations tend to manipulate people. In a discussion about TV Viva becoming a partner in a regional television station, we hear about the contradictions between alternative and mainstream television practices and the members' mixed feelings.

Strengths and Weaknesses: This is a clear and informative documentary that provides an inside account of Brazilian community video. Both the content and technical quality are excellent. The tape is tightly edited and moves clearly and ef-

fortlessly from one theme to another, through interviews and sparse voice-over narration. It is an excellent example of the use of mass media both as a feedback mechanism and to stimulate dialogue. The tape's length is conducive to classroom use.

The tape provides a clear and detailed introduction to some theoretical and political issues of "street" television and alternative video, however some of the issues raised could have been treated in more depth. The documentary style and voice-over narration is a bit dry and conventional, but the clips of TV Viva's less conventional work more than make up for this shortcoming.

Introducing the Tape: The tape could be accompanied by a short essay about the present development of TV Viva and its role and impact in the Recife area. Additional background history about independent and community video in Brazil would be helpful.

How to Use: In my *Communication in Development* course I would use this as an excellent example of how to put program-content control into the hands of the people the television is serving. It would also be an example of how to use television to stimulate dialogue about the issues shown. In my *Social Effects of Communication Technologies* course the tape would illustrate how to use a communication technology to stimulate dialogue rather than just being "top down." (Fett)

In *Introduction to Mass Media* this tape could be used as a starting point for a discussion of the boundaries and points of contact between mass media and alternative media. In *Introduction to Communication* the tape could be used to introduce a discussion of community communication. In *Alternative Media and Society* the tape would be a good introduction to many issues facing alternative media. (Fontes)

This tape provides important background and context for the screening of other Brazilian activist's videos. I would screen it along with tapes by TV Viva and other Brazilian video groups to show how video has been used as a tool of political activism by social movements. (Goldfarb)

Suggested Readings: Burton, Julianne. *Cinema and Social Change in Latin America: Conversations with Filmmakers.*

Burton, Julianne, ed. *Social Documentary in Latin America.*

Fals Borda, Orlando. "Social Movements and Political Power in Latin America," in *The Making of Social Movements in Latin America: Identity, Strategy, and Democracy,* ed. Arturo Escobar and Sonia E. Alvarez, 303–16.

Johnson, Randal, and Robert Stam, eds. *Brazilian Cinema.*

Machado, Arlindo. "Inside Out and Upside Down: Brazilian Video Groups TVDO and Olhar Electronico."

Mattelart, Michele, and Armand Mattelart. *Carnival of Images: Brazilian Television Fiction.*

Pines, Jim, and Paul Wileman. *Questions of Third Cinema.*

Roncagliolo, Rafael. "The Growth of the Audio Visual Imagescape," in *Video the Changing World,* ed. Alain Ambrosi and Nancy Thede.

Saalfield, Catherine. "Pregnant with Dreams: Julia Barco's Visions from Latin America."

Santoro, Luiz Fernando. *A imagem nas mãos: o vídeo popular no Brasil.*

Sarti, Ingrid. "Between Memory and Illusion: Independent Video in Brazil," in *Media and Politics in Latin America: The Struggle for Democracy,* ed. Elizabeth Fox, 157–63.
Level: Junior High School—University

RITO E EXPRESSÃO (Rite and Expression)
Experimental. No Dialogue. 8 min. 1988
Directed by: Eder Santos
Distributed by: Electronic Arts Intermix
Evaluators: María Fernández
Description: Originally an eight-monitor installation, this is an impressionistic evocation of the cultural history of Our Lady of the Rosario Church, a Baroque edifice in the central Brazilian state of Minas Gerais. The church's round shapes and forms suggest both Baroque motifs and African cultural rituals. The artist, Eder Santos, explores tensions between local and global cultures through sound- and image-making. The intervention of personal imagination in the process of image-making is also explored.
Strengths and Weaknesses: The lack of narrative coherence offers a refreshing alternative to traditional formats. Viewers with no background in the arts may find this aspect confusing.
Introducing the Tape: An introduction to the artist and his work would be useful.
How to Use: I would use this tape in my *Latin American Art* classes as part of a section on *Electronic Technologies and Latin American Art.* (Fernández)
Suggested Readings: Hall, Stuart. "The Local and the Global: Globalization and Ethnicity," in *Culture, Globalization and the World-System: Contemporary Conditions for the Representation of Identity,* ed. Anthony D. King.
Level: University

A SANGUE FRIO (In Cold Blood)
Documentary. With Subtitles. 15 min. 1989
Directed & Produced by: TV Viva-Centro Luiz Freire (Rua São Bento 344, Ribeira 53110, Olinda PE; tel: [5581] 429-4109; fax: [5581] 429-4881)
Distributed by: IMRE
Evaluators: David William Foster, Tânia M. Hering, Susan Lozada, Enríque R. Rodríguez, Irwin Stern
Description: This investigative documentary follows the activities of government-sponsored death squads, established in the 1960s to control criminal activity in big cities such as São Paulo, Rio de Janeiro, Belo Horizonte, and Recife. The documentary reveals that poor slum dwellers, including thousands of children, have been the primary targets of the death squads. The tape includes interviews with victims' family members, who express their desire for justice, as well

as comments by the general public, sociologists, and alleged death squadron members.
Strengths and Weaknesses: This realistic documentary discusses an important social problem that continues in Brazil, despite the return to democracy. It offers a balanced viewpoint by including many different perspectives. The public's attitudes that condone the squadrons' activities are quite shocking. The tape is conventional in style, with some docudrama recreations of hit operations.

Evaluators felt that the tape was too graphic, with many violent scenes showing bloodied victims.
Introducing the Tape: U.S. audiences need background on death squads and their resurgence. An introduction should explain that the death squads were established to maintain the status quo for the power elite.
How to Use: The tape effectively shows how human rights abuses carried out by military regimes can continue under "democratic" governments. It would also serve as good background material for U.S. students who believe that reports of such murders are exaggerated. (Foster)

I would use this tape when discussing the similarities and differences of Latin American governments and to demonstrate the power of the military. (Rodríguez)

This tape could be part of discussion on urban violence in Brazil. (Stern)
Suggested Readings: Amnesty International. *Torture in the '80s: A Report on Death Squads.*

Local Brazilian newspapers and magazines: *Veja; O Dia; Manchete.*

Books on military dictatorship, militarism, U.S. intervention in Latin America through military proliferation, and the incompatibility of civil elected government and the military.
Level: Junior High School—University

SANTA MARTA: TWO WEEKS IN THE SLUMS
Documentary. With Subtitles. 54 min. 1988
Directed by: Eduardo Coutinho
Produced by: Iser Video (Rua Prof. Alfredo Gomes 22, Botafogo CEP 22251, Rio de Janeiro RJ; tel: [5521] 265-5747; fax: [5521] 205-4796)
Distributed by: The Cinema Guild
Evaluators: Robert Alvarez, Susan Besse, Angela Carreño, Miguel Huarcaya, Mark Littman, Elizabeth Merena, J. Julian Rívera
Description: Documentarian Eduardo Coutinho offers viewers a chance to observe the dignity, strength, and resolve of many of the people living in the slum of Santa Marta, near Rio de Janeiro. Numerous residents speak candidly about discrimination, police harassment, teenage pregnancy, marital violence, racism, drugs, prostitution, their religious beliefs, educational goals, and child-rearing practices. Despite their problems, almost all feel that there is more opportunity in Rio than in the towns they came from. They speak with pride about their residents' association, which organizes

regular work parties to improve sanitary and physical conditions in the slum. This tape dispels many assumptions about *favela* (shantytown) residents. Despite lack of sanitation, rats, firetrap houses, and crime, these people do not live in complete despair. The film shows them singing, telling jokes, playing soccer, and dancing.

Strengths and Weaknesses: This tape is straightforward in its presentation and comes directly from the people. No narration is used. The natural interviews provide vivid portraits of a broad variety of people and include the points of view of many women. The tape portrays poor people as human, earnest, and mostly hardworking. The residents offer simple yet profound testimonies about their lives and future prospects. Director Coutinho has provided a forum for the residents to speak out and thereby manages to raise a number of important community issues. Through association meetings the tape illustrates the "communal" and "united" aspect of the neighborhood. The video's structure is loose, but in this case mixing interviews with songs and addressing different subjects without warning works well. The footage is well shot and the presentation is suitable for the subject matter.

The tape is a bit long and jumps quickly from topic to topic with inadequate transitions. One reviewer felt that the tape, in trying to cover so many topics, covered nothing in great depth. For example, although violence is a major topic, the interviewees approach the subject very circumspectly, and the military policemen at the entrance to the slum seem apologetic that abuses sometimes occur. Thus, a U.S. audience might not really understand the depth of the problem. A few interviews that were set up in a room with a video monitor appeared staged and controlled.

Introducing the Tape: Viewers need to know how many slums there are in Rio; the geography, size, and population of Rio; and the number of residents in Santa Marta. Questions are left unanswered about the kind of government assistance available and what proportion of Rio's population is poor, middle class, or wealthy. Students would benefit from a description of the migration pattern from rurals areas to the *favelas* of the cities, as well as background on Coutinho's proficiency and recognition as a documentarian (*Um cabra marcado para morrer; Jogo da dívida*). Many other topics could be elaborated upon, such as the problem of drugs, the history and nature of police violence, and race relations in Brazil. Also, a glaring omission in the tape is the lack of mention of AIDS, necessary in any discussion of sexual norms in the 1990s.

How to Use: I would use the tape to illustrate common problems in major cities of Latin America and relate them to conditions in the United States. I would also use the tape to illustrate the social organization of lower-class and economically deprived communities. (Alvarez)

The tape would be useful in elite educational institutions to combat stereotypes about the poor. (Besse)

Suggested Readings: Adler Lomnitz, Larissa. *Networks and Marginality: Life in a Mexican Shantytown.*
Level: University

SAÚBA DOS BONECOS

Documentary.   Without Subtitles.   10 min.   1989
Directed & Produced by: TV Viva-Centro Luiz Freire (Rua São Bento 344, Ribeira 53110, Olinda PE; tel: [5581] 429-4109; fax: [5581] 429-4881)
Distributed by: IMRE Archive (available for viewing only)
Evaluators: Tânia M. Hering, Antônio R. M. Simões
Description: This tape presents the life of a Brazilian toy and puppet maker from the northeast of Brazil, the country's poorest region. The folk artist explains how he became interested in this kind of life and shows fascinating examples of his work. The tape includes excerpts of some of his puppet performances.

Strengths and Weaknesses: The tape is a compelling presentation of a self-taught, probably illiterate folk artist who lives in an impoverished and isolated area. The man and his work are very interesting. Considering his lack of formal education and limited tools, the toys are extremely well made and highly sophisticated. Saúba's representation of the world through his toys reflects much of the popular culture of Brazil, especially in the northeast.

Transitions are not always smooth. The tape would be difficult to use in a *Portuguese Language* class because the artist's Portuguese is not very comprehensible.

Introducing the Tape: An introduction situating the tape in relation to the people and culture of northeastern Brazil is necessary for U.S. viewers.

How to Use: The tape could be used to discuss the cultural component in *Portuguese Language* courses. (Simões)

Students could contrast the toys made by Saúba with the commercial products made in the United States.
Level: Junior High School—University

SECA (Drought)

Documentary.   With Subtitles.   30 min.   1991
Directed & Produced by: TV Viva-Centro Luiz Freire (Rua São Bento 344, Ribeira 53110, Olinda PE; tel: [5581] 429-4109; fax: [5581] 429-4881)
Distributed by: IMRE
Evaluators: Robert Alvarez, Mary Jane Craver, Rosangela Vieira King, Carlos A. Pérez
Description: This video depicts the hard lives of impoverished Brazilians in the northeast (80 percent of Brazil's population). It shows how politicians overwhelm these people with promises before elections and then abandon them. We see President Collor de Melo (who was later impeached) capitalizing on his northeastern background and his understanding of the people in this region as he campaigns in the drought-stricken *sertão,* making promises that he never keeps. He gives rice to the starving population, saying how

much he cares about their needs (each family receives only one portion of rice). The tape ironically illustrates the government's hypocrisy by showing that the state offers gifts of food but not jobs.

Strengths and Weaknesses: The video balances government propaganda and criticism by the people and community leaders. It presents the points of view of both educated and uneducated people. The people candidly explode the myth of the benevolent politician who wants to help the electorate. The government's hypocrisy in using religion as a theme in its interaction with the people is denounced. Many rely on religious faith and their patron saints to cope with their harsh lives. The tape provides good images of living conditions and views of the countryside.

The tape is long, with a somewhat weak story line. One reviewer felt that it provided a superficial explanation of the conditions underlying the poverty and the government's lack of commitment to solve these problems.

Introducing the Tape: Readings or lectures should be given on the socioeconomic and political structures of Brazil (from a historical perspective) to illustrate the uneven distribution of wealth. Ten percent of the population owns 90 percent of the country's wealth. The film can be introduced as depicting the prelude to migration to the urban centers.

How to Use: This is an excellent film to use in discussing the recurring process of rural-urban migration, political distance of the state from ordinary lives, and the economic structure in many Latin American nations. (Alvarez)

In *Adult Education* classes I would show the students this film to demonstrate the importance of choosing elected officials carefully and to show how a devious politician can appeal to the electorate's religious beliefs. In *Portuguese* class we could use the authentic speech in this tape for accent practice and contrast the way educated and uneducated Brazilians speak. (Craver)

I would give a historical overview of Brazilian socioeconomic and political realities, particularly highlighting the role of Brazil's ruling elite in perpetuating the poverty of the majority of the population. I would bring the discussion to the present to show that little or nothing has changed in five hundred years. (Vieira King)

Complementary Films/Videos: Sections of this tape with Collor can be contrasted to the videotape *Campaign Clips of Lula* (Brazil).

Level: University

SEXO NA CLASSE

Documentary. Without Subtitles. 18 min. 1986

Directed by: Angela Freitas

Produced by: SOS Corpo (Rua Major Codeceira 37, St. Amaro, 50100-070 Recife, Pernambuco; tel: [5581] 221-3018; fax: [5581] 221-3947)

Distributed by: IMRE Archive (available for viewing only)

Evaluators: Brian Goldfarb, Susan Lozada, Enríque R. Rodríguez

Description: This documentary addresses the place of sex education in grade school curricula in Brazil. Through interviews with youth and teachers and other adults, it presents a range of viewpoints on a controversial subject. The tape also includes vignettes, directed and performed by students, about teen pregnancy and related problems.

Strengths and Weaknesses: *Sexo na classe* is engaging and creative. Its greatest strength is that it places youth in positions of pedagogical authority, drawing upon and legitimizing their knowledge of the mechanisms of their own education. The tape addresses the importance of sex education as a complex issue that reaches beyond reproduction and family planning to issues of sexuality and identity. It is particularly important during the current AIDS epidemic. The tape is an excellent example of how video can be used as a medium for pedagogical change and intervention.

Introducing the Tape: Viewers could benefit from statistics on teen pregnancy and AIDS among teenagers in Brazil. It would also be helpful to have background on low-budget video production groups such as SOS Corpo and how they get access to equipment, funding, and distribution.

How to Use: I would use this tape to raise questions about what counts as knowledge and how this is determined within educational institutions. The tape would also be useful for talking about the informal channels through which sexuality is taught and learned inside and outside of institutional settings. A viewing of this tape could be productively combined with research projects on the local politics of sexuality curriculum and the history of debates over sexuality and pederasty in educational institutions. (Goldfarb)

Suggested Readings: Agosta, Diana. "Mo' Better News: A Discussion on Media Education."

Fine, Michelle. "Sexuality, Schooling and Adolescent Females: The Missing Discourse of Desire," in *Beyond Silenced Voices*, eds. Lois Weis and Michelle Fine.

Giroux, Henry A. "Radical Pedagogy and the Politics of Student Voice."

Goldfarb, Brian. "Video Activism and Critical Pedagogy: Sexuality at the End of the Rainbow."

Lankshear, Colin, and Peter L. Mclaren, eds. *Critical Literacy: Politics, Praxis, and the Postmodern.*

Schwoch, James, Mimi White, and Susan Reilly. *Media Knowledge: Reading in Popular Culture, Pedagogy, and Critical Citizenship.*

Sedgwick, Eve Kosofsky. "How to Bring Your Kids Up Gay."

Level: Junior High School—University

STORY OF FAUSTA

Feature. With Subtitles. 106 min. 1988

Directed by: Bruno Barreto

Produced by: L. C. Barreto (Av. Franklin Roosevelt, 194-

Gr. 908, Rio de Janeiro, CEP 20021-120; tel: 240-8161; fax: 262-3049)

Distributed by: IMRE

Evaluators: Thomas O. Bente, Susan Besse, Robert DiAntonio, David William Foster, Irwin Stern

Description: This feature film deals with the life of Fausta, an unhappily married Brazilian woman who lives in extreme poverty and works as a maid for a wealthy family. Fausta hates her job and loathes her husband's expectations that she play the role of subservient housewife. She fantasizes that she will buy a piece of land in Campo Grande and go to live there, without her husband. When her husband breaks some bones in his foot and is confined to the house, he becomes even more dependent on her. Fausta's contempt for him boils over. She begins to respond to the advances of a tottering old man who showers her with gifts, takes her on outings every Sunday, and eventually (under Fausta's increasing pressure) agrees to give her his money so they can escape to Campo Grande. Her fantasies are shattered in a final scene when her house is flooded, her few possessions are ruined, and the uselessness of both men is made painfully apparent.

This is the story of a survivor whose hostile social environment determines her selfish, absolutely pitiless nature. The film is loosely structured in order to maximize vignettes of Fausta's unrelenting commitment to her own survival. "Stray dogs never die" is the final speech of the film and the byword of the entire text.

Strengths and Weaknesses: This film provoked contrasting responses from the evaluators. Some found it powerful and compelling, providing an unflinching portrayal of how to survive in Rio's urban jungle. They commented on the interesting view of race and class relations in Brazil, Betty Faria's wonderful acting, the great direction by Barreto, and music by Ruben Blades.

Others, however, felt that the film was weak in its predictability and repetition of bleak human/social circumstances. One evaluator mentioned that it showed the impoverishment of Brazilian popular culture, rather than its richness, and dwelt on people's inability to rise above daily problems. The film's language is strong and the imagery is gross and vulgar in a profoundly disturbing way. It liberally uses foul language and graphic scenes of domestic violence and sex.

Introducing the Tape: Audiences would need some background on modern Brazilian society before viewing.

How to Use: I would use this film as an example of urban social realism and the way in which a Brazilian film can be unrelentingly explicit in a way few American films would dare to be. I would find it interesting to discuss the use of the gross and the vulgar as semiotically productive features. (Foster)

I would use several of the scenes for their realistic dialogues in an intermediate and advanced *Portuguese Language* course. (Stern)

Level: University

TAKING AIM

Documentary.   With Subtitles.   41 min.   1993

Directed & Produced by: Monica Frota (Rua Visconde de Ouro Preto 61/201, Rio de Janeiro, 22250-180; tel: [5521] 266-7066; fax: [5521] 542-6397)

Distributed by: IMRE

Evaluators: George Stoney, Elizabeth Weatherford

Description: *Taking Aim* is a report of the video maker's work with the Kaiapó Indians of the Brazilian rain forest in developing the first Brazilian indigenous media project, *Mekaron Opoi D'joi (He Who Creates Images)*. The tape chronicles the Kaiapós' appropriation of video technology as a political and cultural weapon. Using a combination of archival footage, stills, footage shot by the Kaiapó, and computer animation, director Frota constructs a parodic commentary about the more conventional Western or academic representations of indigenous people. The tape documents how video can be used as a tool to even out the disparities in the relations between the Kaiapó and nonindigenous Brazilians as well as to unite the various Kaiapó groups.

Strengths and Weaknesses: This witty, provocative exploration of issues of power and representation challenges viewers' preconceptions of traditional societies and stereotypes that are often perpetuated by ethnographic film and video. Using irony and humor, the tape challenges viewers to reexamine their presumptions about the capacity of people who choose to live unclothed to manipulate instruments of modern technology. The tape tells its story in an admirable, straightforward fashion. It gives the viewer a good sense of how video technology has become part of the Kaiapós' daily life and manages to capture their attitude toward, and playfulness with, the camera. The tape's structure and method of presentation make it suitable for use in the widest variety of settings, from postgraduate seminars to high school classes studying comparative culture. Its pacing is well suited to the rhythm of an hour-long class period, allowing the presenter an opportunity to stop the tape at several points to invite audience response. The video is truly outstanding in its creative treatment of the subject and should delight the more sophisticated students of *Communication*.

Introducing the Tape: A printed supplement or introduction locating the tribe geographically, providing a bit of its history and describing the relationships among different Kaiapó tribes would be helpful. Also, instructors could relate this project to similar efforts being made by other indigenous people to use video as a social instrument. For example, anthropologist Terry Turner has been active in another video project among the Kaiapó in Gorotive and with other indigenous groups. The Centro de Trabalho Indigenista, directed by Vincent Carelli, is another example (see *Video in the Villages*).

How to Use: In my *Documentary Tradition* class the tape can be used to demonstrate the use of video by citizen producers as a socially relevant means of communication. In

Documentary Production students are encouraged to share their work with the people they are recording. This tape would help me emphasize the importance of "self-image" as an empowering device. It would also be useful in my frequent presentations to adult groups who are being trained to use video as an instrument of social change. In *Citizen Groups Training Workshops* for the use of cable television, the tape would reinforce the idea that content is more important than technical style and that a video should have a useful life well beyond its broadcast date. (Stoney)

Brazil has some excellent case histories, including this one, for looking at how native peoples use video and think about their own representation. (Weatherford)

Suggested Readings: Benton Foundation. *Making Video.*

Benton Foundation. *Using Video.*

Brooke, James. "Conflicting Pressures Shape the Future of Brazil Indians."

Frota, Monica, ed. "The Other's Vision: From the Ivory Tower to the Barricade."

Frota, Monica. "Taking Aim," in *Resolutions,* ed. Michael Renov.

Johnson, Randal, and Robert Stam. *Brazilian Cinema.*

Shohat, Ella, and Robert Stam. *Unthinking Eurocentrism.*

Turner, Terence. *Anthropology and the Politics of Indigenous People's Struggles.*

Turner, Terence. "Defiant Images: The Kayapo Appropriation of Video."

Turner, Terence. "The Kayapo Video Project: A Progress Report."

Turner, Terence. "The Social Dynamics of Video Media in an Indigenous Society: The Cultural Meaning and the Personal Politics of Video-making in Kayapo Communities."

Turner, Terence. "Visual Media, Cultural Politics, and Anthropological Practice: Some Implications of Recent Uses of Film and Video among the Kayapo of Brazil."

Weatherford, Elizabeth. "Native Visions: The Growth of Indigenous Media."

The *Challenge for Change Newsletter* has files that chronicle early experiments in the application of video technology by citizen groups. The National Film Board of Canada library also has several recent evaluations of this work done by Ph.D. candidates in U.S. and Canadian universities.

Community Television Review, the quarterly of the Alliance for Community Media, in which one finds reports of similar uses of media in North America.

Complementary Films/Videos: *Vídeo nas aldeias (Video in the Villages)* (Brazil); *O espírito da TV (The Spirit of TV)* (Brazil).

Level: Junior High School—University

TEMPORADA DE CAÇA (Hunting Season)
Documentary.   With Subtitles.   26 min.   1988
Directed by: Rita Moreira

Produced by: Rita Moreira Produções (Rua Fradique Coutinho 1776, CEP 05416-002, São Paulo; tel: [5511] 813-4354)
Distributed by: IMRE
Evaluators: Robert DiAntonio, John Hays, J. Julian Rívera, David J. Robinson, Michael Shane, Jennifer M. Taylor, Thomas Whigham
Description: This documentary examines the assassinations of gays and transvestites in São Paulo. It presents on-the-street interviews with middle-class Brazilians (most of whom were in agreement with the idea of "cleaning" the streets) and shows the support for gays from the artistic community. The backdrop is the murder of a well-known dancer in São Paulo, purportedly for being gay. Interviews, newspaper clips, portraits of famous gay men, and clips from films depicting gay sex form a collage to plead for an end to this violence. The documentary also shows the links between murders of gays and death squads that are connected to the police.
Strengths and Weaknesses: The film's journalism is accurate and effective, and there is a good cross section of people interviewed. Scenes of deer hunting underscore "deer's" double meaning as a slang term for homosexual. There are long philosophical discourses on the injustices and contradictions of Brazilian society.

Technically this is not a strong production, and the tape has a homemade quality. Some evaluators felt its focus was weakened by rapidly changing scenes and that if it had highlighted one main point (for example, that the government is behind the problem or that the media ignore it), it could have been made stronger. Evaluators had different reactions to a graphic scene incorporating feature film footage of a gay man being stabbed to death. One commented that in this scene the video resorted to violence to expose violence, while another felt it was an effective demonstration of how some Hollywood films promote violence against gay people.
Introducing the Tape: Viewers need general background on modern Brazilian society, the size of the gay population in São Paulo, the transvestite subculture, and the double meaning of the word "deer." Viewers should be told that the assasination of gays is not unique to Rio de Janeiro and is representative of the rest of the country. Links could be made to the death-squad killing of street children.
How to Use: Segments can be used on the high school level in a *Social Studies* course on contemporary issues. (DiAntonio)

The tape would be useful to generate conversation and essays on the topics touched on in the tape, as it shows sharply contrasting opinions on a controversial topic. Students would love to debate this film and its thesis. (Shane)
Suggested Readings: Puig, Manuel. *El beso de la mujer araña (The Kiss of the Spider Woman).*

Gay Sunshine Press in San Francisco puts out several fictional treatments of gay life in Brazil.

Complementary Films/Videos: *A sangua frio (In Cold Blood)* (Brazil)
Level: University

TERRA EM TRANSE (Land in Distress)
Feature.   With Subtitles.   105 min.   1966
Directed by: Glauber Rocha
Produced by: Mapa/Difilm
Distributed by: Festival Films, IMRE Archive (available for viewing only)
Evaluators: Osvaldo Chinchón, David William Foster, Elizabeth Marchant
Description: One of the great art films of the Brazilian *Cinema Novo,* director Rocha's 1967 work is a meditation on the ambiguities of political power, revolutionary ideologies, and the transformative potential of art. It is a satirical film, based on a real-life politician. The political allegory follows its protagonist narrator, a fictional poet, as he recalls the events leading up to his demise.
Strengths and Weaknesses: This film is a cinematographic masterpiece. It is relevant to any discussion of society and art. The work offers a dismantling of political rhetoric and an excellent, surreal vision of Brazilian politics in the 1950s and 1960s through the story of the rise of a populist politician in a remote and poverty-stricken state of Brazil.

The film would require a considerable amount of contextualization to be properly appreciated. As with most political satires, viewers need to know the situation to understand some of the irony and humor. The subtitles are not very clear.
Introducing the Tape: This satirical film requires background knowledge of Brazilian politics of the 1950s and early 1960s to be fully appreciated. A brief political and historical chronology of the period and an introduction to *Cinema Novo* would be helpful.
How to Use: This is a complex art film, and, as such, it cannot be easily used in *History* classes where students and professors have a rather naïve view of film as sociohistorical representation. The chronological fragmentation of the film, the use of flashbacks, and the expressionistic quality of many of the major scenes, leading to multiple allegorical meanings, need to be examined with a secure understanding of cultural texts as interpretation rather than representation. The film is an exercise in self-reflective art and is filled with modernistic devices that would frustrate viewers only interested in its "historical message." Therefore, I would use the film to discuss how modernistic, anti-Hollywood filmmaking provides more complex (if not truer) meanings about historical events than do documentaries, docudrama, and historical fiction. (Foster)

The film is excellent for a discussion of *Brazilian Culture and Politics* of the 1970s. I would use it in any *Literature* or *Culture* course covering that period, and especially in discussions about the relationship between politics and art. (Marchant)

Suggested Readings: Johnson, Randal, and Robert Stam. *Cinema Novo* × 5: *Masters of Contemporary Brazilian Film.*
  Rocha, Glauber. "Cinema Novo vs. Cultural Colonialism," in *The Cineaste Interviews on Art and Politics of the Cinema.*
  Stam, Robert. "Land in Anguish," in *Brazilian Cinema,* eds. Randal Johnson and Robert Stam.
Level: University

TIERRA PARA ROSE (Land for Rose)
Documentary.   With Subtitles.   83 min.   1987
Directed by: Tete Moraes (5521) 239-1422
Distributed by: The Cinema Guild
Evaluators: Silvia Arrom, Paolo Carpignano, Elizabeth Merena, David J. Robinson, Jesikah María Ross, Cliff Welch
Description: *Land for Rose* deals with the history and issues of land reform in post-1964 Brazil. Through the use of historic newsreels and interviews with peasants, politicians, landowners, and economists, the tape documents the struggle of the landless poor for agrarian reform and the forces that operate against them. It details events surrounding land appropriation in Brazil by focusing on a specific land takeover by 1,500 families of the Anoni Ranch in southern Brazil between the years of 1985 and 1987. In 1970, the land had been expropriated and plans made for distributing it among residents, but lawsuits and repression prevented its redistribution. In 1985, when a democratic government replaced the military regime that had been in power for twenty-one years, the peasants decided to force the question by occupying the land and settling on it.

The tape bears witness to the efforts and strengths of the homesteaders as they attempt to make their situation a priority for the government officials. They set up camp in a parking lot near the land-reform office, organize a three-hundred-mile march to Porto Alegre (the state congressional seat), confront the police, and develop a strong sense of community. They achieve a partial victory when 320 families are allowed to stay. The film follows Rose, who moves from the countryside to the city. It portrays her personal path from inaction to action and her questionable death from a hit-and-run accident at a protest march. Following the trials and tribulations of a squatters movement that continued for a decade, the documentary demonstrates the frustrations and complications of rural life and the impact that migration has on communities, families, and individuals.
Strengths and Weaknesses: This film leaves viewers with a strong impression of the trials and tribulations of social movements in contemporary Brazil. It is a fascinating story of brave and resourceful people, powerfully conveying their struggle to build their community. The film contains a wide variety of interviews, including squatters (mainly women), landowners, politicians, and clergy. The film does a good job of contextualizing the case study, historically and nationally, by comparing it to similar movements elsewhere in the coun-

try. The government's inability to expedite change is, unfortunately, familiar. Misunderstandings and lack of communication between state, local, and national bureaucracies lead to confusion, anxiety, and unnecessary hostility.

Some reviewers felt that the film was slow paced and at times repetitive. A few of the interviews seem constructed, and the singing in Portuguese has no translation. At times, the subtitles are difficult to read.

Introducing the Tape: Students need a short history of land reform in Brazil, the power of large agricultural landowners, references to the years of dictatorship, and the political reform now under way. Since the film seems to be dated, an introduction should provide a contemporary context. The tape needs more explanation of the *campamento* (the invaded residential site). The group appears to spring from nowhere, fully organized. There is no background on its leaders, the role of the church, or links to the 1960s peasant unions or to political parties.

How to Use: I would use this as a detailed case study of the attempts by Brazilian landless people to take agricultural development into their own hands. It demonstrates how protests can challenge governmental policies or inaction and graphically describes the hardships such protests involve. Social action is a costly matter! (Robinson)

Excerpts from this film could be used to depict one of the consequences of redemocratization in the 1980s and the way the new social movements drew on previous movements for inspiration and precedent. I might also use it to show the leadership role of women today. (Welch)

Suggested Readings: Biorn Maybury-Lewis, Alan. *The Politics of the Possible: The Brazilian Rural Workers' Trade Union Movement, 1964–1985.*

Sader, Emir, and Ken Silverstein. *Without Fear of Being Happy: Lula, The Workers' Party, and Brazil.*

Stavenhagen, Rodolfo, ed. *Agrarian Problems and Peasant Movements in Latin America.*

Level: University

TODOS OS DIAS SÃO SEUS

Documentary.   Without Subtitles.   30 min.   1991
Directed by: Marcia Meireles and María A. Lemos
Produced by: Comulher-Communição Mulher (Rua Rocha 119–504, São Paulo 01330; tel: [5511] 251-5626; fax: [5511] 660-477)
Distributed by: IMRE Archive (available for viewing only)
Evaluators: Brian Goldfarb
Description: This tape about women and AIDS in Brazil confronts popular misconceptions about how HIV transmitted and who can contract it. The program draws upon the experience of people living with HIV and AIDS and their communities. It combines music, dance, role-playing, and on-the-street interviews to address the complex intersection of social, cultural, and medical issues surrounding HIV and AIDS.

Strengths and Weaknesses: This tape is sensitive to issues of class and ethnicity as they intersect with gender and sexuality. It is an excellent example of camcorder activism in its use of video to educate, organize, and connect communities. While the tape is fairly long, it is all worthwhile. It could be divided into two screenings for classroom use.

Introducing the Tape: It would be helpful to have background on low-budget video production, access to equipment and distribution in Brazil, and how groups such as Colmuher are organized, funded, structured, etc.

How to Use: I would show this tape in conjunction with tapes such as Alex Juhasz and Juanita Mohammed's *We Care: A Video for Care Providers of People Affected by AIDS* and their articles in *Camera Obscura 28*. I would follow up with discussion of the various ways in which video was used to draw on the situated knowledge of communities of people affected by HIV and AIDS. (Goldfarb)

Suggested Readings: Bad Object Choices, eds. *How Do I Look? Queer Film and Video.*

Banzhaf, Marion, the ACT UP/New York Women and AIDS Book Group, et al. *Women, AIDS, and Activism.*

Burton, Julianne. *Cinema and Social Change in Latin America: Conversations with Filmmakers.*

Burton, Julianne. "Women behind the Camera."

Crimp, Douglas, ed. *AIDS: Cultural Criticism/Cultural Activism.*

Juhasz, Alex, and Juanita Mohammed. "Wave in the Media Environment: Camcorder Activism in AIDS Education."

Patton, Cindy. *Inventing AIDS.*

Rubenstein, Anne. "Seeing through AIDS: Media Activists Join Forces with the NYC Department of Health."

Treichler, Paula. "AIDS and HIV Infection in the Third World: A First World Chronicle," in *ReMaking History*, ed. Phil Maríani and Barbara Kruger.

Treichler, Paula. "Beyond *Cosmo:* AIDS, Identity, and Inscriptions of Gender."

Watney, Simon. *Policing Desire: Pornography, AIDS, and the Media.*

Complementary Films/Videos: Alex Juhasz and Juanita Mohammed *We Care: A Video for Care Providers of People Affected by AIDS.*

Level: University

TXAI MACEDO (Txai Macedo)

Documentary.   With Subtitles.   50 min.   1992
Directed by: Marcia Machado
Produced by: Tal Danai and Marci Machado
Distributed by: First Run/Icarus Films
Evaluators: John Hays, Julia Lesage, Sheldon Maram
Description: Deep in Brazil's Amazon rain forest, Antonio Macedo, an associate of martyred Chico Mendes, leads an alliance of Indian and white rubber tappers in a fight against rubber barons, landowners, the logging industry, drug lords, and the corrupt legal system that protects them. The film

vividly reveals the exploitation suffered by inhabitants of the Alto Jurua Reserve and shows the steps Macedo has taken to organize them to defend their rights in the dwindling rain forest. *Txai* (pronounced "tchai") is a term of friendship in the Kaxinawa Indian language, roughly translating to "You are half of me and I am half of you."

Strengths and Weaknesses: This is a descriptive and positive depiction of the struggle of the peoples of the rain forest that would be clearly understood by students. One evaluator appreciated the idea of showing Macedo's life of social dedication, while another felt that there was too much focus on one hero without placing in context enough of the events being depicted.

Introducing the Tape: Background on the rubber industry, the cultures of the rain forest, and Chico Mendes's story would help put the work in context.

How to Use: The tape could be used to discuss the combination of ethnography and social action. (Lesage)

Complementary Films/Videos: *Contrario ao amor* (Brazil)

Level: High School—University

UPDATE BRAZIL

Documentary.   With Subtitles.   15 min.   1986
Directed by: Nancy Marcotte and Colette Loumede
Distributed by: Women Make Movies
Evaluators: Amanda Castro-Mitchell, Teresita Martínez-Vergne, Alida Metcalf
Description: This video documents the 1985 opening of the first Brazilian police station staffed exclusively by women for the purpose of dealing with issues of sexual and domestic violence. Female police and social workers assist women who come to the station, 60 percent from the lower and middle classes of São Paulo. Since then, twenty-five female-staffed police stations have been created. The tape shows that men are not as threatened by female officers and therefore do not resist arrest. Women's organizations in São Paulo are trying to promote changes in legislation to make domestic violence a crime and impose sentences on male aggressors. The video contains interviews with police, victims of sexual violence, and highly placed politicians in São Paulo.
Strengths and Weaknesses: This tape is an inspiring example of women taking control of their own lives. It is excellent for use in courses dealing with global legal issues, gender, and women's studies.

The video does not present information about the nature of the problem nor the origins of the program. More important, the male and military context in which this effort is situated is lost in the film. At times, the voice-over is difficult to hear.

Introducing the Tape: Background on sexual politics, the women's movement, the Brazilian military, and statistics on domestic violence would help introduce the tape for U.S. viewers.

How to Use: The tape is useful for analyzing gender stereotypes in order to study aspects of macho culture, domestic vi-

olence, and legislation, which normally reflect the dominance of a male society. (Castro-Mitchell)

I would use the tape to show students local grassroots efforts that make a difference. The tape also can be used to make a statement regarding the need to empower women legally and socially and the impact of class and race on opportunities for "escape." (Martínez-Vergne)

The tape could motivate a discussion among men and women about the problem of domestic violence against women and strategies developed to deal with it in Brazil. (Metcalf)

Level: High School—University

VARELA EN XINGÚ (Varela in Xingú)

Docudrama.   With Subtitles.   13 min.   1985
Directed & Produced by: Olhar Eletronico/Marcelo Tas (Rua Teodoro Sampaio 833 Sala 13, São Paulo; tel: [5521] 521-1320)
Distributed by: IMRE
Evaluators: Robin Andersen, Catherine Egan
Description: This satirical news report follows fictitious news correspondent Ernesto Varela at the inauguration of a new tribal chief on the Xingú reservation. As clusters of real reporters crowd around to film the celebration rituals for Brazilian news, Varela pokes fun at the television crews' impersonal coverage. Varela's report is stylistically quite different from the traditional news report of such an event. It is shot up close and personal, with other barriers of distance eliminated. Varela invites viewers to go with him and "talk to some Indians." He uses various techniques to remind the audience of the presence of the television camera. At one point, without warning, Varela is unceremoniously pushed aside by the cameraman trying to get closer to the action. The tape includes scenes of the Indians recording their ceremonies for posterity and comparisons of Xingú values and those of the white society.
Strengths and Weaknesses: This is an interesting, engaging treatment that allows the Xingú to speak for themselves and gives some sense of their life. The tape tends to challenge stereotypical views of Indians.

Unless prepared with the knowledge that this is a satirical mock news report shot within a real news event, viewers will not understand the tape. One evaluator felt that the dialogue was rather simplistic. Women are absent from the tape, except for a few distant images.

Introducing the Tape: Students must be told that this is a satirical critique of traditional media coverage. Without an understanding of the Brazilian sense of humor, it may be unclear to U.S. audiences that the air of "noble savage" throughout the film is intentional and part of the tape's satirical bent.

How to Use: The tape could be used at the high school level to raise questions about primitive versus civilized cultures and criticize the traditional role of the mass media.

In a critical viewing exercise, the tape could be played

without preface or with an introductory question: "What is wrong with this report?" The tape could then be replayed and stopped in various places to point out stereotypes, differences from a normal news report, and reverse perspectives offered by the Indians.
Level: High School—University

VÍDEO NAS ALDEIAS (Video in the Villages)
Documentary. With Subtitles. 10 min. 1989
Directed by: Vincent Carelli
Produced by: Center for Indigenous Work (Rua Fidalga 548, Villa Madalena, São Paulo 05432, SP; tel: [5511] 813-3450; fax: [555] 1-212-3692)
Distributed by: IMRE, Video Data Bank, Videographe
Evaluators: Rich Bergeman, Fred Fejes, John Fett, Carlos Fontes, Brian Goldfarb
Description: This tape provides an overview of the "Video in the Villages" project organized by the Centro de Trabalho Indigenista in which different Amazonian Indian tribes have been given video equipment and training. It illustrates how these people use video to record traditional ceremonies for future generations, witness political discussions with Brazilian government officials to record their promises, document their struggles to protect their lands and environment, and communicate with neighboring tribes. The tape shows how video has helped these groups empower, organize, and activate themselves. The center has made a series of documentaries that focus on specific aspects of the indigenous uses of video (see *Spirit of TV, Meeting Ancestors, Pemp, A Festa da Moca, Free for All in Saráre*). All of these tapes are made by or with native video makers to be shown within their tribe and to other native peoples. They also provide foreign viewers with a unique opportunity to observe Indian life from a native point of view.
Strengths and Weaknesses: This is a strong educational documentary about the use and impact of video among Amazonian native tribes, providing a good example of how communication technology could be used as a feedback mechanism. The tape has a clear narrative structure. There is a solid introduction and illustration of the different aspects of the project, as well as clear transitions between themes. The tape is an effective length, conducive to classroom screening and discussion.

Some reviewers felt that the program relies too heavily on a voice-over narration and that the absence of interviews places a certain distance between viewer and the subjects. Therefore, it is important to use this tape in conjunction with others in the series. One evaluator felt that the tape was direct and to the point but had a somewhat utopian interpretation of the indigenous uses of video, noting that it failed to acknowledge forms of dependence that are implicit in the provision of equipment to these groups by nonindigenous anthropologists and videographers.
Introducing the Tape: The tape is self-contained and speaks for itself. Some background on indigenous struggles in the Amazon would be useful.

How to Use: I would use the tape to talk about how video technology can assume different uses in various cultural contexts. (Fejes)

One of the shortcomings of mass media and most new communication technology is that they are generally used for top-down communication only; there is no feedback. Increasingly, video is being used to bring about two-way communication and dialogue. This is an excellent example of how it could be successfully carried out, even by an illiterate audience. (Fett)

In *Alternative Media and Society* this tape could illustrate how the process of making video can be more important than the finished product. It offers a good example of how this kind of community video can be converted into a strong video product suited for wider audiences than those originally targeted. For *Introduction to Communication* classes it could be used as an example of community television in which a message is created by a community member for the community. In *Media Technology, Culture, and Society* it could serve as a starting point for a discussion about the interaction between the use of a medium and its technological characteristics. (Fontes)

I would use this tape to raise questions about the validity of attempts by anthropologists and ethnographic film/video makers to "give voice" to others. (Goldfarb)

In *Anthropology* courses the importance of point of view could be discussed by comparing this tape to ethnographic films made by people outside the community.
Suggested Readings: Crawford, Ian Peter, and David Turton, eds. *Film as Ethnography.*

Fusco, Coco. "Ethnicity, Politics and Poetics: Latinos and Media Art," in *Illuminating Video: An Essential Guide to Video Art,* ed. Doug Hall and Sally Jo Fifer, 304–16.

Karunanayake, Nandana. "Community Radio: A Promising Experiment."

Michaels, Eric. *Bad Aboriginal Art: Tradition, Media, and Technological Horizons.*

Minh-Ha, Trinh T. *Woman, Native, Other: Writing Postcoloniality and Feminism.*

Moore, Rachael. "Marketing Alterity."

Turner, Terence. "The Social Dynamics of Video Media in an Indigenous Society."
Level: Junior High School—University

XICA (Xica)
Feature. With Subtitles. 120 min. 1976
Directed by: Carlos Diegues
Distributed by: IMRE
Evaluators: David William Foster
Description: This film, by the famed director Carlos Diegues, is based on the historical figure of a black slave in the eighteenth century who gains wealth and power by being the lover of an imperial representative. She eventually falls from her position of privilege when her lover is removed from his post. The film is a meditation on the illusory nature

of personal power in the context of a Foucaultian sense of structural power that prevails against individual initiative.

Strengths and Weaknesses: The film is brilliantly shot, and the principal actor, Zezé, is a powerhouse. One evaluator felt that it was probably one of the best Brazilian films in the last ten years.

The weakness of the film is its upbeat ending, changed from the play on which it was based in order to make the film conform to the optimistic political climate of the Brazilian Left during the 1985 transition to democracy. As a consequence, the ending, although well done, is ideologically disconsonant with the underlying theme of unimpeachable political power as wielded by the hegemonic class.

Introducing the Tape: An introduction is not needed, but background on Brazilian history, particularly race and class relations, would enhance viewing.

How to Use: I would use the film as an example of the permanence of certain power structures in the Foucaultian sense and of the illusory nature of representing Brazil as a non-racially-biased society. The use of the colonial setting shows how political oppression has continued throughout Brazil's history. A second facet is the role of women, particularly those inscribed in the dynamics of masculinist power. The film is interesting for its use of erotics as a release from oppression and a tool of the masculinist order. I have discussed the film from the point of view of how contemporary political programs played a role in building the consciousness of a redemocratized Brazil in 1985. (Foster)

Suggested Readings: Araujo, Denise. Article in *Rocky Mountain Review* (1992 or late 1991).

Foucault, Michel. *Discipline and Punish: The Birth of the Prison.*

Johnson, Randal, and Robert Stam, eds. *Brazilian Cinema.*

Johnson, Randal, and Robert Stam. *Cinema Novo × 5: Masters of Contemporary Brazilian Film.*

Level: University

CHILE

LAS ARMAS DE LA PAZ

Documentary.   Without Subtitles.   38 min.   1989
Directed by: Augusto Gongora
Produced by: Nueva Imagen (Jorge Washington 338, Nunoa, Santiago; tel: [562] 498-197)
Distributed by: IMRE Archive (available for viewing only)
Evaluators: Leonor Blum, Rosario Espinal, Joséph A. Gagliano, Frederick M. Nunn
Description: The film depicts events surrounding the 1988 national plebiscite to decide whether the Pinochet regime would remain in power and follows the drama of this step toward democracy after sixteen years of military rule. Several scenes concern the repressive measures the dictatorship took to influence the election results. The tape also includes footage of the overthrow of Allende in 1973 and of the

months immediately preceding the plebiscite. Many scenes present the observations of intensely anti-Pinochet opponents. The film gives almost an hour-by-hour impressionistic account of the voting. It concludes when the results calling for Pinochet to step down are announced and spontaneous celebrations erupt in the streets of Santiago.

Strengths and Weaknesses: This film is particularly good for learning about the details of the plebiscite, the campaign, and the events during the voting period. It vividly captures the drama during vote tabulation and the widespread opposition to the Pinochet regime. An evaluator who was in Chile at the time of the vote attested to the film's accurate representation, commenting on the high quality of the narration and writing.

The film presumes a knowledge of contemporary Chilean politics and provides no context for the 1988 plebiscite. One evaluator felt that the tape was a bit long.

Introducing the Tape: The film must be preceded by discussion or readings that provide information about the Pinochet dictatorship and the years between 1970 and 1988.

How to Use: I would use the film to illustrate the sense of hope and utopia that a transition to democracy brings to many people. (Espinal)

I would use this film following lectures on military rule and civilian resistance. (Nunn)

Suggested Readings: Agüero, Felipe. "Chile: South America's Success Story?"

Aman, Kenneth, and Christina Parker. *Popular Culture in Chile: Resistance and Survival.*

Chavkin, Samuel. *Storm over Chile: The Junta under Siege.*

Sigmund, Paul. *The Overthrow of Allende and the Politics of Chile, 1964–1976.*

Skidmore, Thomas E., and Peter H. Smith, *Modern Latin America.*

Timerman, Jacobo. *Chile: Death in the South.*

Valenzuela, J. Samuel, and Arturo Valenzuela, eds. *Military Rule in Chile: Dictatorship and Opposition.*

Level: High School—University

BLANCA AZUCENA (White Lily)

Documentary.   English Voice-Over.   25 min.   1985
Directed by: David Benavente
Distributed by: First Run/Icarus Films
Evaluators: Julia Lesage, Elizabeth Mahan, Janet Page-Reeves
Description: This program documents the use of video in a Mapuche Indian community adult-education project in Chile. The participants discuss how taking part in the video project affected their relationships with their families and their views of themselves. The video also looks at problems in the community and the resistance that the group encountered from community authorities.

Strengths and Weaknesses: This is a good example of popular, grassroots video. The subjects explain their motivations for joining the program and their deep feelings about the project. They perform a skit that illustrates traditional gender roles and how they can be confronted. The tape ends on a positive note with the participants expressing their feelings of empowerment.

The video does not provide context. Because it is a "home video" that the group made for its own members, it is a bit confusing for outsiders who know little about the alternative-video movement in Chile. The tape can seem slow moving to U.S. audiences, as it reflects the real-life pace of the project. There is an excess of shots of the participants watching their own recorded interviews.

Introducing the Tape: Although the director of the video project provides a brief introduction, more information about the rise of alternative video and its use in grassroots education programs would help viewers unfamiliar with these trends. It would be good to have background on the group—for example, how many tapes they have made and how the project has developed years later.

How to Use: I would use segments of the tape to teach students about using video as an organizing tool and discuss the work involved. (Lesage)

I include a unit on alternative communication in my course *Media, State, and Society in Latin America.* I would use this tape, pointing out its technical flaws, as an example of community video. (Mahan)

Suggested Readings: Gumucio, Alfonso Dagron. *El cine de los trabajadores: manual teorico y practico a la generación de talleres de Cine Super 8.*

Luz Hurtado, María de la. Chapter on the alternative video movement in Chile, in *The Media and Politics in Latin America,* ed. Elizabeth Fox.

Level: High School—University

CAMINO A USMAGAMA

Documentary.   Without Subtitles.   17 min.   1983
Directed by: Marelo Ferrari
Distributed by: IMRE Archive (available for viewing only)
Evaluators: Lynn M. Shirey, Richard D. Woods
Description: Indians from northern Chile narrate this history of their remote and abandoned village in the desert. They explain that they left their homes because of isolation and changing economic times. Years later, they decided to revive their village through a laborious thirty-year construction of a road that connects them with the outside world. After completion, the villagers began to reinhabit their homes and hold a traditional celebration.

Strengths and Weaknesses: A strength of this work is that almost all action and narrative is from a native perspective. The tape is well made and provides an excellent portrait of the villagers. One evaluator felt that the naturalism of the scenery corresponded to the eternal quality of the unidealized Indians.

Another reviewer felt that the story was too anecdotal, without any theme other than community involvement. An-

other commented that men were the main speakers and women were by and large excluded. Nonnative speakers will have difficulty with the rapidity and accent of the Indians' Spanish.

Introducing the Tape: A U.S. audience would benefit from a brief history of Andean Indians before viewing.

How to Use: The tape could be used in *Latin American Civilization* courses. Words could not adequately express the harshness of the environment shown in the tape. Students of advanced *Language* classes might note the regional differences in spoken Spanish. (Woods)

Suggested Readings: Baver, Arnold J. *Chilean Rural Society from the Spanish Conquest to 1930.*
Level: University

CANTO A LA VIDA (Song to Life)

Documentary.   With Subtitles.   48 min.   1990
Directed by: Lucía Salinas
Distributed by: Jane Balfour Films, Women Make Movies
Evaluators: Vera Blinn Reber, Richard D. Woods
Description: "Exile begins when you return home," confesses one of the five returned Chileans who detail their flight after the Pinochet coup in 1973. Among them are Isabel Allende, author of *The House of the Spirits;* Hortensia Bussy de Allende, widow of the martyred president; and folksinger Isabel Parra. For these women, leaving Chile has meant extreme adjustments. Their emotional autobiographies intersect with nightmarish scenes of the Pinochet period, epitomized by the death of the folksinger Victor Jara. In the shared experience of loss and suffering expressed in speech and song, the exiles both condemn Pinochet and manifest solidarity against him. This tape incorporates music, interviews, news footage, and artistic dramatization. Its anti-Pinochet perspective is clear.

Strengths and Weaknesses: The tape deals with all aspects of exile, including the problems one faces when returning home. Its rhythm and poignancy are distinctive, as is its examination of exile from a feminist perspective.

Introducing the Tape: The video provides political and social context in fragmented form. U.S. viewers could use background on the triumph of Allende and his downfall, as well as on the Pinochet dictatorship.

How to Use: I would use this film to discuss *Women in Latin America* and the issue of military governments. (Reber)

This tape could well accompany the standard text for *Latin American Civilization, Tradición y cambio* by Heyck and González-Widel. Half of the contributors to this text are women, and this video emphasizes female reactions to a political system and above all to exile. Any course that includes the writings of Isabel Allende could profit from this tape. (Woods)

Suggested Readings: Agosín, Marjorie. *Scraps of Life: Chilean Arpilleras, Chilean Women, and the Pinochet Dictatorship.*

Allende, Isabel. *The House of the Spirits.* (See bibliography for other works.)

Heyck, Denis Lynn Daly, and María González-Widel. *Tradición y cambio: Lecturas sobre la cultura latinoamericana contemporanea.*

Jara, Joan. *An Unfinished Song: Life of Victor Jara.*

Ladrón de Guevara, Matilde. *Destierro: Diario de una Chilena.*

Level: High School—University

CHILE: SUEÑOS PROHIBIDOS (Chile's Forbidden Dreams)

Documentary.   With Subtitles.   52 min.   1983
Directed by: Delfina Guzmán, Nissím Sharím, and Claudio DiGirolamo
Produced by: ICTUS Theater (Rosal 377-A, Santiago de Chile; tel: [562] 633-3713 or 639-3092; fax: [562] 633-0180)
Distributed by: IMRE
Evaluators: Fortuna Calvo-Roth, Osvaldo Chinchón, Robert DiAntonio, Marlene Gottlieb, Joan A. McGinnis, Elizabeth Mahan, Elaine Torres
Description: This tape presents the daring work of the ICTUS theater group whose plays and videos explore the ways the Chilean dictatorship instilled fear and self-censorship in the population. ICTUS's videos were made available to activists for use in community settings with the objective of helping people who had been anesthetized by the Pinochet regime to recover their "forbidden dreams." Interviews with the principals of the theater company are interspersed with clips of their plays and video productions. One scene takes place in a soccer stadium while a game is being played. At one point the spectators are ordered to cover their eyes and accept the official announcer's version of what is happening in center field. As one spectator sneaks a peek, he sees one of the players protest a referee's call. The player is beaten and pays with his life. The announcer then tells the blindfolded public that the player died of natural causes. The play states that "truth is what you're told, not what you see." The members of ICTUS accuse the dictatorship of destroying the "common memory" of the Chilean people. The tape explains that during the dictatorship ICTUS was allowed to continue its productions. Foreign diplomats were even invited by the government to attend ICTUS's performances to prove that there was freedom of speech in Chile. One of the group's directors explains, "The government feels that we really do no damage. But with art we have a powerful weapon."
Strengths and Weaknesses: This clear and concise tape is moving in its message. Its initial emphasis on the political and historical antecedents of Pinochet's government establishes a context for understanding ICTUS members' commitment to their society. The tape is an excellent introduction to the phenomenon of alternative video in Chile during the Pinochet years. The clips are long enough to convey a sense of the complete productions so non-Chileans have

the opportunity to see what alternative video and theater productions actually looked like. The artists' courageous stand against the repressive system is impressive.
Introducing the Tape: This video could be introduced as a program about the struggles of a theater group working under a dictatorship. The important point is that alternative expressions of culture, politics, and opinion somehow manage to surface in all political situations. While historical background is given in the tape, more information on Allende, Pinochet, and events since the film was made in 1985 would be helpful.
How to Use: For high school, I envision using this documentary in a team-taught period involving our Amnesty International Club, advanced *Spanish* classes, and *Drama* students. (DiAntonio)

In a *Contemporary Literature* course I would use this film to show what life in a military state is like. Then we would examine the difficulties of being a committed artist in a dictatorship, the relationship of art to politics, and the problem of writing between the lines to satisfy censors while still getting the message across. We might even examine the dramatic scenes presented in this film. (Gottlieb)

In a *Spanish Language* class a discussion of the use of art to portray people's ideas could introduce this film. A Spanish vocabulary would facilitate understanding and the discussion after the film. (McGinnis)
Suggested Readings: Lihn, Enrique. *El arte de la palabra.*

Parra, Nicanor. *Chistes para desorientar a la poesía.*

Novels of Isabel Allende. (See bibliography for works.)
Level: High School—University

CIEN NIÑOS ESPERANDO UN TREN (100 Children Waiting for a Train)

Documentary.   With Subtitles.   57 min.   1988
Directed by: Ignacio Aguero
Distributed by: First Run/Icarus Films
Evaluators: Lavina Tilson Gass, Joan A. McGinnis, Danusia L. Meson, Hilda Pato
Description: Children from the slums surrounding Santiago, Chile, participate in a weekly cinematographic workshop under the auspices of the Catholic Church. These children, who have never seen a film, study various techniques involved in cinematography and are creatively involved in making their own film. Teacher Alicia Vega offers the students a stimulating environment in which they can develop an appreciation for, and skill in, one of the most universally viewed art forms. This tape records the exciting hands-on lessons, interspersed with interviews with families. The workshop culminates with the children's trip to the city to see a movie.
Strengths and Weaknesses: This is a delicate and personal film. It is interesting to see what Alicia Vega teaches and how. She has a calm, focused, and inspiring way of dealing with the children. The video shows the children's joy as they learn and

then share this new world with their families. The tape is informative about the socioeconomic conditions in which the children live and gives an eye-opening view of their aspirations. It offers a lyrical commentary about the power of film on the human imagination. While workshop segments serve as the basis of the film, some of the most moving footage is the interviews with the children about their lives. They describe their poverty and fear of the police in a matter-of-fact manner that expresses the conditions to which they are subject.

One evaluator felt that the tape seemed a little long, with unnecessary interviews. Some of the subtitled translations were not accurate.

Introducing the Tape: Viewers should be told that this workshop takes place in Chile, as it is not clearly indicated in the tape. Some background on the military government in Chile at the time (1988) would be helpful.

How to Use: I teach *Spanish* to kindergarten through third grade in a science magnet school. I would tie the showing of this tape into a unit on culture, or cameras and films with a *Science* teacher, or with creative writing in *Language Arts*. There is much to discuss about children in and out of school. (Tilson Gass)

For high school, it would be wonderful to have students to make a "zootrope," or their own video. (McGinnis)

The tape can be used to discuss issues of poverty, access to popular culture and mass media, the use of cinema, and the role of the church in Latin America. A set of questions should be designed for the students. (Meson)

In an *Education* course the tape could be used as an example of how to motivate students in an interactive way by having them use film or video to articulate their vision of themselves and society.

In a *Video Production* class this program could be used to illustrate the importance of grassroots productions, especially in relation to mainstream broadcast media.

Suggested Readings: Castañeda, Tarsicio. *Combatting Poverty: Innovative Social Reforms in Chile During the 1980s.*

Drake, Paul, and Ivan Jaksic, eds. *The Struggle for Democracy in Chile, 1982–1990.*

Hassett, John J., and Grinor Rojo. *Chile: Dictatorship and the Struggle for Democracy.*

Hojman, D. E. *Chile: The Political Economy of Development and Democracy in the 1990s.*

Jelin, Elizabeth, and J. Ann Zammit. *Women and Social Change in Latin America.*

Smith, Brian H. *The Church and Politics in Chile: Challenges to Modern Catholicism.*

Stallings, Barbara. *Class Conflict and Economic Development in Chile, 1958–1973.*

Valenzuela, J. Samuel, and Arturo Valenzuela, eds. *Military Rule in Chile: Dictatorship and Opposition.*

Complementary Films/Videos: *Making Waves,* a documentary about alternative grassroots video production in Bolivia (distributed by IMRE); *Por primera vez* (Cuba), a documentary that addresses how Cuban peasants reacted when they saw a film for the first time (distributed by IMRE); *Scraps of Life* (video) by Marjorie Agosín; *Video in the Villages* (Brazil).

Level: Elementary School — University

CONSUELO (Consuelo)

Feature.   With Subtitles.   105 min.   1988
Directed by: Luis R. Vera
Distributed by: IMRE
Evaluators: Friederike Baumann, Rosario Espinal
Description: An exploration of the meaning of exile, told from the perspective of a young middle-class Chilean. Manuel flees Pinochet's terror and finds refuge in Sweden, leaving his girlfriend Consuelo behind. Although he learns to adapt to life in his host country and forms new relationships, he carries within him the chronic pain of longing for the people he left behind, a pain only his return to Chile can alleviate. After some time Manuel does return home and experiences an equally painful adjustment: Those he loved were as deeply affected by having to adapt to life under Pinochet as he was by making a new life in his host country. The years of separation have turned him into an outsider. Manuel's fate, symbolized by his love for two women (Consuelo and his new Swedish companion), is to remain emotionally divided. Incapable of solving his dilemma, he tries to mend his broken life by uprooting himself once again.

Strengths and Weaknesses: This film addresses in a sensitive and humane manner the meaning of forced exile. It is particularly powerful because it deals with the issue on the level of human relationships, without a strong political or social context. This highlights the universality of the film's main theme, namely, the fate of those who usually are considered the "lucky ones," because they were able to escape with their lives and emigrate to more open societies. The film conveys the split identity of immigrants who struggle to remain connected to the world they left behind but also have a new life in their adopted society.

For some, the largely nonpolitical focus might represent a weakness. The significance of Manuel's class status is not examined. The socioeconomic problems of Chile are suggested but not explicitly addressed or explained. There is no explanation of why Manuel went to Sweden, why Consuelo had no money, or why Manuel's Chilean friends said that life was difficult.

Introducing the Tape: Instructors should present some Chilean socioeconomic and political history to put this story into context. Some concrete background, perhaps some figures, could be provided—for example, the number of refugees from the dictatorships in Argentina, Uruguay, Chile, Central America, etc., and their destinations, particularly European countries and Mexico.

How to Use: I would use this tape to show the impact at the

personal level of moving from one society to another. (Espinal)
Level: University

DIARIO INCONCLUSO (Unfinished Diary)

Docudrama.   With Subtitles.   55 min.   1986
Directed by: Marilu Mallet
Distributed by: Women Make Movies
Evaluators: Osvaldo Chinchón, Robert DiAntonio, Marlene Gottlieb, Chris Holmlund, Rebecca Torres-Rivera
Description: An autobiographical experimental film combining elements of documentary and fiction, *Unfinished Diary* seeks to capture director Mallet's feelings and experiences of political exile by juxtaposing past and present images and using a variety of languages (English, Spanish, and French). Black-and-white newsreels of bombing in Chile, soldiers on the march, and citizens being searched are juxtaposed with color footage of the Canadian environment to which many exiles from Pinochet's dictatorship fled. There are images of Allende's Chile in flames; Mallet's friends, family, and coworkers in Montreal (including Isabel Allende); and, as a kind of a climax and signal of impending divorce, an unscripted argument between Mallet and her Australian filmmaker husband about their relationship and her film. The film emphasizes the linguistic differences between the Spanish-speaking exiles and their French-speaking hosts, the filmmaker, and her husband. The couple's cultural differences create a gap that even their French-speaking child seems unable to bridge.
Strengths and Weaknesses: One of the most intelligent and thoughtful Latin American feminist documentaries, this is a small film that manages to say big things. *Unfinished Diary* is hauntingly beautiful, offering a depth and nuance all too often lacking in documentary and fiction films alike. It gives a cohesive view of how a military coup can create disarray in a society, affecting all its members. The tape communicates beautifully the feeling of alienation and estrangement that the exile experiences. The newsreels of persecution and torture in Chile and the brief scene with Isabel Allende make the film useful as a documentary of the times. One evaluator commented that students of all ages and educational and class backgrounds would like the film if they were helped to feel comfortable exploring experimental works.

For those not open to experimental film, this work may seem confusing unless accompanied by discussion. Also, the language switches can be confusing. One reviewer felt the tape was too long.
Introducing the Tape: The video needs to be introduced as a personal artistic treatment of a subject with universal implications. Historical information on the Popular Unity government and its overthrow, Chilean exiles, and Chilean feminism would be helpful. Audiences should also be told that many Chileans sought refuge in Quebec, possibly because they knew French and there was already a small community of Chilean artists (which grew considerably during the Pinochet years).
How to Use: I would point out and review the scene with Isabel Allende. I would also explain the technique of intertwining three basic plot lines: exile, the problems the couple/family faces, and the difficulties of making a docudrama (fiction versus strict fact). Also the problems of exile could be compared to those of other exiled groups as presented in the stories of Max Aub, Oscar Hijuelos, etc. (Gottlieb)

I use this film in a *Latin American Film* course during a section on films made by women in exile (e.g., Valeria Sarmiento's *El hombre cuando es el hombre* [Costa Rica]). I show this film after Sarmiento's film and before *La historia oficial* (Argentina). Class discussions focus on the different political and aesthetic choices each presents and on the filmmakers' views of how women and men approach history, language, and film. Lectures deal with exiled Chilean filmmakers, the women's movement, and women's organizations in Chile under Pinochet. Earlier lectures and films present the history of the Popular Unity government and its overthrow. (Holmlund)

I would use this after providing information about the military coup in Chile, since so many Chileans went into exile to escape torture and execution. (Torres-Rivera)
Suggested Readings: Miller, Francesca. *Latin American Women and the Search for Social Justice,* as background on feminism in Chile.

Pick, Zuzana. "Chilean Cinema in Exile."

General historical material on Chile, especially the Allende and Pinochet governments.

Novels by Isabel Allende and stories by Max Aub and Oscar Hijuelos. (See bibliography for works.)
Complementary Films/Videos: *La historia oficial (The Official Story)* (Argentina); *El hombre cuando es el hombre (A Man When He is a Man)* (Costa Rica).
Level: High School — University

ESTRELLAS EN LA ESQUINA

Documentary.   Without Subtitles.   25 min.   1988
Produced and Directed by: Nueva Imagen, Claudio Marchant (Jorge Washington 338, Nunoa, Santiago; tel: [562] 498-197; fax: [562] 465-635 or 274-2823)
Distributed by: IMRE
Evaluators: Marcia Dean, Mary Margaret Fogarty, Miguel Huarcaya, María A. Lazarini, Susan Lozada, Deborah Pacini Hernández, Marc S. Roth, Naomi Smith, Jennifer M. Taylor
Description: This documentary portrays youth culture and break dancing in a poor neighborhood of Santiago. Teenage boys on the streets and in their homes discuss dress, music, movements, and influences. Break dancing liberates their minds from the problems of their poor socioeconomic status. The suggestion is that the dancing may save these kids from ruining their lives through the negative expression of energies, such as using drugs to escape their depressing world. The tape presents rap singing, a stylized meeting where two

groups of boys dance, and some graffiti artists at work. The boys discuss how television, U.S. music, and their peer groups have influenced the fad.

Strengths and Weaknesses: This is an interesting and well-done tape portraying hiphop culture with appropriate techniques, such as rapidly repeated images, good special effects, and fast cuts to the rhythm of the music. The interviews are natural and fresh. The camera work is sensitive to important details and conveys hiphop culture's significance to its practitioners, as both resistance and creativity. While the break dancing fad is dated in the U.S., the tape shows how youth actually live in other parts of the world. There is also a parallel with U.S. urban culture. The last five minutes of the tape would be excellent, especially if the words of the rap were available. The technical quality of the tape is quite good for an independent, community-based production, although one reviewer commented that the program had a homemade look. While the boys talk about how break dancing has changed them or about larger social issues, the tape does not put the dancing into the context of their lives. Certain questions about cultural imperialism/appropriation are raised but not addressed. A few reviewers felt that the Spanish was hard to comprehend, so that it would be difficult to use the film in language classes unless it was accompanied by a Spanish transcript.

Introducing the Tape: It would be important to make the connection with this culture's popularity among low-income urban teens in the U.S., and point out that it promoted non-drug, nongang activity. The effects of Latin American social appropriation of U.S. fads and culture are not addressed and should also be discussed.

How to Use: I would use this film with my *Junior High* students, who can really relate to the kids in the video. I would give them a transcript of the rap song to discuss and ask them to relate it to parallels in their own lives. (Dean)

The tape can be used in a course on *Popular Music* and/or *Culture* to raise issues of local appropriation vs. cultural imperialism, and popular culture as resistance. (Pacini Hernández)

I would speak of people living in utterly depressing poverty surrounded by filth and drugs, who look to break dancing in order to rise above their difficult human condition in an attempt to find happiness—that break dancing is spiritual to these teenagers. (Roth)

Level: Junior High School—High School

HASTA VENCER (Until Victory)

Documentary. With Subtitles. 12 min. 1984
Directed & Produced by: ICTUS Theater (Rosal 377-A, Santiago de Chile; tel: [562] 633-3713 or 639-3092; fax: [562] 633-0180)
Distributed by: IMRE
Evaluators: Vera Blinn Reber, Kathleen March, J. Julian Rívera, David Robinson, Rebecca Torres-Rivera
Description: This is a well-documented presentation of the birth and development of a squatters' village in La Granja, outside of Santiago, Chile. The high cost of housing and low salaries made it difficult for many middle-class families to obtain housing. On September 22, 1983, the homeless protested the Pinochet government's failure to meet their needs by organizing a mass squatter action, taking over an empty piece of land. Although the government initially responded with violence, the protesters repeatedly returned and eventually established a squatter settlement. The tape documents life in the settlement over a one-year period. It presents a positive example of how many of the problems faced by homeless people can be eased when people work together. The settlement holds its own elections for community representatives and provides a clinic, schooling for the children, and food for the unemployed. After a time, the government was forced to recognize the settlement and offered the residents land outside of Santiago. They declined the government's offer, saying that the land was too far away from the city for them to commute to work. On November 10, 1984, the settlement met with the brutal repression of Pinochet's *carabineros* (police). In a violent police raid, all males over age sixteen were detained and the leaders were banished and sent hundreds of miles away.

Strengths and Weaknesses: Although the efforts of the community group are eventually crushed, the video effectively demonstrates how groups become empowered and can deal with important social needs when they come together. The photography shows that many of the squatters are from middle- and working-class backgrounds. The program contains an excellent introduction, subtitling, and camera work.

The film is dated and deals with only one community and time period without providing any background on either homelessness, squatting in Latin America, or the political nature of the Chilean government.

Introducing the Tape: U.S. viewers would need information on the military takeover that brought the Pinochet government to power. Also some general background should be provided on Chile under both Allende and Pinochet, the causes of poverty, and the broader issue of squatter settlements in Latin America.

How to Use: I could use this film in *Spanish Language* courses to introduce students to both Spanish, particularly the Chilean accent and expressions, and the social issues of Latin America. (Reber)

In a unit dealing with community organization in a *Social Work* practice course, the tape could show how communities can be organized for their own welfare. (Rivera)

In my course on *Latin American Development* I would use this as an example of the struggles of popular movements during the 1960s to overcome extreme poverty, and the failure of governments to provide low-cost housing in most major cities. I would emphasize the particulars of the Chilean/Santiago case and the context of the military regime. I would also stress the need to look at the details of the physical and social hardships that the squatters had to endure. (Robinson)

I would present this documentary after a lecture concerning either "Big Cities and Housing" or "Pinochet's Dictatorship." (Torres-Rivera)

Suggested Readings: Lloyd, Peter Cutt. *The "Young Towns" of Lima: Aspects of Urbanization in Peru.*

Lobo, Susan. *A House of My Own: Social Organization in the Squatter Settlements of Lima, Peru.*

Level: High School—University

HUELLAS DE SAL

Documentary. Without Subtitles. 16 min. 1990
Directed by: Andres Vargas Danus
Produced by: Grupo Processo (Fernández Concha 85, Nunoa, Santiago; tel: [562] 225-1729 or 209-9147; fax: [562] 209-9495)
Distributed by: IMRE
Evaluators: Miguel Huarcaya, Daniel P. Hunt, Joan A. McGinnis, Elizabeth Merena, Gloria Romero-Downing, Jennifer M. Taylor
Description: This program is a powerful testimony of the lasting impact of the military government in Chile and the trauma resulting from the thousands of disappeared persons. Interviews with the families of the disappeared are combined with footage of demonstrations and funeral processions to honor and rebury the dead. The search for the remains of the missing is still under way ten years later, and mass graves filled with victims of government and death-squad oppression are discovered in the plateau region. The tape follows friends and relatives who continue to dig in the desert sand hoping to find the truth about what happened to their loved ones. On November 1, the Day of the Dead, there is nowhere to lay flowers. The tape contains artfully suggestive shots of the places where victims were arrested and where they were presumably buried.
Strengths and Weaknesses: This is a very emotive piece that evokes the grief and dignity of the survivors of Pinochet's violent regime. The interviews are good and the narration well written and appropriately placed. The film shows very effectively the human responses to militarism and genocide, but it presupposes an audience already familiar with the Pinochet dictatorship. There are some very effective shots of demonstrations, churches, posters being covered with sand, and desperate people searching and hoping, as well as powerful sound effects of wind.

Some evaluators felt the editing could have been better. The rapid speech in Spanish would make it difficult for language students.
Introducing the Tape: U.S. viewers need historical information about the coup d'état that brought Pinochet to power, his relations with the U.S., and U.S. government involvement in the coup and the effects of his regime on the general population.
How to Use: I would use this tape in a course where students need to see the terrible consequences of U.S. intervention or in any course dealing with *Chilean Culture and Literature.*

This film would work well in conjunction with the story of Miguel Littín as retold by García Márquez in *La aventura de Miguel Littín clandestino en Chile*. It would have to be accompanied by an account of the election and murder of Allende and the subsequent terror. (Hunt)

The film can be used to illustrate the fate of the families of those taken away and assassinated. A vocabulary list would facilitate discussion of military rule. My students often make up questions for discussion in cooperative groups. (McGinnis)

The film would be useful in *Latin American Culture and Civilization* courses to bring attention to a dark period of Latin American history. In a *Spanish Conversation* course, the tape could be assigned as an exercise in which the students could listen repeatedly to the speakers to hear different Latin American voices. In a *Latin American History* course it would serve as a historical background to the coup. (Romero-Downing)
Suggested Readings: García Márquez, Gabriel. *La aventura de Miguel Littín clandestino en Chile.*

Skidmore, Thomas E., and Peter H. Smith. *Modern Latin America.*

Timerman, Jacobo. *Prisoner Without a Name, Cell Without a Number.*

Valenzuela, Luisa. *Como en la guerra.*
Complementary Films/Videos: *La Batalla de Chile (The Battle of Chile)* (distributed by New Yorker Films).
Level: University

LA LUNA EN EL ESPEJO (The Moon in the Mirror)

Feature. With Subtitles. 75 min. 1990
Directed by: Silvio Caiozzi
Produced by: Andrea Films (Federico Froebel 1755, Santiago; tel: [562] 209-9031; fax: [562] 204-8988 or 777-0734)
Distributed by: IMRE
Evaluators: Hugo Chapa-Guzmán, Daniel Scroggins, Stephen Webre
Description: With a screenplay by Chilean writer José Donoso and a setting in contemporary Valparaiso, this tape is a tale of domestic tyranny centering on the relationship between an elderly invalid, Don Arnaldo (Rafael Denavente), and his subservient middle-aged son, known only as *Gordo* (Ernesto Beadle). A retired naval officer, Don Arnaldo is contemptuous of modern ways, preferring to dwell in the past as he remembers it, a simpler time when aristocratic values prevailed and the navy occupied a heroic place in Chilean society. Manipulative, demanding, and embittered by his own physical infirmity, the old man uses a system of carefully placed mirrors to maintain surveillance over his son's movements in the small apartment the two share. Gordo, as the nickname ("Fatty") suggests, is overweight, unprepossessing, and a disappointment in general to his father, who misses few opportunities to insult him. Unemployed, Gordo is trapped in a miserable existence by his role as Don Arnaldo's only caregiver and by his financial dependence on the old man's mod-

est pension. The only sources of pleasure in Gordo's tedious life are cooking and his developing romantic attachment to Lucrecia (Gloria Munchmeyer), a fortyish widow living in the apartment below them. Gordo dreams of marrying Lucrecia and opening a seafood restaurant, but both aspirations are unattainable as long as he remains responsible for his father.

Strengths and Weaknesses: This is a well-directed psychological drama that offers a good examination of life in the marginalized middle class of a major South American city. The settings and depictions of cultural behavior and attitudes are authentic, and the cinematography and acting are excellent. The film is particularly strong on atmosphere. The faded opulence of downtown Valparaiso and the darkened interiors of the apartment in which much of the action takes place complement the melancholy mood of the screenplay. The story line is minimal and exists mostly to support the powerful dialogue and character development. The prizewinning study in obsessive dominant-submissive behavior has received high praise from international critics.

One evaluator pointed out that the film has serious limitations for Spanish language classroom use. At least half of the dialogue is conducted in hoarse whispers, with the view of the speakers' faces partially or totally obstructed. Full-face camera shots with well-modulated voices are relatively infrequent.

Introducing the Tape: Because the film contains specific historical and political references, U.S. audiences will want some brief introduction to the modern history of Chile. It is important to note the traditional link between the Chilean navy and the country's sense of national identity. (The navy played a key role in Chile's victory in the War of the Pacific [1879–83], and the national hero, Arturo Prat, was a young naval officer killed in that war.) In this century, the navy has come to be seen as an aristocratic institution and conservator of traditional values. It is also important to explain the role that the navy, along with the other armed forces, played in overthrowing the Socialist government of Salvador Allende Gossens in 1973. The military dictatorship of General Augusto Pinochet is never mentioned explicitly in the film, but it is alluded to and may be taken as a macrocosmic expression of the kind of petty tyranny Don Arnaldo exercises at home.

How to Use: In an *Introduction to Writing for Film and TV* class I would try to illustrate the relationship between character, dialogue, and acting in development of plot. Conflict, even between close family members, can help plot development and highlight character. (Chapa-Guzmán)

Because of the invalid father's obsession with the sea and seafaring life, and because the camera frequently captures the "up to the mountain, down to the beach" movement of many Chilean cities, the film could help U.S. audiences gain some insight into the culture of this South American country, about which they may know very little. (Scroggins)

In *Latin American Studies, Culture,* or *Literature* classes, the film can be used to enourage students to compare/contrast relations between elderly parents and adult children in the United States and Latin American or other Third World countries. It may also be used as an aid to the exploration of two important themes in twentieth-century Latin American literature: tyranny and solitude. (Webre)

Suggested Readings: Cheney, Rev. Theodore A. *Writing Creative Nonfiction: How to Use Fiction Techniques to Make Your Nonfiction More Interesting, Dramatic and Vivid.*

Hintz, Eugenio. *Historia y filmografía del cine uruguayo.*

Loveman, Brian. *Chile: The Legacy of Hispanic Capitalism.*

Sater, William F. *The Heroic Image in Chile: Arturo Prat, Secular Saint.*

Vale, Eugene. *The Technique of Screenplay Writing: An Analysis of the Dramatic Structure of Motion Pictures.*

Level: University

LA MADRE PATRIA (The Motherland)

Experimental.   In English.   7 min.   1987

Directed by: Juan Downey

Distributed by: Electronic Arts Intermix

Evaluators: Deirdre Boyle, John Higgins, Rebecca Torres-Rivera

Description: This is an ironic parable of Downey's native Chile. Returning to Santiago after a long exile, he finds a society in the grip of the military dictatorship of General Augusto Pinochet. In a scenario that suggests the "magical realism" of Latin American fiction, Downey visits the suburban house of his youth and stages a surreal reenactment of the Motherland "giving birth" to a duck, while the crucified Prophet looks on. This overtly symbolic scene is intercut with the spectacle of General Pinochet and his troops in full regalia. In an unsparing indictment of the economic and political reality of the dictatorship, *The Motherland* offers the Prophet as a sacrifice to the goose-stepping ranks of Pinochet's junta. This savage allegory, in which church and state conspire to oppress society and the individual, merges the subjective and the cultural, the autobiographical and the political.

Strengths and Weaknesses: The tape's strength is its originality in form. Presented as a Cubist painting, it has strong visuals and juxtapositions of images.

Some of the symbolism is not clear, and the tape is not easy to understand without background.

Introducing the Tape: U.S. students would need an introduction on the Pinochet regime and the events on which the video is based. Background on Latin American magical realism is also needed.

How to Use: Anyone teaching the *Art of Latin American Film* should seriously consider Downey's work. The artist's symbolic use of religious imagery might make it useful for an adventuresome teacher of religious motifs in secular art. (Boyle)

The tape could be used as a starting point for a discussion of Latin American magical realism, and for a discussion of video as a means of personal/social expression. (Higgins)

The tape could be a first step for a *Literature* or *Advanced Composition* class. (Torres-Rivera)

Level: University

MEMORIES OF AN EVERYDAY WAR

Documentary.   With Subtitles.   29 min.   1986

Directed by: Gaston Ancelovici, Jaime Barrios

Produced by: Cinemateca Chilena, Rene Davila

Distributed by: First Run/Icarus Films

Evaluators: Paul LaReau, Angharad N. Valdivia, Richard D. Woods

Description: The Pinochet regime, which came to power in 1973, waged both physical and psychological war against the Chilean masses. In this powerful film, news footage, clandestine video of political demonstrations, and clips of Pinochet's speeches are intercut with interviews of four people who suffered under the dictator's rule. A former army officer, an actor who lost his son, a young mother whose husband was killed, and an activist priest in the exile city of La Victoria recount their experiences. The film, as a memoir, is unstructured in form, but the end result is a condemnation of the Pinochet government.

Strengths and Weaknesses: A strength of the film is its inclusion of interviews with people from various walks of life. The series of vignettes of the victims of the military regime enables the viewer to link the comments into a single narration, bringing out the universal effects of terrorism.

One evaluator felt it was not always clear who was being interviewed.

Introducing the Tape: Some introductory narration explaining the "suicide" of Salvador Allende and the overthrow of his government would be helpful.

How to Use: This tape explores the cultural, social, economic, and political effects of militarized oppression and shows the resolve of many people when facing such barriers to freedom. (Valdivia)

The tape would be useful in a *Spanish Language* course where students would listen to the Chilean accent. (Woods)

Level: University

NO ME AMENACES (Don't Threaten Me)

Documentary.   With Subtitles.   52 min.   1990

Directed by: Juan Andrés Racz

Produced by: La Mar Films (Gerona 3497, Santiago; tel: [562] 225-3197; fax: [562] 341-4496)

Distributed by: First Run/Icarus Films

Evaluators: Charles Bergquist, Joséph A. Gagliano, Hilda Pato

Description: This documentary deals with Chile's return to democratic political forms after seventeen years of dictatorship. Focusing on the major events of 1988 and 1989, it details the social and political developments that ended the Pinochet dictatorship and restored an elected civilian government. The tape emphasizes the efforts of political leaders on the Left and the Right to promote compromise and reconciliation and ensure a peaceful transition. Presenting the presidential campaign of 1989, the film gives primary attention to Patricio Aylwin and his major opponent on the right, Henri Buchi. Some historical context is provided to illustrate the level of repression during the Pinochet years. The film concludes with a look at important sociopolitical issues confronting Aylwin (who assumed the presidency in March 1990), such as the lack of a strong political center to counterbalance the policy demands of the extreme Left and Right, and the continued threat of military intervention in domestic politics.

Strengths and Weaknesses: This is a visually appealing tape that vividly portrays the strong political involvement of all segments of Chilean society and the hard choices ahead for the country. The commentary provided by several social critics and writers is richly articulate, and at times almost lyrical. The video presents a detailed narrative of political events from 1988 to 1990, introducing viewers to the major political figures who tried to achieve an accommodation to restore democratic government. It captures the flavor of a Latin American election campaign, using campaign images, interviews, and footage of Pinochet's declarations to convey the drama, color, and contradictions. One evaluator commented that the presentation of the different candidates' approaches and "lines" were by themselves a concise lesson in the semiotics of political campaigning. While depicting the repression during the Pinochet years, the film gives a balanced and realistic assessment of Pinochet's leadership and some positive aspects of his rule. Patricio Aylwin is shown as a pragmatic politician who has learned from past mistakes and seeks reconciliation in Chilean politics.

For viewers without sufficient background, the film's imagery can be hard to follow. One evaluator felt that the tape concentrated too much on detailed matters that would not be of concern to U.S. audiences, while not devoting adequate attention to the major sociopolitical issues that faced Aylwin following his election. The significant differences between the presidential candidates are not presented in any depth, so it may be difficult for U.S. audiences to understand why Aylwin won the election. At times, the subtitles are hard to read.

Introducing the Tape: More context and an overview of Allende and the Pinochet dictatorship are necessary for an audience unfamiliar with the context.

How to Use: I would use this in a course I teach on *Modern Latin American History* that includes detailed attention to Chile to wrap up treatment of the whole process of *Twentieth-Century Chilean History*. (Bergquist)

The tape could be used in undergraduate courses in *Twentieth-Century Latin American History* and *United States-Latin American Relations*. It would show students the preoccupation with anticommunism in Latin America during the

1970s and early 1980s, and the resurgence of democratic aspirations since the mid-1980s. (Gagliano)

Suggested Readings: Agüero, Felipe. "Chile: South America's Success Story?"

Dorfman, Ariel. *Death and the Maiden*, a short prizewinning play.

Loveman, Brian. *Chile: The Legacy of Hispanic Capitalism.*

Sigmund, Paul. *The Overthrow of Allende and the Politics of Chile, 1964–1976.*

Timerman, Jacobo. *Chile: Death in the South.*

Valenzuela, J. Samuel, and Arturo Valenzuela, eds. *Military Rule in Chile: Dictatorship and Opposition.*

Level: University

NO ME OLVIDES (Don't Forget Me)

Documentary.   With Subtitles.   13 min.   1989
Directed by: Tatiana Gaviola
Distributed by: Women Make Movies
Evaluators: Elba Birmingham-Pokorny, Sandra L. Cade, James W. Cooper, Grace Leavitt, Angharad N. Valdivia
Description: *No Me Olvides* calls attention to sixteen years of terrible human rights violations and political repression by the military dictatorship in Chile. It documents the August 9, 1988, clash between police and a group of more than three thousand women protesters. The women marched through the streets of Santiago, bearing life-size black cardboard cutouts with the names of "disappeared" persons, demanding answers from the Pinochet regime about their whereabouts. Riot police sprayed the demonstrators and onlookers with fire hoses, knocking down the cardboard shadow figures. Passersby stopped to pick up the broken images. This powerful film deals with the Chilean people's efforts to call attention to the devastating impact Pinochet's repressive government had on every aspect of their lives and on Chile's democratic tradition. Poems and music cry out the pain, voicing the need to protest.
Strengths and Weaknesses: This is a very strong film whose visual aspects need almost no translation. The music paints a picture of sadness and longing, and the somber black silhouettes with names of lost ones create a bleak atmosphere. One of the strongest points of this film is its illustration of how women's participation in the struggle for both political freedom and human rights in Chile reflects their changing role. The film is highly motivating, showing the tremendous impact of people's power to bring about political, economic, and social changes in their societies.

The film lacks general and specific background that would allow those unfamiliar with Latin American and Chilean history and politics to gain a better understanding and appreciation of its message.
Introducing the Tape: Students should be introduced to the situation of the "disappeared" in the military dictatorships of the Southern Cone (Argentina, Uruguay, Chile, and Paraguay). Instructors should give contextual information on

Chilean sociopolitical history and update the film. Although the repression in Chile has eased since the 1988 referendum in which Pinochet lost the "vote of confidence," this tape remains an important historic document of the period.
How to Use: In *Modern Spanish-American Literature* the tape could be used to introduce the works of Isabel Allende, Nicanor Parra, Marjorie Agosín, and others to show how their work reflects and gives symbolic meaning and historical significance to some of the major social, political, and historical upheavals taking place in Latin America today. (Birmingham-Pokorny)

I could use this in the research unit I do with my eighth-grade *Spanish* students. They research a topic and present a video as their final report. This film could be used to pique their interest in a current issue, as well as for examples of effective use of audio to express the emotion of the topic. (Cade)

The tape could be shown to a *High School Social Studies* class prior to having a Chilean guest speaker who lived in Chile during that period. The tape could be used to stimulate students to create questions for the guest. After, they could write an essay on what happened in that period and what they think will happen in the future. (Cooper)

I would use this film in *Spanish-American Culture and Civilization* to illustrate the transition of some of the Latin American nations from dictatorships to democracies and vice versa, as well as to show how the decade of the '70s signaled the institutionalization of military dictatorships in the Southern Cone. (Valdivia)

This tape can be used in conjunction with others that give an overview of Chilean history, particularly in relationship to the military coup of 1973, i.e., *La Batalla de Chile (The Battle of Chile), Chile's Forbidden Dreams.*

In *Political Science* courses this video would exemplify how democratic movements/popular pressures have been instrumental in overthrowing dictatorships.

In *Women's Studies* the tape can stimulate discussion on the changing role of women in Latin American culture.
Complementary Films/Videos: *La Batalla de Chile (The Battle of Chile)* (distributed by New Yorker Films); *Chile: sueños prohibidos (Chile's Forbidden Dreams)* (Chile).
Level: Junior High School—University

PADRE SANTO Y LA GLORIA (Holy Father and Gloria)

Documentary.   With Subtitles.   43 min.   1987
Directed by: Estela Bravo
Distributed by: The Cinema Guild
Evaluators: Joseph A. Gagliano, Glenn J. Kist
Description: The film demonstrates how opponents of the Pinochet dictatorship used the papal visit in April 1987 to draw world attention to repression in their country. Much of the film focuses on the anti-Pinochet activities of Carmen Gloria Quintana during the pope's visit. In 1986, Carmen Gloria was tortured and set on fire for her opposition efforts.

Following medical treatment in Canada, she returned to Chile and was an organizer and active participant in the April 1987 demonstrations. Carmen Gloria sought John Paul II's assistance to end the institutional violence in Chile. The tape includes interviews both with working-class youth, who express opposition and hatred for Pinochet, and with upper-class adolescents who voice support and admiration for him.

Strengths and Weaknesses: The film presents a clear, detailed picture of the opposition to Pinochet that existed in Chile, and how it was organized and manifested during the pope's visit. There are very effective scenes of the papal call for justice at a rally in the national stadium where so many Chileans were detained by the military in 1973—especially strong for viewers familiar with the overthrow of Allende. The scenes showing Carmen Gloria and the demonstration of intense opposition to the dictatorship are particularly poignant. The tape attempts balance by including the contrasting interviews with youth, including the observations of pro-Pinochet students. Some, however, may regard their comments as illustrating a lack of political sophistication among privileged Chilean youth.

The scenes concerning the April 3 disorders are not explained, and the role of Carmen Gloria Quintana as an opposition leader is not treated adequately.

Introducing the Tape: An introduction providing context for the papal visit and the plans of Pinochet opponents is necessary, and some background on the Pinochet years may be important for U.S. viewers. Also, the following information should be presented regarding Carmen Gloria Quintana: Carmen Gloria and a companion, Rodrigo Rojas, were arrested by a military patrol on July 2, 1986. The two young people were carrying paraffin (kerosene), which was apparently intended to be used to start bonfires in the streets to disrupt traffic during antigovernment demonstrations. After arresting the two, the police poured the paraffin on the teens and set them alight. Rojas died on July 4 as a result of severe burns. Carmen Gloria survived, terribly scarred, and was sent to Montreal for treatment. At the time of the pope's visit, she returned to Santiago to meet with him.

How to Use: I would use the tape in my *Twentieth-Century Latin American History* course during the treatment of the growth of democratization in Latin American during the 1980s and early 1990s. After viewing the film, students would discuss how it depicted popular efforts to bring political change in contemporary Latin America. (Gagliano)

This film could be used in *Modern Latin American History*. In the discussion after viewing, I would focus on the following questions: What is the point of view or political perspective of the producers of this film? In what way does the film show class division in Chile? In what way does the film show the importance of the Roman Catholic Church in Chile? The film would give the students a good feel for the tensions that existed in Chile in the late Pinochet era. Another approach would be to show the film prior to any discussion of Chilean history in the period 1970–90, using the events de-picted in the film as the basis for the discussion of that period. (Kist)

Suggested Readings: Agüero, Felipe. "Chile: South America's Success Story?"

Aman, Kenneth, and Christina Parker. *Popular Culture in Chile: Resistance and Survival*.

Arriagada, Genaro. *Pinochet: The Politics of Power*.

Chavkin, Samuel. *Storm over Chile: The Junta under Siege*.

Falcoff, Mark. *Modern Chile, 1970–1989: A Critical History*.

Garretón, Manuel Antonio. *The Chilean Political Process*.

MacEoin, Gary. *Chile, under Military Rule*.

Sigmund, Paul. *The Overthrow of Allende and the Politics of Chile, 1964–1976*.

Timerman, Jacobo. *Chile: Death in the South*.

Valenzuela, J. Samuel, and Arturo Valenzuela, eds. *Military Rule in Chile: Dictatorship and Opposition*.

Level: High School—University

QUE HACER? (What Is to Be Done?)

Feature.   With Subtitles.   90 min.   1992
Directed by: Nina Serrano, Saul Landau, and Raul Ruiz
Produced by: Impact Films
Distributed by: IMRE, Institute for Policy Studies
Evaluators: Saul Landau, Lynn M. Shirey
Description: This spy-story musical follows the experiences of an American Peace Corps volunteer and an undercover U.S. government agent who meet at the time of Salvador Allende's election in Chile (1970). As the volunteer gradually becomes involved with a radical leftist group, the agent uses her to get close to the group and thwart its efforts.

Strengths and Weaknesses: This is a creative treatment of material with interesting camera work, editing, etc. The film evokes the aura of an election in which class conflicts are about to explode in violence and teaches about Chile and politics while remaining upbeat and entertaining. The film mixes actual footage of Allende and political demonstrations of the time with dramatic sequences. Some of the musical scenes, particularly that of the band Country Joe and the Fish, are excellent, while others seem out of place.

There are some confusing results of the editing, which can cause the message to seem unfocused.

Introducing the Tape: For maximum appreciation of the film, students should have some historical background of the U.S. efforts to undermine the election of Salvador Allende. Even without much context, students tend to like this work because of its zaniness.

How to Use: I use the film to teach about *Chile* in the Allende years and as a way to dramatize the meaning of democratic elections within a system that doesn't believe in democracy—unless an election turns out the way it should. I also use the film to show how feature and documentary styles can be intercut to make certain cinematic points. (Landau)

Suggested Readings: Chavkin, Samuel. *Storm over Chile: The Junta under Seige.*

Constable, Pamela, and Arturo Valenzuela. *A Nation of Enemies: Chile under Pinochet.*

Dinges, John, and Saul Landau. *Assassination on Embassy Row.*

Falcoff, Mark. *Modern Chile, 1970–1989: A Critical History.*

Hersh, Seymour. *The Price of Power: Kissinger in the Nixon White House.*

Horne, Alistair. *Small Earthquake in Chile: New, Revised and Expanded Edition of the Classic Account of Allende's Chile.*

Landau, Saul. *The Dangerous Doctrine: National Security and U.S. Foreign Policy.*
Level: University

RETORNADO A CHILE (Returning to Chile)
Documentary.   With Subtitles.   28 min.   1986
Directed by: Estela Bravo
Distributed by: The Cinema Guild
Evaluators: Daniel P. Hunt, Michael Monteón, Frederick M. Nunn, Allen Wells
Description: Focusing particularly on youth, this documentary is about the return in 1985 of a number of families that were forced to flee Chile after Pinochet's 1973 coup. Many of the young people were born in exile or taken out of Chile by their parents at an early age. Their memories and longing for their homeland are explored in the tape. The returned parents and their children are interviewed, as well as the neighbors of people who were detained, "disappeared," or tortured. The film shows the considerable unrest that existed in Chile at the time it was made (twelve years after the military takeover) and how popular resistance to the Pinochet regime was growing. It includes scenes of police breaking up demonstrations and the funeral of one of the demonstrators killed by the police. The result is a passionate plea for human rights and dignity in Chile and for an end to the terror.
Strengths and Weaknesses: This film is well shot and edited. Its strength is the interviews with everyday Chileans, who openly and publicly oppose the dictatorship. There are a number of eyewitness-type shots of the police trying to stifle dissent.

The documentary lacks context. We are introduced rather poignantly to a number of exile families that are returning after all these years, but then we don't follow them through the rest of the film. It is unclear when and where the filming is taking place.
Introducing the Tape: The tape needs to be put in context with background about Chilean history and the Pinochet regime. Some questions to address in the introduction would be: Who was Allende? Who is Pinochet? How long had each been in power? Viewers should be told that interviews take place in a working-class neighborhood and that those detained by the police were arrested for political activity

against Pinochet. To bring the tape up to date, it should be explained that Pinochet was voted out of office in a plebiscite in 1988, but he remained head of the military. Political repression in Chile has lessened, but the scars on the populace are far from healed.
How to Use: I have used García Márquez's account of *La aventura de Miguel Littín clandestino en Chile* in my intermediate *Language* classes. This film would complement that text nicely. I have my students read the text in Spanish and would have them do so before viewing the film. Since it has subtitles, it may not have much value strictly for language acquisition, but it would put faces on the players. It could also be used in conjunction with Isabel Allende's *The House of the Spirits.* (Hunt)

I would show the tape as an example of the feelings and sufferings of the Chilean people in the early 1980s as they fought against political repression and the military dictatorship of Pinochet, pointing out, as the tape does not, that the U.S. was instrumental in putting Pinochet in office and keeping him there. (Monteón)
Suggested Readings: Allende, Isabel. *La casa de los espíritus (The House of Spirits).* (See bibliography for other works.)

Constable, Pamela, and Arturo Valenzuela. *A Nation of Enemies: Chile Under Pinochet.*

Dorfman, Ariel. *Widows.*

García Márquez, Gabriel. *La aventura de Miguel Littín clandestino en Chile.*

Skidmore, Thomas E., and Peter H. Smith. *Modern Latin America.*

Winn, Peter. *Weavers of Revolution: The Yarur Workers and Chile's Road to Socialism.*
Level: High School—University

THE RETURN OF THE MOTHERLAND
Experimental.   In English.   27 min.   1989
Directed by: Juan Downey
Distributed by: Electronic Arts Intermix
Evaluators: Deirdre Boyle, John Higgins, Rebecca Torres-Rivera
Description: A man trying to deal with personal feelings (a love affair) is intertwined with the people's struggle for freedom from military actions in different parts of the world, particularly Chile during the Pinochet dictatorship. The blend of fictional narratives with documentary footage from Pinochet's Chile raises questions about the separation of the personal and the political. The tape includes depictions of the assassinations of Parada, Nabino, and Guerrero, among others, as well as the visit of the pope to Chile.
Strengths and Weaknesses: This tape's strength is its originality. It has strong "fantasy" sequences of personal and fictional narratives.

One evaluator found the tape "too far out," while another felt that, although some symbolism might be lost on some audiences, it was not much of a problem.

Introducing the Tape: U.S. viewers would need some background on the Pinochet regime. Also helpful would be background on video as a form of personal and social expression, and preparation for viewing experimental works.

How to Use: Downey's comparison of the Pinochet regime with that of Hitler through broadcast images would make this interesting for anyone studying *Nazism in Latin America*. The issues of a free press (and broadcast media) in a dictatorship could make this interesting for *Journalism* courses. (Boyle)

For *Video Production* classes the tape would be useful to start a discussion of style and the use of video for personal and social expression. (Higgins)

I would show this as a preparation for *Creative Writing*. (Torres-Rivera)

Level: University

SOLIDARIDAD: FAITH, HOPE, AND HAVEN
Documentary. With Subtitles. 56 min. 1989
Directed by: Edgardo Reyes and Gillian Brown
Distributed by: First Run/Icarus Films
Evaluators: Kendall W. Brown
Description: This tape portrays life under the Pinochet regime and emphasizes how the Vicariate of Solidarity worked to protect dissidents and provide medical care for those who had been tortured. The vicariate generally defied the dictatorship, and its personnel were sometimes arrested and mistreated.
Strengths and Weaknesses: This is a well-produced and well-shot tape, and is valuable in showing the vicariate's opposition to the regime.

The film deals with every aspect of the vicariate's work, including social welfare, food distribution, etc., which are not as useful for U.S. classes; thus excerpts of the program could be more useful.

How to Use: In classes examining *Religion and Politics* the tape presents the example of Chile. Students can research other examples of the church working with the poor in defiance of military or authoritarian governments.
Level: High School—University

SOMOS MAS (We Are More)
Documentary. With Subtitles. 7 min. 1985
Directed by: Pablo Salas and Pedro Chaskel
Produced by: Antu Productions
Distributed by: First Run/Icarus Films
Evaluators: Marc Chernick, Marcia Dean, Paul LaReau, Eliana Moya Raggio, Jennifer M. Taylor
Description: This video documents a 1985 demonstration against the dictatorship organized by women in Santiago, Chile. It depicts peaceful street protesters demanding liberty and democracy, and military and police attempts to suppress their movement with water cannons and tear gas.
Strengths and Weaknesses: The tape shows very graphically what police repression is all about, particularly as it

comes in response to peaceful protest with a deliberately nonprovocative message. The footage of police violence conveys more than a million words could. The tape also powerfully demonstrates the strength of women when they unite in a large group. The video and sound quality is excellent.

The tape has no narration, some of the scenes could use a context, and viewers need an update on events since 1985. One evaluator commented that the tape's message was quickly grasped and the many confrontational scenes could become tedious. Another reviewer felt the video lacked focus.

Introducing the Tape: U.S. students would need general political and historical background. It should be explained that the actions took place during a general wave of protests from 1983 to 1986 that eventually led to the end of the Pinochet dictatorship. It should also be pointed out that although Pinochet was voted out of the presidency in a referendum in 1988, he remained as head of the army, and none of the institutions that perpetrated the repression in Chile were dismantled.

How to Use: This can be used to help students understand spoken *Spanish* as well as to sensitize them to what is and has been going on in South American countries like Chile. It also focuses on the position of the woman, issues of power and control, and the uses of nonviolent demonstrations in the face of violence. The video could be used in a class on *Latin American Women* to show how Chilean women felt the need to challenge the dictatorship and confront the macho values that supposedly protect women. (Dean)

Suggested Readings: Bunster, X. "Surviving Beyond Fear," in *Women and Change in Latin America,* eds. June Nash and Helen Sofa.

P.E.N. Report of Chilean Writers.

Reports on Chile from Amnesty International and Americas Watch.

Level: Junior High School—University

TANTAS VIDAS, UNA HISTORIA (So Many Lives, One Story)
Documentary. With Subtitles. 26 min. 1983
Directed by: Tatiana Gaviloa
Distributed by: Women Make Movies
Evaluators: Sarah Chambers, Rosario Espinal, Michele Geslin Small, Angharad N. Valdivia
Description: Women in a consciousness-raising workshop in a shantytown in Santiago share their experiences as housewives, workers, spouses, and mothers. Through interviews, role-playing, and discussion, they describe to each other and the audience the circumstances of their lives: their work, family, marriage, men, domestic abuse, money, and survival. The underlying message is that through organizing, women can learn that they have much in common.
Strengths and Weaknesses: The testimonial nature of the tape makes it particularly appealing and credible. The women clearly have a relationship of trust with the filmmak-

ers and share their personal stories openly. Viewers get a sense both of the individual personalities of the women and their common problems. Their strength in enduring many hardships is clear, and the workshop's power in bringing them together to discuss, laugh, and support each other is moving and inspiring. The discussion about relationships is especially interesting.

As the tape is purely a documentation of testimonies, it does not contextualize life in a shantytown, nor does it provide background about this neighborhood group and why and how the workshop was organized. One reviewer commented that because the tape is a record of the women's discussion, it is disjointed and confusing. The synthesized subtitles leave out many ideas, a problem inherent in tapes with a lot of dialogue.

Introducing the Tape: Audiences definitely need a preface explaining that the video is about a group of shantytown women who participated in a workshop in Santiago. Some description of living conditions in shantytowns of Latin America would also be helpful.

How to Use: I would use this tape in a *Women's Studies* course to examine the more personal lives of women who consider themselves primarily housewives. I would tell the students to pay particular attention to what the women say about their relationships with men and family. Many of the women have been separated, and some discuss how their husbands/partners treat them better when they are contributing to the household income. (Chambers)

Having discussed issues of poverty, machismo, and exploitation at the workplace, I would use this film to illustrate how women feel about these issues. (Espinal)

Level: High School—Unversity

COLOMBIA

AMOR, MUJERES, Y FLORES (Love, Women, and Flowers)

Documentary. With Subtitles. 58 min. 1988
Directed by: Marta Rodríguez and Jorge Silva
Produced by: Firefret Production (Carrera 8 #65–99, Apto. 101, Bogotá; tel: [571] 249-4316)
Distributed by: Women Make Movies
Evaluators: Silvia Arrom, Susan Besse, Nancy J. Church, Mark Fried, Victor Garatea, Carmen Madariaga-Culver, Stephen P. O'Neill, Angharad N. Valdivia
Description: This film uncovers the appallingly high human costs of the production of flowers in Colombia for export to First World markets. The Harvard-educated U.S. businessman who in the mid-1960s discovered the economic advantages of growing carnations in the rich, flat, well-watered plains surrounding Bogotá has nothing but praise for the Colombian work force and government policies. But intertwined with the "gringo" manager's voice are interviews with the workers, mostly women, powerfully relating their

personal experiences and their hazardous working conditions. Most of the women, who began working in their mid-teens, have had their health seriously compromised by the heavy use of pesticides that are banned in the U.S. and Europe. In case after case, each more moving than the last, the women (and one man) describe their appalling working conditions and the injuries and sicknesses they have suffered: loss of vision, leukemia, epilepsy, bronchitis, asthma, miscarriages, and eczema. Even the soil has been affected by a plant disease that has rendered much productive land useless. These somber and prematurely aged women also tell of difficulties outside their jobs. They work a double shift on the job and at home, and they can't afford adequate housing, food, or clothing (much less medical bills). Additionally, they often suffer physical abuse from their husbands. When the workers struck in 1987 against Bogotá Flowers Ltd. and temporarily occupied the plant, they gained hope from having discovered their strength in unity. But victory ended when they were evicted by tear gas. Unfortunately, due to the filmmaker's untimely death, the tape ends abruptly, just as the documentation of the unionization movement begins.

Strengths and Weaknesses: This is a very powerful, moving, well-produced documentary that vividly brings crucial issues to the attention of people in the U.S.: health hazards, poor working conditions, the role of U.S. multinational corporations, and workers' attempts to organize. It is an interesting and well-done tape that helps people in the U.S. understand how the simple act of buying flowers makes them complicit in this exploitation.

A few evaluators felt the tape should have provided more context and statistics. One found the format somewhat confusing and felt that the tape was a bit long and some aspects outdated.

Introducing the Tape: More contextual information would be helpful, although it is not essential for understanding the messages. Instructors could explain the impact of the spread of commercial agriculture in Latin America since the 1960s. Background about unionization, labor struggles, and the flower industry in general would enhance viewing. Specifically, there is no mention of who owned the land before the flower companies arrived, what happened to those people, and why so many workers are so desperately in need of such miserable jobs. Although the film talks about pregnant workers, it does not make clear what protective laws are on the books and whether they are enforced. An epilogue is also necessary to let the audience know how the unionization movement fared after the tape was made.

How to Use: The film is especially useful in demonstrating the costs of *Development* in Latin America, especially for women and the environment. It raises very difficult questions about what are the ways out, since even if the workers were to succeed in having their union recognized and winning some of their demands, the health issues would not easily, or quickly, disappear. (Besse)

In a *Marketing* course the tape could be used to illustrate business practices, including the exploitation of workers in Third World countries for the benefit of exports to developed countries. (Church)

In a *Social Studies* class I would use this tape to explain to U.S. students how hazardous conditions are created in the Third World in order to satisfy frivolous consumer desires in the U.S. (Garatea)

Since this is in Spanish with English subtitles, an *English as a Second Language* teacher might show the film, have students discuss the issues and create a writing assignment around the tape. Instructors should provide the small language groups with some structured questions. (O'Neill)

Level: High School—University

ANANEKO

Documentary.   Without Subtitles.   54 min.   1991

Directed by: Juan Carlos Borrero

Produced by: Grabacolor Ltd. (Transu 20 #102–09, Bogotá; tel: [571] 269-6136; fax: [571] 368-6945)

Distributed by: IMRE Archive

Evaluators: Maurice P. Brungardt, Osvaldo Chinchón, Joan A. McGinnis, Martha Rees

Description: This tape surveys the culture of the Huitoto and Andoke Indians in Amazonas, an area in southeastern Colombia along the Putamayo River and Ecuadorian border. Native people discuss in both Spanish and their Indian language some of their customs, eating habits, and the curative powers possessed by older members of the community. The film shows daily tasks such as felling a tree, choosing a site to grow food, preparing the land, fixing the yucca (casaba, manioc), fishing, and using coca and relates the Indian explanation for how things are done. Indian myths are offered to explain the specific mechanisms involved in carrying out these tasks. It is clear, for example, that the natives have great respect for the powerful effect coca has in their lives. As they gather the leaves, the narrator explains that they take care of the coca plants as if each were a member of the human family.

Strengths and Weaknesses: The tape provides authentic footage of Indian culture and mythology/storytelling, as well as good insight into the attitudes of an indigenous culture toward nature and how the people coexist in harmony. There are effective visual shots of the Colombian Amazonian area and the techniques employed in slash-and-burn agriculture, yucca preparation, fishing, and the use of coca leaves. The map and native legends are useful.

A couple of evaluators felt the film's pacing in places was slow for general U.S. audiences, particularly the long segments of storytelling. Little explanation is offered as to the importance of these Indian myths and why the tape was made. Much of the footage is without commentary and is not well integrated into the tape.

Introducing the Tape: An introduction should include an overview of the geographical area of the Amazon, plus a little history of coca. More discussion of where and how the Huitoto or Andoke Indians fit into the Indian culture of Colombia is needed. Also more information about the Andoke people, their present situation and past history, as well as background on the filmmakers and purpose of the film would be helpful.

How to Use: The tape could be used to show what native culture and practices are like and how the myths provide these practices with an explanation for why things are done the way they are. Modernization will obviously lead to different practices and explanations that will lead to a further breakdown in these native practices and customs and certainly in their myths. (Brungardt)

I could use this tape to show the linguistic variations in the use of *Spanish* by people in remote areas of a Spanish-speaking nation such as Colombia. For example, at one moment one native uses the article *el* (masculine) before the word *coca* and a moment later he says *la* (feminine) *coca*. (Chinchón)

The film's most interesting aspect is its portrayal of life on the Amazon River. My students might enjoy the legends (in a *Literature* class) and learning about the Indians' use of coca. (McGinnis)

I would use this video to discuss ethnographic material in terms of current events, such as drugs. (Rees)

Suggested Readings: Bushnell, David. *The Making of Modern Colombia. A Nation in Spite of Itself.*

Chagnon, Napoleon A. *Yanomamo, the Fierce People.*

Friede, Juan. *Los Andakí, 1538–1947: Historia de la aculturación de una tribu selvática.*

Murphy, Yolanda, and Robert F. Murphy. *Women of the Forest.*

Reichel-Dolmatoff, Gerardo. *Colombia.*

Level: University

BEHIND THE COCAINE WARS

Documentary.   With Subtitles.   52 min.   1991

Directed by: Patricia Castaño and Adelaida Trujillo

Produced by: Cituurna Producciones (Calle 25C #3–92, Bogotá; tel: [571] 334-1677; fax: [571] 282-4981)

Distributed by: IMRE, Jane Balfour Films

Evaluators: Maurice P. Brungardt, María Fernández, Joséph A. Gagliano, Margarita de la Vega-Hurtado

Description: This documentary analyzes the complex sociopolitical issues confronting Colombia since the 1960s. It is dedicated to journalist Sylvia Duzán, who was assassinated along with three peasant leaders in the Yondó area of Simitarra while the film was being made. The film emphasizes how the government's antidrug campaign, or "Cocaine War," beginning in 1989 has escalated domestic violence and distracted national leaders from instituting pressing social reforms. Focusing on the hinterland community of Yondó, the film describes how reform initiatives of local peasants were stifled by large landowners, international petroleum firms operating in the region, and the military, which claimed the peasants were allied with communist guerrillas.

The film asserts that the Cocaine Wars were used as a pretext by an alliance of the landed oligarchy, drug barons, and military leaders (with funds made available by the U.S.) to fight leftist guerrillas and frustrate the efforts of peasant associations. Political assassinations and intimidation of national leaders by drug barons have also made the Cocaine Wars ineffective. An interview with General Fred Woerner, head of U.S. Special Forces in Latin America, by noted U.S. Latin Americanist Bruce Bagley explores these questions. The argument made is that U.S. military aid to Colombia to fight drug traffickers has increased human rights violations by the Colombian military. The reformers featured in the film recommend funding for local development projects, political pluralism, and using U.S. aid for economic development rather than an anti-drug crusade, in order to address the problems that have created violence and upheaval in the country for more than a generation.

Strengths and Weaknesses: This tape has excellent shots of contemporary Colombian small-town life in the middle Magdalena area, with candid and succinct interviews with Colombian officials and peasant and labor leaders that offer much insight into the complexity of violence in the country. There is a good balance between official rhetoric for the war on drugs and the voices of civilians. An explanation of who is responsible for the violence is more elusive. The film attempts to be unbiased by including many different points of view. In an interview, the U.S. official, General Woerner, discusses the problems inherent in providing Colombia with military assistance and argues for an effort at controlling the drug problem by attacking its demand rather than its supply. The tape is successful in underscoring that violence in Colombia is not only a product of the Cocaine Wars.

This tape is not easy to absorb in only one viewing. Its abrupt transitions and its attempt to cover too much can be confusing for uninformed U.S. viewers.

Introducing the Tape: A brief introduction to Colombia's internal violence and how the cocaine cartels gained their national prominence might be helpful. Also there should be an explanation of the links among the drug barons, the landed oligarchy, and the military.

How to Use: I would use this as an introduction to the issue of violence and civil unrest in Latin America. The complexity of the violence in Colombia demonstrated by this tape works as a good initial model or point of departure for understanding the root causes and larger issues. It would also be a useful counterpoint to some of the simplistic efforts to control the drug problem by increasing military aid to Colombia. (Brungardt)

I would use this tape to illustrate a part of the cultural and political context of Latin America. (Fernández)

I would use this tape in my *Twentieth-Century Latin American History* course to show current issues in a major nation. It would be used as the basis for class discussion on the importance of drug trafficking in the development of Colombia, and its impact on democratic political institutions.

The documentary could also be used in my *United States-Latin American Relations History* course as a basis for discussion of U.S. drug policy in the hemisphere and its effects. (Gagliano)

Suggested Readings: Bergquist, Charles, Ricardo Penaranda, and Gonzalo Sánchez, eds. *Violence in Colombia: The Contemporary Crisis in Historical Perspective.*

Braun, Herbert. *The Assassination of Gaitán: Public Life and Urban Violence in Colombia.*

Bushnell, David. *The Making of Modern Colombia. A Nation in Spite of Itself.*

Dix, Robert. *The Politics of Colombia.*

Hartley, Jonathan. *Politics of Coalition Rule in Colombia.*

Henderson, James D. *When Colombia Bled. A History of the Violencia in Tolima.*

Herman, D. L., ed. *Democracy in Latin America: Colombia and Venezuela.*

Martz, John D. "Colombia at the Crossroads."

Oquist, Paul H. *Violence, Conflict and Politics in Colombia.*

Pearce, Jenny. *Colombia: Inside the Labyrinth.*

Vera, Hernan. "Arpilleras: An Iconography of Contemporary Childhood."

Level: High School—University

CARMEN CARRASCAL (Carmen Carrascal)

Documentary. With Subtitles. 30 min. 1982
Directed by: Eulalia Carrizosa
Produced by: Cine Mujer (Apartado 2758, Avenida 25C #4A24, Oficina 202, Santa Fé de Bogotá; tel: [571] 286-7586; fax: [571] 342-6184)
Distributed by: Women Make Movies
Evaluators: James W. Cooper, Ann K. Coughlin, Marcia Dean, Chris Holmlund, J. Julian Rívera, Michele Geslin Small, Susy Suárez, Angharad N. Valdivia
Description: A respectful study of Carmen Carrascal, an enterprising peasant in the northeastern Colombian highlands who has become renowned for her basket weaving. The film begins and ends with a song composed and sung by Carmen during a period in which she suffered a nervous breakdown brought on by overwork and role conflicts: she is a mother of nine and a talented, hardworking craftswoman. This close look at the daily life and work of a rural woman chronicles Carmen's strength without idealizing her. The tape presents her story in her own words. Carmen relates the circumstances of her life: how she started making baskets despite her husband's early opposition and then eventually taught family and neighborhood women, developing a grassoots basket industry. Carmen discusses her identity as an artisan whose award-winning baskets are sold in government shops to "gringos." Out of the details emerges the difficult life of a remarkable woman who developed her creativity and independence despite many obstacles. Carmen defies the limitations placed on her by gender roles and contributes to both her family's survival and the region's economy.

Strengths and Weaknesses: Carmen speaks openly and from the heart; the women of Cine Mujer (the filmmakers) obviously managed to win her trust. As a result, the film is unassuming but very interesting and powerful. It provides fascinating details of daily life in a very isolated rural area and is quite effective at showing the exploitation of native craftspeople. One of the film's great points is its focus on Carmen's conjectures about what U.S. people do with her baskets. The theme of a valiant, admirable, hardworking human being is relevant to contemporary times and universal, although Carmen comes from a rural area of Colombia. She is a woman right out of the works of Gabriel García Márquez!

One reviewer commented that the tape lacked images of Carmen's husband and family life. Another felt it ended a bit abruptly. The audio, cinematography, and color are not of high quality.

Introducing the Tape: No introduction is necessary; however, information on the lives of peasant women in Latin America in general, and Colombia in particular, would be helpful. Introductions can be geared to highlight environmental, anthropological, or women's issues. Audiences should be advised to pay attention to Carmen's knowledge of horticulture and use of plants, observing her relationship to nature and creativity. "When I showed it to my class I prepared them by saying that heroines are found everywhere and often are of humble origins." (Coughlin)

How to Use: After viewing the tape, students could discuss women's work as defined by society throughout history, including rural and urban differences. They could then write essays and/or discuss Carmen's past and future: how her life will be the same or different from that of her children; how people can be part of nature, or control and shape nature for their needs. (Cooper)

In a unit on the works of Gabriel García Márquez (including *El coronel no tiene quien le escriba, Cien años de soledad, Los funerales de la Mamá Grande*) we read that the women characters of this Colombian author are strong, practical realists. This film is perfect for showing North American students the region and people described by the Colombian Nobel Prize-winning writer. My students viewed and listened to the language of northern rural Colombia. After viewing, they discussed the video with partners (in Spanish). Their homework was to write at least two hundred words about Carmen and their impression of her. My high school students were very impressed with Carmen as a person. They admired her strength of character and industry. The compositions they wrote after viewing were excellent. (Coughlin)

I have used this film in a *Latin American Film* course. The final third of the class was devoted to films by and/or about women. One unit focused on the work of Cine Mujer, the oldest and most prolific Latin American feminist film and video collective. I lectured earlier on Colombian history, politics, and economics and, during the Cine Mujer unit, on women's organizations and positions in Colombia. (Holmlund)

I would use the tape to illustrate folk art in a *Latin American Art* course. Discussion on the nature of folk art vs. art for art's sake would follow. (Suárez)

Those who want to use this tape in *Spanish Language* classes may feel the Spanish is too colloquial. Basic vocabulary about weaving could be introduced to help students learn unfamiliar words. The tape is useful for advanced language students who can become accustomed to Carmen's accent.

Suggested Readings: García Márquez, Gabriel. *Los funerales de la Mamá Grande.*

García Márquez, Gabriel. *No One Writes to the Colonel and Other Stories.*

García Márquez, Gabriel. *One Hundred Years of Solitude.*

Lesage, Julia. "Women Make Media: Three Modes of Production," in *The Social Documentary in Latin America,* ed. Julianne Burton.

Miller, Francesca. *Latin American Women and the Search for Social Justice,* general background on women in Colombia and Latin American feminism.

A short article on Cine Mujer in *Screen.*

Level: Junior High School—University

CARTAS DEL PARQUE (Letters from the Park)
Feature.   With Subtitles.   85 min.   1988
Directed by: Tomás Gutiérrez Alea
Produced by: RTVE
Distributed by: IMRE
Evaluators: Kristine Doll, Kathleen March, Joan A. McGinnis, Virginia Shen

Description: This drama, based on a Gabriel García Márquez story, presents a professional writer of love letters who falls in love with one of his clients. The letter writer lives out his fantasy through his commission. When the suitor proves "unsuitable," the writer continues to send the woman letters and takes the youth's place. García Márquez used his parents' love story as a basis for this work. It is an allegorical defense of love and poetry in an increasingly scientific and technological world.

Strengths and Weaknesses: This is an excellent, romantic tape, with a strong story line. The film also has beautiful music and cinematographic features. The geographic and period setting is particularly well done, and the language is elevated and beautiful. The piece would fit nicely into any level *Spanish Language* or *Literature* course. One evaluator felt the film was slow with little character development, although the richness of each protagonist becomes apparent.

Introducing the Tape: To introduce the tape, the works of García Márquez should be discussed. It might also be useful to explain the custom in which illiterate people hired scriveners to write their personal letters. A great deal of the film's beauty is its extensive quotation of Spain's greatest poets. Audiences unfamiliar with these poems would still appreciate the film but would not understand the subtle nuances of the poetry quoted.

How to Use: In *Spanish* classes I would use this film to reinforce such grammatical points as *tú* and *usted* commands, as well as idiomatic expressions (there are many of them). (Doll)

In a *Literature* class, I would have students read the story, then discuss both the film and written "texts," particularly commenting on cultural images portrayed in the film. I would ask for a written essay about story/film or an extension exercise for writing practice, such as asking the students to create their own love letters. (March)

We were studying the literature of Márquez, and although we didn't read this text, we discussed the story line, the insights into *Latin American Culture* of that time period, and the poetry cited. I prepared a vocabulary sheet, a background sheet on Márquez, and study-guide questions. (McGinnis)

Suggested Readings: Becquer, Gustavo Adolfo. *Rimas.*

Stories of Gabriel García Márquez (see bibliography for selection).

Any poetry by Francisco de Quevedo (see bibliography for selection).

Level: Junior High School—University

ENTRE EL DIABLO Y LOS TIGRES (Between the Devil and the Tigers)

Docudrama.   With Subtitles.   47 min.   1988
Directed by: Vicente Franco
Produced by: Franco Productions (12 Liberty, San Francisco, CA 94110; tel: [415] 282-3069; fax: [415] 282-1798)
Distributed by: Franco Productions
Evaluators: Francine Cronshaw, Roger P. Davis, Glenn J. Kist, Franklin W. Knight
Description: This docudrama, based on the book *Los bombardeos en El Pato* by Alfredo Molano and Alejandro Reyes, portrays the impact of *La Violencia* (1946–62) on the Colombian village of El Pato. The narrator is Carmen, a peasant woman who is arrested by an army patrol while on the way to the market with her two children. She is charged with giving aid to the guerrillas and is held in prison for thirteen months. Carmen explains to her captors that she and her family were caught between the army (the devil) and the guerrillas (the tigers), who come demanding food when the army was not present. The peasants want only to be left alone to work their land undisturbed by political and ideological conflicts. The horror of *La Violencia* is presented to viewers through narration, performance, documentary film, and graphic photos showing the turmoil, peasant marches, and political rallies.

Strengths and Weaknesses: The tape does a good job of presenting both the background of *La Violencia* and its impact on El Pato from the peasants' point of view. It provides insight into the human tragedy of the prolonged violence and suffering of ordinary Colombians. The historical footage of political events is quite strong. One reviewer appreciated Carmen's performance, but others felt she overacted. The Spanish in the tape is very clear for use in *Language* classes.

One evaluator felt the general polemical nature of the film did not aid understanding of the reasons for the war nor did it deal with broader social questions. The Spanish newspaper headlines, in addition to subtitles, are a bit too much to read.

Introducing the Tape: While a sketch of the historical background of *La Violencia* in Colombia is provided, it would be necessary to provide some more detail for viewers who are not familiar with events in Colombia since 1946. A brief introduction should include information about the liberal/conservative struggle, the National Front and the phenomena of *La Violencia* in the small republics.

There are different estimates about the dates that the historical period known as *La Violencia* begins and ends. Most authors concur that the worst episodes of cruelty occurred between 1949 and 1953, but can't agree on the reasons why. Some authors claim that *La Violencia* continues today in a form very reminiscent of the years from 1949 to 1953. The 1965 bombings of the community of El Pato were just one more such action that agricultural communities throughout Colombia suffered systematically, before and after 1958. Viewers could be told that the filmmaker did not intend to put forward the definitive objective analysis of *La Violencia* but to illustrate one woman's personal story, which can be extended to numerous peasants' experiences, not only in Colombia, but throughout Latin America.

How to Use: I would use this tape to explore the relationship of land and labor to politics and the state. Students would be exposed to the horror of violence of a nature new to most of them. Discussion would focus on: Why the option of violence? What do people do if they are caught in such a social situation? Are politics to blame or are they an answer? Discussion also could center on the polemical nature of film. What is left out? Why is the film not a balanced, full analysis? (Davis)

The tape could be used in my *Modern Latin American History* course. In the discussion following the viewing, I would focus on the following questions: How would you define *La Violencia*? What is the attitude shown in the tape of the military toward the peasants? Does this seem realistic to you? In what way does the struggle in Colombia depict the intrusion of the Cold War into that South American country? What other issues might contribute to the violence? (Kist)

I would point out that throughout Latin America during the past fifty years, the peasants have been the most profoundly affected by political change. Their attempts to be neutral in national conflict failed as both sides exploited and harassed them. (Knight)

Suggested Readings: Bergquist, Charles, Ricardo Peñaranda, and Gonzalo Sánchez, eds. *Violence in Colombia: The Contemporary Crisis in Historical Perspective.*

Braun, Herbert. *The Assassination of Gaitán: Public Life and Urban Violence in Colombia.*

Buitrago Salazar, Evelio. *Zarpazo the Bandit: Memoirs of an Undercover Agent of the Colombian Army.*

Bushnell, David. *The Making of Modern Colombia. A Nation in Spite of Itself.*

Kline, Harvey F. *Colombia: Portrait of Unity and Diversity.*

Molano, Alfredo, and Alejandro Reyes. *Los bombardeos en El Pato.*

Oquist, Paul H. *Violence, Conflict and Politics in Colombia.*
Level: University

EL FUTURO ESTA EN NUESTRAS MANOS
Public Service Announcement. Without Subtitles. 14 min. 1992
Directed by: Diego Leon Hoyos
Produced by: Citurna Producciones (Calle 25C #3–92, Bogotá; tel: [571] 282-4981; fax: [571] 334-1677)
Distributed by: IMRE
Evaluators: Richard Boly, Francine Cronshaw, Lavina Tilson Gass, Enríque R. Rodríguez
Description: This series of public service announcements (PSAs) demonstrates environmental consciousness from the perspective of developing countries. The series contains fifteen PSAs created for the Rio Environmental Conference in 1992. Each PSA of approximately twenty to fifty seconds has an ironic twist or surprise ending. All deal with ecological topics: pollution, oil leaks, forest reduction, waste disposal, industrial contamination, and the effect of environmental destruction on medical resources and water supply. Topics are both political (e.g., about industrialized nations dumping garbage in Colombia) and cultural. They draw analogies between things happening in the home and things happening to the outside environment and emphasize how all individuals can and must play an important role in combatting environmental destruction.
Strengths and Weaknesses: The individual spots are well written and produced and are intriguing. In a short and straightforward format they help to illustrate the environmental consciousness or movement from a Third World perspective.

One evaluator felt that the individual PSAs by themselves teach little about culture or language. There is not much factual information and little dialogue. Another evaluator felt the spots were not very imaginative.
Introducing the Tape: The tape needs an introduction and some explanation of the cultural and political values being projected. A comparison between the goals and activities of First and Third World environmentalists would be useful. A graph comparing how much pollution is created by the First and Third World would help viewers understand how First World ecological initiatives might be seen as imperialistic. The 1992 Rio Conference should be described.
How to Use: The tape could be used in *Comparative Studies,* for example comparing U.S. commercials and PSAs to these works. (Rodríguez)

Teachers could use this to begin a lesson, as the motivator for conversation. In *Spanish Language* classes students could write a few sentences in Spanish describing what they understood from the tape. In *Science* classes students could be asked to bring in or write about similar announcements (or the lack thereof) on local television and write to stations to suggest more. (Tilson Gass)

For *Video Production* the PSAs can be used as an innovative example of making a point about social issues without using the traditional documentary genre.
Suggested Readings: Readings on environmental issues, especially from English and Spanish newspapers and magazines.
Level: Junior High School—University

LA LEY DEL MONTE (The Law of the Jungle)
Documentary. With Subtitles. 60 min. 1989
Directed by: Patricia Castaño/Adelaida Trujillo
Produced by: Citurna Producciones (Calle 25C #3–92, Bogotá; tel: [571] 334-1677; fax: [571] 282-4981)
Distributed by: IMRE, Jane Balfour Films
Evaluators: George D. Beelen, Marc Chernick, Francine Cronshaw, Silvia Hyre, Jorge Marcone, J. Julian Rívera, Virginia Shen, Margarita de la Vega Hurtado
Description: This documentary is about the conflict between the environment and development in Colombia, specifically in the Amazon and Macarena regions where "colonists" (modern homesteaders searching for land) have engaged in coca growing. It is an outstanding comprehensive analysis of the overexploitation of the rain forest, including interviews with peasants and footage from the 1950s and 1960s. The film focuses on the role played by the jungles in recent Colombian history and the strong ties between politics, drugs, and development. It explores the causes of the cultivation of coca as a result of the conditions of tenant farmers, the absence of the national government in the region, and the control by the narco-traffic business. The film discusses the guerrilla presence in these areas, as well as political violence generated by the conflict between the guerrillas and the state.
Strengths and Weaknesses: This is a very comprehensive documentary about the narco-traffic business in Colombia and the country's sociopolitical and economic realities. It emphasizes the human element and the international context. The film has excellent visual impact and powerfully conveys the destruction of the environment. It argues effectively that people must do certain things to survive—"the law of the jungle"—and shows that they have been given little choice but to engage in the most recent form of economic development, resulting in a new form of environmental destruction. The film puts these problems into national/international social, political, and economic contexts. The subject of rain forest ecology is accessible to U.S. students.

A few evaluators felt the film touched on too many themes, ranging from the guerrilla violence to the drug wars to peace processes, with images of coca growers mixed with interviews and historical footage. Although it continually returns to the question of environmental destruction and conflicts, the film periodically loses some of its coherence.

Introducing the Tape: U.S. audiences will need a general orientation to the politics and recent periods of violence in Colombia, as well as the different issues of the peace processes, guerrillas, drug cultivators, the drug wars, and the U.S. role and military intervention. Also, some maps are necessary for an understanding of the role played by the jungle in Colombia's life.

How to Use: The film could be used to discuss how simply sending troops to Colombia, Peru, and Bolivia to end drug culture will not work. (Beelen and Hyre)

Before showing the film, concepts like agrarian reform, peasant economy, and a brief overview of *La Violencia* (1949–53) should be introduced. I would provide the students with two items to process while watching the film: 1) What methods do Colombian peasants use in jungle agriculture? 2) Note at least five examples of the relationship between poverty and cutting down the jungle. (Cronshaw)

I would use the film to highlight the impact of violence as a result of the narco-traffic business in my *Latin American Culture and Civilization course*. Also, when I teach *Latin American Literature,* the tape will help students understand the impact of socioeconomic factors in *Literature of the Violence* or *Colombian Literature*. (Shen)

Because the film covers so many subjects, students could be asked to write a list of the social issues explored in the film. Discussion on the various topics, how they interrelate, and their impact on people in the United States could follow.

Suggested Readings: Janvery, Alain de. *The Agrarian Question of Reformism in Latin America.*

Schuyler, George W. *Hunger in a Land of Plenty.*

Level: University

LUCERO

Fiction. Without Subtitles. 25 min. 1988

Directed by: Sara Bright

Produced by: Cine Mujer (Apartado 2758, Avenida 25C #4A24, Oficina 202, Santa Fé de Bogotá; tel: [571] 286-7586; fax: [571] 342-6184)

Distributed by: IMRE Archive

Evaluators: Francine Cronshaw, Michele Geslin Small, Susy Suárez

Description: *Lucero* is the story of the life, dreams, and fears of a preteen girl growing up in poverty in a Colombian city. The viewer glimpses the struggles of her single mother to raise Lucero in a single rented room. Lucero is a latchkey child who has to take care of many of the domestic duties. The major themes are the trials of growing up female in an environment of drugs, violence, and death, while constantly being exposed to the sexual advances of seedy men or idle young machos. These are introduced alongside Lucero's childish dreams of finding her father and enjoying an amusement park as a family. A striking ending hints at a sad but probable future.

Strengths and Weaknesses: With a subtle story line and a great young actress, this is a strong example of the unhealthy environment in which many girls grow up in any city today. The tape presents excellent details of everyday life and is artistic and innovative, employing a surrealistic mode in some scenes. The music adds an effective touch.

One evaluator felt the treatment of some dream sequences was a bit self-indulgent.

Introducing the Tape: The tape is self-explanatory.

How to Use: I would use the tape for a *Women of the Third World* course. It could also be an educational "treat" during midterm week in an *Intermediate Spanish* class, a nice way to blend language teaching and consciousness-raising. (Geslin Small)

The tape could be used in *Women's Workshops*. (Suárez)

In a high school *Social Studies* class it can be used to stimulate urban students to write about and role-play similar situations which they have faced or are familiar with.

Level: Junior High School—University

MILAGRO EN ROMA (Miracle in Rome)

Feature. With Subtitles. 76 min. 1988

Directed by: Lisandro Duque Naranjo

Produced by: RTVE

Distributed by: IMRE

Evaluators: Maurice P. Brungardt, Lourdes Fernández, Daniel P. Hunt, Kathleen March, Joan A. McGinnis

Description: Based on Gabriel García Márquez's "Amores difíciles" (Difficult Loves), this tape is a whimsical story of a father's love for his seven-year-old daughter. The father buys his daughter a present and wants to show it to her, but she wants an ice cream cone instead; the daughter swoons and plays dead and never comes to. The father is crushed by the sudden and unexplainable death of his daughter. A few years later, the church is pushing a new cemetery on its parishioners, forcing them to transplant their loved ones. The father opens his daughter's tomb and finds her body totally fresh and unspoiled (her hair has even grown). The townspeople declare her a saint. With the parish priest, bishop, politicians, and the Colombian state involved, money, power, and international politics override all personal considerations. The layers of these interests get played out in a campaign to make the girl Colombia's first saint. The father takes her body to Rome to begin the beatification process, but, not wishing to have his daughter involved in politics, he spurns the help of the Colombian ambassador. Carrying his daughter around Rome in a box, the father is unable to negotiate the Vatican corridors of power and gets duped in the process. When he returns the kindness of an aspiring Colombian opera singer who befriends him, he unwittingly performs his own miracle, which helps the singer when she auditions for a major role. Finally, with the Italian mortuary police and the Colombian embassy closing in to seize his beloved daughter, the father realizes his own power and remembers the ice cream cone. His daughter wakes up from her deep sleep of twelve years.

Strengths and Weaknesses: This is an extraordinary adaptation, well written, shot, and acted. It is gentle, sparkling, and funny. The tape's light touch belies the stereotype of Colombia as a violent country of overbearing drug traffickers. It is a superb film example of the literary genre of magical realism, a touching portrait of a father's love, and a devastating satire of the worldly ways of the modern church. Politicians, clerics, moneygrubbers, and power seekers are subjected to a refreshing dose of wit and humor, as charlatans are unmasked and revealed for what they are. The acting is not slick, but rather natural and sensitive. The music and operatic scores are perfect audio accompaniments and drive the story energetically forward to its logical conclusion. Although the theme is eerie, the film is very compelling. Much takes place in Rome, but the Colombian-ness is evident.

The style of *Miracle in Rome* may be somewhat slow for U.S. viewers accustomed to the fast pace of North American feature films, yet it accurately captures the style of Colombian life.

Introducing the Tape: No introduction is necessary, but some information on Gabriel García Márquez, magical realism, church-state relations in Latin America, and the Vatican could be useful. Viewers should be told that the word *tintico* is mistranslated in the English subtitle as "a little wine," when in fact it is "a little coffee."

How to Use: The tape is a perfect accompaniment to any class dealing with *Modern Latin American Literature* or artistic expression, and should be included in any course on *Latin American Film.* I would use it as a film example of magical realism, Latin American humor and wit, and Latin American artistic expression. As an example of things Colombian, it is an excellent vehicle for showing subtle nuances and details of Colombian national life that are unobtainable elsewhere. It is great art. (Brungardt)

The film could be used to discuss magical realism in *Latin American Literature* and its relation to Latin American peoples and reality. (Fernández)

We are reading García Márquez's *The General in His Labyrinth* this semester. The video could certainly be shown alongside this or any of Márquez's works. Students would read the text and see the film, and then discuss how Márquez's magical realism works differently in the two media. (Hunt)

I would use this for *Literature* or *Film* classes, *Literature in Translation* courses, and lower-intermediate level *Spanish Language* courses. The screening would be followed by discussion of content and possibly an assigned composition with guided format so as to elicit certain structures. (March)

I present the author and the concept of magical realism along with vocabulary. (McGinnis)

Suggested Readings: Bautista Gutierrez, Gloria. *Realismo mágico, cosmos latinoamericano: teoría y práctica.*

Bushnell, David. *The Making of Modern Colombia. A Nation in Spite of Itself.*

Williams, Raymond L. *The Colombian Novel, 1844–1987.*
Novels and story collections of García Márquez, including: *La hojarasca* (1955); *El coronel no tiene quien le escribe* (1961); *La mala hora* (1962); *Los funerales de la Mamá Grande* (stories, 1962); *Cien años de soledad* (1967); *La increíble y triste historia de la cándida Eréndira y su abuela desalmada* (1972); *El otoño del patriarca* (1975); *Crónica de una muerte anunciada* (1981); *El general en su laberinto* (1989); *El amor en los tiempos del cólera* (1985). (See bibliography for other works.)
Level: High School—University

LA MIRADA DE MYRIAM (Myriam's Gaze)
Docudrama.   With Subtitles.   28 min.   1987
Directed by: Clara Riascos
Produced by: Cine Mujer
Distributed by: Women Make Movies
Evaluators: Francine Cronshaw, Lavina Tilson Gass, Michele Geslin Small, William Glover, Carla Meskill, Stephen P. O'Neill, Angharad N. Valdivia
Description: This is a brief history of one woman's struggle to extricate herself from the grip of poverty and oppression. The tape takes place in a squatters' camp on the outskirts of Bogotá, Colombia. Myriam, the mother of two young children, describes her arrival in the camp after leaving a man who was irresponsible and brutal to make a new life for herself and her children. She and her siblings had been beaten when young, and this produced in Myriam an anger that she carried until she finally left her abusive husband. Myriam discusses her hopes and her involvement in the life of her new community. She is instrumental in creating a day-care center for young children and bringing water to the site. She discusses marital status, the need for a day-care center, community projects, and the critical importance of formal-sector employment for the family's basic security and prospects for social mobility. Clearly she is a strong, independent-minded, and courageous woman.

Strengths and Weaknesses: This is an excellent and realistic piece, a sympathetic picture that is artfully presented without being heavy-handed. It is a story of squatters' survival, struggle, traditions, religion, and education. The tape's most powerful point is that for many people squatter settlements present a hope. The strong community portrayed contradicts all the popular notions of anomie generally used to refer to squatter settlements. The single mother is shown as powerful and the female-headed household as a rational, functional response to environmental social limitations. The tape includes very good footage and details of everyday life. The clear diction in Spanish makes the tape useful for language study, and it is brief enough for classroom use.

Introducing the Tape: It would be useful to have some discussion of slums around Latin American cities and a map locating Bogotá in Colombia. One evaluator suggested a conceptual handout/instructor's sheet to avoid viewers' falling into the trap of pitying Myriam or seeing her as a victim.

How to Use: This video is particularly useful for *Cross Cultural Studies*. In the case of poor people the task should be to discover their basic values and goals, and to give examples of each value or goal from Myriam's perspective. The result will be to systematically derive Myriam's worldview, which is representative of poor Latin Americans. It should be emphasized that they are not purely victims but actors making decisions within a limited range of possibilities. (Cronshaw)

In a *Writing* course the class might view this tape and identify various themes and comment on them in an essay offering solutions. (O'Neill)

I would use the tape for adding to my students' understanding of Latin American culture, as well as for conversational material. For advanced classes students could find stories set in city slums, stories about women who struggle to survive in poverty, then study the historical reasons for the development of slums. (Tilson Gass)

In a *Sociology* or *Women's Studies* class the issues that Myriam confronted, the options she faced, and the decisions she has made should be discussed or written about by students. These issues can be compared to the situation for women from various classes—welfare recipients, low-paid unskilled workers, middle-class housewives/professionals—in the United States.

Level: High School—University

PALENQUE: UN CANTO (Palenque: A Song)
Documentary.   With Subtitles.   48 min.   1992
Directed by: María Raquel Bozzi
Produced by: Casimba Films (10515 Tabor St. #1, Los Angeles, CA 90034)
Distributed by: New Day Films
Evaluators: Francine Cronshaw, Franklin W. Knight, Lori Madden, Lynn M. Shirey
Description: Palenque de San Basilio, a village near Cartagena, Colombia, was founded by runaway slaves who resisted many Spanish attempts to recapture them. This tape presents the townspeople's customs and traditions, their livelihood, and the economic/labor relationship they have had to develop with cities on the coast. Today Palenqueros make their living from agriculture (especially corn), and the women make daily trips to Cartagena to sell their fruit. In straightforward interviews the Palenqueros speak of the racial discrimination and stereotypes they face. One of the visual stereotypes of Cartagena has become the Palenqueras on the beach selling fruit from large basins carried on their heads. They describe their desires for social mobility for their children, who they hope won't have to work out in the sun. The tape demonstrates that many African customs have survived in the town. Each year, their African music festival attracts hundreds from Bogotá and elsewhere.
Strengths and Weaknesses: With a variety of images and voices, the documentary portrays the community and then links it with the coastal city. The tape has extremely candid interviews with the townspeople; the Palenqueros speak for

themselves, discussing stereotypes about blacks. The tape is well edited, with engaging photographs of attractive scenery and slice-of-life shots (such as people working in the fields, pounding corn, etc.). There is an authentic Afro-Caribbean flavor, giving a good feel for the rhythms of life. While the theme is very local, the point can be extended to the wider Caribbean area.

Some music/dance segments seem too long.

Introducing the Tape: This tape should be shown after establishing the historical context of the maroon society during the slave era in Spanish America. An introduction might include a map of Colombia, showing Cartagena and the town of Palenque de San Basilio in Cartagena's hinterland. Another map showing the location of several other *palenques* ("runaway slave communities") during the colonial period and the nineteenth century might be helpful.

How to Use: After comparing North American and Latin American concepts of "blackness" and "racial mixture," I would ask the students to ask themselves the following two questions as they watch the video: (1) How do the Palenqueros perceive their own life chances/opportunities? (2) How do the Palenqueros view race mixture? (Cronshaw)

In *Comparative Culture, Anthropology, Ethnography* courses, this tape could be used to illustrate one of the few remaining maroon villages in the Americas. The visuals are better than, say, similar ones in Jamaica. The description of daily life is not unlike rural activity anywhere in the Caribbean—except in this case the village is in Colombia! (Knight)

Suggested Readings: Borrego, Plá, and María del Carmen. *Palenques de negros en Cartagena de Indias a fines del siglo XVII.*

Curtin, Phillip D. *The Atlantic Slave Trade. A Census.*

Price, Richard. *Maroon Societies: Rebel Slave Communities in the Americas.*

Wade, Peter. *Blackness and Race Mixture,* deals with Colombian race relations, although his target group is blacks on the Pacific Coast (the *Choco*).

Complementary Films/Videos: *Quilombo* (Brazil); *Por los caminos verdes* (distributed by the International Media Resource Exchange)
Level: High School—University

RODRIGO D. (NO FUTURO) (Rodrigo D. No Future)
Feature.   With Subtitles.   92 min.   1989
Directed by: Víctor Gaviria
Produced by: Tiempos Modernos (Calle 14 #85–24, Piso 4, Bogotá; tel: [574] 218-7750; fax: [574] 257-0595)
Distributed by: IMRE
Evaluators: Susana Conde, Francine Cronshaw, Jean Franco, Joan West and Dennis West (excerpted from "Rodrigo D. No Future" in *Cineaste*)
Description: Set in Medellín, Colombia, in the late 1980s, this film is a portrayal of the chaotic and rootless gangs of teenagers that roam the city's working-class barrios. Their

dead-end lives are lived in a continuous and violent present to the raging beat of punk music. The film shows the constraints of these youths' lives: the use of drugs, lack of meaningful employment, and how they see crime as their only option for survival. When the police can find them, they beat, torture, and kill those youths suspected of crimes. Although the protagonist, Rodrigo, dreams of having his own punk band, he never reaches that goal. His alienation from society finally overpowers his skills as a survivor in the dangerous streets of his city, and, in an ultimate act of will, he commits suicide. By the time the film was released, four of the boys who acted in it had been killed in the streets of Medellín.

Strengths and Weaknesses: Powerful and disturbing, this film is a devastating portrayal of the pervasive "lost youth" now typical of Latin American cities. The tie-in to the punk and heavy metal music with which they live adds to the feeling of alienation from mainstream society. The film's style transmits the aimlessness of the young men and, indeed, a crisis of masculinity. Its impact is magnified by the knowledge that some of the actors were killed after the film was shot.

The boys' female counterparts are only briefly sketched; their meager portrayal leaves inevitable questions about the future role of Colombian working-class women. The Spanish dialogue is difficult to follow, as the young men speak in their own coded vernacular, but the subtitles help. One evaluator felt the protagonist, Rodrigo, was not typical—he appears to be clinically depressed after his mother's death and more interested in becoming a drummer than in making money. Rodrigo is also atypical because his father is in the household, and there is no apparent struggle to put groceries on the table, etc.

Introducing the Tape: Viewers should have some prior knowledge of the history of the region and an awareness of the cultural heritage of the population. Instructors could discuss the role of the Medellín cartel and how the city changed from the world's orchid capital in the 1960s to the world's murder capital in the 1980s.

Viewers should be told that since the film's completion, the situation has changed somewhat with the advent of *milicianos,* paramilitary groups whose task is to rid lower-class neighborhoods of the scourge of youth gangs.

How to Use: I would use this film in my *Latin American Film* course, subtitled *Reconfigurations of Family and Nation in Latin America.* A film like this one will be the late 1980s counterpart of Buñuel's *Los olvidados.* It would help illustrate how the political and economic conditions in a country directly affect the conformation of the family. The devastating impact of chaotic economic conditions on the young prefigures the future of the country's social stability. (Conde)

Suggested Readings: Burton, Julianne. *Cinema and Social Change in Latin America: Conversations with Filmmakers.*

Galeano, Eduardo. *Open Veins of Latin America; Five Centuries of the Pillage of a Continent.*

Green, Duncan. *Faces of Latin America.*

King, John. *Magical Reels: A History of Cinema in Latin America.*

Black, Jan Knippers, ed. *Latin America: Its Problems and Its Promise.*

Salazar, Alonso J., and Ana María Jaramillo. "Las bandas juveniles y los procesos de socialización," chapter 7 in *Medellín: Las subculturas del narcotráfico.*

Semana magazine's cover story on the "Culture of Death," no. 408 (February 27–March 6, 1990): pp. 26–33; background on this film is given on p. 33.

Skidmore, Thomas E., and Peter H. Smith. *Modern Latin America.*

West, Dennis, and Joan M. West. "Rodrigo D. No Future."
Level: High School—University

SALSA EN CALÍ

Documentary.   Without Subtitles.   27 min.
Directed by: Carlos Rendon Zipagauta
Produced by: AVC Rainbow (5 Rue de Parme, 1060 Brussels, Belgium; tel: [322] 534-7804; fax: [322] 537-2167)
Distributed by: IMRE Archive
Evaluators: David Bushnell, Francine Cronshaw
Description: This film examines the origins and role of salsa as a dance genre in the city of Calí, Colombia. Although salsa is a product of the Caribbean, many Caleños have wholeheartedly embraced it. Examples of Calí's love of salsa, such as a children's salsa band and a classical ballet troupe performing to salsa music, are highlighted. Various specialists on Afro-Colombian culture provide commentary.

Strengths and Weaknesses: The tape provides positive statements about Latin American culture in general and dance styles in particular. The historical context is quite well done and there are good slice-of-life shots of lower-income lifestyles. The tape includes much good music and nice views of Calí. The Colombian commentators are easy to understand, although one evaluator mentioned that some white commentators seemed uncomfortable discussing African aspects of Calí's culture.

The focus is a bit fuzzy: the title points to salsa music but the commentary dwells on African input to Calí's popular culture without either demonstrating that it is as important as claimed or clearly relating it to salsa. Some dancing vignettes look staged.

Introducing the Tape: Maps, showing the location of Cuba/Caribbean vis-à-vis Calí's southern, interior location, as well as Buenaventura would be useful. Another map showing concentrations of black populations (Atlantic, Pacific Coasts, Valle) would also provide important contextual information.

How to Use: I would only use this tape as a temporary reprieve from heavier topics, and for the nice sounds and scenes of Calí. (Bushnell)

I would explore concepts of the *mestizaje* (popular, low-income) and informal sector, provide background on Caribbean/Cuban salsa music, and explain the concept of the

hacienda and slavery. Then, I would ask students to "process" the film by looking for African influences. (Cronshaw)
Level: High School—University

SECUESTRO (A Story of a Kidnapping)
Documentary. With Subtitles. 92 min. 1993
Directed by: Camila Motta
Produced by: Camila Motta and Barry Ellsworth (874 Broadway, Apt. 1005, New York, N. Y. 10003; tel: [212] 505-1139; fax: [212] 505-1139)
Distributed by: The Cinema Guild
Evaluators: Maurice P. Brungardt, Francine Cronshaw, Grace Leavitt, Donald Mabry, Pamela M. Smorkaloff
Description: This documentary is based on the true story of the kidnapping of Sylvia Motta, a wealthy industrialist's daughter, from the Jesuit Javeriana University in Bogotá, Colombia, on March 28, 1985. The director, Camila Motta, documents the kidnapping of her sister. Their father, Arturo Motta, personally handles the negotiations with the kidnappers. Although advised not to contact the police, he does, and they instruct him in the finer points of negotiating. Negotiations drag on via thirty-second telephone calls, code words, and secretive searches for instructions. How can the kidnappers get their money and not get caught? How can the father retrieve his daughter for the smallest amount of money? The father works with the police but leaves them out of the final successful ransom for 10 million pesos on May 31, 1985. The kidnappers are caught later for another crime, and one of the gang members implicates the others in the kidnapping of Sylvia. This story reveals the complexities of the social struggles and resulting violence in Colombia. The actions of Sylvia, her family, police, and the kidnappers themselves are effectively framed by scholars' discourse on the larger phenomenon of violence in Latin America from 1492 on.
Strengths and Weaknesses: This is a fascinating and honest look at the contradictions of Colombian society—a portrait of affluence and comfort, and the often high price of such a lifestyle in a country of vast economic inequities. It is an authentic, excellent account of the business of kidnapping, in Colombia and how police and victims respond, making some attempt to show balance (both sides have humanity). The film demonstrates the mechanics involved in kidnapping, and provides a convincing analysis of how the father proceeds so the kidnappers do not kill his daughter. One evaluator felt the decision to leave the police out of the final stages of the ransom process had a particularly Colombian ring that enhanced the film's authenticity, as did the extensive footage of Bogotá street scenes. The suspense element is high and the stylistic elements of subtitles, which appear as a ransom note across the screen, are very effective. In general the film's style enhances traditional documentary genre by incorporating dramatization.

One evaluator felt the attempt to put the events into some sort of political or social context was weakly articulated, but commented this ambiguity is probably the best approach given the confused state of affairs in Colombia. Another evaluator found the tape too long and detailed.
Introducing the Tape: Viewers should be told that in Colombia the business of kidnapping is carried out by common criminals in addition to being contracted by guerrilla organizations and organized crime/drug rings. For guerrilla outfits it is a practical means of fundraising along the lines of the Robin Hood concept. The "culture of violence" notion needs to be developed and should be related to the epoch of *La Violencia* because this is the major explanatory factor for why kidnappings are so common in Colombia today. They are so common that specialized antikidnapping detachments have been created by the national police.

There is some confusion in the film over the monetary amounts demanded by the kidnappers and their conversion into U.S. dollars according to 1985 exchange rates. This needs to be clarified.
How to Use: I would probably pair this tape with the Costa-Gavras film *State of Siege* and contrast political, social, and criminal kidnappings. I would also ask students to consider what happens when law and order disappear and much of "civil" society comes to an end. What are the alternatives? When is violence justified? (Brungardt)

Kidnapping for both profit and political reasons is not uncommon in Latin America. This film allows an instructor to demonstrate how and why kidnapping takes place. (Mabry)

The film reminded me very much of Penny Lernoux's *Cry of the People* in the sections where she discusses the absolute divide that separates the social classes and how all classes are "foreigners" inhabiting the same country. Recommended: Chapter 3, "The Awakening." (Smorkaloff)
Suggested Readings: Bergquist, Charles, Ricardo Peñaranda, and Gonzalo Sánchez, eds. *Violence in Colombia: The Contemporary Crisis in Historical Perspective.*

Braun, Herbert. *The Assassination of Gaitán: Public Life and Urban Violence in Colombia.*

Bushnell, David. *The Making of Modern Colombia. A Nation in Spite of Itself.*

Henderson, James D. *When Colombia Bled: A History of the Violencia in Tolima.*

Lernoux, Penny. *Cry of the People.*

Martz, John D. "Colombia at the Crossroads."

Pearce, Jenny. *Colombia: Inside the Labyrinth.*
Level: High School—University

SEGUIMOS ADELANTE (Nothing Will Stop Us)
Documentary. With Subtitles. 52 min. 1990
Directed by: Patricia Castaño, Adelaida Trujillo
Produced by: Cituma Producciones (Calle 25C #3–92, Bogotá; tel: [571] 334-1677; fax: [571] 282-4981)
Distributed by: IMRE, Jane Balfour Films
Evaluators: Ana Caroline Castillo-Crimm, Francine Cronshaw, Margarita de la Vega Hurtado, María Fernández,

Nancy Levy-Konesky, Jorge Marcone, Joan A. McGinnis, Virginia Shen

Description: This documentary portrays the violence perpetrated by drug cartels and drug barons who attempt to suppress the press and buy politicians. The Colombian newspaper *El Espectador,* popularly known as the "conscience of the people," has been a target of terrorism by the drug kings for daring to be outspoken in the pursuit of truth and justice. Terrorist tactics have been used against the newspaper—bribes, threats, and the murders of a main editor and an owner. This video is a view of the drug cartel through the eyes of the paper and its owners (the Cano family). After a brief general commentary on bombing and destruction in Colombia, the program centers on a week in the lives of the family and newspaper workers during a very difficult political period, specifically focusing on their coverage of the drug wars. The film offers pointed advice to consumer countries—they must begin taking responsibility for their drug use.

Strengths and Weaknesses: This film is dramatic, engaging, and credible. It is a very useful informational tool, with an excellent insider view of the cocaine wars. The program presents a dramatic example of how much Colombia (not the government, but the people) is doing in the war against drugs, something which is not always appreciated in the U.S. The film is technically well done, with powerful interviews and articulate speakers.

Many members of the Cano family speak about general issues of the journalism profession, rather than about their concrete campaign against the drug lords. The film could be less laudatory and more informative, providing more context. By using traditional documentary methods, such as objective voice-over narration, it loses some of its creative strength. One reviewer commented that the film favors upper- and middle-class views on Colombia's problems. Another thought the camera work and editing could be better.

Introducing the Tape: As the tape's beginning is somewhat confusing for U.S. audiences unfamiliar with Colombian history, viewers would benefit from a preface introducing the program's objective. Some background, including a discussion of the drug cartel and Medellín, would be useful. An overview of the conflict between drug traffickers and the Colombian government since the mid-1980s (through Escobar's escape from his luxurious "prison" and eventual execution) would be helpful.

How to Use: This film helps students understand the life of people in Colombia who challenge the drug traffickers. It also shows the difficulty of winning against men who have political power and influence, as well as the daily danger of living with powerful enemies. (Castillo-Crimm)

After discussing the "war on drugs" and particularly the aims and goals of the U.S. (an example of the extradition issue), I examine how the drug trade impacts Colombian economics and politics. The money injected into the economy by drug sales is so enormous that it dwarfs traditional activities like coffee exports, manufacturing, and so forth. Also, the

traditional elites who have always controlled economics and politics are overshadowed by the likes of Pablo Escobar and the Cali cartel. (Cronshaw)

It would be very useful in *Political Science* courses on Latin America or drug problems. In *Communications* courses it should illustrate the role of the press and freedom of speech. (de la Vega Hurtado)

In high school *Spanish* classes I would discuss the international problem of drugs and provide a Spanish vocabulary list with guided questions for discussion. After the film students could debate "extradition or no" and/or write compositions on the subject. (McGinnis)

The film would be a very lively example of a typical current life situation in a country victimized by the narco-traffic problem. (Shen)

Level: University

TECNICAS DEL DUELO (Details of a Duel/A Matter of Honor)

Feature.   With Subtitles.   97 min.   1988

Directed by: Sergio Cabrera

Distributed by: First Run/Icarus Films, IMRE

Evaluators: Maurice P. Brungardt, Deborah Pacini Hernández, Thomas Whigham

Description: The film takes place in a small provincial town in 1956, during a period in which Colombia was in a bloody civil war between liberals and conservatives known as *La Violencia.* An Andean town awakens from its traditional routine, as the butcher and the elementary schoolteacher move irrevocably toward a duel to settle "a question of honor" (which remains a mystery throughout the film). Both men are pillars of the community, good friends, and co-leaders of the political opposition. Their impending combat surprises everyone, yet it is understandable, because it is a question of honor. As the two move toward the appointed hour, each works to settle his affairs, making plans for burials and proper liquidations of worldly possessions. The teacher hurries to pay off his debts, while the butcher worries about absolution from the sin he is about to commit. Both must now deal with the two great institutions of Latin American life, the government and the church. The teacher must fill out innumerable forms and pay excessive fees to cover the payment of his debts, while the butcher finds that the priest will not absolve him from future sin without a large donation. The political authorities do nothing to prevent the duel, since they will be free of their two most determined political opponents. The townspeople are more interested in the drama and formalities of the duel than in stopping it. With one combatant unable to secure a pistol, the duel finally comes down to a classic fight to the death with machetes and then bare fists. Finally, the two men realize they are serving their enemies by settling their question of honor, and they stop the fighting.

Strengths and Weaknesses: This is an excellent satire on bureaucracy; small-town life, machismo; the role of "honor" in Latin American society; and political, social, and religious institutions (with the government and the Catholic Church as the targets of most of the ridicule). It is evocative of small-town Latin American life, traditions, and sense of honor and duty that are changing rapidly in modern society. With excellent production values and acting, it is filmed on location in Barichara, Santander, a quaint town with an alluring charm that adds much to the film's authenticity.

The film is slow-paced by Hollywood standards; however, its rhythm reflects the culture in the small town. One evaluator felt it is too much a "comedy of manners," with nuances perhaps too subtle for non-Colombians to appreciate.

Introducing the Tape: Although this story could be set in many Latin American countries, U.S. viewers may need some background about *La Violencia*.

How to Use: I would use the tape to give students a view of small-town life in Latin America, with particular emphasis on political institutions and the Catholic Church. The tape is an appropriate vehicle for discussion of Latin American culture, humor, and points of view. It would make an interesting contrast with the film *Moon Over Parador,* which satirizes Latin American governments at the national level. (Brungardt)

I would use this to illustrate the longstanding, practically pan-Latin conflicts between conservatives and liberals. I would have students identify how liberalism and conservatism are expressed in the film. I would also use it to discuss the concept of honor in Latin America. (Pacini Hernández)

This film looks at the questions of personal honor, politics, and bureaucracy in a lighthearted manner and thus makes them more accessible to U.S. audiences. (Whigham)

Suggested Readings: Bautista Gutiérrez, Gloria. *Realismo mágico, cosmos latinoamericano: teoría y práctica.*

Bushnell, David. *The Making of Modern Colombia. A Nation in Spite of Itself.*

Williams, Raymond L. *The Colombian Novel, 1844–1987.*

Any book by García Márquez or Vargas Llosa (see bibliography).

Anything on recent Colombian history, especially *La Violencia*.

Complementary Films/Videos: *Moon Over Parador* (distributed by Facets)

Level: University

20 MENSAGES INDIGENAS

Documentary.   With Spanish Subtitles.   35 min.

Directed by: Juan Fernando Gutiérrez and Hernan Darío Correa

Produced by: Producciones Audiovisuales (Cra 22 #36–63 Of. 201, Santa Fe de Bogotá; tel: [571] 269-6136; fax: [571] 368-6845)

Distributed by: IMRE Archive

Evaluators: William O. Autry, Maurice P. Brungardt, Francine Cronshaw

Description: This tape presents twenty brief declarations, each less than three minutes long, from the Colombian in-

digenous groups of the Kogi, Puinave, Wayuu, Guainía, Curripaco, Andoke, Guambiano, and Muinane. The Indians protest their marginalization and bad treatment by "whites" and push for greater protection of their environment and culture. Each declaration opens with a nice visual pan of the geographic area in which the Indian groups reside—the Kogi's Sierra Nevada de Santa Marta, for example—with their indigenous music as a backdrop. The tape then cuts to an Indian leader, surrounded by members of the community, declaiming in the native language (Spanish subtitles are provided) and sending a message to outsiders. The Indians identify their major adversaries as the government, missionaries, settlers, and the attitude that Indians "have no culture" that is common among Spanish-speaking Colombians. Their messages contain a continuum of religious, ecological, and cultural considerations. Many try to convince the viewer that, despite negative outside impact, Indians have their own cultures, complete with foods, medicines, and self-government. At times, Indian myths and dress reinforce the distinctive message of each group.

Strengths and Weaknesses: The indigenous messages are short and to the point. The strong photography provides good settings and demonstrates the geographic and Indian diversity in the country. Each leader and scene is effectively identified with name, group, place, and location within Colombia. Messages are delivered in the midst of observable degradation and acculturation of these indigenous peoples. The contrast between highland, coastal, lowland, riverine, and Amazonian Indian groups helps underscore the complexity of modern-day Colombia. The music is appropriate to the various cultural groups.

The tape contains no introductory materials or background about the area. One evaluator felt the declamations of the Indian leaders were somewhat stilted, though direct. At times, the messages are repetitive. Another reviewer pointed out that the Spanish subtitles are more like commentary than serious translations of individuals speaking in their native languages.

Introducing the Tape: For U.S. audiences the tape needs to be introduced with extensive use of maps to show the various terrains where indigenous groups are located (Andean, Sierra Nevada, Guajira peninsula, riverine/rain forest). A quick overview of each indigenous group, their demographics, and a comment about their size and importance in present-day Colombia is needed. Also some information about the significance of the 1991 Constitution would be helpful.

Instructors should point out the indigenous peoples' unity of themes—religious and ecological concerns, and the adverse conditions for cultural survival. Viewers could be told that Protestant missionaries and the Summer Institute of Linguistics (also a mission organization) have led to the greatest cultural disintegration. The Indians' success in maintaining their customs in the face of mainstream Colombian encroachment is reflected in the following order: Sierra Nevada—Kogi; Andean—Guambiano; Guajira Peninsula—

Wayuu; Riverine/rain forest/Amazon—Pauvine, Muinane, all Guainia groups, Andoke, and Curripaco.

Some North American viewers may need a brief preparation to understand the context for the Native Americans' use of coca leaves.

How to Use: I would discuss the environmental degradation in northern South America, the various indigenous societies in the area, and the impacts of modernization on the people and the region. I would instruct the audience to pay close attention to the people, settings, modes of dress, speech, etc., before showing the video. Postvideo screening discussion would concentrate upon language, setting, and visual/verbal indications of acculturation and environmental degradation. (Autry)

I would use the tape to give students a quick tour of Colombian geography and the many Indian groups that inhabit the country. It would help reinforce the point that Colombia, present and past, is made up of many different cultures and peoples, molded by one of the world's most complex geographies. (Brungardt)

I would discuss the concept of *resguardo* (reservation) and why Indians are hostile to them, pointing out the concerns about land use and subsistence patterns. I would also discuss the connection between *Ecology* and *Religion*. Students would explore the differences between groups that use Western dress (those with greatest impact by Protestant missionaries) and those who use ethnic dress (such as Guambiano and Waymu). (Cronshaw)

Suggested Readings: Bushnell, David. *The Making of Modern Colombia. A Nation in Spite of Itself.*

Friede, Juan. *Los Andaki, 1538–1947. Historia de la aculturación de una tribu selvática.*

Reichel-Dolmatoff, Gerardo. *Colombia.*

Level: University

VIENE NACIENDO EN LA CAÑA LA FIBRA

Documentary. Without Subtitles. 21 min. 1988
Directed by: Juan Fernando Gutierrez and Hernan Darío Correa
Produced by: Corfas (Cra 22 #36–63 Oficina 201, Santa Fe de Bogotá; tel: [571] 269-6136; fax: [571] 369-6845)
Distributed by: IMRE Archive
Evaluators: Richard C. Boly, Maurice P. Brungardt, Francine Cronshaw
Description: In this tape Zenú Indian women describe and demonstrate their traditional skills as palm weavers of fine braid, used to make the famous *vueltiado* hat. The distinctive beige-colored hat with its black veins, borders, and patterns is a symbol of the Colombian man, more identified with the rancher than with the Indian, although the roots of its structure and design are indigenous and are documented in pre-Columbian gold figurines. Life for the Zenú Indian literally begins in the rushes with the acquisition of the reeds that will be woven into hats. From a very young age the majority of Indian girls grow up weaving, for the sale of hats brings in

necessary income for food and household supplies. The wild rushes that provide the reeds are now disappearing, and attempts are being made to domesticate and cultivate the plant for hats and other artisan products. This tape documents this Indian artisan activity in the Colombian Indian Reservation of San Andrés de Sotavento in Tuchín, Córdoba, Colombia. Weaving sombreros is a subsistence activity, although some of the women express hope that sending their children to school will eventually lift them out of poverty. The tape emphasizes marketing relationships, especially the role of the intermediary, and the women's attempts to create producer cooperatives to keep more of the earnings.

Strengths and Weaknesses: The tape includes good visual shots of the Indian reservation and its people and of the techniques employed in weaving the hats. The women speak for themselves and there is an excellent explanation and presentation of the importance of the native tradition of hat weaving. Scenes of the mechanics of hat-weaving, the larger purpose and meaning of this artisan activity in Indian life, and the indigenous origins of the hat are the strongest parts of the tape. The video is an appropriate length for classroom use.

The tape, however, does not place this artisan activity and Indian culture within the larger context of Colombia. The spoken Spanish is fast and difficult for nonnative speakers to understand, and the tape's technical quality is not high.

Introducing the Tape: An introduction could include geography, successive maps of South America, Colombia and locations of the Indian reservations mentioned in the video. Instructors should also give a brief overview of regional economics (traditionally a hinterland of Cartagena that now raises cattle, rice, and sugar as major crops). More discussion of where and how this artisan activity fits into the total context of the Indian culture of Colombia would be helpful.

How to Use: I would use the program to show native culture and practices; the mechanics and process of hat weaving; the larger purpose and meaning of this artisan activity in Indian life; and the indigenous origins of the hat. (Brungardt)

After introducing the concept of "informal economy," one can use the sombrero weavers as a good example of rural women's employment opportunities. The slight margin in these women's struggle to survive shows their susceptibility to the exploitative marketing practices of middlemen and the need for women-owned producer selling cooperatives. (Cronshaw)

In a class discussing *Developmental/Environmental Issues* the film could be used as an example of how indigenous cultures are affected by environmental destruction, and the interconnection of human rights and environmental issues.

Suggested Readings: Bushnell, David. *The Making of Modern Colombia. A Nation in Spite of Itself.*

Reichel-Dolmatoff, Gerardo. *Colombia.*

Level: University

Y SU MAMA QUE HACE? (And What Does Your Mother Do?)

Documentary. With Subtitles. 10 min. 1983

Directed by: Eulalia Carrizosa
Produced by: Cine Mujer (Apartado 2758, Avenida 25C #4A24, Oficina 202, Santa Fe, Bogotá; tel: [571] 286-7586; fax: [571] 342-6184)
Distributed by: Women Make Movies
Evaluators: Ann K. Coughlin, Marcia Dean, Michele Geslin Small, Christine Holmlund, Susy Suárez, Angharad N. Valdivia
Description: This satirical ten-minute film uses accelerated footage to show how hard a Latin American middle-class housewife works to get her children and husband ready for school and work every day. Its excellent choice of different music and rhythms contrasts the pleasant leisurely early morning of the husband and the frantic activities of the wife. At the end of the film a little boy asks the son, "And what does your mother do?" He replies, "She does nothing. She stays at home." The implications are devastating at the economic and cultural levels. The film clearly, yet humorously, conveys its message: women's contributions at home are overlooked and denied by society.
Strengths and Weaknesses: This simple, strong, and thoroughly delightful little piece can be understood by all. It raises the issue of the value and lack of appreciation of women's work in the home.

Some viewers may find the film dated and/or technically unsophisticated. One evaluator felt it was a kind of one-joke film, based on a feminist argument made more frequently in the U.S. in the 1970s. Class ramifications are not discussed.
Introducing the Tape: No extra explanations are necessary. Teachers may want to discuss the impact of class differences and contrast Colombian feminism to U.S. feminism.
How to Use: I would use the video as a stimulus for discussion about what a woman does in the home and the value society does/doesn't place on a homemaker's work. Discussion could also be directed to the necessity of having a more equal distribution of household chores in our modern society. I would ask students to write a narrative essay that touched on these points from both a male and female perspective. (Coughlin)

This video could be used as a humorous introduction to *Urban Family Life* in the Hispanic world. Teachers could ask students to compare their views of what their mothers do to this presentation. (Dean)

I have used this film in a course on *Latin American Film*. The final third of the class was devoted to works by and/or about women. One unit focused on the work of Cine Mujer, the oldest and most prolific Latin American feminist film/video collective. I lectured earlier on Colombian history, politics, and economics. During the Cine Mujer unit I spoke about various women's organizations in Colombia. (Holmlund)

The tape could be used in a *Women's Workshop* to stimulate discussion on gender roles and stereotypes. (Suárez)

For *Spanish Language* classes there is not much dialog; however the film is good for listening comprehension prac-

tice and can motivate topics for composition writing exercises.
Suggested Readings: Lesage, Julia. "Women Make Media: Three Modes of Production," In *The Social Documentary in Latin America,* ed. Julianne Burton.

Miller, Francesca. *Latin American Women and the Search for Social Justice*—general background on women in Colombia and Latin American feminism.

Screen—contains a short article on Cine Mujer.
Level: High School—University

COSTA RICA

EL HOMBRE CUANDO ES EL HOMBRE (A Man, When He Is a Man)
Documentary.   With Subtitles.   66 min.   1982
Directed by: Valeria Sarmiento
Distributed by: Women Make Movies
Evaluators: Silvia Arrom, Osvaldo Chinchón, Sandra J. Guardado, Paul J. LaReau, Yolanda Prieto, Angharad N. Valdivia
Description: This very creative and effective tape explores male-female relations in Costa Rica. Tracing gender roles from birth to middle age, it presents the social climate that develops and nurtures the *machista* attitudes toward women. Very frank interviews with men shed light on their views of women and how and why they treat women as they do. Women explain why they allow themselves to be in these situations. The tape focuses particularly on promiscuous male behavior and the resulting double standard in terms of sexual relations. It is a look at Costa Rican machismo in its worst light. There are interviews with men sent to prison for ten or more years for killing their wives or girlfriends; they express little or no remorse, feeling themselves victims of feminine cruelty. Interspersed with the interviews are clips of weddings, fifteenth-birthday coming-out parties, and musical background of popular Mexican songs sung by *charros*. While the tape takes place in Costa Rica, the problem is universal, and much of the content applies to other Latin American and non-Latin American countries.
Strengths and Weaknesses: The tape provides a well-balanced treatment of a complex subject and is humorous as well. It is an excellent, though perhaps stereotypical, treatment of machismo and the relationship between males and females in Latin American culture. The tape brings up universal questions about maleness and the culture that nurtures it. It effectively explores how machismo is developed in men, and how women sometimes unknowingly contribute to it. There is an apparent diversity among the men, women, and children interviewed in terms of age, social class, education, etc. The tape also makes good use of music—old romantic boleros and Mexican *corridos* traditionally associated with male romantic conquests.

Because there is no overall narration to put these perspectives into context, the documentary leans toward generalizations. Some scenes and interviews are also too slow. While the program's beginning is hard to grasp, the end is quite poignant, unexpected, and effective. The translation is poor, with some errors in the subtitles, and some of the dialogue may be inappropriate for more sensitive viewers.

Introducing the Tape: Audiences should be told that this is a documentary about gender roles in Costa Rica. The cut-ins of folklore and 1930s-type mariachi movies with their allusions to the "ideal" romance will not be understood unless discussed beforehand. One evaluator felt that the tape should be put into context to avoid stereotyping. Viewers could be told that these perspectives are more prevalent in rural areas of Latin America and some urban areas, but it should be pointed out that this problem is universal and goes beyond geographic and cultural borders.

How to Use: In *Third World Women* or *Sociology of the Family* I would show the film in the context of the cultural factors that affect the social and economic development (especially of women) of underdeveloped countries. I would try to get the songs translated into English to help students understand how the values and the reality of male dominance permeate cultural expressions. (Prieto)

After viewing and discussing the issues raised by the film, students can write and act out skits dealing with these issues, including some of their own experiences as a basis.

Suggested Readings: Pescatello, Anne, ed. *Female and Male in Latin America*—although dated, this a good collection of articles from different Latin American countries. Many of them provide good historical information that serves as a basis for understanding gender roles today.

Level: High School—University

MADRES NIÑAS (Child Mothers)

Documentary.   With Subtitles.   30 min.   1991
Directed by: Mauricio Miranda
Produced by: Proyecto Chirripo (P.O. Box 1065-2050, San Pedro, Costa Rica; tel: [506] 253-1352; fax: [506] 283-4408)
Distributed by: IMRE
Evaluators: Ann S. Blum
Description: This documentary uses a series of interviews to discuss and dramatize the situation of teenage mothers in Costa Rica today. Discussion includes poverty, education, rape, sexual abuse/incest, availability of medical counseling and treatment, and legal issues.
Strengths and Weaknesses: This is a direct, powerful, and sympathetic work, especially good on the ambivalent or negligent attitude of the legal system and current legal definitions toward the reality of rape and incest. The tape relies heavily on narration and has a somewhat slow and conventional "talking heads" format. Nevertheless, it dramatizes the isolation of thousands of young women from educational and medical benefits and legal protection in Costa Rica today.
Introducing the Tape: Comparative information would be helpful, especially some references to the U.S. and other

Latin American countries with strong welfare-state political cultures, such as Mexico or Cuba.
How to Use: I teach mostly *History* survey courses, but previewed the tape because of its relevance to my own research on orphans and abandoned children in Mexico City in the late nineteenth/early twentieth centuries, which includes an analysis of urban single mothers and their use of available social services. The diversity of teaching contexts in which this film would be very useful makes it a valuable addition to any video library. (Blum)
Level: High School—University

CUBA

A VECES MIRO MI VIDA (Sometimes I Look at My Life)

Documentary.   With Subtitles.   79 min.   1981
Directed by: Orlando Rojas
Produced by: ICAIC (Calle 23 No. 155 Vedado, Havana; tel: [537] 333-862; fax: [537] 333-032)
Distributed by: Center for Cuban Studies, The Cinema Guild
Evaluators: Friederike Baumann, Iris Engstrand, Joan A. McGinnis, Susan Ryan
Description: This is a feature-length documentary about calypso singer, actor, and activist Harry Belafonte. The film explores Belafonte's political involvement with the civil rights movement as well as his development as an artist. At the core of the film are Belafonte's candid and thoughtful reflections on his intellectual, moral, and political formation. These are interspersed with excerpts from his concert in Havana and short scenes from his films. Belafonte discusses his self-understanding as an artist; what it meant for him to grow up as a poor immigrant in Harlem and as a self-educated African American in the confines of racist America; the power of Paul Robeson and W. E. B. DuBois as his role models; and the reasons for his commitment to the civil rights and Indian rights movements. Belafonte is shown not only as a talented artist whose film roles broke with the racist stereotypes prevalent in U.S. movies but also as a human being with a passionate commitment to social justice.
Strengths and Weaknesses: Belafonte articulates the struggle of his intellectual development and self-liberation under the burden of racism with an uncommon openness, lucidity, and freedom. The film shows a side of Belafonte very few people know. His reflections are of great interest as oral history and as a moving document of what it means to grow up poor and black in the U.S.

At times, the choice of film clips seems heavy-handed; this has the cumulative effect of detracting from Belafonte's complex insights in favor of a much more simplistic statement by the filmmakers. The film gets a bit repetitive with many scenes of singing in the same concert in Havana. Some of the subtitles are difficult to read.

Introducing the Tape: Young U.S. viewers may need background about some of the people mentioned in the film: Sidney Portier, Paul Robeson, W. E. B. DuBois, Charlie Parker, and Harry Belafonte. Some introductory information about calypso music would be helpful.

How to Use: The film is useful for presenting the perspectives and feelings of blacks in the U.S. It offers a good history of the changing attitudes from pre-World War II to the 1960s. I would have my students discuss the relationship of Belafonte to the West Indies and U.S. blacks. (Engstrand)

My high school *Spanish* students often do independent research. They could present a paper or panel discussion on the issues covered in the film. (McGinnis)

Suggested Readings: Small biographical sketches of Sidney Poitier, Paul Robeson, W. E. B. DuBois, Charlie Parker, and Harry Belafonte.

Level: Junior High School—University

ACHE MOYUBA ORISHA (Ache Moyuba Orisha)

Documentary. With Subtitles. 42 min. 1990
Directed by: Cristina González Gallardo
Produced by: Televisión Latina (Calle 21 No 1 Esquina a O, Vedado, Havana; tel: [537] 30-0198; fax: 537-33-3476)
Distributed by: IMRE,
Evaluators: David Bushnell, Hugo Chapa-Guzmán, Nancy Levy-Konesky, José-Manuel Navarro, S. Travis Silcox
Description: This tape explores the religion of Santería, a blend of Yoruba beliefs and Catholicism. Unique to Cuba and Haiti, Santería represents the *mestiza* quality of Cuban culture. Through interviews with two *santeros* and a Catholic priest, the tape explains some key concepts of the religion, its pantheon of *orishas,* and its reception in Cuba. The tape presents ceremonial footage of Santería, including attendance at Roman Catholic ceremonies which the followers assimilate with African equivalents.
Strengths and Weaknesses: This interesting documentary contains visually striking ceremonies, and an excellent soundtrack with Afro-Cuban music. The topic itself is one of much intrinsic interest to students and others, and the good narration techniques provide a clear presentation with a great deal of unbiased information. The tape is especially informative about the *orishas.*

A couple of reviewers felt that although the film has a good premise, it was not well developed or technically strong. One found the juxtaposition of interviews of people of opposing views attempted to put them "into conversation," but fell flat and felt manipulative. At times, the subtitles are difficult to read.

Introducing the Tape: U.S. viewers could use some general background on Santería, the Yoruba *orishas,* and the different "paths" such as Palo Monte, Abacua, etc. The equivalences of Catholic and *santero* saints could be introduced in a chart to provide more historical background. Also, an overview of the slave history of Cuba and the resulting Afro-Cuban religion should be discussed.

How to Use: I would feature this in my introductory survey of *Latin American Civilization,* as illustrative of both popular religion and Afro-Latin American culture, and just as applicable or more, to Brazil as to Cuba. (Bushnell)

After showing a Cuban film that makes use of some of these traditions and symbols, such as *Cecilia* or *María Antonia,* I would show this tape to help make sense out of the symbolism. In a *Latin American Studies* type class, I would use this tape in a unit about religion after some reading or an introductory lecture. (Silcox)

I would discuss Yoruba religion and its components, and the present status of these practices in Cuba and the United States, and reflect on the exclusion of blacks from U.S. history as a way to begin remedying a gross historical oversight. (Navarro)

This film can be used as an introduction to the subject of Santería by itself, or as a "warm up" to more general classes dealing with *Cuban or Afro-American Religion.* (Chapa-Guzmán)

It is useful to reinforce or present visual images of a previously studied Santería unit. (Levy-Konesky)

Suggested Readings: Amira, John, and Steven Cornelius. *The Music of Santería: Traditional Rhythms of the Baba Drums.*

Bolívar Aróstegui, Natalia, and Carmen González. *Los Orishas en Cuba.*

Cabrera, Lydia. *Koeko iyawo, aprende novicia: pequeño tratado de regla lucumí.*

Cortéz, Enríque. *Secretos del Oriaté de la religión yoruba.*

Ecún, Obá. *Addimu: ofrenda a los orishas.*

Ecún, Obá. *Ita: Mythology of the Yoruba Religion.*

González-Wippler, Migene. *Santería: African Magic in Latin America; The Santería Experience: Rituals and Spells of Santería; Powers of the Orisha.*

Murphy, Joséph. *Santería: An African Religion in America.*

Pérez y Mena, Andrés Isidoro. *Speaking with the Dead: Development of Afro-Latin Religion among Puerto Ricans in the United States: a Study into the Interpenetration of Civilizations in the New World.*

Vinueza, María Elena. *Presencia arará en la música folclórica de Matanzas.*

Complementary Films/Videos: *Cecilia* (distributed by the Center for Cuban Studies); *María Antonia* (distributed by the Center for Cuban Studies and the International Media Resource Exchange)
Level: University

ALEJO Y LO REAL MARAVILLOSO

Documentary. Without Subtitles. 13 min.
Directed by: Luis A. Fals
Produced by: CINED (7th Ave. No 2802 Miramar, Havana; tel: [537] 237-742 or 237-887; fax: 537-331-697)
Distributed by: IMRE Archive
Evaluators: Hugo Chapa-Guzmán, Marlene Gottlieb,

Daniel P. Hunt, Diane Marting, S. Travis Silcox, Pamela M. Smorkaloff

Description: Through interviews with Alejo Carpentier and dramatized scenes, this tape highlights Carpentier's concept of *lo real maravilloso,* ("marvelous realism.") The tape outlines Carpentier's life and works up to the mid-1970s. Using film techniques similar to those implied by the literary term, it focuses on the prologue from Carpentier's novel, *El reino de este mundo (The Kingdom of this World),* which deals with the Haitian revolution and the notion of cultural syncretism and myth as a force for liberation. The tape explains a bit of the story of the African slave, Macandal, who told his friends he could transform himself into any animal he wished to be. The insurrection in Barbados was inspired by him; even after his death, the slaves believed he was still around. Carpentier's interviews distinguish marvelous realism from magical realism. The tape's conclusion indicates that marvelous realism is a manifestation of the *criollo/mestizo* culture of Cuba.

Strengths and Weaknesses: This clear, concise, and effective tape provides a good definition of the concept, relating it not only to Carpentier's work but also to European sources. The program is well shot and edited, with rare footage; the presence of Alejo Carpentier and his own comments regarding his complex writing are invaluable. The tape is a nice counterpoint to the book's prologue.

While the tape is a good companion to Carpentier's ideas and works, it is a bit highbrow and probably appropriate only for graduate and upper-division *Literature* courses or for readers of Carpentier's works. The film is not terribly attractive: the black-and-white detracts from the *maravilloso* effect. Some of the nature shots and effects seem corny.

Introducing the Tape: A bit more background on the subject of the first Caribbean insurrection which took place in Haiti and its relation to the title of the film, the book, and the subject of *lo real maravilloso* would be helpful.

How to Use: I would use the video in conjunction with any text that uses African myth, and for which the concept of *lo real maravilloso* could be applied. For example, the video would work well with texts by García Marquéz, Toni Morrison's *Song of Solomon,* etc. (Silcox)

I would show this to *Literature* students who were reading one of Carpentier's novels or stories. I might also use it in an upper-division *Literature* course where students were learning to distinguish magical realism from marvelous realism (though I believe it to be a distinction without much of a difference). (Hunt)

I might even use it to supplement a *Latin American Literature* course in which I was unable to treat the work of Carpentier and wanted students to have a basic knowledge of his contribution. (Gottlieb)

I would use the tape in the introductory lectures to all levels of *Latin American Literature* to illustrate the strong links between history and literary creation; also as a requisite before reading any of Carpentier's novels. (Smorkaloff)

I would use this in conjunction with the novel, *El reino de este mundo,* but it could be used with any of Carpentier's novels. (Marting)

Suggested Readings: Augustin, Marie. *Le Macandal: episode de l'insurrection des noirs à St. Domingue /par Tante Marie.*

Carpentier's works including: *El acoso; El reino de este mundo.* ("*The Kingdom of this World*") especially the prologue; *El recurso del método; El siglo de las luces; Guerra del tiempo; Los pasos perdidos; Tientos, diferencias y otros ensayos.*—literary theory. (see bibliography for selected citations)

Giacoman, Helmy F. *Homenaje a Alejo Carpentier: Variaciones interpretativas en torno a su obra, por Fernando Alegría (et al.).*

Gilroy, Paul. *Diaspora Crossings: Intercultural and Transnational Identities in the Black Atlantic.*

Great News from the Barbadoes, or A True and Faithful Account of the Grand Conspiracy of the Negroes Against the English and the Happy Discovery of the Same: with the Number of Those that were Burned Alive, Beheaded, and Otherwise Executed for their Horrid Crimes: with a Short Description of that Plantation. 1676.

Márquez Rodríguez, Alexis. *La obra narrativa de Alejo Carpentier.*

Müller-Bergh, Klaus. *Alejo Carpentier: estudio biográfico-crítico.*

Müller-Bergh, Klaus. *Asedios a Carpentier; once ensayos críticos sobre el novelista cubano.*

Mocega-González, Esther P. *La narrativa de Alejo Carpentier: el concepto del tiempo como tema fundamental: ensayo de interpretación y análisis.*

Morrison, Toni. *Song of Solomon.*

Padura, Leonardo. *Lo real maravilloso, creación y realidad.*

Palermo, Zulma. *Historia y mito en la obra de Alejo Carpentier.*

Speratti-Piñero, Emma Susana. *Pasos hallados en* El reino de este mundo.

Level: University

AMADA (Amada)

Feature.   With Subtitles.   105 min.   1983

Directed by: Humberto Solás

Produced by: ICAIC (Calle 23 No. 155 Vedado, Havana; tel: [537] 333-862; fax: [537] 333-032)

Distributed by: Center for Cuban Studies,

Evaluators: Robert DiAntonio, Daniel P. Hunt, Carlos Pérez.

Description: Based on the novel *La esfinge,* by Miguel de Carrión, the film is set in 1914, the beginning of the sugar boom that lasted a few years beyond World War I. Amada Villalosa is a young woman from a declining aristocratic family that obtained its wealth through the slave trade. She has married Dionisio, a member of the emerging bourgeoisie, to maintain the family's social and economic position, but it is a loveless marriage. Amada's husband is a tyrant and adulterer who manipulates her and her mother to obtain her mother's considerable property. Amada tries to find refuge in a love affair with her cousin, Marcial, an anarchist poet whose ideals of social revolution clash with her own traditional and aristocratic values. But the affair only gives her husband further cause for dividing her from her mother and her property. In desperation, Amada goes to the slums to help nurse some children dying of a contagion. She contracts the disease herself and dies. The film is a powerful indictment of the patriarchal political system and exploitative men like Amada's husband who are able to gain wealth and power by manipulating women and liberals.

Strengths and Weaknesses: The film captures the contradictions of a declining sugar aristocracy with its traditional values, and those of an emerging bourgeoisie exploiting the opportunities available to it during the initial years of U.S. economic and political hegemony. The acting is well done, and the melodramatic story line is clear.

One evaluator felt that the melodrama might not be good for all audiences, especially those who do not enjoy a soap-opera type of plot. Others found the program slow-moving for U.S. audiences.

Introducing the Tape: For someone who is not familiar with Cuban history, many of the references in the film may be obscure. Viewers need some background concerning the events surrounding Mario G. Menocal's presidency, Cuba's relation to the world market, the effects of World War I on the sugar boom of the period, and the results of the "dance of the millions" and its aftermath. Also, a general theme to be incorporated is that of a declining sugar-planter bourgeoisie and the rise of a new elite as the result of U.S. political and economic hegemony on the island. It must be stressed that this new elite was dependent on political office for its economic survival.

How to Use: I would use this tape after lecturing on social classes during the early republic, emphasizing how the declining sugar plantation aristocracy attempted to maintain its social, political, and economic power by marrying members of the emerging elite. The film can be used for a *Latin American* or *Cuban Women* course where the question of women within Latin American or Cuban society and their traditional roles is analyzed. (Pérez)

I might have students watch the film in conjunction with reading novels that share similar themes. Allende's *Casa de las espíritus* tells a similar story with a similar ethos, and Carpentier's novel is set at about the same time, giving an equally incisive portrait of the power structure of patriarchal regimes. Or in a course where we're studying Cuba, I would certainly have students discuss the criticism of conservatism found in the film. (Hunt)

Suggested Readings: Allende, Isabel. *The House of the Spirits.*

Carpentier, Alejo. *El recurso del método.*
Carrión, Miguel, de. *La esfinge; novela.*
Gallegos, Rómulo. *Doña Bárbara.*
Pérez, Louis A., Jr. *Cuba: Between Reform and Revolution.*
Pérez, Louis A., Jr. *Cuba Under the Platt Amendment, 1902–1934.*
Pérez, Louis A., Jr. *Intervention, Revolution, and Politics in Cuba, 1913–1921.*
Level: University

AMOR Y DOLOR

Fiction. Without Subtitles. 5 min. 1990
Directed by: Enrique Alvarez
Produced by: TVE (Calle 108 #29E08 entre 29E y 29F, Maríanao, Havana; tel: [537] 20-9943)
Distributed by: IMRE Archive
Evaluators: Kate Blanas, Alfredo Bushby, Marcia Dean, Miguel Huarcaya, Joan A. McGinnis
Description: This is a visual interpretation and deconstruction of the famous French poem "The Breakfast," by Jacques Prévert. The music sets the tone as we observe a couple eating breakfast together and not communicating at all. The poem expresses how people in couples experience solitude, although they are together. The film juxtaposes a range of cultural and technical elements—television conventions, superimposed text in French, multiple monitors—to pierce the surface of modernity and identity.
Strengths and Weaknesses: Evaluators had mixed responses to the tape. A few reviewers felt it was very nicely done, bringing the poem to life. The Spanish is very clear, and the actions are described by the commentary. Others commented that the video has some interesting composition but does not keep a style. One evaluator felt the tape added nothing to the poem. A strength is the original French poem alongside the visual—almost like a film strip.
Introducing the Tape: It is important to introduce this as an experimental piece.
How to Use: In *Spanish Language* classes, this particular poem works perfectly to illustrate the use of the preterit and action past tense. There is only one imperfect or description past tense. Many of my students have memorized this poem to be proficient in some irregular verbs. They have also performed it with props. (McGinnis)

I would use the video with beginning language students as an introduction to poetry in which students are encouraged to read between the lines and explore human relationships. (Dean)
Suggested Readings: Prévert, Jacques. "Desayuno."
Level: University

LA BELLA DEL ALHAMBRA (The Beauty of the Alhambra)

Feature. With Subtitles. 108 min. 1989
Directed by: Enrique Pineda Barnet

Produced by: ICAIC (Calle 23 No. 155 Vedado, Havana; tel: [537] 333-862; fax: [537] 333-032)

Distributed by: Center for Cuban Studies, IMRE

Evaluators: Donald S. Castro, Darién J. Davis, Robert DiAntonio, Rick Langhorst, Hilda Pato, Currie Kerr Thompson, Margarita de la Vega Hurtado

Description: The Machado dictatorship is seen through the eyes of Rachel, a woman who remembers her struggle and sacrifices to become a "star" burlesque entertainer at the Alhambra, a popular club for men only. Many scenes from the burlesque musical theater of Cuba are intermingled with scenes from Rachel's life as she rises from obscure poverty to acclaim. The viewer is painfully aware of the limited options available to women at this time in history, yet the protagonist is determined to perform on her own terms. The film is full of political references providing a credible historical representation of the late 1920s and early 1930s.

Strengths and Weaknesses: This is an impressive film with a visually arresting, historically faithful, and very interesting narrative. It sensitively explores the social situation of this marginal but culturally very significant world. The film re-creates Cuban life in the 1920s, commenting on the political situation under Machado and U.S. involvement with the Cuban oligarchy in a subtle but powerful manner. The traditional Cuban music is wonderful and completely relevant. A number of evaluators commented that the film was stylistically well done, with first-rate acting and technical details.

One reviewer found the plot somewhat melodramatic and the ending weak. Another felt the acting was poor at times. The Spanish conversation is rapid and may be difficult for non-native speakers to understand. The tape contains some nudity.

Introducing the Tape: This is a feature film with many "cultural aspects" that viewers not familiar with Cuban history may not grasp. An introduction to the musical theater of Cuba and to the political atmosphere around the time of Machado would be helpful. The film opens with two actors, one has a painted blackface and is referred to as "Blackie." This overtly racist caricature would have to be explained/discussed, especially when screening the video in high school classes.

How to Use: In a course on *Latin American Film,* the video is useful for revealing the atmosphere of the burlesque, sexually suggestive musical theater of Cuba earlier this century. (Langhorst).

The tape could be used as an out-of-class assignment. Perhaps clips could be used to illustrate the political savagery of Machado. There are several vivid scenes. (Davis)

Suggested Readings: Aguilar, L. E. *Cuba 1933: Prologue to Revolution.*

Level: High School—University

CANTAR AL SOL

Documentary.   Without Subtitles.   59 min.

Directed by: Daniel Touron

Produced by: Video Cultura (Calle 19 No. 560 esq. a C, Vedado, Habana 4; tel: [537] 33-2302 or 33-2469; fax: 537-22-7771)

Distributed by: Center for Cuban Studies, IMRE Archive

Evaluators: John Chasteen, Kim Kowalzcyk, Jorge Rodríguez-Florido

Description: This tape documents the daily life, struggles, music, and dance of Haitian residents in eastern Cuba. It begins with a mythic narration ("The drum is a tree that talks . . .") then is organized, for the most part, around a series of specific individuals presenting their stories. The Haitian religion (Voodun) is portrayed, with a streak of Cuban Santería.

Strengths and Weaknesses: This is a recent and unique source on Cuban-Haitian culture; the Haitians' personal interviews make it a real testimonial work. It is quite provocative, with artistic narration and choreography. Some highlights of the Festival of Caribbean Culture are included, and Cuban-Haitian music is emphasized.

The Spanish language in the film will be difficult for lower-level language students but is a good illustration of the Cuban accent for advanced students.

Introducing the Tape: A general introduction about the cultural elements presented in the film (such as Santería, Candomble, Voodun) would be helpful for U.S. students. Viewers may need to be prepared for the depiction of an Afro-Caribbean ritual including quite shocking scenes in which live animals are torn apart. One evaluator pointed out that syncretic cults have been unjustly portrayed as barbaric within our culture, thus this scene poses something of an interpretive problem. At any rate, it is strong material capable of confirming negative suppositions of cultural relativism. The sacrifice scene, while disturbing, is also valuable and thought provoking.

How to Use: I would use this tape in any discussion of the Haitian contribution to *Afro-Cuban Culture.* (Rodríguez-Florido)

In a course on *African Musical and Dance Traditions in the New World,* this tape could illustrate the durability and centrality of these traditions to the culture of the Caribbean. (Chasteen)

Suggested Readings: Moreno Fraginals, Manuel, ed. *Africa in Latin America: Essays on History, Culture, and Socialism.*

Materials on religious syncretism in the Caribbean would be an important accompaniment for this film.

Level: University

CHAPUCERIAS (Sloppy Work)

Documentary/Comedy.   With Subtitles.   11 min.   1987

Directed by: Enrique Colina

Produced by: ICAIC (Calle 23 No. 155 Vedado, Havana; tel: [537] 333-862; fax: [537] 333-032)

Distributed by: Center for Cuban Studies, IMRE

Evaluators: Jules Benjamin, Nancy J. Church, Donald W. Davey, Jorge Rodríguez-Florido, Roger A. Sánchez-Berroa, Margarita de la Vega Hurtado

Description: This humorous short documentary about the variety of situations in which sloppiness detracts from the Cuban quality of life is a satirical comment on people's bad work habits. The very technique of the filmmaker is at times intentionally sloppy: beginning credits are placed at the end and letters are askew, with finger and thumbprints all around. The tape intersperses diverse elements (a tongue-in-cheek television program, excerpts from old movies, spontaneous interviews with outraged workers and consumers, and film clips showing sloppy work) to create a certain helter-skelter effect. The mixture of these elements and the film's comic overtone make it a unique and creative example of the documentary form. It is a constructive criticism of the lack of a work ethic and pride in work in contemporary Cuba.

Strengths and Weaknesses: This documentary looks at a universal problem in a humorous way. Both analytical and instructional, it is full of rhythm and irony. The satirical bent of the film is well reflected in the filmmaking style, and the use of humor to make hard-hitting, poignant comments is very effective. One reviewer felt the tape would be very useful for instilling good work habits. English translations and subtitles are good.

One evaluator felt the tape was not very serious, mentioning that it never probed the roots of the problem. Although the problems take place within a socialist-structured economy, the causes are chalked up more to human nature. Other reviewers saw this as a strength, noting that such problems are also prevalent in capitalist economies.

Introducing the Tape: A statement of the film's purpose and a comment on the filmmaker's technique may help viewers place the satire into perspective and understand the piece more quickly.

How to Use: I would use the tape to provoke reactions among students in a *Conversational Spanish* class. (Rodríguez-Florido)

In a *Film Studies* or *Communication* class this would be a good example of a creative documentary. (de la Vega-Hurtado)

I would show the tape as an adjunct to the part of my *Hispanic Cultural Perspectives* course dealing with attitudes toward work. (Davey)

In a *Comparative Culture* class, students can use the tape to compare work ethics in socialist and capitalist economies.

I would use the tape as a humorous lesson in doing your best work. (Church)

Level: High School—University

CLANDESTINOS (Underground)

Feature. With Subtitles. 103 min. 1987
Directed by: Fernando Pérez
Produced by: ICAIC (Calle 23 No. 155 Vedado, Havana; tel: [537] 333-862; fax: [537] 333-032)
Distributed by: Center for Cuban Studies, IMRE,
Evaluators: Marilyn Jiménez, Carlos Pérez, S. Travis Silcox, Elaine Torres, Margarita de la Vega Hurtado

Description: This feature, dedicated to those who died in the struggle against the dictatorship of Fulgencio Batista, captures the struggle of an urban revolutionary group in Havana from 1956 to 1958. It is the tragic story of underground rebels working to overthrow the dictatorship. Ernesto, the calculating and cautious leader, unexpectedly finds romance when he is nursed back to health by a comrade, Nerieda, after being shot in a police struggle. His own dedication to secrecy, however, cannot prevent the blunders of other underground members, and the hideout he shares with Nerieda is discovered. Ambushed, he decides to save Nerieda's life at the expense of his own and surrenders the pregnant Nerieda to the police. He is shot to death while Nerieda watches in horror.

The film focuses on a seldom-studied area of Cuban history, the urban guerrilla struggle against Batista. Through its characters, it examines the reality of a life underground and the personal sacrifices involved. It illustrates how an individual's personal life must be subsumed to the political struggle, and it explores women's roles in this type of protracted guerrilla struggle.

Strengths and Weaknesses: The film demonstrates the participation of the urban sectors and middle class in the struggle to overthrow Batista. Its plot is easy to follow, and the entertaining format makes it extremely accessible, allowing viewers to empathize with its characters. With strong acting and direction, the film was very popular in Cuba.

A few evaluators mentioned that the historical and political content of the film was not readily apparent because the romantic, melodramatic subplot takes most of the attention. One reviewer felt that the female characterization was predictable and that the acting and direction were not consistent.

Introducing the Tape: An introduction to Batista and the historical development and political situation in Cuba would clarify the content. Also, the urban participation, the rural movement as well as the role of Cuban women in this struggle must be emphasized.

How to Use: I would use this tape when lecturing on the struggle to overthrow Batista in order to illustrate to the students that the struggle against Batista was one undertaken not only by the rural guerrillas of the 26th of July movement, but also by the urban sectors. After the film, we would discuss the relationship between the personal and the political in revolutionary movements. In a short essay, I would have the students apply Ernesto "Che" Guevara's precept about a revolutionary's concept of love to the film. If it is to be used for a course on *Latin American* (or *Cuban*) *Women,* the changing role of women during a revolutionary struggle should be analyzed. (Pérez)

I would use this in a *Latin American Film* class as an example of Cuban national filmmaking and a successful blending of politics and entertainment. (Silcox)

This tape can be used in conjunction with *Viva la república,* a collection of historical footage depicting various epochs of Cuban history (including the Machado/Batista eras).

Suggested Readings: Bonachea, Ramón L., and Marta San Martín. *The Cuban Insurrection, 1952–1959.*

Dorschner, John and Roberto Fabricio. *The Winds of December.*

Kling, Merle. "Cuba: A Case Study of a Successful Attempt to Seize Political Power by the Application of Unconventional Warfare," pp. 42–52.

Padula, Alfred L., Jr. "Financing Castro's Revolution, 1956–1958." pp. 234–246.

Pérez, Louis A., Jr. *Cuba: Between Reform and Revolution.*

Special Operations Research Office. *Case Study in Insurgency and Revolutionary Warfare: Cuba, 1953–1959.*

Complementary Films/Videos: *Viva la república* (distributed by the International Media Resource Exchange)
Level: High School—University

COMO UNA SOLA VOZ (Like One Voice)
Documentary.   With Subtitles.   10 min.   1988
Directed by: Miriam Talavera
Produced by: ICAIC (Calle 23 No. 155 Vedado, Havana; tel: [537] 333-862 fax: [537] 333-032)
Distributed by: Center for Cuban Studies, The Cinema Guild
Evaluators: Sandra L. Cade, Hugo Chapa-Guzmán
Description: This video moves from rehearsals to performances by several female vocalists including Sonia Silvestre, Lucecita Benítez, and Sara González at the Festival del Caribe.
Strengths and Weaknesses: The tape is full of vivid performances and wonderful music with good pacing and photography. It is a very interesting look at musicians at work, discovering their balance with each other.

Background is not provided, and performers are not identified.
Introducing the Tape: An introduction identifying the performers who are not known internationally would be very useful. It would also be helpful to have the lyrics and history of any folkloric songs.
How to Use: The tape could be used simply as an introduction to the feel and sound of Caribbean music. (Chapa-Guzmán)
Suggested Readings: Bilby, Kenneth M. *The Caribbean as a Musical Region.*

Brouwer, Leo. *La música, lo cubano y la inovación.*

Gómez, Jorge. *Canciones de la Nueva Trova.*

Sealy, John. *Music in the Caribbean.*
Level: High School—University

EL CORAZON SOBRE LA TIERRA
Feature.   With Subtitles.   95 min.   1985
Directed by: Constante Diego
Produced by: ICAIC (Calle 23 No. 155 Vedado, Havana; tel: [537] 333-862; fax: [537] 333-032)
Distributed by: Center for Cuban Studies

Evaluators: Edgar G. Nesman, Jorge Porras, Virginia Shen, Thomas Whigham
Description: This is the story of the struggles of peasants to found a rural cooperative in eastern Cuba. It shows one man's efforts to work with the cooperative while accepting his own past. The cooperative is given the name of his son, who was killed in the Ethiopian war.
Strengths and Weaknesses: This is a touching story about an authentic struggle to start a production cooperative. It uses local people as actors and is well produced and thought out. A significant number of scenes are filmed at night, which gives the feeling of obscurity and bitterness. It is a stark portrait of contemporary socialist Cuba that shows the need for agricultural cooperatives and the essential role of peasants in their formation.

A couple of evaluators commented that there were too many dark, slow scenes with long dialogues. One felt the tape would not be clear unless put into the Cuban context.
Introducing the Tape: An introduction to the Cuban Revolution and Cuban society would put the tape in context. Background on the political and social structures in Latin America, specifically in Cuba, would be helpful.
How to Use: When we talk about *Contemporary Latin American History,* specifically social-economic changes, I would present this film to talk about how efforts have been made by the peasants to make progress. (Shen)
Suggested Readings: Writings on contemporary Cuban society (see bibliography)
Level: University

CUANDO PIENSO EN CHE
Documentary.   Without Subtitles.   47 min.   1987
Directed by: Alberto Ortiz de Zárate
Produced by: Videocultura (Calle 11 esq 4, Apto 14217, Habana; tel: [537] 33-542)
Distributed by: Center for Cuban Studies,
Evaluators: Carmen Chávez, Donald W. Davey, Robert DiAntonio, José Pérez
Description: In 1987, an Italian journalist interviewed Fidel Castro about Che Guevara. The interview is interspersed with a montage of photos and film and some modern-day shots of Havana. Fidel reminisces about Che's exceptional intellectual qualities and the impact Che had on the Cuban Revolution. He recalls that from the beginning, Che insisted on returning to South America and Fidel promised him he could. Che undertook many different tasks during the early years of the Cuban Revolution, including serving as director of the Cuban National Bank. Recounted also is Che's sojourn in Africa and the events that led up to his death in the mountains of Bolivia. The tape ends with a moving speech by Fidel in the Plaza de la Revolución, in which he praises Che.
Strengths and Weaknesses: This is an authentic interview with one of Che's closest associates. The information is wonderful and provides a good definition of what Fidel and Che meant by communism. The mixture of interviews with pho-

tos and film footage is appropriate. The tape will provide younger students who don't remember Che Guevara with an excellent introduction. It includes rare archival film and photography.

Fidel is a bit long-winded at times, and the tape overly doctrinaire. One evaluator found the musical background melodramatic and a bit irritating.

Introducing the Tape: Background on Che Guevara and Fidel Castro is necessary. Those familiar with the history of Castro and his revolution will find the tape much easier to follow. Also, the idea of "storytelling" should be explained.

How to Use: When presenting *Twentieth-Century Cuba,* I would put on ten or fifteen minutes of the tape just to bring the textbook to life. (Davey)

I would show a clip and discuss the "art" of storytelling. I would do an analysis of Castro's and Guevara's charismatic qualities. (Chávez)

Suggested Readings: Contemporary Latin American history books focused on revolutionary forces in the 1960s.

Any biography of Che Guevara.

Complementary Films/Videos: *Una foto que recorre el mundo (A Photo that Goes Around the World)* (Cuba)

Level: University

CUATRO MUJERES, CUATRO AUTORES

Documentary. Without Subtitles. 14 min. 1983
Directed by: Luis Felipe Bernaza
Produced by: ICAIC (Calle 23 No. 155 Vedado, Havana; tel: [537] 333-862; fax: [537] 333-032)
Distributed by: Center for Cuban Studies, IMRE Archive
Evaluators: Hugo Chapa-Guzmán, Susy Suárez
Description: Pablo Milanés and Silvio Rodríguez, two well-known representatives of the Latin American *nueva trova* ("new song movement"), interpret songs about women written by themselves or other Cuban composers (including Sindo Garay, author of "Perla Marina" and Manuel Corona, author of "Santa Cecilia"). The songs are named after four women who personify Cuba, the revolution, Latin culture, and the Muses.

Strengths and Weaknesses: With beautiful music and a great rendering by two of Cuba's most renowned artists, this short music video deserves to be seen at least once by everyone. The imagery on the last song is superb. The poetry is an example of the magnificent work of Silvio Rodríguez.

The filler video (some cards moving about the frame) seems unrelated and does not add much to the musical performances.

Introducing the Tape: Some introduction to the *nueva trova* in Latin America would be helpful.

How to Use: I would combine this piece with short stories by the boom writers, music from Brazil's Tropicalismo, Violeta Parra and Atahulpa Yupanqui, and Latin American poetry and film. (Suárez)

Subtitles of the lyrics would be nice for audiences that don't understand Spanish. The tape could be shown in a *Spanish Language Laboratory.* (Chapa-Guzmán)

Suggested Readings: Casaus, Victor. *Silvio, que levante la mano la guitarra.*

Gómez, Jorge. *Canciones de la nueva trova.*
Level: University

CUBA VA: EL RETO DE LA NUEVA GENERACION
(Cuba Va: Challenge of the Next Generation)

Documentary. With Subtitles. 60 min. 1993
Directed by: Gail Dolgin and Vicente Franco
Produced by: Cuba Va Video Project (12 Liberty St., San Francisco, CA 94110; tel: [415] 282-1812; fax: [415] 282-1798)
Distributed by: The Cinema Guild
Evaluators: Joel C. Edelstein, Terry Karl, Kim Kowalczyk, Margot M. Segura
Description: This documentary takes a critical look at Cuba's social and economic situations today, through the eyes of its youth. The video provides interviews with young people; their discussions and arguments about the economic situation, the government, and the political system; and the responses of those in authority to youth subcultures such as rock, rap, hard core, and reggae.

Strengths and Weaknesses: This is an exceptionally well done, youth-oriented presentation of the pros and cons of Fidel Castro's regime today. The tape captures a realistic and balanced expression of Cuba's youth regarding the benefits of the revolution, internal difficulties, and hope for the country's future. The documentary is especially strong in that it lets Cubans speak for themselves and gives audiences an opportunity to hear them. With beautiful camera work; fast-paced, strong editing; engrossing music and dancing; and a presentation of diverse views, the tape brings Cuba out of the haze of ideological contention, showing the society as a human enterprise. One evaluator pointed out that the tape is unique in documenting the thoughts and feelings of Cuban youth (who are exceptionally articulate), and it provides probing insight into the contemporary crisis of Cuba.

Introducing the Tape: Background on the history of Cuba-U.S. relations would be useful.

How to Use: I would use the tape to introduce my students to Cuban society and the nature of Cuba's current political and economic difficulties, as well as to explore the situation and perspectives of Cuban youth. (Edelstein)

I would present this film as an example of social experiment where there is a measurable outcome. This film is important because it gives a firsthand view of the lives of those young people who have, or have not, benefited from the Cuban Revolution, its ideals, and the implementation of its policies and programs. (Segura)

I would probably use excerpts from this video and intersperse them with a lecture, or show part of the video and have the students write in class about what they saw. The conversations between the students are particularly well-suited to this type of activity. (Kowalczyk)

Suggested Readings: Guevara, Ernesto. *Reminiscences of the Cuban Revolutionaries.*

Huberman, Leo, and Paul M. Sweezy. *Introduction to Socialism.*

Kozol, Jonathan. *Children of the Revolution.*

Randall, Margaret. *Cuban Women Now: Afterward 1974.*

Rius. *Cuba for Beginners: An Illustrated Guide for Americans (and their Government).*

Venceremos Brigade. Educational Commission. *Health Care in Cuba: Only the People Can Perform Miracles.*

Wald, Karen. *Children of Ché: Childcare and Education in Cuba.*

Level: High School—University

DE CIERTA MANERA (One Way or Another)
Documentary/Feature. With Subtitles. 79 min. 1974
Directed by: Sara Gómez
Produced by: ICAIC (Calle 23 No. 155 Vedado, Havana; tel: [537] 333-862; fax: [537] 333-032)
Distributed by: Center for Cuban Studies, IMRE
Evaluators: Susana Conde, Mary Jo Dudley, Juan Espadas, Christine Holmlund, Christine List
Description: A revolutionary love story combining elements of fiction and documentary, this film examines the roots of machismo and the changing relationships between women and men in early 1960s Cuba. The main story deals with the growing relationship between Yolanda, a schoolteacher, and Mario, a bus factory worker. The plot unfolds in the midst of the destruction of the old and the establishment of the new order of the Cuban Revolution (symbolized in the tearing down of a marginal neighborhood and the building of a new housing project). The film illustrates the difficulties of changing the codes of conduct from a male-based philosophy to a "revolutionary" philosophy and the conflicts that arise when confronting the status quo with a new form of thinking. It analyzes the successes and shortcomings of the revolution regarding racism, sexism, and class-based prejudices. Subsections of the film provide documentary footage of the Abacua cult, poverty under Batista, the destruction of old Havana slums, etc. Most of the footage was filmed in actual factories, schools, and neighborhoods, where workers, teachers, students, and ordinary people represented themselves. The film's ideological bent is clear; it gives the revolutionary philosophy in a strong moral fashion. The director, Sara Gómez, died when the editing of the film was almost completed, and two other Cuban filmmakers, Tomás Gutiérrez Alea and Julio García Espinosa, finished the undertaking.
Strengths and Weaknesses: Gómez's film is deservedly one of the most acclaimed Cuban films to look at the impact of the revolution on individuals and daily life. Gómez is also of interest as the only Cuban woman director to make a feature film during the 1970s–80s. The film's experimental style, combining sociodrama and documentary footage, pre-sents a woman's perspective and documents the early years of the revolution. The film appears, and is, in some ways dated, yet its core analysis of machismo is still valid, and the Brechtian mix of documentary and fiction is still intriguing. Some students will find the film confusing because it mixes genres, but class discussion can clarify why such mixes were key to Cuban "imperfect cinema." Although the film can seem overly propagandistic, reviewers felt that for those who persist, the tape illustrates interesting points about the dilemmas involved in changing the philosophy of the Cuban people in the revolutionary process.
Introducing the Tape: A brief background on the history and cultural heritage of the population would be helpful. Discussion should include Afro-Cuban religion, Santería, as well as references to the Abacua and other elements of West African culture. An introduction to the conflicts of the Cuban government as it confronted changing from a "male" orientation to a "revolutionary" view would be useful. It would be important to present both the U.S. and the Cuban perspectives in the study of twentieth-century Cuba. Also some discussion of Cuban "imperfect cinema" would be appropriate.
How to Use: My course on *Latin American Film* is subtitled *Reconfigurations of Family and Nation in Latin America.* I would be particularly interested in analyzing with my students the representation of women in this film, the relationship of parents to both young and adult children, the developing love relationship between Mario and Yolanda, the issues of machismo and feminism, and the method of changing the configuration of a neighborhood through the participation of the people that change affects. This film is interesting in its technique, which is quite different from the seamless Hollywood continuity editing. Technique and theme are consistent however, since the apparent imperfection in the telling reflects the ideological basis on which it rests. (Conde)

I would use this tape in *African American Cinema* and *Latino Media* courses I teach to show issues of sexism and racism in a Pan-African and Pan-Latin American context. (List)

I have used this film in *Introduction to Film, Women's Studies* and *Latin American Film* classes, lecturing on Cuban history in general, the history of Cuban film, the changing roles of women in Cuba, and on "imperfect cinema." Ample critical material exists in English which explains cultural differences. (Holmlund)

Now, twenty years after the film was made, the task of changing sexist mentality discussed in the film could be contrasted to the present-day reality of male/female relations in Cuban society.
Suggested Readings: Black, Jan Knippers, ed. *Latin America. Its Problems and Its Promise.*

Chanan, Michael. *The Cuban Image: Cinema and Cultural Politics in Cuba.*

Galeano, Eduardo. *Open Veins of Latin America. Five Centuries of the Pillage of a Continent.*

García Espinosa, Julio. *For an Imperfect Cinema: Cuba, 1969.*

Green, Duncan. *Faces of Latin America.*

Kaplan, E. Ann. *Women and Film.*

King, John. *Magical Reels. A History of Cinema in Latin America.*

Kuhn, Annette. *Women's Pictures*

Lewis, Oscar. *Men, Women, Neighbors Living the Revolution: An Oral History of Contemporary Cuba.*

Skidmore, Thomas E., and Peter H. Smith. *Modern Latin America.*

West, Dennis. "Reconciling Entertainment and Thought: An Interview with Julio García Espinosa."

Level: University

DE DONDE SON LAS CANTANTES

Documentary.   Without Subtitles.   32 min.   1976
Directed by: Luis Felipe Bernaza
Produced by: ICAIC (Calle 23 No. 155 Vedado, Havana; tel: [537] 333-862; fax: [537] 333-032)
Distributed by: Center for Cuban Studies, IMRE Archive
Evaluators: Rebeca Harclerode, Grace Leavitt, Joan A. McGinnis, Jorge Rodríguez-Florido, Roger A. Sánchez-Berroa
Description: The film tells the history of the Cuban *son* and of the famous musical group Trio Matamoros, with interviews and film clips from the 1950s and the 1960s. It includes several musical numbers, as well as a good amount of information on Cuban history, beginning with the fight for independence at the end of the nineteenth century. There are conversations with two of the members of the trio (Siro and Cueto) and recordings of talks with the third member (Miguel Matamoros), as well as interviews with Matamoros's widow and other personalities. The tape presents the relationship of the *son* with poetry, as practiced by Nicolás Guillén, who also appears in an interview.
Strengths and Weaknesses: This is an excellent introduction to a very important segment of Cuban music. It is a strong depiction of the music and artwork of the period.

Some evaluators found the story line difficult to follow. It's not clear if the primary focus of the tape is the *son* or the Trio Matamoros. Viewers need a background in Cuban history to appreciate the film. Some of the interviewees are a little difficult to understand, but the film provides a good amount of information on a topic not readily available otherwise.
Introducing the Tape: An introduction should include historical context about Cuba, and background on Caribbean music trends and concepts (e.g., *cumbia, son*). Viewers should be told of the importance of the contribution of the Trio Matamoros to the history of Cuban music.
How to Use: I would use the tape in a course on *Latin American Music* or in a course on *Cuban Poetry* (especially Afro-Cuban poetry). The tape can lead to discussions about the relationship between poetry and music or just about the origin

of the modern Cuban music including (*décima, son, mambo,* and *guaguancó*). (Rodríguez-Florido)

I would use this film in conjunction with a unit on *Latin Music and Dance,* or possibly as part of a unit on Cuba (but the main emphasis of the film is on the music). (Leavitt)

The tape could be complemented by biographical/historical background, a vocabulary list and study-guide, as well as poetry by Nicolás Guillén inspired by the music. (McGinnis)
Suggested Readings: Moreno Fraginals, Manuel, ed. *Africa in Latin America.*

Poetry by Nicolás Guillén (see bibliography).
Level: High School—University

EL DIALOGO (The Dialogue)

Documentary.   With Subtitles.   60 min.   1979
Directed by: Estela Bravo and Karen Ranucci
Distributed by: IMRE
Evaluators: Silvia Arrom, Glenn J. Kist, Luis Martínez-Fernández, S. Travis Silcox, Allen Wells
Description: In 1978, after almost twenty years of complete isolation from their homeland, seventy-five representatives of the Cuban exile community defied both the U.S. government and extremist Cuban exile groups by traveling back to Cuba to meet with Fidel Castro and discuss the opening of relations. Three main points were agreed upon: Cuban exiles would be allowed to return home to visit their families; older Cubans could be permanently reunited with family members in either the U.S. or Cuba; and all political prisoners held since the beginning of the revolution would be set free. This documentary shows the emotional effects of separation endured by Cubans in Cuba, the U.S., and Puerto Rico and documents the consequences of the "dialogue" on each of these communities. The dialogue paved the way for the release of four thousand political prisoners from Cuba and the visits of over one hundred thousand exiles to Cuba.

Interviews with exiles from different age groups, socioeconomic circumstances, and locations (Miami, New York City, New Jersey, and San Juan) provides viewers with a sense of the variety of emotions these exiles felt about their country after Castro's victory in 1959 and how they saw themselves and their respective conditions. While the people provide many different reasons for their flight, the unifying elements in the exile community are love of the homeland and the desire to return to Cuba some day. The dialogue also led to violence within the exile community. Those supporting the dialogue and wanting to return to visit their families were branded as pro-Castro and communists by those who were opposed to any accommodation with the Castro government. Many dialogue participants had their lives threatened, and two were murdered for their participation in this process.
Strengths and Weaknesses: Interesting and informative, the tape provides good background to the 1990s events in Cuban-U.S. relations. It is an emotionally poignant story, well told by the filmmakers. The audience gets a real sense

of how difficult this issue is—how it divides families and drives a wedge between the Cuban people. Students will respond to this kind of film precisely because it relies on interviews with everyday people who feel very ambivalent about how political disagreements have kept them away from their family and culture. The film is most useful in portraying the diversity and plurality of thought among the Cuban exile community in the U.S. It shows them to be factory workers as well as owners and gives voice to the progressive Cuban exile community, the right-wing community in its Miami and New Jersey strongholds, and those exiles who viewed the dialogue as a way to reunite families. The voice-over translations are unusually strong, keeping with the vocal patterns of the speakers.

While it is very clear that the filmmakers support the dialogue, they aren't heavy-handed about it. However, opponents of Castro are not always shown in the most flattering light. The scope of the interviews produce a clear bias against those in opposition to the dialogue. One evaluator felt that more attention should have been paid to the vexations and other humiliations endured by those Cubans who made the very difficult decision to leave their homeland. The link between the Puerto Rican exile community and that of the U.S. is not sufficently developed. Also, the documentary treats a specific moment in time and needs to be updated.

Introducing the Tape: Brief but adequate background is provided for the exodus from Cuba from 1959 though 1963. The tape presents the period shortly before the massive Mariel boatlift. Students would need to be updated on this event. It can be explained that in part, Mariel was a consequence of the dialogue in that Cubans previously isolated from their families in the States were now attracted to the consumer goods they brought which were not available on the island.

The dialogue needs to be set in the context of the efforts of the Carter administration to improve relations with Castro. The explanation of who issues visas both to Cubans wanting to leave their country and to exiles wanting to visit Cuba is not clear to people unfamiliar with the baroque diplomatic situation. Cuban exiles are heard shouting "end the blockade," but the U.S. blockade of Cuba is not explained. Instructors should underscore that fact and explain that the Cuban reality has changed dramatically since 1980, particularly since the collapse of the Soviet Union.

How to Use: The film is useful in showing the very complex human issues surrounding a revolutionary experience and a massive political exodus. I would use it in conjunction with Christine García's novel *Dreaming in Cuba.* (Martínez-Fernández)

I teach a first-year seminar on the Cuban Revolution. The tape would be perfect for that class. It could also be used in a class on *Revolutionary Movements in Modern Latin America* or *Sociology* classes on *Immigration.* I would use this in conjunction with other materials related to how Cuban exiles have tried to cope with the revolution. I might use *Dreaming in Cuba* or some material on U.S./Cuban relations for context. (Wells)

I plan to use this video in conjunction with the films *55 Hermanos, Lejanía, El super,* and Estela Bravo's 1992 *Miami—Havana* in a unit dealing with the human face of U.S./Cuban relations. (Silcox)

The tape could be used in my course in *Modern Latin American History.* Because of its length, I would probably assign it for out of class viewing. In the subsequent discussion, I would focus on the following questions: How would you characterize the socioeconomic background of the Cuban exile community? What were the divisions that existed within the exile community? What impact did the exiles' return to Cuba have on Cuba as well as on the Cuban exile community in the United States? (Kist)

Suggested Readings: Center for Cuban Studies. "Emerging Voices of Dissent from Jorge mas Canosa's CANF Right-Wing Exile Party Line" in *Cuba Update.*

Didion, Joan. *Miami.*

García, Christine. *Dreaming in Cuba.*

Geyer, Georgie Anne. *Guerrilla Prince: The Untold Story of Fidel Castro.*

Pérez, Louis. *Cuba: Between Reform and Revolution.*

Portes, Alejandro, and Alex Steick. *City on the Edge: The Transformation of Miami.*

Portes, Alejandro and Alex Steik. *Masters of Survival.*

Quirk, Robert E. *Fidel Castro.*

Rieff, David. *The Exile: Cuba in the Heart of Miami.*

Sayles, John. *Los gusanos.*

Szulc, Tad. *Fidel: A Critical Portrait.*

Novels by Reinaldo Arenas

Songs by Silvio Rodríguez and other Cuban singers.

Complementary Films/Videos: *Lejanía* (Cuba); *El super* (U.S.A./Cuba); *Miami-Havana; 55 hermanos*

Level: University

DUEÑO DEL TIEMPO

Documentary.   Without Subtitles.   24 min.   1989

Directed by: Julián Gómez

Produced by: CINED (7th Ave. No 2802 Miramar, Havana; tel: [537] 237-742 or 237-887; fax: 537–331-697)

Distributed by: IMRE Archive

Evaluators: Hugo Chapa-Guzmán, Diane Marting, Danusia L. Meson

Description: This black-and-white film is a portrait of the life and works of Eliseo Diego, one of the most important Cuban poets of this century and a member of the group *Orígenes* and the journal with the same name. Diego reminisces about his childhood and adolesence, and several scenes show old Havana and his childhood home. Diego describes the literary themes that are of importance to him and discusses what it means to be a poet within the context of the urban revolution. He reads several poems including "En la calzada de Jesús del Monte," perhaps his best known work. Cintio Vitier, a famous Cuban critic, and other interviewees discuss Diego's work and intellectual companions.

Strengths and Weaknesses: This is a straightforward, sincere, and interesting film documenting the life and work of Eliseo Diego, an internationally recognized Cuban poet. The scope of the film is useful because it includes his life and work in a cultural as well as a political context. The filmmakers also mention the intellectuals who worked on *Orígenes,* one of the most important literary journals of its time. Audiences have the opportunity to listen to the voice of the poet as he reads, hearing the cadence of the words as Eliseo Diego wished them to be intoned. The language and references are not for beginning Spanish students without good, long subtitles and accompanying materials. But for an advanced class reading Diego's work, the interviews and readings are very good.

The film fails to identify Diego until almost midway into the film, nor does it identify other people interviewed.

Introducing the Tape: Viewers need to be introduced to Eliseo Diego and his importance to Cuban poetry and literature. Diego and all others interviewed or mentioned should be identified (i.e., Cintio Vitier, Lezama Lima, Fina García Marruz) by name, profession and how they contribute to an understanding of Eliseo Diego's work.

Background on Cuban culture and history in the twentieth century would be very helpful.

How to Use: The film would be most appropriate for specialized, university level *Literature* or *Writing* classes. It can be used to contextualize poetry read by students (either before or after the reading). The students could then discuss the relationship between the written word and the discussions of literature heard in the film narrative. (Meson)

I would only use this in a graduate course in which I was teaching Eliseo Diego, and then I would not use this to introduce his work, but rather at the end to summarize what we have studied. (Marting)

Suggested Readings: Books of poetry by Eliseo Diego including: *Divertimientos, En las oscuras manos del olvido, En la calzada de Jesús del Monte, Por los extraños pueblos, Muestrario del mundo: o libro de las maravillas de Boloña, Versiones, Nombrar las cosas, A través de mi espejo, Inventario de asombros, Soñar despierto* (see bibliography).

Bejel, Emilio. *Escribir en Cuba: entrevistas con escritores cubanos 1979–1989.* (A book on Cuban poetry which includes an interview with Eliseo Diego and another with Cintio Vitier).

Bejel, Emilio. "La poesía de Eliseo Diego"

García-Carranza, Araceli. *Bibliografía de Eliseo Diego.*

"Especial: Eliseo cumple setenta y La Gaceta lo felicita."

Fleites, Alex. "Fragmentos de una nueva conversación en la Penumbra."

Matas, Julio. "El espacio ideal de la memoria: la poesía de Eliseo Diego."

Quintero, Aramis. "Las extrañas lindes."

Seinz, Enrique, ed. *Acerca de Eliseo Diego*

Seinz, Enrique. "Eliseo Diego: definición de un poeta."

Seinz, Enrique. "Sitios, cosas, memorias."

Vitier, Cintio. "Recuento y alabanza de Eliseo Diego."

Level: University

EL ESPECTADOR (The Spectator)

Experimental.   No Dialogue.   6 min.   1989
Directed by: Enrique Alvarez
Produced by: TVE (Calle 108 #29E08 entre 29E y 29F, Maríanao, Havana; tel: [537] 209-943)
Distributed by: IMRE
Evaluators: Kate Blanas, Mary Jane Craver, John Higgins, Miguel Huarcaya, Joan A. McGinnis
Description: This is an experimental video in which the spectator and the television spectacle are in confusion. To the music of Gregorian chants, we watch a man watching a television screen, unblinking and unable to tear his eyes away. He is scarcely able to turn off the set before the television character shoots him. He then discovers that he is inside the television set, watched by another viewer, who is also ultimately on the television screen with news in the background. The spectator is spectacle for another spectator, and so on, bringing up the question of who is watching whom.
Strengths and Weaknesses: This is an innovative, well-done piece, with a strong visual message. The sounds, the suspense, and the underlying message are powerful. Viewers will have no problem understanding the film, as there is not a word spoken, except on the television background.

One evaluator felt that the tape is a bit abstract for all but *Art/Film/Video* classes, saying many audiences wouldn't know what to "do" with it. Another commented that the tape tries to show how television violence impresses young minds negatively but uses the same medium and is very suggestive.
Introducing the Tape: Viewers should be told this is an experimental work exploring the impact of television.
How to Use: The tape could be used to spark discussion of how cultural perception is reflected in the media. (Higgins)

This is a useful piece to motivate discussion of the media and "mind control." As another film (*Chile's Forbidden Dreams*) states so well, we "dream what others want us to dream." Viewers become automatons living another's life. The tape would be a good vehicle to present specialized vocabulary in *Spanish* classes. (McGinnis)
Level: University

ESTETICA (Aesthetics)

Documentary/Comedy.   With Subtitles.   11 min.   1984
Directed by: Enrique Colina
Produced by: ICAIC (Calle 23 No. 155 Vedado, Havana; tel: [537] 333-862, fax: [537] 333-032)
Distributed by: Center for Cuban Studies, IMRE
Evaluators: Jules Benjamin, Marlene Gottlieb, Daniel P. Hunt, Rick Langhorst, Angharad N. Valdivia, Margarita de la Vega Hurtado
Description: This humorous tape shows how the Cubans

beautify their lives by ornamenting themselves and their environment. It is an ironic documentary about the definition of taste and aesthetics as applied to everyday life in Cuba. A variety of people recite their notions of beauty, in everything from hairstyles to the home, fashion, houses, and trucks. The examples given are often extravagant, making the film quite entertaining. Businessmen talk about how they decorate their shop windows, brochures, and advertisements to make them appealing. Restaurant owners present examples of "food art." Many people suggest that some goods on the market are so ugly/distasteful that they can't be sold.

Strengths and Weaknesses: This lively, funny documentary is cleverly edited, with a catchy sound track and footage of neobaroque decoration of buses, houses, clothes, etc. Clearly directed to correct "problems" in the social functioning of Cuban society, the film is a good example of an instructional documentary. There are a variety of ethnic groups represented, and a good opportunity to see the "everyday" man and woman on the street in Cuba. One evaluator stated that this film shows that Castro's socialism was far from dreary in the 1970s when this film was made.

Because of its quick pace and jumps from comment to comment, the tape can seem fragmented. The rapid spoken Spanish is quite difficult for nonnative speakers to understand. Also, some of the translations of songs are not accurate. Many signs and billboards that would add to the understanding of the film are not translated.

Introducing the Tape: A brief introduction about the use of the film as social propaganda in Cuba might be in order.

How to Use: For a *Film Studies* class, the tape's useful to show the use of humor, music, and clever editing. For a *Communications* class, I would use it as an example of how to provide information on problems to a wide audience. (de la Vega Hurtado)

This tape is short and interesting enough to present in any *Spanish* class to give a quick view of daily life, culture, speech, and music in Cuba. (Langhorst)

I might show brief cuts of it so that my students could meet the common people of Cuba seeing that "they put their pants on the same as we do." It also could be used in advanced level *Spanish language* classes for the purpose of illustrating the Cuban accent. (Cade)

In a *Spanish Language* course, I would interrupt the film from time to time to discuss signs and comments made by the characters (to review or teach vocabulary). In a *Spanish Conversation* class we might also discuss the central theme of commercial art and how it differs from more traditional or classic art. We might also comment upon the Cuban music which accompanies the film. (Gottlieb)

In *Spanish Conversation and Composition,* the students would view the film, then I would ask them to write an essay in which they compared their own view of decoration with that enjoyed by the Cubans. In *Latin American Literature and Civilization,* I would use the film to show that the neo-

baroque is not simply a literary fashion, but rather permeates all levels of Latin American culture. (Hunt)

Suggested Readings: Stories by Alejo Carpentier (see bibliography for selection).

Novels by Cabrera Infante (see bibliography for selection).

Level: High School—University

EXPORT TV: ANATOMY OF AN ELECTRONIC INVASION

Documentary.   With Subtitles.   27 min.   1990

Directed by: Rafael Andreu and Monica Melamid

Produced by: RAMM (Insurgente Sur 2355, Suite 3, San Angel, México D.F. 01000; tel: [525] 550-8520 or 550-8551; fax: [525] 661-8310)

Distributed by: The Cinema Guild

Evaluators: Elizabeth Mahn, S. Travis Silcox

Description: This documentary explores TV Martí—the broadcasting mechanism created by the U.S. government as a result of the passage of the Television Broadcasting to Cuba Act, which mandates the broadcast of U.S. propaganda to Cuba. Clearly oppositional, this video makes a case for the futility and injustice of this U.S. effort, examining the legal, technical, political, and social aspects of TV Martí. The tape explores Cuban reactions to this affront to sovereignty, including the range of options available for jamming the signal and retaliating against U.S. stations. Finally, it suggests that the result is a potential for increased animosity and expanded conflict.

Strengths and Weaknesses: The tape explains a complicated situation with great clarity, making even the technical aspects understandable. It begins with a consideration of important questions regarding international communications regulation: borders and national sovereignty and the doctrine of free flow of information. It offers a range of views critical of the TV Martí initiative, some of which might be surprising—for example, an official of the U.S. National Association of Braoadcasters and a representative of a Cuban American group.

While the tape is successful in portraying TV Martí as an outrageous, illegal waste of time and money, it does leave the impression of being one-sided. It attempts to demolish the arguments of those who favor such ventures but does so without presenting them. One evaluator commented that the argument could be even stronger with a couple of earnest voices from the Cuban American community asserting the efficacy of, and need for, TV Martí, juxtaposed ironically and effectively with the powerful legal and technical arguments against it. Also, the tape leaves viewers with questions regarding the actual impact of TV Martí.

Introducing the Tape: The tape is self-explanatory and needs no introduction to be understood.

How to Use: "I would use the video as a case study or example of a current international situation of nonarmed aggression. This tape is also useful as an educational video for clubs or events having to do with Cuba. (Silcox)

Level: High School—University

UNA FOTO QUE RECORRE EL MUNDO (A Photo That Goes Around the World)

Documentary. With Subtitles. 13 min. 1981
Directed by: Pedro Chaskel
Produced by: ICAIC (Calle 23 No. 155 Vedado, Havana; tel: [537] 333-862; fax: [537] 333-032)
Distributed by: Center for Cuban Studies, IMRE
Evaluators: Carmen Chávez, Enrique R. Rodríguez, S. Travis Silcox
Description: Photographer Alberto Korda recounts his feeling at the moment he snapped the famous photo of Ernesto "Che" Guevara. "As my finger pressed down on the trigger," Korda recalls, "I sensed that I had just captured an important historic moment." This memorable image took on a life of its own. As the portrait of Che to be remembered and revered, the photo circulated internationally and was used as a symbol of inspiration by the Left. This documentary is a fast-paced collage of images following this photo as it was used to represent liberation and human rights struggles in demonstrations worldwide.
Strengths and Weaknesses: This inspiring and powerful film deals with an inherently interesting story idea. It is also thought-provoking regarding the uses of representation. The music by Nacha Guevara, "Yo te nombro," is very effective, and the editing extremely well crafted. The tape's short length makes it ideal for classroom use.

One evaluator felt the interviews included are not as effective, as their length is disproportionate to the quickly edited collage segments.
Introducing the Tape: The video assumes knowledge of the life and death of Che Guevara. U.S. viewers need background on Che and his role as revolutionary hero, which inspired revolutionary movements worldwide. Prior to viewing, students should have studied the history of liberation movements in the Western hemisphere since Simón Bolívar; the Cuban Revolution, and its effects on the Western hemisphere, especially in Latin America.
How to Use: I would show the documentary and then study how the images influence the viewer. It is useful to illustrate how the idea of a "revolutionary hero" is threatening to the "status quo." We would describe and define "revolutionary hero." (Chávez)

The film would highlight the impact Che had, and has, on liberation struggles worldwide. I would use it to introduce students to one of Latin America's most important leaders since Simón Bolívar. In teaching a *Language Arts* course, I would use it to study Che's impact in Latin America. The lyrics to the song that accompanies this film could also be studied. (Rodríguez)

In any type of course dealing with cultural production, this video could be used to generate thought-provoking discussion of the use and appropriation of symbols within movements. The question that is unasked and unanswered in the video is: what does "Che" represent and how do people with different cultures and agendas use the image? (Silcox)
Level: University

GALLEGO (Gallego)

Feature. With Subtitles. 12 min. 1987
Directed by: Manuel Octavio Gómez
Produced by: ICAIC (Calle 23 No. 155 Vedado, Havana; tel: [537] 333-862; fax: [537] 333-032)
Distributed by: Center for Cuban Studies, IMRE Archive,
Evaluators: David Bushnell, Nancy Levy-Konesky, Christine List, Kathleen March, Eliana Moya-Raggio, Gerardo Piña
Description: Based on the novel by Cuban author Miguel Barnet, this film is the story of a Galician boy forced to emigrate to Las Indias America (Cuba) for employment. The boy sincerely wants to succeed through hard work but is consistently disappointed. He remains optimistic and true to his friends and ideals. The film explores the financial and personal problems he faces living in Cuba as the years pass. The boy remains a stranger in his new land—Spain is in his blood. The personal story of the protagonist takes place against a backdrop of politics and corruption in Cuba between the 1930s and the 1960s. We follow the boy's point of view as an immigrant and his disinterested view of the political happenings. The story covers almost fifty years of Cuban history and provides an excellent view of the relationship of this poor Spanish immigrant to revolutionary change.
Strengths and Weaknesses: This is an exceptional film—a great character study and view of history and its effects on the individual. It is poignant, sensitive, accurate, and entertaining, without losing sight of the underlying tragic reality. Although fiction, the film is symbolic of the experiences of many Galician emigrants, and the events depicted are completely plausible. The Galicians and Cubans are portrayed realistically; the film does a great job of explaining the political conservatism of immigrants, while also showing the protagonist's ability to adopt a more progressive viewpoint through identification with his Cuban daughters. The film covers a broad sweep of Cuban history from a critical but not overtly polemical perspective. There are good views of old Havana.

The film is too long to show in most single-class sessions. Also, Cuban Spanish is often difficult for the nonnative Spanish speaker to understand. One evaluator felt the characters' motivations and actions are not quite developed enough.
Introducing the Tape: Some background on what Galicia is—the language, culture, national identity, and economic situation—would improve U.S. viewers' understanding greatly. Also, the film presumes a basic knowledge of Cuban history, thus viewers may need some background on Cuba in the 1930s to 1960s as well as during the Spanish Civil War.
How to Use: I would use *Gallego* for *Spanish Civilization* classes to exemplify the historical situation of Galicia and

provide explanations of the context of both Cuba and Spain, so that it is clear the film has many documentary elements and is not just an individual fictional representation. (March)

The film could be used in a *Film Studies* course, to illustrate point of view (since the protagonist is only able to be involved in revolutionary movements in Spain). History is filtered through his own national consciousness, obscuring his understanding of the Cuban struggle. I would also use this film to discuss filmmaking approaches to history. (List)

I would provide a brief explanation with a condensed background of the history between Cuba and Spain and have the students read the novel by Barnet. We would discuss the differences between the novel and film. (Piña)

I would use the tape in my course on *Twentieth-Century Latin America,* in the section on prerevolutionary Cuba—emphasizing that the presentation of modern Spanish immigration would also be applicable to Argentina and other countries. I would probably fast-forward through the Spanish Civil War to fit it into two fifty-minute class periods. (Bushnell)

Suggested Readings: Barnet, Miguel. *Gallego.*

Chanan, Michael. *The Cuban Image: Cinema and Cultural Politics in Cuba.*

Level: University

GREGORIO Y EL MAR (Gregorio and the Sea)

Documentary.   With Subtitles.   27 min.   1989

Directed by: Mady Samper

Produced by: Tropical Media and TV Latina (Carrera 1 #72–41 (Apto. 104), Bogotá; tel: [571] 255-0645)

Distributed by: Filmmakers Library

Evaluators: Elba D. Birmingham-Pokorny, Joan A. McGinnis, Daniel C. Scroggins

Description: This film offers the viewer a rare glimpse of the life and experiences of Gregorio Fuentes, the character who served as inspiration for Ernest Hemingway's novel *The Old Man and the Sea.* It is an exquisitely shot, lyrical evocation by the ninety-year-old Fuentes, who was a fishing companion and friend to Hemingway during his twenty-year stay in Cuba. The film combines brilliantly colored scenes of the Cuban waterfront with black-and-white newsreel footage and still photographs in a montage reflecting the structure of an old man's recollections. An imaginative soundtrack consisting of Gregorio's on-camera and off-camera narrative, selections from Norberto Fuentes's book *Hemingway en Cuba,* and well-chosen musical selections add to the film's beauty.

Strengths and Weaknesses: In every sense, the film is an artistic gem, a worthy tribute to Hemingway, a piece of cinematic poetry. Its strongest points are the many views of the island, as well as the warm and colorful personality of Gregorio and his friends. The off-camera reading of selections from *Hemingway en Cuba* are very well done.

The mixture of fantasy versus reality is confusing at times. Also, the references to Hemingway and his literature need to be more explicit. For language students, the poor articulation of the aged Gregorio will be a problem. Too frequently he speaks from off camera, and his speech is so indistinct that only the most advanced students will be able to follow the Spanish. Yet, evaluators agreed that the film is so well done that it could be used in an advanced conversation class as a point of departure, in spite of Gregorio's unclear articulation.

Introducing the Tape: A very brief introduction about Hemingway in Cuba would be helpful. Presenters should explain that he was proficient in Spanish. A geographical, historical, and literary background would help students gain more from this film. A vocabulary list would be useful for a *Spanish Language* class.

How to Use: Reading *The Old Man and the Sea* (in either Spanish or English) in conjunction with seeing this tape would be helpful. Students could then write essays on "solitude." (McGinnis)

I would use this film to help students gain an insight into Cuban culture, as well as to test students' understanding of spoken Spanish. (Birmingham-Pokorny)

Suggested Readings: Fuentes, Norberto. *Hemingway en Cuba.*

Hemingway, Ernest. *The Old Man and the Sea.*

Level: High School—University

HANDS OFF CUBA, TV TEACH-IN I & II

Docudrama.   With Subtitles.   60 min.   1992

Directed by: Cathy Scott and José Martínez

Produced by: Deep Dish (339 Lafayette Street, New York, NY 10012; tel: [212] 473-8933; fax: [212] 420-8223)

Distributed by: Deep Dish, IMRE Archive

Evaluators: George D. Beelen, Susana Conde, Virginia Shen

Description: Through a series of interviews with well-known Cuban authors, lawyers, activists, and people in the street, this tape makes a strong argument for the end of the U.S. economic embargo against Cuba. Since the Soviet Union withdrew its aid, the welfare of the country has been threatened on several fronts. Among the challenges that Cuba faces is a 40 percent decrease of oil shipments and inadequate quantities of medical supplies. Fewer than 5 percent of existing sugar mills are currently operative. Thousands of government employees have been laid off, and electricity is turned off for hours every day. To confront these problems, Cubans have formed farm collectives, where people from the city travel to the country to help with the planting and harvest; city neighborhoods have organized community gardens; and a new and burgeoning bicycle industry has developed as the bicycle has become the most popular and effective way of dealing with the gas shortage. The video comments on the efforts of numerous associations in the U.S. working for Cuba's sociopolitical autonomy. It encourages opposition to the U.S. Congress's Cuban Democracy Act, the Mack amendment, and the Guarini bill, measures that will tighten the blockade and further limit trade with Cuba. On the other hand, the program encourages support for Congress's Weiss bill, which would exempt food and medical goods from the embargo, and the Berman bill, which would allow U.S. citizens to travel to Cuba.

Strengths and Weaknesses: The film does an excellent job presenting the theme of a call for Cuba's autonomy from the U.S. The arguments among Cuban teenagers about their country's economy are very effective and convincing. The openness of the journalist who states the case for more freedom of expression in Cuba is welcome, as is the explanation that opposition to the embargo has differing and even conflicting motivations. The film makes excellent use of music. Each section of the film lasts thirty minutes, which is an ideal length for classroom instruction and discussion.

Introducing the Tape: Audiences should know, however succinctly, the history of Cuba. The teacher or presenter of this film should emphasize the political situation in Cuba in the twentieth century, its role in the 1960s and 1970s as a model for liberation against U.S. hegemony in other Latin American countries, and the pivotal events that explain Cuba's current economic predicament. The film is clearly pro-Castro and against U.S. imperialism and would need to be discussed within that context.

How to Use: In the advanced *Spanish Language* course that I teach, I would complement the study of Latin American culture, politics, and ideology by introducing a brief outline of Cuban history and then presenting the film as a contrast to the common fare that students are likely to receive from the U.S. news media. (Conde)

I could use the tape to discuss the results of the Cuban Revolution from the point of view of Cubans who believe in Castro. (Beleen)

In *Communication* classes, the clearly Cuban point of view of the tape can be contrasted to U.S. news reports about Cuba.

Suggested Readings: Benjamin, Medea. *No Free Lunch: Food and Revolution in Cuba Today*

Black, Jan Knippers, ed. *Latin America: Its Problems and Its Promise.*

Castro, Fidel. *The World Economic and Social Crisis.*

Galeano, Eduardo. *Open Veins of Latin America: Five Centuries of the Pillage of a Continent.*

Green, Duncan. *Faces of Latin America.*

Skidmore, Thomas E., and Peter H. Smith. *Modern Latin America.*

Smith, Wayne. *The Closest of Enemies: A Personal and Diplomatic History of U.S.–Cuban Relations since 1957.*

Level: High School—University

HASTA CIERTO PUNTO (Up to a Point)
Feature. With Subtitles. 75 min. 1983
Directed by: Tomás Gutiérrez Alea
Produced by: ICAIC (Calle 23 No. 155 Vedado, Havana; tel: [537] 333-862; fax: [537] 333-032)

Distributed by: Center for Cuban Studies, IMRE Archive, New Yorker Films
Evaluators: Gerard Aching, Carol Becker, Susana Conde, David William Foster, Nancy Levy-Konesky, Alicia Ramos
Description: In *Hasta cierto punto,* a filmmaker named Oscar plans to explore the subject of machismo. He and his crew choose the port of Havana, where they believe they will find a greater level of machismo among the workers, however enlightened they may be in their revolutionary awareness. Oscar's own machismo is put to the test when he falls in love with the woman on whom he bases his protagonist. He and the attractive worker Lina start a romantic relationship that jeopardizes Oscar's marriage. Disagreements among the crew, Oscar, and the film's director prompt the abandonment of the project. Lina finally leaves Oscar, quits her job, and decides to start anew in Santiago. This film is a direct descendant of other Cuban revolutionary films—*De cierta manera, El otro Francisco, Memorias del subdesarrollo,* and sections of *Lucía*—and chronicles the director's search for different "reading" levels in a film, already theorized by Gutiérrez Alea in his essay *The Viewer's Dialectic.*
Strengths and Weaknesses: Evaluators' reaction to this film was quite mixed. Some thought quite highly of it, finding the exploration of more subtle machista attitudes and behaviors and women's responses particularly engaging. Cuban culture is reflected throughout the film, and these reviewers were impressed by the cultural self-questioning. The acting performances were also well received. The film intersperses the use of documentary and fictional plot development with measured success. This strategy, by now, is the signature of Cuban revolutionary film, markedly distinct from Hollywood cinema.

A few evaluators found the film a failed but somewhat interesting attempt by Marxist discourse to incorporate feminism through a love story. They felt that the film was ultimately predictable and boring.

Introducing the Tape: U.S. viewers would benefit from some historical and cultural background of the region. Information on what programs have existed in Cuba to provide equal rights for women, and how women have (or have not) moved into positions of social and political power should be discussed.

How to Use: I would be particularly interested in analyzing with my students the representation of women in this film, the relationship of husbands and wives, extramarital relations, the developing love relationship between Oscar and Lina, the issue of machismo and feminism, and the intervention of class differences in dealing with the subject of machismo. This film is interesting in its technique, which is quite different from the seamless Hollywood continuity editing. Technique and theme are consistent, however, the apparent imperfection in the telling reflects the ideological basis on which it rests. (Conde)

I would probably use some snippets in a larger and more culturally productive contexts, whether literary or film based, dealing with personal rights in Cuba. I would also be interested in contrasting the consciousness over women's rights with the dreadful record of the Castro government in the area of gay/lesbian rights. (Foster)

The film would be useful in a *Cuba* seminar to show various degrees of machismo and feminine response. (Levy-Konesky)

Suggested Readings: Black, Jan Knippers ed. *Latin America: Its Problems and Its Promise.*

Chanan, Michael. *The Cuban Image: Cinema and Cultural Politics in Cuba.*

Green, Duncan. *Faces of Latin America.*

Gutiérrez Alea, Tomás. "The Viewer's Dialectic," in *Reviewing Histories: Selections from New Latin American Cinema.* Edited by Coco Fusco.

King, John. *Magical Reels: A History of Cinemas in Latin America.*

Skidmore, Thomas E., and Peter H. Smith. *Modern Latin America.*

Complementary Films/Videos: *De cierta manera (One Way or Another)* (Cuba); *El otro Francisco (The Other Francisco)* (Cuba); *Memorias del subdesarrollo (Memories of Underdevelopment)* (Cuba); *Lucía* (Cuba)

Level: University

HASTA LA REINA ISABEL BAILA EL DANZÓN
(Even Queen Isabel Dances the Danzón)

Documentary.   With Subtitles.   20 min.   1991

Directed by: Luis Felipe Bernaza

Produced by: ICAIC (Calle 23 No. 155 Vedado, Havana; tel: [537] 333-862; fax: [537] 333-032)

Distributed by: Center for Cuban Studies, IMRE

Evaluators: Elba D. Birmingham-Pokorny, Donald W. Davey, Marlene Gottlieb, Susan Griswold, Roger A. Sánchez-Berroa, S. Travis Silcox

Description: This documentary/comedy examines the mixture of Hispanic customs and traditions with the African culture that permeates every aspect of Cuban life. It follows a spiritist, Marta González, who is visited from time to time by the spirit of Queen Isabel of Spain. The filmmaker attempts to speak with Queen Isabel through the spiritualist medium, to ask her the questions of the Cuban people. Many people in the street are questioned to gain insight into their personal impressions of the historical role the queen played in conquering the New World. They are asked, "Do you believe in spirits? What would you ask Isabella if you had the chance?" People offer many questions—what would the queen do about Cuba's transportation problems, pollution, the hole in the ozone layer? The film looks at the belief in the supernatural within the context of a socialist revolution. It is a self-reflective satire of Cuban and Afro-Cuban popular beliefs and of how Cubans appear to turn everything into dance. There are many scenes of Yoruba ceremonies, a recitation of Nicolás Guillén's famous poem "Sensemaya," and excellent scenes of Galician dances on the streets of Havana (often performed by mulatto men and women).

Strengths and Weaknesses: This is a charming short, with clear visual images, excellent scenes of old Havana, and a diversity of people interviewed. Strong points include wonderful music and dance scenes, humorous interview comments, and very comprehensible and linguistically interesting Spanish. The filmmaker takes advantage of the then upcoming quincentennial to explore the multicultural and multiethnic diversity of the Cuban culture, as well as the opposing views of the event. The film is an excellent example of how documentaries can incorporate other genres.

One evaluator felt the film presents things so convincingly that students might believe it is more serious than it really is. Another felt that much of the inside humor (for example, use of famous Cubans in the on-the-street interviews or references to contemporary Cuban problems) would be lost on U.S audiences. The film presupposes a certain level of knowledge about Santería and the problems facing contemporary Cuba. The Cuban Spanish can be difficult for language students.

Introducing the Tape: It should be pointed out that the film is tongue-in-cheek. It might be important to explain a little about the history of Cuba, Queen Isabel's historical role, the problems in contemporary Cuba, the Yoruba/Santería influence and spiritism.

How to Use: In *Language* classes, I would prepare an introduction and some vocabulary before showing the film a couple of times. Then, there would be discussion, questions and answers, and opinions. (Sánchez-Berroa)

I would use this film to illustrate the richness and diversity of the Cuban culture, and to make students aware of the diverse ways the quincentennary was perceived by the Cuban people and by most people throughout Latin America. (Birmingham-Pokorny)

In a *Latin American Culture* course, the film is useful to illustrate syncretism and African heritage in the Caribbean. It is also good for a *Film* course as an example of a very successful short which mixes genres and uses comedy to make serious points. (Griswold)

I would show the film to my *Spanish* majors and discuss the conflict and confluence of Hispanic and African cultures in Cuba and other Caribbean countries. We might examine the language of the film (the Cuban colloquialism, pronunciation, etc.) and study the Guillén poem in its relation to the film's basic theme. I would also discuss the so-called "Black Legend" of the conquest and how it is treated in the film. (Gottlieb)

Suggested Readings: Cabrera Infante, Guillermo. *Three Trapped Tigers.*

Hartell, Joanna—interviewed Director Luis Felipe Bernaza in *Cine Acción.* The article focused in part on this film.

Critical studies of Afro-Cuban Literature.

Poetry by Emilio Ballagas, Nicolás Guillén; Stories by Lydia Cabrera (see bibliography for selection).
Level: University

HEREDIA
Documentary.   Without Subtitles.   23 min.   1990
Directed by: Jorge L. Chagoyen Lucas
Produced by: CINED (7th Ave. No 2802 Miramar, Havana; tel: [537] 237-742 or 237-887; fax: 537–331-697)
Distributed by: IMRE Archive
Evaluators: Melvin S. Arrington Jr., Hugo Chapa-Guzmán, Marlene Gottlieb
Description: This black-and-white documentary honors the life and writings of poet José María Heredia. Heredia is highly regarded as one of the first romantic poets of Latin America. The film commemorates the 150th anniversary of Heredia's death, and includes interviews, re-creations of scenes from the poet's life, and selected readings from his best-known works. It touches on aspects of the Cuban *independista* movement and Heredia's participation, with some interviews made with Salvador Arias. Also interviewed is Heredia's great-granddaughter. Against backdrop scenery of Cuba and Niagara Falls, the tape is a noncritical presentation of a revered national figure.
Strengths and Weaknesses: This is an interesting introduction to the life and work of the poet. It does a good job of surveying Heredia's life and work, emphasizing the salient points of his poetry and placing it in historical context.

While one evaluator felt the photography is good and romantic, others found it neither original nor stimulating. One mentioned that the commentary is dull at times and the critical assessment of Heredia's poetry somewhat inflated. More contextual information is needed.
Introducing the Tape: A short biography of Heredia is necessary for viewers to benefit from the tape.
How to Use: The tape could be used as an introduction to nineteenth-century Spanish American romanticism, or in a course which included any readings on Heredia. (Chapa-Guzmán)

I would use this video as a supplement to class discussion of Heredia's life and poetry. Students would follow a printed text of the poetry as they hear it on the video. (Arrington)

I probably would ask students to view the tape on their own in the library, since it really doesn't require any specific commentary on the part of the instructor. It is a good introduction to a poet before studying his work in depth. In a survey course, the tape might be assigned in lieu of a lecture on the poet. (Gottlieb)
Suggested Readings: Chacón y Calvo, José María. *Estudios heredianos.*

Cipriano de Utrera, Fray. *Heredia.*

Díaz, Lomberto. *Heredia, primer romántico Hispanoamericano.*

Esténger, Rafael. *Heredia: La incomprension de si mismo.*
Gobierno del Estado de Mexico. *José María Heredia.*

Heredia, José María—poems including "En el Teocalli de Cholula."; "Niagara."; "Himno del desterrado."; "A Cuba" (see bibliography for selected works).
Level: University

HOLA HEMINGWAY (Hello Hemingway)
Feature.   With Subtitles.   105 min.   1984
Directed by: Manuel Pérez
Produced by: ICAIC (Calle 23 No. 155 Vedado, Havana; tel: [537] 333-862; fax: [537] 333-032)
Distributed by: Center for Cuban Studies, IMRE Archive
Evaluators: Carmen Chávez, Susan Griswold, Joan A. McGinnis
Description: Taking place in prerevolutionary Cuba, this is the love story of Larita and Víctor, a poor Cuban couple interested in the advancement of their society. Larita works for her intellectual advancement, while Víctor works toward forming a student political association. Larita is introduced to the *Old Man and the Sea* by Hemingway, which serves as a powerful motivating force for her. Her success in school places her in a competition to win a scholarship to study in the U.S. The dream Larita cherishes of extricating herself via education from her impoverished and powerless life in prerevolutionary Cuba seems nearly within her grasp. Larita also risks losing Víctor and her family. The film depicts her loss of innocence and intellectual empowerment as she comes to understand why and how her dream is impossible and, indeed, the wrong dream.
Strengths and Weaknesses: A fine film—well crafted, coherent, moving, and very accessible for U.S. audiences. It provides important glimpses into family life in the era of Batista and employs powerful symbolism.

There are a number of translation errors in the subtitles that might make the film a bit difficult for nonnative speakers to understand.
Introducing the Tape: A brief introduction to Hemingway's biography, particularly his time in Cuba, would be useful.
How to Use: I would have students read excerpts of *The Old Man and the Sea* in Spanish. We should discuss the aspirations of young people and how they would handle frustrations. An important aspect is the sacrifices of Larita's family, especially of her grandmother and mother. For the male point of view, we would examine how a man would feel being the only male among five females. Vocabulary and questions would be provided and elicited from students or cooperative groups. (McGinnis)

I would use this tape to show the conflicting roles women have in Hispanic society. Also, to illustrate that the economic support that women provide in the family, by sewing, cooking for others, etc., is often overlooked. This video shows the importance placed on education by the young in Cuba, and explains how the youth came together to form student organizations to put pressure on the Batista government. I would also use this video to show how Cuban culture influenced Hemingway. (Chávez)

The film could be used in a study of *Literature and Film, Cuban Revolutionary Film* and the role of *Women in Hispanic Cultures* (as well as the depiction of women in *Hispanic Film*). (Griswold)

Suggested Readings: Hemingway, Ernest. *The Old Man and the Sea*.

Readings on Hemingway, Cuba, the Batista era, etc.

Complementary Films/Videos: *Gregorio y el mar (Gregory and the Sea)* (Cuba)

Level: High School—University

UN HOMBRE DE EXITO (A Successful Man)

Feature.   With Subtitles.   109 min.   1987

Directed by: Humberto Solás

Produced by: ICAIC (Calle 23 No. 155 Vedado, Havana; tel: [537] 333-862; fax: [537] 333-032)

Distributed by: Center for Cuban Studies, IMRE Archive,

Evaluators: Fortuna Calvo-Roth, Luis Martínez-Fernández, José-Manuel Navarro, Carlos Pérez, Currie Kerr Thompson

Description: This is the story of two upper-class brothers, Javier and Darío, who participate in the struggle to overthrow Machado during his dictatorship in the 1930s. Darío is a revolutionary true to his ideals, while Javier is a social climber and opportunist. Javier charts his way to the top through alliances with dictators and politicians, becoming a government informer and eventually a congressman during the Batista regime. He causes his brother's murder and his mother's subsequent suicide. The film traces twentieth-century Cuban history until 1959 through the life of Javier, exploring the trajectory of a political and economic class that benefited from Cuba's neocolonial relationship with the U.S. With the revolution, this class would lose their privileged position as the masses became the foundation of the new society. Leading themes in the film include the accommodation of the Cuban elite and the Catholic Church to the dictatorial governments in Cuba before 1959 and the achievement of success through betrayal. The film points out the U.S. influence on Cuban internal politics, as well as the corruption that was part of the system.

Strengths and Weaknesses: This film gives a very good account of some of the major events that led to the Cuban Revolution. The narrative is easy to follow, once the viewer situates the characters in their proper context. The cinematography and acting are professionally done. The film's full spirit is complemented by a successful blend of the music popular during each of the decades chartered by the film, from 1932 to 1959.

Some evaluators felt that the script is overly ambitious, attempting to cover too extensive a period of Cuban history, with too many characters for audiences to keep track of. This weakens the focus on the psychological contrast between commitment and opportunism. One evaluator found the ending of the film a bit confusing.

Introducing the Tape: The film presupposes knowledge of Cuban history. Students should be introduced to the events (1924–59) both national and international, in order to have an understanding of the context of the various years that the narrative covers. Developments leading to the Machado dictatorship should be examined. The theme that should be developed is the behavior of the political and economic elites during this period and their lack of scruples as they used every opportunity for self-aggrandizement. The role of the U.S. in contributing to this state of affairs must also be examined.

How to Use: After studying the period 1924–59 I would show this tape and discuss it. I would emphasize the role of social class as being one of the determinant factors in the political and social choices that one makes. We would further explore how one should have a sense of social responsibility when making individual choices. We would explore these issues by contrasting Javier and Darío and exploring their ideology and choices. After this, I would have the students write a five- to seven-page paper on how the film reflects social reality before the revolution. (Pérez)

This film could be used in conjunction with Luis E. Aguilar's *Cuba 1933* to illustrate the connections between the "revolution" of 1933 and Castro's revolution. The film would make a good introduction to the topic of the Cuban revolution. (Martínez-Fernández)

Suggested Readings: Aguilar, Luis. *Cuba, 1933: Prologue to Revolution*.

Farber, Samuel. *Revolution and Reaction in Cuba, 1933–1960: A Political Sociology from Machado to Castro*.

Pérez, Louis A. Jr. *Cuba: Between Reform and Revolution*.

Pérez, Louis A. Jr. *Cuba under the Platt Amendment*.

Wood, Dennis B. "The Long Revolution: Class Relations and Political Conflict in Cuba, 1868–1968."

Level: High School—University

EL HOMBRE DE MAISINICU (The Man from Maisinicu)

Feature.   With Subtitles.   12 min.   1973

Directed by: Manuel Pérez

Produced by: ICAIC (Calle 23 No. 155 Vedado, Havana; tel: [537] 333-862; fax: [537] 333-032)

Distributed by: Center for Cuban Studies, The Cinema Guild

Evaluators: Fortuna Calvo-Roth, Marvin D'Lugo, Paul J. LaReau

Description: This film is based on a true story. In 1963–64, following the failed Bay of Pigs invasion, Alberto Delgado, a secret agent for the Cuban security forces, manages to infiltrate a band of counterrevolutionaries that is involved in terrorist activities in Cuba. After nearly fourteen months of successfully working as an undercover agent, Delgado's real identity is discovered by the counterrevolutionaries. He is tortured and murdered. The government forces then pursue each of the principals in the counterrevolutionary group.

Strengths and Weaknesses: With an interesting plot, the narrative gives an uncommon view of some of the counterrevolutionary activities in Cuba during the first decade of the new regime. Some of the action sequences are especially well photographed.

Evaluators found the distinctions between rebel revolutionary forces and counterrevolutionary forces confusing at times. The use of multiple narratives and flash-forwards makes it difficult to follow. Delgado's real identity as a counteragent, while suggested throughout, is divulged only at the very end. A couple of reviewers felt that the basic thrust of the film is overtly propagandistic, similar in tone and style to certain Cold War, anticommunist works of the 1950s in the U.S. (e.g., *I Led Three Lives*).

Introducing the Tape: The significance of the historical period in question needs to be well established in order for the U.S. audience to appreciate the political significance of the story. Background about the Cuban Revolution, the work of the Committees for the Defense of the Revolution, and the terms associated with those for and against the revolution need to be explained (e.g., "bandits" and "banditry" refer to subversives and counterrevolutionaries, and G2 is the Cuban equivalent of the KGB or CIA).

How to Use:. This tape would supplement courses dealing with revolutions in Latin American and the Cuban Revolution in particular. (LaReau)

In *Communications* classes, the film could be compared/contrasted to U.S. spy films from the Cold War era.

Level: University

IGNACIO PIÑEIRO

Documentary.   Without Subtitles.   20 min.   1977
Directed by: Luis Felipe Bernaza
Produced by: ICAIC (Calle 23 No. 155 Vedado, Havana; tel: [537] 333-862; fax: [537] 333-032)
Distributed by: Center for Cuban Studies, IMRE
Evaluators: Rebeca Harclerode, Grace Leavitt
Description: On the fiftieth anniversary of the musical group Septeto Nacional with Ignacio Piñeiro, this film takes a look at Cuban music since 1925 and the development of the popular Cuban dances—particularly *la rumba* and *el son*. The tape explains how this group was responsible for creating a fusion of culturally acceptable "salon" music and *rumba*. Various members of the Septeto Nacional talk about Ignacio Piñeiro's influence on Cuban music. There are many songs interspersed with scenes from old films and current (1970s) scenes and conversations with Piñeiro's contemporaries.
Strengths and Weaknesses: The footage and the information are of particular interest as they are not commonly available to U.S. audiences. The musical numbers mesh very well with the narrative.

The narrative jumps around and is very anecdotal. The clips of people dancing date the film (1970s), which is a drawback only with adolescent viewers.
Introducing the Tape: A glossary pertaining to the types of dances and other terms would make a good accompaniment, as most U.S. audiences would not be familiar with some of this vocabulary.

How to Use: The tape would be useful as part of a unit on *Music of the Caribbean,* or *Latin American Music and Dance.* (Leavitt)
Suggested Readings: Hijuelos, Oscar. *The Mambo Kings Play Songs of Love.*
Level: Junior High School—University

LA INFATIGABLE SANTIAGO

Documentary.   Without Subtitles.   27 min.   1984
Directed by: Luis Felipe Bernaza
Produced by: ICAIC (Calle 23 No. 155 Vedado, Havana; tel: [537] 333-862; fax: [537] 333-032)
Distributed by: Center for Cuban Studies, IMRE
Evaluators: Reed Anderson, Silvia Arrom, David J. Robinson, Lynn M. Shirey
Description: This is a patriotic portrait of the city of Santiago de Cuba, renowned for the solidarity of its citizens, especially during the Cuban Revolution. Older townspeople share memories of the time, remembering sons who were killed and people who opened their doors to escaping revolutionaries. The tape glorifies the popular struggle of the 1950s insurgency against Batista in Santiago and includes archival film footage and photographic records.
Strengths and Weaknesses: Unique perspectives on the city are provided by personal, seemingly spontaneous narratives by people who experienced Cuba before, during, and after the revolution. These narratives are accompanied by a more or less official history of the city. The tape is very well edited, humorous, and entertaining (with good music).

One evaluator felt that some of the stories told by the people are interesting, but in general the film is amateurish and might be too detailed for a non-Cuban audience. The Spanish is colloquial and thus not easy to understand. Photos are not captioned, and very few of the people interviewed are clearly identified. The film's appeal would be limited to students of twentieth-century Cuba, popular resistance against Batista, or of the city of Santiago.
Introducing the Tape: All historical figures and speakers need to be identified, especially the famous people unknown to U.S. viewers.
How to Use: The tape could be used to reflect the revolutionary impact of Fidel Castro, et al., on the evolution of Cuban society, exemplified in the case of Santiago de Cuba. (Robinson)

I might use clips of the film, a few interviews, to show how widespread popular support was for the revolutionaries. (Arrom)
Suggested Readings: McManus, Jane, ed. *From the Palm Tree: Voices of the Cuban Revolution.*
Level: University

IRE A SANTIAGO

Documentary.   Without Subtitles.   14 min.   1964
Directed by: Sara Gómez

Produced by: ICAIC (Calle 23 No. 155 Vedado, Havana; tel: [537] 333-862; fax: [537] 333-032)

Distributed by: Center for Cuban Studies, The Cinema Guild, IMRE

Evaluators: Elba D. Birmingham-Pokorny, David Bushnell, Hugo Chapa-Guzmán, Marilyn Jímenez, Diane Marting, José-Manuel Navarro

Description: This black-and-white piece is a gentle, loving portrait of Santiago de Cuba and its people. It provides a view of Cuba as a picturesque country—a product of an earthy mix of black and criollo people. The film meanders through the history of the port of Santiago de Cuba, with historical clips showing the end of the eighteenth century when Haitian slave owners fled with their slaves to Cuba after the Haitian revolution. The film takes a tour of the city and ends with a few "must see" places. Included are Cuban dance, music, food, architecture, and Carnival. The personal quality of the film is so intense that viewers can feel the heat of the Santiago streets and the *calor* of the people.

Strengths and Weaknesses: This entertaining, short piece is touristy but not preachy, with nice photography, music, and images of difficult-to-find urban culture. The filmmaker captures not only the history but also the spirit of the people of Santiago. It is a good introduction to Cuba's social life, customs, and popular music and provides an opportunity to view a city that retains more of its early architecture than Havana. One evaluator felt the tape's style of shooting, editing, and informal voice-over commentary make it perhaps the most striking "free cinema" documentary ever produced in Cuba.

A few evaluators mentioned that the tape is "too happy," with everyone constantly smiling. It does not comment on the political situation. One reviewer remarked that the tape is too short and disorganized to make a substantial point and that the narrator's ironic tone undermines the film.

Introducing the Tape: This video sets out to prove the importance of Santiago in Cuba's history, but this intention would be lost without knowing the context. Viewers need to be given information about the history of Havana's domination of the rest of the country.

How to Use: I could use the tape in conjunction with a contemporary novel that dissects the nostalgia for this "lost" Cuba, or an introductory course on *Cuba* or *Latin American Culture* where I talked about the Boom, a marketing phenomenon in literature. (Marting)

The tape could be used together with Carpentier's *The Kingdom of this World,* because it illustrates the legacy of the Haitian Revolution. It might be useful as well as a short glimpse of the development of Caribbean cities. (Jiménez)

It could be used as a warm-up to any particular topic which I need to stress, ethnic relations or Afro-American music. (Chapa-Guzmán)

Suggested Readings: Carpentier, Alejo. *El reino de este mundo.*

Casal, Lourdes. *Revolution and Race: Blacks in Contemporary Cuba.*

Entralgo, Elias José. *La liberación étnica cubana.*

Fuerzas Armadas Revolucionarias, Dirección Política, Sección de historia. *Historia de Cuba.*

Guerra Ramiro y Sanchez, et al. *Historia de la nación Cubana.*

Manuel, Peter, ed. *Essays on Cuban Music: North American and Cuban Perspectives.*

Sarduy, Severo. *De dónde son los cantantes?*

Poems by Nicolás Guillén (see bibliography).

Level: University

UNA ISLA PARA MIGUEL

Documentary.   Without Subtitles.   20 min.   1968

Directed by: Sara Gómez

Produced by: ICAIC (Calle 23 No. 155 Vedado, Havana; tel: [537] 333-862; fax: [537] 333-032)

Distributed by: Center for Cuban Studies, IMRE

Evaluators: David Bushnell, Darién J. Davis, José-Manuel Navarro, Enrique R. Rodríguez, Susan Ryan, S. Travis Silcox

Description: This black-and-white tape looks at the life of young Cuban boys at a correctional institution—a revolutionary tool for the integration of many marginalized and delinquent youths in Cuba. The Isle of Pines (Isla de los Pinos), later renamed the Isle of Youth (Isla de la Juventud), serves as a penitentiary/reform school for delinquent boys (ages 13–17) who are not guilty of serious crimes. The school attempts to inculcate a sense of pride and community in this sector of the population, which was ignored by the prerevolutionary regimes. The tape presents scenes of activity at the work/training camp and interviews with school administrators and boys to give the social context for why they are there and what the revolution is doing to help them. Through the case study of Miguel, the tape documents the counselors' and community members' process of assessing and approaching problems. Miguel is eventually able to solve his own problems and conforms.

Strengths and Weaknesses: This is a fine film by an important filmmaker, Sara Gómez, to whose work U.S. viewers have little access. It shows an aspect of Cuban society rarely seen in the U.S. and is effective for comparative studies about how problems such as delinquency are assessed and solved in Cuba and the U.S. The film shows the Cuban practice of having young adults who are accused of infractions judged and sentenced by their peers, presenting an alternative to the criminal justice system to which U.S. viewers are accustomed. The tape shows the sense of hope and revolutionary zeal on the part of many adults and young people from the very beginning of the Cuban Revolution. It is a good example of the Cuban Revolution's social programs, favorably presented in a low-key manner.

The Cuban Spanish dialect is difficult to follow, and the

film is dated. One evaluator felt the theme is not well introduced at the beginning, and the editing and organization can make it confusing.

Introducing the Tape: U.S. audiences need to know about Cuba's history and its relation with the United States. U.S. viewers should be told how various U.S. presidencies have responded to Cuba—for example, the embargo. An introduction to the Cuban Revolution would help, in addition to information about the historical role of the Isle of Pines and the historic problem of delinquency among teenagers in Cuba. Also, the goal of the correctional institute—to encourage work and study—should be stated up front.

How to Use: I would use this film when discussing problems shared by Cuba and the U.S. under different forms of ideology. One task for students would be to list problems shared and compare and contrast the politics of each, including the various community and government reactions. (Rodríguez)

After the introduction and screening, the discussion would focus on the alternatives which are offered to the usual reformatories. (Navarro)

I would use this as another example of Gómez's work, in addition to her film *One Way or Another.* (Ryan)

Suggested Readings: Chanan, Michael. *The Cuban Image: Cinema and Cultural Politics in Cuba.*—section on Gómez

Elder B. "Report on Cuba's First Symposium on Politics, Ideology and Law."

Evenson, Debra. *Revolution in the Balance: Law and Society in Contemporary Cuba.*

Lesage, Julia. "Dialectical, Revolutionary, Feminist: One Way or Another."

"The Dialectics of Race and Class: One Way or Another," in *The New Latin American Cinema: A Continental Project.* Ed. Zuzana Pick.

Readings on criminal justice in contemporary and prerevolutionary Cuba

Complementary Films/Videos: *De cierta manera (One Way or Another)* (Cuba).

Level: University

JAU (Bow Wow)

Documentary/Comedy.   With Subtitles.   22 min.   1986
Directed by: Enrique Colina
Produced by: ICAIC (Calle 23 No. 155 Vedado, Havana; tel: [537] 333-862; fax: [537] 333-032)
Distributed by: Center for Cuban Studies, IMRE
Evaluators: Jules Benjamin, Marlene Gottlieb, Margarita de la Vega Hurtado
Description: This creative film is shot from the perspective of a German shepherd on the streets of Havana. It is a comic portrayal of the idiosyncrasies, foibles, and hypocrisy of the human species, as seen from the obviously superior point of view of a dog. The documentary begins with a dogcatcher chasing after the dog, following him around town as he observes human behavior. Interviews that exemplify people's

strange and excessive behavior toward their pets are intercut with the German shepherd's reactions. The dogcatcher eventually catches the dog, which then escapes at the very end, providing a circular structure to the film.

Strengths and Weaknesses: This is an extremely funny and entertaining film. The creative mix of "staged" scenes with documentary footage and well-crafted editing and soundtrack present a humorous perspective of a dog's life. Cuban music accompanies the scenes.

Introducing the Tape: The film needs no introduction.

How to Use: In an *Advanced Conversational Spanish Language* course, I would stop the film from time to time to examine the signs, shops, etc. to review vocabulary. Then we would discuss, in Spanish, the message of the film, what aspects of human behavior were being ridiculed, etc. In a *Literature* class, we would see the entire film and discuss the inverted roles of human and animal and how this affects the viewer's impression (the importance of perspective in communicating a message). I might even compare and contrast the film with other films, such as *Lassie* or *Oliver,* the cartoon version in which dogs play the roles. In *Civilization* courses, the tape could be used to show life in Havana—there are numerous scenes from everyday life: signs, shops, transportation, etc. (Gottlieb)

Suggested Readings: Bakhtin's theories of the carnivalesque.

Cervantes Saavedra, Miguel de. *El casamiento enganoso y colloquio de los perros; novelas.*

Complementary Films/Videos: *Falsas Historias* (available in the International Media Resource Exchange Archive)

Level: Junior High School—University

LOS JIBAROS (The Wild Ones)

Feature.   With Subtitles.   94 min.   1973
Directed by: Daniel Díaz Torres
Produced by: ICAIC (Calle 23 No. 155 Vedado, Havana; tel: [537] 333-862; fax: [537] 333-032)
Distributed by: Center for Cuban Studies
Evaluators: Carol Becker, Daniel C. Scroggins, Currie Kerr Thompson, Margarita de la Vega Hurtado
Description: *Los Jíbaros* is set in the Escambray mountains of Cuba in 1960. The characters are small farmers and cattlemen trying to adjust to a new life in Cuba after Batista. Two hunting partners find that they are on opposite sides of the political spectrum. One allies himself with the revolution, and the other with the counterrevolutionaries. Wild dog hunting becomes a parable for popular response against counterrevolutionary groups. The film combines many of the clichés of old Westerns, including a drunken brawl, gunfights, cows, and a hero astride a white horse, with reminiscences of *Moby Dick.*

Strengths and Weaknesses: This film is quite well made, with strong acting and cinematography and an interesting script with an intriguing focus. It contains wonderful footage of Sierra de Escambray and of rural Cuba at an intriguing moment in history—material that is not easily accessible to U.S. viewers. The parable of the wild dogs works quite well.

One evaluator felt that the tape is quite predictable. Another thought that the plot covers many issues and is not coherent enough. The regular use of dialectical speech will be difficult for nonnative speakers.

Introducing the Tape: An introduction to the Cuban Revolution is necessary. A very brief chronology of events in Cuba in the five years preceding 1960 would be very helpful, as would a thumbnail explanation of the concept of the literacy campaign in revolutionary Cuba and agrarian reform.

How to Use: The film would be appropriate for any course dealing with the Cuban Revolution including *History* courses on *Social Revolution in Latin America*. It would also be suitable for *Latin American Civilization* courses. In both instances students would rely primarily on the English subtitles. I would like to use it in advanced *Oral Studies Language* courses to equip students to deal with regional differences in spoken Spanish. (Scroggins)

This work could be used as an example of Cuban/New Latin American Cinema's use of fictional genres to construct history. (de la Vega Hurtado)

Level: University

LEJANIA (Parting of Ways)

Feature.   With Subtitles.   94 min.   1985

Directed by: Jesus Díaz

Produced by: ICAIC (Calle 23 No. 155 Vedado, Havana; tel: [537] 333-862; fax: [537] 333-032)

Distributed by: Center for Cuban Studies, The Cinema Guild

Evaluators: Robert DiAntonio, Alicia Ramos, Currie Kerr Thompson, Margarita de la Vega Hurtado

Description: A Cuban woman who went into exile in the U.S. returns to Cuba after many years to see the son she left behind. She comes back with suitcases filled with clothes and appliances. The mother is upset to find that her son has married a divorced woman with a child and that his wife is mulatto. She fails to reconnect with her alienated son.

Strengths and Weaknesses: This is a sensitive film about how the revolution divided Cuban families. The Cuban refugee/immigrant story, so common in the U.S., is presented from the point of view of those left on the island. The film has good dramatic structure and poetic sensibility, portraying the pains of exile and family separation. It is a compelling story of family conflict and guilt, complete with wonderful views of the city of Havana.

Although it is true that many of those who remained in revolutionary Cuba felt betrayed by family members who left, the complexity of those relationships is not explored in this film. A couple of evaluators felt the film was one-sided, presenting those Cubans who stayed on the island as having less

materialistic values than their U.S. counterparts. Another felt it was uninspired.

Introducing the Tape: Some historical background about the Cuban Revolution, Fidel Castro, and the present political situation would be useful for U.S. viewers. The various waves of emigration from Cuba should be explained.

Viewers could be told that before 1959, many poor Cubans, including many blacks, fled the poverty and repression of the Machado and Batista dictatorships. Immediately after the revolution, the majority of exiles were white, upperclass professionals or businessmen who lost much of their fortune as a result of the revolution. In 1979, thousands of Cubans with family in the United States were picked up at Mariel Bay by family members with boats. As a result of the current economic crisis in Cuba, many artists and professionals, once loyal to the revolution, have left (many on rafts) to find better economic conditions.

How to Use: The film would be useful to depict the conflicts of those who emigrate from their homeland and can be used in conjunction with *El super* to show the counterpoint of perspectives of those who left and those who remained behind. (DiAntonio)

The complexity of emotions resulting from exile, both for those who leave and those who remain behind, can be examined with students. A critical viewing exercise could have students discuss how these complexities are oversimplified by the film.

Complementary Films/Videos: *El super (The Super)* (U.S.A./Cuba); *El diálogo (The Dialogue)* (Cuba)

Level: University

LUCIA (Lucía)

Feature.   With Subtitles.   16 min.   1968

Directed by: Humberto Solás

Produced by: ICAIC (Calle 23 No. 155 Vedado, Havana; tel: [537] 333-862; fax: [537] 333-032)

Distributed by: Center for Cuban Studies, IMRE, New Yorker Films

Evaluators: Patricia Aufderheide (excerpted from *Cross-cultural Film Guide*), Carol Becker, Nancy Levy-Konesky, Christopher Ortiz, Alicia Ramos

Description: *Lucía* is an anthology film, three separate stories related by the common theme of women in revolution. It tells the stories of three Lucías, one in 1895, when the Cubans fought for independence from the Spaniards (a situation that resolved with U.S. intervention and purchase of Cuba from Spain); in 1933, when Cuban popular resistance against the dictator Geraldo Machado resulted in failure; and in the early 1960s—in the aftermath of the victory of the revolution led by Fidel Castro. They are women from three different classes; the first is upper class, the second is from the middle class, the third is working class. They have three different ranges of potential action and responses. Each story is hung on a love drama. In the first, the woman has an affair with a Spanish soldier, in which she must betray her own family. In the second, a young woman abandons her family and class to go underground with her soon to be slain husband; in the third, a young wife learns how to read and write and work in collective agriculture, in spite of a traditionally macho husband who tries to keep her in the house.

"The events of each life portrayed focus around issues of politics, feminism and gender battles. Solás, the director, explains that he made women the protagonists because 'women are traditionally the number one victims in all social confrontations. The woman's role always lays bare the contradictions of a period and makes them explicit.' . . . Lucía was extremely well received in Cuba, won many international awards, and is now an international classic. (Aufderheide)

Strengths and Weaknesses: Fabulously done! This is a gorgeous film—interestingly shot, with wonderful camera work and acting. . . . "The film demonstrates vividly and with great creativity the relationship between form and content. The style of each segment is distinctive and appropriate both to the tale and to evoking the epoch." (Aufderheide) It is extremely useful in tracing women's roles through time in a particular culture.

The film's third segment is by now outdated and doesn't represent current life in Cuba.

Introducing the Tape: Teachers could provide a bit more background about the Cuban/Spanish war and Cuban political history for each of the time periods.

How to Use: "It is valuable to demonstrate how history always searches out a 'usable past'; for discussion of the relationship between form and content; and as an example of engaged cinema that is also a narrative, psychologically engaging one." (Aufderheide)

I could use this in my class for issues of *Gender Politics* and just as a well-made film dealing with art and life. (Becker)

In a *Seminar on Cuba,* I present the history in three periods which coincide to the three segments of Lucía. It is highly effective. (Levy-Konesky)

Suggested Readings: Aufderheide, Pat. *Cross Cultural Film Guide.*

Burton, Julianne. *Cinema and Social Change in Latin America: Conversations with Filmmakers.*

Chanan, Michael. *The Cuban Image: Cinema and Cultural Politics in Cuba.*

Level: High School—University

MACHITO (Machito: A Latin Jazz Legacy)
Documentary. With Subtitles. 58 min. 1987
Directed by: Carlos Ortiz
Distributed by: First Run/Icarus Films
Evaluators: Susan Altgelt, Rebeca Harclerode, Joan A. McGinnis, Hilda Pato
Description: This rhythmic documentary narrates the life and music of one of the premier band leaders of the Latin jazz movement, Frank "Machito" Grillo. The tape includes vintage film clips and recordings of over four decades of

Latin music—the fusion of Cuban rhythms and American jazz. The development of Afro-Cuban jazz is traced from its origins in the *barracones* ("barracks") of the black sugar plantation workers to the nightclubs of New York City, with Machito as one of its great exponents. Cuban-born Machito came to the U.S. and played with some of the greatest Latin musicians: Tito Puente, Willie Colón, Ray Barreto. He also recorded albums with Charlie Parker and Dizzy Gillespie. The film includes scenes and performances of conga, rumba, bebop, mambo, bamba, salsa, and the original "break dancing" in some of the greatest clubs of the 1940s and 1950s in New York. Latin and jazz greats share their memories of Machito, whose interview is at the center of the film.

Strengths and Weaknesses: This is a professional and interesting documentary that clearly describes the history of, and brings important recognition to, this uniquely Latin and Afro-Cuban music. The music and vintage clips in the tape are wonderful! The tape shows the centrality of the music for people of the Caribbean, regardless of race, and how it survives and continues to be a unifying force.

One evaluator felt the video seemed a bit long.

Introducing the Tape: The tape provides a historical context and needs no introduction, but students could benefit from some background on the Cuban *son* and its influence in Spanish Harlem.

How to Use: Any *Spanish Language* course should definitely include music . . . I have had students illustrate Latin music and dance by singing, dancing, playing, musical instruments. Lyrics to some of the songs would be useful for a "sing along." (McGinnis)

I would simply show this film as a superb example of Hispanic culture and its contribution to U.S. culture. (Harclerode)

In *Comparative Cultures,* the relation of this music to today's music, such as rap, could be explored.
Level: High School—University

UNA MAS ENTRE ELLOS (One More Among Them)
Documentary. With Subtitles. 31 min. 1989
Directed by: Rebeca Chávez
Produced by: ICAIC (Calle 23 No. 155 Vedado, Havana; tel: [537] 333-862; fax: [537] 333-032)
Distributed by: Center for Cuban Studies, The Cinema Guild, IMRE
Evaluators: Elba D. Birmingham-Pokorny, Ann K. Coughlin, Irene Matthews, Susy Suárez
Description: This film mixes documentary footage with dramatic biographical reconstruction to tell the story of Tania, an Argentine woman who migrated to Cuba in the early days of the revolution. Tania was trained to do intelligence work on behalf of the Cuban Communist Party in various Latin American countries, including Bolivia, where she prepared the arrival of Che Guevara. She was later killed with him. The tape deals primarily with Che Guevara's Bolivian

campaign. The viewer is able to obtain a more complete picture of Tania through the voices and narrations of many of her friends.

Strengths and Weaknesses: This is an excellent docudrama showing the early stages of the revolution. The film has a relative importance in relationship to Cuba shortly after the revolution—the strongest period of the exportation of the revolution. It is clear that Latin America and Cuba were caught in a trap between the two superpowers and their own needs and political realities. The film provides interesting information about the work of the Cuban communists in various countries during the 1960s.

The film's eclectic structure received mixed reviews—it is attractive but confusing. The abundance of information about Che Guevara seriously undermines the importance of Tania. One evaluator disliked the music and found the acting melodramatic.

Introducing the Tape: This is a tape that should be seen within the context of other Latin American guerrilla movements, i.e., Chile, Argentina, Guatemala, El Salvador, etc. U.S. viewers would need to know the history of the Cuban Revolution and the Cold War era.

How to Use: I would use this video for listening comprehension in my *Spanish Language* classes. It also would be useful when we study events of the twentieth century in Latin America. (Coughlin)

The tape could be used in a *Latin American Art* class. Most of the work of Latin American artists is political in context. The ideology that the young woman Tania expresses, and the struggle she finds herself in, are important in understanding the sentiments portrayed in much of the art work of the sixties, seventies, and eighties. (Suárez)

Suggested Readings: Guevara, Ernesto. *Reminiscences of the Cuban Revolutionaries.*

Any histories of the Cuban Revolution or biographies of Tania, Che, etc.

Level: University

MAS VALE TARDE QUE NUNCA (Better Later Than Never)

Documentary/Comedy.   With Subtitles.   10 min.   1986
Directed by: Enrique Colina
Produced by: ICAIC (Calle 23 No. 155 Vedado, Havana; tel: [537] 333-862; fax: [537] 333-032)
Distributed by: Center for Cuban Studies, IMRE
Evaluators: Jules Benjamin, Jorge Rodríguez-Florido, Roger A. Sánchez-Berroa, Margarita de la Vega Hurtado
Description: With a humorous perspective and clever editing, this documentary presents a series of interviews on the problems of lack of punctuality in Cuba, particularly concerning work. Although treated satirically, lateness is seen as a social evil that adversely affects the Cuban economy and culture. There is also amusing commentary on the tyranny of the clock and the attempt of Cubans to retain a "laid-back" attitude.

Strengths and Weaknesses: This is an incisive analysis of social problems caused by individual habits and the security that workers in socialist Cuba enjoyed—no workers were ever fired from their jobs, no matter how bad their performance. The film has visual and musical rhythm, proving that a "dry subject" can be made entertaining. The examples are very real and poignant.

Because of its quickly edited, comical portrayal, the tape can seem "lightweight" unless accompanied by a more serious analysis of the issues. There is little Spanish dialogue for language practice.

Introducing the Tape: It would be helpful to U.S. viewers to contextualize the tape within present conditions in Cuba, particularly looking at the Cuban government's decision to reverse the policy of never firing workers.

How to Use: This piece could be used in a *Film Studies* class as an example of its genre. (de la Vega Hurtado)

For *Language* classes, it would be helpful to provide a brief summary in Spanish before watching and to compare the concept of time and use of the subjunctive in the Hispanic world and in the U.S.A. I would stop the tape at various points to elicit explanations of what is occurring in various scenes. (Sánchez-Berroa)

This tape could be used in a *Spanish Conversation* class to motivate discussion of what happened, the consequences of doing a bad job or being late, etc. (Rodríguez-Florido)

In *Cinema/Video* studies, this tape provides an excellent example of creative documentary making. The tape could be paused to point out which scenes are true documentation and those which have been set up for filming. Also, the use of juxtaposition for humorous effect can be studied.
Level: High School—University

MEMORIAS DE SUBDESARROLLO (Memories of Underdevelopment)

Feature.   With Subtitles.   97 min.   1968
Directed by: Tomás Gutiérrez Alea
Produced by: ICAIC (Calle 23 No. 155 Vedado, Havana; tel: [537] 333-862; fax: [537] 333-032)
Distributed by: Center for Cuban Studies, IMRE
Evaluators: Gerard Aching, Patricia Aufderheide (excerpted from *Cross Cultural Film Guide*), Robert DiAntonio, Nancy Levy-Konesky, Carlos Pérez, Rebecca Torres-Rivera
Description: Based on a book by Edmundo Desnoes, *Memories of Underdevelopment* is an international classic that represents a complex sociopolitical study of a once-wealthy Cuban man who remains in Havana after his family leaves for the United States in 1961. Director Gutiérrez Alea deftly mixes documentary, fantasy, and fiction narrative in a film that takes the viewer inside the mind of a man caught between capitalist and revolutionary worlds. Sergio is an indecisive spectator of life. He muses cynically about the contradictions in underdevelopment, and on outings idly girl watches. Cut off from the world he knew, he attempts to

reenter through relations with women of various social classes. Through these relationships and his general sense of inertia, the viewer sees Sergio's perspective on the aftermath of the Cuban Revolution.

Director Gutiérrez Alea explained that the goal of his film was to foster self-criticism on the part of the spectator. "Sergio is not someone to imitate—he lacks a series of obvious virtues—but he is contradictory, and because of that the spectator first identifies with him, than questions him. His attitudes accord with values of the dominant society until the revolution: he is a petit-bourgeois who dresses well, has a good apartment, pretty women, a certain level of education. Because of this, first there's an identification, which slowly transforms into criticism." (Aufderheide)

Strengths and Weaknesses: This film provides an extremely forceful, dramatic, and interesting view of existential difficulties, matched by equally intriguing camera work and experimentalism. Postmodernity and underdevelopment clash fruitfully here. There is interesting footage of post-Castro Cuba with a view of Cuban life in the early 1960s as well as a fascinating tour of Hemingway's home in Cuba and reflection on his relationship to the Cuban people. This thought-provoking work points to class differences and the shift of power, analyzing the role to be played by wealthy and educated Cubans in the new state. One evaluator felt the strongest point of the film is that it offers a glimpse into the profound changes a person must undergo when confronted with a society in transition. It has a universal theme as it explores the alienation of the individual in contemporary society. Another evaluator commented that the film presents an objective and fair view of the situation after Castro's takeover.

The film's intentionally discontinuous structure and juxtaposition of images, using the cut-up technique of incorporating newsreel footage and film clips, may distract and confuse U.S. viewers unfamiliar with this cinematic strategy. Although the film encourages viewers to reflect, U.S. students familiar with a linear narrative and action movies may consider the film slow and introspective and would need an introduction for better understanding. There is a strong sexual content in the film and some nudity, which can distract the viewer from the basic story.

Introducing the Tape: Viewers may need to be introduced to the director's film technique, which may be unfamiliar to a U.S. audience. Also necessary is a presentation of the relationship between Cuba and the U.S. during Fulgencio Batista's regime, as well as an explanation of the disintegration of that relationship after 1960. A discussion of the events surrounding the Bay of Pigs, the Cuban exodus, and the October missile crisis would contribute to a better understanding of the main character's reflections.

How to Use: I used this film in a *Seminar on Cuba* to bring the revolution close to individual lives—to show how various socioeconomic levels were affected by the revolution, to

personalize it, and show it in a less idealized context. (Levy-Konesky)

The film is particularly useful for a course on the *Cuban Revolution* and its aftermath for the arts there. Also for *Women's Studies*. (Aching)

For *Latin American Literature:* first have students read the novel by Edmundo Desnoes then compare and contrast it to the film. (DiAntonio)

I would use this tape after lecturing on the radical policies that Cuba's revolutionary government undertook in the face of growing U.S. and counterrevolutionary threats. I would explain the relationship between the individual and the masses, and how during a period of revolutionary change one cannot remain complacent and indecisive on the sidelines, but must become an active participant in that process. In the post-viewing discussion, we would examine the main character's relationship to his society and the relationship of the students with their own society. We would proceed to see if that sense of alienation characteristic of a capitalist society had been transcended by Cuba's revolutionary society. I would introduce the topic of the revolution's attempt to create *una nueva conciencia* ("a new consciousness") and *un hombre nuevo* ("new man") through the revolutionary process, struggling against bourgeois values and vices. (Pérez)

Suggested Readings: Burton, Julianne. *Cinema and Social Change in Latin America: Conversations with Filmmakers.*

Chanan, Michael. *The Cuban Image: Cinema and Cultural Politics in Cuba.*

Desnoes, Edmundo. *Memories of Underdevelopment.*

Downing, John, ed. "Four Films of Tomás Gutiérrez Alea." *Film & Politics in the Third World.*

Gutiérrez Alea, Tomás. "The Viewer's Dialectic." In *Reviewing Histories. Selections from New Latin American Cinema.* Ed. Coco Fusco.

Johnson, Leland J. "U.S. Business Interests in Cuba and the Rise of Castro."

King, John. *Magical Reels: A History of Cinemas in Latin America.*

Myerson, Michael. *Memories of Underdervelopment. The Revolutionary Films of Cuba.*

Padula, Alfred L. "The Ruin of the Cuban Bourgeoisie, 1959–1961."

Pérez, Louis A., Jr. *Cuba: Between Reform and Revolution.*

Welch, Richard E. Jr. *Response to Revolution: The United States and the Cuban Revolution, 1959–1961.*

Wyden, Peter. *The Bay of Pigs: The Untold Story.*

Level: University

MIRTA AGUIRRE

Documentary.   Without Subtitles.   21 min.   1990
Directed by: Jimmy R. Sariol Carballo
Produced by: CINED (7th Ave. No 2802 Miramar, Havana; tel: [537] 237-742 or 237-887; fax: [537] 331-697)
Distributed by: IMRE Archive

Evaluators: Daniel C. Scroggins, S. Travis Silcox
Description: This black-and-white tape outlines the professional career of Cuban author Mirta Aguirre. Made as an educational documentary, it is traditional in its approach. The tape covers the period from the 1930s, when Aguirre's political involvement against Machado forced her into exile in Mexico, through her prizewinning books and professorship in literature at the University of Havana, to her death in 1980.
Strengths and Weaknesses: The tape's strength is the chronology of this important feminist revolutionary's writings and activities, including scenes of Cuban children reciting her poetry in memory of Camilo Cienfuegos and Che Guevara. The Spanish is clear and accessible to undergraduate students from the sophomore level and up.

While the tape is informative and clear, evaluators found the presentation stagnant and technical quality poor. It is composed primarily of two "talking head" interviews with professors José Antonio Portuondo and Vincentina Antuña, who often reads from prepared notes.
Introducing the Tape: As Aguirre may not be a well-known literary figure in the U.S., viewers need to be exposed to at least four or five of her poems before seeing the program.
How to Use: I would use the tape to provide insight into the *Literature of the Cuban Revolution* and the cultural and social goals and accomplishments of the leaders of the revolution. (Scroggins)
Suggested Readings: Aguirre, Mirta. *Perfil histórico de las letras Cubanas.* (incomplete at the time of her death).

Other works by Mirta Aguirre (see bibliography).
Level: University

LA MUERTE DE UN BUROCRATA (Death of a Bureaucrat)

Feature.   With Subtitles.   85 min.   1966
Directed by: Tomás Gutiérrez
Produced by: ICAIC (Calle 23 No. 155 Vedado, Havana; tel: [537] 333-862; fax: [537] 333-032)
Distributed by: Center for Cuban Studies, IMRE
Evaluators: Robert Alvarez, David Bushnell, Fortuna Calvo-Roth, Rick Langhorst, Nancy Levy-Konesky, Daniel C. Scroggins
Description: This is a black comedy/satirical critique of bureaucracy during the early period of the Cuban Revolution. It follows the antics of a woman who tries to collect her dead husband's pension. The husband, who worked in a factory that made plaster busts of Marx and other revolutionary heroes, invented a machine that increased productivity, churning out thousands of busts per hour. He unfortunately got caught up in the machine and met an untimely end. Singing his praises at his funeral, his friends decide to bury him with his identification card, as a tribute to his true proletarian heroism. After his burial, when his wife tries to collect his pension, she is told it is impossible without the identity card. The film comically leads us through a labyrinth of brain-dead bureaucracy and follows the efforts of the woman's nephew, a

dutiful socialist youth, to help her obtain the widow's pension. The nephew is forced to exhume his uncle's corpse to retrieve the work card. Endless lines to obtain signatures and stamps, and mountainous government forms attended by bored, unthinking employees utterly frustrate attempts to rebury the deceased proletarian. Finally, the nephew is carted away in a straitjacket after strangling the cemetery administrator.
Strengths and Weaknesses: This highly entertaining, well-done film is universal and timeless. It is full of humor, poking fun mainly at the unimaginative bureaucracy but also making some good-natured digs at revolutionary rhetoric and symbolism. The film provides a good picture of Cuba during this period. The Spanish language is exceptionally clear, making it suitable for use in mid-level language classes.

One evaluator felt that the film wears a little thin before the end but continues to be valid. At times, the humor is slapstick. Some of the written text in the film is difficult to read.
Introducing the Tape: A few introductory words of explanation concerning the depth and resilience of the bureaucratic tradition, particularly in underdeveloped countries would be helpful. Problems with bureaucracy are universal, regardless of economic/social circumstance. It should be pointed out that although this film is critical of government bureaucracy, it was produced by the national film institute of Cuba (ICAIC) and represents an attempt at self-criticism. It is also one of the classics of revolutionary Cuban cinema. The film's director, Tomás Gutiérrez Alea, made other Cuban "greats" such as *Memories of Underdevelopment* (also in the 1960s) and *Strawberry and Chocolate* (1993) (the story of the friendship between a homosexual and a straight "communist" youth).
How to Use: The film would be useful in a course about postrevolutionary Cuba. It could also be used in a *Spanish Language* course because of the clarity of the spoken language and the accuracy of the English subtitles. (Scroggins)

I have shown this film in a seminar on Cuba to depict, in an entertaining way, the realities of a bureaucratic government that has lost touch with the needs of the people, and how this impacts the lives of the citizens. (Levy-Konesky)

I might use this as a mid-semester change of pace and tone in *Latin American History,* to illustrate the points made above (and also to illustrate autonomy enjoyed by Cuban filmmakers at certain stages of revolution). (Bushnell)

For *Anthropology* classes, this is an excellent spoof on the institutional parameters faced by the ordinary person. It illustrates in some degree the importance of kin ties in Latin American society (i.e., the nephew helping his aunt retrieve the work card) and plays on a significant dialectic—the importance of continued survival in a bureaucratic state and death. (Alvarez)

The tape is useful for giving an overview of the bureaucratic stagnation of Cuba, seen comically. One could also expound a bit on burial customs. Probably better as a "cinema week" tape than for classroom. (Langhorst)

Suggested Readings: Halperin, Maurice. *The Rise and Decline of Fidel Castro: An Essay in Contemporary History.* — Bureaucracy and Castro
Complementary Films/Videos: *Memorias de subdesarrollo (Memories of Underdevelopment)* (Cuba); *Strawberry and Chocolate* (distributed by Miramax Films)
Level: High School—University

MUJER TRANSPARENTE (Transparent Woman)
Feature. With Subtitles. 82 min. 1990
Directed by: Hector Veitia, Mayra Segura, Mayra Vilasis, Mario Crespo, Ana Rodriguez
Produced by: ICAIC (Calle 23 No. 155 Vedado, Havana; tel: [537] 333-862; fax: [537] 333-032)
Distributed by: Center for Cuban Studies, IMRE
Evaluators: Alfredo Bushby, Osvaldo Chinchón, Susana Conde, Mary Jo Dudley, Victor Garatea
Description: In this film, cinematic vignettes made by different directors present five quite different women in contemporary Cuba. Each of these female-centered narratives focuses on the search for personal fulfillment. Isabel, a dutiful, albeit discontented, wife and the mother of two teenagers, has just been promoted to an assistant's position at work. Adriana is an older woman, nostalgic about her youth but unable to act on her wishes. Julia, separated from her husband, finds no satisfaction in an affair with an ex-student and longs to work through the problems in her marriage. Zoe, a young and free-spirited art student, eschews traditional school and personal responsibilities. And Laura, whose friend Ana left for Miami after the revolution, reflects on her two failed marriages and Ana's role in her life. When Ana comes back for a short visit, Laura tries to recapture the friendship that was cut off when Ana left Cuba. These five women's experiences reveal the universal nature of their feelings and their relationships with those around them.
Strengths and Weaknesses: The film provides an accurate portrait of Cuban society, particularly women's issues. The stories are interesting, intense, and extremely informative. One evaluator suggested that the film would dispel many stereotypes U.S. audiences have about women in Latin America. Although the film may seem at first to lack cohesiveness, a common theme emerges from the individual stories: the search for identity and the value of relationships in personal fulfillment.

One evaluator felt the film was too long for classroom use and suggested showing it in segments for discussion.
Introducing the Tape: Although not explicitly feminist, this film centers on the need to reevaluate the role of women in Cuban society. An overview of the different positions assigned to women in various sectors of society and historical periods is necessary when introducing this film.
How to Use: In *Latin American Film: Reconfigurations of Family and Nation in Latin America,* I would emphasize the role of women in Latin American societies. (Conde)
I would use this tape in a *Spanish Conversation* class. The Spanish is clear and the situations are conducive to interesting discussions. (Chinchón)

I teach second-semester *Spanish,* which includes a week dedicated to cultural activities. This week I would show the students the film (without subtitles). We would talk about what they understood about the differences between Cuban and North American societies as shown in the film. I would give them a writing assignment in which they would discuss any issue related to the film. (Bushby)
Suggested Readings: Black, Jan Knippers ed. *Latin America. Its Problems and Its Promise.*
Burton, Julianne. *Cinema and Social Change in Latin America: Conversations with Filmmakers.*
Green, Duncan. *Faces of Latin America.*
King, John. *Magical Reels: A History of Cinemas in Latin America.*
Masiello, Francine. *Between Civilization and Barbarism. Women, Nation, and Literary Culture in Modern Argentina.*
Miller, Francesca. *Latin American Women and the Search for Social Justice.*
Skidmore, Thomas E., and Peter H. Smith. *Modern Latin America.*
Books by Betty Friedan, Germaine Greer.
Level: University

NGANGA KIYANGALA (Nganga Kiyangala, Congo Religion in Cuba)
Documentary. With Subtitles. 33 min. 1991
Directed by: Tato Quiñones and Luis Soto
Produced by: Television Latina (Calle 21 No. 1, Esquina a O, Vedado, Havana; tel: [573] 30-0198; fax: [573] 33-3476)
Distributed by: IMRE
Evaluators: Rosemary Brana-Shute, Danusia L. Meson, José-Manuel Navarro, Edgar G. Nesman
Description: This film presents the history, rites, and practices of Nganga, the Bantu-based belief system of the slaves brought to Cuba from the Congo region of Africa. Nganga is one of three or more sects in Cuba that are more African than Christian in belief, rituals, music, and dance. The film focuses on the actions performed by a *palero* during his morning devotion to the Nganga, in which a ritual offering is placed in a sacred receptacle. Ethnographer and writer Miguel Barnet explains much about the rites, ritual objects, symbols, signs, art, dance, vocabulary, and music. He and the narrator, Luis Cabrera, briefly discuss some of the differences between the Lucumi (*Yoruba/Santería*) and *Abakua* beliefs. Barnet points out that the Africans brought to Cuba have greatly influenced its culture, and their contributions must be included in any comprehensive definition of the island's culture.
Strengths and Weaknesses: This program introduces viewers to Nganga with excellent footage and nicely integrated music. It presents the role of the Bantu religion, distinguishing it from the better-known Yoruba religion (referred to as Santería). The tape is unique in covering this vital element of

Cuban life and helps to rewrite Cuban history "from the bottom up"—particularly important since there is little written history of this aspect of Cuban culture. It shows clearly the prevalence of Nganga beliefs among certain segments of the Cuban population.

While the tape presents important material, evaluators felt it was more declarative than analytical and lacked clear cultural and historical context, leaving reviewers with many questions. The participants, their background, and the location of the filming are not identified. There is little statistical data about the practices and how many people participate in the rituals. Although some information is presented about the Nganga gods, the film does not talk about other individuals within the belief system or comment on gender roles, specifically the role of women. There is no discussion with practitioners about their beliefs and no contrast with the Catholicism of most Cubans. Transitions between scenes are not always smooth.

Introducing the Tape: Viewers would benefit from a brief introduction to the Africans' history in the New World. Use of the film would be enhanced by an overview of the differences between Bantu and Yoruba peoples during the time of the slave trade and the roles played by each in Cuba and by a survey of Congo theogony. Background should address the following questions: During which specific period of slavery was Nganga imported? How is Nganga practiced? What roles do the priests play? etc. Viewers should also be told that Miguel Barnet is a well-known anthropologist and highly respected author and specialist on African influences in Cuba.

How to Use: This is one example of the important cultural impact and continuing attraction of African practices in a New World society. (Brana-Shute)

Before showing the tape, I would ask the students to discuss religious beliefs and practice in the U.S. and ask them to talk about what they know, if anything, about religion in Africa and in Cuba. I would then show the film. After viewing, I would divide them into groups, and provide each group with questions to answer based on the material in the film. I would also assign a story by Lidia Cabrera and ask them to discuss the story in terms of what they saw in the film. (Meson)

This tape could be used when dealing with *Religion in Latin America,* and the African influence in contemporary society. (Nesman)

This tape could be shown with the complementary film *Ache mayuba orisha* to contrast the two religions. First, instructors could provide an introductory overview as outlined above. Then, they could discuss the role of Bantu and Yoruba slaves in Cuba, analyze the role of religion in slave life, and discuss the present status of these religious practices. I would conclude with a discussion of these films as examples of the new Cuban historiography. (Navarro)

Suggested Readings: Bastide, Roger. *African Civilisations in the New World.*

Bastide, Roger. *The African Religions of Brazil: Toward a Sociology of the Interpenetration of Civilization.*

Bejel, Emilio. *Escribir en Cuba: entrevistas con escritores cubanos 1979–1989.* Has interviews with Miguel Barnet and Manuel Moreno Fraginals

Cabrera, Lidia. *Reglas de Congo: Palo Monte y Mayombe; La regla de Santo Cristo en buen viaje; El Mote: Igbo, finda, ewe orisha vititi nfinda: notas sobre las religiones, la magia, las supersticiones y el folklor de los negros criollos y el pueblo de Cuba* (see bibliography).

Montejo, Esteban. *Biografía de un cimarrón (The Autobiography of a Runaway Slave).*

Moreno Fraginals, Manuel. *The Sugarmill: The Socioeconomic Complex of Sugar in Cuba 1760–1860.*

Guillén, Nicolás. "La balada de los dos abuelos" ("The Ballad of the Two Grandfathers"), a poem found in many anthologies of Latin American literature (see bibliography for other works).

Herskovitz-Frazer, classics on African religion in the New World.

Ortiz, Fernando. *Los bailes y el teatro de los negros en el folklor de Cuba.*

Ortiz, Fernando. *Los negros esclavos.*

Complementary Films/Videos: *Ache mayuba orisha* (Cuba)
Level: University

UNA NOVIA PARA DAVID (A Girlfriend for David)
Feature.   With Subtitles.   100 min.   1985
Directed by: Orlando Rojas
Produced by: ICAIC (Calle 23 No. 155, Vedado, Havana; tel: [537] 333-862; fax: [537] 333-032)
Distributed by: Center for Cuban Studies, The Cinema Guild
Evaluators: Paul J. LaReau, Currie Kerr Thompson, Elaine Torres
Description: This is the story of a young man from the countryside who goes to Havana to study at the university. The film shows how David, naive and idealistic, interacts with the other students, whose superficial values and selfishness frequently betray the ideals of the revolution. The one exception is Ofelia, a homely girl who keeps these ideals alive and with whom David eventually falls in love. Intertwined are the relationships of the other students, their stereotypically sexist attitudes, and the pressure they put on David to go out with prettier girls. The ending is bittersweet: David runs after Ofelia to confess his feelings while his classmates watch and express their derision.
Strengths and Weaknesses: Evaluators agreed that the film was well acted and produced. The love story centers around the ideals of the Cuban Revolution and the equality of women. It shows the culture of machismo and the high value it places on superficial qualities. While one evaluator found this an evenhanded and sensitive film about confronting individuality at an early age, others' assessments of the script ranged from "somewhat cliché" to "extremely dogmatic."

Introducing the Tape: To fully appreciate the film and its message, some background about the Cuban Revolution, its ideals, and its anti-U.S.-imperialism ideology is necessary.
How to Use: This would be a good introductory film in the study of the culture of machismo in Latin America. (LaReau)

I could use this in a *Spanish-American Civilization* course to show how similar the thinking of Cuban university students is to that of their U.S. counterparts, despite three decades of revolutionary efforts. (Thompson)
Level: University

ORACION (Prayer)
Video Poem.   With Subtitles.   11 min.   1983
Directed by: Marisol Trujillo
Produced by: ICAIC (Calle 23 No. 155, Vedado, Havana; tel: [537] 333-862; fax: [537] 333-032)
Distributed by: Center for Cuban Studies, The Cinema Guild, IMRE
Evaluators: Melvin S. Arrington Jr., Lynn M. Shirey
Description: Film clips and stills of the famous Marilyn Monroe at various stages of her life alternate with graphic depictions of poverty, oppression, exploitation, and other politically charged issues from the 1960s. The only narration over these black-and-white images is the poem "Oración por Marilyn Monroe" ("Prayer for Marilyn Monroe") read by its author, Nicaraguan priest, poet, and activist Ernesto Cardenal. The producers, who share Cardenal's perspective, powerfully combine the spoken word with visual effects and issue a call for intervention on behalf of all those who suffer under an unjust system. Thus, Marilyn Monroe becomes a metaphor for victims of exploitation of any kind.
Strengths and Weaknesses: This moving reading by the poet is very powerful—a classic. The images effectively convey the producers' message.

Technically speaking, this is a primitive production: The background music is overly simplistic; credits are difficult to read; some images flash by too quickly; and the exclusive use of black-and-white photography lessens the impact of some of the images.
How to Use: I would use the video to help stimulate discussion of Cardenal's poem. The tape also lends itself to a discussion of a variety of social, economic, and political issues affecting Latin America, in addition to the specific problems addressed by Cardenal's poem. (Arrington)

The film can be presented as a good example of how the New Latin American Cinema reflected the growing revolutionary, anti-imperialist movements of the 1960s.
Suggested Readings: Cardenal, Ernesto, *Apocalypse and Other Poems,* contains the English version of the poem that inspired this video.

Cardenal, Ernesto. "Oración por Marilyn Monroe."
Level: University

OTRA MUJER (Another Woman)
Feature.   With Subtitles.   98 min.   1986

Directed by: Daniel Díaz Torres
Produced by: ICAIC (Calle 23 No. 155, Vedado, Havana; tel: [537] 333-862; fax: [537] 333-032)
Distributed by: Center for Cuban Studies, IMRE Archive
Evaluators: Julia Lesage, Luis Martínez-Fernández, Elaine Torres, Margarita de la Vega Hurtado
Description: This rural drama begins with the homecoming of a small-town soldier who spent time fighting against counterrevolutionary forces. It addresses the readjustment problems faced by returning veterans and the prevailing attitudes of machismo. Juan González finds his former job as a trucker is no longer available, and his brother pressures him into accepting a position as the town storekeeper. Complications arise from Juan's lack of management experience and the peculiar bookkeeping system imposed on all stores by the new revolutionary government. Frustrated and angered by these new feelings of inadequacy, Juan reestablishes an affair with a former mistress, leaving his wife without a husband and the community stranded without a storekeeper. His wife eventually takes over the store but is denounced by the Communist Party when she takes some groceries home after a storm. At an annual Party-sponsored ceremony, she is given a turtle, the icon for poor management. Humiliated, she decides to quit. Meanwhile, her husband faces problems with his new common-law wife. In the end, the wife decides to continue as storekeeper and confront her problems.
Strengths and Weaknesses: This well-acted film provides a good portrayal of life in a small town during the early years of the revolution. It presents the problems associated with the transition from a capitalist to a socialist system. The surprising and interesting ending makes it evident that the story is about a woman struggling to maintain her identity during a time of crisis and not about her husband beset by mixed emotions.

The three main characters are somewhat stereotyped, if not caricatured: Juan is the rough macho type; Eugenia is the devoted wife/mother/revolutionary; Delfina is the aloof lover. One evaluator felt the tape was pedantic; another saw it as surprisingly traditional in its style and its ideas about women.
Introducing the Tape: Viewers should be told that the film is set in 1965 during the early years of the revolution. Many attitudes associated with the old system lingered.
How to Use: I would ask my students to pay attention to the changes brought about by the revolution in the economy, labor organizations, values, and culture. One way of framing the discussion would be to ask the students which aspects of continuity and change are represented by each character in film. (Martínez-Fernández)
Suggested Readings: Castro, Fidel, Vilma Espin, et al. *Women and the Cuban Revolution: Speeches and Documents.*

Holt-Seeland, Inger. *Women of Cuba.*
Level: University

EL OTRO FRANCISCO (The Other Francisco)
Feature.   With Subtitles.   100 min.   1974
Directed by: Sergio Giral
Produced by: ICAIC (Calle 23 No. 155, Vedado, Havana; tel: [537] 333-862; fax: [537] 333-032)
Distributed by: Center for Cuban Studies, IMRE, New Yorker Films
Evaluators: Susana Conde, Currie Kerr Thompson, Margarita de la Vega Hurtado
Description: This film is a revisionary look at Suárez Romero's novel, *Francisco,* laying bare the ideological underpinnings of the nineteenth-century book. The deconstruction of the romantic abolitionist work is realized by juxtaposing scenes taken from the novel, a story about the love between the black slave Francisco and the mulatto slave Dorotea. In documentary fashion, the voice-overs describe the actual conditions of slaves in the sugar mills in nineteenth-century Cuba and the profit motive of the abolitionist movement promoted by British capitalist Richard Madden.
Strengths and Weaknesses: The film invites a critical rereading of abolitionist literature. It is well made, and the idea of reworking a well-known literary work by filming opposing versions of the same sequence is intriguing.

Some evaluators felt the film was a bit heavy-handed, aspiring to reveal "the" truth while seeking to discredit the original work. There are many arguments against slavery in the nineteenth century, and while the film adds a valid dimension—the economic perspective—it presents this as the only truth. At times, the dialect is difficult to understand.
Introducing the Tape: The only introduction necessary would be some knowledge of the history of the region and awareness of the cultural heritage of the population. In studying nineteenth- and twentieth-century Cuba, it would be important to present both the U.S. and Cuban perspectives.
How to Use: In my course, *Latin American Film: Reconfigurations of Family and Nation in Latin America,* I would encourage students to screen this work on their own, and would suggest comparisons with other Cuban films that deal with slavery or that contrast different epochs of Cuban history, e.g., *La última cena (The Last Supper)* (Cuba). (Conde)
Suggested Readings: Black, Jan Knippers, ed. *Latin America. Its Problems and Its Promise.*

Burton, Julianne. "Marginal Cinemas and Mainstream Critical Theory."

Chanan, Michael. *The Cuban Image: Cinema and Cultural Politics in Cuba.*

Galeano, Eduardo. *Open Veins of Latin America. Five Centuries of Pillage of a Continent.*

Green, Duncan. *Faces of Latin America.*

King, John. *Magical Reels: A History of Cinemas in Latin America.*

Skidmore, Thomas E. and Peter H. Smith. *Modern Latin America.*

Complementary Films/Videos: *La última cena (The Last Supper)* (Cuba)
Level: University

LOS PAJAROS TIRANDO A LA ESCOPETA (Tables Turned)
Feature.   With Subtitles.   90 min.   1984
Directed by: Rolando Díaz
Produced by: ICAIC (Calle 23 No. 155, Vedado, Havana; tel: [537] 333-862; fax: [537] 333-032)
Distributed by: Center for Cuban Studies, The Cinema Guild,
Evaluators: Donald W. Davey, Robert DiAntonio, Marvin D'Lugo, Roger A. Sánchez-Berroa
Description: This film offers a humorous look at a family situation in working-class Havana, including a tongue-in-cheek treatment of machismo and feminism, with a little propaganda thrown in for good measure. Emilio and Magdalena are planning to get married but have already begun to have sexual relations. One afternoon, the couple's lovemaking is interrupted by the surprise return of Emilio's widowed mother, Hilda, who has brought a man to the house. The younger couple takes refuge under the bed, only to discover that Hilda's amorous partner is none other than Magdalena's widower father, Felo. Emilio is incensed by what he sees as his mother's perverse conduct. When he sees Felo later, he insults his future father-in-law and tries to break up his mother's relationship with the older man.

The tables are turned on Emilio when Magdalena discovers she is pregnant and must get married in a hurry. Now it is Felo's turn to disapprove of the actions of the younger generation. After the hasty wedding, Magdalena moves in with Emilio and his mother. A new series of arguments erupts between the young couple due to Emilio's machista attitude, and Magdalena throws her husband out of the house. Hilda, meanwhile, finds herself annoyed with Felo, who has calmed down and invites his son-in-law to live with him. A recurring question in the film is "Will the baby be a boy or a girl?" The difficulties are resolved and peace is made when Magdalena gives birth to two baby girls.
Strengths and Weaknesses: The film offers a thoughtful study of machismo with good acting. It also depicts generational conflicts, an equally important theme in Cuban society. These easily recognizable issues and the light comedy genre make the film fun and easy to follow. Stylistically, *Los pájaros* appears to be an attempt at subverting conventional genre films by exaggerating generic features and stereotyped characters. Some evaluators found this to be overdone and the plot obvious. One reviewer felt the use of the musical group to narrate the story was particularly ingenious, although not original. Others felt the constant background singing wore thin. The film would be useful for studying the Cuban accent.
Introducing the Tape: Though the theme of persisting machista attitudes has particular meaning in the context of

Cuban society, this film plays heavily on broader stereotypes of male attitudes and female responses and can thus be understood and appreciated outside its specifically Cuban context. No introduction is necessary.

How to Use: I would use this in a survey of *Latin American Cinema* to illustrate the ways in which some filmmakers seek to undermine conventional genre films by over-defining the genre for comic effect. The film is also an interesting illustration of narrational experimentation. It follows on the pattern already explored by Humberto Solás in *Lucía* and Pastor Vega in *Portrait of Teresa* to narrate through song. Finally, though not a particularly powerful example, the film illustrates ways in which issues of female status are addressed in Cuban cinema. (D'Lugo)

I would show the film, then have students discuss and write compositions comparing the subjects as they appear in the film and as we know them in this country. (Sánchez-Berroa)

Complementary Films/Videos: *Lucía* (Cuba); *Retrato de Teresa (Portrait of Teresa)* (Cuba)

Level: High School—University

PAPELES SECUNDARIOS (Supporting Roles)

Feature. With Subtitles. 110 min. 1988

Directed by: Orlando Rojas

Produced by: ICAIC (Calle 23 No. 155 Vedado, Havana; tel: [537] 333-862; fax: [537] 333-032)

Distributed by: Center for Cuban Studies, IMRE

Evaluators: Lourdes Fernández, Jorge Porras, Virginia Shen

Description: This feature deals with actors, actresses, and the life of the stage. Its focus is a Havana theater group that is putting on a classic Cuban play. The film portrays the complicated relationships between the group's director (an older actress), the director of the play, the actors, and a government representative auditing the group's finances. Present-day performers are haunted by stars of the past, and theatrical roles are intermingled with everyday life. The film addresses the personal search for freedom and self-confidence, fears of aging and loss of power, and the difficult relations between culture and politics.

Strengths and Weaknesses: The film gives a very good sense of the advantages and disadvantages of artistic production in a socialist milieu. The acting is generally very good. The conflicts and intrigues are well presented through characters who embody diverse problems.

At times, when acting and reality are juxtaposed, it is difficult to understand the story line. One evaluator felt the film was a bit pretentious, especially in its humorless pastiche-like quotation of famous films. The film may reach a limited audience.

Introducing the Tape: A short explanation of government involvement in artistic production in Cuba would be helpful. Background on Latin American culture and the arts is necessary.

How to Use: After showing the film, I would promote a discussion on the relations between government and art in a socialist context, trying to point out the criticisms the film makes about cultural politics. Also, I would discuss the existential aspects of the tape and its implications for power and sex relations. (Fernández)

When we talk about theatrical theory and acting, I would use the tape to show how life (reality) is related to acting (fantasy) and the way the director presents it. (Shen)

The tape could be used in extra-curricular *Language* activities as part of a *Latin American Film* series. (Porras)

Level: University

PEDRO CERO POR CIENTO

Documentary. Without Subtitles. 20 min. 1980

Directed by: Luis Felipe Bernaza

Produced by: ICAIC (Calle 23 No. 155, Vedado, Havana; tel: [537] 333-862; fax: [537] 333-032)

Distributed by: IMRE

Evaluators: Lavina Tilson Gass, S. Travis Silcox

Description: This documentary is the predecessor to the successful stage play and film *De tal Pedro tal astilla*. It tells the story of cattle manager Pedro Acosta, better known as Pedro *Cero por ciento* ("Zero percent") because in his model farming practices he has not lost any of his dairy cows. The documentary is humorous and masculine, and Pedro Acosta emerges as a character of folk wit.

Strengths and Weaknesses: This is a wonderful portrait of a man who loved and cared for his animals. His sincerity and the joy he takes in his work are evident throughout the film. The tape includes fascinating glimpses of rural Cuban life and animal husbandry. There is a terrific night scene of a cow giving birth. One evaluator felt the tape's best moment was when Pedro says that if he were able to read, he could do more.

One reviewer commented that a kind of male locker-room humor guides the film. The Cuban rural accents are difficult for Spanish language students to understand.

How to Use: I would use the documentary in conjunction with the feature fiction film, *De tal Pedro tal astilla,* to show the movement from documentary to feature. (Silcox)

In advanced *Spanish* courses, the tape can be used for cultural enrichment and speaking practice in discussion to follow. It is very useful for hearing regional dialect. (Tilson Gass)

Complementary Films/Videos: *De tal Pedro tal astilla* (Cuba)

Level: University

EL PIROPO

Documentary. Without Subtitles. 10 min. 1978

Directed by: Luis Felipe Bernaza

Produced by: ICAIC (Calle 23 No. 155, Vedado, Havana; tel: [537] 333-862; fax: [537] 333-032)

Distributed by: Center for Cuban Studies, IMRE

Evaluators: Donald W. Davey, Rick Langhorst, Roger A. Sánchez-Berroa

Description: A short, funny, macho-in-the-street view of the none-too-politically correct *piropo* (the humorous, flattering, or crude remark made by men to women who pass by). A sort of nerdy narrator comes on and, in classroom fashion, gives some background on the *piropo,* listing its fundamental characteristics. Many entertaining *piropo*s are heard. Two women say they like them; other women become tongue-tied when asked why women don't do the same to men, and an older woman fondly remembers her husband's *piropos* when they were younger. The film shows the different style of life in the Caribbean and contextualizes the *piropo* in terms of the intense street life in Havana. The jump-cut interviews give a good sense of the variety of ethnic backgrounds in Cuba, as much as an interesting look at Cuban fashion of the time.

Strengths and Weaknesses: This is an informative and amusing tape. It provides a good look at the variety of people in urban Cuba. A mixed group of women and men are interviewed, providing material for language practice in hearing different Spanish speakers.

The film's weakness is that it cuts very quickly from one interview to another and does not attempt to develop any kind of political view of the *piropo.* It only touches the surface of how women feel about the *piropo.*

Introducing the Tape: A thorough explanation of this cultural phenomenon would be necessary before screening the tape. Viewers could be told that the tape portrays the *piropo* as a historical masculine appreciation of women, not as a vulgar catcall; its roots are even traced back to the Bible. However, many people consider *piropos* offensive and politically incorrect. U.S. viewers could be asked to consider the different points of view about *piropos* while watching the tape.

How to Use: In advanced *Spanish Language* classes, the tape could be used to give an introduction to the way Spanish is spoken in Cuba. The different short interviews give the chance to hear many speakers. . . . The tape could bring up interesting discussions about the *piropo* and the way men and women see their roles in Latin American societies. It does very little to address these questions, preferring to deal humorously with the subject. I would use the tape primarily to introduce the notion of the *piropo* and to allow students to hear Cuban Spanish. (Langhorst)

In a *Sociology* course, the *piropo* could be looked at in relation to machista culture.

In a *Women's Studies, Sociology, Cultural Studies,* or advanced *Spanish Conversation* courses, the cultural and political dimensions of the *piropo* could be discussed.

Level: High School—University

PLAFF! (Plaff!)

Feature.   With Subtitles.   98 min.   1988
Directed by: Juan Carlos Tabío
Produced by: ICAIC (Calle 23 No. 155 Vedado, Havana; tel: [537] 333-862; fax: [537] 333-032)

Distributed by: Center for Cuban Studies, IMRE,
Evaluators: James W. Cooper, Donald W. Davey, Lourdes Fernández, Susan Griswold

Description: The central mystery of this hilarious comedy is who is throwing eggs (splat!) at Conchita, a widow struggling in conflictive relationships with her son; her new daughter-in-law; her suitor, Tomás; and her neighbors. Conchita is consumed by her fears. Although an old woman tells her that the eggs have great power and she must leave the house and move in with Tomás, Conchita is afraid of being betrayed once more. Witchcraft and superstition add to her depression, and only after she is literally frightened to death does a practitioner of Santería uncover the mystery of the eggs.

This film parodies everyone and everything, including filmmaking in general and this work in particular. The story line is persistently interrupted by all sorts of filmmaking pratfalls and feigned technical problems. The director addresses the viewers in person to explain why an important scene was not shot; a supposedly missing first reel turns up and is shown at the end; cues are given on screen; missing props are tossed in from the wings, etc.

Strengths and Weaknesses: This is a humorous and entertaining film. Its self-reflective techniques prompted diverse responses from evaluators ranging from "A marvelous film! . . . the most purposefully anti-Hollywood classical style imaginable" to "confusing . . . throughout the film the viewer wonders if these technical problems are tongue-in-cheek, or whether they actually had the nerve to debut a film that looks like it was put together by a twelve-year-old in a garage. An excellent example of bizarre, off-the-wall film-making." The fast-paced Cuban Spanish makes the film more appropriate for advanced language students.

Introducing the Tape: The film provides an excellent opportunity to introduce and discuss cinematic self-parody. Also, a discussion of Cuban traditional rituals, common superstitions, the concept of neighborhood witches, and the persistence of these beliefs despite revolutionary politics would help introduce the film.

How to Use: The film's illustration of various aspects of middle-class life in a socialist country provides sociological and cultural interest. After watching the tape, students can write about the film's critique of bureaucracy and traditional beliefs and its interesting treatment of fear; they can reflect on the significance of the eggs and who is throwing them and consider and comment on the cinematic style. (Cooper/Fernández)

In a *Cinema Studies* or *Film/Video Production* course, the film is an excellent example of techniques of self-reflexivity and self-parody.

Level: High School—University

EL PODER POPULAR EN CUBA

Documentary.   Without Subtitles.   30 min.   1990
Directed by: Patricia Boero

Distributed by: IMRE Archive

Evaluators: Hugo Chapa-Guzmán, Darién J. Davis, Glenn J. Kist

Description: This tape explains the political process in Cuba today, claiming that it is a participatory democracy, despite its government by one official Communist Party. The narrator takes us on a tour of the political process at the local, regional, and national levels and portrays the functioning of grassroots democracy. The popularly elected municipal assemblies, institutionalized by the Cuban Constitution of 1976, are responsible for local economic, educational, social, and legal matters. In addition, these municipal assemblies select representatives to the provincial assemblies and to the national assembly. The tape includes footage of the actual election process and debates of the municipal assemblies, both urban and rural. Cubans from diverse backgrounds are interviewed about the electoral process.

Strengths and Weaknesses: This well-organized and informative tape presents a clear picture of the workings of "people's power" in revolutionary Cuba. Actual footage from the local, regional, and national assemblies is effective, and interviews with Cuban workers add an important personal dimension to what would be considered propaganda by many.

The major weakness of this tape is that it only shows a prosperous, happy Cuba. There is no indication of the economic deterioration Cuba has experienced in recent years or of the repression of political dissent. In general, evaluators agreed that the tape uncritically made a case for democracy (although there is some implicit criticism of the bureaucracy). One evaluator felt the film was unconvincing and looked like a well-designed propaganda tool.

Introducing the Tape: An introduction providing a brief background on the Cuban Revolution, developments in Cuba from 1959 to the mid-1970s, and the purpose of the 1976 Cuban Constitution would be helpful for U.S. audiences. There should be an explanation of how the Communist Party is organized locally, regionally, and nationally and the limits of power in Cuba.

How to Use: The tape could be used as an introduction to practical politics. I would ask students to analyze the aspects of the representative democracy presented. (Chapa-Guzmán)

I would use this film in *Modern Latin American History* course as an out-of-class assignment. In the discussion after the viewing of the film, I would focus on the following questions: What is the point of view or political perspective of the producers of this film? What is the purpose of "people's power" in Cuba? Is "people's power" effective? (Kist)

Suggested Readings: Azcri, Max. *Cuba: Politics, Economics, and Society.*

Geyer, Georgie Anne. *Guerrilla Prince: The Untold Story of Fidel Castro.*

Harnecker, Marta. *¿Cuba, dictadura o democracia?*

Horowitz, Irving Louis, ed. *Cuban Communism.*

Mesa-Lago, Carmelo. *Cuba in the 1970s: Pragmatism and Institutionalization.*

Pérez, Louis A., Jr. *Cuba: Between Reform and Revolution.*

Szulc, Tad. *Fidel: A Critical Portrait.*

Timerman, Jacobo. *Cuba: A Journey.*

Level: University

LA POESIA DE NICOLAS GUILLEN

Documentary. Without Subtitles. 30 min. 1974

Directed by: Ambrosio Fornet

Produced by: CINED (7th Ave., No. 2802, Miramar, Havana; tel: [537] 237-742 or 237-887; fax: 537–331-697)

Distributed by: IMRE

Evaluators: Hugo Chapa-Guzmán, Marlene Gottlieb, Diane Marting

Description: This documentary introduces viewers to the complex poetry of Nicolás Guillén. It includes interviews with the author as well as footage of him reading his work. Using black-and-white lithographs from Mialhe and a disjointed editing style, the video creates a feel for Guillén's poetry, which tends to use fragmented statements. The tape places his work in biographical, historical, and political context, discussing how his poetry was influenced by the regimes of Machado and Batista and the death of his father for political reasons.

Strengths and Weaknesses: This is an excellent introduction to Guillén's work. It is well produced and interesting both visually and thematically. Traditional Cuban music provides the background sound. One evaluator felt the tape's best feature was the footage of Guillén himself, although it is brief and somewhat staged. The readings of Afro-Cuban poetry are also particularly effective.

The tape presumes viewers have background knowledge. One evaluator found the experimentation interesting but somewhat confusing. Another commented on its propagandistic quality, while others found it tedious in places. Some photos and figures from Cuban history and literature are not explained. At times, it isn't clear whether the film is discussing Machado or Batista.

Introducing the Tape: The audience should have some biographical background on Guillén and historical information on Cuba from the early twentieth century to the present and should be updated on recent events, including Guillén's death. One evaluator suggested pointing out to viewers the didactic quality of the tape, although it is quite evident from the tape itself.

How to Use: The tape can be used in classes on *Cuban Literature and Poetry* of the twentieth century, or any course that might use the blending of cultures to produce a new synthesis. (Chapa-Guzmán)

I would only use this tape in an advanced course in *Literature* that devoted quite a bit of time to Guillén, but it would be useful to show Guillén's popularity and centrality in Cuba after the revolution. I would prepare the students for the showing by discussing his political poetry and explaining the adulatory tone. (Marting)

I might ask students to view the tape on their own as an introduction to the poet before studying his work in depth. The tape might even substitute for a class lecture on the poet, especially in survey courses or *Latin American Civilization* courses where a general and somewhat superficial acquaintance with literature is sought. In a *Poetry* course, I would isolate the scenes in which Guillén comments upon his poetry, and would play his own readings of the poems so we can discuss his use of rhythm and emphasis. (Gottlieb)

Suggested Readings: Ramírez Alderete, and Ada Nilda. *El sonido y el ritmo en la poesía de Nicolás Guillén.*

Augier, Angel I. *Nicolás Guillén.*

Dawes, Neville. *Prolegomena to Caribbean Literature.*

Fernández Retamar, Roberto. *El son de vuelo popular.*

Hays, H. R. *Nicolás Guillén and Afro-Cuban Poetry.*

Mansour, Mónica. *Poesía negra de America, antología.*

Poetry of Nicolás Guillén and other Afro-Antillian poets such as Luis Palés Matos, Manuel del Cabral, and Emilio Ballagas (see bibliography).

Level: University

POLVO ROJO (Red Dust)

Feature.   With Subtitles.   105 min.   1981

Directed by: Jesús Díaz

Produced by: ICAIC (Calle 23 No. 155, Vedado, Havana; tel: [537] 333-862 fax: [537] 333-032)

Distributed by: Center for Cuban Studies

Evaluators: Richard Boly, Fortuna Calvo-Roth, Carmen Chávez, Marvin D'Lugo, Luis Martínez-Fernández

Description: A docudrama of the Communist government's efforts to operate a high-tech nickel and cobalt plant reluctantly left in Cuba by a U.S. multinational firm. The tape exposes the industrial problems connected with the first years of the Cuban Revolution: Experts flee and revolutionaries have to cope without spare parts and know-how in plant operation. Set in a mining town in Oriente, the film relates these themes by following the personal story of José Arias, who left his family to fight with the revolutionary insurgents and was believed dead. When José returns to his hometown, he finds his wife, Fabiana, has remarried an engineer at the plant. Fabiana plans to move to Miami with her new husband and two children.

The film brings together several key issues of the early moments of the revolution, among them the nationalization of the high-tech nickel mine and the clashes between the mining company's old management and the new administration composed of soldiers and workers.

Strengths and Weaknesses: This is a sensitive depiction of the emotional and ethical problems of Cubans caught in a struggle over family, economics, and political allegiances during the early years of the revolution, and the managing of the day-to-day operation of the country. The tape presents the divisions among the different factions of Cuban society: the church and "the revolutionary," those educated in the U.S., and the Cuban military. It deals with U.S. intervention in

Cuba within the professional community and the effects the *Americanos* have on the Cuban population. One evaluator noted the film's interesting perspective, that of Cubans who were forced to leave Cuba. Another reviewer appreciated that the tape showed the impact of the revolution on mining rather than in the usual agricultural setting.

Evaluators felt the film seemed contrived and propagandistic, stating that while emotional conflicts were presented, they were resolved in an unconvincing manner. Some found it too long and the soundtrack difficult to understand at times.

Introducing the Tape: Viewers need a brief historical summary of the first couple of years after 1959. Presenters should discuss the escalation of tensions between the United States and Cuba from 1959 to 1962. Background should cover the historical depiction of the flight of technical and professional people from Cuba and the impact of that flight on the country. The opening sequences need to be explained, as well as details of the triumphant return of the Sierra Maestra rebels.

How to Use: In my *Latin American Culture* course or a short course on *Cuban History,* I would give a historical framework, show U.S. film clips from the same period, and contrast different points of view (U.S. vs. Cuban) showing how the same historical event can be contrasted depending on the perspective. (Chávez)

This film might work well in a *Seminar on Cuban Film* to show the variety of treatment of history. As indicated above, the historical representation of the immediate post-Batista period is interesting in the way it dramatized the emotional/political conflicts. I would also emphasize the way in the 1980s that the problematic theme of national identity is treated as a historical problem, with the Cuban national continually aligned, in this film, with the family. (D'Lugo)

The film would be a very good source to convey notions about the struggles of a revolutionary regime that tries to maintain its economy without access to North American parts, technology, and natural resources. I would ask my students to enumerate the manifestations of dependence and how the new regime overcame them. (Martínez-Fernández)

Suggested Readings: Burton, Julianne. *Cinema and Social Change in Latin America: Conversations with Filmmakers.*

Welch, Richard. *Response to Revolution: The United States and the Cuban Revolution, 1959–1961.*

Level: University

PURO SABOR

Documentary.   Without Subtitles.   52 min.

Produced by: ICRT (26 nro. 301 Esquina 26, Vedado, Havana; tel: [537] 309-6565; fax: [537] 36-048)

Distributed by: Center for Cuban Studies,

Evaluators: José-Manuel Navarro, Jorge Rodríguez-Florido, S. Travis Silcox

Description: This is a magical tour of Cuba's top contemporary musical masters, giving a rollicking view of the vivacious, upbeat music for which Cuba is famous. Included are Grupo Sierra Maestra, Grupo Dan Den, Jacqueline Castel-

lanos, Charagon de Reve, Laye, Rumba Havana, Grupo Raison, Orquesta Original de Mazanilla, and Septeto Nacional.
Strengths and Weaknesses: As U.S. audiences rarely have the chance to hear, let alone see, these performers, this tape is a treat. The music is wonderful!

The video's production qualities are not high. The tape may bore some viewers if shown in its entirety and could instead be presented in segments. Grupo Sierra Maestra, Grupo Dan Den, and Orquesta Original de Mazanilla probably have the highest name recognition in the U.S.
How to Use: I would use the music to show an important aspect of Cuban culture—its diverse population and especially its Afro-Cuban background. (Rodríguez-Florido)

I would give a quick introduction to the history of salsa, then follow with the screening of the film, and discussion. (Navarro)

In a *Musicology* class, in addition to looking at the performers, the instruments, and the musical craft involved, I would point out the governmental support for the arts that enabled such large ensembles to work. (Silcox)
Suggested Readings: Boggs, Vernon. *Salsiology: Afro-Cuban Music and the Evolution of Salsa in New York City.*
Level: High School—University

RETRATO DE TERESA (Portrait of Teresa)
Feature. With Subtitles. 103 min. 1979
Directed by: Pastor Vega
Produced by: ICAIC (Calle 23 No. 155, Vedado, Havana; tel: [537] 333-862; fax: [537] 333-032)
Distributed by: Center for Cuban Studies, IMRE
Evaluators: Patricia Aufderheide (excerpted from *Cross Cultural Film Guide*), Susana Conde, Carmen Madariaga Culver, Margarita de la Vega Hurtado, Richard D. Woods
Description: Teresa is a woman who exemplifies the problems of Cuban women under the revolution: They have done a lot for the revolution, but what has the revolution done for them? Teresa has three sons and a traditional, rather suspicious husband. She also has a factory job and is a dedicated, harassed revolutionary worker who takes on the job of cultural secretary at the factory despite misgivings that she won't be able to handle her many responsibilities. The new responsibilities increase her husband's jealousy and infantilism and make her feel increasingly inadequate. She throws her husband out after an ugly scene, and he returns to his mother's house. Teresa is left shouldering the day-to-day burdens of managing life under the revolution. (Aufderheide)
Strengths and Weaknesses: This was one of Cuba's most popular films because it empathetically focused on a pervasive problem. Internationally the film has come to be regarded as emblematic of the best in Cuban cinema. It is viewed generally as an explicitly feminist film that questions the position of women in society. The story superbly focuses on women-to-women relationships and emphasizes the paradox of the traditional/liberated role of females. One

evaluator appreciated the film's good dramatic structure and clear expression of ideas: Women's lives cannot change with new laws under socialism; they must bring about these changes by their own actions. All background sound in the film is organic, thus viewers' emotions are not led by the music.

A couple of evaluators found the film almost contrived in its efforts to present the varying roles of females. One felt the film was best at showing the inequalities still existing in revolutionary Cuba.
Introducing the Tape: Some background on the history of the Cuban Revolution since 1959 would be helpful. The film can be introduced with the following: In 1974, the Cuban government promulgated its Family Code, under which both partners in a marriage must share in household and child-rearing chores, and both are entitled to the same sexual prerogatives. Five years later, director Pastor Vega illustrated in *Portrait of Teresa* the sexual inequality still pervasive in Cuban society.
How to Use: In *Latin American Film: Reconfigurations of Family and Nation in Latin America,* I would analyze with my students the representation of women in the film, the relationship of men and women, the issue of legislation vs. cultural practices, and the comparison of U.S. and Cuban societies on these issues. (Conde)

For *Spanish* classes, the film is superb for illustrating the Cuban accent. (Woods)
Suggested Readings: Aufderheide, Patricia. "Cuba Vision: Three Decades of Cuban Film," in *The Cuba Reader,* edited by Philip Brenner et al.

Black, Jan Knippers. *Latin America. Its Problems and Its Promise.* 157–168.

Burton, Julianne. "Portrait of Teresa," in *Magill's Survey of Cinema: Foreign Language Films,* ed. Frank N. Magill.

Burton, Julianne. "Seeing, Being, Being Seen: *Portrait of Teresa* or Contradictions of Sexual Politics in Contemporary Cuba."

Chanan, Michael. *The Cuban Image: Cinema and Cultural Politics in Cuba.*

Green, Duncan. *Faces of Latin America.*

King, John. *Magical Reels: A History of Cinemas in Latin America.*
Level: University

EL ROMANCE DEL PALMAR
Feature. Without Subtitles. 92 min. 1938
Directed by: Ramón Peon
Produced by: ICAIC (Calle 23 No. 155, Vedado, Havana; tel: [537] 333-862; fax: [537] 333-032)
Distributed by: Center for Cuban Studies
Evaluators: David William Foster, Marilyn Jiménez, Daniel C. Scroggins
Description: *El romance del Palmar,* starring Rita Montaner, is an old-fashioned musical melodrama with a dozen or more songs, among them pieces by Ernesto Lecuona. The

film includes such enduring favorites as "La Guajira" and "El Manisero." In the simple plot, Montaner, as a beautiful farmer's daughter, is lured off to the bright lights and night life of pre-Castro Havana by a villainous nightclub owner eager to exploit her musical talents and personal charms. Fortunately, true love in the person of a fellow performer rescues her from the clutches of evil and leads to a reconciliation with her doting parents.

Strengths and Weaknesses: The strengths of this classic Cuban film are its musical pieces, best appreciated by viewers who enjoy nostalgia. The musical score presents some of the great classic songs of Gonzalo Roig, Lecuona, etc. There are some interesting glimpses of life in the Cuban countryside, particularly the tobacco-growing regions. When seen through a 1990s sensibility, the film also shows how women became victims of a society that denied them economic opportunities other than the low-paying, routine work of the tobacco fields or factory.

At least 40 percent of the dialogue will be unintelligible to any except Cuban speakers because of the jokes and *piropos* perhaps known only to Cubans and the dialect of the *guajiro* and comic characters. Snippets of dialogue could be used in some language classes, but the film as a whole could not. The tape would probably appeal to Cubaphiles or Cuban-Americans but is of limited use for others. One evaluator felt that the film was commercial fluff typical of the 1940s, but it was worth watching the whole film just to see the final dance routine.

How to Use: I would use this in a *Latin American Film* course to show the type of musical melodramas that were produced by Latin American producers before the 1960s. In a course on *Cuban Culture* or *Literature,* it is an interesting counterpoint to the portrayal of Cuba in the forties and fifties in the works of Cabrera-Infante, among others. It would also work well with the second part of the film *Lucía.* (Jiménez)

I would use only clips to illustrate this type of Latin American filmmaking, especially the final dance sequence and probably some of the opening sequences in the tobacco fields—there are some good local-color bits. (Foster)

Level: University

SE PERMUTA (House for Swap)

Feature. With Subtitles. 105 min. 1984
Directed by: Juan Carlos Tabío
Produced by: ICAIC (Calle 23 No. 155 Vedado, Havana; tel: [537] 333-862; fax: [537] 333-032)
Distributed by: Center for Cuban Studies, The Cinema Guild
Evaluators: James W. Cooper, Jorge Porras, Jorge Rodríguez-Florido
Description: This humorous film set against the backdrop of Cuba's housing shortage involves an interfering mother who attempts to control her daughter's social life. The mother trades apartments with someone in a "better" neighborhood so that the daughter meets and gets engaged to the "right

type" —a Cuban bureaucrat with influence. The mother next arranges a five-way house trade so that they can all live together. The daughter, however, falls in love with a black architect and breaks off her engagement, and all the deals fall apart.

Strengths and Weaknesses: The film provides insight into housing arrangements in socialist Cuba. It is a clever, very well acted, believable comedy about an interfering mother. The film also parodies the Cuban bureaucracy, depicting it as causing moral treachery among friends, free love, and material greed.

The dialogue is fast, and one evaluator felt that some of the adult scenes and language were unnecessary.

Introducing the Tape: An introduction to Cuba and Latin America in general is suggested, as well as some background on the phenomenon of house swapping in Cuba. A familiarity with the socioeconomic status of various Havana neighborhoods and the general geography of the island would be helpful.

How to Use: I could use this in a course on *Afro-Hispanic Culture* to show the relationship between blacks and whites under Castro. Also it can be used in an *Urban Planning* class to show different housing arrangements in Havana. Finally, the soap-opera character of the documentary helps to elicit conversation and discussion in a *Spanish Conversation* class. (Rodríguez-Florido)

I would show fifteen to twenty minutes and discuss various aspects of the video, particularly real estate transactions in the U.S. as compared to those in a socialist country. Students could develop notes on culture and values they see in the video and contrast them with the U.S. (Cooper)

Level: University

LA SEGUNDA HORA DE ESTEBAN ZAYAS (Esteban Zaya's Second Time Around)

Feature. With Subtitles. 105 min. 1984
Directed by: Manuel Pérez
Produced by: ICAIC (Calle 23 No. 155, Vedado, Havana; tel: [537] 333-862; fax: [537] 333-032)
Distributed by: Center for Cuban Studies
Evaluators: Fortuna Calvo-Roth, Marvin D'Lugo, Jorge Rodríguez-Florido
Description: In December 1956, after the landing of Fidel Castro's revolutionary band in Oriente Province, Estéban Zayas, a local workman in a sawmill, finds himself in an emotional dilemma. Having once been deeply involved in the anti-Batista movement, he prefers now to remain outside of political intrigues. His principal interests lie in Lidia, a beautiful young married woman, and in Elena, who is closer to his age but seems to hold less attraction for him. Estéban's conflict intensifies when a man named Luis shows up at his cabin and asks him to collaborate with his old political ally, Víctor Sánchez. Estéban refuses at first, but eventually he becomes involuntarily involved with the revolutionary movement when Sánchez comes in person to seek his help. Es-

téban reluctantly allows Sánchez to stay and, ironically, is brought in for interrogation by the local military leader, Captain Valdivia. Valdivia suspects Estéban of collaboration with the insurrectionists and takes him prisoner. At last, Estéban's old revolutionary zeal is rekindled. He finds he cannot remain uncommitted, even though commitment could cost him his life.

Strengths and Weaknesses: This is a well-acted and suspenseful drama, a vivid document of an important period in Cuban history. The protagonist's parallel emotional and political conflicts are realistically and convincingly portrayed. The historical and political background gives contemporary audiences insight into the nature of rural life under Batista. The film also demonstrates Latin American machismo and other cultural and family values. It is well photographed and attractive.

One evaluator felt Estéban's character was underwritten and that the protagonist didn't hold the viewers' interest fully. The action drags a bit.

Introducing the Tape: Background would be needed on the Cuban situation between 1956 and 1958 (the time of Castro's revolt and the defeat of the Batista government in January 1959). An initial prefatory note is necessary on the significance of the landing of the *Granma* in 1956.

How to Use: In an *Introduction to Latin American Cinema,* the film might be a useful illustration of the effort to combine issues of national history into traditional movie genres, in this case the adventure/spy/combat film. On a more interesting level, the film would be useful in a course on *Cuban Cinema* to contrast the efforts to deal with national history within popular genres, specifically, the way the history of the revolutionary struggle is treated as the individual's ethical problem and thereby addresses a contemporary audience. The class might look at how a number of films of the 1980s (Fernando Pérez's *Clandestinos* and *Hello Hemingway* and Jesus Díaz's *Polvo Rojo,* for example) use material from the 1950s to address the individual spectator as citizen in the 1980s. (D'Lugo)

I can use this tape in any course on *Latin American Culture* or *Cuban History* because its content leads to an understanding and discussion of Cuban history/culture. In an advanced *Spanish Conversation* class, the film can lead to a discussion of important themes, such as machismo, friendship, loyalty, dictatorship, etc. (Rodríguez-Florido)

Suggested Readings: Tomás, Hugh. *Cuba: The Pursuit of Freedom.*

Complementary Films/Videos: *Clandestinos (Underground)* (Cuba); *Hola Hemingway (Hello Hemingway)* (Cuba); *Polvo rojo (Red Dust)* (Cuba)

Level: University

LA SEMILLA ESCONDIDA (The Hidden Seed)

Documentary. With Subtitles. 20 min. 1985
Directed by: Lázaro Buria
Produced by: ICAIC (Calle 23 No. 155, Vedado, Havana; tel: [537] 333-862; fax: [537] 333-032)

Distributed by: Center for Cuban Studies
Evaluators: Lavina Tilson Gass, Enrique R. Rodríguez
Description: A Cuban teacher narrates his experiences working to get young people involved in a school band. Some glimpses of the students' lives at home and in school are included, as well as some samples of their music. In one scene, an adolescent male is "acting out." The teacher realizes the young man has low self-esteem because people tease him about his large ears, and his family decides to remedy this with plastic surgery. After surgery, the youth focuses on his studies and changes C's and D's to A's and B's—success for the young man, his family, the community, and the Cuban Revolution. Music is also a key element in the boy's success. The teacher organizes a musical adventure in which the children take their instruments to an island and are allowed to play their hearts out.

Strengths and Weaknesses: This tape deals with many issues: peer pressure, low self-esteem among youth, alternative educational philosophies, and government policy. The teacher seems very sincere, and the music is excellent. The tape is brief and clear, leaving time for discussion. It encourages critical thinking and the formation of hypotheses and conclusions.

One evaluator noted that the teacher mentioned something specific about all of the children except the Afro-Cubans. Another commented that the music being played by the children seemed in part to be dubbed and not actually played by them. The subtitles are not direct translations but rather "idea equivalents," which does not make the film useful for language practice at early levels. For some viewers, the tape may seem propagandistic.

Introducing the Tape: An introduction to the different styles of Caribbean music would be useful.

How to Use: This video can be used for listening comprehension and conversation in advanced *Spanish* classes. Also, for motivating youngsters to do something extraordinary. The tape is useful for fun, for the sound and story are upbeat. In *Education* courses, it could be used with future teachers to discuss the extra-academic roles that teachers take on. (Tilson Gass)

In *High School* classes, the tape can enrich students' understanding of Cuba—understanding "global citizenry." I would use it as an enriching resource when comparing, contrasting, and drawing conclusions from information. (Rodríguez)

Level: Elementary School—University

LOS SOBREVIVIENTES (The Survivors)

Feature. With Subtitles. 12 min. 1979
Directed by: Tomás Gutiérrez Alea
Produced by: ICAIC (Calle 23 No. 155, Vedado, Havana; tel: [537] 333-862; fax: [537] 333-032)
Distributed by: Center for Cuban Studies, IMRE Archive
Evaluators: Fortuna Calvo-Roth, David William Foster, Franklin W. Knight, Kathleen March, José Pérez

Description: This is the story of an upper-class Cuban family that isolates itself from the Cuban Revolution after 1959, expecting it to last only a short time. The family refuses to change and moves from stagnation to deterioration to eventual self-destruction, and even cannibalism. This is a symbolic portrayal of the degradation and disappearance of this class. Based on a fictional text by Benítez Rojo, the story portrays a microcosm of differing reactions to the revolution and underscores the social structures that the process deconstructs, along with accompanying mentalities.

Strengths and Weaknesses: This is a very good film with overtones of Buñuel's portraits of upper-class mentalities in the process of advanced decay (as in *Exterminating Angel* or *Viridiana*). The film becomes increasingly expressionistic.

One evaluator commented that the film was "not pleasant" and may be difficult for U.S. viewers to receive. There is a clear, necessary political perspective that, though not heavy-handed, may not appeal to all viewers and might alienate certain groups. A couple of reviewers felt the plot was confusing, with a good deal of black humor but not much reflective analysis.

Introducing the Tape: An introduction should include a general explanation of prerevolutionary and postrevolutionary Cuban society and the ideology and emotions of the Cuban population. Also, information on Benítez Rojo's life and work would be helpful. The filmography of director Gutiérrez Alea should be mentioned, as he has made some important Cuban films, including *Memories of Underdevelopment, Death of a Bureaucrat,* and, most recently, *Strawberry and Chocolate,* a groundbreaking film about the friendship of a homosexual and a straight Communist Party youth.

How to Use: In *Cinema Studies,* the film could be placed in a tradition of cultural versions of a decaying oligarchy—Buñuel's *Viridiana* and literary texts like Cortázar's *La casa tomada* or Donoso's *El obsceno pájaro de la noche.* (Foster)

In a *Cuban Cinema* unit, this film can be viewed in the context of other works by director Gutiérrez Alea.

Due to its length, I would assign the film for out-of-class viewing, with instructions for subsequent class discussion and/or essay. (March)

Suggested Readings: Cortázar, Julio. *La casa tomada.*

Donoso, José. *El obsceno pájaro de la noche.*

Complementary Films/Videos: Gutiérrez Alea's *Memorias de subdesarrollo (Memories of Underdevelopment* (Cuba), *La muerte de un burócrata (Death of a Bureaucrat)* (Cuba), and *Strawberry and Chocolate* (distributed by Miramax Films), Buñuel's *Exterminating Angel* (distributed by Facets and the International Media Resource Exchange), *Viridiana* (distributed by Facets)

Level: University

SONES CUBANOS (Cuban Sounds)

Documentary. With Subtitles. 95 min. 1980
Directed by: Luís Felipe Bernaza, Constante Diego

Produced by: ICAIC (Calle 23 No. 155, Vedado, Havana; tel: [537] 333-862; fax: [537] 333-032)
Distributed by: Center for Cuban Studies, IMRE Archive
Evaluators: Elba D. Birmingham-Pokorny, Carmen Chávez, Ann K. Coughlin, Nancy Levy-Konesky, Joan A. McGinnis
Description: This compilation examines the Cuban *son* from its early origins to the present, showing its social and political message and its far-reaching impact on both the Latin and American music scenes. *Sones Cubanos* is a collection of five documentaries: *Ignacio Piñeiro, Felix Chapotin and Miguelito Cuni, Con sabor a caña, tabaco y ron, De dónde son los cantantes,* and *Con la misma pasion.* Musicians' lives and work are portrayed through interviews with them or those who knew them.

Strengths and Weaknesses: The collection provides a good understanding of the *son* and a rather complete picture of the African influences on Cuban music. The filmmakers follow the evolution of the Cuban *son* from the countryside to the city and up to the United States. The commentary is very interesting from the point of view of language (accent, syntax, choice of words, etc.) and information about Cuban music. The musicians perform wonderfully rich and exciting pieces, and the live footage of Cuba is excellent.

The film appears to have been made a long time ago. For a non-Cuban, the language and accent will be difficult to understand. This is both a plus (good practice) and a minus (some students may be discouraged). The first documentary includes the words and music of Ignacio Piñeiro, the Cuban innovator of the *sones* music of the twenties and thirties. It is a bit dated and students will have a little difficulty taking it seriously. The fourth documentary is somewhat long. The fifth documentary should follow a description of the *son* and an introduction to the major figures in Cuba. The collection is particularly appropriate for audiences interested in music and/or Cuba.

Introducing the Tape: A brief introduction to the importance of the *son* in Cuban history is needed, as well as some background on the Caribbean in the 1920s and 1930s. Also, it would be interesting to discuss how this music is used to send a political message and compare this with U.S. music.

How to Use: I would use this film to introduce students to the richness of the Cuban musical tradition, to help them develop an understanding and appreciation for the Afro-Cuban contributions to Cuban culture as a whole. (Birmingham-Pokorny)

I would use it as an illustration that music is a definite part of the culture of a people. I would introduce students to the various instruments as well as: *rhumba, salsita, guajiro/a, son, clavos,* and *maracas.* (McGinnis)

I would show the tape in short segments or have it playing between classes. It is great for students who love music and would also be excellent for an *Afro-American Culture* class. My Cuban students would enjoy it very much. (Coughlin)
Level: University

STONE'S THROW FROM CUBA, SAMPLE OF CUBAN TELEVISION

TV.   With Subtitles.   60 min.   1990
Directed by: ICRT
Produced by: Dee Dee Halleck, Monica Melamid
Distributed by: Center for Cuban Studies, IMRE
Evaluators: Elba D. Birmingham-Pokorny, Fortuna Calvo-Roth, Ann K. Coughlin, Marvin D'Lugo, Angharad N. Valdivia
Description: This is a four-hour collection of samples of typical programs from Cuban television, providing U.S. viewers with an electronic window into Cuban culture as presented on national television. Different types of programs such as soap operas, police shows, sit-coms, and documentaries on diverse topics are included, giving insight into the culture, politics, and entertainment of socialist Cuba. There is a wide variety in this sample.
Strengths and Weaknesses: Overall, this is a superb compilation series, although some segments are more effective than others. Among the most successful programs is the soap opera, *Los abuelos se rebelan* (Rebelling Grandparents), which uses humor to capture aspects of intergenerational conflict and everyday values and depicts Cuban social problems (e.g., housing shortages, rationing cards) in a natural way. *Cuando yo sea grande* (When I Grow Up) follows a child as he/she dreams of a particular career. The absence of the violence, sexually explicit subjects, and commercialism that pervade children's programs in the U.S. is impressive. Other shows offer revealing insights into Cuban society and television programming and have scattered moments of brilliance. Special mention should be made of *No porque lo dice Fidel Castro,* which apparently was not part of the regular television programming. This video about homosexuality in Cuba was made by a non-Cuban student at Cuba's international film school and touches on an important theme of social marginalization. Groups of young people openly and candidly express themselves about their views and prejudices. The impression is that, although discrimination exists in the society, the government is not oppressive.

The audience for this somewhat dated compilation video is limited; it would interest people especially attracted to the study of Cuban history and culture, sociology, or media studies but would not hold the average high school student's attention for long. At least two of the samples seem stridently propagandistic—*Veredicto en la Habana* (The Verdict in Havana), a documentation of the trial of General Arnaldo Ochoa, who was found guilty of drug trafficking and executed; and the report on *Televisión Martí,* U.S. broadcasts aimed at Cuba that are the equivalent of Radio Free Europe.
Introducing the Tape: In general, much of this material can be screened without an introduction, as prefaces have already been added to the tapes. Viewers might benefit from more detailed information about the social and political contexts that gave rise to certain programs (e.g., the foreign perception of Cuban state policy as homophobic). U.S. audiences will re-quire some background for *Veredicto en la Habana;* and the *Televisión Martí* program, while accurate in terms of its political assertions, needs to be acknowledged as a propagandistic text directed, unlike the earlier pieces, at a U.S. audience. Commentary about the experimental narrative nature of some of the programs would help orient viewers.
How to Use: I would use this film to introduce my students to all aspects of Cuban society after the revolution, as well as to U.S. interventionist politics in the Caribbean. The tapes are excellent as examples of spoken Spanish, and for helping students develop an understanding and appreciation of the richness of the Cuban culture and society. (Birmingham-Pokorny)

I am particularly interested in the soap operas and in *No porque lo dice Fidel* as supplementary texts for a *Cuban Film* course. These tapes could be viewed outside of class as examples of the social problems of marginalization described in major feature films from Cuba. (D'Lugo)

I think the program would work best as part of an exhibit. (Valdivia)
Level: University

LA ULTIMA CENA (The Last Supper)

Feature.   With Subtitles.   120 min.   1976
Directed by: Tomás Gutiérrez Alea
Produced by: ICAIC (Calle 23 No. 155, Vedado, Havana; tel: [537] 333-862; fax: [537] 333-032)
Distributed by: Center for Cuban Studies, IMRE
Evaluators: Peter Bakewell, Elba D. Birmingham-Pokorny, Donald W. Davey, Judith Elkin, Iris Engstrand, Mark Fried, Christine List, Carlos Pérez, Susan Ramírez
Description: The horror, brutality, and religious hypocrisy of the slave system are brilliantly brought to life in this account of an alleged incident set on a Cuban sugar estate in the mid-1790s during Holy Week. The plantation owner (the Count) washes the feet of twelve slaves and invites them to dine with him in imitation of Christ's last supper with his disciples. During the meal, the Count becomes increasingly drunk and expounds Christianity to the slaves, particularly the notions of salvation, paradise, and the attainment of perfect happiness through suffering. The slaves are bewildered by this treatment, and the Count promises that the next day, Good Friday, there shall be no work on the estate. Early the next morning, the Count leaves, and the slave administrator (mayoral), a brutal man who recently cut off a slave's ear to punish him for trying to escape, summons the slaves to work as usual. He knows the owner has declared the day a holiday, but he also knows that the cane must be cut to keep sugar production at the level the owner wants. The slaves rebel, setting fire to the estate and killing the mayoral. At first, the Count refuses to intervene, but then, incited by the burning and the death of the mayoral, he hunts down and kills all but one of the ringleaders.
Strengths and Weaknesses: The film lays bare the plantation system that was implemented once Cuba became the

world's primary sugar producer in the late eighteenth century. The filmmaker intelligently and artistically combines legends, folklore, and religion to document the painful and dehumanizing experience of slavery and to criticize the many abuses and crimes committed in the name of religion. The film is a powerful indictment of Spanish colonialism and the social hierarchy imposed—by both church and state—on blacks and Indians. The film is well acted, with good cinematography and realistic sets. The narrative is very easy to follow, but under this simplicity lies a complexity that instructors can explore with students. Many issues are tackled—race, class, religion, etc.—that can be further explored in the context not only of Cuban history but of Latin American history in general. The dialogue is vitally important, as it juxtaposes two worldviews, the African and the European. The clearly articulated Spanish is useful for language classes.

Some evaluators commented that a few scenes were too long and the music was somewhat "hammy." One reviewer felt that the film was a bit pretentious, with some overly obvious symbolism. Another thought it was too anti-Spanish.

Introducing the Tape: The audience should understand the importance of the Haitian slave rebellion of 1791 in the context of Latin American history. Its ramifications were felt in the development of the world market economy, as Cuba replaced St. Domingue as the primary sugar producer. This shift drastically affected Cuba's ideological, political, social, and economic development through the nineteenth and twentieth centuries.

How to Use: I would have students read materials on the *History of Cuba,* the slave trade, and the role of the church. The film would follow the lecture and discussion. (Elkin)

The film gives a good idea about the Cuban opinion of Spanish control and provides an excellent example of slave life—beliefs, desires of blacks. (Engstrand)

I would show this film to illustrate the points about colonial Catholicism mentioned above. (Bakewell)

In *Spanish Language* class, the tape can be used to introduce students to the different versions of spoken Spanish, to help them gain a better understanding of Latin American history, culture, and politics, and to teach them about the African presence in Latin America. (Birmingham-Pokorny)

As the film is long for classroom use, I would probably present two or three of the most dramatic scenes on separate days in order to bring the institution of slavery in Latin America to life. (Davey)

I would use this tape after lecturing on the impact of the British occupation of Havana and the Haitian revolt, on Cuba's becoming a major economic actor on the world market. Also, I would discuss the development of capitalism and the world market at the end of the eighteenth and early nineteenth century. We would then analyze the plantation system and the various components that went into its operation. After watching the film, we would take up the aspect of race and class and how these eighteenth-century events gave rise to Cuba's subsequent socioeconomic and political dependency on the United States. (Pérez)

Suggested Readings: Downing, John D. H., ed. "Four Films of Tomás Gutiérrez Alea" in *Film and Politics in the Third World.*

Freyre, Gilberto. *The Masters and the Slaves— Caza Grande and Senzala: A Study in the Development of Brazilian Civilization.*

Gilbert, Jorge. *Cuba: From Primitive Accumulation of Capital to Socialism.*

Gutiérrez Alea, Tomás. "The Viewer's Dialectic," in *Reviewing Histories: Selections from New Latin American Cinema,* ed. Coco Fusco, 178–96.

Hall, Gwendolyn Midlo. *Social Control in Slave Plantation Societies: A Comparison of St. Domingue and Cuba.*

James, C. L. R. *The Black Jacobins: Toussaint L'Ouverture and the San Domingo Revolution.*

Knight, Franklin W. *Slave Society in Cuba during the Nineteenth Century.*

LeRiverend, Julio. *Economic History of Cuba.*

Lux, William R. "French Colonization in Cuba, 1791–1809."

Moreno Fraginals, Manuel. *The Sugar Mill: The Socioeconomic Complex of Sugar in Cuba 1760–1860.*

Pérez Jr., Louis A. *Cuba: Between Reform and Revolution.*

Sánchez Crespo, Osvaldo. "The Last Supper," in *Reviewing Histories: Selections from New Latin American Cinema,* ed. Coco Fusco, 197–200.

Smallwood, Lawrence. "African Cultural Dimensions in Cuba."

Level: High School—University

VALS DE LA HABANA VIEJA (Old Havana Waltz)

Feature. With Subtitles. 84 min. 1989
Directed by: Luis Felipe Bernaza
Produced by: ICAIC (Calle 23 No. 155, Vedado, Havana; tel: [537] 333-862; fax: [537] 333-032)
Distributed by: Center for Cuban Studies, IMRE
Evaluators: Robert DiAntonio, Marvin D'Lugo, Francia Espinosa, Marilyn Jiménez
Description: This is the comic tale of a mother's attempt to celebrate her daughter's fifteenth birthday with a formal *quinceaños* extravaganza, despite the objections of her husband and daughter. Soledad, a dressmaker, and Epifanio, a projectionist in a movie theater, live in the old section of downtown Havana with their fifteen-year old daughter and younger son. Soledad, who never had a fifteenth birthday party of her own, wants one for her daughter, Odry. Epifanio thinks it would be a foolish extravagance and would rather spend the money on a new color television set. The plot revolves around Soledad's efforts to organize the gala while keeping her plans secret. She enlists the help of her female friends, who set up a spy network complete with codes and passwords. They use an ambulance to deliver the piano and order a cake made out of six hundred eggs. After a series of

comical complications, including the parents' temporary separation over the party dispute, all the difficulties are resolved. The story ends with Odry's elaborate fifteenth birthday party taking place as planned. The film presents the conflict of the traditional and the new in a good-humored way, poking fun at the mores of Cuba's revolutionary society, as well as at the contradictions of bourgeois ideology.

Strengths and Weaknesses: The film is quite funny in parts and does not take itself or its subject very seriously. A frivolous narrative on the surface, it provides some interesting insights into male-female relations in general and husband-wife relations in particular. The struggle between the husband's pragmatism and the wife's desire for some romantic illusion to enliven the family's otherwise drab existence could be read as an allegory of much of Cuban life in recent years. The on-location photography of the streets and neighborhoods provides an authentic sense of everyday life in Old Havana. The older women in the film are a wonderful cross-section of social types, perhaps demonstrating the true nature of neighborliness in Cuba. This film would appeal to high school students, as it concerns the problems of a young woman, her friends, and her parents.

One evaluator felt that the film had some imaginative narrative devices but then fell into an all-too-predictable pattern of plot and narration approximating the genre of U.S. television sit-coms. Another reviewer found the film quite boring.

Introducing the Tape: Some knowledge of the Cuban situation after the revolution would be useful, especially the types of educational institutions (school-farms, etc.) that were set up after the revolution. Some of the humor relies on the viewers' familiarity with the difficulties in transportation and the length of lines in Cuba. It would be useful to explain that the *quinceañera* is the coming-out party when a fifteen-year-old girl is formally presented to society, a tradition adopted from the Spanish upper class. Many Cuban exiles in the U.S. still have elaborate *quinceaños* parties. It is no longer just a tradition of the upper class. Many middle-class families go deeply into debt to "properly" present their daughters. In revolutionary Cuba, *quinceaños* celebrations have been seen as "bourgeois," but, as the film demonstrates, some traditions die hard.

How to Use: I would use this very straightforwardly for the enjoyment of the plot. The character of the mother is interesting because it would be easy for students to identify with her single-minded pursuit of a goal that no one else wants. The film also raises questions of how, though the goals of a society may change, individuals can continue to be caught up in the structures of a desire that run counter to social roles. This is a more subtle point, however, and needs to be teased out of the film by the instructor. This film would go well with others that portray the rite of the *quinceañera* in a serious manner. (Jiménez)

In a *Spanish Conversation* course, I would juxtapose the depiction of females (mother and daughter) with the depiction of mothers and daughters in other Cuban films, such as Tabío's *Plaff!* or *Se permuta,* for example. In a course on *Latin American Film,* I would introduce this work as an example of the variety of female characters who are central to the cultural narrative developed in Cuban cinema. Though this film is considerably less representative of dominant film trends, its very frivolousness suggests a unique image of everyday life that other, more "serious" Cuban films lack. In a *Women's Studies* course on female roles and representations in Latin America, it needs to be recognized that the image of women in this film are not entirely consistent with those usually depicted in Cuban films, i.e., the fifteenth-birthday aspect. (D'Lugo)

Suggested Readings: Randall, Margaret. *Cuban Women Now: Interviews with Cuban Women.*

Complementary Films/Videos: *Plaff!* (Cuba); *Se permuta (House for Swap)* (Cuba)

Level: High School—University

VAMPIROS EN LA HABANA (Vampires in Havana)
Animation.   With Subtitles.   80 min.   1987
Directed by: Juan Padrón
Produced by: ICAIC (Calle 23 No. 155, Vedado, Havana; tel: [537] 333-862; fax: [537] 333-032)
Distributed by: The Cinema Guild
Evaluators: James W. Cooper, Marvin D'Lugo, Jorge Porras

Description: This animated feature takes place in Havana in 1933, during the Machado dictatorship. Pepito (the film's hero) is a vampire and the grandson of Count Dracula, although he does not know it. His uncle, Werner Amadeus Dracula, developed a potion that enables vampires to tolerate daylight and has been feeding it to his nephew since Pepito was five. The plot involves two interconnected story lines. In one Werner Amadeus's plan to distribute his potion, free of charge, to vampires around the world is challenged by two opposing vampire groups—a business consortium from Dusseldorf and a mob from Chicago. Both groups are on their way to Havana to get rid of Werner and his potion. At the same time, Pepito is working with an underground network of spies and insurrectionists to overthrow the Machado dictatorship.

Strengths and Weaknesses: This entertaining film has excellent visuals and very readable subtitles. It appears to be a very witty reworking of the capitalist-socialist struggle. The concept of good and bad vampires—those willing to help others and those motivated by base capitalistic instincts—is quite clever. So is the linguistic play on Spanish accents, which adds humor. The spoken language makes the film easy for advanced language students to understand, and the simple plot and visuals make it suitable for beginners.

The story is a bit long and at times confusing. One evaluator found the format childish but the content purposeful. Another found the treatment of women sexist and stereotyped.

Introducing the Tape: The film is totally comprehensible without an introduction; however, classes could be given background about Hispanic history, culture, and politics, specifically the Machado dictatorship.

How to Use: I would provide my *High School* students a sense of geography so they can relate Cuba to Europe. Then, I would have them retell the vampire story and ask how they would relate the mob/underworld to a vampire tale. Then, I would follow up with similar parody on a current issue/problem that could be told as a myth parody. (Cooper)

In a course on *Cuban Cinema and Popular Culture,* the film could be shown with Alea's *Death of a Bureaucrat,* which incorporates animated segments. Both films make use of the cartoon genre to engage a popular audience. (D'Lugo)

For an advanced *Spanish Language* class, instructors could point out the idiomatic expressions used in the film, particularly the *Cubanismos,* unique to Cuban Spanish.

Complementary Films/Videos: *La muerte de un burócrata (Death of a Bureaucrat)* (Cuba)

Level: High School—University

VECINOS (Neighbors)

Documentary/Comedy.   With Subtitles.   15 min.   1985

Directed by: Enrique Colina

Produced by: ICAIC (Calle 23 No. 155, Vedado, Havana; tel: [537] 333-862; fax: [537] 333-032)

Distributed by: Center for Cuban Studies, IMRE

Evaluators: Jules Benjamin, Jorge Rodríguez-Florido, Margarita de la Vega Hurtado

Description: This documentary/comedy examines the real and potential problems that can develop among neighbors. It is a light though not unserious look at the difficulties of living together, such as noise and messiness, especially regarding garbage disposal. The camera angles are often voyeuristic, giving the viewer a feeling of spying on neighbors. Although shot in Havana, the tape reflects problems that occur in socialist and capitalist economies alike.

Strengths and Weaknesses: This is a very articulate and convincing demonstration of day-to-day frictions. It is well done and profound, providing a frank, fun, and rhythmic look at human relations on a daily level. The tape also demonstrates the needs of neighborhood councils in socialist Cuba. It is very approachable, with no cultural barriers.

Introducing the Tape: The film needs no introduction.

How to Use: The tape could be used in a *Film* class as an excellent example of an entertaining instructional documentary. (de la Vega Hurtado)

The tape could be used to show daily life in revolutionary Cuba. (Benjamin)

It would be a humorous tool to stimulate conversation in an advanced *Spanish* class, especially relating it to our own experience with neighbors. (Rodríguez-Florido)

Level: High School—University

Y TENEMOS SABOR (So Sweet)

Documentary.   Without Subtitles.   30 min.   1968

Directed by: Sara Gómez

Produced by: ICAIC (Calle 23 No. 155, Vedado, Havana; tel: [537] 333-862; fax: [537] 333-032)

Distributed by: Center for Cuban Studies, IMRE

Evaluators: David Bushnell, John Chasteen, Margarita Pont, Roger A. Sánchez-Berroa

Description: This black-and-white film is organized around discussing and demonstrating a series of instruments (especially percussion) used in more traditional Afro-Cuban music. It provides information about the origin and use of urban musical instruments and dance music and concludes with a Latin jazz session.

Strengths and Weaknesses: The film is an excellent demonstration of musical instruments and styles, with rich visual images intelligently incorporated. It provides a very good history of the instruments in Cuban music and will be of special interest to aficionados of Caribbean music.

While the true enthusiast will find this film quite valuable, other viewers may not. The tape is a little difficult to understand at times. The jazz session, meant to indicate the contemporary vibrancy of these musical ideas, seems dated, and some of the lyrics are hard to understand.

Introducing the Tape: Time and geographical location of the tape should be identified. U.S. viewers should be told that the development of Afro-Cuban music is very important because of the strong influence it has exercised over the whole circum-Caribbean region. Some introductory comments are necessary, as many U.S. high school students tend to believe that these segments represent an entire country or even all of Hispanic America. Also, viewers will need an introduction to the Cuban expressions, which are not familiar in other Spanish-speaking countries.

How to Use: I would use the tape to teach students the different dances and instruments of Cuba. Also, it could be used to illustrate the Indian influence in Latin American music. (Pont)

In my *History* courses, I would have to strain to find an appropriate spot to put this in, but would try nevertheless. (Bushnell)

Suggested Readings: Ortiz, Fernando. *La africanía en la música folklórica de Cuba.*

Level: Junior High School—University

YO SOY JUANA BACALLAO

Documentary.   Without Subtitles.   10 min.   1989

Directed by: Miriam Talavera

Produced by: ICAIC (Calle 23 No. 155, Vedado, Havana; tel: [537] 333-862; fax: [537] 333-032)

Distributed by: Center for Cuban Studies, The Cinema Guild

Evaluators: Rebeca Harclerode, Ulises Mejías, Michael Shane

Description: This is a short biographical sketch of Cuban singer-performer Juana Bacallao, including images of her nightclub performances and interviews on the development of her career and the revolution's impact on it. Juana Bacallao speaks briefly about herself and then sings "Yo soy Juana Bacallao" and "Mata siguaraya."

Strengths and Weaknesses: The tape is short but well constructed. It discusses the role of the artist in the revolution, and, while it promotes the Cuban Revolution, it doesn't overwhelm viewers with propaganda. The spoken Spanish is a good representative of a Caribbean accent.

One evaluator felt that the film was too short and its thesis unclear.

Introducing the Tape: Viewers need some background on Juana Bacallao and her career. The context of Cuban rhythms should be established. Some familiarity with Cuban art (music, film) would be helpful.

How to Use: The tape could be used in a *Spanish Language* class to show students typical Caribbean speech patterns. (Shane)

In a *Latin American Film* class, I would use this film to show the difference between what the Cubans conceived as revolutionary entertainment, and the entertainment industry that we know. (Mejías)

Complementary Films/Videos: *Sones Cubanos* (Cuba)
Level: University

YO TAMBIEN TE HARE LLORAR (I'll Make You Cry Too)

Documentary/Comedy.   With Subtitles.   15 min.   1984
Directed by: Enrique Colina
Produced by: ICAIC (Calle 23 No. 155, Vedado, Havana; tel: [537] 333-862; fax: [537] 333-032)
Distributed by: Center for Cuban Studies, IMRE
Evaluators: Jules Benjamin, Donald W. Davey, Margarita de la Vega Hurtado
Description: This is a documentary/comedy about the need for customer service and efficiency in a well-managed society. It uses humor, music, and interviews to convey its message. Cubans argue with one another and/or criticize the quality of work and services. The public complains of long delays and lazy workers who can't be fired. One woman suggests using a firm hand to deal with "deadbeats"; another suggests unannounced inspections. Workers say they get no respect and don't have enough time, spare parts, or raw materials. Music with appropriate lyrics provides a counterpoint.
Strengths and Weaknesses: This is an entertaining and creative portrayal of daily life in Cuba in the 1980s. Many people's responses, while addressing a serious topic, are very amusing. The camera work and editing are extremely well done.

The tape is a superficial treatment of the topic and avoids the more profound social and political issues.
Introducing the Tape: Viewers would need to understand the intentions of the socialist economy and social system to understand better the failings that are pointed out in the tape.
How to Use: I would show this as an adjunct to the part of my *Hispanic Cultural Perspectives* course dealing with attitudes toward work. (Davey)

In a *Comparative Societies* class, students could compare the problems touched on in the tape (in socialist Cuba) to their own experiences or observations (in the capitalist U.S.A.).

Economics students can discuss why such problems occur and possible solutions.

In *Film/Video Production* courses, the piece can be used as a creative example of the documentary approach.
Level: High School—University

DOMINICAN REPUBLIC

EL PODER DEL JEFE (The Power of the Generalissimo)

Documentary.   With Subtitles.   60 min.   1991
Directed by: René Fortunato
Distributed by: J&N Distribution
Evaluators: Silvia Arrom, Rosario Espinal, Joséph A. Gagliano
Description: This tape uses newsreel footage and still photographs to trace the rise and early dictatorship of Rafael Trujillo in the Dominican Republic. It emphasizes that the United States military occupation of the island nation from 1916 until 1930 facilitated the rapid advancement of Trujillo in the U.S.-created national guard. The narrative relates that U.S. military and State Department officials viewed Trujillo as a leader who would stabilize Dominican politics while protecting U.S. investments and guaranteeing repayment of the nation's sizable foreign loans. Trujillo's control of the military and his cooptation of church, business, and academic leaders are depicted as key factors in the consolidation of his authoritarian rule. The tape follows the dictatorship up until 1937 massacre of Haitians residing in the Dominican Republic and ends by identifying major national figures who aided the dictator in stifling opposition.
Strengths and Weaknesses: This detailed account of Trujillo's rise to power includes excellent and rare footage from the 1920s and 1930s. It uses many photographs of prominent Dominican leaders, as well as stills showing the capital and Santiago at the time. The program also includes background on Trujillo's youth and excerpts from his early political speeches, enabling viewers to hear his voice.

Evaluators felt that for general North American audiences the tape contained excessive detail about the violence during the 1930 and 1934 elections. One reviewer felt that the tape did not provide enough context for the viewer to understand how Trujillo came to power and held it for so long. Another reviewer found the tape overly polemical, simplistically emphasizing the U.S. role while minimizing domestic issues. The film includes photos of approximately twenty-five prominent leaders who helped strengthen Trujillo's authoritarian rule, but the narrative provides no specific examples of how and why their support was significant. The film ends abruptly with the 1937 massacre of Haitians.

Introducing the Tape: U.S. viewers will need general background on the Dominican Republic, particularly the period from 1915 to 1940 and Trujillo's rise to power. An introduction should also include a clearer outline of the 1930 and 1934 elections and the violence that followed each. Trujillo's political and military opponents should be identified. Viewers should be updated about subsequent events in the Dominican Republic and Trujillo's assassination in 1961.

How to Use: I would use this tape to illustrate the rise of a dictator to power, and to illustrate the role of U.S. foreign policy in supporting/installing dictators to power in the Caribbean. It would also be useful in examining an important period in the history of the Dominican Republic. (Espinal)

An edited version or segments of this tape would be used: (1) in discussion of the United States interventions in the Caribbean, Central, and South America during the early twentieth century; (2) in considering the effects of the World Depression on Latin America. The Trujillo dictatorship would be discussed by students as a case study in the growth of authoritarian rule in Latin America during the 1930s. (Gagliano)

Suggested Readings: Atkins, C. and Larman Wilson. *The United States and the Trujillo Regime.*

Crassweller, Robert. *Trujillo: The Life and Times of a Caribbean Dictator.*

Diedrich, Bernard. *Trujillo: The Death of the Goat.*

Galíndez, Jesús. *The Era of Trujillo.*

Ornes, German. *Trujillo: The Little Caesar of the Caribbean.*

Wiarda, Howard. *Dictatorship and Development: Methods of Control in Trujillo's Dominican Republic.*

Level: University

ECUADOR

ALLPAMANDA, POR LA TIERRA (Allpamanda, For the Land)

Documentary.   With Subtitles.   47 min.   1992
Directed and Produced by: Alberto Muenala (10 de Agosto 619 y Checa, Quito; tel: [593] 292-0410; fax: [593] 292-0231)
Distributed by: CIMR, Fabian Muenala, IMRE Archive
Evaluators: Gary S. Elbow
Description: This film was made by the Indigenous Organizations of Pastaza Province. It follows the April 1992 peasants' protest march from Puyo (the capital of Pastaza in the Amazon) to Quito to lobby for land grants to Indian groups and "plurinationalism" in Ecuador to recognize and preserve Indian culture. The march was part of the Columbus quincentenary protest.

Strengths and Weaknesses: This is an interesting film because it was made by the Indians; however, it is not techni-

cally strong. The march footage is too long and repetitive for U.S. audiences. The tape would be hard to understand for someone who is not familiar with the Indian protest movement in Ecuador.

Introducing the Tape: Instructors would need to introduce the concept of plurinationalism—the idea of giving Indian cultures equal recognition with Spanish culture in the state apparatus. Some discussion of the Indians' land demands would be necessary as well.

How to Use: I would use this tape as an example of how the Indians in Latin America are becoming more sophisticated and militant in demanding rights from the State. It is a nice example of native population/state relations that are evolving in some countries. I would discuss these issues before showing the film. The film then could be used to generate class discussion of the problem—Can the state be induced to give up territory and power to the Indians? Can the Indians handle the power? Can they protect the land if they get it? (Elbow)

The film can be used in conjunction with materials on the peasant rebellion in Chiapas, Mexico, to draw parallels between how indigenous peoples are confronting the state in various parts of Latin America.

Suggested Readings:

Kimmerling, J. *Amazon Crude.*

Menchú, Rigoberta. *I, Rigoberta Menchú: An Indian Woman in Guatemala.*

Uquillas, Jorge. "Social Impacts of Modernization and Public Policy, and Prospects for Indigenous Development in Ecuador's Amazonia," in *The Human Ecology of Tropical Land Settlement in Latin America,* ed. D. A. Schumann and W. L. Partridge, 407–31.

Whitten, N. *Sacha Runa: Ethnicity and Adaptation of Ecuadorian Jungle Quichua.*

Level: University

AMAZANGA (Amazanga, Heaven for Earth)

Documentary.   With Subtitles.   56 min.   1991
Directed by: Basile Sallustio
Produced by: Jungle Films (Rue Hollebeek 9, B-1630, Linkebeek, Belgium; tel: [322] 734-5905; fax: [322] 521-9108)
Distributed by: CIMR, IMRE Archive
Evaluators: Rebeca Harclerode, Julia Lesage
Description: This tape shows the use of small airplanes in the Amazon River Basin, U.S. religious missionaries' control over these flights, and the need for local organizations to have their own plane. The film starts out at a Congress of Indigenous Peoples in Quito, Ecuador. The president of Ecuador speaks about giving Amazon territory to the Indians. The importance of air transportation is discussed in connection with the Indians' hope to buy a plane collectively in order to be more independent of the evangelists. There is discussion of missionaries imposing their beliefs on the people, colonial competition for land and resources, and industrial disregard for environmental pollution. Through-

out the film, a vague argument is made in favor of native autonomy.

Strengths and Weaknesses: The tape is very clear and well made. It shows different tribes and language groups and provides a good analysis of the situation, although it depends on voice-overs. One evaluator felt that the film's overall purpose was not clear and that it was pro-Indian and anti-everyone-else in tone.

Introducing the Tape: U.S. viewers could use information about the tribes and language groups included.

How to Use: I would use this tape in the cultural aspect of my *Spanish Language* class, as I try to expose students to the people in the various places that the language is used. I would ask the class to answer questions regarding the diverse forces affecting the Indians' lives and also have them identify some of the language being used by the narrators. (Harclerode)

I would teach about using video to present an argument, and discuss the pre-production planning that would have to go into an ambitious project like this—one that covers people in so many areas. (Lesage)

Level: University

ASI PENSAMOS (This Is What We Think)

Documentary. With Subtitles. 29 min. 1984
Directed by: Camilo Luzariaga
Produced by: Grupo Cine (Av. America 3269 y San Gabriel, Quito; tel: [593] 256-6845)
Distributed by: First Run/Icarus Films
Evaluators: Jules Benjamin, Roger P. Davis, Jorge Marcone, Carlos A. Pérez

Description: This is the story of a former *hacienda* in Pillachiquir, located near Cuenca, Ecuador. The peasants have organized themselves into an association and now cultivate the land communally. There are scenes showing community members doing their daily routine at work and at home and discussing their efforts to organize against the local landlord despite government apathy and declining harvests. They speak of how their way of life has improved since they organized and about their particular struggle to preserve ancient traditions and a fragile environment while modernizing their lives and raising their productivity. The film presents Amerindian views on property, social organization, ecology, economics, and government. The villagers talk about the oppression of peasants by landlords, politicians, and society at large. They discuss the options open to peasants: migration and association at a national level.

Strengths and Weaknesses: This is an excellent visual portrayal of an Amerindian community, refreshingly presented from the peasants' point of view. The tape gives the Amerindian leaders an opportunity to make a statement to the state, nation, and/or outsiders about their community's political thought and the politics with which they want to be associated. The tape covers many topics: home and work routines, clothing, family, music, traditions, etc. The camera is unobtrusive, and the images and narrative work well together, with the background indigenous music maintaining theme and mood. The tape has a dramatic energy derived from the story of a murdered village leader. One evaluator considered the tape's lack of narration and its understatement to be strengths. Another felt that it was persuasive because the peasants' words are optimistic but not utopian.

The subtitles are difficult to read at times.

Introducing the Tape: Additional information on the scope of the Ecuadorian agrarian reform would be helpful.

How to Use: Instructors could use this tape to start an in-depth discussion on a number of themes: *hacienda* labor obligations, deforestation and drought, reforestation and social forestry, migration, and women's roles in agriculture. (Pérez)

The tape is a very useful document to prove that "traditional" societies are not frozen, but very much alive and far from being a living piece of a museum. I would use this film in my *Introduction to Latin America, Colonial Latin America, Modern Latin America,* and *Topics in Latin America* classes to focus upon the Amerindian peoples as a distinct body of peoples in Latin America, as a society and societies which offer different ways of "doing" economics, political organization, family, and society. I would use the film to raise questions about how indigenous societies/peoples adapt to "modern" surroundings and even change those surroundings. The film has elements that address ancient historical themes and modern topical issues. (Davis)

The tape could be used as an example of nonrevolutionary peasant self-mobilization. (Benjamin)

Suggested Readings: Icaza, Jorge. *Huasipungo: The Villagers.*

Redclift, M.R. *Agrarian Reform and Peasant Organization on the Ecuadoran Coast.*

Whitten, Jr., Norman E. *Sicuanga Runa: The Other Side of Development in Amazonian Ecuador.*

Level: High School—University

HIELEROS DEL CHIMBORAZO (Icemen of Chimborazo)

Documentary. With Subtitles. 21 min. 1980
Directed by: Gustavo Guayasamin
Produced by: (Edificio Yuraj Pirca, Calle Carlos Iba #176, Quito; tel: [593] 221-5789; fax: [593] 240-2363)
Distributed by: CIMR, First Run/Icarus Films
Evaluators: William O. Autry, Jorge Marcone, Carlos A. Pérez, Susan Ramírez

Description: This documentary tells the story of Ecuadoran peasants who make their living by bringing ice from the glaciated peak of Mount Chimborazo in the Andes to a number of small towns nearby. The icemen have been doing this work for centuries but still meet with discrimination. The video follows the people on a journey to secure ice, depicting the hardships they face. All the preparations for the trip are shown, along with the actual cutting or harvesting of the ice. Upon the icemen's arrival in a village, it becomes clear that their ancient trade and ways of life have been displaced by machine-made ice, now plentiful and cheap. The tape depicts the reaction of one iceman as he realizes that his way of life has been destroyed by modernization.

Strengths and Weaknesses: This film is beautiful and touching. It is an excellent testimony to the extreme poverty and isolation of these particular peasants from the highlands, or *puna*. The story line is reasonably easy to follow.

One reviewer felt the tape did not provide enough information and context so its message was not necessarily well defined. The iceman's Spanish will be very difficult to understand for all but the most fluent speakers, because of his accent and the anger and frustration in his speech. Thus, the tape is not useful for Spanish language instruction. Also, some English subtitles do not match the Quechua or the Spanish speech.

Introducing the Tape: The tape needs to be put into context for a U.S. audience. Viewers should be told in what era this is taking place. Do the icemen have any other ways of earning a living? Some background on the indigenous cultures and peasants of the Andes might be helpful and would enhance understanding and appreciation of the ethnic differences depicted.

How to Use: I would use this feature in courses dealing with the impact of modernization on peasant cultures. First, I would provide background on Andean societies of Ecuador/Peru—particularly emphasizing differences in ethnic and rural/urban aspects of these societies—then provide a specific introduction to the video, telling audiences what to look for and expect. The tape would be followed by discussions about the impact of modernization, and what might be done to assist these societies in the transition, as their ways of life are destroyed. (Autry)

I would present this within a discussion on peasant livelihood and the roles people have to play to diversify their economy in order to survive. This is a nice way to start considerations on the informal sector. (Pérez)

Suggested Readings: Heath, Dwight B., ed. *Contemporary Cultures and Societies of Latin America.*

Potter, Jack M., May N. Díaz, and George M. Foster, eds. *Peasant Society: A Reader.*

Level: High School—University

TIEMPO DE MUJERES (Time of Women)
Documentary.   With Subtitles.   20 min.   1988
Directed by: Mónica Vasquez
Produced by: (Casilla 3520, Quito)
Distributed by: Women Make Movies
Evaluators: Florence E. Babb, Sarah Chambers, Rick Langhorst, Janet Page-Reeves, Angharad N. Valdivia

Description: In Santa Rosa in the Cuenca region of Ecuador, as in many rural communities in Central and South America, many men migrate to the cities or to the United States in search of work. The women are left behind to take care of the children and assume the burden of running the community. This tape depicts the village women working in a wide variety of tasks, including communal projects. In interviews, the women speak of the pain of separation from their husbands and sons, and one discusses her impressions of the U.S. They all express great sadness and loneliness but seem determined to carry on.

Strengths and Weaknesses: The film is very effective in driving home an understanding of the mass exodus of men from Latin America to the United States and how difficult it is for those left behind, primarily women and children. It is a good view of rural life and how women are holding agricultural communities together. The film explores both the daily work of the women (the economic aspect) and their expressive side (the psychological and cultural aspects). It is also effective in showing community relations and villagers working together. The film is very useful in humanizing the migration experience of families and permitting U.S. audiences to see the other side of immigration—what happens to the families and communities left behind.

Some evaluators felt the video lacked cohesion and development and was sometimes hard to follow as it moved from one topic and scene to the next. Another felt the male narrator gave a machista perspective on the condition of women living without men. The Spanish is difficult to hear in places and the subtitles are minimal.

Introducing the Tape: U.S. viewers could use some background on Ecuador, the rural sector and migration, and gender division of labor. The tape does not elucidate the causes of the flight of the male labor force, nor does it show how the problem might be addressed. It would be useful to provide context on migration, to explain why there are no longer work opportunities for men in the countryside, and why few women migrate. It is not clear from the tape whether the only problem is unemployment or whether the peasants also face losing their land.

How to Use: If I were using the film to examine *Peasant Communities* or *Migration,* I would ask students ahead of time to think about how migration to the U.S. affects the community in Latin America. Few of the women are actually interviewed, so if I were using it in a course on *Women,* I would tell students to pay particular attention to what women are doing, as well as what they are saying. Then I would ask them in what ways they think the women's lives have changed because of the migration of the men. (Chambers)

I would find the tape useful in teaching women's roles in *Cross Cultural Perspectives,* and *Gender and Development Studies.* It is good on the changing gender division of labor as consequences of labor migration and relates well to the study of underdevelopment. (Babb)

Suggested Readings: Bourque, Susan, and Kay Barbara Warren. *Women of the Andes: Patriarchy and Social Change in Two Peruvian Towns.*

Deere, Carmen Diana. "Changing Social Relations of Production and Peruvian Peasant Women's Work."

Nash, June, and Helen Safa, eds. *Women and Change in Latin America.*

Phillips, Lynne. "Women, Development, and the State in Rural Ecuador," in *State Policy and Women in Latin America and the Caribbean,* ed. Carmen Diana Deere.

Weismantel, Mary J. *Food, Gender, and Poverty in the Ecuadoran Andes.*

Weiss, Wendy. "The Social Organization of Property and Work: A Study of Migrants from the Rural Ecuadoran Sierra."

Level: High School—University

LA TIGRA (The Tigress)

Feature.   With Subtitles.   80 min.   1990
Directed by: Camilo Luzuriaga
Produced by: Grupo Cine (Av. America 3269 y San Gabriel, Quito; tel: [593] 256-6845)
Distributed by: International Film Circuit
Evaluators: Emperatriz Arreaza-Camero, Susana Conde, Paul J. LaReau, Nancy Levy-Konesky, Margarita de la Vega Hurtado
Description: This film of love, power, magic, and revenge is based on the novel by José de la Cuadra. It opens with Don Clemente Suárez Caseros presenting a formal complaint to the police department against Francisca Miranda, "the tigress," who keeps her sister, Sarita, locked up in her room. The rest of the film is a flashback.

After their parents are killed, Francisca Miranda and her two sisters reign over a jungle outpost in the Amazon region of Ecuador. Francisca earlier witnessed her father's execution by bandits trying to take over his land, and she now uses her sexuality to exert power and keep control over their farm. The three sisters also own the only bar and store in the region, where they dance with the clientele and often choose one customer for the night. The sisters control not only peasants living nearby but also travelers to the region. The local *curandero* ("witch doctor"), whom Francisca regularly consults, predicts that for the sisters to keep their property, the youngest, Sarita, must remain a virgin.

Sarita soon tires of her sister Francisca's domination. One day, a local merchant, Don Clemente Suárez Caseros, comes to the farm and invites Sarita to the local fiesta. Don Clemente's motivations are questionable: Is he really in love, or is he just interested in the sisters' farm and business? When Sarita and Don Clemente decide to get married, Francisca "the tigress" opposes them, and Don Clemente enlists the aid of the police. The "tigress" kills a policeman, and reinforcements are called in. In the final battle, a voice calls the tigress back to the forest. She rises up but is shot. The film closes as her spirit runs through the forest, returning to nature as a manifestation of the eternal feminine.

Strengths and Weaknesses: This prizewinning film is strong and original, with sensual beauty, powerful music, and a forceful narrative. It contains impressively luscious images of Amazonian life, underscored by an evocative musical soundtrack. The women are independent and strong, not dominated by machismo.

The story is very allegorical and can be confusing. Many scenes jump between fantasy and reality, present and past, dream and consciousness, and fact and witchcraft. Evaluators had mixed reactions to the film's pacing: one found it slow-moving, others felt it appropriate for its genre. One evaluator commented that the pervasive feeling of unbridled sensuality was effective but often too self-conscious. The strong sexual images and situations would not be appropriate for screening in high school classes.

Introducing the Tape: An introduction providing historical background for the story or the literary source is necessary, as is information on magical realism. Viewers could be told that the film re-creates the myth of "the superwoman" as she could exist only in a tropical, macho culture. Francisca Miranda possesses a sensual beauty that she uses liberally to maintain dominance over everyone around her, including her lovers and her two sisters. The film takes place midway between fantasy and reality, the territory inhabited in literature by magical realism. Audiences also may be interested to know this was the second feature film ever to come out of Ecuador.

How to Use: I would use his film as an example of the role played by women—as makers of their own destiny—in the *New Latin American Cinema,* highlighting their aggressiveness and decision to resolve their own circumstances. (Arreaza)

Suggested Readings: Burton, Julianne. *Cinema and Social Change in Latin America: Conversations with Filmmakers.*

Gibbs, V. "Latin American Film."

King, John. *Magical Reels: A History of Cinemas in Latin America.*

López, A. "Setting Up the Stage."

Sklar, Robert, and Charles Musser, eds. *Resisting Images: Essays on Cinema and History.*

Various readings in *IRIS,* no. 13 (Summer 1991).

Level: University

YAPALLAG

Fiction.   Without Subtitles.   23 min.   1989
Directed by: Alberto Muenala
Produced by: Corp. Rupai (10 de Agosto 619 y Checa, Quito; tel: [593] 292-0410; fax: [593] 292-0231)
Distributed by: CIMR, Fabian Muenala, IMRE
Evaluators: Marcia Dean, Miguel Huarcaya, Joan A. McGinnis, University of Pittsburgh Group (María Consuelo Acosta, John Frechione, Shirley A. Kregar, Nichole Parker, Lynn Young, José Zavallos)

Description: This video adaptation of a Quechuan Indian oral folktale tells the story of a simple-minded peasant in a little town of the Ecuadorean Sierra. The peasant's wife sends him off with several assignments, but he never does anything right. This is a humorous sketch of a "bumbling idiot" who speaks with animals and does silly things but somehow, despite his simple nature, comes out on top.

Strengths and Weaknesses: The film contains interesting cinematography and authentic coverage of the Otavalo area. A few evaluators found it difficult to make sense of the story, other than as a comedy. One felt the acting was poorly directed.

Introducing the Tape: The film needs to be accompanied by an explanation of the folktale. This tape was made by a group of Quéchua artists using nonprofessional actors and is the first effort to use dramatization to capture the oral folk tradition on tape. A common theme in these oral tales is that life seems simple on the surface but that underneath there is a hidden twist or complexity that is revealed. For example, one Indian tradition is to give something to a buyer and receive the payment later. In the film, the simpleton "sells" some scarves to the statues in a church. When he returns for his money, the scarves have been removed. To get his payment, he breaks the church collection box. The "simplicity" is that the man got what he was owed; the twist is that the church robs the people and the peasant's act of restitution is completely justified.

Level: University

EL SALVADOR

RETURN TO AGUACAYO
Documentary.   With Subtitles.   18 min.   1987
Directed by: Celeste Greco (165 Magnolia Street, San Francisco, CA 94123; tel: [415] 474-2477)
Distributed by: Educational Film/Video Project, Facets
Evaluators: Rebeca Torres-Rivera
Description: A member of a U.S. church-sponsored delegation to El Salvador narrates this documentary. It briefly shows Operation Phoenix, a military action ordered by the government of El Salvador in July 1986 that bombarded a wide area (Aguacayo) occupied by peasants. The results were 22 people dead and 213 missing. The purpose of this action was to eliminate peasants who, it was believed, supported the guerrillas. The survivors were sent to a refugee camp, but most wanted to return to their own territory. The U.S. church delegation sought and received permission to help them. On their way back, the villagers were denied reentry to their territory by the military. Ultimately, through the efforts of international organizations, the peasants were able to return.

Strengths and Weaknesses: The images and their pacing depict step by step all the frustration experienced by the people. There is too much emphasis on the actions of the church (but perhaps this was inevitable as the tape was made by the church delegation).

Introducing the Tape: Historical background concerning the economic, political, and social situation in El Salvador would be useful.

How to Use: The tape could be shown after a lecture on repression in Central America. Students could debate the role of the church in the war in Central America.

Level: High School—University

TIEMPO DE VICTORIA (Time of Victory)
Documentary.   With Subtitles.   60 min.   1989
Produced by: Sistema Radio Venceremos
Distributed by: Third World Newsreel
Evaluators: Carol Becker, Rebeca Torres-Rivera
Description: This tape, made by the guerrilla film unit of Radio Venceremos, traces the gradual involvement of the peasants and workers of El Salvador in the FMLN (Frente Farabundo Martí de Liberación Nacional), their struggle against government forces, and the continually escalating U.S. intervention. It depicts the creative uses the "People's Army" makes of limited, primitive resources in its campaign to eliminate the abysmal gap between the haves and the have-nots. The victory implied in the title is expressed in the growing strength of the masses and in government's loss of power owing to the downfall of José Napoleón Duarte and his death from cancer. The FMLN guerrillas' motto, "We make war to win peace," synthesizes this victory.

Strengths and Weaknesses: The tape offers an excellent historical sequence with dramatic images from original footage. The chronological editing is quite effective. The scene of the massacre carried out by government forces at Archbishop Oscar Romero's funeral is particularly impressive.

The tape uses the most conventional forms of documentary production. Reviewers felt the interpretation was not very interesting and was a bit too long.

Introducing the Tape: A brief history of the conflict in El Salvador and an update on the present situation would be important.

How to Use: I would show the tape after a lecture on El Salvador, to reinforce words with visual images. (Torres-Rivera)

Level: University

GUATEMALA

BROKEN SILENCE: RIGOBERTA MENCHU
Documentary.   With Subtitles.   30 min.   1992
Directed by: Felix Zurita
Produced by: Alba Films (Apartado P-278, Las Piedrecitas, Managua, Nicaragua; tel: [505] 265-0021)
Distributed by: Films for the Humanities, First Run/Icarus Films, Jane Balfour

Evaluators: Joséph A. Gagliano, Diane Marting, Cliff Welch

Description: This tape features interviews with Rigoberta Menchú, the Guatemalan human rights activist and recipient of the 1992 Nobel Peace Prize. She speaks of the Quiché people, the cultures of indigenous peoples, and their struggles for recognition, human rights, land, cultural preservation, and political power. Menchú speaks as a woman and about women's position in these struggles. Focusing on the genocidal repression of Guatemala's indigenous population, the film shows Menchú's efforts to call world attention to the human rights violations, as well as her attempts to end discriminatory and racist policies in her native land. The film includes scenes from various rallies of indigenous people, including the Second Encounter of Indigenous Peoples of the Americas, held at Quetzaltenango, Guatemala, in 1992. It also includes a counterhistory of the Conquest as Menchú urges unity among Native Americans throughout the Western Hemisphere in order to find effective strategies for ending five centuries of oppression of the Indians by Europeans and persons of mixed races. Menchú is shown as especially concerned with the rights of indigenous women in the Americas.

Strengths and Weaknesses: The tape demonstrates Rigoberta Menchú's charisma. Her moving and often poetic manner of expression is captivating. The piece is well filmed, clear, and thorough in presenting her arguments regarding the demands of the Indians. There is a nice critique of those who enjoy Indian folk traditions but can't stand Indians as people. Menchú's Spanish is easy to understand, and the subtitles are clear and effective. Several scenes illustrate unique aspects of Guatemalan Indian culture. The tape is also quite brief, which makes it easier to use in classes.

The tape does not include much depth or background. Lacking general context, it does not explain major issues in race relations stemming from economic and sociopolitical concerns. Some may find the tape flawed in that it fails to present other opinions. There are no spokespeople for Menchú's opponents.

Introducing the Tape: A historical overview of Guatemalan policies concerning indigenous peoples and the U.S. relationship to these policies, as well as some background on the Quiché people, would make the tape more comprehensible for U.S. viewers who are unfamiliar with Guatemala's political and socioeconomic development.

How to Use: I would use this tape in my undergraduate *Central American and Caribbean Island Nations* and *Twentieth-Century Latin America* courses to demonstrate sources of conflict in contemporary Central America in general, and Guatemala in particular. (Gagliano)

I use Menchú's memoir, and this tape would be useful to update her views and show her in action, speaking and organizing in Guatemala. (Welch)

After reading her book, I would show the tape to open a discussion on the social function of literature—how it can change minds and societies. (Marting)

Suggested Readings: Ashabranner, Brent K. *Children of the Maya.*

Carmack, Robert M., ed. *Harvest of Violence. The Maya Indians and the Guatemalan Crisis.*

Cambridge History of Latin America, vol. 8—chapter on Guatemala since 1930.

Diéguez, María Luz. "La 'polifonía' como imperativo feminista: Desmitificación, subversión, y creación de nuevas voces narrativas en Esther Tusquets, Paloma Díaz Más, Carolina María de Jesús y Rigoberta Menchú."

Feal, Rosemary Geisdorfer. *Spanish American Ethnobiography and the Slave Narrative Tradition: Biografía de un cimarrón and Me llamo Rigoberta Menchú.*

Handy, Jim. *Gift of the Devil: A History of Guatemala.*

International Work Group for Indigenous Affairs. *Guatemala 1978: The Massacre at Panzos.*

Martínez-Echazabal, Lourdes. "Testimonial Narratives: Translating Culture While Narrowing the Genre Gap Translation."

Menchú, Rigoberta. *I, Rigoberta Menchú: An Indian Woman in Guatemala.*

Rice-Sayre, Laura P. *Witnessing History: Diplomacy versus Testimony.*

Salazar, Claudia. "Rigoberta's Narrative and the New Practice of Oral History."

Smith, Carol A., and Marilyn Moors. *Guatemalan Indians and the State, 1540 to 1988.*

Whisnant, David E. "La vida nos ha enseñado: Rigoberta Menchú y la dialéctica de la cultura tradicional."

Level: High School—University

GUATEMALA: CAMINOS DEL SILENCIO
(Guatemala: Roads of Silence)

Documentary. With Subtitles. 28 min. 1987

Directed by: Felix Zurita

Produced by: Alba Films (Apartado P-278, Las Piedrecitas, Managua, Nicaragua; tel: [505] 265-0021)

Distributed by: The Cinema Guild

Evaluators: Robert Claxton, Audrey Cournia, Susan Douglass, Carlos A. Pérez, Kathleen Ross, Rebeca Torres-Rívera

Description: In the past thirty years, the army in Guatemala has killed 90,000 civilians, and 36,000 have been "disappeared." In 1981, the military began an extermination campaign against the peasants: 120,000 Indians escaped to Mexico, while thousands were captured and put in work camps. Whole tribes fled to the mountains. This video, made in 1987, shows how the persecution continues, despite a new government. Tens of thousands of Indians have retreated into the mountains and have learned to organize for survival: they sow, harvest, establish schooling for the young people, and are always ready to flee when the military forces approach. The tape provides much information on the systems of agriculture and social organization developed by these people. The filmmakers interview people in the forest performing everyday tasks and escaping from Guatemalan army operations.The soundtrack consists of native instruments.

Strengths and Weaknesses: The video deals with a vitally important issue—the growing worldwide refugee stream—from the point of view of the indigenous people. It not only depicts the political issues but also shows some aspects of the Guatemalan indigenous people's lives and mores. The tape shows the difficulties the Indians must face in surviving with no outside aid under the constant pressure of the genocidal policies of the Guatemalan government. The tape is clearly sympathetic to the Indians.

A few reviewers commented that the video lacked interviews with the government and/or army. Some subtitles are a bit difficult to read.

Introducing the Tape: U.S. audiences could use background on the political situation in Guatemala and when and why this persecution started. Also, a brief update on Guatemalan history is necessary. Particularly important is a discussion of what has happened to Indian rights since 1987, when the film was made.

How to Use: Although it is obvious that one could first and foremost use this in a course to describe the fate of indigenous groups in Latin America, the possibilities that this film presents are many. I certainly would use it to discuss human adaptation and ecology (adaptation encompasses biological factors, but also social, economic and political factors). This film shows how peasants have been able to switch agricultural production so that it reflects the limitations and possibilities of a context regulated by war. (Pérez)

I would use this film to illustrate the problem of native Indians in Central America, as well as their ability to be self-sufficient in a life-threatening situation. (Douglass)

This film would be excellent to introduce students to the problems which refugees face, and to explain the nature of guerrilla and counterinsurgency warfare in less-developed countries. Also, the results of the application of "national security" doctrine. (Claxton)

After viewing the tape in my *High School Social Studies* class, students would research how Western media present information on this issue. Students might also write letters to the U.S. State Department and the Guatemalan government, as well as their own legislations, expressing their opinions on how the government treats these people. (Ross)

Suggested Readings: Menchú, Rigoberta. *I, Rigoberta Menchú: An Indian Woman in Guatemala.*

Complementary Films/Videos: *Broken Silence: Rigoberta Menchú* (Guatemala)

Level: Junior High School—University

THE LONG ROAD HOME
Documentary.   With Subtitles.   30 min.   1992

Directed by: Andrea E. Leland
Produced by: Andrea E. Leland Productions (1200 Judson, Evanston, IL 60202; tel: [708] 864-7746; fax: [708] 864-8454)
Distributed by: New Day Films
Evaluators: Walter R. and Marilyn Adams, Leonor Blum, David J. Robinson
Description: This is an account of a Guatemalan Indian, Maya Konjubal, whose family fled first to Mexico then to the United States during the political violence of the early 1980s. Ricardo narrates how he and his parents fled because of the repression under the U.S.-supported regime of Rios Montt. Ricardo, the eldest son, relates how, after he graduated from high school, he and his parents fled to Chiapas, on the Guatemalan-Mexican border, and were reunited with his relatives at a refugee camp. The refugees discuss the difficulties of obtaining food and finding jobs and their desire to return to Guatemala. The documentary ends in 1992, before the January 1993 return of many refugees to their homeland.

Strengths and Weaknesses: This is an excellent portrayal of typical forced migration of Guatemalans to escape military torture and repression. It is one of the few films depicting life in the refugee camps. The tape presents important issues: the destruction of old villages and the establishment of "new villages" (prison camps for peasants) and the migration of "illegals" into the U.S. It incorporates a good mixture of video clips and still photos and presents very emotional case histories.

The tape does not contain enough background. It ends before the resettlement process, which would have been important to include. One evaluator felt there were a few dull segments.

Introducing the Tape: A thorough introduction is necessary, including, a short history of Guatemala between 1954 and the 1990s, particularly focusing on the situation in the 1980s; an explanation of why so many Indians fled to Mexico and the U.S.; and the Arias Peace Plan and its effects.

How to Use: I would use this tape to show that one way the peasantry has dealt with their problems with harsh governments is by escaping via emigration, also to illustrate the consequences for other countries (Mexico and the U.S.). (Robinson)

The tape would be useful in courses on *Contemporary Latin America* and *Cultural Anthropology* to convey the importance of cultural identity and cultural adjustment under imposed change. (Adams)

Suggested Readings: Handy, Jim. *Gift of the Devil: A History of Guatemala.*

Jonas, Susanne, Ed McCaughan, and Elizabeth Sutherland Martinez, eds. *Guatemala: Tyranny on Trial, Testimony of the Permanent People's Tribunal.*

Schlesinger, Stephen C. *Bitter Fruit: The Untold Story of the American Coup in Guatemala.*

Level: High School—University

META MAYAN II (Meta Mayan II)
Experimental.   No Dialogue.   20 min.   1981
Directed by: Edin Vélez
Distributed by: Electronic Arts Intermix
Evaluators: William O. Autry, Deirdre Boyle, Susan Griswold, Christine List
Description: This is an experimental, expressionistic, visual portrayal of the Guatemalan Mayan people and their ways of life in the Guatemala highlands during the 1970s and 1980s. The tape includes scenes of indigenous peoples in the markets and other settings important in everyday life. The soundtrack is only ambient sound, with the exception of an NBC news broadcast voice-over about a 1980 incident when Mayans occupied the Spanish embassy and were burned alive by the Guatemalan army. The majority of the images are in slow motion—including Mayan people walking, running, at worship, in the marketplace, in processions, etc. This is director Edin Vélez's personal vision and has the feel of an outsider's view. Vélez wants to capture the spirituality of the people but can do little more than observe from behind the camera. Therefore he foregrounds the sense of distance by taking shots of Mayans staring back at him, and slowing the images down.
Strengths and Weaknesses: This is an excellent experimental work highlighting the problem of taping a culture that is not the filmmaker's own. It is very interesting visually, with little intellectual content. There is a stunning and loving rendering of color and faces in close-up.

Although the scenes are beautiful and are indicative of the strong Mayan influence on the Guatemalan culture, the tape provides no narration or background. Many students in the U.S. do not have either the historic or the current-events knowledge of Guatemala that would make these images convey their full impact and the intent of the videographer; thus an instructor's introduction is necessary. While some evaluators felt the tape was useful for showing the beauty and richness of the Mayan culture, one reviewer felt it would not be appropriate for anthropology or social science classes unless used in conjunction with more informative tapes, because it tends to mystify the Mayan culture.
Introducing the Tape: U.S. viewers should be told that this is an experimental, impressionistic film. An introduction to film aesthetics would be very useful. Some historic and current-events background on Guatemalan and indigenous peoples would also be important. Those studying about Rigoberta Menchú could be informed that her father was one of the peasants burned alive in the Spanish embassy.
How to Use: I use this tape in my courses in *Video Criticism* and *Media Criticism*. I think it could be used well in *Journalism* courses to demonstrate a nonverbal critique of news misinformation. It would also be useful to classes in *Latin American Studies* where the history and culture of Guatemala is under discussion. Of course, it is a must for any *History of Video Art* course because Vélez was a pioneer of the video "essay." (Boyle)

Before showing the video, we'd have discussion and background about the Maya in Guatemala; recent events and their historical background since the 1930s; the Catholic/Protestant Church and evangelicals in Guatemala; and the relationship between Guatemala, the U.S., and Mexico. After the tape, discussion would center upon the violation of human rights and the plight of refugees. (Autry)

I would use the tape to illustrate the problems of documenting cultures that you do not understand, and as an example of developing ways to honestly reflect personal impressions of foreign cultures rather than presenting your footage as "expert" knowledge. (List)
Suggested Readings: Lovell, W. George. "Surviving Conquest: The Maya of Guatemala in Historical Perspective."

Newsletters of the *Liga Maya Internacional* c/o Casa Guatemala, 4554 N. Broadway, Chicago, IL.
Level: Elementary School—University

RESISTIR PARA VIVIR (Struggling for Our Lives)
Documentary.   With Subtitles.   20 min.   1991
Directed by: Felix Zurita
Produced by: Alba Films (Apartado P-278, Las Piedrecitas, Managua, Nicaragua; tel: [505] 265-0021)
Distributed by: CIMR, EPICA, IMRE Archive
Evaluators: William O. Autry, Friederike Baumann, Wayne S. Osborn
Description: This film examines the plight of displaced Indians in Guatemala during the civil war of the 1980s and shows the role of a liberation-theology church in their midst. The tape documents the bishop of Quiché's first visit to Indian refugees in their jungle hideout at Petén. The Indians are survivors of the genocidal massacres by the Guatemalan army, which destroyed their home communities. The bishop is confronted with accounts of the horrendous injustices these Indian campesinos had to suffer, as well as their dignity and life-affirming strength, stemming from a deep sense of justice and community and their all-pervasive religious faith. The tape is as much a testimony to the 1982 state policy of Indian genocide and the continued persecution as to the qualities of the victims. It also gives a portrait of the bishop's spiritual progression from fear to committed defense of his suffering flock.
Strengths and Weaknesses: The film provides outstanding insights into the plight and strength of the Quiché Indians facing death and destruction at the hands of Rios Montt. The power of the film lies in its documentation of the brutal army massacres of defenseless human beings, the dignified strength of Quiché Indians in the face of horrors and unimaginable struggles, the immense distance between the church hierarchy and the grassroots followers, and why people of conscience in the church cannot avoid confrontation with a brutally repressive state. Interviews with the women are particularly good, as are the priest's comments.

The lack of background or political context detracts from the strong visual presentation. Apart from gathering evidence of systematic army massacres, the film mainly chronicles the bishop's visit. The emphasis on Christian faith is heavy, and one reviewer felt that at times the focus was too much on the religious service itself. While one evaluator felt the tape did an excellent job of taking the viewer inside the Indians' experience, another commented that the perspective throughout is that of outside visitors who literally drop in from a helicopter for a short encounter with the Indians. The sound quality is poor in some sections, and there are abrupt cuts.

Introducing the Tape: An introduction providing Guatemalan historical and political context is necessary for U.S. audiences. Instructors should present maps showing regions and communities that were affected and provide data on Guatemalan state policy in the 1980s, particularly the Rios Montt regime, and approximate numbers of murdered and displaced. This would give the proper context without taking away from the raw quality of the testimonials.

One evaluator felt that it would be useful to point out that the video is somewhat self-serving on the part of the Guatemalan church hierarchy, as the Guatemalan church has done little, either verbally or actively, to aid or prevent the suffering.

How to Use: This tape could be used in my *Central American Modern History* class when we consider the events in Guatemala since 1954. It would give the students a concrete sense of the plight of the Indians in the ideological struggle of the Cold War. (Osborn)

Initial discussion would include background about the Maya in Guatemala, recent events and their historical context since the 1930s, the Catholic/Protestant church and evangelicals in Guatemala, the role of the U.S. in this problem, and the nature of the U.S.-Guatemala relationship. After the video, discussion would center upon the violation of human rights and the plight of those caught between the government and the guerrillas. I would also introduce discussion of the role of non-Guatemalan companies and the labor of the Indians as major disruptive and contributing forces to this problem. (Autry)

Suggested Readings: Berryman, Phillip. *Liberation Theology.*

Handy, Jim. *Gift of the Devil: A History of Guatemala.*

Lovell, W. George. "Surviving Conquest: The Maya of Guatemala in Historical Perspective," 25–57.

Menchú, Rigoberta. *I, Rigoberta Menchú: An Indian Woman in Guatemala.*

RIGOBERTA (Rigoberta)

Documentary.   With Subtitles.   15 min.   1985
Directed by: Rebeca Chávez
Produced by: ICAIC (Calle 23 No. 155, Vedado, Havana; tel: [537] 333-862; fax: [537] 333-032)
Distributed by: The Cinema Guild, IMRE
Evaluators: Elba D. Birmingham-Pokorny, Ann K. Coughlin, Grace Leavitt, Irene Matthews

Description: Nobel Peace Prize recipient (1992) Rigoberta Menchú speaks about her life and the rebels' cause in Guatemala in the 1970s and 1980s. Menchú, a representative of her Quiché tribe and many indigenous peoples from the mountains, tells a story of exploitation, violence, and survival. The tape denounces the pain and suffering of Menchú and her people and the many obstacles that made her cultural assimilation into mainstream Guatemalan society extremely difficult. It describes the persecution she and her family endured and her remarkable courage. Intercut are village scenes, including a marketplace, and images of the capital city.

Strengths and Weaknesses: From the short interview with Rigoberta Menchú, one is impressed by her intelligence, strength, sadness, and determination. The film is a strong and effective reconstruction, well photographed and well paced. It makes economical use of documentary footage from past to present—news stories and "folkloric" shots—contextualizing the straight "talking head" presentation of Rigoberta. The most outstanding moments are those that pertain to the tragic death of members of Menchú's family. The scenes of the beautiful textiles and of a woman making tortillas are valuable, but the rather violent scenes of fighting may be upsetting for secondary school audiences. In general, the tape conveys a simple, clear message—it is propagandistic but also poetic. The length is good for classroom use.

Introducing the Tape: U.S. audiences could use background on the history of Guatemala. An introduction to Rigoberta Menchú and her winning of the 1992 Nobel Peace Prize would be helpful.

How to Use: The tape can provide an excellent introduction to Rigoberta Menchú, who she is and what she represents. The tape might make North American students more aware of what is going on in other American countries, especially Guatemala. (Coughlin)

I would use this as a supplementary text in my course on *Latin American Women Writers* or in *Narratives of Conquest* to lend veracity to the reading of *I, Rigoberta Menchú*. I also might use the tape as an example of mixed media documentary. (Matthews).

I would show this as part of a unit on the Central American republics, which includes a discussion of the numbers of immigrants to the United States due to political repression in their own countries, as well as a discussion of U.S. foreign policies in Central America. A good accompanying film might be *El Norte.* (Leavitt)

The tape could be used as an excellent vehicle for making students aware of the social and political reality of Latin America. In particular, the tape can be used to illustrate the impact that U.S. economic and military policies have on the life of the general population. (Birmingham-Pokorny)

Suggested Readings: Kattan-Ibarra, Juan. *Perspectivas culturales de hispanoamérica.*

Menchú, Rigoberta. *I, Rigoberta Menchú: An Indian Woman in Guatemala.*

Zan, Julio de, et al. *América: Conflicto, construcción, y desafío.*
Complementary Films/Videos: *El Norte*
Level: High School—University

SANTIAGO ATITLAN: CANTO DE UN PUEBLO
Documentary.   Without Subtitles.   60 min.   1991
Directed by: Froylan Rascon Cordova
Produced by: COMPA (Av. Cuauhtemoc # 1021–4, Col Del Valle, México 03100 D.F.; tel: [525] 575-3036; fax: [525] 575-6854)
Distributed by: IMRE
Evaluators: Marilyn and Walter R. Adams, Ulises Mejías, Susy Suárez
Description: This is the history of a village in highland Guatemala, as told by its indigenous inhabitants. The people of Santiago de Atitlán, a town battered by death squads and the Guatemalan military, plead for control of their community. In an effort to regain their autonomy and dignity, they get permission to police themselves and remove the army from their town. The video also shows religious practices, ceremonies, and folklore.
Strengths and Weaknesses: This is an ethnographically very rich piece, with beautiful videography and indigenous music. A great strength of the tape is its narration by the townspeople.

One evaluator felt parts of the tape were too long and others might be confusing to those unfamiliar with Guatemala.
Introducing the Tape: An introduction to the political history of Guatemala is important for U.S. viewers.
How to Use: This tape can be integrated into courses that address the ritual life of the Maya and courses dealing with textiles. (Suárez)
Suggested Readings: Menchú, Rigoberta. *I, Rigoberta Menchú: An Indian Woman in Guatemala.*
Level: High School—University

EL TAMBORON DEL INDIO PASCUAL ABAJ
Experimental.   Without Subtitles.   7 min.   1991
Directed by: Luis Argueta
Produced by: Morningside Movies, Inc. (362 W. 123rd Street, Ground Floor, New York, NY 10027; tel: [212] 316-3760; fax: [212] 316-3926)
Distributed by: Morningside Movies
Evaluators: Elba D. Birmingham-Pokorny, Susan Griswold, Carlos A. Pérez
Description: Ernesto Mérida recites a poetic story, describing and lamenting the violent massacre of the Quiché Maya five hundred years ago and in subsequent violent episodes. The poetic adaptation and artistic rendering are based on one of José Calderón Salazar's short stories, inspired by the written history and the oral folklore of Guatemala.
Strengths and Weaknesses: This is a beautiful story, very clearly articulated. Its strongest point is the way in which the filmmaker explores the issues of the uninterrupted persecu-

tion and genocide of the Guatemalan Indian in light of the quincentenary.

The tape has a conventional, slow approach in conveying its message. Beyond a few sound effects, there is only one image, that of the narrator talking to the camera. This gives a sense of intimacy but at the same time loses the visual potential of the theme.
Introducing the Tape: It should be made clear that the massacre of Indians the film refers to did not take place in one incident but represents a general trend. A historical context of the repression and systematic extermination of Indians in Guatemala and Latin America is needed. The tape also requires an introduction to the Popul Vuh.
How to Use: I would use this film to introduce my students to some of the social issues affecting the marginal groups in Latin American society, and also to introduce students to spoken *Spanish, Folklore,* and *Indian Legends and Myths.* (Birmingham-Pokorny)

This film could be used to teach the elements of poetry (how metaphors are created, how sounds convey feelings). But also as an introduction to the movement among artists to adopt social causes. (Griswold)
Suggested Readings: Menchú, Rigoberta. *I, Rigoberta Menchú: An Indian Woman in Guatemala.*
Level: High School—University

TEJEDORAS DEL FUTURO (Weaving the Future)
Documentary.   With Subtitles.   28 min.   1988
Directed by: Sonia González
Distributed by: Women Make Movies
Evaluators: Ana Carolina Castillo-Crimm, Graciela Michelotti, Vera Blinn Reber
Description: This video focuses on the contemporary role of indigenous women in Guatemala and the struggle for human rights. Although women first became politically active in a 1925 workers' strike and benefited from the Guatemalan Revolution (1944–45), women's opportunities have been decreased by the current oppressive government and the undeveloped nature of the economy. The government's human rights violations led to one out of seven Guatemalans leaving their villages, while the detention and death of men forced women to support their children with low-paying unskilled jobs. Although some women have "disappeared" or joined the guerrilla movement, others are participating in unions, widows' organizations, refugee groups, and mutual support groups to assure a future for their children and themselves. Mayan women have begun to weave the future to assure real democracy and the end of injustice.
Strengths and Weaknesses: This film has some excellent photography, musical background, and thought-provoking interviews. It shows the accomplishments of women in Guatemala in the last three decades. Fitting well into a fifty-minute class period, it provides a limited understanding of the position and role of the indigenous population in Guatemala.

The film offers little historical context on either the traditional role of the Guatemalan indigenous population or the revolution of 1944. It covers different periods, but weak editing and continuity make it somewhat confusing. One evaluator felt the focus on women seemed superfluous and that the real focus is on the need to continue to organize against the current Guatemalan government to assure social reform.

Introducing the Tape: To appreciate this film, viewers must have already been exposed to the history of political changes in Guatemala. An introduction should include a general historical background that would help students understand why this film is relevant and how it fits into other historical changes in Guatemala and Central America. Background on the Guatemalan indigenous population, the revolution of 1944, and the present evolution in government would be useful.

How to Use: I would precede the viewing with extensive coverage of Guatemala's history, and a detailed study of the role women have played in Latin American history. The book *I, Rigoberta Menchú* gives a clearer and more detailed view of life for Guatemalan women, and if used with the film, would provide the background which the film lacks. (Castillo-Crimm)

Suggested Readings: Menchú, Rigoberta. *I, Rigoberta Menchú: An Indian Woman in Guatemala.*

Level: High School—University

TODOS SANTOS CUCHUMATAN: REPORT FROM A GUATEMALAN VILLAGE (Todos Santos Cuchumatan: Report From a Guatemalan Village)

Documentary. English Voice-Over. 41 min. 1982
Produced & Directed by: Olivia Carrescia
Distributed by: First Run/Icarus Films
Evaluators: Susan Altgelt, Marshall Eakin, Nancy Levy-Konesky, Dennis West (excerpted from *Hispania Journal*)
Description: The village of Todos Santos is the subject of this powerful portrayal of traditional Indian life in the Guatemalan highlands. The tape presents a short historical introduction then explores the region's social and economic realities. Interviews with the Mam people of Todos Santos document the tragic social changes taking place. The film explores the impact of modernization on the lives of the Mam Indians in the community. Once self-sufficient, the villagers are now forced to migrate to the lowlands to find work in the cotton plantations. On November 1 and 2, however, poverty and frustration are forgotten amid the preparations for the annual celebration of All Saints' Day and the Day of the Dead. The film vividly describes the social turmoil that was a precursor to the severe repression and violence in the region in the 1980s.

Strengths and Weaknesses: This deeply respectful and important tape provides an overview of the life of the Guatemalan Indians and the problems they face, particularly the impact of migrant labor on their lives. The photography and the scenery are beautiful, and the interviews are excel-

lent. Historical and socioeconomic explanations are succinct and understandable without being overly didactic.

Introducing the Tape: Some background is needed to understand the relationship between plantation labor demand on the coast and land scarcity in the highland villages.

How to Use: I would use the tape in a course on *Central American History* to show students the life of Indians in contemporary Guatemala. It could be used in a course on contemporary *Latin American Sociology* to depict the life of Indians. (Eakin)

Suggested Readings: Menchú, Rigoberta. *I, Rigoberta Menchú: An Indian Woman in Guatemala.*

Oakes, Maud. *The Two Crosses of Todos Santos: Survivals of Mayan Religious Ritual,* a classic ethnographic study of religion in the Todos Santos, depicts the village as it was in the mid-1940s.

Schlesinger, Stephen, and Stephen Kinzer. *Bitter Fruit: The Untold Story of the American Coup in Guatemala,* a well-documented account of the U.S.-inspired overthrow of the government of Jacobo Arbénz in 1954.

West, Dennis. *Hispania Journal.*

Complementary Films/Videos: *Todos Santos: The Survivors* (Guatemala); *Mayan Voices: American Lives* (distributed by First Run/Icarus Films).
Level: High School—University

TODOS SANTOS: THE SURVIVORS

Documentary. With Subtitles and English Voice-Over. 58 min. 1989
Produced & Directed by: Olivia Carrescia
Distributed by: First Run/Icarus Films
Evaluators: Silvia Arrom, Gary S. Elbow, Carolyn Shapiro
Description: A documentary filmmaker returns to the village where she made a previous film to assess the impact of the guerrilla-military conflict of the 1980s. Interviews with survivors of the 1982 massacres, interspersed with scenes from daily life, give a good picture of how the massacres have affected the community and changed people's lives. The tape provides excellent background on the history of Guatemala and the socioeconomic conditions of the indigenous people. Included are segments on the effects of migration to Guatemala City and Mexico, the creation of civil patrols, seasonal migration to the Pacific Coast, and the relationship of civil unrest to the rise of Protestantism in the village.

Strengths and Weaknesses: This is a beautiful, moving film, with striking cinematography, including an effective use of masks and fire to recount the massacre. The story is largely told by the people of Todos Santos, whose words give an authenticity to the accounts of events during the 1980s. There is interesting dialogue about migration to the capital city, Evangelical influence, victimization of Indians by the Left and Right, and the Indians' insistence on not choosing sides. The film has far greater use than simply to point out the impact of the civil unrest on Todos Santos, because it contains many examples of forces for change that are largely universal.

The film is slightly dated (1987). While the Spanish is clear for nonnative speakers, the subtitles during the first ten minutes are difficult to read.

Introducing the Tape: Viewers could use some more context, especially historical background on the region. It might be helpful to give some information about the politics of the period and the violence that so profoundly affected this town.

How to Use: If I wanted to stress the impact of the military conflict, I would probably give a one- to two-hour preliminary survey of background, with emphasis on the exploitation of the Indians, beginning with the conquest. The article by Lovell cited in the bibliography would be an excellent model. One could deal with so many of the topics that are raised in the film, such as changes in Indian life. Students could play the role-playing game "Bullets or Ballots," based on Guatemala (available from the Roosevelt Center for American Policy Studies in Washington, D.C.). Another approach would be to show Olivia Carrescia's first film, *Todos Santos Cuchamatán: Report from a Guatemalan Village,* before showing the more recent film to compare the two and discuss changes in the community. (Elbow)

I would ask students to role-play—what would their responses be to the guerrillas, to the army, to their situation? What alternatives did the Todos Santos inhabitants have? I would take some of the people's statements and ask the students to explore the implications in these statements—what it reflects of the history, the economy, the indigenous philosophy. (Shapiro)

Suggested Readings: Americas Watch. *Human Rights in Guatemala: No Neutrals Allowed,* one of several reports by independent organizations that document human rights violations by both guerrillas and government.

Asturias, Miguel Angel. *Leyendas de Guatemala.*

AVANCSO, *Assistance and Control: Policies toward Internally Displaced Populations in Guatemala,* a brief report on the treatment of Guatemalan internal refugees who return to their homes from mountain hiding places.

Barry, Tom. *Roots of Rebellion: Land and Hunger in Central America,* links control of land to civil unrest in Central America.

Black, George. *Garrison Guatemala,* a good review of the early years of conflict, now somewhat dated.

Booth, John A. "Socioeconomic and Political Roots of National Revolts in Central America," a comparative analysis of recent civil unrest in Guatemala, El Salvador, and Nicaragua.

Cambranes, J. C. *Coffee and Peasants: The Origins of the Modern Plantation Economy in Guatemala, 1853–1897,* an excellent historical account of the process by which Indian villages lost their communal lands to coffee estates.

Carmack, Robert M., ed. *Harvest of Violence: The Maya Indians and the Guatemalan Crisis,* a collection of case studies of the impact of civil unrest on Guatemalan Indian villages written primarily by anthropologists.

Cultural Survival's catalog of books, and its quarterly and papers.

Dennis, Philip A., Gary S. Elbow, and Peter L. Healer. "Development under Fire: The Playa Grande Colonization Project in Guatemala."

Fried, Jonathan L., M. E. Gettleman, D. T. Levenson, and N. Peckenham, eds. *Guatemala in Rebellion: Unfinished History,* a collection of background documents on the history of violence against Indians in Guatemala.

Garrard Burnett, Virginia. "Protestantism in Rural Guatemala, 1872–1954," a study of the rise of Protestantism in the country that now has the largest proportion of Protestants in Hispanic America.

Handy, Jim. *Gift of the Devil: A History of Guatemala,* very strong on events of the twentieth century.

Jonas, Susanne, Ed McCaughan, and Elizabeth Sutherland Martinez, eds. *Guatemala: Tyranny on Trial, Testimony of the Permanent People's Tribunal;* victims of the violence report in their own words.

Lovell, W. George. "Surviving Conquest: The Maya of Guatemala in Historical Perspective," a succinct review of the history of European-Indian contact in Guatemala that focuses on the Indian ability to adapt and survive in the face of adversity.

Manz, Beatriz. *Refugees of a Hidden War: The Aftermath of Counterinsurgency in Guatemala,* details the impact of violence on Indian communities in three key areas of the country.

Melville, Thomas, and Marjorie Melville, *Guatemala: The Politics of Land Ownership,* a historical account of the development of patterns of land ownership in Guatemala.

Menchú, Rigoberta. *I, Rigoberta Menchú: An Indian Woman in Guatemala,* moving testimonial by the 1992 Nobel Peace Prize winner, a Quiché Indian woman from Guatemala.

Montejo, Victor. *Testimony: Death of a Guatemalan Village,* an eyewitness account of army attack on a small village in the Todos Santos region.

NACLA Report on the Americas

Salvado, Luis Raul. *The Other Refugees: A Study of Nonrecognized Guatemalan Refugees in Chiapas, Mexico.*

Schlesinger, Stephen, and Stephen Kinzer. *Bitter Fruit: The Untold Story of the American Coup in Guatemala,* a well-documented account of the U.S.-inspired overthrow of the government of Jacobo Arbénz in 1954.

Simon, Jean-Marie. *Guatemala: Eternal Spring, Eternal Tyranny,* a photographer's lavishly illustrated account of events in Guatemala during the 1970s and 80s.

Complementary Films/Videos: *Todos Santos Cuchumatán: Report from a Guatemalan Village* (Guatemala); *Mayan Voices: American Lives* (First Run/Icarus Films)

Level: High School—University

WINDS OF MEMORY
Documentary.   With Subtitles.   51 min.   1992
Directed by: Felix Zurita
Produced by: Alter Cine (53–71 Esplande, Montreal, Canada, H21 2Z8; tel: [514] 273-7136; fax: [514] 273-8280)
Distributed by: First Run/Icarus Films, Jane Balfour
Evaluators: George D. Beelen, Susan Douglass, Gary S. Elbow, Sylvia Hyre, Glenn J. Kist, Edgar G. Nesman
Description: The film provides a review of recent political unrest in Guatemala, with emphasis on class differences and attitudes. It begins with footage of the massacre of Indians by the military in Santiago Atitlán. In 1980, Santiago Atitlán, a center of the indigenous culture, had a population of 14,000 Quiché-speaking descendants of the ancient Mayas. In the ensuing decade, over 2,000 Indians were murdered and another 1,000 were "disappeared." Much of the loss of life is attributed to the attack in 1981 by General Benedicto Lucas García during his efforts to pacify the countryside by punishing population centers that supported guerrilla groups. In an interview some ten years after the event, General Lucas García claims that he loves the people and did nothing to harm them. He explains that his goal is to make their lives easier and says that the massacre that occurred was really the fault of the mayor, who set it up by summoning the population and placing the children in the front ranks of the crowd that was confronting the soldiers. Lucas García goes on to blame the influence of Cuba. The film depicts other results of the military's pacification campaign, such as the discovery and opening of mass graves. It shows communities of resistance and guerrilla camps in the mountains of the north and continues with excellent interviews with representatives of the ruling classes and military. A courageous member of the Catholic clergy is seen visiting the Indian guerrillas and condemning the military persecution. There is also skillful discussion of problems such as land distribution, working conditions on the estates of the wealthy, and the presence of foreign investment in Guatemala.
Strengths and Weaknesses: This is an excellent portrayal of the endurance of the Mayan culture in Guatemala and the struggles of the indigenous people, particularly over the past ten years. The interviews with General Lucas García and Sandoval Alarcón are excellent for revealing upper-class and military attitudes toward the Indians. Interviews with wealthy Guatemalans of European descent are contrasted with those of Indian community residents to demonstrate the social conflict in Guatemala. There is also a variety of scenes from diverse Indian villages. The juxtaposition of parties, celebration, and images of death and destruction is very powerful and moving.

The film fails to place the events of the 1980s in an adequate historical context. The very complex and long-standing reasons for the guerrilla movement and Indian resistance are not presented clearly. More background on the problems of land alienation, exploitation of Indian labor, etc., is necessary. Also, the film does not really address the validity of the charge that the Mayan communities were supporting the guerrillas.

Introducing the Tape: The film requires some background on the civil unrest in Guatemala and Central America to bring out more clearly the reasons for the guerrilla movements and Indian resistance. Readings of Booth's article (see below) or other materials on the Guatemalan revolution would be helpful. While the film mentions General Efraín Rios Montt, more information is needed about his role in the events of the mid-1980s. An explanation about the long-standing struggle of the indigenous peoples would be helpful, as unfamiliar viewers may get the impression that the violence against these communities began in the 1980s. The role of the clergy and the concept of liberation theology are also important to explain. The opening footage of tourists in Chichicastenango is excellent, but discussion may be necessary to clarify the film's point that tourists come to appreciate the Mayan ruins, while the descendants of the Mayans who built them are victims of systematic genocide.
How to Use: I would use this film for ninth-grade *Global Studies* classes to show the contrast between the powerful and the powerless. The film gives an excellent picture of the geography of this nation, as well as life in the cities and the forests. (Douglass)

In introductory *Latin American Studies,* I would present the film after discussion of problems in Guatemala/Central America. Students could read Claribel Alegría's book on El Salvador, *Luisa in Realityland,* or *I, Rigoberta Menchú* on Guatemala. In the discussion after viewing, I would ask questions about attitudes of the wealthy revealed in the film (racism toward Indian culture, etc.) and about why the Indians are perceived as a threat. This might be related to ideas about racism in the U.S. One might also want to ask students to think about how the Indians might take actions to improve their own situation (very idealistic, but it would get students to think about the relative hopelessness of the Indians' situation). The "Bullets or Ballots" game would be a useful strategy for this film (see comments on *Todos Santos: The Survivors*). (Elbow)

In my course in *Modern Latin American History,* I would use this as a way of illustrating one of the sources of conflict in Central America. Discussion questions could easily focus on such issues as the sources of social conflict in Guatemala, the endurance of the indigenous peoples, the forced acceptance of Spanish culture by the Mayas, or application of the dependency theory to Guatemala. (Kist)
Suggested Readings: Alegría, Claribel. *Luisa in Realityland,* a book on El Salvador

Anderson, Marilyn. *Granddaughters of Corn: Portraits of Guatemalan Women.*

Barry, Tom. *Guatemala: A Country Guide.*

Bizarro Ujpán, Ignacio. *Campesino: The Diary of a Guatemalan Indian.*

Bizarro Ujpán, Ignacio. *Son of Tecún Umán: A Maya Indian Tells His Life Story.*

Fried, Jonathan L., et al. *Guatemala in Rebellion: Unfinished History.*

Gleijeses, Piero. *Shattered Hope: The Guatemalan Revolution and the United States 1944–45.*

Immerman, Richard H. *The CIA in Guatemala: The Foreign Policy of Intervention.*

Krauss, Clifford. *Inside Central America: Its People, Politics and History.*

LaFeber, Walter. *Inevitable Revolutions: The United States and Central America.*

Menchú, Rigoberta. *I, Rigoberta Menchú; An Indian Woman in Guatemala.*

Montejo, Victor. *Testimony: Death of a Guatemalan Village.*

Smith, Carol A., and Marilyn Moors, ed. *Guatemalan Indians and the State, 1540 to 1988.*

Woodward, Ralph Lee. *Central America, a Nation Divided.*

Level: Junior High School—University

GUYANA

A MONTH FOR THE ENTERTAINMENT OF SPIRITS

Documentary.   With Subtitles.   30 min.   1991
Directed by: Kean Gibson
Produced by: Kean Gibson (Apt. A 58 Husbands Heights, St. James, Barbados; tel: [809] 424-5321; fax: [809] 425-1327)
Distributed by: University of California at Berkeley
Evaluators: Barbara Roos
Description: This tape contains footage of several different ceremonies demonstrating African continuities in a Guyanan community, including references to multicultural influences. Spirit possession is evidenced in some of the ceremonies.
Strengths and Weaknesses: The tape is well organized, and the carefully placed narration unobtrusively explains what is shown. The tape provides a good deal of information and is well paced. The participants in the ceremonies seem unselfconscious, with the exception of a visitor from the United States who seems to be playing to the camera toward the end of the tape.

While the tape covers much material, some of what is shown remains unexplained. In particular, the final section concerns a dance from the Congo, and, unlike the rest of the tape there is little information to guide viewers. The editing is very basic.
Introducing the Tape: An introduction should provide some economic, social, and historical context for the film. Information about the people featured in the video and how many participate in these ceremonies, a map locating the region, and some explanation of the final dance would enhance understanding.
How to Use: In a *Multicultural* course for freshmen I would

ask students to be alert for all evidences of diverse cultural influences that they can detect (the voice-over narration mentions only a few of them). (Roos)
Level: High School—University

HAITI

HAITI: KILLING THE DREAM

Documentary.   With Subtitles.   56 min.   1992
Directed by: Rudi Stern, Babeth, Katharine Kean
Produced by: Crowing Rooster Arts (P.O. Box 1944, Canal Street Station, New York, N.Y. 10013; tel: [212] 431-7408; fax: [212] 431-3816)
Distributed by: Crowing Rooster Arts, Jane Balfour Films, IMRE Archive
Evaluators: George D. Beelen, Silvia Hyre, Lester D. Langley, Vera Blinn Reber, Pamela M. Smorkaloff
Description: This powerful documentary traces the history of U.S. imperialism and indifference in the Caribbean and South America, portraying the poverty and violence that ravage the beautiful country of Haiti. The film presents a stark look at the country whose nineteenth-century origins as the world's first independent black republic have been obscured by decades of harsh repression. The documentary allows the desperate Haitian people to speak for themselves through interviews and through their exiled leader, Jean-Bertrand Aristide, Haiti's first democratically elected president. It traces Aristide's tortuous rise and fate (there have been five attempts on his life) and suggests that Haiti's repression has been historically enhanced and, in part, supported by the United States.

In the wake of the 1986 flight of Jean-Claude (Baby Doc) Duvalier, Haiti's poor and oppressed were given hope with the emergence of Aristide, a priest elected president in December 1990 with a whopping 67 percent of the vote. However, despite his popular appeal, Aristide was opposed by the U.S. government. He set up literacy programs, AIDS education, and land reform and concentrated on narrowing the awesome gap between the vast numbers of poor and the handful of super-rich who paid no taxes and were virtually a law unto themselves. In the eyes of the military, Aristide sealed his fate when he requested that several generals resign. The military carried out the coup d'état ousting Aristide only seven months into his presidential term. *Haiti: Killing the Dream* shows that the country, ruled by a succession of dictatorships, is the poorest and most vulnerable in the Western Hemisphere, with about 75 percent of its adult population illiterate and unemployed. The film ends appropriately with a protest against the fact that fleeing Haitian refugees are being turned back by the U.S. government to face whatever the military might have in store for them. An official from a refugee center claims that racism is at the center of the U.S. policy that returns desperate Haitians and welcomed fleeing Cubans with open arms.

Strengths and Weaknesses: The video presents the basic social and political realities of modern Haiti and provides useful historical context for the current situation up until 1993. There is a good integration of stills, movie footage, and music. The documentary is very detailed and successful in highlighting aspects of the crisis not usually touched on in the U.S.'s mainstream media. One evaluator felt the tape provided a balanced view of Haiti and of U.S. relations with Haiti. Another commented that, although it seeks to be even-handed, providing opposing views on controversies, the film's perspective is clearly one of support for Aristide and opposition to U.S. policies and the Bush administration.

Introducing the Tape: As the documentary provides a detailed history of Haiti, no introduction is necessary. However, students would need to be updated on events since the completion of the film in 1992. After years of exile, Aristide was returned to Haiti in 1994 by the U.S. military. Most of the former Haitian police and *Ton Ton Macoutes,* or secret police, were not disarmed by the U.S. military occupation force, and although the human rights situation has improved in Port-au-Prince, the capital, the same military forces are still in control, particularly in the countryside.

How to Use: In a *Latin American Survey* class the film could be used to introduce twentieth-century Haiti, with a particular focus upon the instability and lack of modernity. (Beelen and Hyre)

This video would be useful in my *Latin American Survey* course during the last week of class, where we discuss issues such as the role of the military, underdevelopment, the failure of U.S. foreign policies to support democratic governments, and U.S. interventions in Latin America. I would use it at the end of the week to emphasize issues that we had been discussing during the week. (Reber)

The program could be used as an introduction to a session on modern issues of *Caribbean History* and especially U.S. interests. (Langley)

I think the film would be seen to greater advantage if preceded by a viewing of the film *Krik? Krak!,* which focuses on the Duvalier regime. (Smorkaloff)

Suggested Readings: Aristide, Jean-Bertrand. *In the Parish of the Poor: Writings from Haiti.*

Knight, Franklin W. *The Caribbean.*

Langley, Lester D. *The United States and the Caribbean in the Twentieth Century.*

Wilentz, Amy. *The Rainy Season: Haiti since Duvalier.*

Complementary Films/Videos: *Krik? Krak!* (Haiti)
Level: University

KRIK? KRAK! (Krik? Krak!)

Experimental/Documentary. With Subtitles. 78 min. 1990
Directed by: Jac Avila and Vanyoska Gee
Produced by: Mountain Top Films (98 E. Broadway #3, New York, N.Y. 10002; tel: [212] 226-4093)
Distributed by: Facets, IMRE

Evaluators: Leslie Desmangles, Glenn J. Kist, Frank Laraque, Luis Martínez-Fernández, Claus Mueller, Pamela M. Smorkaloff, Thomas Whigham, Dessima Williams
Description: This imaginative, impressionistic film provides a sociohistoric overview of Haiti under the Duvalier regimes, primarily from the point of view of the rural peasantry. Neither a historical chronology nor an analysis, the film forms an impression of the Haitian people's feelings as they face a slavelike existence and build resistance to its horrors. Through the creative use of fiction film clips and newsreels of U.S. intervention in the 1920s, the film traces Haiti's history through the fall of Jean-Claude Duvalier, attempting to establish a causal relationship between foreign domination and the Duvaliers' human rights violations. Viewers witness the terrible economic and living conditions and the political oppression in the country under François (Papa Doc) Duvalier and Jean-Claude (Baby Doc) Duvalier. The Haitian people are portrayed as a gentle and often optimistic population facing apparently hopeless conditions. We see the operation of the *Ton Ton Macoutes* (Haiti's renegade secret police), the dependency on foreign corporations, and the boat people's futile attempts at escape to the United States. The conflict with the neighboring Dominican Republic, the use of *vudou* to control the populace, the influence of the cold war, and the use of anticommunist rhetoric to label Duvalier's opponents are also presented. The film intermeshes a hallucinatory magical reality in the social realist evocation of the people's activities. It unveils allegorical visions of their ancestral freedom quest haunting their stream of consciousness and inspiring dissent.

Strengths and Weaknesses: Visually shocking and musically hypnotic, the gripping *Krik? Krak!* "comes from the heart of Haiti," claims President Aristide. Made in the tradition of Haitian marvelous realism, the film is very useful for U.S. audiences who may not be aware of the level of violence during political turmoil in Haiti. It demonstrates how the country's past is alive in the present national consciousness, giving viewers an impressionistic understanding of life in Haiti. The excellent camera work shows the enormous gap between rich and poor and the negative impact of the U.S. policy. Some of the footage shows actual events; some shows reenactments. The film, however, presents not only a very thorough, compelling examination of oppression but one of resistance and its historical roots in Toussaint L'Ouverture (the precursor of Haiti's independence) and Boukman through the present. It tells the story of a courageous people in a continuous struggle for their dignity and freedom.

Some evaluators commented that although the nonlinear style conforms to the popular stream of consciousness in Haiti, it could be confusing to U.S. viewers and should be introduced.

Introducing the Tape: Viewers accustomed to traditional linear documentaries may need pointers to orient them to the film. They should be told that the film is not intended to give a detailed history of Haiti nor to provide answers but rather to create an impressionistic feeling for what life is like in Haiti and how the past and present merge.

Background briefly tracing the historical development of the country including the Duvalier regimes, the racial politics in Haiti, and recent events would be very useful.

How to Use: In my *Modern Latin American History* course I would focus on how little things have changed in Haiti before, during, and after the Duvalier regimes. (Kist)

Krik? Krak! is perfect for getting students to realize: (a) the complexity of development process in the Third World; (b) the role of symbolic structures in everyday life and in the politics of liberation and oppression; and (c) the gap between Western and non-Western value structures and perceptions of reality, and to a lesser degree, the power of nonlinear documentaries. (Mueller)

The film could be used in a course I teach on the history of the Dominican Republic to illustrate the real story of conditions in Haiti and to dispel Dominican bias toward Haitians. (Smorkaloff)

I would show sections of it to expose a class to cultural realities and to state repression. (Williams)

U.S. students often find it difficult to visualize life for a proud but impoverished people; this film builds just such an understanding. (Whigham)

Suggested Readings: Aristide, Jean-Bertrand. *In the Parish of the Poor: Writings from Haiti.*

Bellegarde-Smith, Patrick. *Haiti: The Breached Citadel.*

Chomsky, Noam. *Year 501, The Conquest Continues.*

Davis, Wade. *The Serpent and the Rainbow.*

Denning, Melita. *Vodoun Fire: The Living Reality of Mystical Religion.*

Desmangles, Leslie Gerald. *The Faces of the Gods: Vodou and Roman Catholicism in Haiti.*

Ferguson, James *The Dominican Republic: Beyond the Lighthouse.*

Ferguson, James. *Papa Doc, Baby Doc: Haiti and the Duvaliers.*

Greene, Graham. *The Comedian.*

Healy David. *Gunboat Diplomacy in the Wilson Era, 1915–1916.*

Herskovitz. *Life in a Haitian Valley.*

James, C. L. R. *The Black Jacobins: Toussaint L'Ouverture and the San Domingo Revolution.*

Lawless, Robert. *Haiti's Bad Press: Origins, Development, and Consequences.*

Lemoine, Maurice. *Sucre amer. (Bitter Sugar: Slaves Today in the Caribbean.)*

Leyborn, James. *The Haitian People.*

Metraux, Alfred. *Voodoo in Haiti.*

Montague, Ludwell L. *Haiti and the United States, 1714–1938.*

Nicholls, David. *From Dessalines to Duvalier: Race, Color, and National Independence in Haiti.*

Thoby-Marcellin, Phippe. *Canape Vert.*

Trouillot, Michel-Rolph. *Haiti. State Against Nations: The Origins and Legacy of Duvalierism.*

Weinstein, Brian, and Aaron Segal. *Haiti: Political Failures, Cultural Successes.*

Wilentz, Amy. *The Rainy Season: Haiti since Duvalier.*

Any serious book dealing with liberation theology in Latin America.

Level: High School — University

HONDURAS

ELVIA: THE FIGHT FOR LAND AND LIBERTY
Documentary. With Subtitles. 27 min. 1988
Directed by: Rick Tejada Flores and Laura Rodríguez
Produced by: Global Exchange, Laura Flynn (2141 Mission St., San Francisco, CA 94110; tel: [415] 255-7296)
Distributed by: Global Exchange, IMRE
Evaluators: Anna R. Adams, Silvia Arrom, Cynthia Radding, Carolyn Shapiro, Angharad N. Valdivia
Description: This powerful and personal documentary tells the story of Elvia Alvarado, a peasant woman who has been struggling for years to enforce an agrarian reform law that has been on the books since 1972. A single mother of six who has been arrested and tortured, Elvia is a leader with incredible perseverance and energy. The tape provides some historical background on the need for agrarian reform in Honduras, explaining the dependence on export crops, the powerful military, and conditions imposed by U.S. aid. It also gives a perspective on social issues in the country: the lack of education, medicine, and technical knowledge, as well as women's need to stand up to macho attitudes and/or physical abuse. Traditional agricultural methods (e.g., the digging stick) and some of the stark realities of poverty and military oppression in the Honduran countryside are depicted. Through interviews with landowners and government officials, the tape provides a variety of perspectives.
Strengths and Weaknesses: Elvia's story is an excellent portrayal of a rural woman leader. This moving, personal portrait clearly articulates the strong message that change is needed. The sequence of interviews with peasants, government officials, and landowners is very effective. The tape shows that the landowning classes use the label "communist" to demonize those who seek social justice.

One evaluator felt that the tape's analysis was shallow (stating that poverty does not inevitably lead to revolution). Another, on the other hand, felt the tape clearly showed that the peasants understand that they must unite and organize to effect any change. The tape is a bit outdated, specifically in its reference to the contra war going on during this period in neighboring Nicaragua.
Introducing the Tape: Instructors could begin with an explanation of the political economy of monocultural export nations like Honduras and the history of U.S. political, economic, and military domination of the region. Also, viewers need to know the date and context of the agrarian reform law. Some background on Honduras' relationship to the U.S. and

Nicaragua during the contra war would place the segment on this topic in context.

How to Use: The tape could be used to accompany the book *Gringo, Don't Be Afraid,* which I use often in my classroom, for discussions on peasant struggles and revolution in Central America. It could also be used in a *Women's Studies* course talking about women and politics. (Adams)

The tape would be well received by students because it is slick, short, and powerful. It would need considerable discussion to counter its simplistic analysis, but this could be done within a fifty-minute class period. (Arrom)

I would use the tape to illustrate the harsh conditions prevailing in Central American countries for the majority of their population; the capacity of peasants to organize in the face of fearsome military repression; and the way one woman has organized her people around class issues which concern both men and women vitally. (Radding)

The tape could inspire discussion about how to change social situations—What techniques are used? How is what Elvia's does similar to the work of César Chávez, Chico Méndez, or the U.S. civil rights movement? Students could study the lives of other women, like Rigoberta Menchú, and enact role-plays by debating their side with others representing landowners. (Shapiro)

Suggested Readings: Alvarado, Elvia. *Gringo, Don't Be Afraid: An Honduran Woman Speaks from the Heart: The Story of Elvia Alvarado.*

Menchú, Rigoberta. *I, Rigoberta Menchú: An Indian Woman in Guatemala.*

Cultural Survival's books, quarterly, and papers.

Level: High School—University

MOSQUITIA HONDUREÑA (Mosquitia Hondureña)

Documentary. With Subtitles. 30 min. 1992
Directed by: Roberto Miranda
Produced by: Chirripo (Apto. Postal 1065–2050, San Pedro, Costa Rica; tel: [506] 253-1352; fax: [506] 225-2307)
Distributed by: IMRE
Evaluators: Charles Brockett, Gary S. Elbow
Description: This is a portrayal of the everyday life and problems of the Mosquitia Indians in the Mosquitia region of Honduras. The tape focuses on the people's education, isolation, and relationship with the Honduran government. Featured are interviews with a schoolteacher, a community leader, a shaman, an herbalist, and an agronomist.
Strengths and Weaknesses: This film documents a little-known subgroup of the Miskito. One evaluator mentioned that, while there are several films and books about the Nicaraguan Miskito, this seems to be the only program that deals with the Honduran Mosquitias. There are some nice area shots of the Mosquitia village and landscape and beautiful photography of the people, especially the children.

The tape provides little background and does not present much information about the people's way of life (although there is quite a bit on pressures for change). One evaluator

felt the tape was slow moving. Another commented its objective was unclear—is it to point out how the Honduran government has ignored the Mosquitia?

Introducing the Tape: An introduction on the Mosquitia is definitely needed. The film provides only the basic demographic facts. It would be useful to contrast the Honduran group with the Nicaraguan Miskito, who were very much disrupted by the Sandinista revolution and subsequent civil war.

How to Use: I might use the tape with an older film, *Turtle People,* that deals with the Nicaraguan Miskito, to discuss the different recent histories of the two groups—relatively peaceful for Hondurans, and war-torn for the Nicaraguans. The film would also make a nice point of departure for discussing the relations between Indians and the state—what should the state be doing and what shouldn't it do for the Indians? (Elbow)

Suggested Readings: Dennis, Philip A. "The Costeños and the Revolution in Nicaragua."

Hale, Charles R. "Inter-ethnic Relations and Class Struggle in Nicaragua's Atlantic Coast: An Historical Overview," in *Ethnic Groups and the Nation State: The Case of the Atlantic Coast in Nicaragua,* eds. CIDCA/ Development Study Unit, pp. 35–57.

Nietschman, Bernard. *Between Land and Water: The Subsistence Ecology of the Miskito Indians, Eastern Nicaragua.*

Nietschman, Bernard. "Hunting and Fishing Focus Among the Miskito Indians, Eastern Nicaragua."
Level: University

LATIN AMERICA

BARROCO (Barroco)

Feature. With Subtitles. 108 min. 1989
Directed by: Paul Leduc
Produced by: Opalo Films
Distributed by: International Film Circuit
Evaluators: Thomas O. Bente, Fortuna Calvo-Roth, Lori Madden, Robert J. Morris, Roger A. Sánchez-Berroa
Description: *Barroco* traces the emergence of contemporary Latin American and Caribbean culture through the historical and musical encounters among native Mayan and Aztec populations, Spanish colonialists, and imported African slaves. It does so without more than a sentence or two, relying instead upon music to tell the story of conquest and eventual accommodation. Inspired by Alejo Carpentier's *Concierto Barroco,* the film is structured like a concert in four movements and includes a wide range of music, using pieces and rhythms from *Ave Maria,* Candomblé, danzón, Vivaldi, rhumba, Bach, opera, Silvio Rodríguez, and Pablo Milanés. This dreamlike interpretation attempts to express the philosophical and conceptual parameters of the Latin American baroque. The syncretic nature of the baroque is presented by way of "witnesses" to the encounter of the Old and New

Worlds, to the blending, now the *mestización* of peoples, religions, and forms of expression including the artistic, musical, and physical. A surrealistic montage of scenes and historical moments suggests the conflict, mixing, and coexistences characterizing the indigenous, white European, and black African elements in the Caribbean and Latin America. The brutality of the conquest and cruelty of the Europeans is constant. After reminders that Spain is itself a *mestiza* nation (as in the case of the Hispano-Arab), the film ends with the clear message that the *barroco,* whether Spanish or Latin American, is a broad-based, highly energetic, and sensitive blending of human beings and our forms of expression.

Strengths and Weaknesses: A very rich and imaginative film, with strong visual images and nice samples of dance woven into the cultural history. The success of the film depends on the viewer's preexisting comprehension of the baroque. It can be a powerful pedagogical aid for advanced students with at least a basic grasp of the concept. Anyone with some exposure to baroque expressions is likely to have a powerful response to the film.

The film is very surrealistic and obscure. The lack of linear chronology and explanation of characters and their metamorphosing roles could be disorienting for U.S. viewers with no background. Since there is very little dialogue, the film is not for those wishing to emphasize language studies.

Introducing the Tape: Students need to be prepared with information about the nature of Latin American baroque before seeing the film. The surrealism and images of Caribbean history should also be introduced to students. Background on Alejo Carpentier and his *Concierto Barroco* would also be useful.

Suggested Readings: Carpentier, Alejo. *Concierto Barroco.*

Level: University

BURIED MIRROR/CONFLICT OF THE GODS

Documentary.   In English.   58 min.   1991
Directed by: Christopher Ralling and Carlos Fuentes
Produced by: Quinto Centenario España
Distributed by: IMRE
Evaluators: Sharon Sieber

Description: This documentary, narrated by Carlos Fuentes, is a nontraditional treatment of the history of the conquest of the New World. The tape challenges colonial assumptions of superiority and demonstrates the juxtaposition of Indian gods and Catholic doctrine in modern Mexico and Latin America. Providing a chronological account beginning with Cortez's conquest of Mexico and the reconstruction of contemporary Aztec society, the film propels the viewer into this world from the point of view of the indigenous peoples.

Strengths and Weaknesses: This is a superb documentary that fills a slot previously ignored in the presentation of the cultural history of Mexico and Latin America. The material is heightened significantly by Carlos Fuentes's powerful and rhetorically skilled delivery. It is vibrantly interesting and very well put together and will definitely appeal to U.S. au-

diences. The video's multidimensional aspects make it useful for many different academic disciplines.

Introducing the Tape: The tape contains much historic background and needs no specific introduction.

How to Use: The tape could be used in an *Intermediate Spanish Language* class to show how language is a vehicle for culture; in an *Advanced Spanish Language* class it could show how the study of different linguistic systems involves the understanding of different systems and structures of beliefs and values. In an *Anthropology* class it would be useful to introduce new students to an alternative treatment of ancient and sophisticated pre-Columbian history. The tape would be equally pertinent in a *History* class for its juxtaposition of the history of values and the reconstruction of history from alternative points of view—that of the clergy, the official voice of authority; and the underdogs, the native people who were condemned to live as slaves under the auspices of Christianity. In a *Literature* class the tape would be useful to demonstrate the importance of the history of ideas. I would show how the understanding of the subconscious or racial consciousness of a particular people is fundamental to the understanding and appreciation of their art and literary production. (Sieber)

Level: High School—University

BURIED MIRROR/THE AGE OF GOLD

Documentary.   In English.   58 min.   1991
Directed by: Paul Newington and Carlos Fuentes
Produced by: Quinto Centenario España
Distributed by: IMRE
Evaluators: Lavina Tilson Gass, David J. Robinson, Engracia A. Schuster

Description: This tape is one of a series adapted from Carlos Fuentes's book *The Buried Mirror. The Age of Gold* deals with the early years of contact between Spain and America, portraying the development of sixteenth- and seventeenth-century Spain and its New World colonies. The tape describes the impact of silver bullion on Spain and Europe. It provides multiple views of the world via literature and painting and describes the consequences of interchange of crops and products between East and West.

Strengths and Weaknesses: With superb photography and excellent commentary, this is an incredible overview of the history of the Spanish-speaking Americas. It is entertaining to watch and very informative.

One evaluator felt the tape was rather slow and pedantic and that some of Fuentes's connections were romanticized and difficult to follow. For high school and college language courses, the tape may need to be shortened, but for courses dealing strictly with culture, it is excellent.

Introducing the Tape: The tape is self-explanatory and needs no introduction.

How to Use: I would use this tape to demonstrate the impact of Spain on the New World, and the countereffect of the opening of the New Worlds on Europe. (Robinson)

I would show some parts in my *Advanced Spanish Language* courses and use the book *The Buried Mirror* as a textbook. It is easy to read, inspirational, and not very long. The tape would be a reinforcement. Classroom discussions would follow. (Gass)

Suggested Readings: Fuentes, Carlos. *The Buried Mirror: Reflections on Spain and the New World.*

Galeano, Eduardo. *Open Veins of Latin America: Five Centuries of the Pillage of a Continent.*

Level: High School—University

BURIED MIRROR/UNFINISHED BUSINESS
Documentary.   In English.   58 min.   1992
Directed by: Michael Gill
Produced by: Quinto Centenario España
Distributed by: IMRE
Evaluators: Stephen K. Ainsworth, Rosario Espinal
Description: In Part Five of the *Buried Mirror* series, Carlos Fuentes narrates an examination of the reality of Latin American experience and existence. The film begins in Spain and uses the complexity of Spanish society, as well its contradictions, as a tool for understanding the Americas. Fuentes and his camera crew travel throughout Spain and the Americas to capture the sights and sounds important to convey his message.
Strengths and Weaknesses: The video is an eloquent and cogent argument for the benefits of cultural pluralism. Fuentes is one of the premier intellectuals of the twentieth century. He and the producer clearly have vast knowledge of Spain and the New World, and it is a pleasure to witness his discussion. The film is of very high technical quality, with no expense spared.

The objective of the work is to provide a reflection on Spain and the New World, yet the film moves so quickly across such broad material that some of the connections and logic seem forced or unclear. For example, the film never explains what Mussolini or Picasso had to do with poverty, urbanization, Indians, dictatorship, or art in Latin America.
Introducing the Tape: U.S. viewers need some background knowledge of Latin American history.
How to Use: Race is a dominant theme, as is cultural conflict, in Latin American and U.S. history. I would use this film to present the argument that, in spite of the conflict and suffering that has occurred in the creation of the multiracial, multicultural societies of the Americas, racial and cultural differences are ultimately positive and strengthening dimensions of the societies of the Americas. (Ainsworth)
Suggested Readings: Galeano, Eduardo. *Open Veins of Latin America: Five Centuries of the Pillage of a Continent.*
Level: High School—University

GALEANO: MEMORIA, MITO, DIOS, MENSAJE
Documentary.   Without Subtitles.   24 min.   1991
Directed by: Ataulfo Tobar
Produced by: CEDEP (La Isla No. 416 y Cuba, 1171 Quito; tel: [593] 252-5521; fax: [593] 254-2818)
Distributed by: IMRE

Evaluators: Emperatriz Arreaza-Camero, Rosario Espinal, Juan Espadas, Deborah Pacini Hernández, Gerardo Piña, Ann Marie Stock
Description: Eduardo Galeano gives a beautiful lecture about the reinterpretation of Latin American history. He reflects on the five hundred years since Columbus, offering his perspectives on memories and history, myth and reality, and God. Galeano criticizes the official history, the "*machos, ricos, blancos, and militares*" of the European conquering culture. He touches on the themes of racism, sexism, and homophobia. Bringing out the hidden history of the indigenous people and Africans in Latin America, Galeano emphasizes the value of pre-Columbian civilizations and the beauty of African practices in America. He makes the point that what must be commemorated in 1992 is the resistance of the oppressed. Intercut with Galeano's speech are images from Latin America to help provide context.
Strengths and Weaknesses: The strength of this tape is Galeano's gift as a powerful, compelling, and extraordinarily articulate lecturer and storyteller. The language is passionate and poetic. He presents a different vision of the "official story" of Latin America.

The format is not very imaginative and at times is amateurish, but this is overcome by the force of Galeano's personality. While one reviewer liked the musical background, another felt that European art and music subverted Galeano's focus on African and indigenous people's resistance. Another commented that at times the accompanying images of Latin America seemed somewhat contrived as illustrations of what Galeano was saying. One evaluator felt Galeano's discourse was too extremist and radical and ignored the positive influence of Spain.
Introducing the Tape: An introduction to Galeano and his work would be useful for those unfamiliar with him. Viewers of the tape would also benefit from a brief introduction to Latin American history, particularly the colonial years.
How to Use: I would present this film as an introduction and example of the search and research for the unofficial history of Latin America. (Arreaza-Camero)

I would use it to illustrate the efforts societies make to survive when facing hostility and the significance of cultural practices in premodern societies. (Espinal)

The tape would be useful in discussing the quincentennial. (Pacini-Hernández)

This tape could provide a context for courses on the *Literature, History,* or general *Culture of Latin America.* I would then have students read from Galeano's writings to explore his treatment of history and collective memory. (Stock)

This tape is ideal for a discussion in a *Conversational Spanish* course. I would have students read some of the chronicles (XVI Century) and *Memorias del fuego* by Galeano. (Piña).
Suggested Readings: *Cultural Survival's* quarterly, books, and papers

Galeano, Eduardo. *Open Veins of Latin America: Five Centuries of Pillage of a Continent.*

Galeano, Eduardo. *We Say No.*

Galeano, Eduardo. *Memory of Fire,* (3 Parts: Genesis, Faces and Masks, and Century of the Wind).

Gutiérrez, Gustavo. *A Theology of Liberation.*

NACLA reports.

Level: University

HOME OF THE BRAVE

Documentary.   In English.   53 min.   1986

Directed by: Helena Solberg Ladd

Produced by: International Cinema Inc. (200 West 90th St., Suite 6H, New York, NY 10024; tel: [212] 877-2972; fax: [212] 877-3462)

Distributed by: The Cinema Guild, International Cinema

Evaluators: Graciela M. Castex, Kim Kowalczyk, Kathleen March, Virginia Shen, Susy Suárez

Description: This tape documents the first opportunity that Native Americans had to present their concerns to the international community through the United Nations. The Indians of North, Central, and South America speak out on their common problems and today's threats to their traditional identities. They discuss the encroachment of whites on lands of Native American peoples: environmental damage, economic exploitation, cultural and linguistic discrimination, and destruction. Also discussed are paternalism, lack of comprehension, and the clash of tradition and progress.

Strengths and Weaknesses: This is a good example of indigenous organizations and their slow integration into the modern state and international sphere. The film does an excellent and sensitive job depicting the discrimination and sufferings of indigenous peoples of both North and South America. The tape's focus is broad, and the different indigenous groups are compared and contrasted. The call for solidarity is very powerful, and the historical and current issues affecting this population are treated with sensitivity and accuracy. The tape makes clear that the world can no longer ignore the issues addressed.

Some of the material is dated, yet it is very useful to illustrate early processes. One evaluator felt the program was too long.

Introducing the Tape: The tape is self-contained and needs no introduction.

How to Use: The tape can be used as an introduction to the issues related to Native Americans. It is an excellent documentary that can generate much class discussion. (Castex)

In *Literature* classes (I teach *Literatura Indigenista* in Spanish) I would combine film viewing with class discussion, in conjunction with works by and about indigenous peoples (in Spanish or in English translation). (March)

I taught a course on *Latin American Literature* in the fall of 1993 in which I introduced *Latin American Indian Literature* of José María Arguedas and also mentioned the Indian literature of Miguel Angel Asturias and others. This tape would definitely serve as an excellent highlight of Indian ways of living, and their thoughts, sufferings, and perception of traditions, which are reflected in their literary works. (Shen)

This is a very good film to contrast the level to which the indigenous people have organized themselves since the documentary was made. It even seems naive compared to the level of political savvy that Indian organizations have achieved. I would use the tape in the *Minority Achievement Program* to illustrate various minority groups and the resources used by marginalized groups to push their agenda forward. (Suárez)

Level: High School—University

NIÑOS DEUDORES (Children in Debt)

Documentary.   With Subtitles.   43 min.   1985

Directed by: Estela Bravo

Distributed by: The Cinema Guild

Evaluators: George D. Beelen, Brian Goldfarb, Silvia Hyre, Michael Monteón, Richard Stahler-Sholk

Description: Shot in Bolivia, Colombia, Peru, and Argentina, *Children in Debt* provides an insightful combination of personal and structural accounts of the foreign debt and the effects of economic austerity programs on the poor, especially children. The filmmakers argue that children in Latin America are born with a burden that ensures that the majority will live difficult and impoverished lives. Included are interviews with people on the street (including homeless children), a priest, workers in an orphanage, and employees of a social welfare agency who protest ongoing cutbacks. The film depicts the contrasts of rich and poor and places the resulting drug abuse and prostitution cultures in their social context. It asserts that the U.S. spends significant amounts of money on arms at home and abroad to maintain this status quo.

Strengths and Weaknesses: The tape uses a balance of personal accounts and factual information to present an accessible yet complex description of economic imperialism in Latin America. There are moving interviews with children, and the images of slums and street children have emotional impact. Examining how the debt is experienced by various communities and age groups across four nations, the tape demonstrates that the problem is vast and institutionalized.

There is, however, little discussion of how the debt developed or what can be done about it. One evaluator felt the tape's appeal to a notion of childhood innocence challenging the exploitative nature of international finance implies that there are innocent and non-innocent victims of economic imperialism.

Introducing the Tape: Some background is necessary on how the debt was created. Viewers could use a brief introduction referring to the post-1982 debt crisis, capital outflow, and the economic downturn in Latin America since that time, as well as information on the economic and social impact of the International Monetary Fund's adjustment programs. As scenes from a variety of countries are presented, a few sentences summarizing the impact of debt-related austerity in each country would be helpful.

How to Use: This tape could be used to show the devastating effects of huge debt. (Beelen and Hyre)

I would use the video to aid students in a discussion of the economic imbalance between the Northern and Southern Hemispheres, its history and the mechanisms through which it is maintained, and national and international approaches to its solution. In addition, I would direct students to consider how concepts such as innocence, youth, and development, drawn from a discourse of psychology, intersect with ideologies of world economic development both in this tape and in popular media representations. (Goldfarb)

The tape could be used as a depiction of inner-city poverty. (Monteón)

I could use this in a course on *Debt and Democracy in the Third World* to supplement a week on *Austerity vs. Human Needs*. The film would not provide analysis or much empirical information, but it would help bring home the human implications of what might otherwise seem like a technical issue. (Stahler-Sholk)

The Debt Game, a tape that gives a detailed technical analysis of the debt from a Third World perspective, would be an effective complement to this program.

Suggested Readings: Ambrosi, Alain, and Nancy Thede, eds. *Video the Changing World.*

Burton, Julianne. *Cinema and Social Change in Latin America: Conversations with Filmmakers.*

Burton, Julianne. *The Social Documentary in Latin America.*

Burton, Julianne. "Don (Juanito) Duck and the Imperialism of Patriarchal Unconscious." In *Nationalisms and Sexualities,* ed. by Andrew Parker et al.

Burton, Julianne. "Women behind the Camera."

George, Susan. *A Fate Worse than Debt.*

Hansen, Edward. *The Human Condition in Latin America.*

Jesus, Carolina María de. *Child of the Dark: The Diary of Carolina María de Jesus.*

Lernoux, Penny. *Cry of the People.*

Pines, Jim, and Paul Willeman. *Questions of Third Cinema.*

Rocha, Glauber Pedro de Andrade. "El manifesto del 'cinema novo': La estetica del hambre."

Roddick, Jackie. *The Dance of the Millions: Latin America and the Debt Crisis.*

Saalfield, Catherine. "Pregnant with Dreams: Julia Barco's Visions from Latin America."

Schuyler, George W. *Hunger in a Land of Plenty.*

Complementary Films/Videos: *O jogo da dívida (The Debt Game: Who Owes Whom?)* (Brazil)

Level: High School—University

ONWARD CHRISTIAN SOLDIERS
Documentary.   With Subtitles.   52 min.   1989
Directed by: Gaston Ancelovici and Jaime Barrios
Distributed by: First Run/Icarus Films
Evaluators: Robin Andersen, Juan Espadas, Jorge Marcone, Richard D. Woods

Description: Fundamentalist Protestants now number 35 million in Latin America, and religious broadcasters spread their message from HCJB radio in Ecuador to TV Rio in Brazil. This video attempts to unravel the complexities of the Protestant Evangelical movement's penetration into Latin America, focusing on three Evangelical sects and liberation theology in Ecuador and Brazil. Powerful footage of exorcisms, baptisms, and preachers is mixed with testimonials of the converted, those who preach, and those who oppose the influence. This is augmented with historical and sociological analysis of the religious traditions and social upheavals that provide the context for the spread of fundamentalism. Population shifts from country to city create instability within families and communities, especially among the poor; the resulting sense of loss and anxiety explains the appeal of religion's soothing message. The political implications are vast: authoritarian rule goes unchallenged and unthreatened.

Strengths and Weaknesses: This is a balanced educational tape with perspectives from both the Evangelicals and their critics, such as the Catholic clergy, sociologists, Indian activists, and historians. The tape has great analytical depth, revealing the complexities of an often simplified situation. The historical practices of the Catholic Church and its role in establishing and maintaining Spanish domination are contrasted to the present uses of the Evangelical message—especially the promise of wealth and prosperity as if by magic—and the growing U.S. influence. The footage of Jimmy Swaggart is chilling, including his meeting with Chile's General Pinochet. The competition between Catholicism and Fundamentalism for the souls of the indigenous population is nicely contrasted with the voices of indigenous peoples seeking independence and control of their own spirituality. The tape shows that what makes the Evangelical message so powerful is the promise of progress, technology, and modernization and the Evangelicals' use of radio and television to penetrate even the most remote areas. One evaluator commented that the tape captures the enthusiasm and perhaps the naiveté of the Evangelical movement, interpreting it as a new form of imperialism.

The tape includes a great deal of material, and at times the organization might confuse the viewer. A number of evaluators mentioned points not emphasized in the film (see above). One evaluator commented that the documentary fails to prove its premise that Evangelical churches effectively "put people to sleep" in the political sense.

Introducing the Tape: A U.S. audience may already know about Fundamentalist Protestants. This tape is about religious Fundamentalism in another context, from the perspective of the institutions affected by the Evangelical forces. Viewers should be told that although the Evangelical success may be seen as an act of imperialism, it is a phenomenon that challenges established powers and/or ideological trends (from the Left and Right) in Latin America. The film does not focus at all on the Protestant movement in Latin America. Therefore, students should be told that mainstream Protestants have been in this area since the early nineteenth century. Also they should be prepared to note the similarities between conservative Roman Catholics and Fundamentalist Protestants.

How to Use: The tape is an excellent example of long-form informational video to show *Communications* students that the medium can be used for information purposes. (Andersen)

In *Latin American Culture and Civilization* the tape could be used to illustrate U.S. cultural imperialism. (Espadas)

Suggested Readings: Martin, David. *Tongues of Fire: The Explosion of Protestantism in Latin America.*

Nelson, Wilton M. *Protestantism in Central America.*

Serrano Elías, Jorge. *La participación del Cristiano en la vida pública.*

Stoll, David. *Is Latin America Turning Protestant?: The Politics of Evangelical Growth.*

Complementary Films/Videos: *A su nombre (In His Name)* (Latin America).

Level: High School—University

A SU NOMBRE (In His Name)

Documentary.   English Narration with Subtitles.   25 min. 1985

Directed by: Jan VanBilson and Dirk Vandersypen

Produced by: Euro Video (Torres Adalid 511 Dto. 508, Col. del Valle, 03100, Mexico D.F., Mexico; tel: [525] 523-6395; e-mail: 74173.3013@compuserve.com)

Distributed by: IMRE

Evaluators: Robin Andersen, Craig Auchter, Juan Espadas, Rosario Espinal, J. Julian Rívera, Miguel Huarcaya, Daniel P. Hunt

Description: A chilling investigative documentary about the growth of conservative fundamentalism in Central America, especially in Guatemala and Honduras. The tape draws out the connections between the Christian Fundamentalist Evangelical movement and the U.S. military policies in Central America, particularly the Reagan administration's support of the Nicaraguan contras. In the 1980s, the religious movement found a foothold and became a growth industry in Central America. U.S. counterinsurgency policies were also being put in place in this period. Extreme anticommunism propelled this religious-military complex. Evangelicals with ties to the U.S.-based Christian Broadcasting Network (CBN) preached blind faith in God, the acceptance of military power, and the rejection of reformist social and political action. By demonizing Nicaragua, these sects created a peasant populace ready to defer its rewards until the afterlife. In Guatemala in 1982, the rise to power of General Rios Montt (a devout Evangelical) solidified the connection between right-wing military power and fundamentalism. The tape shows how the authoritarian and oppressive elements benefit from a population that is converted to a religious faith that equates communism with the devil and the military with salvation.

Strengths and Weaknesses: The visual juxtapositions in the editing reveal the contrast between the poverty of the peasants and the well-fed, well-dressed fundamentalist, preaching that "faith will save you." Television's power to promote religious messages and the role of CBN are beautifully illustrated by the words of an American who says "TV should invade the privacy of houses, including bedrooms, for religious purposes." But most effective is a segment at the municipal dump in Guatemala City that sustains three thousand people. A truckful of fundamentalists arrives in the midst of this human misery. They ask who is sick and "cure" hundreds of desperate people by placing their hands on their foreheads and saying, "In the name of Jesus Christ, get well." The weak and ragged scavengers are given a meal once every two weeks but no medicine. The preacher returns to a first-class hotel and a luncheon given by his supporters—rich businessmen. The tape uses footage of the religious leaders themselves effectively to show their disturbing philosophy.

Most of the analysis and understanding of the issues is imparted in the "voice of God"narrative style. There are almost no interviews with the peasants themselves; their ideas, impressions, needs, and feelings are absent. The tape needs to be updated, particularly in reference to the war in Central America. The English subtitles leave out much of what is said in Spanish.

Introducing the Tape: Since this piece was completed in 1986, it is now somewhat outdated and should be introduced as a vehicle for understanding the murderous applications of anticommunism in Central America in the 1980s. A few words to update and contextualize the information for the present would be useful, or the tape could be presented as a historical piece. Sample question: "since 1986, Communism has lost the fangs fashioned for it by right-wing hysteria. Have the Evangelicals lost ground as a consequence, or simply shifted the burden of guilt elsewhere?"One evaluator felt explanation was needed about why the Evangelicals attracted more followers than the Catholic Church. Also, some background is necessary on the role of Catholicism in the region, the actual situation of the different religions in the zone, and the religious dimensions of the conflict.

How to Use: In *Communications and Journalism* classes the tape is a great example of hard-hitting, long-form investigative reporting for broadcast, the kind that is so rare now on mainstream television. The video is interesting for its form, and its points are well made. It imparts information as well as impressions of U.S. military policies and the uses of religious fanaticism to propel those policies. One segment is a news story about right-wing fundamentalist Pat Robertson (who ran in the 1988 U.S. presidential race) visiting a Nicaraguan contra camp in Honduras. Seeing this ordinary news piece in the context of this report is very effective. (Andersen)

This is a very good film for discussing the relationship of church and politics in contemporary Latin America. (Espinal)

In our survey of *Latin American Culture and Literature* it would make a good introduction to the problem of U.S. interventionism beyond the level of government. I would preface it with readings in recent history in the region, probably Skidmore and Smith's *Modern Latin America.* (Hunt)

Suggested Readings: Anfuso, Joséph, and David Sczepanski. *He Gives—He Takes Away: The True Story of Guatemala's Controversial Former President Efraín Rios Montt.*

Berryman, Phillip. *The Religious Roots of Rebellion: Christians in Central American Revolutions.*

Matthiessen, Peter. *At Play in the Fields of the Lord.*

Skidmore, Thomas E., and Peter H. Smith. *Modern Latin America.*

Readings from NACLA *Report on the Americas,* issues on Guatemala, Honduras, and conservative religion.

Level: University

MEXICO

ABRIL, EL MES MAS CRUEL

Documentary. Without Subtitles. 34 min. 1993

Directed by: Boris Goldenblanc

Produced by: Universidad de Guadalajara/Daniel Varela—Centro de Arte Audiovisual, Lerdo de Tejada 2071, entre Marsella y Chapultepec, CP 44150, Guadalajara, Jalisco, Mexico; tel/fax: [523] 615-8470)

Distributed by: IMRE

Evaluators: Rebeca Harclerode, John Hess, Daniel P. Hunt, Ulises Mejías

Description: Taking its name from the first line of T. S. Eliot's *The Waste Land,* this documentary examines the sewer explosion in Guadalajara on April 22, 1992, in which hundreds were killed or wounded and thousands were left homeless. This disaster was caused by the national Mexican petroleum company, PEMEX. The event itself is impressionistically reenacted in an artistic rendition that frames the film. The body of the tape consists of interviews with survivors, officials, and social scientists exploring the causes and consequences of the tragedy. The film reveals the extent of the Mexican government's complicity in creating such dangerous conditions and its failure to provide replacement housing and compensation for the victims. The tape shows people protesting the lack of government action to aid families or identify the cause of the disaster. It exposes how authorities expelled residents from condemned structures without offering alternative housing and how the government, in attempting to clean up quickly with bulldozers, actually killed more victims trapped in the rubble.

Strengths and Weaknesses: The film has good production values. One evaluator stated that it is one of the few documentaries that seems to do everything just about right.

Another evaluator felt that some artistic effects detracted from the tragic, emotional accounts of the people involved

and that the tape tended to victimize its subjects by emphasizing their suffering and helplessness. Even the causes of the explosions were depicted as abstract, incomprehensible, and out of reach.

How to Use: In *Comparative Politics* this incident could be compared to other environmental disasters of recent years, especially focusing on the lack of government and industry accountability.

Suggested Readings: Castañeda, Jorge. *Utopia Unarmed: The Latin American Left after the Cold War.*

Rosenthal, Alan, ed. *The Documentary Conscience: A Casebook in Film Making.*

Rosenthal, Alan. *New Challenges for Documentary.*

Skidmore, Thomas E., and Peter H. Smith. *Modern Latin America.*

Level: High School—University

ALMA PUNK (Punk Spirit)

Fiction. With Subtitles. 57 min. 1992

Directed by: Sarah Minter

Produced by: Sarah Minter (Quintana Roo 93–1 Col. Roma 067, México D.F.; tel: [525] 574-6421)

Distributed by: IMRE Archive (available for viewing only)

Evaluators: Danny J. Anderson

Description: *Alma Punk* is a fictionalized tape that uses real teens to act out its story. Alma is an adolescent who lives alone in Mexico City. Her mother, who is living and working somewhere in California, writes to her from time to time. The mother encourages Alma to consider moving to California since she will fit in with other adolescents in the punk culture there. The film traces Alma's financial and personal dilemmas. She is six months behind on her rent and the landlady is pressuring her. The tape shows her interactions with other members of the punk culture, in which there is a marked social division between genders. Men take advantage of Alma, whereas female peers are supportive. Alma gets involved with a group of women trying to stage a play and publish a fan newsletter. Eventually she returns home to find that she has been evicted and all of her belongings are scattered on the tenement patio. She then begins her journey through Mexico City and on the California border. The film closes with Alma climbing the fence to enter the United States illegally. The tape includes brief nudity.

Strengths and Weaknesses: The video provides an interesting image of a seldom-studied sector of Mexico City, the youth punk culture.

The production and acting are not professional, although the overall concept is good. The dialogue relies heavily on Mexico City punk slang of the 1980s, which makes it unsuitable for Spanish language classes. Some of the story lines are underdeveloped and require viewers to fill them in.

Introducing the Tape: Viewers could be told that, although the idea of Mexican punk culture may sound exotic to some viewers, the story is a rather typical tale of young girl who grows up too fast and leaves in search of a better life.

How to Use: In a *Sociology* class this could be used to study urban subcultures or the spread of punk culture internationally. The detail in the film of a Polish pen pal who is also writing a punk fan newsletter establishes an interesting web of relationships. Obliquely, the film exemplifies problems about family, economic situations, and migration that might be of interest in a *Social History* class. In a *Film* class this could be an example of a docudrama. The issues of context, characterization, and film structure are quite interesting. I would use the film as both an example of a specific subculture and an explanation of how and why this punk subculture exists and its relation to broader social issues of the 1980s in Mexico. (Anderson)

Suggested Readings: Monsiváis, Carlos. "Muerte y resurrección del nacionalismo mexicano."

Studies in Latin American Popular Culture, numerous published articles on contemporary rock in Mexico.

Level: High School—University

AMAS DE CASA (Housewives)

Docudrama.   With Subtitles.   5 min.   1984
Produced & Directed by: Collectivo Cine Mujer
Distributed by: IMRE
Evaluators: Anna R. Adams, Silvia Arrom, Rob Huesca, Angharad N. Valdivia
Description: *Amas de casa* is an excellent example of how video can be used as an empowerment tool by marginalized people. The tape is not a complete program, but rather a short documentation of a role-play situation in which women in a poor tenement in Mexico City confront a well-dressed lawyer who tries to hand an eviction notice to a tenant. The organized neighborhood women come to her defense and run him out. In real life many women feel they have no option but to leave and are afraid to fight back. Seeing this non-threatening role-play situation helps to allay their fears and enables them to take action. When they watch the tape, they begin to see their own strength and understand that when they join together with the other women in the neighborhood, they are no longer powerless.

Strengths and Weaknesses: The role-play scene is quite realistic. The women are very convincing in their portrayal, and their strength in solidarity and common purpose is clear. The tape is a good example of the application of drama and video as empowerment strategies.

The tape documents only the role-play and will be confusing without an explanation of its context and purpose.

Introducing the Tape: Viewers should be told that the purpose of making the video was to empower the residents and prepare them to support each other and resist eviction. Some brief background on the realities of tenement life would be useful.

How to Use: This tape is useful for any class that deals with popular movements or poverty. (Huesca)

This could be used in an *English as a Second Language* course. After viewing the tape, students could discuss their own feelings of powerlessness and the social issues they confront. The students could write and act out skits about the issues discussed.

Level: Junior High School—University

AMOR A LA VUELTA DE LA ESQUINA (Love around the Corner)

Feature.   With Subtitles.   86 min.   1985
Directed by: Alberto Cortez
Distributed by: IMRE, Latina
Evaluators: Sharon Sieber, Stephen Webre
Description: This is a depressing tale of petty crime and prostitution set in a modern Mexican city. The story begins when María escapes from prison and ends when she is recaptured by the authorities. Upon her escape, María returns to the streets to make a living as a prostitute. The great love interest in her life is the unreliable and often absent truck driver Julian, who hauls contraband for a living. María also develops a lesbian relationship with a fellow prostitute, Marta. María keeps a journal, but the film shares little of her inner life, except in a brief fantasy sequence in which she imagines herself as a model in *Penthouse* magazine.

Strengths and Weaknesses: This film offers a moving portrayal of street life in a modern Mexican city, reminiscent of Luis Buñuel's *Los Olvidados.* The settings and cultural situations are authentic, the direction is competent, and the acting is convincing.

The narrative itself is episodic, almost picaresque in its structure, and eventually leads nowhere except back to prison for María. The minimal story line exists primarily to support character development. Unlike the Buñuel film, *Amor a la vuelta de la esquina* makes no attempt to explain how María became the way she is.

Introducing the Tape: This film deals frankly and explicitly with sexual matters and thus may not be appropriate for all audiences.

How to Use: This film would be useful in courses that deal with *Modern Latin American Society,* particularly the impact of modernization and urbanization on women. It is important for instructors to note, however, that the conditions the film portrays are universal in modern cities, rather than unique to Latin America or Mexico. (Webre)

Level: University

BESAME MUCHO

Feature.   Without Subtitles.   98 min.   1944
Directed by: Eduardo Ugarte
Distributed by: IMRE
Evaluators: Robert DiAntonio, José-Manuel Navarro, Margarita Pont
Description: This black-and-white film in the style of the Hollywood musicals of the 1940s and 1950s presents a producer's and musicians' struggles to become famous on a radio show. It deals with honor and how true love helps the aspiring actors overcome their struggles. The film is comedic

and uses many of the standards of classic Mexican humor: bons mots, witty dialogue, switched identities, musical parodies, and music, including some classic songs such as *"Bésame mucho."*

Strengths and Weaknesses: This is an entertaining comedy that captures an era. It is highly produced and interesting for its portrayal of the ambiance and attitudes of an earlier time.

The film is quite dated, but that is its charm.

Introducing the Tape: None is needed.

How to Use: I would use this film to present the influence of African music and culture in *Latin American Music and Culture.* (Pont)

Level: University

CHICHEN ITZA (Chichén Itzá)

Documentary.   With Subtitles.   30 min.   1991

Directed by: Gonzalo Infante

Produced by: OMAC Video (Miguel de Quevedo 296, Coyoacán CP 04000, México D.F.; tel: [525] 554-0883 or 658-3171; fax: [525] 659-8895)

Distributed by: IMRE, Latina

Evaluators: Melvin S. Arrington Jr., William O. Autry, John Hays

Description: Part of the series *Ciudades del México antiguo* (Cities of Ancient Mexico), this video documents how the ancient city of Chichén Itzá, Yucatán, developed and changed. The program opens with a short historical introduction combining drawings and actual views of the city. The major portion of the video consists of a re-creation of daily life and sacred rituals during the time of the Maya and the Itzá, the conquering peoples who changed the name of the city to Chichén Itzá. The producers speculate on an alliance between the Maya and the Itzá, comparing these two groups to the divine brothers in the sacred myths.

Strengths and Weaknesses: This is a realistic, scholarly, and accessible tape. It has visually strong presentations, with excellent re-creations of ancient times, especially of the ball game and the sacrifice. The photography is wonderful and provides views of the major structures and of the stone carvings at the ball court.

The leader of the tape, before the initial title and story line, is long and somewhat confusing. Also, there are some errors in the subtitles, particularly in the leader.

Introducing the Tape: The presentation would be enhanced if the audience had some historical information about the area and the role of *Chilam Balam* (the diviner) in Mayan culture and society.

How to Use: This tape introduces students to the geography and architecture of Chichén Itzá and exposes them to Mayan sacred rituals. (Arrington)

Unlike traditional presentations which portray Chichén Itzá as a city invaded by Toltecs in the eleventh century, this video stresses the cultural influences they brought from central Mexico. The dramatic device employed to show the struggle between the old faith and the new is through the character of *Chilam Balam,* the Mayan diviner. This video provides an interesting format for discussions of cultural change. (Autry)

Suggested Readings: Barrera Vásquez, Alfredo, and Silvia Rendón, trans. *El libro de los libros de Chilam Balam.*

Coe, Michael D. *The Maya.*

Coggins, Clemency C., and Orrin C. Shane III. *Cenote of Sacrifice: Maya Treasures from the Sacred Well at Chichén Itzá.*

Roys, Ralph L. *The Book of Chilam Balam of Chumayel.*

Schele, Linda, and David Freidel. *A Forest of Kings: The Untold Story of the Ancient Maya.*

Tedlock, Dennis. *Popol Vuh: The Mayan Book of the Dawn of Life.*

Level: High School—University

CON EL ALMA ENTRE LOS DIENTES

Documentary.   Without Subtitles.   36 min.   1981

Directed by: Jaime Riestra

Produced by: Instituto Nacional Indigenista (Av. Revolución, 1227, Col. Alpes, México D.F., 01010; tel: [525] 593-2875; fax: [525] 651-7342 or 593-5967)

Distributed by: IMRE Archive (available for viewing only)

Evaluators: Friederike Baumann, Robert C. Williamson

Description: This is an illuminating documentary on the culture and economic relationships in the Totonac community of Pantépec, Puebla, Mexico. Against the backdrop of *Todos santos* (All Saints Day) celebrations and burial rites, emerges the sadly universal story of the Indian *campesinos'* (peasants') struggle to confront the looming danger of spiritual and cultural extinction. By juxtaposing interviews with successful mestizo elite with testimony by *campesinos,* the reality behind the slow death of the Indian community becomes clear. Wealth and political control is gained by a few who deprive the majority of the means for survival. With economic and political avenues closed to them, and their land base disappearing, Indians feel powerless to change their fate.

Strengths and Weaknesses: This film succinctly presents the central dilemma of Indian communities everywhere. Equally important, the film offers us the rare chance to learn how Totonacs themselves perceive their situation. There are authentic illustrations of peasant life, including fiestas, funerals, and coffee growing.

Some viewers may find the film slow paced. Some of the anthropological footage and abrupt cutting may distract the uninitiated viewer.

Introducing the Tape: Presenters may want to provide background and emphasize the particular relevance of the tape in light of the 1994 Zapatista insurrection in Chiapas, which drew international attention to the issues raised by Indians.

Suggested Readings: Leon-Portilla, Miguel, ed. *Aztec Image of Self and Society: An Introduction to Nahua Culture.*

Menchú, Rigoberta. *I, Rigoberta Menchú: An Indian Woman in Guatemala.*

Weckmann, Luis. *Herencia medieval de México. (The Medieval Heritage of Mexico)*.
Level: University

CONCHEROS SOMOS
Documentary.   Without Subtitles.   26 min.   1992
Directed by: Eduardo Herrera
Produced by: IXTACA Producciones (Aptdo Postal 20–325, México D.F., 01090)
Distributed by: IMRE Archive (available for viewing only)
Evaluators: Reed Anderson, Rebeca Harclerode, Robert C. Williamson
Description: This a beautiful documentation of a Mexico City performance of the Concheros dances, part of a genre called the *danzas de la conquista*. Musicians and dancers are filmed in the various ritual locations where their annual performances are held in November, culminating at the *Basílica de la Virgen de Guadalupe*. A narrator guides the viewer with explanations from sacred and secular texts relevant to the meaning of the dances and the costumes' symbolism.
Strengths and Weaknesses: This engaging tape presents beautifully filmed native dances and excellent musical accompaniment comprised of field recordings. The video makes good use of historical and religious texts to illustrate the tradition and meaning of the dances. The narration is clear and accessible to nonnative speakers.
Introducing the Tape: An introduction should provide more context regarding the dancers' traditions and history. Viewers could be told that the Concheros speak about their tradition and obligations because the dances make sense only within a complex system of symbolic content and belief. Dancing is part of a ritual, not just a performance; being a Conchero means being part of a brotherhood, not just a dancer. The dancing has devotional meaning, and the Concheros fulfill a certain number of obligations throughout the year; for example, they must dance on particular dates in each of their four sacred sanctuaries: *La Villa de Guadalupe; Los Remedios; Amecameca;* and *Chalma,* which are related to the cardinal directions (north, west, east, and south, respectively). The Concheros also have military degrees: the chief of each group of dancers is the *capitán;* the one who carries the banner or *estandarte* is the *alférez;* the woman in charge of receiving and blessing all the dancers before they enter the circle is *la malinche.* Viewers may be interested to know that many groups from the *Danza de Concheros* have emigrated to Europe.
How to Use: The tape could be used to discuss aesthetics in preliterate societies. (Williamson)
Suggested Readings: Adams, Richard E. W. *Prehistoric Mesoamerica.*

Morley, Sylvanus Griswold, and George W. Brainerd. *The Ancient Maya.*

A history of Mexico and anything on the anthropology of Mexico
Level: University

LOS CONFINES
Feature.   Without Subtitles.   80 min.   1987
Directed by: Mitl Valdez
Produced by: UNAM
Distributed by: IMRE, Latina
Evaluators: Daniel P. Hunt
Description: Based on two short stories by Juan Rulfo and a part of his *Pedro Páramo,* this film explores themes of violence, poverty, and hopelessness in a small pueblo of north central Mexico. In the first story, a poor man kills the owner of a hacienda in a dispute over grazing rights and years later is hunted down by the dead man's son. In the second, when a sick man's brother comes to his aid, his wife and his younger sibling fall in love. Their passion must remain unrequited as they help the ailing husband make a penitential pilgrimage and then die. The third story follows the narrator of *Pedro Páramo* as he wanders into hell (set in rural northern Mexico). He spends time with an incestuous brother and sister who turn out to be ghosts.
Strengths and Weaknesses: This film is beautifully conceived and shot. It attempts to be faithful to Rulfo's fragmentary and ambiguous literary style and thus is difficult to follow for audiences not familiar with his writing.
Introducing the Tape: It would be useful to read and discuss Juan Rulfo's stories before viewing.
How to Use: I would have students read the Rulfo works depicted here first, then show the film. We would then discuss the possibilities offered and limitations encountered in each medium. (Hunt)
Suggested Readings: Brushwood, John Shibbs. *Mexico in its Novel; A Nation's Search for Identity.*

Brushwood, John Shibbs. *Narrative Innovation and Political Change in Mexico.*

Rulfo, Juan. *Obra completa: el llano en llamas, Pedro Páramo, otros textos.*

Rulfo, Juan. *Pedro Páramo.*

Rulfo, Juan. *Inframundo: The Mexico de Juan Rulfo.*
Level: University

CONOZCO A LAS TRES (I Know All Three)
Feature.   With Subtitles.   55 min.   1983
Directed by: Maryse Sistach
Produced by: Zafra A. C., Macuca Films
Distributed by: IMRE, Latina
Evaluators: Teresita Martínez Vergne, Stephen Webre
Description: This is the story of three friends, single women who live and work in a Mexican city. Magazine editor Ana is a single parent separated from her abusive husband; she meets and falls in love with Pablo, a gentle and apparently sensitive newspaper reporter. Their relationship appears ideal until Ana suspects she is pregnant and finds herself unwilling to tell Pablo for fear that he will abandon her. Artist Julia pines for her love, Juan, who has left her, and schoolteacher María is raped and has a humiliating encounter with Mexico's sexist criminal justice system. The dialogue fo-

cuses largely on the concerns of single women, such as job and physical security, and especially relationships with men. The feminist consciousness of the three grows during the film but in some ways reflects ambivalence. The film ends with a brief fantasy sequence in which Ana, Julia, and María amuse themselves by imagining a world in which gender roles are reversed.

Strengths and Weaknesses: This film offers a good examination of sexual attitudes in contemporary Mexico and, by extension, any other Latin American or traditional Third World society. The three women touch on aspects of being female that are of interest to feminists in the United States: motherhood, work, sexuality, and friendship. The settings and the depictions of cultural behavior and attitudes are authentic. The tape will fit perfectly into a typical fifty-minute class period.

The story line is minimal and exists mostly to support the dialogue and character development; nothing is resolved. One evaluator found the script poor. Production values in general are not high. There is partial nudity in the love scenes and a masturbation scene.

Introducing the Tape: U.S. audiences should be asked to think about how problems of sexism and the victimization of women in a traditional patriarchal society, such as Mexico, are similar and different in the United States. In particular, the concept and strong impact of machismo must be explained as it pertains both to men's expectations of themselves and to their concept of women. The problem for the three protagonists in *Conozco a las tres* is that their place in Mexican society is new and ambiguous. As self-supporting middle-class career women, they have no niche in the traditional gender scheme, which assigns all females to one of three fixed categories, virgin, wife, or whore, and which assumes that any decent woman is protected/supported by a man.

How to Use: This film may be used to encourage students to compare/contrast the situation of women in the United States and in Latin America or other Third World societies. Issues for discussion might include society's attitudes toward marriage, careers, rape, responsibility for contraception, abortion, and other gender-related questions. (Webre)

Suggested Readings: Franco, Jean. *Plotting Women: Gender and Representation in Mexico.*

Ramos-Escandón, Carmen. *Presencia y transparencia: la mujer en la historia de México.*

Level: University

CONTRA CORRIENTE (Against the Current)
Documentary. With Subtitles. 50 min. 1990
Directed by: Carlos Mendoza
Produced by: Canal 6 de Julio (Medellín 33, 3er piso, Colonia Roma, 06700 México D.F.; tel/fax: [525] 511-2349)
Distributed by: IMRE
Evaluators: Danny J. Anderson, Hilda Pato, José Pérez, Jorge Porras

Description: The documentary explores the flagrant human rights violations in Mexico around the issue of voting and electoral fraud. It focuses on the period since the 1988 elections, the most contested since the Mexican Revolution, and the triumph of the Partido Revolucionario Institucional (PRI) candidate Carlos Salinas de Gortari. The tape includes interviews with opposing political groups and live scenes of street demonstrations and violence. Numerous well-known Mexican intellectuals and professionals are interviewed: Mariclaire Acosta, Bernardo Batiz, Jorge Castañeda, Miguel Concha, Nestor de Buen, Luis de la Barreda, Emilio Krieger, Lorenzo Meyer, Carlos Monsiváis, Veronica Ortiz, and Rodolfo F. Peña. A narrator considers the various manifestations of electoral fraud, repressive police power, responses to the 1990 Americas Watch report, and the recent creation of human rights organizations in Mexico. The tape concludes with the metaphor of a salmon swimming upstream (*contra corriente*) and losing the strength to sustain life.

Strengths and Weaknesses: The tape provides interesting information and covers a wide range of viewpoints.

Some speakers are identified only by a list at the beginning of the tape, so it would be difficult for many viewers to know who is talking and from what social position. The production quality is uneven, with some technical problems. One evaluator felt the tape was interesting, but partial and proselytizing.

Introducing the Tape: Viewers need to be told who is being interviewed and the position each represents. An update regarding the most recent elections and political situation in Mexico would be useful.

How to Use: In a *Culture* or *Literature* course the tape could be used to emphasize the nature of state repression in Mexico. It also would complement political novels or a study of the history of the PRI, the state party, and its gradual decline as Mexican elections have become increasingly fraudulent and competitive. (Anderson)

The video could be used to study human rights violations in Mexico. (Pérez)

Suggested Readings: Basañez, Miguel. *La lucha por la hegemonía en México 1968–1980.*

Pastor, Robert A., and Jorge Castañeda. *Limits to Friendship: The United States and Mexico.*

Level: University

CRONICA DE UN FRAUDE (Chronicle of a Fraud)
Documentary. With Subtitles. 60 min. 1988
Directed by: Carlos Mendoza
Produced by: Canal 6 de Julio (Medellín 33, 3er piso, Colonia, Roma, 06700 México; tel: [525] 511-2349)
Distributed by: IMRE
Evaluators: Glenn J. Kist
Description: Clearly hostile to the Partido Revolucionario Institucional (PRI) and its monopolistic control of Mexico's political system, this tape documents the flagrant fraud committed in the Mexican presidential election of 1988. Most of

the tape consists of footage shot at political demonstrations and rallies on behalf of the candidates opposed to the PRI and its then candidate, Carlos Salinas de Gortari. Scenes of police interfering with the political rallies are shown. Snatches of campaign speeches of Cuauhtémoc Cárdenas and other opposition candidates are included. The tape also shows the recovery of presidential ballots that had been partially destroyed and thrown into a landfill.

Strengths and Weaknesses: This is a good summary of the criticisms leveled against the PRI during the 1988 presidential election. It provides an in-depth look at the opposition candidates and the popular campaign practices in Mexico.

The excessive detail limits the audience for this tape to those familiar with, and interested in, Mexican politics. Not much background is provided for any of the candidates.

Introducing the Tape: An introduction to the political system in Mexico would be necessary. Students should also be updated about events of the 1994 election, including the Zapatista uprising in Chiapas, the assassination of PRI candidate Colosio, and the subsequent victory of PRI candidate Zedillo.

How to Use: The tape could be used in a course in *Mexican History*. Because of its length, I would assign it for out-of-class viewing. In the discussion that would follow, I would focus on the following questions: What, according to the documentary, are the root causes of fraud in the Mexican political system? What are the programs of the opposition candidates? Are the charges of corruption and fraud that are made in the documentary convincing to you? (Kist)

Suggested Readings: Camp, Roderic A. *Politics in Mexico.*

Gil, Carlos B. *Hope and Frustration: Interviews with Leaders of Mexico's Political Opposition.*

Meyer, Michael C., and William L. Sherman. *The Course of Mexican History.*

Oster, Patrick. *The Mexicans: A Personal Portrait of a People.*

Riding, Alan. *Distant Neighbors: A Portrait of the Mexicans.*

Level: University

DE ACA, DE ESTE LADO (From Here, From This Side)
Documentary. With Subtitles. 20 min. 1988
Directed by: Gloria Ribe
Produced by: Ribe Asociados (Aguayo 3–19, Col. del Carmen, Coyoacán 04100, México D.F.; tel: [525] 554-8851)
Distributed by: Women Make Movies
Evaluators: Patricia Aufderheide (excerpted from *Cross Cultural Film Guide*), Oscar Flores, Robert Haskett, Chon Noriega, Jennifer M. Taylor
Description: This documentary collage begins with a collection of opposing stereotypes, first of North Americans as seen from Mexico and then of Mexicans as seen from the United States (primarily in classic Mexican film clips). Next it provides a brief summary of Mexico's recent quest for modernization, centered on the "Mexican Miracle" set off by

the discovery of massive new sources of oil in the 1970s. The film provides a cautionary tale of what can happen when a nation becomes dependent on exporting raw materials to a market controlled by outsiders and consequently develops a massive foreign debt coupled with ruinous interest payments. The film links Mexico's foreign policy positions on U.S.-sponsored conflicts in Central America to its economic dependency on the United States. Directed to a Mexican audience, the tape expresses the need to reenvision cross-cultural relations, emerge from an inferiority complex vis-à-vis the United States, assume responsibility for Mexico's own economic problems, and reimagine, in conjunction with the United States, the international arena as a single space inhabited for mutual benefit. The tape ends with a call for an alternative path towards national growth, prosperity, and self-determination, though it is not clear just what this should be.

Strengths and Weaknesses: The film has a distinctly Mexican perspective and argues that the people of Mexico, and Latin America in general, are not (or should not be) objects, but rather agents of their own present and future. Among the film's strengths are some compelling visuals, coupled with a thought-provoking narrative based on the writings of Octavio Paz. The film employs innovative documentary strategies; it has an effective juxtaposition of images that work well with the narration and music.

A couple of evaluators felt the tape made a laudable attempt to cover many topics, at times with superficial results. One reviewer found it interesting but somewhat didactic. The film's emphasis on the cold war is somewhat dated.

Introducing the Tape: Some audiences may need background on the concepts and philosophical language used. An update on the North American Free Trade Agreement (NAFTA) and recent developments in U.S.-Mexico relations would be helpful.

How to Use: The tape could be used in *Spanish Language* classes to present the Latin American point of view regarding economic problems. (Flores)

This film would be useful to spur discussion in a *Mexican History* or *Economics* course, specifically in a unit dealing with the "Mexican Miracle" and international/U.S. relations. The film could be used in the same way in a more general *Latin American History* survey, in *International Relations,* or in *Mexican/Latin American Culture* classes. (Haskett)

Suggested Readings: Aufderheide, Patricia. *Cross Cultural Film Guide.*

Meyer, Michael, and William L. Sherman. *The Course of Mexican History.*

Mora, Carl J. *Mexican Cinema: Reflections of a Society.*

Oster, Patrick. *Mexicans: A Personal Portrait of a People.*

Paz, Octavio. *The Labyrinth of Solitude; The Other Mexico; Return to the Labyrinth of Solitude; Mexico and the United States; The Philanthropic Ogre.*

Raat, W. Dirk, and William H. Beezley, eds. *Twentieth-Century Mexico.*

Reavis, Dick. *Conversations with Moctezuma: Ancient Shadows over Modern Life in Mexico.*

Riding, Alan. *Distant Neighbors: A Portrait of the Mexicans.*

Rodríguez, Richard. *Days of Obligation: An Argument with My Mexican Father.*

Schmidt, Henry C. *The Roots of lo Mexicano: Self and Society in Mexican Thought, 1900–1934.*

Schnitman, Jorge A. *Film Industries in Latin America: Dependency and Development.*

West, Dennis. "Mexico." In *World Cinema since 1945,* ed. William Luhr.

Level: University

DE TODOS MODOS JUAN TE LLAMAS

Feature. Without Subtitles. 108 min. 1978
Directed by: Marcela Fernández Violante
Produced by: UNAM
Distributed by: IMRE, Latina
Evaluators: Currie Kerr Thompson, Stephen Webre
Description: Set in rural Mexico during the Cristero Rebellion (1926–1929), this is the story of General Guajardo, a veteran of the revolutionary wars of the 1910s, who is now a regional military commander. The Mexican Revolution has made Guajardo wealthy and influential, but as time passes, the process corrupts him, and he becomes alienated from his wife and children. The film begins as the revolutionary policies of President Plutarco Elías Calles (1924–1928) provoke a popular, clergy-led rebellion in the countryside. Aggravating the situation is the constant threat of U.S. intervention to protect foreign property interests. In addition, personal ambitions are in play, as various generals aspire to presidential succession. As Guajardo maneuvers to ensure his own advancement in such perilous times, he repeatedly betrays his family, friends, and revolutionary ideals. As the film closes, he has survived and prospered, but he is alone and unloved.
Strengths and Weaknesses: This professionally crafted film successfully evokes the political and military atmosphere of 1920s Mexico, with authentic settings and historical context. The screenplay develops Guajardo's character and shows his gradual change, while supplying the necessary historical background. The direction is effective and lively, and the photography takes advantage of Mexico's rural and small-town scenery.

Evaluators liked the acting performances for the most part, although one felt some of the supporting characters could have been a little more developed. Another reviewer felt the pacing was slow at times.
Introducing the Tape: U.S. audiences will need a substantial introduction to early twentieth-century Mexico, including a basic overview of the major events of the Mexican Revolution, from the outbreak of the rebellion against Porfirio Díaz in 1919 through the Calles presidency. Because of their centrality to an understanding of Guajardo's behavior, it is particularly important to stress the issues of land redistribu-

tion, foreign control of mineral resources (Calles's politics concerning U.S. mining interests), and church-state relations. Although the film is not about the Cristero Rebellion per se, it cannot be fully appreciated without an understanding of this event.
How to Use: The film could easily be used in a *Civilization* or *Spanish Language* class. In *Cinema Studies* I would focus less on the content than the cinematography and how this film relates to other cinema in Spain and Latin America. We would study the film in the context of books on film theory and texts dealing with contemporary cinema in Latin America. (Thompson)

Any course on modern *Mexico* must address the controversy over the meaning of the Mexican Revolution. To what extent has this historical process made good on its initial promises? *De todos modos Juan te llamas* is valuable as a Mexican attempt to come to grips with this problem though the medium of film. The central issue the film addresses is the effect of power on revolutionary leaders. The universal question of why revolutions that begin as authentic movements for freedom end by establishing tyrannies applies not only to the Mexican experience but to other modern revolutions. Colonel Bonilla, the idealist who remains loyal to his uncle, Guajardo, despite his increasing disenchantment with Guajardo's behavior, sums it up best when he says that the struggle has turned out to be not as simple as it once appeared: "The enemy is fighting for what you thought was your cause, and you find yourself fighting for what the enemy wanted in the first place." John Steinbeck took a similar approach to the Mexican Revolution in his screenplay for Elias Kazan's *Viva Zapata!* (1951), a film that might be used with this one in a comparative exercise. The film may also be used to facilitate classroom debate over the nature of the Cristero Rebellion itself. Traditional accounts have dismissed the Cristeros as religious fanatics wedded to the status quo and opposed to the popular will. This film casts them in quite a different light and with a good deal more sympathy. (Webre)
Suggested Readings: Bailey, David C. *Viva Cristo Rey: The Cristero Rebellion and the Church-State Conflict in Mexico.*

Bordwell, David. *Making Meaning: Inference and Rhetoric in the Interpretation of Cinema.*

Dulles, John W. F. *Yesterday in Mexico: A Chronicle of the Revolution, 1919–1936.*

Meyer, Jean. *The Cristero Rebellion: The Mexican People between Church and State, 1926–1929.*

Level: University

DOÑA HERLINDA Y SU HIJO (Doña Herlinda and Her Son)

Feature. With Subtitles. 90 min. 1969
Directed by: Manuel Antin
Distributed by: Cinevista Video, Facets
Evaluators: Rosangela Vieira King, Laura Elisa Pérez
Description: This is a film about negotiating male homosexuality within conventional, middle-class Mexican culture

of the late 1960s. Expertly manipulating gender stereotypes, Doña Herlinda graciously trades a matronly benevolence and indulgence for her son's discreet accommodation of his homosexuality. The film is a fascinating look at the contradictions of Mexican middle-class culture and the homosexuality embedded within it.

Strengths and Weaknesses: Evaluators had quite divergent opinions of this film. One felt that although the film seemed a bit dated, representing a specific middle-class Mexican culture of that time, it was quite important in representing homosexuality as a kind of hidden norm behind the appearances of conventional propriety. This reviewer commented, however, that the film erroneously suggests that Doña Herlinda, a saccharine dictatorial matriarch, is ultimately the culprit behind a hypocritical patriarchal and heterosexist culture. Another evaluator felt that the film's explicit illustrations of homosexual acts made it unsuitable for classrooms.

How to Use: I would use the film to discuss Mexican culture of the late 1960s and 1970s, specifically that of the conventional middle- and upper-middle class. *Doña Herlinda and Her Son* narrates one story of how that culture accommodates homosexuality (male) as long as it conducts itelf "discreetly," that is, maintains appearances of heterosexuality, family loyalty, and heterosexist patriarchy. (Pérez)

Suggested Readings: López Páez, Jorge. *Doña Herlinda y su hijo, y otros hijos.*

Level: University

EN ALAS DE LA FE (On Wings of Faith)

Documentary.   With Subtitles.   27 min.   1991
Directed by: Antonio Noyola and Rafael Rebollar
Produced by: Consejo Nacional para las Artes (San Francisco 1514 Col. Del Valle, México CP 03100, México; tel: [525] 575-5840; fax: [525] 575-4335)
Distributed by: IMRE Archive (available for viewing only)
Evaluators: William O. Autry, Elba D. Birmingham-Pokorny, Robert Haskett, José-Manuel Navarro
Description: A brief look at the festival in honor of San Miguel, as celebrated in two villages in the Nahuatl-speaking Sierra Norte de Puebla, Mexico—San Miguel Tzinacapán, and Cuezcatlán, (the municipal seat). Interviews with and by local residents provide information about regional historical traditions and customs and the rivalry between the two communities over the possession of a large image of San Miguel. The main focus of the film is a series of dances staged by each community for the festival: in Tzinacapán the dances of the Santiagos, Toreadores, Migueles, Negritos, and Quetzales; in Cuezcatlán, the Huahuas and the most visually stunning of all, the Volador. The processions and dances portray a uniquely Mexican expression of Catholicism, a syncretic blending of the indigenous traditions of Mesoamerica with the Spanish expression of Roman Catholicism. By means of the religious dances, the survival of tradition in the rural communities is contrasted with the undeniable modernity of the urban areas.

Strengths and Weaknesses: The tape's native-centered perspective and its use of indigenous language are compelling. There are also stunning visuals; the display of beautiful dresses, dances, and music is captivating.

There is no narrative explaining the dances and traditions portrayed. Also, some translations of the Nahua are general.

Introducing the Tape: Viewers need a geographical setting, as well as background on religious syncretism and the blending of Mesoamerican and Hispanic traditions. Also some introduction to Mexican fiestas that celebrate *santos* (saints) would be helpful, as would an explanation of the dances and traditions contained in the tape.

How to Use: I would introduce the tape with a discussion of Mesoamerican religion, particularly Nahua and Totonaco beliefs and features, and continue with a discussion of the Catholic cult of the saints. The blending of the two traditions is depicted in the video, along with town rivalries and disagreements. Postvideo discussions would center upon syncretism and linguistic features of the tape. (Autry)

In my *Indigenous History* course I would lecture briefly on the origins and the nature of the dances to be pictured, as well as some of the other points raised in the film. A discussion of such issues as cultural survival and mixing would then follow. (Haskett)

Suggested Readings: Brandes, Stanley H. *Power and Persuasion: Fiestas and Social Control in Rural Mexico.*

Cordry, Donald Bush, and Dorothy M. Cordry. *Costumes and Textiles of the Aztec Indians of the Cuetzlan Region, Puebla, Mexico.*

Fergusson, Erna. *Fiesta in Mexico.*

García Martinez, Bernardo. *Los pueblos de la sierra: El poder y el espacio entre los indios del norte de Puebla hasta 1700.*

Ingham, John M. *Mary, Michael, and Lucifer: Folk Catholicism in Central Mexico.*

Johnston, Edith. *Regional Dances of Mexico.*

Nutini, Hugo G. *Todos Santos in Rural Tlaxcala: A Syncretic Expressive and Symbolic Analysis of the Cult of the Dead.*

Pettit, Florence H., and Robert M. Pettit. *Mexican Folk Toys: Festival Decorations and Ritual Objects.*

Reavis, Dick J. *Conversations with Moctezuma: Ancient Shadows over Modern Life in Mexico.*

Sayer, Chloe. *Costumes of Mexico.*

Sedillo, Mela. *Mexican and New Mexican Folk Dances.*
Level: University

ENAMORADA

Feature.   Without Subtitles.   93 min.   1947
Directed by: Emilio "El Indio" Fernández
Produced by: Clasa Films Mundiales
Distributed by: IMRE
Evaluators: Susana Conde, Mark Fried, Ann Marie Stock
Description: This 1947 classic of the golden age of Mexican cinema, starring María Félix and Pedro Armendáriz, deals

with the tumultuous time of the Mexican Revolution. Juar-ista General José Juan Reyes arrives in Cholula with his troops and roughs up the local landed gentry for money and supplies. Among them is Carlos Peñafiel, a proud conserva-tive landowner who wants nothing to do with the revolution, and his daughter, Beatriz, who is engaged to a foreigner. In the few initial exchanges between Beatriz and the heavy-handed general, the grounds for their feud and the initiation of the terms of their relationship are established. In the end, Beatriz does not marry but follows José Juan Reyes into bat-tle, like a good, typical Mexican *soldadera* (soldier fol-lower), while her father, her well-bred foreign fiancé, and the parish priest watch in silence.

Strengths and Weaknesses: This classic film is part of di-rector Fernández's program of films extolling the virtues of the Mexican Revolution. It offers insight into many aspects of the Mexican Revolution and Mexican "official" culture. Although the story line is predictable and melodramatic and the characters stereotyped, the acting is first-rate, the cine-matography is excellent, and it presents an accurate portrait of small-town life during the revolution. This is a must-see for film students, because it is an example of the classic pe-riod of filmmaking in Mexico at its height.

Introducing the Tape: A brief summary of Mexican his-tory encompassing the era of Porfirio Díaz and the subse-quent revolutionary period would help in grounding this film. Also, an introduction to the period of Mexican clas-sic film would be useful. María Félix's legendary roles as the strong woman, as opposed to Dolores del Río's roles, for example, would add interest to the presentation of this film.

How to Use: I would use the tape to emphasize the role of *Women in Latin American Societies,* in different sectors over different historical periods. (Conde)

In a unit on the *Mexican Revolution* I would use the film to spark discussion on the following topics: how the revolu-tion was lived in small towns; the ideology of revolutionar-ies; the role of religion; and the evolving interpretation of the revolutionary over the twentieth century. (Fried)

I would use this film to illustrate features of *Mexican Clas-sic Cinema,* pointing out the similarities to Hollywood con-ventions in the western and the melodrama from that time. It also serves as an example of the acting of María Félix and the directing of Emilio Fernández. (Stock)

Suggested Readings: Black, Jan Knippers, ed. *Latin Amer-ica. Its Problems and Its Promise.*

Fuentes, Carlos. "Orchids in the Moonlight." In *Drama Contemporary, Latin America,* Plays by Manuel Puig et al., eds. Mario Peter Holt and George Woodyard.

Green, Duncan. *Faces of Latin America.*

King, John. *Magical Reels: A History of Cinemas in Latin America.*

Mora, Carlos. *Mexican Cinema: Reflections of a Society.*

Skidmore, Thomas E., and Peter H. Smith. *Modern Latin America.*

Sommer, Doris. *Foundational Fictions: The National Ro-mances of Latin America.*
Level: University

ESPACIOS DE JUAN RULFO
Documentary.   Without Subtitles.   49 min.   1993
Directed by: Oscar Menéndez (Presidente Carranza 52–8 Altos, Coyoacán Centro 04100, México; tel: [525] 659-4562)
Distributed by: IMRE Archive (available for viewing only)
Evaluators: Marlene Gottlieb, Richard D. Woods
Description: This tape is an introduction to the life and works of the Mexican novelist and short-story writer, Juan Rulfo. It is primarily narrated by a critic, who tells of Rulfo's life and work against the backdrop of scenes of the Mexican landscape. There are interviews with the author himself, as well as commentary from several critics of his work. Long selections are read and reenacted from his stories. Emphasis is placed on "Luvina," *"La cuesta de los comadres,"* and *Pe-dro Páramo,* with images of its pervasive loveless landscape.
Strengths and Weaknesses: The scenes from the Mexican countryside that accompany the narrative are magnificent. The interviews with Rulfo are useful, and the readings of the stories are well done and emphasize the realistic, popular, oral aspect of Rulfo's work.

Evaluators felt that although, in a sense, the visuals cap-tured the mythical "Luvina," the technical craftsmanship was not strong. The tape tends to be long and monotonous, de-pending too heavily on the "talking head" format. The spo-ken Spanish is rapid and unclear.

Introducing the Tape: Viewers need an introduction to, and some familiarity with, the work of Juan Rulfo, as the tape is more a commentary and dramatic reading of selections.

How to Use: I would first study the work of Rulfo in class. We would read *Pedro Páramo,* as well as several of the short stories in *El llano en llamas.* I would then use the tape to il-lustrate the rural areas of Mexico in which Rulfo's stories take place. The readings from the stories aid in demonstrat-ing the oral nature of his prose. Finally, we would view the interviews with Rulfo. In short, rather than show the entire tape from beginning to end, I would first isolate portions of the tape then use the entire tape as a kind of summary for our study of Rulfo. (Gottlieb)

Suggested Readings: González Boixo, J. C. *Claves narrati-vas de Juan Rulfo.*

Harss, Luis. *Los nuestros,* interview with Rulfo.

Munguía Cárdenas, Federico. *Antecedentes y datos bi-ográficos de Juan Rulfo.*

Rulfo, Juan. *Obra completa: El llano en llamas, Pedro Páramo, Otros Textos.*

Rulfo, Juan. *Inframundo: El México de Juan Rulfo.*

Rulfo, Juan. *Pedro Páramo.*

Taggart, Kenneth M. "Juan Rulfo." *Dictionary of Mexican Literature,* pp. 610–12, ed. Eladio Cortes.
Level: University

FRIDA (Frida)
Feature.   With Subtitles.   108 min.   1987
Directed by: Paul Leduc
Distributed by: IMRE
Evaluators: Robert Alvarez, Susan Douglass, David William Foster
Description: Leduc's film is an abstract, fictionalized portrait of Frida Kahlo's recollections of her life from her deathbed, with excellent pseudodocumentary material. The references to Kahlo's early life are in sharp contrast to the trials of her tragic health problems, caused by an accident in 1926. Kahlo's strong will is evident. Her artistic talent emerges and develops amid a great deal of pain. Also illustrated are Kahlo's relationship with her husband, Diego Rivera, her involvement with Trotsky, and her commitment to political causes (particularly the communist movement) despite her illness.
Strengths and Weaknesses: This powerful film captures Frida Kahlo's person, both in spirit and physically, and offers insights into her relationship with Diego Rivera. The film examines an important period in Mexican and Latin American history, the influence of the Communist Party of Mexico, the presence of Trotsky, and the role of art and artists in the political arena. The film uses symbols of Mexican revolutionary Zapata, the Mexican Revolution, World War II, and Hitler to portray the political climate of the time. Evaluators appreciated the film's abstract form, which follows no chronology and uses little dialogue.

One evaluator felt the film lost something by focusing only on Kahlo's life while ignoring her artwork. Others felt it was a bit long for U.S. audiences. The film's psychological interpretation and abstractions make it more suitable for college than high school courses.
Introducing the Tape: An introduction to Frida Kahlo's life and relationship with Diego Rivera is necessary, as the film moves back and forth in time sequences. Some contextualization about the Mexican sociopolitical climate, the Mexican Revolution, the Communist Party of Mexico, and the role of Trotsky would be helpful.
How to Use: Overall this is a film that uses Frida's life to depict an important period of historical change in Mexico. (Alvarez)

Since Kahlo is now virtually an icon in regards to the role of women in masculinist societies, I have used the film to discuss the question of aggression against the female body and the struggle to render an adequate representation of the body outside hegemonic artistic conventions. The fact that the filmmaker is a man opens up the question of men in feminism. Also, the film is fascinating for its representation of Kahlo's sexuality, including her lesbianism, which can be discussed in terms of sensationalism vs. representational honesty. (Foster)
Suggested Readings: Herrera, Hayden. *Frida, a Biography of Frida Kahlo.*

The Metropolitan Museum of Art's catalog to the show "Mexico," which included a great deal of Kahlo's work.

Zamora, Martha. *Frida Kahlo: The Brush of Anguish.*
Level: University

UNA ISLA RODEADO DEL AGUA (An Island Surrounded by Water)
Fiction.   With Subtitles.   25 min.   1985
Directed by: María Novaro
Distributed by: Women Make Movies, Latina
Evaluators: Sandra Boschetto-Sandoval, Lynn M. Shirey
Description: This is a feminist political depiction of a young girl's search for her mother, portrayed in a sensitive, nondogmatic style. The film takes place around the time of the 1968 killings of university students by Mexican authorities. Edith's mother had left her with a godmother some fourteen years earlier in a small coastal island town in western Mexico and had gone to the mountains of northern Mexico to join her husband, a guerrilla leader opposing the Partido Revolucionario Institucional (PRI) government. Edith's search for her mother appears frustrated, yet it leads to her self-discovery. Through a journey of recollection, she embraces the strong bond with her mother's invisible presence. Verbal abuse by classmates and peers seems to strengthen Edith's resolve. The final scene provides an ambivalent but poignant conclusion as Edith, alone on her fifteenth birthday, has her photo taken against a fake seashore backdrop, in lieu of the traditional *quinceañera* (coming-out party).
Strengths and Weaknesses: This is a lyrical, impressionistic short film that subtly allows viewers to compile fragments into meaning. It is beautifully made, with little dialogue and long evocative camera shots depicting the mood of the character and the island or town.

One evaluator noted that the plot was puzzling and the ending abrupt.
Introducing the Tape: Viewers should be told that ambiguity is an inherent and relevant aspect of this film. The political overtones are highlighted at its end within the context of a guerrilla group opposed to the Mexican PRI. Some political background would be helpful—for example, an examination of women's roles within a revolutionary resistance movement. Some background on the 1968 student massacre and the PRI government's rule would also be necessary.
How to Use: I would use this tape in conjunction with literary texts by Hispanic women writers, especially those less known or experimental. The film is short enough to provide for easy playback and accessibility. We would discuss the creative process of Latin American women writers and film directors and the motivating force behind individual works. We would also look at the problems faced in writing or filming and the strategies that have enabled these women to reach their goals. (Boschetto-Sandoval)

In *Sociology, Social Work,* or *Psychology* courses the film can be used to stimulate discussion or essays examining family and the impact of its absence on children's emotional development.

Suggested Readings: Correas de Zapata, Celia, ed. *Short Stories by Latin American Women: The Magic and the Real.*

García Pinto, Magdalena. *Women Writers of Latin America: Intimate Histories.*

Picon Garfield, Evelyn. *Women's Voices from Latin America: Interviews with Six Contemporary Authors.*
Level: University

L.E.A.R. (League of Revolutionary Artists and Writers)
Documentary.   With Subtitles.   30 min.   1987
Directed by: Yvette Nieves Cruz
Distributed by: The Cinema Guild
Evaluators: Danny J. Anderson, Donald W. Davey, Lewis A. Tambs, Allen Wells
Description: This documentary includes a collage of interviews with the remaining members and supporters of the organization League of Revolutionary Writers and Artists (L.E.A.R.). L.E.A.R. existed between 1934 and 1938, during the presidency of nationalist Lázaro Cárdenas, and brought graphic artists, muralists, writers, and musicians together in the struggle against imperialism and fascism. In these interviews, numerous men and women look back on the organization and its purposes and activities and provide a behind-the-scenes account of the heyday of mural painting with Diego Rivera, the activities of the Taller de Gráfica Popular, the Mexican support for left-wing struggles in Cuba (Julio Antonio Mella) and Nicaragua (Sandino), the nationalization of the oil industry, and the Mexican view of the Spanish civil war. Praise of, and support from, President Lázaro Cárdenas (1934–1940) are featured. L.E.A.R. eventually went into decline when leftist orthodoxy turned into excessive bureaucracy (1938).
Strengths and Weaknesses: The well-integrated, nostalgic recollections of participants and supporters of L.E.A.R. are picturesque and interesting. The interview clips are rich, because those interviewed lived through this heady time, when the members of L.E.A.R. really believed they could fight and win the struggle for a better society. In a real and wonderful way, they still carry that sense of commitment with them. The tape also highlights the international aspect of their involvement with Cuban, Nicaraguan, and Spanish struggles, in contrast with the usual emphasis on Mexican nationalism during this period. The tape includes good historical photos and film footage of Sandino, Siqueiros, Rivera, Kahlo, Mella, Cárdenas, and Vasconcelos. It touches indirectly on several hot topics in contemporary Mexican scholarship (e.g., the assassination of Julio Antonio Mella, the Mexican Left, Sandino in the 1930s, and the Spanish civil war).

U.S. viewers would need substantial background to appreciate this documentary, because there is no historical, artistic, or literary context given. There is no narrator and only a few still photographs to break up the barrage of oral histories. The tape provides little discussion of the relationship between L.E.A.R. and the Mexican government, a key

point given the government's sponsorship of the arts during the early stages of the revolution. Sectarian differences within the Left are also not mentioned. One evaluator felt the subject matter in general was quite esoteric and narrowly focused. As is often the case in tapes with long dialogues, the subtitles are greatly summarized and lose much of the flavor of the language.
Introducing the Tape: U.S. viewers would need background about this period in Mexican history, the league, and its activities during these years. Also, key historical, artistic, and literary figures should be identified. An introduction that explains the Popular Front, the civil war in Nicaragua, U.S. interventionism, communist infiltration, and the clash between Joseph Stalin and Leon Trotsky would help set the context.

U.S. viewers should be told that the Mexican Communist Party stopped supporting Sandino because he was not orthodox enough for them. Sectarian differences within the Left should be discussed.
How to Use: The tape could be useful in contextualizing a figure like Diego Rivera in *Art History,* revealing the ideological currents of the 1930s for a *Literature* class, or talking about the specific kind of leftist politics among intellectuals in a *Social/Cultural History* course. I teach both *Mexican Literature* and *Mexican Culture* and could easily use this kind of a video to tie together the music, mural painting, and literature of the 1930s. It would be particularly helpful in communicating the air of enthusiasm among the L.E.A.R. and the rather wide ideological range of leftism. (Anderson)

I would use the film in an *Intellectual and Cultural History* course to demonstrate the idealism and talent of the artists and writers of the 1930s. (Tambs)

This tape can be used in conjunction with a discussion of the mural movement in Mexico, showing slides of the murals and the feature film, *Frida.* I would lecture on the role of the revolutionary Left in Mexico during the 1920s and 1930s. The students would also need context on the presidency of Lázaro Cárdenas from 1934 to 1940, which in many ways abandoned this cooperative. (Wells)
Suggested Readings: Hamilton, Nora. *The Limits of State Autonomy: Post-Revolutionary Mexico.*

Herrera, Hayden. *Frida: A Biography of Frida Kahlo.*

Knight, Alan. "Revolutionary Project, Recalcitrant People." In *The Revolutionary Process in Mexico: Essays on Political and Social Change, 1880–1940,* ed. Jaime E. Rodríguez, pp. 224–67.

Meyer, Michael, and William L. Sherman. *The Course of Mexican History.*

Any reading on the Mexican muralists, e.g., Diego Rivera.

Any reading about the postrevolutionary period or the presidency of Lázaro Cárdenas would provide context.
Complementary Films/Videos: *Frida* (Mexico); *Reds* (the U.S. film distributed by Facets).
Level: University

LOLA CASANOVA

Feature. Without Subtitles. 91 min. 1948
Directed by: Matilde Landeta
Distributed by: IMRE, Latina
Evaluators: Alvaro Félix Bolános, Currie Kerr Thompson
Description: The film is based on the novel by Francisco Rojas González about the Indians of Sonora. Lola Casanova receives an Indian child captured during a raid to keep as a servant. She treats him kindly, and her kindness is repaid when she is captured and forced to live with the Indians. Ultimately, she falls in love with an Indian and bears his child. The couple represents the union of the two cultures through *mestizaje* (racial mixing).
Strengths and Weaknesses: The film is professionally made and has an engaging script. One evaluator mentioned that the film can only be appreciated as a period piece. From a contemporary perspective, it will seem primitive, stereotyped, and overly sentimental.

There is no authenticity in its presentation of indigenous culture. The "native" dances are actually European ballet. The film celebrates the illusion of a new mestizo Mexico that combines civilized, white Euro-Americans with barbaric Native Americans.
Introducing the Tape: Viewers need to have background on Latin American culture, the place of the golden age of Mexican cinema in film history, and its relationship to Hollywood cinema of the time.
How to Use: The tape is useful for a *History of Latin American Film* and a history and critique of minority stereotypes in *Latin American Culture.* (Bolános)

I would have the students discuss how it relates to other films of the period, particularly in its development of the plot and the cinematography. In *Film* class we would study the film in the context of books on film theory and texts dealing with popular cinema in Latin America. (Thompson)

Instructors can use the stereotyped images of indigenous culture in the film to engage students in a discussion of questions of representation and media.
Suggested Readings: Bordwell, David. *Making Meaning: Inference and Rhetoric in the Interpretation of Cinema.*

Rojas González, Francisco. *Lola Casanova.*
Level: University

LUCHA LIBRE (Lucha Libre)

Documentary. With Subtitles. 22 min. 1991
Directed by: José Martínez
Produced by: Deep Dish TV (339 Lafayette St. New York, NY 10012; tel: [212] 473-8933; fax: [212] 420-8223)
Distributed by: Deep Dish TV, IMRE
Evaluators: Silvia Arrom, Angela Carreño, Daniel P. Hunt, Enrique R. Rodríguez
Description: This documentary follows the efforts of Mexican folk hero and human rights activist "Super Barrio." Super Barrio disguises himself as a freestyle wrestler, takes advantage of media opportunities, and parodies hegemonic cultural forms, such as music videos, in order to expose social injustice of all kinds. In particular, he defends the poor against forced eviction from their homes. Super Barrio stages a wrestling match between himself, as representative of popular justice, and a character representing the Mexican government. The government is seen as an invidious force, manipulating television, assisting in the corruption of landlords, selling justice, and ignoring the needs of the poor. Super Barrio organizes local neighborhoods to resist city officials, real estate speculators, and the police. He also speaks out against policies such as the North American Free Trade Agreement (NAFTA) and against human rights violations practiced by the U.S. Border Patrol.
Strengths and Weaknesses: The authentic footage of the city's poor neighborhoods captures the scope of the squalor throughout Mexico City. The satiric portrayal of the powerful is adroit.

The sound and editing are uneven. One evaluator found Super Barrio a colorful character, but felt that only a Mexican audience would appreciate his mission. Another found the tape dated and clichéd.
Introducing the Tape: Some introduction to the history of urban development and poverty in twentieth-century Mexico would be necessary for most U.S. students. Background on Cardenas, Octavio Paz, NAFTA, and the debt crisis and austerity measures in Mexico City should be included, as well as information on the grassroots urban movement that developed after the 1985 earthquake. To avoid having U.S. viewers blame the victims, the film could be supplemented with an introduction to the causes of urban migration and the ubiquity of squatters' districts and the struggle for squatters' rights throughout Latin America. Instructors could compare urban issues in Mexico city to those in U.S. cities.
How to Use: In my *Spanish Language* course I first gave an introduction to the problem of *desalojamiento* (displacement) and the almost total powerlessness of the poor to defend themselves against developers. I also discussed the popularity of wrestling and its importance in establishing folk heroes. I had the students watch the video twice, first for general impressions, then again closely, stopping the tape frequently to ask questions in Spanish or to make further comments. We then discussed the program in Spanish, and a few of the students chose to respond to the program in a longer composition. The tape is good for language classes because Super Barrio speaks slowly and clearly, and the dialogue is backed up by relevant footage. (Hunt)

This film is useful for comparing U.S. urban centers with Latin America urban centers and the similarities and differences of problems. Teachers can present the issue through discussion, introduce the film, and hand out questionnaires for further discussion. (Rodríguez)
Suggested Readings: Lewis, Oscar. *The Children of Sanchez: Autobiography of a Mexican Family.*

Poniatowska, Elena. *Hasta no verte Jesús mío,* captures

the urban culture and the yearning for a strong political advocate.

   Skidmore, Thomas E., and Peter H. Smith. *Modern Latin America*.

Level: High School—University

MARA ACAME (Mara Acame: Cantor and Curer)
Documentary.   With Subtitles.   47 min.   1982
Directed by: Juan Francisco Urrusti
Produced by: Instituto Nacional Indigenista (Av. Revolución, 1227, Col. Alpes, México D.F., 01010; tel: [525] 593-2875; fax: [525] 651-7342 or 593-5967)
Distributed by: IMRE Archive (available for viewing only)
Evaluators: Sandra L. Cade
Description: The film follows the daily sacred ritual activities of Don Agustin Montoya de la Cruz "Tepu," a noted Huichol shaman who is seen as a healer, cantor, and interpreter of dreams. This man is a directive force within his society, since he is considered the wise one, the one who can guide, protect, and ensure health. His healing ceremonies and rituals of *wimacuarra* and *tatneirra* are described.
Strengths and Weaknesses: This is an excellent view of the life in rural Jalisco, including the gathering of food and medicinal plants, and the preparation for, and performance of, religious rituals. There is a moving scene in which the *curandero* (faith healer) prays with those who come seeking help.

   The map at the outset does not set the scene well, and the sound of corn being harvested can be distracting.
Introducing the Tape: The definition and role of a *curandero* should be explained to audiences.
How to Use: At the college or advanced high school level, I would show this film as one of a series in which we explored religious experiences from various cultures. I would inquire if the prayer scene had parallels in other religious experiences. (Cade)
Level: University

MARÍA CANDELARIA (María Candelaria)
Feature.   With Subtitles.   99 min.   1945
Directed by: Emilio Fernández
Produced by: Clasa Films Mundiales/Manuel Barbachano (Atletas No.2, Colonia Country Club, Mexico D.F.; tel: [525] 544-0029/30; fax: [525] 689-3157)
Distributed by: IMRE
Evaluators: Michael Shane, Stephen Webre
Description: Filmed in 1943, this is a classic Mexican tragedy about an outcast indigenous woman who becomes a victim of circumstance. Already ostracized by the villagers in Xochimilco, María Candelaria (played by Dolores del Río) is barely surviving with the help of her fiancé when she becomes ill with "the fever." Her desperate boyfriend breaks into the local store to get quinine and is subsequently arrested and jailed. A sophisticated painter (Alberto Galán), who specializes in scenes of Indian life, discovers María Candelaria, who embodies for him the essence of Mexican beauty. María

agrees to pose for him in return for his assistance in providing bail. Before the painter finishes his work, however, María realizes she cannot continue with the project. Another indigenous woman takes her place, modeling nude, and the painter completes the piece. When the villagers see the painting, they assume the body is María's and stone her to death.
Strengths and Weaknesses: This is one of the great classics from the golden age of Mexican cinema. Beautifully photographed in black and white, the story is simple and well developed, and the acting and directing are memorable. Although the film romanticizes peasant life to a certain extent, it offers a candid exposure of some of the less agreeable aspects of rural communities.

   One evaluator pointed out that Dolores del Río is a fine actress and a beautiful woman, but (as is typical of the casting of the era) is too European in appearance to fit the painter's enthusiastic description of María Candelaria as a woman of the pure Mexican race with the beauty of the ancient Aztec princesses.
Introducing the Tape: U.S. audiences will want an introduction to the peculiar geography of Xochimilco, with its canals and its *chinampa* (floating-garden system of agriculture). Also some explanation of the racial/ethnic makeup of the Mexican population would be useful, with particular emphasis on the distinction between mestizos and Indians. Viewers would benefit from learning a little about the history of prejudiced attitudes toward the Indian in Mexican society.
How to Use: I would use this as entertainment followed by discussion and/or written composition. It is not an anthropological study but will stimulate students to think about the cultural differences long in existence between upper-class Mexicans and marginalized indigenous peoples. (Shane)

   In courses on *Latin American Culture and Society* students may be encouraged to ponder realities of peasant life. The film illustrates the role of gossip and informal modes of social discipline in face-to-face societies. It also portrays the peculiar status of cash in a subsistence economy. Cash is always in short supply, and, while not necessary for daily life, it is absolutely essential as a linkage to the outer, official world. It is the storekeeper's insistence that María Candelaria's debt be paid in cash, rather than in flowers or vegetables, that is at the root of her problem. Cash is also necessary to buy a wedding dress, pay a physician, or bail Lorenzo Raphael out of jail. (Webre)

   Students in *Film History* or *Mexican History* courses could be invited to place the film in its own historical context, as a revolution. Important themes from this period are the idealization of the Indian and the exaltation of science over superstition, which is developed in the film in the depiction of both the quinine distribution program and the confrontation between the medical doctor and the folk healer. The film's sympathetic treatment of the village priest and of religious observances in general may be taken to reflect the church-state reconciliation that is usually dated to 1940.

Suggested Readings: García Riera, Emilio. *Historia documental del cine mexicano.*
Level: High School—University

MEXICO: A VUELO DE PAJARO
Documentary.   Without Subtitles.   28 min.   1990
Directed by: Eduardo Herrerra
Produced by: Copal, José Manuel Pintado (Manzanillo No. lll Esq. Tepic, Col. Roma CP 06760, México D.F.; tel: [525] 574-6864; fax: [525] 264-6651)
Distributed by: IMRE Archive (available for viewing only)
Evaluators: Gary S. Elbow, Rebeca Harclerode
Description: A group of young Mexican men and women attempts to fly from the southern tip of Baja California to the Yucatán in two single-motored ultralight aircraft. The film shows the thrills of the expedition in three segments: *Baja California; Sobre volcanes, desiertos y lagos;* and *El Sureste.*
Strengths and Weaknesses: The tape has excellent aerial views of Mexico. The footage of Baja California and the Yucatán is especially striking.

Evaluators felt the tape placed too much emphasis on the adventure of flying and did not supply much information regarding Mexico beyond geography.
How to Use: This tape could be used to introduce a course on the *Geography of Mexico.* I would first present students with a map that shows the route followed and point out the places that are featured in the tape. I also would discuss with students the different landscapes that are illustrated. (Elbow)
Suggested Readings: West, R. C., and J. P. Augelli. *Middle America: Its Lands and Peoples,* chap. 2.
Level: Junior High School—University

MI QUERIDO TOM MIX (My Dear Tom Mix)
Feature.   With Subtitles.   90 min.   1991
Directed by: Carlos García Agraz
Produced by: Instituto Mexicano de Cine (Tepic 40, CP 06760, Mexico D.F. tel: [525] 574-4902; fax: [525] 574-0712)
Distributed by: IMRE, Latina
Evaluators: Daniel P. Hunt, S. Travis Silcox, Ann Marie Stock
Description: Based on a script written at a scriptwriting workshop led by Gabriel García Márquez, this charming film spoofs the conventions of the silent western in a love story with heroes and villains. An old, unemployed cowboy actor rides into a northern Mexican village. An aging woman obsessed with the films of a western cowboy hero, Tom Mix, presumes that her dreams have been fulfilled and her hero has arrived to sweep her away from her mundane life. When the local law is unable to stop a gang of thieves and killers, the actor and the woman team up and in comic fashion overcome all odds and stop the criminals. Finally, the woman experiences a happy ending with her own Tom Mix as they ride off together into the sunset.

Strengths and Weaknesses: This film received mixed evaluations. Some reviewers found it a captivating, poignant, and funny story with interesting characters, excellent acting, high production quality, and an impressive mix of film styles. One evaluator appreciated the casting of the hero and heroine as dispossessed and lonely seniors.

Other evaluators found the film slow paced (despite its action sequences), with a predictable sentimental plot and occasional bad acting.
How to Use: The tape would provide a delightful addition to introductory *Spanish Language* courses where the students depend heavily on subtitles. I would simply show the film in class and comment on language use from time to time and then require the students to write a character sketch in Spanish of one of the protagonists. (Hunt)

In a *Film* class the tape could be used as an example of the colonized gaze of the Hollywood convention of the western. (Silcox).

I would use *Tom Mix* in a *Latin American Film* course to challenge notions of films as national products. While the film was produced in Mexico, the tale underlines the importance of Hollywood films in Latin America. (Stock)
Suggested Readings: Stock, Ann Marie. *On Location in Costa Rica,* a doctoral dissertation.
Level: High School—University

MONTE ALBAN (Monte Alban)
Documentary.   With Subtitles.   30 min.   1991
Directed by: Gonzalo Infante
Produced by: OMAC Video (Miguel De Quevedo 296, Coyoacán CP 0400, México D.F.; tel: [525] 554-0883; fax: [525] 659-6942)
Distributed by: IMRE
Evaluators: Daniel C. Scroggins
Description: This program is part of the series *Ciudades del México antiguo* (Ancient Cities of Mexico). Photos, paintings, and a reenactment of the excavations carried out by Alfonso Caso in the 1930s introduce the viewer to the astonishing past of Monte Albán and its discovery.
Strengths and Weaknesses: The strong points are the visual rendering of an important archeological site, the presentation of some of the artifacts, and the re-creations of the poetic force that the site exercised over Alfonso Caso. The material presented is more poetic than factual. The film is not as informative as it could have been for students of Mexican culture. Camera work is good, and special credit is due for the original musical score. The Spanish is clear and accessible to undergraduate students from the sophomore level up, and the program has unusually good English subtitles.
Introducing the Tape: U.S. audiences would benefit from a brief orientation to the Monte Albán program.
How to Use: I would use *Monte Albán* to demonstrate the importance that the indigenous past has for the heirs of the Mexican Revolution. The film displays, perhaps unintentionally, the magic hold that the ancient cultures had or have

on some Mexican intellectuals of the twentieth century. (Scroggins)

Level: University

LOS MOTIVOS DE LUZ

Feature.   Without Subtitles.   94 min.   1985

Directed by: Felipe Cazals

Produced by: Hugo Scherer

Distributed by: IMRE Archive (available for viewing only)

Evaluators: Sandra Boschetto-Sandoval, Currie Kerr Thompson, Stephen Webre

Description: This deeply moving film, based on a real-life story, is set in a contemporary Mexican city. Luz, a simple country woman living in a recently formed shantytown, is arrested and accused of having murdered her four small children. A feminist lawyer and a psychologist are interested in her case and, after speaking with Luz, become convinced that she is innocent. Under interrogation, Luz is distracted and unresponsive and is initially classified as being of subnormal intelligence. Through interviews with the female psychologist, flashbacks to scenes from her life in a brutalizing environment, and interrogations of other principals, Luz's story unfolds, and a more complex reality emerges. As we piece together her peculiar worldview, traditional rural beliefs find no easy accommodation in psychological models borrowed from modern, secular societies. The murder of the children is an apparently inexplicable act for which a possible frightening explanation begins to emerge.

Strengths and Weaknesses: This professionally done feature film explores its subject in an interesting and thought-provoking manner. It provides a sensitive and powerful portrayal of the central character and the material and spiritual worlds in which she lives. The screenplay, direction, and acting are all of high quality, and the settings and the cultural attitudes presented are authentic. The Spanish sound recording is also of high quality. The film affords insight into several contemporary problems: the clash between traditional and modern systems of beliefs and values; rural-to-urban migration; life, politics, and social control in marginal urban settlements; the condition of women in Mexican society; and the relationship between poverty, on the one hand, and family instability and domestic violence, on the other.

The extensive use of flashbacks makes the narrative difficult to follow at times.

Introducing the Tape: U.S. audiences will need a substantial introduction to Mexican folk beliefs concerning the supernatural, and in particular *brujería* (witchcraft), *nahualismo* (the possession of human bodies by maleficent animal spirits) and *mal de ojo* (the evil eye, a form of curse or spell). Students of Spanish language will benefit from familiarization with Mexican popular speech.

How to Use: I would use the tape in conjunction with an *Advanced Seminar in Foreign Literature and Film:* a critical study of the political and aesthetic uses of language in literature, film, and other selected arts from Hispanic language communities. Around the integrative theme (language and power), students will study several subthemes such as racism, sexism, and the experience and abuse of personal power. (Boschetto-Sandoval)

For a *Cinema* class the focus of the questions would be less exclusively on the content and would include cinematography, as well as how the film relates to other testimonial cinema in Spain and Latin America. We would study the film in the context of books on film theory (for example, David Bordwell's *Making Meaning: Inference and Rhetoric in the Interpretation of Cinema*) and texts dealing with testimonial cinema in Latin America. (Thompson)

The film can also facilitate discussion of a number of issues associated with *Gender*. For example, how are gender roles and obligations defined in different cultures and social classes? Students may be encouraged to compare Luz's attitude toward her relationship with Sebastian (her abusive and unfaithful lover, and the father of three of the murdered children) with that of the educated, middle-class women who come to her defense. (Webre)

The film can be used to explore many themes in contemporary Latin America. In particular, students may be challenged to consider the standards by which modern Western society defines "normal" intelligence and behavior and how what is considered "normal" may vary from culture to culture. The film may be used also as an illustration of how apparently inexplicable (mad) behavior can make sense once the cultural attitudes underlying it are understood. Students may wish to view the Argentine films *Hombre mirando al sureste* and *Gerónima* for other Latin American inquiries into the adequacy of modern psychiatry.

Suggested Readings: Bordwell, David. *Making Meaning: Inference and Rhetoric in the Interpretation of Cinema.*

Foucault, M. *Discipline and Punish: The Birth of the Prison.*

García Márquez, Gabriel. *Chronicle of a Death Foretold.*

Jelin, Elizabeth, ed. *Women and Social Change in Latin America.*

Complementary Films/Videos: *Gerónima* (Argentina); *Hombre mirando al sureste (Man Facing Southeast)* (Argentina).

Level: University

LA MUJER DE NADIE (Nobody's Woman)

Feature.   With Subtitles.   80 min.   1935

Directed by: Adela Sequeyro

Distributed by: IMRE, Latina

Evaluators: Alicia Borinsky, Kim Kowalczyk, Stephen Webre

Description: Its action beginning literally on a dark and stormy night, this pioneering feature film by Mexico's first woman director is the story of the lovely but unfortunate Ana María (Adela Sequeyro), who is driven from her home by her villainous stepfather. Three young men find her in the street and, overcome by pity, agree to give her refuge in a house they share. Up until this moment, painter Marcelo (Mario

Tenorio), poet Leonardo (José Eduardo Pérez), and musician Rodolfo (Eduardo González Pliego) had lived peaceably together, contentedly producing paintings, poems, and songs. By mutual agreement, they had excluded women from their household, but their compassion for Ana María leads them to break that pact, with predictable results. Marcelo, Leonardo, and Rodolfo all become infatuated with the young woman, and each dedicates a work of art to her. Ana María, for her part, is attracted to Marcelo, causing the other two friends to become jealous. The three companions recognize that the woman's presence has changed their own relationship, but none is willing to expel her. Finally, the impasse is resolved by an admirable act of self-sacrifice. Ana María writes them a letter and, while they are at the market, leaves their home.

Strengths and Weaknesses: This is a good example of early Mexican filmmaking. While the story is not particularly sophisticated, the narrative structure is clear and confidently handled. There is some clever camera work, including close-ups and some interiors shot through a fireplace with a roaring fire. Not far removed from the era of the silents, the film has melodramatic qualities and relies more heavily on facial expressions and bodily gestures than on dialogue to convey emotions. To relieve the tedium of what is not much of a story, the film employs humor liberally. Many of the comic episodes are slapstick in nature, but one of the finest sequences in the entire work is a humorous bit in which the three artists con the local storekeeper into purchasing one of Marcelo's paintings. The film is an excellent example of a highly stereotyped idea of women.

In general, evaluators found the film predictable and outdated for today's U.S. students, except in a *Cinema* class, as it was made by the first Latin American woman film director.

Introducing the Tape: Information about the history and importance of this film and its director would be helpful.

How to Use: The film may have value in *Film Studies* and *Women's Studies* courses. Its use is limited for Latin Americanists because it has little or no specifically Latin American cultural content. It moral message, the selfless nature of true love, is universal rather than characteristically Mexican. The film may be useful in courses on the early history of filmmaking in the region. In courses on *Women's Studies* and related matters it might be used as a case study on the depiction of gender roles in the Mexican media. What will students make of the bachelors' attitude toward women in general and toward Ana María in particular? Why is it assumed that Ana María's role in the household must automatically become that of cook, cleaner, and decorator? How will students evaluate Ana María's behavior at the end of the film? Why should she have been willing to sacrifice her own happiness, when Rodolfo and Leonardo made it clear that they were willing to step out of the picture? An interesting writing exercise might be to invite students to create alternate endings and provide justifications for them. (Webre)

Level: University

MUSEO NACIONAL DE ANTROPOLOGÍA

Documentary. Without Subtitles. 39 min. 1992

Directed by: Roberto Ramonda

Produced by: OMAC Video (Miguel De Quevedo 296, Coyoacán CP 04000, México D.F.; tel: [525] 554-0883/658-3171; fax: [525] 659-6942)

Distributed by: IMRE

Evaluators: William O. Autry

Description: This video provides an excellent overview and introduction to one of the finest anthropology museums in the world, Mexico's Museo Nacional de Antropología. It provides a description of the layout and rooms that comprise the museum in Chapultepec Park, Mexico City. Various vistas of important archaeological sites are also included to enhance the presentation of the museum's exhibitions.

Strengths and Weaknesses: The tape is visually strong and contains excellent description and commentary.

Unfortunately, the video ignores the ethnographic exhibits on the museum's second floor, consequently weakening the link between present-day Mexico and its archaeological past. Reflecting the emphasis of the museum, the video presents regional developments at the expense of chronological ones.

How to Use: I would discuss the geography of Mexico and provide a brief overview of chronology (since the video emphasizes regions over temporal developments) in order to enhance comprehension. I would include brief discussions of the regional cultures so that the class would be able to grasp various names as they are mentioned on the tape. After showing the tape, I would go over the chronology and regional cultural developments and relate the developments within each region to the overall prehistoric developments within all Mesoamerica. (Autry)

Suggested Readings: Artes de México. *Museo Nacional de Antropología.*

Bernal, Ignacio et al. *Museo Nacional de Antropología de México.*

Coe, Michael D. *México.*

Sanders, William T., and Barbara J. Price. *Mesoamérica: The Evolution of a Civilization.*

Level: University

MUSEO NACIONAL DE HISTORIA

Documentary. Without Subtitles. 39 min. 1992

Directed by: Roberto Ramonda

Produced by: OMAC Video (Miguel De Quevedo 296, Coyoacán, CP 04000, México D.F.; tel: [525] 554-0883; fax: [525] 659-6942)

Distributed by: IMRE

Evaluators: Roger P. Davis

Description: This promotional tape of the museum takes the viewer to Mexico City's Chapultepec Castle, which houses the museum, and presents shots of the park, the building, the interior rooms, the furniture, artifacts, and the artwork of the historical displays. The tape reviews the history of the site and building and presents an exhaustive inventory of the museum art work.

Strengths and Weaknesses: The tape gives viewers an aesthetic sense of the museum, which contains historical murals from the conquest to the end of the Mexican Revolution and *costumbrista* painting of local culture. Lovely complementary shots of the park and building are included.

Introducing the Tape: The tape needs an introduction that can order the chronology and boil down the wide variety of painters/paintings, themes, and scenes.

How to Use: I would present this tape for an impression. Students would see this only after we had dealt with *Mexican History* and historical themes and personalities so that as the film quickly moved along they would be able to recognize items. The tape would add color and dimension to the history discussed in class. (Davis)

Suggested Readings: Meyer, Michael C., and William L. Sherman. *The Course of Mexican History.*

Riding, Alan. *Distant Neighbors: A Portrait of the Mexicans.*

Level: High School—University

MY FILMMAKING, MY LIFE

Documentary.   With Subtitles.   30 min.   1990
Directed by: Patricia Díaz
Distributed by: Women Make Movies
Evaluators: Rebeca Harclerode, Irene Matthews, Susan Ryan

Description: This is a documentary on the life of Matilde Landeta, Mexico's earliest and most significant woman film director. Landeta, a lucid, funny, and charming old lady, describes her struggle to become a director in the male-dominated golden age of the Mexican film industry (the 1940s to the 1950s). She offers a pragmatic, totally unnostalgic reflection on this period. Interwoven with the interview are clips of her three feature films: *Lola Casanova* (1948), *La Negra Angustias* (1949), and *Trotacalles* (1951).

Strengths and Weaknesses: The tape does a fine job of explaining Landeta's struggle and the period in which she did her work. There is excellent narration by the protagonist, as well as interesting historical footage and photographs of family members and production sets.

The image quality of the video interview does not compare to the quality of the film clips. Also, some of the English narration is difficult to understand.

Introducing the Tape: Some general context to Latin American filmmaking, specifically the importance of the golden age of Mexican film history, could be useful to viewers.

How to Use: I would use the film to accompany the texts in a *Mexican Women Writers* course or as a central text in a course I give on *Women's Film*. (Matthews)

I would use the tape to introduce Landeta's work and as a way of discussing the obstacles women faced in entering the commercial cinema in Latin America. (Ryan)

Suggested Readings: King, John. *Magical Reels: A History of Cinemas in Latin America.*

Mora, Carlos J. *Mexican Cinema: Reflections of a Society.*
Level: University

LA NEGRA ANGUSTIAS (Angustias: The Black Woman)

Feature.   With Subtitles.   85 min.   1949
Directed by: Matilde Landeta
Distributed by: IMRE
Evaluators: John Hess, Cynthia L. Stone, Currie Kerr Thompson

Description: This Mexican classic, by the pioneering director Matilde S. Landeta and adapted from the novel by Francisco Rojas González, is based on the life of a mulatto woman who served as a colonel under Emiliano Zapata during the revolution of 1910–1916. The film centers on the struggle of Angustias to overcome the sex and race barriers to full participation in the fight for social justice. As a young girl, Angustias recoils from the traditional role of female as victim and comes to identify with her father, the legendary bandit Anton Ferreira. Harassed by the villagers for rejecting marriage, she is eventually forced to flee after committing murder as a defense against rape. Tougher than most of the men inspired by her revolutionary fervor, Angustias faces her most pronounced spiritual crisis when she falls in love with a fair-skinned aristocrat who teaches her to read and write. In contrast to other strong female characters who typically renounce nonfeminine behavior at the end of most films, Angustias overcomes her momentary lapse and returns to her revolutionary ideals with renewed vigor.

Strengths and Weaknesses: This film is engaging as a historical period piece. It is an early Latin American film directed by a woman who attempts to establish a parallel between sexual and racial discrimination. The film is particularly bold in its approach to gender issues. From a 1990s perspective, the critique of racial stereotyping comes across with less force, in large part because Angustias and her father are played by white actors with their skin painted black. For its period (1940s Mexico), the film has an engaging and original plot and professional cinematography. It should, however, be viewed only as a period piece and will not hold up if viewers approach it with the expectations they bring to a contemporary film. The sound quality is poor, and frequent use of colloquialisms can be confusing for novice language students.

Introducing the Tape: The tape needs to be placed in the contexts of both Mexican cinema and Mexican history. Viewers should be told that director Matilde Landeta, with the support of her brother Eduardo, was able to maintain artistic control over the production of the film and thus it is refreshingly daring in its approach to gender issues.

How to Use: This tape could be used in a *Film* class as an example of Mexican cinema of the late 1940s. It is one of three films by Mexico's first female director and has some interesting feminist touches. (Hess)

I would have the students discuss how the film relates to others of the period. (Thompson)

The film could be used as supplementary material for particularly dedicated students interested in pursuing issues of *Women in Film, Classical Mexican Film,* or *Cinema and Revolution.* (Stone)

Suggested Readings: Bordwell, David. *Making Meaning: Inference and Rhetoric in the Interpretation of Cinema.*

King, John. *Magical Reels: A History of Cinemas in Latin America.*

Plazaola, Luis. "Matilde S. Landeta." In *Cine y mujeres en America Latina: directoras de largometrajes de ficción,* pp. 211–31.

Rich, B. Ruby, "An/Other View of New Latin American Cinema."

Rojas González, Francisco. *La negra Angustias.*

Level: University

THE NEW TIJUANA

Documentary. With Subtitles. 58 min. 1990
Directed by: Frank Christopher and Paul Espinosa
Produced by: KPBS-TV (5200 Campanile Dr., San Diego, CA 92182-5400; tel: [619] 594-5996; fax: [619] 265-6417)
Distributed by: University of California Extension Center
Evaluators: Julia Lesage, Richard D. Woods
Description: One-hundred-year-old Tijuana is the ostensible subject of this film. History, industry, beautification at the expense of the poor, *maquiladoras* (foreign-owned factories), beauty contests, journalism, and, above all, Mexican regional politics comprise a panoramic view of this popular border city.
Strengths and Weaknesses: The interviews with a variety of Mexicans of all classes lend both interest and authenticity to the film. The program has high production values and unusual historical footage. It can be easily viewed in segments.

The film relies too heavily on narration, although it is intelligently done. A disproportionate amount of time is spent on details of Mexican politics, and discussion of drug lords is omitted. One evaluator felt the tape was shot with an outsider's eye and lacked intimacy.
Introducing the Tape: Viewers need background knowledge of the U.S.-Mexican border. An overview showing the ten border cities from Brownsville-Matamoros to San Diego-Tijuana would provide some needed context. Also, information about the people's lives from their own point of view would be helpful.
How to Use: This is a great example of the ideology of a documentary that is made by the Public Broadcasting System (PBS). The omissions are glaring and need to be pointed out. (Lesage)

My most appropriate course for the film is *Latin American Civilization.* Tijuana's problems relate to urbanization in all of Latin America. (Woods)
Suggested Readings: Carrillo, Jorge, and Alberto Hernández. *Mujeres fronterizas en la industria maquiladora.*

Demaris, Ovid. *Poso del mundo: Inside the Mexican-American Border from Tijuana to Matamoros.*

Price, John A. *Tijuana: Urbanization in a Border Culture.*
Complementary Films/Videos: *Amor, mujeres, y flores (Love, Women, and Flowers)* (Colombia)
Level: University

1992

Documentary. Without Subtitles. 50 min. 1993
Directed by: Carlos Mendoza and Norma Madrid
Produced by: Canal 6 de Julio (Medellín 33, 3er piso Col. Roma, 06700 México D.F.; tel: [525] 511-2349; fax: [525] 208-2062)
Distributed by: IMRE
Evaluators: Ulises Mejías
Description: This is an analysis of the neoliberal government's attempt to change the constitution during 1992 to make it possible for Salinas de Gortari to be reelected. The tape shows the opposition of the lower classes in Mexico.
Strengths and Weaknesses: This is a thorough, challenging, and denunciatory documentary.

The production values are not high.
Introducing the Tape: The viewers should have some basic knowledge of modern Mexican politics.
How to Use: I would use the tape as an example of independently produced, critical video work. It provides an alternative viewpoint to mainstream media. (Mejías)
Level: University

NO LES PEDIMOS UN VIAJE A LA LUNA (We Are Not Asking for the Moon)

Documentary. With Subtitles. 58 min. 1986
Directed by: Mari Carmen de Lara
Distributed by: First Run/Icarus Films, Latina
Evaluators: Silvia Arrom, Ann S. Blum, Sandra L. Cade, Allen Poor
Description: This documentary follows the seamstresses who survived the collapse of their downtown workshop in the 1985 Mexico City earthquake. The callousness of the Mexican government and the clothing factory owners to the workers' plight leads the seamstresses to form an independent union. They first confront their employers and the police, who forbid them to search the ruins for other survivors or bodies. Although persecuted by the police and discouraged by "official" labor groups, the women set up cooperative workshops, continue to organize, and demand recognition from the state. The tape is a dramatic documentation of class and gender empowerment.
Strengths and Weaknesses: This fascinating and well-paced story demonstrates the seamstresses' determination and the terrible discrimination they suffered at the hands of the Mexican government. Authentic voices clearly communicate the women's awakening of consciousness. Visually and linguistically interesting interviews represent a wide variety of people. The Spanish language is extremely clear and slow enough for intermediate-level Spanish students to understand.

The hand-held camera work and rough-cut documentary style occasionally make the tape visually confusing. One evaluator felt the tape was slow, with too much time spent on the earthquake and not enough on the organization that emerged. There is also not enough context provided for U.S. viewers. The subtitles have many errors, and some speech is marked slang when it is perfectly acceptable standard Spanish.

Introducing the Tape: Some background on the earthquake and its aftermath is necessary for U.S. audiences. An introduction should include the role of the Mexican state in coopting union organization and political independence. Information about women in the informal economy and urban manufacturing would also be helpful. Viewers need to be told about the significance of the union and how radical these women's demands are in the Mexican context. These themes are developed throughout the documentary but never from the larger historical perspective.

How to Use: I would use this tape in a course on the *Social History of Mexico* or *Development Economics* to illustrate the position of women in economic development, in manufacturing, and the informal economy. This would be a useful film for teaching about *Women's Political Mobilization* or *Urban Political Cultures*. It would work well in a *Sociology* context on urban Latin America and would serve superbly to illustrate current NAFTA-related issues concerning the conditions of work and the exploitation of low-wage female labor in Mexico. The diversity of teaching uses of this film, as well as its stark power, makes it an extremely valuable addition to a teaching video library. (Blum)

In *Spanish III* I would provide a list of idiomatic expressions and other phrases (e.g., *trabajar con las uñas* [to work or produce something with no resources]) to listen for. There are also opportunities to focus on imperative verb forms and preterit vs. imperfect. I would ask students to write paragraphs based on what they understood from the documentary. In *Spanish IV/V* I would use this as part of a unit on the *Labor Movement,* connecting it with readings on NAFTA. Role-playing, using the film and other research, would be a part of the unit. The tape would also make an excellent resource for classes studying the *International Labor Movement.* (Cade)

Suggested Readings: Beneria, Lourdes, and Martha Roldan. *The Crossroads of Class and Gender: Industrial Homework, Subcontracting, and Household Dynamics in Mexico City.*

Wilson, Fiona. *Sweaters: Gender, Class, and Workshop-Based Industry in Mexico.*

Level: High School—University

NUESTRO TEQUIO (Our Tequio)
Documentary. With Subtitles. 10 min. 1984
Produced & Directed by: La Assemblea Zapoteca (Apartado Postal 1137, Oaxaca)
Distributed by: IMRE
Evaluators: Gerard Aching, Carol Becker, Nancy J. Church, J. Julian Rívera, Marc S. Roth, University of Pittsburgh group—María Consuelo Acosta, John Frechione, Shirley A. Kregar, Nichole Parker, Lynn Young, José Zevallos

Description: This short video, made by the Indians themselves, shows how the Mexican Zapotec Indians in a remote village in Oaxaca state band together to fix the roof of a community building. *Tequío* (communal work) is an Indian tradition predating written history. The tape demonstrates how the villagers use their own resources to get things done, while the government refuses to provide them with these services. It explains that residents work illegally in the United States and use a portion of their incomes to purchase the supplies needed for the community project. A meeting depicted at the video's end shows the tradition in which the participants of the tequío have a public meeting where anyone who wishes can comment on the project and/or the process of completing it.

Strengths and Weaknesses: The tape contains a clear introduction, good cinematography, strong continuity, and an authentic feeling of the culture and ambience of the community. It conveys the geographic remoteness of the village, surrounded by vast mountains, as well as the local Indian culture, foods, and music, without appearing staged.

The tape says little about the individuals involved, particularly the leaders, or about the process used to bring people together or why the film was made.

Introducing the Tape: Viewers need to be told that a group of young Zapotecs made this tape for their community to help generate pride and preserve their tradition of regular collective work, a tradition that is slowly being lost. The background music is traditional Zapotec music used especially on festive occasions. An explanation of the present state of the municipal building would also be helpful, as would background about Oaxacan ethnic groups and their cultures, specifically the Zapotecas (and the language used in the tape).

How to Use: This could be used as a motivational tape to show how a community can work together to accomplish a seemingly overwhelming task. It also shows the traditional roles of men and women. (Church)

I could use the video in the *Ethnicity* course I teach in the social work program to show specific aspects of community life and culture of ethnic groups in their own country. It could show the potential for similar cooperative strategies in U.S. communities where the groups settle. (Rivera)

Tequío would be introduced and described as an example of Indian traditions that predate discovery and conquest. The time involved for each family as a commitment to community life and well-being would be discussed following the film. The women's role and food and its preparation would also be discussed. (University of Pittsburgh group)

Suggested Readings: Simpson, Lesley Byrd. *Many Mexicos.*

Wolf, Eric Robert. *Sons of the Shaking Earth.*

There are excellent monographs available on the Zapotecas.
Level: University

NUEVO MUNDO

Feature.   Without Subtitles.   95 min.   1976
Directed by: Gabriel Retes
Produced by: Rio Mixcoax (Coapa North 45, Col. Toriello Guerra, Tlalpan, México D.F., CP 14050; tel: [525] 665-6417; fax: [525] 665-9123)
Distributed by: IMRE, Latina
Evaluators: Alvaro Félix Bolános
Description: This is the story of the heartless evangelization effort in the New World, which faces a relentless Indian resistance. The brutality of the Spanish colonization (including harsh exploitation, military repression, genocide, and destruction of native culture) is provocatively presented. Treachery, politics, contempt for native cultural expressions, and European arrogance are demonstrated in a Spanish priest's effort to control an Indian uprising. The priest creates a syncretic Spanish-Indian Virgin icon that allegedly will save the Indian population from the physical extermination the Viceroy is contemplating.
Introducing the Tape: Viewers would benefit from a short introduction about the Spanish commitment to impose their religious beliefs on the rest of the world as part of an expansionist imperialistic project in the sixteenth and seventeenth centuries.
How to Use: The tape could be shown after studying texts like Las Casas' *Brevísima Relación* or Cabeza de Vaca's *Los Naufragios*. (Bolanos)
Suggested Readings: Casas, Bartolomé de las. *Brevísima relación de la destrucción de las Indias.*

Nuñez Cabeza de Vaca, Alvar. *Los naufragios.*
Level: University

LA OFRENDA (The Day of the Dead)

Documentary.   With Subtitles.   50 min.   1990
Directed by: Lourdes Portillo and Susana Muñoz
Produced by: Xochitl Films (981 Esmeralda St., San Francisco, CA)
Distributed by: Direct Cinema Limited, Xochitl Films
Evaluators: Sandra L. Cade, Miguel Huarcaya, Daniel P. Hunt, Grace Leavitt, Chon Noriega, Janet Norden, J. Julian Rivera
Description: *La ofrenda* explores the traditional rituals and celebrations related to the dead in Mexico and among U.S. Latinos. Family members of those who have died make offerings and conduct rituals in the cemetery, at home, and on the streets of the community on specific dates, particularly All Saints Day and the Day of the Dead. The film includes the folk parades and the colorful Day of the Dead altars and costumes, introducing both the artistic skeletons of J. G. Posada and the sculpted figures of local artisans. Moving from celebrations in Mexico to those in San Francisco, the tape bridges the ancient past and its Indian beliefs (preserved in stone ruins and oral tradition) with the twentieth century. Psychologists explore the value of today's celebrations as a way to connect people to their cultural past.

Strengths and Weaknesses: This is a beautiful film, rich in customs and colors. It is a lyrical exploration of cultural practices/rites within a binational perspective. *La ofrenda* effectively shows the interplay of such cultural elements as religion, folklore, music and art, and a philosophical way of viewing death as part of life among Mexican peasants (for example, candies are made in the shape of skulls and coffins and people can laugh about death). The film is beautifully shot and thoughtfully put together to explain a cultural concept completely different from that of the mainstream U.S. The detailed narration makes the program interesting, and the interviews are illuminating. There are inserts of reflections about death by Octavio Paz that are valuable because they explain the Mexican ways of dealing with death. The second half of the tape, which is shot in San Francisco, represents an abrupt shift in style and tone but at the same time manages to relate to the change in setting for the transplanted celebration of the Day of the Dead.

One evaluator both loved the film and was frustrated by its attempt to do too many things.
Introducing the Tape: A short introduction about the concepts of death among native Mexicans could be useful for audiences unfamiliar with the native customs. The film can also stand alone.
How to Use: I concentrated on the grandmother scenes with my sixth graders. We wrote poems about our dead loved ones and placed them on an altar we had decorated with marigolds and *velitas* (candles). We made marzipan *calaveras* (skeletons) and little pop-up coffins. In the past, I have also used another film that showed Pedro Liares at work in greater detail, and we made our own *calaveras*. (Cade)

I could use the tape in a *Social Work Ethnicity* course to show the attitude of Hispanic groups about death and dying and how to make use of it in working with members of those groups in moments of crisis. (Rivera)
Suggested Readings: Garro, Elena. *Los recuerdos del porvenir.*

Lowry, Malcolm. *Under the Volcano,* novel and film.

Revueltas, José. *El luto humano.*

Rulfo, Juan. *Pedro Páramo.*

Taussig, Michael. *The Devil and Commodity Fetishism in South America.*

Turner, Victor Witter. *The Ritual Process: Structure and Anti-structure.*

Yañez, Augustín. *Al filo del agua.*

Instructions for making figures from marzipan and *calaveras* from balloons and paper mâché. *Teachers' Discovery* catalogs have kits for pop-up coffins and wonderful *papeles cortados* (paper cut-outs).
Complementary Films/Videos: *Si Dios nos da licencia (If God Allows Us)* (Mexico).
Level: Elementary School—University

PALENQUE: EL EXPLORADOR (Palenque: The Explorer)

Documentary.   With Subtitles.   30 min.   1991

Directed by: Gonzalo Infante
Produced by: OMAC Video (Miguel A. De Quevedo 296, Coyoacán CP 0400, México D.F.; tel: [525] 554-0883/658-3171; fax: [525] 659-6942)
Distributed by: IMRE
Evaluators: Robert C. Williamson
Description: Part of the series *Ciudades del México antiguo* (Cities of Ancient Mexico), this is an excellent presentation of Palenque and its meaning. In this docudrama, scenes go from past to present, illustrating a ritual offering by men and women at the Temple of the Sun representing the interrelationship of humans and the gods who arranged life on earth and in the universe.
Strengths and Weaknesses: This is an engaging film with high production qualities. The clear narration makes it useful for Spanish language practice.
Introducing the Tape: No introduction is necessary.
How to Use: The film could be useful in discussing the meaning of aesthetics in preliterate societies. (Williamson)
Suggested Readings: Adams, Richard E. W. *Prehistoric Mesoamerica*.
   Aveni, Anthony F. *Conversing with the Planets: How Science and Myth Invented the Cosmos*.
   Morley, S. et al. *The Ancient Maya*.
Level: University

PEDRO PARAMO (Pedro Páramo)
Feature.   With Subtitles.   108 min.   1966
Directed by: Carlos Velo
Produced by: Clasa Films Mundiales (Atletas No.2, Colonia Country Club, Mexico D.F.; tel: [525] 544-0029/30; fax: [525] 689-3157)
Distributed by: UCLA Archives
Evaluators: David William Foster
Description: Based on Juan Rulfo's novel, this film provides an incisive and complex portrait of the *caudillo* (boss). As such, it is one of the most powerful characterizations of patriarchal society in Latin American culture.
Strengths and Weaknesses: The overall quality of the story is the video's greatest strength.
   Literal-minded students may find the magical-realist discourse confusing. Also, the film tends to weaken some of Rulfo's narrative complexity.
Introducing the Tape: Viewers would benefit from a brief overview of the Mexican Revolution and the question of land-ownership in Mexican revolutionary ideology, which Rulfo is always deconstructing.
How to Use: I would use this tape primarily as a portrayal of patriarchal structures; of the destruction of society by the vengeful phallic center of a society that refuses to accept his primacy; the role of women as bearers of the phallic order and as the objects of its wrath when that order breaks down; the interlocking relationships between the phallic patriarchy and questions regarding sociocultural identity, self-expression, and a microcosm of Mexican history. (Foster)

Suggested Readings: Mora, Carl. J. *Mexican Cinema: Reflections of a Society*.
   Rulfo, Juan. *Pedro Páramo*.
Level: University

PELEA DE TIGRES: UNA PETICION DE LLUVIAS NAHUA (Tiger Fights: A Nahua Petition for Rain)
Documentary.   With Subtitles.   60 min.   1987
Directed by: Alfredo Portilla and Alberto Becerril
Produced by: Instituto Nacional Indigenista (Av. Revolución, 1227, Col. Alpes, México D.F., 01010; tel: [525] 593-875; fax: [525] 651-7342 or 593-5967)
Distributed by: IMRE Archive (available for viewing only)
Evaluators: William O. Autry, Kendall W. Brown
Description: Each spring in the fiesta of Santa Cruz, the Nahua villages of Acatlán and Zitlala (in Guerrero, Mexico) stage tiger fights as a religious ritual to ensure adequate rainfall for their crops. Men don masks and padded clothing and then beat each other with fists or clubs. The harder they fight, the greater the sacrifice to appease the gods. Villagers supplicate the Virgin Mary and the sacred stone, a combination of Christian and indigenous religious beliefs. This video documentation portrays the people performing ritual oblations, feasting and fasting, and making their masks, some of which are animal-like and others Spanish-looking. The tape also alludes to the dilemma posed by those villagers who no longer have any respect for the fights and even ridicule them.
Strengths and Weaknesses: This documentary provides an excellent visual presentation and narration of the entire celebration.
   The film, however, lacks the context necessary for interpreting the events recorded. The tape is a bit long, and the sequence of events is somewhat confusing until it unfolds during the fiesta. Some of the subtitles are difficult to read.
Introducing the Tape: An outline or summary of events in the tape should be presented as an introduction. Also, background on religious syncretism and Nahua religion, as well as a map showing the location of the villages, is necessary for U.S. viewers.
How to Use: I would introduce the area and indigenous peoples of Guerrero, describe their rain-propitiation ceremonies, and include some information about Nahua language and religion. Discussion would center upon religious syncretism, Nahua language presentation, and various structural elements of the entire ceremony. The *Atzatziliztli* communal ceremony is widely known from central Mexico, but there are variations in its presentation in the region. The video also highlights various ethnic boundaries and markers between the towns that could be discussed. (Autry)
   I would spend course time discussing what resulted when the Spaniards imposed Christianity on indigenous cultures. Excerpts from the video would illustrate the resulting syncretism. I would then discuss the degree to which the villagers had adopted Christian practices, to what extent they

preserved their indigenous culture, and what the video revealed about village life in contemporary Mexico. (Brown)
Level: University

EL PIEL DEL SIGNO

Documentary. Without Subtitles. 30 min. 1990
Directed by: Antonio Noyola and Rafael Rebollar
Produced by: Consejo Nacional para Artes (San Francisco 1514, Col Valle, CP 03100 Mexico D.F.; tel: [525] 575-5840; fax: [525] 575-4335)
Distributed by: IMRE Archive (available for viewing only)
Evaluators: Rebeca Harclerode, Cynthia Radding
Description: This is a well-conceived documentary of the Tarahumara (Rarámuri) Indian people of the Sierra Madre Occidental (Chihuahua) in northern Mexico. It uses the *Semana Santa* (Easter Holy Week) ceremonials as the leitmotif. The people are shown painting their bodies for ceremonial dancing, symbolic of the Christian Easter story, particularly Judas's role in Christ's crucifixion. The Tarahumara are shown preparing a traditional drink made out of corn that is used during the festivities. The tape includes footage of visits to Tarahumara homes and conversations with Tarahumara men about the ceremonies and their daily life, subsistence farming, and conflicts with the white people.
Strengths and Weaknesses: The tape's strength is its use of an anthropological approach and time line through the Holy Week ceremonials. The original music is well integrated.

The film spends almost as much time idling on nature as it does focusing on the people and their ceremonies. The spoken language is mainly Rarámuri, with a little Spanish.
Introducing the Tape: U.S. students would need an introduction to the background of Sierra Madre religious ceremonials, which combine indigenous and Catholic elements. A brief history of the Tarahumara people, where they live, etc. would be necessary.
How to Use: I would use this tape to illustrate the integrated nature of work and religion in contemporary Indian cultures. (Radding)

The tape provides a good example of the influence of Catholicism on Indian cultures.
Suggested Readings: Merrill, William. *Rarámuri Souls: Knowledge and Social Process in Northern Mexico.*

Waters, Frank. *Book of the Hopi,* writings on the Tarahumara Indians.
Level: University

POPOL VUH: THE CREATION MYTH OF THE MAYA

Animation. With Subtitles. 60 min. 1989
Directed by: Patricia Amlin
Produced by: One Frame at a Time (2515 Regent St., Berkeley, CA 94704; tel: [510] 548-5560; fax: [510] 848-6442)
Distributed by: University of California—Berkeley
Evaluators: William O. Autry, Marlene Gottlieb, John Hays
Description: This is an excellent animation of the Quiché

Mayas' creation myth that uses illustrations from classic-period Mayan pottery to convey its story. The tape introduces the world and cosmology of the Quiché Maya through the actions of the Hero twins and their struggle to overcome the lords of the underworld.
Strengths and Weaknesses: This is a creative and well-executed version of the Quiché Popol Vuh, drawn from authentic ceramic and codex documents. The photography is excellent, and the background music is the perfect accompaniment for the reenactment of scenes. The myths are recounted in a clear, entertaining way, and the tape simplifies a complex Mayan worldview.

One evaluator felt that the tape was long and became tedious after a while and that it should be shown in two or three sessions.
Introducing the Tape: U.S. students should be told that this is the Mayan bible and that it therefore attempts to explain creation and natural phenomena.
How to Use: First, the class would either read or talk about the function of the Popul Vuh and other bibles. Then I would show the tape in various parts, concentrating on one myth at a time, interrupting the viewing of the tape for class discussion to compare Mayan beliefs to Christian, Semitic, and Oriental beliefs. In a *Civilization* course we would view each portion of the tape twice: first for the mythical content, then to examine the artwork used as a backdrop. We would also comment upon the music. (Gottlieb).
Suggested Readings: Asturias, Miguel Angel. *Leyendas de Guatemala.*

López Portillas, Miguel. *La literatura de los Mayas.*

Any version of the Bible and the Koran.

Books on pre-Columbian Art.
Level: High School—University

QUE SI QUEDE HUELLA

Documentary. Without Subtitles. 27 min. 1991
Directed by: Rafael Rebollar
Produced by: Consejo Nacional Para Artes (San Francisco 1514, Col. de Valle, CP 03100, México D.F.; tel: [525] 575-5840; fax: [525] 575-4335)
Distributed by: IMRE Archive (available for viewing only)
Evaluators: Elba D. Birmingham-Pokorny, José-Manuel Navarro
Description: This film is an introduction to the dances and culture of the Zapotec Indians in the Mexican state of Oaxaca. It provides a contrastive look at some of the traditional costumes of Tehabtepect, including parts of a wedding filmed in 1931 and a popular fiesta in 1990. Themes explored are survival and changes and tradition and modernity. The tape highlights the prominent role of women during the celebration of the fiesta.
Strengths and Weaknesses: This is a good presentation with interesting camera play between the 1990 wedding in color and the black-and-white version done by filmmaker Sergei Eisenstein in 1931. The regional particularities of the event capture the attention of the viewers.

Introducing the Tape: Viewers could benefit from a quick historical sketch of the dances and Zapotecs. Some background on Sergei Eisenstein would also be of interest to viewers.

How to Use: After viewing, the instructor could engage students in a discussion of the film, the survival of pre-Columbian traditions, and their melding with Hispanic cultural traditions. Students could be encouraged by the instructor to discuss the survival of similar traditions in their own cultural milieu. (Birmingham-Pokorny)

Level: University

QUERIDO DIARIO

Animation.   With Subtitles.   12 min.   1992

Directed by: Sarah Minter

Produced by: Sarah Minter, Maria Teresa Uriarte de Labastida, and Elvira García (Quintana Roo 93–1 Col. Roma 06760, México D.F.; tel: [525] 574-6421)

Distributed by: IMRE

Evaluators: Ann K. Coughlin, Lavina Tilson Gass, James A. Lewis, Elinor Melville

Description: In this creative animation a young girl goes on a school field trip to the ruins of Teotihuacán. She meets a pre-Columbian boy named Agua, who takes her for a visit into the past to see how the wall decorations in the temple were made and to catch glimpses of what life was like in these times. When the girl awakens from her dream and rejoins her classmates, Agua's request echoes in her mind: "Estrella, no nos olvides" ("Star, don't forget us").

Strengths and Weaknesses: This appealing story is told with a sense of mystery, providing an interesting vehicle for viewers to learn about the past. The animation contains excellent and charming depictions of the ruins at Teotihuacán.

At times the soundtrack is unclear. Agua's voice is difficult to understand because it is made to sound as if coming from an echo chamber. One evaluator felt the animation was not highly sophisticated and the story line was predictable.

Introducing the Tape: U.S. students would benefit from some introductory information about Teotihuacán, as well as pre-Columbian Mexican civilizations.

How to Use: In my *High School Spanish Language* classes the tape could be used for a discussion of time and cross-cultural understanding. (Coughlin)

I would show this as part of a unit on *Pre-Columbian History*. It could be used in advanced *Spanish Language* classes for listening comprehension, conversation, and cultural enrichment. (Gass)

I would use the tape to provide my students with an entertaining opportunity to hear spoken Spanish and to obtain a visual concept of what the ancient cities of Mexico looked like and how wall paintings were made by Native Americans in Mexico. (Lewis)

Level: First Grade—University

LA RADIO QUE SE VE

Documentary.   Without Subtitles.   30 min.   1992

Directed by: Cristina Barajas Rocha and E. Fernández

Produced by: COMPA (Av. Cuauhtémoc # 1021–4, Col. Del Valle, 03100, México D.F.; tel: [525] 575-3036; fax: [525] 575-6854)

Distributed by: IMRE

Evaluators: María Fernández, William Herzog

Description: This is a documentary of the anniversary broadcast of the radio program *Del campo y de la ciudad* (From Country and City) in Mexico City that works on integrating the city with rural areas of the country. Peasants from various areas of Mexico bring their opinions, concerns, music, and humor to the daily two-hour show. The tape is an example of educational and participatory popular radio.

Strengths and Weaknesses: This is a good documentary covering grassroots, participatory local radio. It incorporates an interesting mix of program elements. At times, the editing is a bit abrupt and unprofessional.

How to Use: For classes dealing with *Popular Communication,* the tape shows an example of popular radio in action.

Level: University

LOS REBELDES DEL SUR

Documentary.   Without Subtitles.   63 min.   1992

Directed by: Ramon Aupart

Produced by: Cine Film SA (Saturnino Herrán 35, San José Insurgentes, México D.F.; tel: [525] 598-2870; fax: [525] 611-2763)

Distributed by: IMRE

Evaluators: Kim Kowalczyk, Stephen Webre

Description: This is a historical documentary about the role that the followers of rebel Emiliano Zapata (1879–1919) played in the Mexican Revolution. Zapata's cause was land redistribution, and his struggle was limited largely to the southern state of Morelos and its immediate environs. The film integrates background narrative and contemporary footage with interviews conducted in 1980 with surviving Zapatista veterans Faustino Aquino, Francisco Bandas, Alejandro Quintana, Longinos Rojas, Aurelio Rosales, and Faustino Sánchez, most of whom have since died. The principal issues developed in the film are the social origins of the Zapatista revolt and the human experience of exploitation and guerrilla warfare.

Strengths and Weaknesses: This is an excellent documentary on the revolution, as seen through the eyes of the men who fought in it. The film makes good use of firsthand testimony and effectively employs split-screen images to juxtapose the "talking heads" of the aged informants with contemporary photographs and film clips.

Unfortunately, the script lacks continuity; the significance of the visuals is not always explained; and the veterans tend to enunciate unclearly, so that much of what they say is difficult to understand.

Introducing the Tape: U.S. viewers will want a basic narrative overview of the Mexican Revolution, and of the Zapata revolt in particular. Some introduction to the social and ethnic peculiarities of the Morelos region is also desirable.

How to Use: I would show excerpts of this tape. The interviews of the veterans would be useful in helping students understand the *Mexican Revolution*. I would use parts of the video also in my *Literature* classes to help my students grasp works written about the revolution. (Kowalczyk)

The film may be used to stimulate student discussion of the social character and regional complexity of the Mexican Revolution, especially its ethnic and class dimensions. The veterans' testimony offers interesting clues to peasant self-identity, which may be invoked in any examination of the revolution as a nationalizing experience. For example, what significance is there to the fact that the interviewees refer to their class enemies, the landowners, as *gachupines* (an offensive colonial-era term for Spaniard) and to themselves as *Indios* or *Mexicanos?* The Hollywood version of the Morelos revolt can be seen in Elia Kazan's *Viva Zapata!* An interesting exercise would be to have students compare the images of the peasant rebel presented in the two films. (Webre)

Suggested Readings: Knight, Alan. *The Mexican Revolution.*

Womack, John, Jr. *Zapata and the Mexican Revolution.*

Level: University

REFLECION

Experimental.   Without Subtitles.   5 min.   1989
Directed by: Gustavo Domínguez and María Morfino
Produced by: Universidad de Guadalajara (Av. Hidalgo #1296, SHCP, 44100 Guadalajara, Jalisco; tel: [523] 625-5723; fax: [523] 626-0248)
Distributed by: IMRE
Evaluators: Janet B. Norden
Description: This is an artistic study of memory as an animated painting. A workingman and a boy are presented in changing positions around a table.
Strengths and Weaknesses: This visual poem has interesting, haunting images. The spoken Spanish is clear.
Introducing the Tape: No information or factual data should be demanded of this artistic work.
How to Use: This tape could be used for some of the advanced *Spanish* classes, or for free viewing in a lab situation. (Norden)
Level: University

REVOLUCION LATINOAMERICANA

Music Video.   Without Subtitles.   5 min.   1992
Directed by: José Antonio Latapi (Jojutla No. 44 Tlalpan, México D.F. 14000; tel: [525] 655-4618; fax: [525] 662-1703 or 573-9286)
Distributed by: IMRE Archive (available for viewing only)
Evaluators: María Fernández
Description: The rock group "The Rastrillos" incite Latin Americans to revolution in a song entitled "*Revolución Lati-

noamericana.*" Images stress Latin American social realities from *mestizaje* to foreign intervention. This is an appropriation and transformation of Music Television (more commonly known as "MTV") for social purposes.
Strengths and Weaknesses: The camera work is impressive. However, the long instrumental musical sequences could be shorter.
How to Use: I would use this tape to illustrate the appropriation and transformation of North American and European artistic forms by Latin Americans. (Fernández)
Suggested Readings: Olalquiaga, Celeste. *Megalopolis,* chapter entitled "Tupiconopolis."
Level: University

EL SECRETO DE ROMELIA (Romelia's Secret)

Feature.   With Subtitles.   100 min.   1988
Directed by: Busi Cortes
Produced by: Instituto Mexicano de Cine (Tepic 40, CP 06760, Mexico D.F. tel: [525] 574-4902; fax: [525] 574-0712)
Distributed by: IMRE, Latina
Evaluators: Melvin S. Arrington Jr., Daniel C. Scroggins
Description: This adaptation of Rosario Castellanos's short novel *El viudo Román* is a suspenseful tale of *machista* vengeance in contemporary Mexico (1988), where ancient codes of honor and contemporary lifestyles collide. The matronly Romelia returns with her recently divorced daughter and her granddaughters to the provincial town of her birth to liquidate an estate left to her by *el viudo Román.* Román had married the adolescent Romelia after the death of his beloved first wife, who had had an affair with Romelia's older brother. After the wedding night Román returned the disgraced Romelia to her family, claiming, despite her protestations of innocence, that she was unworthy to live in his house because she was not a virgin; Romelia was accused of an incestuous affair with the same brother. Romelia's single night of wedded bliss, the only night she ever spent with a man, left her pregnant with the daughter who accompanies her.

Romelia's story and secret are revealed by means of the diary entries of her recently deceased husband, Carlos Román, and through a series of flashbacks. The film treats the powerful themes of incest, suicide, guilt, and denial. It also underscores the conflict between traditional moral values and evolving social attitudes.
Strengths and Weaknesses: The film contrasts women's lifestyles in present and previous generations, and makes good use of flashbacks. The acting, direction, and camera work make it excellent for use in the language classroom. Well-articulated, carefully modulated speech, with full-face views of the speakers, predominates throughout the film, with only a few exceptions.

One evaluator found the plot convoluted and the use of darkness to create a gloomy atmosphere overdone. The film takes for granted a certain familiarity with postrevolutionary Mexico that is not typical of U.S audiences.

Introducing the Tape: There are some references that should be explained to U.S. audiences in advance: land reforms, the old estates, the *india,* Lázaro Cárdenas, landowners' obligation to provide schools and teachers for the workers, etc. Also, some kind of program notes identifying the characters and their relationships to each other, as well as introducing Rosario Castellanos and the themes covered in her works, would be helpful.

How to Use: The film could be used in two ways: to teach *Language* and to teach *Literature.* If I were using it to teach language at the college sophomore or junior level, I would prepare a small amount of supporting materials for the students, such as short transcriptions of critical dialogues, brief vocabulary lists, and questions in Spanish for students to answer as they view the film in order to focus their attention on important information. To teach literature, I would have students study the Castellanos text before seeing the film. (Scroggins)

Suggested Readings: Castellanos, Rosario. "El viudo Román" in *Los convidados de Agosto.*

Level: University

SI DIOS NOS DA LICENCIA

Documentary.   Without Subtitles.   27 min.   1991
Directed by: Luis Lupone
Produced by: Consejo Nacional para Artes (San Francisco #1514, Col. Valle, CP 03100, México D.F.; tel: [525] 575-0677)
Distributed by: IMRE Archive (available for viewing only)
Evaluators: Pamela Voekel, Robert C. Williamson, Richard D. Woods
Description: Interwoven with scenes from Sergei M. Eisenstein's 1935 masterpiece, *Viva México,* this documentary turns the camera on preparations for Day of the Dead festivities in the small town of San Juan Atzingo in the state of Mexico. The tape highlights the community's long history and continued identification with its indigenous past. Preparations begin on October 21, and on October 31 the Indians spread flower petals to guide the dead. The activities culminate on November 2. Images of lamenting adults placing offerings and burning incense suggest the serious nature of the ceremony. A town official describes a pre-Hispanic musical instrument (a *teponaztle*) housed in the church as "the heart of our town," and the staffs carried by the colonial-era community are still revered. The film presents the Day of the Dead as the creative amalgamation of the traditional and unabashedly modern elements that compose it; plastic tea services and soccer cleats are offered along with the flowers associated with death before the arrival of the Spanish.

Strengths and Weaknesses: This is a visually alluring tape with ostensibly unrehearsed scenes of Day of the Dead altars and prayers. The realistic images speak for themselves, directly carrying their message to the viewer, annotated only with dialogue and Spanish translation when necessary.

One evaluator commented that the events in the tape were not explained and the purpose of intercutting Eisenstein's black-and-white footage was not clear.

Introducing the Tape: Some background on the Day of the Dead ceremonies and what is happening in the video is necessary for viewers.

How to Use: The tape could be used in *Anthropology* courses to illustrate how different cultures respond to the universal truth of death. (Voekel)

The tape could be useful in the meaning of aesthetics in preliterate societies. (Williamson)

I would use this tape mainly in my course on *Latin American Civilization.* Only upper-division students could understand the Spanish subtitles. (Woods)

Suggested Readings: Adams, Richard E. W. *Prehistoric Mesoamerica.*

Carmichael, Elizabeth, and Chloe Sayer. *The Skeleton at the Feast: The Day of the Dead in Mexico;* contains a good bibliography.

Zazueta, Jesús Angel Ochoa. "El día 2 de Noviembre"

Morley, Sylvanus Griswold, and George W. Brainerd. *The Ancient Maya.*

Complementary Films/Videos: *La ofrenda (The Day of the Dead)* (Mexico).

Level: University

LA TERCERA RAIZ

Documentary.   Without Subtitles.   27 min.   1992
Directed by: Rafael Rebollar
Produced by: Consejo Nacional para Artes (San Francisco 1514, Col. Valle, CP 03100, México D.F.; tel: [525] 575-0677; fax: [525] 575-4335)
Distributed by: IMRE Archive (available for viewing only)
Evaluators: Elba Birmingham-Pokorny, José-Manuel Navarro, Robert Williamson
Description: Part of a series entitled *Los caminos de lo sagrado* (Paths of the Sacred), this film explores a rarely mentioned aspect of Mexico's culture and history: the nation's African cultural roots. It presents the dances, beliefs, folklore, and dramatizations enacted by members of the Costa Chica community in the Pacific Coast states of Oaxaca and Guerrero. The tape demonstrates that African-based folk dances are still performed by descendants of African slaves. It also includes a reconstruction of the conquest of Mexico as seen from the perspective of the conquered.

Strengths and Weaknesses: The video makes an engaging, effective presentation of the dances, including some explanation. It is an excellent example of the mutual exchange between the indigenous and African cultures.

Introducing the Tape: A quick, historical presentation of the role of Africans in the history of Oaxaca and Guerrero is definitely needed. More interpretation of the dances and honorific titles used in the dialogue would enhance viewing.

How to Use: I would use this film to introduce students to the richness of the African presence in Latin America. (Birmingham-Pokorny)

The tape could be useful in teaching the meaning of aesthetics in preliterate societies. (Williamson)

Suggested Readings: Adams, Richard E. W. *Prehistoric Mesoamerica.*

Chang-Rodríguez, Eugenio. *Latinoamérica, su civilización y su cultura.*

Morley, S. et al. *The Ancient Maya.*

Complementary Films/Videos: *Teotihuacán, Monte Albán* (distributed by IMRE).

Level: University

TLC: DETRAS DE LA MENTIRA

Documentary. Without Subtitles. 50 min. 1993
Directed by: Carlos Mendoza and Norma Madrid
Produced by: Canal 6 de Julio (Medellín 33, 3er Piso, Roma, CP 06700, México D.F.; tel: [525] 511-2349; fax: [525] 208-2062)
Distributed by: IMRE Archive (available for viewing only)
Evaluators: Carlos R. Delgado, Richard Stahler-Sholk
Description: This critical documentary on NAFTA from a Mexican perspective presents an interesting combination of satire and serious academic discussion. Its purpose is to review the major arguments against the treaty. Political figures of opposition parties (Partido Acción Nacional, Partido de la Revolución Mexicana), economists, and members of the academic community (including José Luis Calva) are interviewed. Their positions are contrasted in a negative and deriding but humorous way with the empty rhetoric of official advertisements. The video makes use of mock television news, game shows, and cartoons. This is where rational discourse meets caricature and comic strips. It attempts to relate anti-NAFTA sentiment with the general civil unrest due to electoral fraud and government repression. A subtheme is the deception in the government's use of mass media to shape popular perceptions of political issues favorable to those in power.
Strengths and Weaknesses: This critique, covering a wide range of themes and distinct Mexican perspectives on NAFTA, will be novel for many U.S. audiences. The film is skillfully organized, and those interviewed are well informed and articulate. Economic data is presented clearly and concisely, and the use of satire is sophisticated and well placed. In general, the images support the arguments.

Some of the materials used are more effective than others. One evaluator found the cartoons silly and one interviewee's technical language inaccessible for most audiences. Another evaluator mentioned that sections dealing with the broader issues of civil unrest were confusing.
Introducing the Tape: Instructors should discuss the relationship between anti-NAFTA sentiment and the broader problem of antigovernment feeling due to electoral fraud and general official repression. Also, the Mexican political figures depicted in the film should be identified. It would

be useful to give a brief review and update on recent highlights of Mexican politics, including the ratification of NAFTA, the Chiapas rebellion, the assassination of Partido Revolucionario Institucional (PRI) presidential candidate Colosio, and the subsequent election of PRI candidate Zedillo.
How to Use: I would use this film in any course related to *U.S.-Mexico Relations.* Clear policy issues are discussed, as well as the decision-making process in Mexico. The film gives students unofficial Mexican perspectives on current issues. (Delgado)
Suggested Readings: Cavanagh, John, et al. *Trading Freedom: How Free Trade Affects Our Lives, Work and Environment.*

Grinspun, Ricardo, and Maxwell A. Cameron, eds. *The Political Economy of North American Free Trade.*
Level: University

13 JUEGOS EL FUEGO (13 Games of Fire)

Documentary. No Dialogue. 28 min. 1991
Directed by: José Manuel Pintado
Produced by: Copal (Manzanillo No. lll Esq. Tepic, Col. Roma CP 06760, México D.F.; tel: [525] 574-6864; fax: [525] 264-6651)
Distributed by: IMRE Archive (available for viewing only)
Evaluators: William O. Autry, Donald W. Davey
Description: This video, without narration or dialogue, presents thirteen rubber-ball games, played in various areas of Mexico, that reveal continuity with pre-Hispanic ball games. The games are interspersed with drawings and statues from ancient times, contrasting past and present. There are glimpses of Teotihuacán and the ball field at Chichén Itzá. The players are modern-day Indians and other Mexicans. The balls are various sizes and are propelled by the hand, elbow, hips, and a hammerlike device. One game is played by women who propel a ring forward with a stick. Oaxaca, Michoacán, and Yucatán are three areas represented in the tape.
Strengths and Weaknesses: The various forms of the rubber-ball games are visually well represented. The tape would be of interest to sports fans or civilization teachers/students.

The tape lacks narration, so, without an introduction, viewers have no idea what they are watching and only the vaguest idea what culture or area is being represented. There is no discussion of pre-Hispanic ball games, so there can be no idea how much divergence or similarity is represented in the present-day games. Often the objectives and rules of the games are unclear.
Introducing the Tape: This tape needs an introduction providing a discussion of pre-Hispanic ball games and an overall geographic focus, as well as background for the thirteen presentations and their relation from past to present. A map showing which cultures are being illustrated would also be useful.
Suggested Readings: Scarborough, Vernon L., and David R. Wilcox, eds. *The Mesoamerican Ballgame.*

Stern, Theodore. *The Rubber-Ball Games of the Americas.*
Sweezey, William R. "La Pelota Mixteca."
Level: High School—University

TROTACALLES

Feature. Without Subtitles. 101 min. 1951
Directed by: Matilde Landeta
Distributed by: IMRE, Latina
Evaluators: Sandra M. Boschetto-Sandoval
Description: This black-and-white film dating from the early 1950s by director Matilde S. Landeta (Mexico's only woman film director of the time) recounts the story of two sisters: one a good but naive prostitute, the other a "bad," high-society dame who marries an older man for financial security after her sister's boyfriend jilts her. The film portrays *machista* society's denigration of women and the underworld life of prostitution in a somewhat melodramatic but scathingly feminist manner. Presented side by side, the romantic prostitute and the unscrupulous married woman evoke not merely the unchanging dichotomized stereotypes of the Latin eternal feminine but also the tragic and limiting roles allowed to women who permit themselves the luxury of romantic illusion and male dependency for self-fulfillment. The film ultimately suggests that women in love with men are condemned to suffer both spiritual and physical prostitution. Important lessons are learned and harbored in the sisterhood of women, yet ultimately the film offers no formal resolution, only a tragic melodramatic ending. The female characters are definitely more complex than the male characters, who are portrayed primarily as a pimp, a Don Juan, and a condemning father/husband.
Strengths and Weaknesses: The film includes strong women character portrayals. The black-and-white imaging adds significance to its almost allegorical portrayals of good and evil. The lighting is also effective.

The film's weaknesses are its unambiguous development and climax, poor sound quality, and choppy structure.
How to Use: I would use the film as an adjunct to a course on *Women in Latin American Literature* to portray in visual form how imaging of women by authors and directors exploits the treatment of women in Latin society. (Boschetto-Sandoval)

In *Cinema Studies* classes the film can be used as an example of early Mexican cinema, focusing particularly on the fact that it was made by a woman director treating a feminist theme.
Suggested Readings: Miller, Beth Kurti, ed. *Women in Hispanic Literature: Icons and Fallen Idols.*

Virgillo, Carmelo, and Naomi Lindstrom, eds. *Women as Myth and Metaphor in Latin American Literature.*
Level: University

TROUBLED HARVEST

Documentary. With Subtitles. 30 min. 1990
Directed by: Sharon Genasci and Dorothy Valesco

Distributed by: Women Make Movies
Evaluators: Anna R. Adams, Lester D. Langley, Elinor Melville, Cliff Welch
Description: This is an analysis of Mexican migrant farmworkers' main concerns in California and Oregon at the end of the 1980s. The tape discusses how the workers' health is affected by poisonous pesticides and how immigration laws break up their families. While clearly supportive of better conditions for farmworkers, the program tries to be balanced. It includes interviews with farmworkers, Delores Huerta (vice president of the United Farm Workers), a farm labor representative, and various experts and officials.
Strengths and Weaknesses: This well-produced, succinct film covers many issues, including immigration, pesticides, child care, and unionization. It emphasizes the case of workers in Oregon, rather than California. The interviews with farmworkers and organizers are interesting, and the tape provides extensive background. The sections on immigration and pesticides are the best developed, and there is a concise assessment of fundamental health issues associated with Southwest agribusiness.

A couple of evaluators commented that the tape was not of the highest quality. Another mentioned that it failed to offer any solutions and that some aspects are a bit outdated.
Introducing the Tape: It would be useful to update viewers on recent developments in farm labor and immigration issues.
How to Use: I would use this in a course on *Latinos in the United States* accompanied with readings on border issues, perhaps with the video *The Wrath of Grapes,* which also illustrates the disregard for Mexican workers' lives and the efforts of the United Farm Workers to organize against this poisoning. (Adams)

I could use this tape in both *U.S. Labor History* and *Environmental Studies* at both undergraduate and graduate levels. (Melville)

In my class we talk a lot about farmworkers and their organizations. I might not use this, since neither unions nor collective action is emphasized as a possible means of resolving the workers' problems. On the other hand, for the uninitiated (as many students are), it exposes the hazards farmworkers face each day. (Welch)
Complementary Films/Videos: *The Wrath of Grapes* (distributed by the United Farm Workers, P.O. Box 62, La Paz, Keene, CA 93531, [805] 822-5571.)
Level: High School—University

UXMAL (Uxmal)

Documentary. With Subtitles. 33 min. 1992
Directed by: Gonzalo Infante
Produced by: OMAC Video (Miguel De Quevedo 296, Coyoacán CP 04000, México D.F.; tel: [525] 554-0883; fax: [525] 659-6942)
Distributed by: IMRE
Evaluators: Gary S. Elbow, David J. Robinson

Description: This dramatization recounts Frederick Catherwood's experiences with John Lloyd Stephens in the 1840s, exploring and etching the Mayan ruins and paintings of northern Yucatán. The tape features Uxmal, Labna, and other Puuc-style sites.

Strengths and Weaknesses: This is an interesting attempt to recreate one of the seminal investigations of early Mayan archaeology. Catherwood's etchings are still valuable for their recording of many now eroded or destroyed building façades and stelae. This film recounts Catherwood's experiences in his own words (translated into Spanish).

The film has some serious anachronisms. For example, in 1840, Catherwood listens to opera recordings on a gramophone that couldn't have been invented for another forty years, and the filming takes place in restored ruins (Catherwood and Stephens had to hire Indians to clear brush and forest from the ruins to record the details of architecture and art). One evaluator felt the first segment detracted from the overall piece and commented that the film was dull at times.

Introducing the Tape: Ideally, students would read all or part of Stephens's *Travels in Yucatan.*

How to Use: I would have students read parts of *Travels in Yucatan* before showing the film. Discussion would center on the value of the work of these men for Mayan archaeology and history. There are some interesting anecdotes that might accompany the discussion, such as when Stephens bought the Mayan site of Copán in Honduras for a few dollars. The story of how the archaeologists did a great deal of inadvertent damage to sites by burning off the brush that covered them serves as a good example of how well-intentioned people can damage the sites they are hoping to preserve. (Elbow)

I would use the tape to demonstrate how the "others" in Mexico were represented by these archaeological travelers/reporters/explorers in the mid-nineteenth century. (Robinson)

Suggested Readings: Coe, Michael. *Breaking the Maya Code.*

Stephens, John Lloyd. *Incidents of Travel in Yucatan.*

Wauchope, Robert. *They Found the Buried Cities.*

Level: University

VIDEO EN TRANSFERENCIA

Documentary. Without Subtitles. 16 min. 1993

Directed by: Guillermo Monteforte, Daniela Cremoux, Javier Samano

Produced by: Centro Nacional de Video Indigenista (Circuito La Cascada, Fraccionamiento La Cascada, Oaxaca, 68040; tel./fax.: [529] 515-3715)

Distributed by: IMRE Archive (available for viewing only)

Evaluators: Brian Goldfarb

Description: This tape documents a number of media training programs that have been instituted in indigenous communities throughout Mexico. It discusses examples of distinct uses of video being implemented by rural indigenous communities, among them educational video, video for political organizing, and video for broadcast (to counter the tendency to underrepresent or misrepresent rural life within mainstream Mexican television).

Strengths and Weaknesses: This is a fairly conventional documentation of a topic that is unfamiliar to most Western audiences. It is an effective length for classroom screening and discussion.

Introducing the Tape: Viewers should be told that this is not a completed program, but rather a sample tape demonstrating the video training programs that are being organized. The program was produced for internal use within Instituto Nacional Indigena as documentation of a proposal to continue work on the indigenous project.

How to Use: In *Communications* courses this could be used to discuss the relationship between community video production and strategies of broadcast and narrowcast. (Goldfarb)

Suggested Readings: Ambrosi, Alain, and Nancy Thede, eds. *Video the Changing World.*

Burton, Julianne. *Cinema and Social Change in Latin America: Conversations with Filmmakers.*

Downing, John D. H., ed. *Film and Politics in the Third World.*

Fusco, Coco. "Ethnicity, Politics and Poetics: Latinos and Media Art." In *Illuminating Video: An Essential Guide to Video Art,* eds. Doug Hall and Sally Jo Fifer, pp. 304–16.

Mattelart, Armand. *Multinational Corporations and the Control of Culture: The Ideological Apparatuses of Imperialism.*

Michaels, Eric. *Bad Aboriginal Art: Tradition, Media, and Technological Horizons.*

Minh-Ha, Trinh T. *Woman, Native, Other.*

Roncagliolo, Rafael. "The Growth of the Audiovisual Imagescape." *Video the Changing World,* eds. Alain Ambrosi and Nancy Thede.

Complementary Films/Videos: *O espiritu da TV (The Spirit of TV)* (Brazil); *Vídeo nas aldeais (Video in the Villages)* (Brazil); *Making Waves,* popular video in Bolivia (distributed by IMRE).

Level: University

NETHERLANDS ANTILLES

KANTIK'I MAISHI: SONGS OF SORGHUM

Documentary. With Subtitles. 58 min. 1992

Directed by: Joan Kaufman

Produced by: Newton Television Foundation (21 Van Wart Path, Newton, MA 02159; tel: [617] 527-1974; fax: [617] 527-3081)

Distributed by: University of California—Berkeley

Evaluators: Friederike Baumann, Elizabeth Mahan

Description: This is a beautiful exploration of sorghum harvest festivals in Bonaire and Curaçao, depicting the interweaving and transformation of African and European cultural practices. The film explores the impact of modernization in the form of oil and tourist industries on these local traditions. The celebrations derive their meaning from the collective harvest of sorghum, once the main staple of the islands, and are expressed in songs and dances that have their roots in the African homelands of their slave ancestors. In Bonaire, the migration of the young generation to service jobs in the cities is eroding rural life; only the few who remain can keep the culture alive with families and friends, while individual folk artists attempt to preserve the knowledge of the past. In urban Curaçao, the government has become the promoter of the culture of the festival. Dissociated from its original meaning, it is celebrated by folkloristic groups who are trained in government-sponsored workshops. This exposes the fundamental dilemma: local culture, kept alive because it is a valuable commodity in the international tourist trade, turns into a spectacle largely devoid of meaning. At the same time, the tradition is continued only because workshops provide a medium in which teachers pass on practices to a new generation and infuse tradition with new meaning.

Strengths and Weaknesses: Well-crafted and multilayered, the film presents complex themes, such as the cost of modernization, cultural transformation, etc., in an easily accessible manner. It contains interviews with a wonderfully diverse cast of characters, such as peasant farmers, folksingers, academics, and male and female officials. The film demonstrates sorghum's significance to the traditional peasant economy of Bonaire, shows how the harvest festivals link African and European practices, and portrays how the more "modern" Curaçao lost its version of the festival and replaced it with the workshop "reconstruction." The music is wonderful, and students with some familiarity with Spanish will have the thrill of being able to decipher some of the Papiamento language.

Introducing the Tape: The narration provides an adequate introduction to Dutch colonialism.

How to Use: I would use this tape in my introductory course on *Latin America* to illustrate the formation and transformation of Afro-Latin cultures. (Mahan)

Level: High School—University

NICARAGUA

ALSINO Y EL CONDOR (Alsino and the Condor)
Feature.   With Subtitles.   89 min.   1983
Directed by: Miguel Littín
Distributed by: Facets, IMRE
Evaluators: Patricia Aufderheide (excerpted from *Cross Cultural Film Guide*), John Higgins, Daniel P. Hunt
Description: This film rewrites the Nicaraguan folktale of the boy who wanted to fly as the story of a boy living through the brutality of Somoza's war on the Nicaraguan people and

the corresponding rise of the Sandinistas. Alsino takes a ride in a helicopter belonging to a U.S. military adviser and then decides that he would rather fly under his own power. When he jumps from a tree and tries to fly, he cripples himself, then goes off to join the Sandinista resistance. Alsino's wounded body and his desire to fly are powerful metaphors in the film's anti-interventionist message. When the U.S. adviser oversteps his authority to avenge the death of a mercenary friend, he underestimates the skill and organization of his adversary and is killed in a battle with the Sandinistas. (Aufderheide)

Strengths and Weaknesses: This allegorical film is a landmark in adversarial cinema. Alsino, symbolizing the people, wants freedom, not the foreign substitute (helicopter). His own efforts (individualistic solutions) fail, but when he joins the struggle, his dreams come true. The film addresses the role played by U.S. military advisers abroad, particularly in Central America. With excellent acting and camera work, it overwhelms viewers with a sense of a child's awe of the world. Action sequences are handled well, as are the personal interactions, with a successful portrayal of conflicting personal loyalties. *Alsino* was well received throughout Latin America and was an Academy Award nominee for Best Foreign Language Film of 1982. Since the film is in both English and Spanish, many scenes allow for language lessons.

The film can seem a bit slow-paced for U.S. audiences.

Introducing the Tape: Viewers should have some historical background on the Sandinista revolution and the Contra war as well as some familiarity with magical realism.

Background on Latin American *Nuevo Cine* could include the following introductory comments. "Diverse in style, form, subject matter, and responding to the particular social and political realities of each country, the *Nuevo Cine* productions shared some commonalities. They were typically authorial works, produced outside commercial cinema; they were marked by a strong passion to probe social reality and reveal popular culture; they were often oppositional to regimes that, in this period, were often military or military-controlled. Producing works that were internationally heralded, while often bitterly contested and even censored at home, this movement became one of the hallmarks of the vibrancy of modern Latin American culture. . . . *Alsino* was made as a coproduction between Cuba, Mexico, and Costa Rica, and was widely seen as a filmic expression of Third World solidarity." (Aufderheide)

One evaluator commented that the confusion encountered in screenings of this film with U.S. students had more to do with the audiences than the film itself, explaining that most U.S. students have been so thoroughly exposed to U.S. anti-Sandinista propaganda, and are so unfamiliar with the events, that they mix up the Sandinista communists with the Contra rebels. Even after an introduction and reminders, many students continue to read the Somozistas as communists.

How to Use: I would show this film to U.S. students to help them to see people in the Third World as humans, rather than objects of study. The film complements articles read in class about conflicts, lifestyles in the developing world, and U.S. influence. (Higgins)

In *Language* courses I stop the film at certain points to discuss elements of language use. For example, we stop where the bird man dislocates the bird's wing to examine the way he tells Alsino about it. Many students also enjoy the film's lessons in swearing, since exchanges between Spanish speakers and English speakers occur in a couple of key scenes. The U.S. adviser's Spanish is good for language study, as he speaks slowly with a gringo accent and makes some typical errors with the language that students can pick out. In *Culture* courses I simply show the film, and we discuss its historical implications. (Hunt)

Students could be introduced to the *Nuevo Cine* that was produced from the late 1950s through the 1970s.

Suggested Readings: Armes, Roy. *Third World Film Making and the West.*

Asturias, Miguel Angel. *Viento fuerte.*

Aufderheide, Patricia. *Cross Cultural Film Guide.*

Aufderheide, Patricia. "Latin American Cinema and the Rhetoric of Cultural Nationalism: Controversies at Havana in 1987 and 1989," *Quarterly Film Review* 12 (1991): 64-78.

Chanan, Michael. *Twenty Five Years of New Latin American Cinema.*

García Márquez, Gabriel, "Alsino & the Condor." In *Cultures in Contention,* eds. Douglas Kahn and Diane Neumaier.

García Márquez, Gabriel. *La aventura de Miguel Littín clandestino en Chile.*

King, John. *Magical Reels: A History of Cinemas in Latin America.*

Ramírez, Sergio. *To Bury Our Fathers: A Novel of Nicaragua.*

Rushdie, Salmon. *The Jaguar Smile: A Nicaraguan Journey.*

Schnitman, Jorge A. *Film Industries in Latin America: Dependency and Development.*

Skidmore, Thomas E., and Peter H. Smith, *Modern Latin America.*

Level: Junior High School—University

AQUI EN ESTE ESQUINA (Here on This Corner)
Television Program.   With Subtitles.   5 min.   1985
Produced by: SSTV
Distributed by: IMRE
Evaluators: Robin Andersen, Oscar Flores, Robert Huesca.
Description: This is a segment of an alternative/popular television game show made by Sandinista TV. Each week, the filmmakers took TV cameras to different neighborhoods where local residents participated in a variety of competitions and displays of talent. This tape sampler consists of three segments. The first and most compelling piece is a children's dance contest. The overwhelming applause suggests there is no dispute about the winner. The second segment

presents two men singing a Mexican *corrida*-style folk song about Sandino. The third is an arm-wrestling bout between two women. The winner of two out of three matches receives two thousand cordobas. The host is a real showman.

Strengths and Weaknesses: This is a wonderful example of the game show format done spontaneously and at minimal cost. It contrasts with the gaudy and commercialized production of U.S. game shows. Also, the participants are unmistakably "real people," unlike the doctored versions of U.S. commercial television's "scripted authenticity." No attempt is made to mask the political nature of the show. This is excellent entertainment, especially the music, and the added voice-over introduction in English is useful.

This is only a fragment of the program, though enough to give the audience a sense of the show. A full version of the program is also available.

Introducing the Tape: Viewers should be familiar with the "populist" Sandinista government and understand that this show is a reflection of populist television.

How to Use: In *Cross-Cultural Studies* and *Communications* classes the contrast to U.S. game shows could be studied.

In *Political Science* and *Sociology* courses the phenomenon of popular television during the Sandinista administration could be seen as a reflection of its populist/revolutionary platform.

Level: Elementary School—University

BANANERAS (The Banana Company)
Documentary.   With Subtitles.   15 min.   1982
Directed by: Ramiro Lacayo
Produced by: Instituto Nicaraguense de Cine
Distributed by: First Run/Icarus Films
Evaluators: Charles Bergquist, Jorge Marcone, Joan A. McGinnis
Description: This tape provides a look at a foreign-owned banana company in Nicaragua, emphasizing worker exploitation. Interspersed with newsreel footage detailing the modernization in banana harvesting are interviews with the impoverished laborers, talking about their living and working conditions. The irony is graphic, with images of the company owners living well in other countries, juxtaposed with barefoot workers pulling banana-filled sledges.

Strengths and Weaknesses: This is an impressive depiction of the working conditions on banana plantations. There are powerful contemporary images of primitive working conditions juxtaposed with the footage of Somoza's bourgeois lifestyle. The picture of exploitation and waste is strong, with images of bananas being thrown into the sea to keep the price inflated.

One evaluator felt the tape failed to convey the structural context of the banana industry. For example, to what extent did the industry evolve from direct foreign ownership to subcontracting with Nicaraguan capitalists?

Introducing the Tape: Viewers need some background on the history and economic structure of the banana industry. They should be alerted to the relatively small scale of Nicaragua's banana industry as compared to the industries in Honduras and Costa Rica.

How to Use: I would use this film in conjunction with a study of literature (mentioned below) providing a previewing questionnaire about *Bananeras,* the role of the "banana republics" in U.S. economic development. After viewing, they would write a composition from the point of view of a banana company owner or one of the workers. (McGinnis)

Suggested Readings: Galeano, Eduardo. *Open Veins of Latin America: Five Centuries of the Pillage of a Continent.*

García Márquez, Gabriel. *No One Writes to the Colonel and Other Stories.*

García Márquez, Gabriel. *One Hundred Years of Solitude.*

Schlesinger, Stephen C. *Bitter Fruit: The Untold Story of the American Coup in Guatemala.*

Pablo Neruda's poem on the United Fruit Company (see bibliography for selection of his works).

Level: High School—University

EL HOMBRE DE UNA SOLA NOTA (The Man of a Single Note)

Fiction.   No Dialogue.   14 min.   1988
Directed by: Frank Piñeda
Produced by: Incine/Camila Films (Apdo. Postal P 193, Managua; tel: [505] 222-5517; fax: [505] 222-4606)
Distributed by: IMRE Archive (available for viewing only)
Evaluators: Susan Ryan
Description: A man leaves his apartment to go to work, a job that consists of playing a single note on his clarinet in a symphonic composition with an orchestra. To reach the concert, he must pass through streets filled with soldiers searching citizens, burning and demolished buildings, and other scenes implying civil strife. After work, the man returns home and goes to bed.

Although never explicitly stated, the references in the film are to Nicaragua before the revolution. The experimental narrative uses no dialogue or voice-over and can be interpreted in several ways, among them: that some sectors of society are oblivious to what happens around them and continue their lives, or that art (music) will continue despite political turmoil.

Strengths and Weaknesses: The tape is technically proficient, with good cinematography and use of sound. However, the theme is a bit obvious and simplistic, given the complexity of the situation in Nicaragua.

Introducing the Tape: The film is meant to be open ended, to allow audiences to draw their own conclusions. It seems the filmmaker wanted to refer not only to Nicaragua, but to other repressive political situations in Latin America; thus it might not be appropriate to have a prologue that refers too specifically to Nicaragua.

How to Use: I would use the film as an example of short nar-

rative filmmaking (as opposed to documentary or newsreel) in a relatively new film industry. It could also be shown as another way of creating a political cinema through images as opposed to more direct documentary practices. (Ryan)
Suggested Readings: "From Revolution to INCIME." In Julianne Burton's *Cinema and Social Change in Latin America: Conversations with Filmmakers.*
Level: University

PANAMA

ALGO DE TI (Something of You)

Music Video.   No Dialogue.   5 min.   1985
Directed by: Luis Franco
Produced by: Boa Productions (Apdo 87–1528, Panamá 7, Panamá; fax: [607] 25-420)
Distributed by: IMRE
Evaluators: Robin Andersen, Marcia Dean, Enrique R. Rodríguez
Description: This is a surreal, evocative music video that implies that all members of society are complicit through their silence in the violence perpetrated by military dictatorships. The video opens as soldiers break in on a couple who are enjoying an intimate evening at home. The man is dragged away to an island inhabited by various characters: a prostitute, nun, lawyer, journalist, undertaker, etc. He is kept in a cell, and the dreamlike structure of the video then overwhelms the narrative. Edited fragments of different scenes are repeated in an accelerating sequence. Presented in a playful, music-video style, the action suggests obscurely that anyone can become the victim in this situation. As the various characters rise out of a coffin (presumably the prisoner's), they dance, enjoying the benefits of society, almost celebrating the prisoner's death. Flashes of a young boy watching cautiously from behind the scenes appear throughout. The eeriness of this silent observer is a reminder of the silent conscience of society. At one point, the prisoner's *compañera* (companion) appears and manages to slip him a letter. As he reads it in his cell, her spirit dances caressingly around him. Suddenly the scene is transposed, everyone else is in the cell, while the prisoner and his *compañera* dance freely outside (they are the ones free at heart, while the others are really the prisoners). When the camera pulls back, the cell opens and all are set free. An outline of a military figure appears over the scene, slamming a cell door on the brief moment of freedom. The elusive figure of the young boy pops up and the frame freezes, holding the haunting expression of his face, one that demands an explanation.
Strengths and Weaknesses: This is an interesting experimental video that evokes feelings of the surreal nature of human repression, violence, and individual responses.

While creative and artfully presented, the tape fails to narrate in any coherent way. The symbolism is vague, and without an introduction, it is unclear what is going on. The title song, "Algo de ti," while wonderful music in and of itself, bears little relation to the visual narrative.

Introducing the Tape: Viewers would need an understanding of the state of political affairs in Panama, particularly relating to the rule of Manuel Noriega. The video is a reminder that military dictatorships will endure as long as they are not beaten back by popular protest. The scene near the end in which everyone is freed symbolizes the "democratic" period that existed after Noriega, the former military strongman, used his might to be "elected" president. This democratic "freedom" is a façade that is always watched over by the military "big brother." Repression will continue as long as people remain silent. North American viewers should also be introduced to magical realism.

How to Use: This is interesting video for its evocative imagery and editing style. It could be used in a *Production* course as an example of well-made music video with a message. (Andersen)

Because of its short length, the tape could be shown in its entirety to students without an introduction. Using their impressions as the basis for the discussion, as well as the political and historic context in which the tape was made (i.e., the end of the Noriega regime), the tape could be played again, this time stopping to point out the possible meanings of the symbols used.

Suggested Readings: Literature on magical realism.

Complementary Films/Videos: *Que bom te ver viva (How Nice to See You Alive)* (Brazil); *Chile: sueños prohibidos (Chile's Forbidden Dreams)* (Chile).

Level: University

CARRUSEL (Carousel)

Music Video. No Dialogue. 6 min. 1989
Directed by: Eduardo Harker
Produced by: Ex-Productions (Calle 61 Oeste, Royal Plaza Bld, Apt. 3B, Panamá; tel: [507] 267-222; fax: [507] 267-039)
Distributed by: IMRE
Evaluators: Elba D. Birmingham-Pokorny, Marcia Dean, Jorge Porras
Description: This music video examines conformity. All people in the film wear large red noses. When the hero's nose falls off accidentally, people respond to him with horror. The tape follows the hero's progressive awakening to his situation; at first he hides, but then he comes to terms with his liberation from all forms of social entrapment. The tape presents the carousel as a metaphor for life.
Strengths and Weaknesses: Technically well-produced with excellent use of music, colors, and pacing to convey its message, the tape would easily stimulate discussions on conformity.
How to Use: The tape would be effective for introducing students to the artistic value of myths and symbols. (Birmingham-Pokorny)

The tape could be used with students in a *Spanish* class to motivate them to talk about conformity, peer pressure, and personal reactions. (Dean)

In a *Video Production* course the tape can be used as an example of an effective use of the music video genre to convey social messages.
Level: Junior High School—University

THE PANAMA DECEPTION

Documentary. With Subtitles. 91 min. 1992
Directed by: Barbara Trent
Produced by: Empowerment Project (3403 Highway 54 West, Chapel Hill, NC; tel: [919] 967-1963; fax: [919] 967-1863; e-mail: project@nando.net)
Distributed by: Empowerment Project, IMRE, Jane Balfour
Evaluators: Ana Caroline Castillo-Crimm, Joséph A. Gagliano, Robert Haskett, Luis Martínez-Fernández
Description: This powerful documentary, narrated by Elizabeth Montgomery, exposes the underside of the U.S. invasion of Panama in 1989. The film offers a scathing critique of U.S. actions before, during, and after the invasion, presenting the perspectives of Panamanian people, opinions of former U.S. political and military policymakers, and a critical examination of diverse U.S. mass-media coverage. The documentary calls into question the stated objectives of the invasion to arrest Manuel Noriega for drug trafficking, to protect American lives, and to restore democracy to Panama. Instead, it claims that the invasion's aim was to prevent Noriega from enforcing the Panama Canal Treaty, which would return control of the canal and the Canal Zone to Panama in the year 2000. The film asserts that by undermining the effectiveness of the Panama Defense Force to provide security for the canal, the United States attempted to maintain a substantial military presence beyond 1999. It argues that the United States was determined to retain its bases in Panama to have a proximate site for staging operations against anticipated conflicts in the Andean region in the twenty-first century. The film discusses how U.S. propaganda distorted objectives, the number of civilian casualties, and the extent of damage during the conflict and the lack of American aid in assisting Panamanian reconstruction. Charges are also made that the United States used the invasion to test new weapons, many of them far in excess of the amount of force needed for the operation. Finally, the film offers a running critique of the ethnocentric reporting of the mainstream U.S. media, as well as the obstacles to publicizing the truth that were created by the U.S. military and government.
Strengths and Weaknesses: This Oscar-winning work is a well-paced, forthright, and well-documented critique of the events in Panama and the United States before, during, and after the attack. It builds on historical facts to make a solid analysis and a clear and cogent argument. The film presents an alternate vision of the invasion, giving important voice to the victims and refugees. Skillfully shot and edited, it is visually compelling, sometimes disturbing or even horrifying. Graphic evidence demonstrates the extent of the casualties

and damage in Panama. The interviews with experts from Panama and the United States are excellent, and there is good treatment of Panama's domestic politics since 1989. The film presents an evenhanded view by including answers offered by the U.S. government and commentary from the newly installed Panamanian government. The musical accompaniment is also well done.

Some critics might find the film one-sided or propagandistic. This is true to the extent that it is consciously offering a counterpoint to the official story and makes no pretense at being objective. One evaluator felt that the central thesis is supported more with speculation than hard evidence. Others found that the polemical tone hampers a balanced analysis.

Introducing the Tape: A review of U.S. involvement in Latin America in general, and Panama in particular, during the nineteenth and early twentieth centuries would make the film easier to understand. For the sake of balance, some more information should be made available to the audience about the actions that made Noriega so odious to many of his compatriots. An understanding of the geographical importance of Panama and the canal to the U.S. government and economy is also important.

How to Use: The film is an example of the U.S. view that it needs to retain a presence in Central America to stop the drug flow from Colombia, Bolivia, and Peru. I would use it to show the thinking of U.S. military and political leaders in developing plans on how to deal with Latin American countries. (Castillo-Crimm)

I intend to use this tape in my *United States-Latin America Relations* undergraduate course. Because of its length, it will be shown in two segments when the course considers U.S.-Latin American relations during the 1980s and 1990s. The film will be used to demonstrate varying perspectives on recent U.S. policy in Latin America. It will also serve as the basis for discussion of recent U.S. policy and its effects. The film may also be used for the same purposes in my course on *Central America and the Caribbean Island Nations.* (Gagliano)

I would screen this film for two reasons: to provide an alternate reading of the invasion of Panama, and to stimulate debate about the U.S. role in Latin America, its assumptions, and its consequences. Of the courses I currently teach, it would work best in the twentieth-century term of the *Latin American Survey* or in the *History of Central America,* in which I already include the issue of the canal, Noriega, and the U.S. invasion. (Haskett)

A way to set up the discussion of this good film would be to ask the students to read examples from several media of the coverage of the December 1989 events. Clippings from *Time,* the *New York Times,* etc., could be placed on reserve for this purpose. Another possible angle for discussion could be to ask the students to compare the justifications for operation "Just Cause" with those used by Spanish conquerors in their "Just War" five centuries earlier. (Martínez-Fernández)

Suggested Readings: Agee, Phillip. *The Truth behind the U.S. Invasion of Panama.*

Buckley, Kevin. *Panama: The Whole Story.*

Cameron, Ian. *The Impossible Dream: The Building of the Panama Canal.*

Crane, Philip M., with an introduction by Ronald Reagan, *Surrender in Panama: The Case against the Treaty.*

Dinges, John. *Our Man in Panama: How General Noriega Used the United States—and Made Millions in Arms and Drugs.*

Greene, Graham. *Getting to Know the General: The Story of an Involvement.*

Independent Commission of Inquiry on the U.S. Invasion of Panama. *The U.S. Invasion of Panama: The Truth behind Operation "Just Cause."*

Kempe, Frederick. *Divorcing the Dictator: America's Bungled Affair with Noriega.*

Koster, R. M., and Guillermo Sánchez. *In the Time of the Tyrants: Panama, 1968–1990.*

LaFeber, Walter. *The Panama Canal: The Crisis in Historical Perspective.*

La Feber, Walter. *Inevitable Revolutions.*

Levine, Isaac Don. *Hands Off the Panama Canal.*

MacDonald, Scott B. *Mountain High, White Avalanche: Cocaine and Power in the Andean States and Panama.*

McCullough, David G. *The Path Between the Seas: The Creation of the Panama Canal.*

Millett, Richard. "Looking Beyond Noriega," pp. 46–63.

Moffett, George D., III. *The Limits of Victory: The Ratification of the Panama Canal Treaties.*

Ropp, Steve C. *Panamanian Politics: From Guarded Nation to National Guard.*

Ryan, Paul B. *The Panama Canal Controversy: U.S. Diplomacy and Defense Interests.*

Level: High School—University

PARAGUAY

LA CLASE DE ORGANO (The Organ Lesson)
Fiction.   No Dialogue.   10 min.   1989
Directed by: Juan Carlos Maneglia
Produced by: Trabajar y Compartir (Meli Rockhold Peña, P.O. Box 945, General Santo 415, Asunción; tel: [595] 23-160-9198; fax: [595] 98-140-2383; e-mail: ccpa@pla.net.py)
Distributed by: IMRE
Evaluators: Gerard Aching, Rick Langhorst, Deborah Pacini Hernández
Description: In this comedy of manners, repressed passions in the proper household spring to life at the touch of an organ. A proper mother escorts a debonair organ teacher into the room where her sultry daughter will be given music lessons. When the overly zealous, prying mother closes the door, fingers begin to play all over the organ. Images of wild love scenes follow while the organ continues to be played. Is

this passion real, or a product of the mother's imagination? Viewers are titillated but not told; the ending is left open to interpretation.

Strengths and Weaknesses: This short, imaginative tape, without dialogue, communicates moods and actions through its creative camera work, acting, and musical soundtrack. The piece highlights the way women are oppressed by social norms. There is humor in the "did they or didn't they?" dilemma.

Evaluators commented that while the tape is entertaining, it may have limited use in the classroom.

Introducing the Tape: Teachers (particularly in high schools) should be alerted that some scenes are sexually graphic, although there is no nudity.

How to Use: The tape could be used to show a Latin American critique of oppressive social norms. (Pacini Hernández)

Although there is no dialogue, the tape's short length and provocative plot make it useful for motivating writing and discussion in *Language and Writing* classes. Students could be asked to interpret the story and compose essays imagining what happened before and what will happen after the tape ends.

In a *Video Production* class the tape could be shown as a good example of a creative fictional piece that communicates without words.

Level: University

PARAGUAY: THE FORGOTTEN DICTATORSHIP
Documentary.   With Subtitles.   27 min.   1988
Directed by: Patricia Boero
Distributed by: The Cinema Guild
Evaluators: Elba D. Birmingham-Pokorny, Ana Caroline Castillo-Crimm, Robert Claxton, Jerry Cooney, Iris Engstrand, Joan A. McGinnis, Kathleen March
Description: This film offers an overview of the political situation in Paraguay in the late 1980s, just before the fall of dictator Stroessner. Interviews with people from various socioeconomic and ideological backgrounds offer a view of what thirty-eight years of Stroessner's regime has meant to the Paraguayan people and society. The film contrasts the comments of Stroessner and his supporters with scenes and interviews with the poor, clerics, and students. It calls attention to the growing sense of disillusionment and discontent expressed by the younger generations, women's groups, and peasants with the repressive policies of Stroessner's regime. The anti-Stroessner view covers the religious and political problems inherent in the system. The film makes a limited attempt to provide an evenhanded view by describing how the wealthy fare under this government and the successes of such projects as the Itaipú Dam. However, it shows that while there is material progress, human rights are regularly violated. The program is particularly useful in projecting the potential future problems with the end of the Stroessner regime.
Strengths and Weaknesses: The tape provides an excellent historical overview of the period, with good cinematography, maps, diverse and organized interviews, and a powerful message by comparisons. It captures the active role played by women's groups, young professionals, and, above all, peasants in the struggle for social and agrarian reforms, the acquisition of political freedom, and the protection of human rights. The tape also includes Paraguayan folk music.

Like many videos on Paraguay, the tape concentrates on Asunción almost to the neglect of the Guaraní-speaking countryside where over 60 percent of Paraguay's population lives. One evaluator felt that it presents a somewhat shallow analysis of why the Stroessner dictatorship was so strong and long-lived. While the tape is good on the opposition to Stroessner, it neglects the great political force in Paraguay, the army. It does not present the tension between the *tradicionalistas* and *militantes* in the Colorado Party.

Introducing the Tape: Any U.S. audience would need an introduction including a brief description of Paraguay as well as the social and political system of that nation prior to and during the Stroessner era. Instructors should discuss how Stroessner could be successful for so long. The role of the army should be explained. Viewers should be updated and told that Stroessner fell from power, and why.

How to Use: I will use this film to illustrate the transition in the early twentieth century of some of the Latin American nations from dictatorship to democracy and from democracy to dictatorship. The best example of the latter can be seen in the cases of Chile, Uruguay, and Paraguay. This film will also be extremely helpful to show the historical role that women, peasants, and students have played in the Latin American society as catalysts of social and political change. I would use this film in a *Contemporary Latin American Fiction* course to illustrate how the Latin American novel reflects some of the most salient political, economic, cultural, and historical events shaping Latin Americans' conceptions of their reality. (Birmingham-Pokorny)

I would definitely use this film in my survey of *Modern Latin America* to point out the ability of a dictator to maintain power for so long and the variety of opinions about Stroessner expressed by Paraguayans. (Castillo-Crimm)

I would provide an introductory discussion of the methods of perpetuating dictatorship. I would discuss my own personal recollections of a visit to Paraguay when Stroessner was still president. After the video, we would have a discussion of content followed by a lecture on Paraguay since the fall of Stroessner. (Claxton)

I would show the film after having presented information on Paraguay or having assigned student research. After showing it, I would promote discussion and analysis of contradictions the film portrays. I would definitely supplement with references to Guaraní. (March)
Suggested Readings: Lewis, Paul H. *Paraguay under Stroessner.*

Wiarda, Howard J. *American Foreign Policy toward Latin America in the 80s and 90s.*
Level: University

PERU

BOCA DEL LOBO (The Lion's Den)
Feature.   With Subtitles.   100 min.   1988
Directed by: Francisco J. Lombardi
Produced by: Inca Films
Distributed by: IMRE
Evaluators: Carmen Chávez, Marvin D'Lugo, Roger P. Davis, Luis Martínez-Fernández, José Pérez
Description: This film graphically depicts how the Peruvian *campesinos* (peasants) are caught between the *Sendero Luminoso* (Shining Path) and the military hierarchy. Based upon actual events from 1980 to 1983, the film seeks to portray the abuses committed by the soldiers against the local population. The story revolves around a Peruvian military unit of a dozen men and an officer who are sent to garrison a small Amerindian community of Chuspi, near Ayacucho, after a raid by the Shining Path. The military reoccupies a government building, restores the national flag, and tries to reestablish the authority and symbols of the national government with the local leaders. Unseen guerrillas undermine these efforts. The building is spray-painted with symbols of the guerrillas and the flag is torn down. Ultimately, there is an armed assault on the barracks while the officer and a squad are out on patrol. Following the death of the original officer, the new lieutenant takes a hard line against the guerrillas and the community. Violent incidents and misunderstandings increase the tension that finally leads to an insanely calculated massacre of dozens of the villagers.
Strengths and Weaknesses: This excellent film paints a moving picture of life in the Indian communities and is a gripping depiction of the corruption and sadism of the Peruvian army. It is also quite graphic in its depiction of the ways in which the Sendero Luminoso ruled the Peruvian countryside. The film makes an informed presentation of the complexity of guerrilla warfare, the cultural distance and tension of urban-rural values, and machismo confronting complex situations where it does not function. The symbolism emphasizes the conflict between icons, the symbols of nationalism and local identities of the Amerindian communities. The program is technically accomplished.

One evaluator felt the film is a heavy-handed criticism of the military and its counterinsurgency methods, with dialogues that are not well developed. Another felt that the plot constructs an ethically ambiguous position for the audience. Viewers find themselves siding with the Sendero against the army. Since the Sendero never appears, and its objective or ideology is not clarified, the uninformed audience is left with a skewed notion of the "good guys" and the "bad guys." In truth, there are no good guys in the film except for the long-suffering indigenous population.
Introducing the Tape: U.S. viewers need to have a historical/political background about the army's fight against the Sendero to understand the significance of the struggle in the film. A brief introduction should include the history of the guerrilla movement in Hispanoamérica; an introduction to the Sendero Luminoso, its goals, methods, and ideology; and the government's struggle to control territory and maintain legitimacy of national authority. Background on life in Peru and elements of terrorism would be helpful.
How to Use: I have used this in a *Latin American Culture* course to show the problems of the military in Peru, specifically the hierarchy that exists, and to expose how the peasants are the ones who suffer because they are caught in the middle. I would ask students to read Hernando de Soto's *The Other Path* to connect economic development to political struggle. (Chávez)

This film would be useful for my *Modern Latin American History* and *Introduction to Latin America* classes, especially to discuss *Revolution in Latin America*. It is good for displaying the themes of Amerindian culture; military/state culture; complexity of nation building; individuals confronting reality in the context of Latin America; and problems in contrast to the United States. (Davis)

I would use this tape as the basis of a discussion on the ways in which dominant Hollywood-style cinema deforms and distorts the representation of cultural conflict in Latin American society. I would ask the class to consider the problematic nature of specific types of representation: (a) the class focus of the tape, (b) the impossible antagonism between army and Sendero as codified by the narrative, (c) the ambiguous ending and its possible decoding by various types of audiences in Latin America and the United States. (D'Lugo)
Suggested Readings: Blanco, Hugo. *Land or Death: The Peasant Struggle in Peru.*

Mariátegui, José Carlos. *Seven Interpretive Essays on Peruvian Reality.*

Palmer, David Scott, ed. *The Shining Path of Peru.*

Reid, Michael. *Peru, Paths to Poverty.*

Soto, Hernando de. *The Other Path: The Invisible Revolution in the Third World.*

Tarazona-Sevillano, Gabriela, and John B. Reuter. *Sendero Luminoso and the Threat of Narcoterrorism.*

Vargas Llosa, Mario. *The Real Life of Alejandro Mayta.*
Level: University

LA CIUDAD Y LOS PERROS (The City and the Dogs)
Feature.   With Subtitles.   135 min.   1985
Directed by: Francisco Lombardi Pery
Distributed by: IMRE
Evaluators: Patricia Aufderheide (excerpted from *Cross Cultural Film Guide*), Eliseo Picó, Lynn M. Shirey, Mitchell L. Whichard
Description: A political allegory based on a Mario Vargas Llosa novel, this film portrays life in a Peruvian military school for boys, where the corruption of the military is learned and practiced. Theft, cheating, and brutality are common. The plot plays out the boys' conflicts. Power and order are in the hands of a clique of older, stronger boys whose

leader is a brutal bully. When one of the cadets is killed, another youth tries to expose the secretive acts of the clique by destroying the bullying leader.

Strengths and Weaknesses: This well-crafted drama evokes the roots of a brutal military culture. Unlike the novel, the film is chronologically straightforward, with an uncomplicated narrative. It has an excellent cast, story, direction, camera work, and editing and was well received by a national and international public. Director Lombardi is the most successful commercial filmmaker in Peru.

One evaluator felt that the film is a bit slow at the beginning but builds to a compelling story. There may be too much brutality in the video for junior high school use.

Introducing the Tape: The film is straightforward and needs no particular introduction to understand its message.

How to Use: This tape is an excellent example of *Latin American or Hispanic Cinema*. Its value to U.S. audiences is that it offers a cultural perspective on Peruvian life alien to North Americans. At the same time, the film's look at life among youth in a military school may strike some chord about areas where our own military cultures overlap. (Whichard)

In *Social Studies* and *Political Science* courses this film could be used to motivate essays on subjects such as militarism, power, machismo, and peer pressure.

Suggested Readings: Aufderheide, Patricia. *Cross Cultural Film Guide*.

King, Johna. *Magical Reels: A History of Cinemas in Latin America*.

Lewis, Marvin A. *From Lima to Leticia: The Peruvian Novels of Mario Vargas Llosa*.

Oviedo, José. *Mario Vargas Llosa: La invención de una realidad*.

Vargas Llosa, Mario. *The Time of the Hero*.

Vargas Llosa,. *La ciudad y los perros*.

Level: University

CON SU ALMA INDIA, PERO

Documentary.   Without Subtitles.   16 min.   1992

Directed by: Rosa Montalvo

Produced by: Video Y Sociedad (Av. Aramburu 904 Surquillo, Lima 34; tel: [5114] 423-019)

Distributed by: IMRE

Evaluators: Grace Leavitt, Naomi Smith

Description: The film is about the festival of the Virgen Carmen in the village of Paucartambo, Peru, which celebrates renewal of life and a settling of old debts. There are scenes of the preparations, processions, and ceremonies, as well as the foods and dances associated with the festival. The film emphasizes the theme that despite the Spanish-forced adoption of outward forms of religion, dance, etc., the basic indigenous spirit remains.

Strengths and Weaknesses: The film contains much music and dance and is most valuable from that perspective. Its narrative is well written; however, some points are repetitive.

Introducing the Tape: U.S. viewers could use an introduc-

tion to the tradition of satire and humor and the use of masks in Peru.

Level: University

DESAPARECIDOS (The Disappeared Ones)

Music Video.   With Subtitles.   17 min.   1985

Produced & Directed by: Rodolfo Pereira

Distributed by: IMRE

Evaluators: Susan Altgelt, Paul J. LaReau, Jorge Marcone, Eliana Moya Raggio, David P. Werlich

Description: This is a powerful, graphic music video documenting the plight of the people of Ayacucho, Peru, caught in the violence between the Peruvian Army and the Shining Path. Actual testimonies from families whose loved ones have disappeared and are presumed murdered are interlaced with the song, "Desaparicidos," by Ruben Blades. The lyrics poetically describe the horrors and helplessness felt by people who have had loved ones disappear. Although the tape is set in Peru, the lyrics could be applicable to any of the Latin American countries that have suffered military dictatorships.

Strengths and Weaknesses: This is a strong, emotional portrayal of people living through hell. There are images of grieving interviewees and actual footage of atrocities committed by the army. It is a moving, sad, and powerful presentation aided by excellent production values. The tape successfully blends music video and documentary genres.

One evaluator felt that while the tape allows the viewers to feel the pain and suffering of the victims of political violence, it is too short to do justice to the topic. It does not contain enough historical background and should be used in conjunction with more informative materials. Although the tape treats the Shining Path's violations of human rights, it is far more critical of the security forces. The tape's end contains graphic images of decaying corpses.

Introducing the Tape: The tape has a clear introduction, but information on the problem of the disappeared and context about the Shining Path would aid in understanding the complexity and difficulty of the tragic human rights abuses in Peru.

How to Use: I would use the tape to begin a discussion of the problems of the "disappeared" and insurrection in Peru. (Higgins)

The tape would provide insights into the life of indigenous people in modern times and could be used in listening comprehension exercises in my *High School Spanish Language* class. (LaReau)

Suggested Readings: Americas Watch. *Peru under Fire: Human Rights since the Return to Democracy*.

Palmer, David Scott, ed. *The Shining Path of Peru*.

Level: High School—University

GREGORIO (Gregorio)

Docudrama.   With Subtitles.   59 min.   1984

Directed by: Alejandro Legaspi and Stefan Kaspar

Produced by: Grupo Chaski (Casablanca, Melecon Grau 929, Chorrillas, Lima 9; tel: [5114] 670-7220; fax: [5114] 300-603)

Distributed by: IMRE, PICS

Evaluators: Patricia Aufderheide (excerpted from *Cross Cultural Film Guide*), Elba D. Birmingham-Pokorny, Carmen Chávez, Susana Conde, Victor Garatea

Description: This tape traces the devastating transformation of a young peasant boy into one of the thousands of children who live on the streets of Lima. The establishing shots situate the viewer in the beautiful landscape of the high Andes. Jacinto (Gergorio's father) is advised by his father not to go to Lima, where his search for a better life will only cause him grief. Jacinto reminds him that, according to the Quechua custom, his younger brother will inherit the family's lands and he will be left with nothing. Jacinto moves his family to the city but soon after loses his new job. The family is forced to live in a squatters' camp two hours from Lima, where Jacinto falls ill and dies. Juana, Gregorio's mother, washes clothes for well-to-do families, and Gregorio shines shoes.

Gradually, Gregorio learns the life of the streets and gets involved in dangerous activities with the other street children. When Juana begins a new relationship, Gregorio stays away from home more and more. Juana futilely and desperately tries to keep track of her son as he becomes more independent. Gregorio joins a gang of petty thieves, and the boys are arrested after a pickpocketing incident. Gregorio manages to escape and offers his mother the money. She refuses, knowing it must have been stolen. Gregorio leaves home and uses the money on a spending spree. Later, the other boys involved in the robbery find him and beat him up. Throughout the film, Gregorio narrates his experiences, revealing sorrow but no particular remorse or conviction that anything could change, leaving viewers with an understanding of his limited options.

Strengths and Weaknesses: The film stars a nonactor whose experiences were similar to Gregorio's, giving it the feel of a documentary. Its use of the real slums, streets, and people of Lima contributes to a strong sense of authenticity. Gregorio's direct-address segments are also particularly effective. The film powerfully calls attention to Peru's social and political problems, as well as to the perennial marginalization of the poor, the Indian, and the homeless in the major metropolitan cities of Latin America. It focuses on the appropriation of idle government land by homeless peasants and poor city dwellers, failed agrarian reforms, and endemic unemployment. The scene changes, from the serenity and beauty of the Andes to the confusion and squalor of the city, are striking.

A few evaluators found the film slow at times.

Introducing the Tape: Viewers should be given some knowledge of the history of the region and awareness of the cultural heritage of the population. The contrast between the Quechua Indian traditions and those of the Spanish population should be studied and discussed. A brief outline of the massive migration of the Peruvian peasants from rural areas to the city, as well as the history of the violent clashes between the peasants occupying idle government land and the Peruvian armed forces, should also be included. Students should be prepared for the use of time in this film, as its pace reflects real life and does not move as quickly as U.S. television or Hollywood films. They also could be told that the film was made by a film collective whose mandate is to raise consciousness and create popular education in and around Lima.

How to Use: Students could discuss the implications of the following facts reported to Patricia Aufderheide: (1) The producers originally wanted the film to end happily, with Gregorio spending his windfall in some socially useful way, perhaps buying something for his family. But the film's main informant, the street child who played Gregorio, said he would never do that. (2) According to members of Grupo Chaski, who often accompanied the film's screening, middle-class audiences often criticize the film for harping on the ugly and depressing sides of national reality, while in the slums, audiences often get engrossed in the main character's problems, with heated discussions afterwards of how he ought have solved them. (Aufderheide)

I would use this tape to illustrate the traumatic moral, economic, social, and psychological impact that life in the city has on the peasants, as well as to help students explore the tremendous economic gap that exists between the upper classes and the poor. This film will also be extremely helpful to the students' understanding of failed social and agrarian reforms in Latin America. (Birmingham-Pokorny)

This film could be used in conjunction with the book *Civilización y barbarie: vida de Juan Facundo Quiroga.* (Chávez).

In teaching *Latin American Film: Reconfigurations of Family and Nation,* I would focus first on the Quechua heritage of the inhabitants of the Andean regions and the challenge that the arrival of the Spanish and Catholic cultures presented to them. A study of the economic conditions of the area would also foster an understanding of the conflicts facing Peruvian society today. (Conde)

The film could be used to explain the innate desire of all humans to better their condition and to explain the exploitation of children in the world. (Garatea)

Suggested Readings: Aufderheide, Patricia. *Cross Cultural Film Guide.*

Black, Jan Knippers, ed. *Latin America. Its Problems and Its Promise.*

Galeano, Eduardo. *Open Veins of Latin America. Five Centuries of the Pillage of a Continent.*

Green, Duncan. *Faces of Latin America.*

King, John. *Magical Reels: A History of Cinemas in Latin America.*

Skidmore, Thomas E., and Peter H. Smith. *Modern Latin America.*

Level: High School—University

MALABRIGO (Malabrigo)

Feature.   With Subtitles.   87 min.   1986
Directed by: Alberto Durán
Distributed by: The Cinema Guild
Evaluators: Alfredo Bushby, Marvin D'Lugo, Susan Griswold

Description: This is a film noir mystery set in Malabrigo, a fishing port on Peru's coastal desert. The town has been steadily dying since the afternoon the first boat came home without fish. A woman arrives by bus in this tense, forbidding place. She has come to join her husband, an accountant at the local fish-meal factory. But he is not waiting for her as expected. Her anxious wait gradually turns into a desperate search, leading her into the web of deceit, betrayal, and murder that has engulfed the town and her husband.

Strengths and Weaknesses: The film is beautifully edited, with a sleek narrative flow and excellent tracking shots. This produces an interesting narrational texture that adds to the initial sense of mystery and intrigue. Filmed in Puerto Chichama and Huanchaco, the film presents an accurate portrayal of Peruvian society and a fascinating array of characters: the exile Spanish hotel owner, his Cuban wife, her lover, the corrupt police commissioner, the newspaper correspondent, etc.

The film can seem slow by U.S. commercial film standards.

How to Use: I would screen the film without subtitles and conduct two kinds of discussions: (1) What did the students understand (purely language based)? (2) What did they think about the film? (Bushby)

In a *Spanish Conversation* course the narrative enigmas could be used to involve students in the activity of describing action, character, motivation, and setting. (D'Lugo)

The film would be interesting to use in a comparative study with a classic film noir piece. (Griswold)
Level: University

ME DEJARON MUERTO AHI

Documentary.   Without Subtitles.   15 min.   1991
Produced by: Inst. Comunicacion Y Desarrollo, Manuel Gómez 634 Lince, Lima [5114] 715-930; tel: [5114] 714-979)
Distributed by: IMRE Archive (available for viewing only)
Evaluators: Richard C. Boly, Joséph A. Gagliano, Rebeca Harclerode, Susan Ramírez, David P. Werlich

Description: This 1991 documentary is a balanced discussion of human rights abuses in Peru by both the Sendero Luminoso (Shining Path) and the military. It includes interviews with peasants, security personnel, human rights advocates, and victims of abuse, most notably journalist Gustavo Goriti, an authority on the Shining Path. The tape briefly describes the objectives of the Maoist Senderistas, and compares their terrorism and violence with that of Pol Pot in Cambodia. It focuses on the strategies of the Peruvian military since 1982 to crush the Shining Path. The film implies that the Peruvian military adopted strategies that were used by the United States in Vietnam and during the "dirty war" in Argentina. The graphic scenes demonstrate the extreme human rights violations by the Peruvian military, as well as Senderista violence, in both rural and urban communities. While most of the victims have been peasants caught in the middle of the conflict, many important community leaders also have been assassinated. The war has taken on racial aspects, since most of the victims have been Quechua-speaking Indians from the mountain regions. The film makes the case that little is made of the death of the victims because they are Indian. It ends by showing the victims of Peru's dirty war, which has taken more than twenty-three thousand lives (as of 1991), lists more than five thousand disappearances, has created fifty thousand orphans, and has led to mass migrations from the hinterland.

Strengths and Weaknesses: This is a well-constructed albeit traditional-style documentary with graphic footage and a strong message. There is some balance in the presentation, as it shows the effects of both military repression and Shining Path terror on the peasants, the primary victims of Peru's dirty war. The video has excellent production values, including Spanish subtitles for interviews with *campesinos* (peasants) whose accents are difficult to understand.

The film assumes a knowledge of twentieth-century Peruvian development. The historical context provided is superficial. While showing Alan García's role in supporting the military repression from 1985 through 1989, the film glosses over Alberto Fujimori's position during the 1990 presidential campaign. Some of the people interviewed are not identified. The tape is more appropriate for the college level, as there are haunting images of dead and exhumed corpses. One reviewer felt that a chronology of purported army massacres of Indians during the twentieth century is misleading and inaccurate, while others thought that the two-sided placement of the blame was more realistic than a one-sided condemnation of the Sendero.

Introducing the Tape: The film requires some introduction to provide a more detailed context about the plans and significance of the Shining Path. Viewers should be given information about Alberto Fujimori's position during the 1990 presidential campaign. Also, additional information about any reform measures that have been undertaken to counter the Shining Path and military policies should be presented. An update on the situation since the capture of Sendero leader Abimael Guzmán is also necessary.

How to Use: The tape could be used in a discussion of civil wars, using Peru as an example. Instructors could lecture on contemporary Peru, then use the film to illustrate points. (Ramírez)

I would use this film in my *Latin American History* survey or my advanced course on Peru to supplement readings and lectures on the Shining Path. The film would make a good springboard for discussion of the complex problems of human rights violations in Peru. (Werlich)

This program can be used together with the feature film *La boca del lobo* to give more context to the presentation of the Sendero Luminoso in the film.

Suggested Readings: Americas Watch. *Peru under Fire: Human Rights since the Return to Democracy.*

Masterson, Daniel M. *Militarism and Politics in Latin America: Peru from Sánchez Cerro to Sendero Luminoso.*

McClintock, Cynthia, and Abraham Lowenthal, eds. *The Peruvian Experiment Reconsidered.*

Palmer, David Scott, ed. *Shining Path of Peru.*

Complementary Films/Videos: *La boca del lobo (The Lion's Den)* (Peru).

Level: University

MISS UNIVERSO EN PERU (Miss Universe in Peru)

Documentary.   With Subtitles.   29 min.   1985

Directed by: M. Barwa, F. Barrieto, and F. Espinoza

Produced by: Grupo Chaski (Casablanca, Malecon Grau 929, Chorrillas, Lima 9; tel: [5114] 670-722; fax: [5114] 300-603)

Distributed by: IMRE, PICS, Women Make Movies

Evaluators: Gerard Aching, Susan Besse, Victor Garatea, John Higgens, Carmen Madariaga-Culver, Jorge Marcone, Laura Elisa Pérez, Janet Page-Reeves

Description: A powerful video that chronicles the 1982 Miss Universe Pageant in Peru and juxtaposes those images with the real life of indigenous Peruvian women, the tape shows the opulence and "white" features of contestants in the media-saturated world of advertising and glamour and the faces of women from poor neighborhoods viewing the television pageant. Interspersed are interviews with Peruvian reporters and feminists who protested the pageant and were subsequently beaten by the police. The connections between business interests and the pageant are explored, as well as the objectification of women and the government's attempts to showcase modernity internationally while the majority of Peruvian women's lives are not benefited.

Strengths and Weaknesses: This is a solid traditional-form documentary with extremely effective symbolism and juxtaposition of the absurd and the real. The use of women watching the pageant on television is particularly powerful. The tape gives important attention to class and race polarization that leads to radically different definitions of womanhood and feminity. It also provides excellent examples of how cultural imperialism works at many different levels and raises questions about the role of media in colonizing relations between countries.

One reviewer felt that the presentation of the differences between disenfranchised women and women in the pageant was too heavy-handed and commented that while the documentation of the plight of indigenous women is good, the government position is less clearly stated. Another reviewer felt that more images of the *campesino* and poor women would have been better. The tape is a bit dated.

How to Use: This would be a good tape for classes in *Cultural Studies, Latin American Studies,* and *Women's Studies.* It would be a film with which one could begin a course in order to point out the basic binomial conflict. (Aching)

The tape could be used to show how women all over the world are trying to gain equality. (Garatea)

There are many interesting and powerful images and dialogue that could be most useful in a variety of different classes. I plan to use the tape in my *Spanish Conversation* class. (Marcone)

In *Women's Studies* the tape could be used to explore the production and exportation/imposition of culturally constructed notions such as gender, particularly within the context of unequal First/Third World power relations. (Pérez)

In courses about *Latin American Women* the tape would be useful to discuss differences in feminine/feminist consciousness among women of different classes and ethnic groups. It could also be useful in courses on *Latin America* to discuss issues of cultural imperialsm.

Level: High School—University

MUJERES DEL PLANETA (Women of El Planeta)

Documentary.   With Subtitles.   30 min.   1982

Directed by: María Barea

Produced by: Faust Films

Distributed by: Women Make Movies

Evaluators: Silvia Arrom, Sarah Chambers, Robert Haskett, Angharad N. Valdivia

Description: This film looks at the lives and struggles of women in a squatter settlement near Lima, Peru, through the eyes of Rosa, a member of a women's self-help solidarity organization. In the film, Rosa and others describe the initial takeover of the land by the squatter families, their struggle with police, and the continuing conditions they face. Most important, the tape details the ways in which women and men of the community are organizing themselves (with the help of a female schoolteacher) to learn about and fight for their rights. It shows the women in meetings, marches, literacy class, and the neighbohood.

Strengths and Weaknesses: The film provides compelling, and at the same time disturbing, images of what it is like to live in a squatter shantytown. It has a sincere, unmediated quality. Though made in 1982 and set in Peru, this visual image is unfortunately a universal one. The film is also important in that it gives a human face to the poor, showing their daily lives and the dire conditions in which they live. Throughout, the film portrays them as human beings with great dignity and the will, desire, and ability to act as agents of their own future. The tape articulates the triple oppression that women experience and clearly shows their leadership role in the new social movements (grassroots efforts to improve urban conditions and to fight for justice). It also recognizes pleasure as an essential human need, something that is not often addressed.

The film is a bit slow-moving, with a few repetitive scenes and little context provided. The connections between seg-

ments are not smooth, and some scenes are a little hard to follow. One reviewer would have preferred more direct, personal testimonies.

Introducing the Tape: The tape is basically straightforward. However, a contextual background on issues of migration, the nature of urban poverty in Peru, the establishment of shantytowns, and the growth in grassroots
movements would enhance understanding. The film could be
brought up to date by describing some of the self-help programs that have borne fruit in Peru but which came under attack by such groups as the Sendero Luminoso (Shining Path).

How to Use: I would use this film in either a *Women's Studies* or *Contemporary Politics* course to focus on the emergence
of new social movements since the 1970s and on the leadership role women have taken in them. I would ask students to
consider why women are playing such a role. Why are they
particularly interested in issues such as housing, urban services, and education? It would be interesting to complement
the film with another that shows more of the personal side of
women's lives (like *Tantas vidas, una historia* [Chile]).
(Chambers)

In the twentieth-century section of my *Latin American
Survey* the film would be a useful addition to the materials I
present regarding urban poverty and grassroots efforts for
self-help. In my upper-division *Indigenous History* course
the film could be used to demonstrate not only the conditions
and pressures of life that confront indigenous migrants (and
especially women) from the highlands to the coastal cities
but also their efforts to take charge of their own lives. (Haskett)

Suggested Readings: Americas Watch. *Peru under Fire:
Human Rights since the Return to Democracy.*

Andreas, Carol. *When Women Rebel: The Rise of Popular
Feminism in Peru.*

Bunster, Ximena, and Elsa M. Chaney. *Sellers and Servants: Working Women in Lima, Peru.*

Cathelat, Marie-France, and Teresa Burga. *Perfil de la mujer peruana, 1980–1981.*

Collier, David. *Squatter Settlements and the Incorporation of Migrants into Urban Life: The Case of Lima.*

Dietz, Henry A. *Poverty and Problem-Solving under Military Rule: The Urban Poor in Lima, Peru.*

Dietz, Henry A., and Richard J. Moore. *Political Participation in a Non-Electoral Setting: The Urban Poor in Lima,
Peru.*

Jelin, Elizabeth, ed. *Women and Social Change in Latin
America.*

Lewis, Robert Alden. *Employment, Income, and the
Growth of the Barriadas in Lima, Peru.*

Lloyd, Peter Cutt. *The "Young Towns" of Lima: Aspects
of Urbanization in Peru.*

Lobo, Susan. *A House of My Own: Social Organization in
the Squatter Settlements of Lima, Peru.*

Quijano, Anibal. *Dominación y cultura: lo cholo y el conflicto cultural en el Perú.*

Reid, Michael. *Peru, Paths to Poverty.*

Stein, Steve. *Populism in Peru: The Emergence of the
Masses and the Politics of Social Control.*

Stokes, Susan C. "Politics and Latin American's Urban
Poor: Reflections from a Lima Shantytown."

Complementary Films/Videos: *Tantas vidas, una historia
(So Many Lives, One Story)* (Chile).

Level: High School—University

NI LECHE, NI LA GLORIA (Bitter Milk)

Documentary. With Subtitles. 42 min. 1987
Directed by: Alejandro Legaspi and Stefan Kaspar
Produced by: Grupo Chaski (Casablanca, Malecon Grau
929, Chorrillas, Lima 9; tel: [5114] 670-722; fax: [5114]
300-603)
Distributed by: IMRE, PICS
Evaluators: John Hays, Graciela Michelotti-Cristóbal, Janet
B. Norden, Susan Ramírez, David J. Robinson, Aaron Vinck
Description: Based on a book by Manuel Lajo, this film documents the monopoly and economics of the evaporated-milk
industry in Peru. It traces the history of the Carnation company from its establishment to its nationalization by the Peruvian government. This is a superb study of how the
transnational corporation, Nestlē (the parent of Carnation),
influenced the economic and social fabric of Peru, gained its
monopoly status, affected wages and workers' rights, and
deftly used the media and advertising to promote the perception that powdered milk was better than breast milk. The film
illustrates the paradox of having such an expensive product
as canned milk in so poor a country; how land used exclusively for raising cows obliges peasants to purchase basic
foodstuffs from distant markets; and how Peruvian children
drink tea and coffee while powdered milk is packaged in
fancy wrappings and sent out of the country. The film describes the "Glass of Milk" policy that aimed to solve this
problem and includes former president Alan García's speech
announcing the government nationalization of the Carnation
company. The film ends with an open question about the possibilities of this policy being fully carried out.

Strengths and Weaknesses: The film effectively portrays
the level of poverty of the people affected by the system. The
filmmakers limit their editorializing, yet their bias in favor of
the oppressed is clear. The technical aspect of Carnation milk
processing is contrasted to the fact that most Peruvian children never drink the costly processed milk. The film is well
written and historically accurate. It combines poignant documentary footage with creative editing. Brilliant juxtapositions powerfully depict the tragic impact of this monopoly.

While one evaluator found the pacing somewhat slow, another felt that this allowed the viewer to get a sense of life in
the Andean highlands.

Introducing the Tape: Viewers would need some background regarding the normal standard of living in Peru, in order to make comparisons to others' lives. Also, a map showing the Arequipa and Chiclayo areas would be helpful. The

dates of the presidencies mentioned and the role of the government need to be clarified.

How to Use: The tape could be used in *Spanish Language* courses to expose students to Andean culture and economic problems caused by international companies. (Michelotti-Cristobál)

I would use the tape to teach the *Development of Underdevelopment.* I would assign a theoretical piece and show the film as an example, followed by discussion. (Ramírez)

I would use this film in my *Development* course. It is one of the best portrayals that I have ever seen of the invasive nature of a transnational company and how it affects a national pattern of development and changes customs, perceptions, lifestyles, wage rates, job markets, and regional growth. (Robinson)

Suggested Readings: Chicote, Ronald H., and Joel C. Edelstein, eds. *Latin America: The Struggle with Dependency and Beyond.*

Lajo, Manuel. *Food Processing in Peru, with Particular Reference to Milk and Balanced Poultry Feeds: Case Studies on Technology and Development in the Food Processing Sector.*

Level: University

EL PUENTE DE ICHU

Documentary.   Without Subtitles.   50 min.   1972
Directed by: Kurt Rosenthal
Produced by: Panorama Producciones (Producción de Cine y TV, Lima; tel: [5114] 370-100)
Distributed by: CIMR, IMRE Archive (available for viewing only)
Evaluators: Lynn M. Shirey, David P. Werlich
Description: In this film, the villagers in the Andean Department Cuzco of Peru build a new suspension bridge over the Apurímac River. The structure is entirely made of Ichu bunch grass, probably just as it was in pre-Columbian times. The film, while focusing on this project, provides an excellent overview of rural village life. Local customs, such as coca-leaf chewing and potato cultivation, are described, and the importance of precolonial tradition is emphasized.
Strengths and Weaknesses: This is an intimate portrayal of rural life in the Andes. It presents material on agricultural techniques, folk religion, traditional medicine, and village labor organization. The film focuses much attention on peasant women crafting ropes. Footage of the ropemaking is fascinating, as are visuals of women spinning yarn and weaving. Viewers have an opportunity to hear the indigenous Quechua language spoken. The mountain scenery and Andean music add beauty and color to the film.

The tape provides geographic introduction to the area. How the bridge is actually finished is not clear because the story deviates to other local customs.
How to Use: I would use this film in my *Latin American History Survey* or advanced course on Peru to introduce students to peasant life. (Werlich)

Suggested Readings: Ferris, H. B. *The Indians of Cuzco and Apurimac.*

Meyerson, Julia. *'Tambo: Life in an Andean Village.*

Salas, Portilla, and Pedro Hernán. *Apurimac, el perfil de un pueblo olvidado del Perú.*
Level: University

SOBREVIVIENTE DE OFICIO (Occupation Survivor)

Documentary.   With Subtitles.   10 min.   1982
Directed by: S. Kaspar, O. Carpio, and J. Portocarrero
Produced by: Grupo Chaski (Casablanca, Malecón Grau 929, Chorrillas, Lima 9; tel: [5114] 670-722; fax: [5114] 300-603)
Distributed by: IMRE
Evaluators: John Hays, Graciela Michelotti-Cristóbal, Susan Ramírez, Aaron Vinck, David P. Werlich
Description: This film is a brief portrait of an unemployed young man who washes auto windows at a busy intersection in Lima. He is an artist at his trade. As he works, he plays with his tools, imitating the tricks of a soccer player. He addresses the camera directly, sharing his dreams and hopes for a better life for his child. The film is edited to a musical score to create the effect of a choreographed ballet.
Strengths and Weaknesses: This well-produced piece is respectful, forceful, and sympathetic. It is a strong statement about one of Latin America's greatest problems: underemployment/unemployment. The filmmaker's presentation does not obligate the audience to pity the subject, although his situation would merit pity.

One evaluator felt that the tape provides little insight into the plight of the "informal" workers, as this window washer is unique.
Introducing the Tape: Students should be told that the film takes place in Peru and should be given some background on issues of the informal economy, unemployment, homelessness, and the ineffectiveness of any existing government programs to combat these problems.
How to Use: I would use the tape to discuss the use of inappropriate technology and the resultant unemployment. (Ramírez)
Suggested Readings: Soto, Hernando de. *The Other Path: The Invisible Revolution in the Third World;* an influential book about the informal sector in Peru.
Level: Junior High School—University

TUPAC AMARU (Tupac Amarú)

Feature.   With Subtitles.   95 min.   1984
Directed by: Federico García
Produced by: ICAIC (Calle 23 No. 155, Vedado, Havana; tel: [537] 333-862 fax: [537] 333-032)
Distributed by: IMRE Archive (available for viewing only)
Evaluators: Donald J. Mabry, Luis Martínez-Fernández
Description: The film traces the Tupac Amarú rebellion of 1780–1781 in Nueva Castilla, Peru. It examines the trials and

executions of Tupac Amarú and other Indian leaders following their capture by Spanish forces. The film asserts that this was an abortive social revolution, the first in the New World. The actual trials serve as the central narrative line, with flashbacks to episodes leading to, and taking place during, the mass rebellion.

Strengths and Weaknesses: This is a useful recreation of the original rebellion. The film is quite clear. The period's complexity, including the Indian/state and church/state tensions, and the creation of the creole elite are well developed. Most scenes were filmed on location in Cuzco and Lima, with excellent footage of costumes and household interiors in the style of the period.

The narrator assumes a markedly pedagogical tone at times. **Introducing the Tape:** The film gives enough historical context that an introduction is not necessary.

How to Use: This tape could be used as a means to demonstrate the complexity of the original Tupac Amarú rebellion and the nature of Spanish rule. (Mabry)

I would use this film as part of the course unit covering the tensions produced by the Bourbon reforms and as a background to the wars of independence. It would also be of use in discussing how native Andean culture had changed since the conquest and why Peru became a bastion of loyalism during the wars of independence. (Martínez-Fernández)

Suggested Readings: Fisher, John. *Government and Society in Colonial Peru: The Intendant System, 1784–1814.*

Juan, Jorge, and Antonio Ulloa. *Noticias secretas de América.*

Level: University

LAS VENAS DE LA TIERRA

Documentary. Without Subtitles. 52 min. 1990
Directed by: José Antonio Pontugal
Produced by: CADEP (Calle Saphi No. 808, Cuzco; tel: [518] 428-021; fax: [518] 425-731)
Distributed by: CIMR, IMRE Archive (available for viewing only)
Evaluators: Kendall W. Brown, David J. Robinson, David P. Werlich
Description: The peasants of Mollepata (a village in the Andean department of Cuzco) work communally to restore an old neglected irrigation canal linking a glacial lake with their village. The villagers need to reconstruct and reclaim old canal systems for the community to help solve economic and sociocultural problems caused by a drought. This tape documents the project and intersperses references to Andean deities in an attempt to show how the canals and water are tied to traditional religious practice. There is also interesting footage of La Estrella, a hacienda and sugar mill owned by former president (1930–1931) David Samanez Ocampo.

Strengths and Weaknesses: The tape provides a comprehensive overview of peasant life in the Andes, including folk religion and folk medicine. There is wonderful mountain scenery and Andean music.

One evaluator felt that there is too little exposition and explanation of anthropological and ethnic references. The film does not have strong production values.

Introducing the Tape: Some explanation for a U.S. audience is necessary, as references to places, deities, and cultural practices are not explained. Viewers should be told that while the peasants in this film may look like full-blooded Indians to U.S. viewers, they are mestizos and are quite Westernized by Andean standards.

How to Use: The tape could be used to demonstrate how cultural meanings in Andean societies pervade all aspects of life. (Robinson)

I would use this film in my *Latin American History* survey or my specialized course on *Peru* to introduce students to peasant life. (Werlich)

Suggested Readings: Meyerson, Julia. *'Tambo: Life in an Andean Village.*

Valderrama Fernández, Ricardo. *Del tata mallka a la mamá pacha: riego, sociedad, y ritos en los Andes Peruanos.*
Level: University

LA VIDA ES UNA SOLA (You Only Live Once)

Feature. With Subtitles. 84 min. 1992
Directed by: Marinne Eyde
Produced by: Kusi Films (Godofredo García 140 San Isidro, Lima 27; tel: [5114] 226-005; fax: [5114] 402-838)
Distributed by: Films Transit, IMRE
Evaluators: Richard C. Boly, Carlos Pérez, Susan Ramírez, Lynn M. Shirey, David P. Werlich, Thomas Whigham
Description: A village in the Peruvian Andes is caught between the tyrannies of the terrorist group Sendero Luminoso (Shining Path) and the Peruvian military. The film opens as an indigenous community festival is interrupted by the arrival of three members of the Sendero, posing as university students. They begin their organizing activities among the community of Rayopampa, and in the process, one member, Aurelio, falls in love with Florinda, a young Indian woman. After the Sendero members leave the town, the military arrives and demands that the community not associate with terrorists. The community is not free from the military's plunder, as we see soldiers leave laden with provisions taken from the community.

Sendero militants return at night, painting slogans and leaving a red flag. In an assembly, the community decides that it does not want to side with either the Sendero or the military. The Sendero leader threatens Teodorio, the town leader, with death if he does not resign. When he seeks help from the military, the military commander orders him to take down the flag and erase the graffiti himself as proof of the community's allegiance to the nation. When the Sendero members arrive, they execute Teodorio as an example, then forcibly educate and organize the community politically, preparing it for armed struggle. As Sendero leaves the town, they take many of the community's young people with them, including Florinda.

When the military arrives, those suspected of collaborating with Sendero are taken away. Subsequently, there is a confrontation between Sendero and the military. At the end of the battle, the military discovers that some of the guerrillas were from Rayopampa and promises revenge on the town. The guerrillas force Florinda to execute an individual who tried to escape during the battle. After the execution, Florinda escapes and returns home, where she finds her village destroyed and empty. When she finds her family hiding in the surrounding mountains, her father orders her to leave, fearing Sendero or the military will kill them all if she is found. Florinda is told she cannot return until Rayopampa thrives again.

Strengths and Weaknesses: The film takes a strong, critical approach towards this subject matter. It does not glorify the military nor Sendero, but in an evenhanded manner exposes the havoc that both create. It is clear that these external forces are destroying the internal logic and structure of the Indian community that has sustained indigenous peoples through five hundred years of colonial exploitation and oppression. The film also demonstrates the prominent role of women in the Sendero's ranks. It is particularly clear for a U.S. audience because of the easy-flowing narrative and uncomplicated character types. With good production qualities, it presents beautiful scenery and a believable portrait of an Andean village. Much of the dialogue lends itself to further examination of pivotal issues in the study of Andean society and history.

Evaluators felt that many times the film presents stereotyped characters and romanticizes the Indian community. The Hollywood technique of situating a personal situation (the love affair) in the midst of what is a political and social struggle interrupts the flow of the community's narrative and detracts from the film. However, this film strategy does, perhaps, make the film more accessible to U.S. audiences.

Introducing the Tape: Audiences should be familiar with some of the background of the present guerrilla war in Peru. They should be introduced to the tactics used by the Sendero to organize the communities and the government reprisals that this has engendered. Viewers should be told that although the insurgency movement of the Sendero Luminoso has its unique characteristics, this film encapsulates many of the problems existing in other countries, such as Guatemala, that have a large indigenous communal population that is being devastated by the counterinsurgency tactics employed by the military. The organization by the state of the Civil Defense Committees, or peasant patrols, should be studied. Although having roots in the communities, they have been used by the state in its counterinsurgency struggle against the Sendero. Background on the historical relationship of the Indian communities with the Peruvian state and society is also necessary. The film makes it appear as if the Indian community lived in relative isolation and harmony prior to the intrusion of the guerrilla war. This assumption should be challenged by the instructor.

How to Use: I would use this tape when discussing contemporary Peru. After focusing on the 1968 military coup and the subsequent return to civilian rule in 1980, we would study the contradiction and conflicts that the military government's land reforms left in the countryside. We would also discuss the Peruvian student movement of that period and the rise of the Sendero Luminoso, under the leadership of Abimael Guzmán (a university professor), who rose from the movement's ranks. After viewing the film, I would engage the students in a discussion of the military's role in the repression of the communities as a counterinsurgency strategy. We would then analyze the relationship of the Indian communities to the state as well as the question of ethnicity and nationalism. (Pérez)

I would lecture on resistance to modernization and Hispanization by native peoples and then show the film. (Ramírez)

This film would be useful in my *Latin American History Survey* or my advanced course on Peru, to supplement lectures and readings on the Shining Path insurgency. It could also provide background for discussion of the problems of human rights abuse. (Werlich)

Suggested Readings: Americas Watch. *Peru under Fire: Human Rights since the Return to Democracy.*

Anderson, James. *Sendero Luminoso: A New Revolutionary Model?*

Burt, Jo-Marie, and Aldo Panficihi. *Peru: Caught in the Crossfire.*

Degregori, Carlos Iván. *El surgimiento de Sendero Luminoso: Ayacucho 1969–1979.*

"Fatal Attraction: Peru's Shining Path," *NACLA Report on the Americas.*

Isbell, Billie Jean. *The Emerging Patterns of Peasants' Responses to Sendero Luminoso.*

Isbell, Billie Jean. *The Text and Contexts of Terror in Peru.*

Kruijt, Dirk. *Perú, entre Sendero y los militares: seguridad y relaciones, civico-militares, 1950–1990.*

Masterson, Daniel M. *Militarism and Politics in Latin America: Peru from Sánchez Cerro to Sendero Luminoso.*

McClintock, Cynthia. "Sendero Luminoso: Peru's Maoist Guerrillas."

Palmer, David Scott. *The Shining Path of Peru.*

Poole, Deborah, and Gerardo Renique. *Peru: Time of Fear.*

Tarazona-Sevillano, Gabriela, with John B. Reuter. *Sendero Luminoso and the Threat of Narcoterrorism.*

Complementary Films/Videos: *La boca del lobo (The Lion's Den)* (Peru).

Level: University

PUERTO RICO

LA BATALLA DE VIEQUES (The Battle of Vieques)
Documentary.   With Subtitles.   40 min.   1986
Directed by: Zynida Nazario

Distributed by: The Cinema Guild
Evaluators: Nancy Levy-Konesky, María Ramírez, Virginia Shen
Description: This film provides a historical overview of the Puerto Rican island of Vieques and the sociopolitical and economic repercussions of the presence of the U.S. Navy base on a major portion of the island. It presents the resistance of the people of Vieques, particularly the fishermen, to the navy's bomb-dropping and target-practice operations on the island.
Strengths and Weaknesses: This clear and well-organized film uses outstanding production techniques to personalize the problems of the people of Vieques and present the injustices committed against them. It is realistic and interesting from a historical and cultural perspective, providing good background with documentary footage and newspaper clippings.

The film's editing is a bit disjointed.
Introducing the Tape: None necessary.
How to Use: This tape could be used in my *Seminar on Puerto Rico* to illustrate U.S. presence there. It thoroughly presents the side of the Vieques residents in this conflict. (Levy-Konesky)

When we talk about *Contemporary Latin American History* in my *Latin American Culture and Civilization* course, I would use the tape to show the U.S.-Latin American relationship in the past and present. (Shen)
Suggested Readings: Any history book that includes information about the Spanish-American War or the history of Puerto Rico.
Level: High School—University

MANOS A LA OBRA (The Story of Operation Bootstrap)

Documentary.   With Subtitles.   59 min.   1983
Directed by: Pedro Rivera and Susan Zeig
Distributed by: The Cinema Guild
Evaluators: César Ayala, Jerry W. Cooney, Glenn J. Kist, Nancy Levy-Konesky, María Ramírez
Description: This documentary presents an in-depth, highly critical look at the government-sponsored program of industrialization, which transformed Puerto Rico from a monocultural island, dependent on sugar exports, into the urban, highly industrialized society it is today. After the World War II, the local government offered tax exemptions to multinational corporations to attract U.S. private capital. The process was called Operation Bootstrap (*Operación Manos a la Obra*). This video covers the historical development of Puerto Rico from 1898 through the early 1980s, offering interesting footage from the 1930s to the present and interviews with prominent figures who were involved with the island's program of industrialization. Among the most outstanding figures interviewed are Teodoro Moscoso, the main architect of Operation Bootstrap; Juan Saenz Corales, the pro-independence leader of the Confederación General de Trabajadores; and Luis Ferre, the island's foremost industrialist and a leader of the pro-statehood party.

The documentary focuses on the contradictions generated by Operation Bootstrap. The general interpretation is based on the dependency theory of development. It asserts that the island prospered, but at the cost of massive, state-sponsored emigration of the population and massive sterilization of the women. Unemployment rates in Puerto Rico are typically at least twice the national unemployment rate of the United States. Per capita income is far below that of the poorest state of the union, and high crime rates have caused the disappearance of public space. Petrochemical industries came to the island in the mid-1960s, but they did not generate the number of jobs expected in the initial forecasts. When they closed operations in the mid-1970s, they left the entire southern coast of the island polluted. A Puerto Rican generation put its hands to work and built the Caribbean's most profitable (for the foreign multinational corporations) and dynamic economy. The children of this generation are now jobless and have been forced to emigrate to survive. The film is clearly in favor of socialism and nationhood for Puerto Rico.
Strengths and Weaknesses: The tape is an honest look at the realities of the promotion of industrialization for export that occurred in Puerto Rico. It provides a good summary of the political, social, and economic developments in Puerto Rico since the War of 1898. As an educational tool, it is invaluable because of its straightforward format and intelligible narrative. Archival research provides it with excellent footage from the 1930s to the 1980s. One evaluator felt that this is the best available one-hour-long explanation of the reality of Puerto Rico in the second half of the twentieth century.

The filmmakers have an obvious sympathy for the Puerto Rican laborers and a clear antipathy for the producers of Operation Bootstrap, yet they fail to posit any alternatives to that economic program other than a romantic treatment of nationalism. One evaluator felt that the film puts too much emphasis on the poverty and misery in Puerto Rico. The various film techniques used may also be confusing for some audiences. The tape is now ten years old and somewhat dated. At times, the subtitles are difficult to read.
Introducing the Tape: A modern history of the island would be useful. Viewers could be told that in the 1930s the collapse of the price of sugar during the Great Depression caused extreme hardship in Puerto Rico, particularly in the countryside communities. Sugar was the island's main export. Revenues from sugar sales provided islanders with the capacity to buy imports, including food. In the late 1930s Luis Muñoz Marín and the Popular Democratic Party, founded in 1938, introduced a program to dismantle the sugar industry, carry out a partial agrarian reform, and diversify the island's economy. During World War II the program had to be abandoned as the island returned to sugar production to supply the United States and the Allies' war effort. It was during this period that the first factories were built in

Puerto Rico, at government expense, to produce inputs needed in government projects, especially roads and infrastructures necessary to supply the twenty-six U.S. military bases on the island. After the war, the local government turned to attracting U.S. private capital, particularly by offering tax exemptions. This process began in 1947 and continues to this day. Viewers could also be updated on recent developments in Puerto Rican political history.

How to Use: In a *Survey of United States History* course I would probably assign the documentary to be viewed out of class. In the discussion that would follow, I would focus on these questions: Did the presence of the United States in Puerto Rico have a positive or negative impact on the island's development? Explain how the directors of the tape have applied the dependency theory to the development of Puerto Rico. (Kist)

In my *Spanish Practicum/Seminar on Puerto Rico* I would use this tape to visually present the political turmoil in Puerto Rico from the 1930s to today. These are themes that we study in depth in class. The film helps to give students a clear image of the history. (Levy-Konesky)

Suggested Readings: Carr, Raymond. *Puerto Rico: A Colonial Experiment.*

Level: High School—University

LA OPERACION (The Operation)

Documentary.   With Subtitles.   40 min.   1982
Directed by: Ana María García
Distributed by: The Cinema Guild
Evaluators: Marilyn Jiménez, Nancy Levy-Konesky, Jorge Porras, S. Travis Silcox, Susy Suárez
Description: This is an in-depth investigation of the population control programs directed against Puerto Rico by the United States from the 1950s to the 1970s, including the widespread use of female sterilization. In Puerto Rico, the country with the highest rate of sterilization in the world (one third of the whole population), women often consented to the operation without knowing it was permanent. Statistics and interviews show the negative results of such practices and complaints that U.S. health officials abused or neglected women's rights by omitting information. They suggest that this was done to avoid a revolution of the underclass in a country where the United States exploited the Puerto Rican workforce and U.S. companies thrived. The filmmakers demonstrate how colonialism affects women in ways peculiar to their gender. In a poignant moment, two women who have been given an experimental version of the Pill (with much higher dosages of estrogen than finally approved) realize that they are guinea pigs; their facial expressions change as they recognize that they are being treated like animals.
Strengths and Weaknesses: The film is a strong, compelling, well-presented narrative with detailed historical background (including Operation Bootstrap, Muñoz Marín's presidency, the Puerto Rican economy, etc.). The film makes excellent use of newsreel footage and interviews. Ultimately,

the tape is a powerful indictment of U.S. policy toward Puerto Rico. One evaluator mentioned that although almost a decade old, and hence somewhat dated, this film always stuns the U.S. students who see it.

One evaluator felt that the bias precluded understanding the history of this project. The questions of who favored sterilization, who opposed it, and why are not answered. The film is presented in a traditional documentary format without much creativity in style.

Introducing the Tape: Viewers will want to know what the situation is today; thus a postscript is essential. Further history of the project would also be useful.

How to Use: I have used this tape in different classes to present the issue of sterilization and population control. It also provides an interesting lead-in for discussions of the abortion issues today and the nature of the choice in pro-choice. (Jiménez)

I would use this documentary in *Women's Studies* courses to show how women become the focus in development strategies to globalize the world's capitalist economy. It would be interesting to use this video in conjunction with works on birth control and population control that developed alongside eugenicist movements (including the work of Sanger). It shows that reproductive rights include freedom from coerced or forced sterilization. (Silcox)

I have used this tape during *Latino Heritage Month* and during *Puerto Rico Day* in November. (Suárez)

Suggested Readings: Ostoloza Bey, Margarita. *Política sexual en Puerto Rico,* provides a wider context of the relationship between colonialism and sexism in Puerto Rico; she mentions the film but questions its uncritical acceptance of the independentista ideology that associates women with the bearers of tradition and the future of the race.

Level: High School—University

LA PARTICIPACION DE MUJERES EN SALUD

Documentary.   Without Subtitles.   30 min.   1989
Directed by: Yamila Azize and Emilio Rodríguez
Produced by: Estudios de la Mujer (Colegio Universitario de Cayey, Cayey, PR 00736)
Distributed by: IMRE Archive (available for viewing only)
Evaluators: Frederick M. Nunn, J. Julian Rívera, Roger Sánchez-Berroa, Linda Whiteford, Susan Wood
Description: This video provides an overview of Puerto Rican women in the medical field since the late nineteenth century. The tape includes still photographs and interviews.
Strengths and Weaknesses: This tape is well researched and effective. It provides thorough historical background, with excellent use of archival photographs. The music and narration are excellently integrated. The tape can be used for health information and women's issues. The spoken Spanish is clear, making it useful for language classes.

One evaluator found the tape slow paced and predictable. Another pointed out that the topic is extremely specific and of less general interest.

Introducing the Tape: Viewers could use an introduction to traditional women's roles in Puerto Rico.

How to Use: In *Spanish Language* classes I would show small, two-to-four-minute segments, followed by discussion of vocabulary and historical facts. (Sánchez-Berroa)

I would use this to show the relationship between women's status and access into the medical profession, using Puerto Rico as an example of common patterns in both North and South America. (Whiteford)

Level: University

PUERTO RICO: A COLONY THE AMERICAN WAY

Documentary. With Subtitles. 27 min. 1982
Directed by: Diego Echeverría
Produced by: Terra Productions (588 Broadway, Suite 804, New York, NY 10012; tel: [212] 226-3170; fax: [212] 226-2561)
Distributed by: The Cinema Guild
Evaluators: Kim Kowalczyk, Virginia Shen
Description: This tape examines Puerto Rico's relationship with the United States, focusing on the Puerto Rican 1988 gubernatorial race. The video contrasts the different factions: those who wish to see Puerto Rico an independent country, those in favor of statehood, and those who want it to remain a U.S. territory.
Strengths and Weaknesses: The tape discusses the relationship between Puerto Rico and the United States from diverse perspectives in an organized and systematic manner. The themes are clear and accessible.
Introducing the Tape: An introduction should inform viewers that although the tape deals with the 1988 election, the same political issues and divisions are pertinent today in Puerto Rico.
How to Use: I would show this tape as a springboard for discussion of U.S. involvement in Puerto Rican affairs. (Kowalczyk)

When I teach *Latin American Literature* I would use this tape to enhance discussion of U.S.-Puerto Rican relations and how the relationship is reflected in literature. This tape summarizes the concerns of many Puerto Rican writers regarding the dependence of Puerto Rico on the United States. (Shen)

Level: High School—University

VISA PARA UN SUEÑO (Visa for A Dream)

Documentary. With Subtitles. 28 min. 1990
Directed by: Sonia Fritz
Distributed by: East Village Exchange
Evaluators: Rosario Espinal, Henry Funes, Eliana Moya Raggio, Janet B. Norden, Aaron Vinck
Description: This documentary follows women who migrate from the Dominican Republic to Puerto Rico in search of better educational and employment opportunities. The women express animated and valuable perspectives on their arrival, adjustments, and longing for the homeland. They also discuss their views about Dominican men and their own overall aspirations in life.
Strengths and Weaknesses: This tape brings to the forefront the critical situation of many people from the Dominican Republic. Its interview format provides succinct information from a woman's point of view. The program moves quickly, beginning with a clear and artistic introduction, set to the theme song "Visa for a Dream," performed by a popular Dominican singer, Juan Luis Guerra. Included are effective images of the culture and an interesting contrast between the Dominican Republic and Puerto Rico.

Evaluators felt that there were too many street scenes and interviews and that the pacing and editing are uneven at times. One reviewer was disappointed by the lack of historical background and follow-through regarding the issue of Dominicans using Puerto Rico as a base for emigration to New York City.
Introducing the Tape: Although some historical information is provided, viewers could use additional background on U.S.-Dominican relations, specifically, U.S. intervention, CIA activities on the island, economic misdevelopment of the island, migration between the two islands and the U.S. mainland, and the present situation of Dominican communities in the United States and their relationship to their homeland.
How to Use: I would use this video to illustrate a series of reasons for female migration. (Raggio)

Using real-life examples, this tape provides an understanding of why people emigrate.
Suggested Readings: Nash, June, and Helen Safa. *Women and Change in Latin America.*
Level: High School—University

UNITED STATES (U.S. LATINOS)

A BAILAR: JOURNEY OF A LATIN DANCE COMPANY

Documentary. In English. 30 min. 1988
Directed by: Catherine Calderón
Distributed by: The Cinema Guild
Evaluators: John Chasteen, Roger A. Sánchez-Berroa
Description: This film traces the career of a New York dance troupe from its conception in the mind of choreographer and dancer Eddie Torres to its debut performance at New York's renowned Apollo Theater. Although there are a number of brief interviews, most of the footage is devoted to the dancers during several practices sessions and on the night of the performance. One of the high points is the troupe's audition with salsa great Tito Puente, in which Torres seems genuinely nervous.
Strengths and Weaknesses: This is a wonderful film, with generally high production values and an engaging, unpretentious style. It is an informative, cultural piece about popular dancing, and the performances are excellent.

The specific focus of the tape limits its audiences. It contains no Spanish dialogue.

Introducing the Tape: The tape stands on its own; however, an introduction discussing the significance of such a dance company to the Latino community could be helpful.

How to Use: In a course on the *Social History of Popular Dance in Latin America* this video could be used to illustrate salsa and mambo. (Chasteen)

This tape could be integrated into almost any class for fun or an alternative to usual class activities. (Sánchez-Berroa)

Suggested Readings: Hijuelos, Oscar. *The Mambo Kings Play Songs of Love.*

Anything on the migration of Cuban musicians to New York in the 1950s and 1960s and on their interaction in New York with African American jazz musicians resulting in the creation of salsa music.

Level: University

ANA MENDIETA: FUEGO DE TIERRA (Ana Mendieta: Land of Fire)

Documentary.   With Subtitles.   49 min.   1987
Directed by: Nereyda García and Kate Horsfield
Produced by: Video Data Bank (37 South Wabash, Chicago, IL 60603; tel: [312] 263-0141; fax: [312] 899-5172)
Distributed by: Video Data Bank, Women Make Movies
Evaluators: Carol Becker, Elba D. Birmingham-Pokorny, Diane Marting, Gerardo Piña, Alicia Ramos
Description: This excellent documentary examines the life and work of the Cuban-born environmental sculptor Ana Mendieta, who met an untimely death in New York at the start of her career. Structured around the memoirs of the Mendieta family, the video gives a sense of Ana's development as an artist and as a person displaced as a child from Cuba. The tape analyzes the impact of Ana's uprooting from Cuba and of life in orphanages, facing discrimination and isolation in the U.S. Midwest town where she grew up. It also shows the influences of Afro-Cuban music, folklore, and myths on her art. The tape lovingly presents artifacts and still pictures of Ana's childhood and interviews family, friends, and art critics about her relationship with Cuban and U.S. cultures, her feminism, and her artistic legacy.
Strengths and Weaknesses: This video is a wonderful tribute; it presents an in-depth analysis of the artist and her art, with fascinating artistic concepts and a touching story of Mendieta's life. Technically, the tape is well done, with excellent use of interviews, photos, and footage to convey the importance of Mendieta's contribution to the arts. It also sheds light on the struggles of a young woman artist for self-expression.

One evaluator felt that this could be a stronger and more artful piece but acknowledged that it is a useful portrait.

Introducing the Tape: It should be explained that Ana was one of the thousands of children sent from Cuba to the United States in the early days of the revolution, as a result of the CIA's Operation Peter Pan. In the early days of the revolution, rumors were spread in Cuba that the communist regime would send all its children to the Soviet Union for training. Fearful parents sent their children to the waiting arms of the operation's conduit, a Catholic church based in Miami. Also, some information about the direction Mendieta's art took at the time of her death could be added. For *Women's Studies* and *Latin American Culture* classes, definitions and a brief history of conceptual and performance art would be needed. For *Art History* classes context would be needed on recent Cuban history. An introduction could include information about Mendieta's death and the mystery behind it. She fell or was pushed from the balcony of her New York City apartment. Her husband, there at the time, was acquitted of the murder charges against him.

How to Use: I could easily use this tape in my *Art* classes for students interested in the process of becoming an artist. (Becker)

This documentary is extremely helpful in any course dealing with *Afro-Hispanic Literature* insofar as it helps students understand the tremendous impact of African culture on the literature, arts, music, language, and culture of Latin America and the Caribbean. (Birmingham-Pokorny)

Suggested Readings: Rasmussen, Waldo, ed. *The Latin American Arts of the Twentieth Century.* This catalog of the 1993 exhibition at the Museum of Modern Art contains some information on Mendieta.

Level: University

AREPA COLOMBIANA EN NUEVA YORK

Documentary.   Without Subtitles.   16 min.   1992
Directed by: Roberto Arevalo (44 Washington St. #817, Brookline, MA 02146; tel: [617] 739-1376)
Distributed by: Roberto Arevalo
Evaluators: Maurice P. Brungardt, Graciela M. Castex, Grace Leavitt, Suzanne Oboler, J. Julian Rívera, Roger A. Sánchez-Berroa
Description: After some brief general remarks on Latin American communities in the United States, the tape focuses on the point of view of a vendor of *arepas* (Colombian corn-based snacks) on the streets of New York City. He speaks about his experiences and how he came to select this work as a way to survive. The tape includes scenes of the Colombian neighborhood of Jackson Heights, as well as brief unrehearsed interviews with a stream of customers as they stop to buy an *arepa*. The customers speak about their reasons for emigrating, and how eating *arepas* reminds them of home and loved ones. The documentary demonstrates the struggle for survival of this Latino community and the ways that cultural continuity are maintained in immigrant life. The vendor earns his livelihood, maintains a little bit of Colombia in New York, and in the process enriches the culture of the United States.
Strengths and Weaknesses: This is a useful video on the role of food in cultural continuity and daily life in a working-

class New York City community. It provides authentic scenes of life in Little Colombia. The tape successfully expresses views of Latino people and culture in the United States. Set to cheerful Colombian folk music from the coast, it conveys some of the nostalgia of things left behind but is not bitter about the new beginning and the immigrant struggle to earn a living and survive. The video provides wonderful practice for Spanish students, displaying a variety of accents and vocabulary. In general, the Colombian accent is easy for U.S. students to understand, although a few speakers' accents are less clear for nonnative speakers.

One evaluator felt that the tape gets a bit repetitious.

Introducing the Tape: Viewers could use an introduction regarding the Colombian community, as well as other immigrants in the United States. Also useful might be a brief definition of what an *arepa* is and the place of *arepas* in Colombian cuisine. Are they national, regional, or class-based snacks?

How to Use: I would use the tape to show how Latin American immigrants that come to the United States bring with them certain traditions and patterns of life, such as their food, that enrich and add to our own. (Brungardt)

This is a wonderful example of how immigrant groups bring the material culture of their country to the receiving society. (Castex)

I would use the tape in my *Ethnicity Social Work* course with emphasis on the life of Hispanic immigrants in the United States. (Rivera)

Suggested Readings: Bautista Gutiérrez, Gloria. *Realismo mágico, cosmos Latinoamericano: teoría y práctica.*

Bergquist, Charles, Ricardo Peñaranda, and Gonzalo Sánchez, eds. *Violence in Colombia: The Contemporary Crisis in Historical Perspective.*

Bushnell, David. *The Making of Modern Colombia. A Nation in Spite of Itself.*

Martz, John D. "Colombia at the Crossroads."

Pearce, Jenny. *Colombia: Inside the Labyrinth.*

Level: Junior High School—University

ARROZ, FRIJOLES, Y SALSA (Rice, Beans, and Salsa)

Docudrama. In English and Spanish with Subtitles in Both Languages. 24 min. 1992

Directed by: Nelson J. Ginebra

Produced by: El Azul Más Profundo Filmworks (36 Ashley Way, Myersville, MD 21773; tel: [301] 293-2226; fax: [301] 293-3450)

Distributed by: El Azul Mas Profundo Filmworks

Evaluators: Virginia Shen

Description: In this film, four diverse Latin Americans gather for lunch and get involved in a heated intracultural debate triggered by actual news footage of the May 1991 Mount Pleasant riots in Washington, D.C. After their tension results in physical conflicts, the men go to different rooms to reevaluate their viewpoints regarding their own identities as well as the delicate road to assimilation. The tape explores intracultural prejudice, self-negation, and attitudes towards immigrants.

Strengths and Weaknesses: The diverse points of view are clear and well presented.

How to Use: When I next teach *Chicano Theater,* I would like to use this tape to highlight the intracultural aspects of the Mexican Americans as well as their loss and search for identities. (Shen)

In an *English as a Second Language* class students could write compositions about their own or their family members' immigration and cultural identities/experiences.

Level: University

BABALU (Babalu)

Experimental. In English; Spanish Portions Not Subtitled. 10 min. 1980

Directed by: Tony Labat

Distributed by: Electronic Arts Intermix

Evaluators: Jules Benjamin, Marlene Gottlieb, Enrique R. Rodríguez, Pamela M. Smorkaloff

Description: In a powerful collusion of traditional and pop-cultural mythologies, video maker Labat confronts his Cuban heritage and identity and critiques the representation of this culture by the mass media. Donning theatrical face paint and a wig, Labat transforms himself into an icon of Babalu, the Afro-Cuban folk god. His use of Babalu as a cultural metaphor is steeped in irony; to millions of Americans, Babalu is the theme song of Cuban bandleader Ricky Ricardo on television's *I Love Lucy.* In other sequences, Labat deconstructs the stereotypical gestures and objects (macho posturing, jai alai, maracas) that are used by the media to signify Latin culture.

Strengths and Weaknesses: This well-made and visually interesting tape is one of the early works by Labat, a talented video artist. It creatively portrays the African influence on Cuban culture.

Labat's tapes are extremely experimental and often obscure. Audiences not familiar with video art or Cuban exile could find this piece confusing.

Introducing the Tape: Viewers should be told that this is a satirical, experimental work dealing with Cubans in the United States. Students need to be introduced to the African Yoruba belief systems and structures, as well as to how the African formation influences the religious beliefs of many Latin American countries. Background on the Cuban exile experience and an introduction to cinematic symbolism and experimental video forms would be helpful.

How to Use: After viewing this tape, students could discuss the interplay of cultures in the film with the Afro-Caribbean poetry of Guillén or Ballagas, particularly noting musicality, linguistic interchange, presence of African religious symbols, and sensuality. (Gottlieb)

In *Media Studies, Transnationalism,* or *Migration Studies* the tape can be used to explore issues of identity and acculturation and the role of mass media.

Suggested Readings: González, José Luis, and Mónica Mansour. *Poesía negra de America: (antología)*

Mansour, Mónica. *Poesía Afro-Antillana.*

Books on Yoruba or Santería and the Cuban exile experience.

Poetry of Guillén or Ballagas (see bibliography for selection).

Level: University

EL BARRIO CANTA CON JOHNNY COLON (El Barrio Sings with Johnny Colon)

Documentary.   In English; Spanish Portions Not Subtitled. 30 min.   1987

Directed by: Eric Peña

Distributed by: Deep Dish TV

Evaluators: Elba D. Birmingham-Pokorny, Lourdes Fernández

Description: Dr. Carlota Suárez interviews the prominent Latino musician, singer, and composer Johnny Colón about the creation and goals of his school of music, founded in East Harlem, New York, in 1963. The tape documents the tremendous impact the school has had on Hispanic youth by offering a role model and an alternative to drugs, crime, and dropping out of high school.

Strengths and Weaknesses: The interview conveys the message of Johnny Colón's School of Music, and depicts an exciting community project. The musical performances by the groups adds an entertaining dimension to the message.

The tape's production quality is not high.

Introducing the Tape: None necessary.

How to Use: I would use this tape to introduce students to the prominent Hispanic presence in the United States, as well as to the richness of the Hispanic culture. This film also is extremely helpful in illustrating positive ways in which the Hispanic communities in the United States are dealing with the issues of drug abuse and school dropouts. (Birmingham-Pokorny)

Level: Junior High School—University

THE BIKE

Fiction.   With Subtitles.   11 min.   1991

Directed by: Gary Soto (43 the Crescent, Berkeley, CA 94708; tel: [510] 845-4718)

Distributed by: Gary Soto

Evaluators: Susan Lozada, Debbie Reyes

Description: Rudy, a Mexican American boy about ten years old, takes off on his bicycle for wacky adventures around his neighborhood. His mother forbids him to go down a certain block where "the dog will bite your behind," but his friend's magic trick frees him from the consequences of disobeying her.

Strengths and Weaknesses: The film realistically depicts a single-parent family. The characters are believable, and the acting and overall quality of the tape are excellent. The fantasy quality makes the video enjoyable viewing for young

audiences. Southern Californian children or Mexican children in the Southwest will particularly relate to it.

The ending is abrupt and could be confusing.

Introducing the Tape: This is a fun piece that speaks for itself and needs no introduction. Viewers could be told the ambiguous ending leaves it open for personal interpretation.

How to Use: I would use the film in *Language Arts* class for story writing, script/play writing, to stimulate students' writing of their own autobiographical stories. (Lozada)

In a *Junior High School Family Relations* unit the tape could be introduced by saying, "Sometimes parents advise you because they are trying to help you steer away from dangerous situations." (Reyes)

After viewing, students could be asked to write essays on: (1) their own parents' advice that has been helpful to them; (2) advice that they disagreed with or objected to.

Suggested Readings: Twain, Mark. *The Adventures of Huckleberry Finn.*

Level: Third Grade—University

BREAK OF DAWN

Documentary.   In English.   100 min.

Directed by: Isaac Artenstein

Produced by: Cinewest (700 Adella Lane, Coronado, CA 92118)

Distributed by: IMRE

Evaluators: David William Foster

Description: This docudrama, set in the 1940s, presents the story of the first Mexican American radio star. Owing to racial prejudice, he is framed for the sexual abuse of a minor and sentenced to jail.

Strengths and Weaknesses: A strength of the film is its treatment of a historical incident that unrelentingly portrays an abuse of justice; however, the whole matter is depicted in soap opera fashion.

Introducing the Tape: The film is self-explanatory.

How to Use: I would focus on the use of the soap opera genre as the major feature of the film and stress what is gained in terms of an unconfused representation of social injustice and what is lost in terms of the actual dynamics of power and the problems of a minority person's access to power. (Foster)

Level: High School—University

CAFE NORTE Y SUR (Cafe North and South)

Fiction,   With Subtitles.   30 min.   1988

Produced & Directed by: María Victoria Maldonado (P.O. Box 1165, Cooper Station, New York, NY 10276)

Distributed by: Victoria Maldonado, MacArthur Library Collection

Evaluators: Elba D. Birmingham-Pokorny, Graciela M. Castex, Carlos R. Delgado, Richard Stahler-Sholk

Description: In this fictional narrative set in New York's Lower East Side, Marpesa, a South American immigrant, helps run a cafe that serves as a meeting place for other Latin American immigrants. Favio, an alcoholic artist and the cafe owner, is romantically involved with Marpesa and pressures her for a commitment, but the young woman resists. The appearance of her longtime friend, Giovani, a South American Indian, arriving to participate in a conference for indigenous peoples, exacerbates her hesitation about whether to put down roots in New York. The rivalry between Favio and Giovani for the young woman's affections mirrors Marpesa's internal conflict between her Spanish and Indian roots. A theme throughout the film is the possibility of returning to Latin America in search of meaning and fulfillment. With its multiethnic clientele and South American/Native American dancers and musicians, the cafe encapsulates North and South and provides the metaphorical milieu for Marpesa's dilemma. Music from Peru, Ecuador, Bolivia, Colombia, the Caribbean, and even the Sioux Nation serves as a backdrop for the unfolding conflicts as a vehicle of cultural identity.

Strengths and Weaknesses: The filmmaker combines diverse media to convey the process of the search and reaffirmation of cultural identity. The portrayal of the characters' relationships is strong. The piece explores the link between cultural identity manifested in music, language, and art and individuals' awareness and self-esteem. The music is beautifully presented as a mosaic of different expressions and forms.

A few evaluators thought that the message of the story may seem unclear to U.S. viewers and that the tape could use more narration and character development.

Introducing the Tape: The cultural dilemma faced by Marpesa (outlined above) should be discussed with viewers.
How to Use: I would use the film to help students understand the opposing views held regarding the commemoration of Columbus's arrival in the New World and the multiethnic and multicultural nature of the Latin American society. It is also useful for helping students develop a better understanding and appreciation of the Latin American arts—music, dance, and other forms of visual art. (Birmingham-Pokorny)

This film could stimulate classroom discussion on the issues facing many immigrants who are living a *norte/sur* (north/south) existence. (Castex)

The film could be used to show how urban life affects individuals, particularly their sense of community and self, as well as to demonstrate the variety of Latin American cultural expressions. (Delgado)
Level: University

CASA PRIMAVERA
Documentary. Without Subtitles. 36 min. 1992
Produced & Directed by: Roberto Arévalo (44 Washington St., #817, Brookline, MA 02146; tel: [617] 739-1376)
Distributed by: Roberto Arevalo
Evaluators: David Bushnell, Grace Leavitt, J. Julian Rívera, Roger Sánchez
Description: This video provides a view of a culturally based treatment approach for Hispanic psychiatric patients in

Boston. It shows how specific elements of the Hispanic culture are integrated into the center's activities and provides evidence that patients respond well to this approach. The tape consists of interviews with clients and conversations with the directors and staff. A detailed explanation of the program emerges.

Strengths and Weaknesses: This tape effectively shows clients and staff members in a setting that appears real, convincing, and worthwhile. It provides examples of the application of cultural elements to the treatment of mental patients and important information about a socially oriented project in a U.S. Hispanic community.

Some evaluators felt that the tape was a bit too detailed and repetitious, with a lack of progression. Some clients are difficult to understand and should have been subtitled.
How to Use: The *Ethnicity* course in *Social Work* could use the tape to teach specific treatment approaches for Hispanic patients. (Rívera)
Complementary Films/Videos: *Garden of Hope,* about alternatives used in psychotherapy treatment in Cuba (distributed by IMRE).
Level: University

CHICANA (Chicana)
Documentary. In English. 23 min. 1979
Directed by: Sylvia Morales
Produced by: Sylvan Productions (12034 Washington Pl., Los Angeles, CA 90066; tel: [310] 391-0070)
Distributed by: Women Make Movies
Evaluators: Sarah Chambers, Eliana Moya Raggio, Suzanne Oboler, Pamela Voekel
Description: In this moving and empowering documentary, director Sylvia Morales weaves together vintage photos and drawings, interview footage, and Mexican murals to produce a visually stunning rendition of Chicana history. After briefly discussing the stereotypical roles for Mexican women, the film provides their more complex reality throughout history. Following a long history of Mexican and Chicana struggle to define the pre-Hispanic past as part of their own process of identity formation, Morales highlights the matriarchal roots of the Americas. The superbly crafted, fast-paced film then introduces the many heroic Mexican and Chicana women who have struggled for social justice in Mexico and the U.S. Southwest. It identifies women who played key roles in well-known historical periods: Sor Juana Iñez de la Cruz, Independence hero Joséfa Ortiz de Domínguez, union leader Lucia González Parsons, the revolutionary Dolores Jiménez y Muro, and the United Farm Workers' Dolores Huerta. The tape emphasizes women's participation in the labor force and in political struggles.

Strengths and Weaknesses: This is an empowering and inspirational film. It retells history from a woman's point of view, showing the continuities in women's conditions across national boundaries (U.S.-Mexico). A rich visual experience, it makes excellent use of art, sculpture, and photography, with impressive illustrations taken from pre-Columbian art and spectacular works of Diego Rivera, José Clemente Orozco, David Alfaro Siqueiros, Juan Cordero, and others. Photographs from the nineteenth and twentieth centuries are also fascinating. One evaluator appreciated the common treatment of greater Mexico, since few in the United States recognize the Spanish-American history of the U.S. Southwest.

The film may try to cover too much material in a short time, at the expense of some idealization, especially of the pre-Columbian period. At times it generalizes because of brevity, though for classroom purposes brevity is a strength. The tape may be a bit confusing, as it assumes basic knowledge of the histories of the U.S. Southwest and Mexico, moving quickly from one historical period to the next and back and forth over the border. Also, the tape needs to be updated.

Introducing the Tape: Viewers could use some background on the history of the U.S. Southwest and Mexico. To maintain historical accuracy, they should be told that many of the murals shown were not painted during the period they are depicting but rather in the postrevolutionary period.

How to Use: I would use this in a course on either *Women* or *Mexican History.* Students could focus on how examining the experiences of women broadens our understanding of historical events. I would also ask students to examine the extent to which women directly challenge their roles in society. (Chambers)

I would assign readings on Chicano history and include this tape in class when discussing current conditions. (Oboler)

This film could be used to discuss why history is always a contested terrain and how groups struggle to represent themselves and their history as part of more contemporary battles. This could lead into a larger discussion of how groups forge identities and whether Chicana identity is contested or fractured along the lines of class or region. (Voekel)

Suggested Readings: Anzaldúa, Gloria. *Borderlands/La Frontera: The New Mestiza.*

Arrom, Silvia Marina. *The Women of Mexico City, 1790–1857.*

Castilla-Speed, Lillian. *The Chicana Studies Index: Twenty Years of Gender Research, 1971–1991.*

Fernández-Kelly, María Patricia. *For We Are Sold, I and My People: Women and Industry in Mexico's Frontier.*

Franco, Jean. *Plotting Women: Gender and Representation in Mexico.*

Gutiérrez, Ramón A. *When Jesus Came, The Corn Mothers Went Away: Marriage, Sexuality, and Power in New Mexico, 1500–1840.*

Jensen, Joan M., and Darlis A. Miller, eds. *New Mexico Women: Intercultural Perspectives.*

Keller, Gary D., Rafael J. Magallan, and Alma M. García. *Curriculum Resources in Chicano Studies: Undergraduate and Graduate.*

Macias, Ana. *Against All Odds: The Feminist Movement in Mexico to 1940.*

Meier, Matt S. *Bibliography of Mexican-American History.*

National Association of Chicano Studies. *Chicana Voices: Intersections of Class, Race, and Gender,* papers for the 1984 conference.

Noriega, Chon A., ed. *Chicanos and Film: Essays on Chicano Representation and Resistance.*

Ruiz, Vicki L. *Cannery Women, Cannery Lives: Mexican Women, Unionization, and the California Food Processing Industry, 1930–1950.*

Segura, Denise. "Labor Market Stratification: The Chicana Experience." In *From Different Shores: Perspectives on Race and Ethnicity in America,* ed. Ronald Takaki.

Level: High School—University

EL CORRIDO (El Corrido)

Fiction.   Parts in both Spanish and English.   68 min.   1989

Directed by: Luis Valdez

Produced by: Teatro Campesino (P.O. Box 1240, San Juan Bautista, CA, 95045; tel: [408] 623-2444; fax: [408] 623-4127)

Distributed by: Teatro Campesino

Evaluators: Alberto J. Carlos, Osvaldo Chinchón, Rene González, Suzanne Oboler

Description: The Teatro Campesino players present a political drama about Mexican laborers and the traditional *corrido* music. A group of farmworkers is recruited to go fruit picking and travel by truck to a farm a long distance away. During the trip, a young, fast-talking Chicano tries to impress those in the truck with his facility in speaking English but instead alienates some of them, who call him a *pocho* (someone of Mexican origin who acts more like an American in his use of language and habits). Before arriving at their destination, the young Chicano undergoes a transformation when he is given a guitar by an older worker who teaches him a few of the songs (*corridos*) of old Mexican tradition.

One *corrido* performed in the film tells the story of José Pelado Rascuache, a migrant worker who leaves Mexico for the United States and is exploited as an undocumented rural worker. He marries and has four children. His entire family works in the fields as scab labor. The family later moves to the city and then breaks apart. The father eventually dies in the welfare office, the children forget their roots and go to jail and to war in Vietnam.

Strengths and Weaknesses: This is a well-written, intelligent piece in which the actors demonstrate their dazzling and varied talents. They sing, play, dance, mimic, exaggerate, underplay, and use satire. The tape clearly demonstrates the importance of the *corrido* and oral tradition in Mexican American culture and history. Included are examples of *corridos* and musical traditions from Mexico and the U.S.-Mexican border. The excellent story line serves as political commentary and satire. It introduces topics such as cultural shock/transition, acculturation, assimilation, the bicultural mobile existence, economic exploitation of the migrant worker community, adaptation to an urban environment, the intergenerational differences between first and second generations, machismo, and abuse.

One evaluator felt that the tape was too long and repetitious, with a number of predictable situations and the same *corrido* music repeated. Another reviewer felt that the peculiar mixture of Spanish and English spoken by the Mexican Americans could make the tape difficult to use in Spanish language classes.

Introducing the Tape: An introduction should include an overview of the history of Mexican Americans and Mexican emigration to the United States. Viewers should be told that the Spanish spoken by some of these Mexican Americans does not correspond to the standard Spanish spoken by Mexicans and other Spanish Americans. The places where English words have been incorporated into the spoken Spanish could be noted as examples of the blending that occurs with cultural contact. For example these farmworkers talk about *picar frutas,* influenced by the English verb to "pick."

How to Use: This tape, complemented by appropriate pages from Acuña's book, could be used to describe living conditions for Mexican Americans in the period from roughly 1900–1960. I would ask students to learn something about the Mexican *corrido,* using Américo Paredes' *With His Pistol in His Hand* and by viewing the *corrido* tape made for the Public Broadcasting System (PBS) with Linda Ronstadt, the Valdez brothers, etc., to compare the two representations. (Carlos)

I would use this tape in conjunction with articles on *Mexican Immigration* and perhaps to organize a role-play and debate on the various points of view in the *corrido.* (Oboler)

In a *High School* class students could be asked to write their own *corrido* in reference to the struggles they or their relatives may have faced when migrating to the United States.

Suggested Readings: Acuña, Rodolfo. *Occupied America,* chap. 6.

Paredes, Américo. *"With His Pistol in His Hand," a Border Ballad and Its Hero.*

Level: Junior High School—University

DESPUES DEL TERREMOTO (After the Earthquake)
Fiction.   In Spanish and English.   23 min.   1991
Produced & Directed by: Lourdes Portillo (981 Esmeralda St., San Francisco, CA 94110)
Distributed by: Women Make Movies, Third World Newsreel
Evaluators: Florence Babb, Richard C. Boly, Susan Ryan
Description: The film is set in San Francisco in 1976. Irene, a young Nicaraguan woman working as a maid, awaits the arrival of her fiancé, Julio, whom she hasn't seen since the 1972 earthquake in Nicaragua. Dramatic tension arises when Julio visits, and it is apparent that they have grown apart. He has become politicized after torture by the government at home. Julio

disturbs the complacency of the exile community with a slide show containing horrible scenes from their homeland.
Strengths and Weaknesses: This is a well-acted, strong story that effectively portrays Irene's daily life, work relationships, and the difficult questions that Julio raises. The film is simple (not pretentious), fluid, and compact.

One evaluator mentioned that the only drawback is the tape's short length, which limits an in-depth development of issues. The film is dated, since the clothes and surroundings clearly are set in the 1970s. Also, the country of origin is not stated.

Introducing the Tape: A brief introduction contextualizing the tape could be useful. Background should indicate that the country of origin is Nicaragua, with information on the earthquake's date, the extent of the destruction, the period of Somoza's rule, and the Sandinista Revolution. Also some discussion of the number of Nicaraguans in the United States and why they emigrated would be helpful.

How to Use: This tape could be used in a course on *Latin American Economy and Society* for debating political issues in Nicaragua. In a course on *Latinos in the United States* the film could stimulate discussion about the dichotomy of these communities both in cultural and political terms. (Babb)

The film would be useful in terms of discussing the problems of exile, the desire to maintain traditions while still adapting to the new situation. It would be useful also for a discussion of women filmmakers and their attempts to look at gender issues in a broader political context. (Ryan)

Suggested Readings: Booth, John A. *The End and the Beginning: The Nicaraguan Revolution.*

Walker, Tom. *Land of Sandino.*

Level: University

DISTANT WATERS
Fiction.   In English with Spanish Portions Subtitled.   29 min.   1990
Produced & Directed by: Carlos Avila (8051 Lincoln Blvd. #5, Los Angeles, CA 90045; tel: [213] 215-0878; fax: [213] 221-4564)
Distributed by: Carlos Avila
Evaluators: Joan A. McGinnis, Jorge Porras
Description: This critically acclaimed, award-winning film tells the bittersweet story of a Chicano boy growing up in 1943 Los Angeles. The story, which has both comedic and dramatic elements, is set against the backdrop of the zoot suit riots and segregated swimming pools. The story includes scenes depicting cultural friction and racial strife and focuses on the impact that segregation has on the young protagonist and his family. The film's black-and-white photography and visual style are reminiscent of the neorealist films of the 1940s and 1950s.
Strengths and Weaknesses: This is a well-acted, insightful story with humorous incidents and good music. It presents a positive view of the Chicano community and stresses the importance of the family.

Introducing the Tape: The tape needs an introduction to Chicano culture in the U.S. Southwest and some information about immigration. Young viewers would benefit from an introduction to the era of zoot suits and a definition of *pachuchos*.

How to Use: I would provide background on this era or have students research zoot suits and *pachuchos*. The film could introduce a discussion of discrimination and racial tensions and possible solutions. (McGinnis)

I would use this in *Spanish Language* courses for listening comprehension and in *Culture* courses about Mexican Americans in the United States. (Porras)

The tape's themes can be compared and contrasted to those of modern times, particularly focusing on racism.
Level: High School—University

DOLORES (Dolores)

Fiction.   In Spanish and English.   45 min.   1988
Directed by: Pablo Figueroa
Distributed by: The Cinema Guild
Evaluators: Mary Jo Dudley, Joan A. McGinnis, Susy Suárez
Description: Based on extensive research and interviews with battered Latina women, this docudrama addresses the issue of domestic violence in the U.S. Latino household. It is based on the story of Dolores, a women who finds herself caught in the web of trying to please everyone in her family and avoid violent reactions on the part of her husband. The video shows how the husband's machismo has intimidated both Dolores and her daughter into continual fear of physical abuse and alienated the son, who resents his father's conduct.
Strengths and Weaknesses: This video makes a strong argument about the pressures on Latina women in relationships where the woman is dominated primarily by her husband and secondarily by her family in general. Designed to raise awareness and stimulate discussion, it addresses issues including domestic violence, fidelity, and family pressure, and presents a situation that is not uncommon for women. The photography, story line, and suspense are effective. The tape graphically touches on the themes of machismo and "life is a dream" of Calderón de la Barca. Dolores's dream is a veritable nightmare from which she is forced to awaken.

The weakness of this tape is that it may reinforce negative stereotypes of Latino men, and thus it must be preceded with an introduction. The tape graphically depicts the effects of a relationship of domination and domestic violence and may be too violent for young viewers. One evaluator felt the acting was weak.
Introducing the Tape: The preface should explain that the situation presented does not apply to all Latino families and that it portrays a relationship of male-female domination resulting in domestic violence that crosses race and class lines. It also depicts the pressures that can be placed on young men (Latinos and others) to live up to macho expectations.
How to Use: This tape is relevant for a course on *Contem-*

porary Topics in Latin America and for *Transnational Communities,* in which we explore the situation of Latinos in the United States. The tape requires both an introduction and a follow-up discussion. Its brevity makes it manageable for classroom viewing. (Dudley)

I would discuss domestic violence and ask students to consider the situation from the viewpoint of the opposite gender. (McGinnis)
Suggested Readings: Barca, Calderón, de la. *La vida es sueño. (Life Is a Dream).*
Level: High School—University

DRUGS ON THE LOWER EAST SIDE

Documentary.   In English.   20 min.   1983
Directed by: Educational Video Center
Produced by: Educational Video Center (55 E. 25 Street, New York, NY 10010 (tel: [212] 725-3534; fax: [212] 725-6501)
Distributed by: Educational Video Center
Evaluators: Rebeca Harclerode, Christine List
Description: Made by a group of New York City high school students about their neighborhood, this documentary follows drug users and pushers, offering an intimate look at these usually anonymous people. The tape shows the community demonstrating against the drug users. Through interviews, people involved in different aspects of the drug trade explain why they sell drugs. With 50 percent unemployment in their community, it is not surprising that young people turn to the drug trade for a living. The tape ends by portraying the home life of one dealer, who ends up by leaving town because of a threat to her life.
Strengths and Weaknesses: This tape is a good example of community-based filmmaking. Because the filmmakers are part of the community portrayed, the tape investigates the drug culture in a New York neighborhood with an authenticity and insight rarely seen in the mainstream media. The tape has a good introduction. It is short and to the point.

The amateur-style camera work may alienate some viewers, but if understood within the context of how and by whom the tape was made, it does not present a problem.
Introducing the Tape: Viewers should be told that this work was made by a group of high school students in a community media program about an issue of concern to them.
How to Use: In *Spanish* and *Social Studies* classes I would compare and contrast the two largest Hispanic groups in the United States (Puerto Ricans and Mexicans). I would discuss their reasons for coming to this country as well as some of the problems they encounter as a minority in this society. (Harclerode)

In a *Communications/Video Production* course I would use this tape as an example of guerrilla filmmaking and community-based production at its best. (List)

The tape ends abruptly, which could inspire role-play and essays concerning the future for young people in poor urban neighborhoods.

In a *High School Social Studies* unit on *Urban Studies* this would be an excellent tool to begin discussion and essays on urban problems and possible solutions.
Level: Junior High School—University

ENTRE AMIGOS (Between Friends)
Fiction.   In English.   26 min.   1990
Directed by: Severo Pérez
Produced by: Ideas in Motion, Lynn Adler (2600 10th St., Suite 430, Berkeley, CA 94708; tel: [510] 843-3884; fax: [510] 841-2833)
Distributed by: Churchill Films
Evaluators: Susana Conde, Susan Lozada, Jorge Porras
Description: The script of this educational fiction film, sponsored by the San Francisco Department of Public Health, is based on a report about the infection of Latino people with the acquired immune deficiency (AIDS) virus through casual sex. The story takes place in the Mission District of San Francisco, where most of the Latino population of the city is concentrated. Monica lies to her sick mother and skips junior high school regularly to go to parties where sex and drugs are the main form of entertainment. Her friend Gloria, portrayed as not too square but responsible, attends one of the parties and rejects the scene. At the party, Monica gets into an argument with a young man who feels that she should have sex with him because he gave her drugs. Gloria and her friends take Monica home. There they all find out that Monica's mother has AIDS and has been taken to the hospital. A health clinic counselor advises Monica of the risks she is taking by using drugs and having unprotected sex.
Strengths and Weaknesses: This is a well-done, dramatized message for Latino teenagers. The acting by the teens is completely convincing, and the message is one that most young people can relate to. Important information about condoms, safe sex, drugs, and machismo is given in a nondidactic manner.

One evaluator felt the tape could have been more complete and varied.
How to Use: In a *High School Health* or *Social Studies* class students could be asked to reflect on the experiences of people they know with AIDS.
Level: Junior High School—High School

ESPERANZA (Esperanza)
Fiction.   In English with Spanish Portions Subtitled.   53 min.   1985
Directed by: Sylvia Morales
Produced by: Jean Victor (12034 Washington Pl., Los Angeles, CA 90066; tel: [213] 390-2282)
Distributed by: Sylvia Morales
Evaluators: George Beelen, Silvia Hyre, Danusia L. Meson, Suzanne Oboler, Wayne S. Osborn, Engracia Schuster, Pamela Voekel
Description: Set in Los Angeles, this film provides a searing look at the destructive consequences of U.S. immigration pol-

icy on the lives of a refugee family from Chiapas, Mexico. Esperanza, a young teenage girl, has recently arrived in Los Angeles with her mother and six-year-old brother, Miguel, in hopes of joining their father, a migrant worker. The family struggles with poverty, the difficulty of communicating with the English-speaking world, loss of family members, discrimination, alienation, fear of the immigration police, and the desire to return to Mexico. Their worst fears are realized when the mother is turned in by a neighbor and picked up by immigration officials. The children are left alone and are befriended by a young Chicano boy named Ricky. Esperanza and Miguel set off to find their father, who is working in a city north of Los Angeles. They show great creativity and resourcefulness by selling tamales to earn the money needed for the bus trip. When a policeman enters the bus station, Miguel runs in fear, and their plans abruptly end. The children are taken away to an unknown destiny, presumably to be deported back to Mexico.
Strengths and Weaknesses: This is a compelling docudrama that humanizes the immigrant experience. It stands out, as there are few videos that explore the theme of immigration from a child's point of view. Truly an engrossing story, the tape holds the viewers' interest and is fast-paced enough for younger audiences. It effectively and empathetically conveys the plight and desperation of the children and is an accurate portrayal of the circumstances that many undocumented immigrants must face. While profiling one family, the tape generalizes beyond the individual story to the broader issues of cultural assimilation, the downward mobility of political refugees in the United States, and U.S. immigration policy. It is sensitive, professionally done, and particularly useful for junior high and high school students.

The tape seems to have been designed as a trigger for discussion, as it offers no suggestions for solutions to the problem. One evaluator felt that it is slow moving and repetitive at times.
Introducing the Tape: An introduction concerning the situation of undocumented workers and families and the Immigration and Naturalization Service (INS) is needed. Discussion of California Proposition 187, its reflection of conservative anti-immigrant sentiment, implications for undocumented immigrants, and questionable constitutionality would put the tape in more recent context. The tape could also stimulate a discussion among students about what they might do if something similar happened to them.
How to Use: I could use this film to discuss multiculturalism and immigration in *U.S. History* courses. (Beelen)

Students could read a short story by a Mexican American writer, a description of the history of Mexican immigration to the United States, and a current newspaper account of what is occurring at the border. They could then see the video for a more personalized version of what the numbers and statistics are conveying. (Meson)

I would use the tape as part of a lesson in culture, primarily as an example of how poor Latin Americans struggle in their own countries as well as in the United States. (Schuster)

The film could be used as an introduction to the study of U.S. immigration policy, Chicano-Mexican relations in the urban context, and the experiences of immigrant families. (Voekel)

Suggested Readings: Anaya, Rudolfo. *Aztlan: Essays on the Chicano Homeland.*

Carrera, John Wilshire. *Immigrant Students: Their Legal Right of Access to Public Schools: A Guide for Advocates and Educators.*

Cisneros, Sandra. Several works of fiction describing the Mexican American experience (see bibliography for selection).

Cockcroft, James. *Outlaws in the Promised Land: Mexican Immigrant Workers and America's Future.*

Conover, Ted. *Coyotes: A Journey through the Secret World of America's Illegal Aliens.*

Cruz, Pablo. *Pablo Cruz and the American Dream: The Experience of an Undocumented Immigrant from Mexico.*

Davis, Marilyn P. *Mexican Voices, American Dreams: An Oral History of Mexican Immigration to the United States.*

Fernández, Celestino. *The Border Patrol and News Media Coverage of Undocumented Mexican Immigration during the 1970s: A Quantitative Content Analysis in the Sociology of Knowledge.*

First, Joan McCarty. *New Voices: Immigrant Students in U.S. Public Schools.*

Heer, David M. *Undocumented Mexicans in the United States.*

Hundley, Norris, Jr., ed. *The Chicano.*

Lewis, Oscar. *The Children of Sanchez: Autobiography of a Mexican Family.*

McWilliams, Carey, *North from Mexico: The Spanish-Speaking People of the United States.*

Nathan, Debbie. *Women and Other Aliens: Essays from the U.S.-Mexico Border.*

Prago, Albert. *Strangers in Their Own Land.*

Reimers, David M. *Still the Golden Door: The Third World Comes to America.*

Schorr, Alan Edward. *Refugee and Immigrant Resource Directory, 1990–1991.*

Valdez, R. Burciaga, Kevin F. McCarthy, and Connie Malcolm Moreno. *An Annotated Bibliography of Sources of Mexican Immigration.*

The University of Texas at Austin Benson Latin American Collection stocks updated guides on Mexican immigration to the United States. To obtain a free copy, write to: Series Editor Ann Hartness, The Benson Latin American Collection, SRH 1.109, Austin, Texas 78713–7330.

Villareal, Roberto, and Norma Hernández. *Latinos and Political Conditions: Political Empowerment for the 1990s.*

Villaseñor, Víctor. *Rain of Gold.*

Level: Junior High School—University

1492 REVISITED

Documentary.   With Subtitles.   28 min.   1992

Directed by: Paul Espinosa

Produced by: Paul Espinosa (5200 Campanile Dr., San Diego, CA 92182-5400; tel: [619] 594-5996; fax: [619] 265-6417)

Distributed by: University of California Extension Center

Evaluators: María Fernández

Description: This tape contains statements from artists, scholars, and curators who participated in the exhibition "Counter Colon-Ialismo," a visual arts exhibit that reexamined the Quincentennial. The exhibit investigates the construction of history and brings out alternative views that have been silenced.

Strengths and Weaknesses: An intelligent treatment of interesting and provocative subject matter. The camera work and editing are well done.

Introducing the Tape: The tape is self-explanatory and needs no introduction to be understood.

How to Use: I would use this tape as the basis for a discussion of how histories are written and what kinds of historical narratives are favored by scholars. I would also use it for a discussion of how art might contribute to the writing of history. (Fernández)

Suggested Readings: Tedlock, Dennis. "Torture in the Archives."

White, Hayden. *Tropics of Discourse: Essays in Cultural Criticism.*

Level: University

GLOBAL DISSENT

Documentary.   In English with Spanish Portions Subtitled. 30 min.   1991

Directed by: Tony Avalos

Produced by: Gulf Crisis TV Project/Deep Dish (339 Lafayette St., New York, NY 10012; tel: [212] 473-8933; fax: [212] 420-8223)

Distributed by: Deep Dish

Evaluators: Suzanne Austin Alchon, Glenn J. Kist, Donald J. Mabry, Richard Stahler-Sholk

Description: This tape provides a global perspective on U.S. foreign policy and foreign intervention, focusing specifically on the early 1990s. Taking the Gulf War as a point of departure, it examines the groundswell of protest in the United States and around the globe against the emerging New World Order. There is footage of demonstrations, speeches, and interviews with activists, as well as scenes of U.S. military interventions and poverty in the United States and the Third World.

Strengths and Weaknesses: The tape generated mixed responses from the evaluators. One evaluator felt that it provides an important counterpoint to the U.S. government's attempts to portray universal consensus behind its foreign policy in the post-cold war era. Another commented on the great introduction and powerful images that capture students' attention.

Other reviewers felt the tape is one-sided, calling it "left-wing propaganda." It does not place the events or comments of the speakers in any context. The video asserts, yet does not prove, that the majority in the Third World opposed the Gulf War, and that the war was simply a capitalist conspiracy fostered by the United States for its own economic and political gain. Some of the material in the video is already outdated (e.g., on the war in El Salvador and U.S. bases in the Philippines).

Introducing the Tape: Instructors should place the video in context, making clear that the producers of the film were a collective of independent video makers who were opposed to the U.S. invasion of Iraq during the Gulf War. The information about El Salvador and the Philippines needs to be updated. An introduction to the North American Free Trade Agreement (NAFTA) and U.S. involvement in Haiti and Somalia would also add important information.

How to Use: I would use this tape in my *Latin American History* survey to give students an overview of U.S. interference around the world and to generate discussion. I showed this to several students and we had a great discussion. (Austin Alchon)

I would use the tape to discuss U.S. foreign policy and the New World Order. (Stahler-Sholk).

Suggested Readings: Broad, Dave, and Lori Foster, eds. *The New World Order and the Third World.*

Chomsky, Noam. *Deterring Democracy.*

Icaza, Jorge. *Huasipungo. The Villagers, a Novel.*

Menchú, Rigoberta. *I, Rigoberta Menchú: An Indian Woman in Guatemala.*

Peters, Cynthia, ed. *Collateral Damage: The "New World Order" at Home and Abroad.*

Skidmore Thomas, and Peter Smith. *Modern Latin America.*

Walker, Thomas. *Nicaragua: Land of Sandino.*

Woodward, Bob. *The Commanders.*

Level: University

HISTORIAS PARALELAS (Home Is Struggle)
Documentary. With Subtitles. 37 min. 1992
Produced & Directed by: Marta Bautis (505 East 6th St., Apt #3, New York, NY 10009; tel: [212] 673-8065)
Distributed by: Women Make Movies
Evaluators: Elba D. Birmingham-Pokorny, Kate Blanas, Martha Rees
Description: This tape documents the life experiences of four Latin American women immigrants in their countries of origin and in the United States. By means of flashbacks and personal testimony, the tape explores the impact that the patriarchal system and the U.S. interventionist policies have had on: (1) the lives of these women; (2) the social, economic, cultural, and political oppression of the Latin American people; and (3) the political destiny of Latin American society. The interviews of the immigrant women are interspersed with scenes acted out by actors/actresses portraying the traditional roles of women.

Strengths and Weaknesses: The tape defines the women's dissatisfaction with the roles society has assigned them. The role of women as catalysts for social, economic, political, and historical change is documented. The tape renders homage to the tremendous strength and courage of Latin American women in the face of sexual and economic exploitation and political repression.

Some reviewers felt that the tape failed to contrast the lives of these four women in the United States with life in their own countries. One evaluator thought that without an introduction, the tape could be seen as overemphasizing the "woman as doormat" role.

Introducing the Tape: The principal audience for *"Historias Paralelas"* is Latinas and Latin American women. The tape's main objective is to present women as active participants in the transformation of their lives. The shared stories can be used as topics for analyzing and discussing the tape.

For other audiences, instructors may want to provide some background on the social and political situation in the countries being mentioned, and in Latin America in general. A study guide for this tape will soon be available. For information, contact the distributor.

How to Use: I plan to use this tape to call students' attention to some of the factors responsible for the disappearance of the extended family and the role of women in Latin American society. It can also help raise students' awareness of the impact of U.S. interventionist policies in the socioeconomic, political, cultural, and historical reality of both the Latin American and U.S. societies, particularly regarding the demographic changes taking place within the American society. This tape will also be extremely helpful in a *Phonetics* course to acquaint students with the differences existing in the Spanish spoken in Chile, Argentina, the Dominican Republic, and Nicaragua. (Birmingham-Pokorny)
Level: High School—University

LA IDEA QUE HABITAMOS (The Idea We Live In)
Documentary. Mixed Language, Parts in English and Spanish. 19 min. 1990
Directed by: Pilar Rodríguez
Produced by: Anarca Films (Grama 111, El Rosario Coyoacán, México D.F.; tel: [525] 618-2781)
Distributed by: Women Make Movies
Evaluators: Emperatriz Arreaza-Camero
Description: This experimental film is a reflection on the meaning of "home." Is it four walls? A sheet for a roof? A garden? A womb? The filmmakers use different poems to explain their diverse concepts of home.
Strengths and Weaknesses: With excellent camera work and editing, the film makes an effective match of images and poems. The tape contains English and Spanish, but sections are not translated for single-language viewers.
Introducing the Tape: A brief introduction to concepts of ethnicity, gender, and class in the United States would be useful.

How to Use: I would present this film in a class that deals with ethnicity, class, and gender in the United States and how the concept of "container," "home," and "universe" is permeated by the ethnic experience in this country. (Arreaza-Camero)

Suggested Readings: Anzaldua, G. *Borderlands: La frontera: The New Mestiza.*

Anzaldua, G., ed. *Making Face, Making Soul—Haciendo Caras: Creative and Critical Perspectives of Women of Color.*

Cisneros, Sandra. Short stories and novel (see bibliography for selection).

Bhabha, Homi K., ed. *Nation and Narration.*

Minh-Ha, Trihn Thi. *Woman, Native, Other: Writing Post-Coloniality and Feminism.*

Level: High School—University

IN THE SHADOW OF LAW

Documentary.   In English and Spanish.   58 min.   1987
Directed by: Paul Espinosa
Produced by: Paul Espinosa (5200 Campanile Dr., San Diego, CA 92182-5400; tel: [619] 594-5996; fax: [619] 265-6417)
Distributed by: University of California Extension Center
Evaluators: Osvaldo Chinchón
Description: This documentary, produced by KPBS-TV of San Diego in 1987, presents the portraits of several undocumented immigrants and their long legal procedures to avoid deportation back to Mexico. The U.S. Immigration and Naturalization Service (INS) deals with the cases of four different families who migrated illegally to the San Diego area. These families may remain because they had children born in the United States. However, they must prove that they resided in the United States from 1972 until 1986, the time of the amnesty provision passed by the U.S. Congress. One portrait follows Amalia, a single mother who has no proof that her adult son was born in the United States. Amalia gave birth at home, fearing she would be turned over to the INS by the hospital.
Strengths and Weaknesses: A strong point of this documentary is the truthful testimony of these immigrants. They reveal their aspirations and fears for themselves and their children and the uncertainty of living in the shadow of the law. They speak in clear Spanish and in a candid, engaging manner. The introduction and translation of passages in Spanish are also excellent.
Introducing the Tape: Instructors could discuss the film in light of the 1994 California Proposition 187 and its ramifications for undocumented immigrants.
How to Use: After viewing the film, *Spanish Language* or *English as a Second Language* students could write an essay, letter, or diary entry from the point of view of an undocumented immigrant.
Complementary Films/Videos: *Esperanza* (U.S.A.).
Level: High School—University

KIKIRIKI (Kikiriki)

Experimental.   In English.   11 min.   1983
Directed by: Tony Labat
Distributed by: Electronic Arts Intermix
Evaluators: Jules Benjamin, Enrique R. Rodríguez, Pamela M. Smorkaloff, Angharad N. Valdivia
Description: In a fragmented, staccato composition, *Kikiriki* explores cultural dislocation, alienation, and media representation of the immigrant as "other." Structured as a journey in which video maker Labat leaves the lush, romanticized beauty of home and stumbles onto land after a long sea voyage, this work confronts the bewildering process of adaptation and displacement. Vibrant hand-held Super-8 film footage of the streets of Havana and Miami is contrasted with negative mass-media stereotypes. Negative images include headlines of a hijacking to Havana by a Cuban, television images of the *Marielitos* (Cuban boat people) as bloodthirsty ex-convicts. Using split screens, quick cutting, and pastiche, Labat juxtaposes mass-media images, real narratives of culturally marginalized men and women, and ironic visual metaphors.
Strengths and Weaknesses: The tape is well crafted and visually fascinating. Its political stance is purposely ambiguous.

Labat's tapes are extremely experimental and often obscure and confusing. The ironic humor is geared to other Cuban Americans; thus many things would be lost on outsiders.
Introducing the Tape: Viewers should be told that this is a satirical, experimental work dealing with Cuban immigrants in the United States. An introduction to experimental media forms and video art would be helpful.
Level: University

LATINO IMAGES

Documentary.   In English with Spanish Portions Subtitled. 58 min.   1988
Directed by: Yvette Nieves Cruz and Susana Aikin
Produced by: Deep Dish TV (339 Lafayette St. New York, NY 10012; tel: [212] 473-8933; fax: [212] 420-8223)
Distributed by: Deep Dish TV
Evaluators: Robin Andersen, Graciela M. Castex, Sandra J. Guardado, Laura Elisa Pérez, Nancy Saporta Sternbach
Description: In interviews, diverse Latino/Latina video producers discuss their experiences, creative inspirations, social purposes, and future plans. Juxtaposed with their comments are video segments of their works. The compilation of extremely rich material leaves viewers with a heightened sense of, and appreciation for, the diverse Latino/Latina heritage and the struggle for acceptance and understanding within the dominant U.S. culture. Represented in the over twenty videos of varied genres are: Chicano poetry; Puerto Rican immigrants; music instructors in New York City; old Nicaraguan men recounting encounters with Sandino; women strikers in Oakland mixed with a Mercedes Sosa

song, "Trabajando"; urban housing problems and issues of community; a critique of images of Latinas in the mass media (intercut with footage of Carmen Miranda); an analysis of a beer advertisement and its objectification of women; a Salvadoran peasant rally with an explanation of U.S. policy; and, finally, a brilliant segment on Guatemala, using Edin Vélez's *Meta Mayan II,* which employs a television newscaster's voice over powerful images of Guatemalan women.

Strengths and Weaknesses: This is a creative, informative, and effective treatment of issues of multiculturalism, focusing on Hispanic Americans in the United States. The range of cultural diversity represented is compelling. The quality of the interviews is impressive: the men and women articulate the nature of their work and experiences and, refreshingly, the sense of social and cultural purpose they bring to that work. They present interesting and touching life stories. The tape contains a richness in its depiction of history that can expand to a discussion in the classroom about the treatment of history.

The film contains so much information in different formats that it may be overpowering for a single viewing with some audiences. There is no central focus, and the structure can be confusing without an introduction. The video clips are also of mixed quality; some are more articulate and informative than others. One evaluator felt that many of the interviews with the producers were more successful than the clips of their work.

Introducing the Tape: A summary of the tape's format is necessary to avoid viewer confusion. Audiences should be told that the video segments of various genres are samples of the interviewed artists' works. Beyond that, the tape stands on its own as an introduction to the work and issues of U.S. Latino/Latina video art as oppositional cultural practice.

How to Use: This tape is useful for a number of different topics: as independent and experimental video, testimonial art, the rich multiculturalism in the United States, accomplished women and Latino video producers, Latin American traditions, and U.S. foreign policy. It also contains some wonderful video graphics done by the tape producers, Deep Dish TV, and effectively exemplifies some alternative advertising for nonprofit organizations. (Andersen)

I would first discuss the history of immigrants and their fate in this country and bring the class up to date on recent issues. The postviewing discussion would include an analysis of the images, asking students how artists use juxtaposition, irony, language, and acquired images to create their statements. (Guardado)

Complementary Films/Videos: *El X; Alambrista; The Ballad of Gregorio Cortez, Zoot Suit* (distributed by El Teatro Campesino), to illustrate how Latino artists are dealing with their history.

Level: High School—University

THE LEMON GROVE INCIDENT

Docudrama. In English with Spanish Portions Subtitled. 58 min. 1985

Directed by: Frank Cristopher

Produced by: Paul Espinosa (5200 Campanile Dr., San Diego, CA 92182-5400; tel: [619] 594-5996; fax: [619] 265-6417)

Distributed by: The Cinema Guild

Evaluators: René Arbelado Gonzáles, Paolo Carpignano, Iris Engstrand, Elizabeth Merena, Chon Noriega

Description: Director Espinosa reconstructs the history of the first successful desegregation case in the United States. In a small California town in 1930, white school administrators tried to segregate their school and send the Mexican American children to an inferior building for their classes. The Mexican American parents organized, filed a lawsuit, and, after a very tense trial, won their case. *The Lemon Grove Incident* combines scripted reenactments and documentary interviews with participants recalling their experiences as children. Both local and national contexts are mentioned as factors contributing to the climate of racism, including President Hoover's repatriation programs and the introduction of the Bliss bill in California. This is a story of a successful civil rights struggle, twenty years before *Brown v. Board of Education.*

Strengths and Weaknesses: The tape has an interesting and effective mix of ethnographic text, oral histories of actual participants, and dramatic recreations. It is simply written and clearly addresses segregation problems and solutions, demonstrating the strength of organizing. Like much of the Chicano experience, the event portrayed in the tape was an invisible moment in U.S. history. In general, it is an excellent overview of race relations and educational policy.

Some evaluators felt that the acting is flat but the film is adequate, standard educational television fare (made for KPBS-TV in San Diego) with period costuming that gives an authentic ambience. For a younger audience, the tape provides a relevance and immediacy to the story that would otherwise be entirely lacking. Transitions between documentary parts and dramatic scenes are not always smooth.

How to Use: In *Sociology, Education, U.S. History,* or *Mexican-American History* classes, the tape can be shown to illustrate themes of desegregation and civil rights.

Level: Junior High School—University

LIFE IN THE G: GOWANUS GENTRIFIED

Documentary. In English. 20 min. 1988

Directed by: Héctor Sánchez

Produced by: Educational Video Center (55 E. 25 Street, New York, NY 10010; tel: [212] 725-3534; fax: [212] 725-6501)

Distributed by: Educational Video Center

Evaluators: Rebeca Harclerode, Christine List, Suzanne Oboler

Description: This autobiographical, student-produced video illuminates the neighborhood gentrification process in the 1980s and its effects on the hopes and dreams of young Puerto Ricans for their future. It includes interviews with residents, real estate agents, businessmen, community organizers, and activists. Héctor Sánchez talks about the housing projects where he grew up and interviews his mother, Ada Sánchez, who describes the changes in society that have taken place since she arrived from Puerto Rico. A community organizer discusses the rise in rents, the gentrification that squeezes out the community of poor residents, and how the American dream of living well is out of reach for Hispanics and African Americans. The tape suggests that the only solution is for the community to unite and fight displacement.

Strengths and Weaknesses: This is a well-produced student video that is particularly interesting because of its teenage point of view on gentrification.

One evaluator felt that the tape gives only a cursory look at the causes and problems of gentrification. The technical quality is a bit amateurish; however, in the context of high school student-made work, it does not present a problem.

Introducing the Tape: An introduction should explain that the tape is about the gentrification of one student's neighborhood, the Gowanus area in Brooklyn, New York. Viewers should be told that the documentary was made by high school students in a community video program.

How to Use: In a *High School Video Production* class this tape could be used as a successful example of how students could use video to express the realities of their life and make connections to broader social issues faced by their community. Students could then discuss issues that are of concern to them and how they could use video to address these issues.

The tape can also be used to stimulate student writing, comparing or contrasting their own lives/living situations with those of the student in the tape.

Level: Junior High School—University

LOST IN THE TRANSLATION
Experimental.   In English.   8 min.   1984
Directed by: Tony Labat
Distributed by: Electronic Arts Intermix
Evaluators: Jules Benjamin, Graciela M. Castex, Enrique R. Rodríguez, Pamela M. Smorkaloff
Description: In this elusive exploration of identity, marginalization, and difference, video maker Labat constructs a nonlinear narrative from fragmented images and sounds that have been decontextualized and thus "lose something in the translation." Layering the fictive and the real, he stages scenes, including an artist's model imitating the pose of Ingres's Odalisque, and repeats words and images to confound meaning. In an ironic play on anonymity, black strips are placed on television "talking heads" to conceal the subjects' identities. Through associative imagery and ruptured narratives, Labat creates a collage of disorientation and otherness, replicating the mediated experience of "a bad joke told in a foreign language."
Strengths and Weaknesses: The tape is well made and vi-

sually provocative. Issues about language are creatively presented.

Labat's tapes are extremely experimental and may be confusing if they are not put into a social context.
Introducing the Tape: Viewers should be told that this is a satirical, experimental work dealing with Cuban immigrants in the United States. An introduction to experimental video forms and cinematic symbolism would be helpful.
How to Use: The tape could be used in a *Video Production* class as an example of experimental work.
Level: University

MAYAMI: BETWEEN CUT AND ACTION
Experimental.   With Subtitles.   8 min.   1986
Directed by: Tony Labat
Distributed by: Electronic Arts Intermix
Evaluators: Jules Benjamin, Enrique R. Rodríguez, Pamela M. Smorkaloff
Description: In this experimental work, artifice and reality, identity and disguise, representation and transformation are woven through a powerful pastiche of theatrical performance, mass-cultural appropriation, and fragmented narrative. Deconstructing an episode of television's *Miami Vice* that features crude representations of Hispanic drug dealers, video maker Labat constructs a multilayered psychological drama of converging realities. In the studio space between "cut" and "action," artists Tony Oursler and Winston Tong provide commentary. Playing out a tragic drama with dolls, Tong also tapes his eyelids down and applies makeup, transforming himself from Asian to Caucasian, male to female. In a final confrontation of identity, Tong steps through the enlarged television image, devoid of masks or makeup.
Strengths and Weaknesses: The tape is highly produced and visually stunning.

Labat's works are extremely experimental and may be seen as obscure and confusing without an introduction.
Introducing the Tape: Viewers should be told that this is a satirical, experimental work dealing with aspects of immigrants' experiences in the United States. An introduction to experimental forms and video art would be helpful.
Level: University

MI PECADO ES QUERERTE (My Sin Is Loving You)
Fiction.   In English.   22 min.   1988
Directed by: Esther Durán
Produced by: David Ranghelli (375 W. 55th St. #2J, New York, NY 10019; tel: [212] 315-5607)
Distributed by: Esther Durán, IMRE
Evaluators: Florence Babb, Elba D. Birmingham-Pokorny, Sandra J. Guardado, Carmen Madariaga-Culver, Angharad N. Valdivia
Description: This film depicts the laborious and isolated existence of Emilia, a working-class, urban, Latina housewife in the United States. Emilia's detached attitude towards her husband and children suggests deep unhappiness and a fatal-

istic resignation. She vicariously experiences her dreams of romance and adventure through the female protagonist of her favorite soap opera. The film intermixes the fantasy world of the television program with the reality of the Emilia's daily life, exploring the profound sense of dissatisfaction and acute feelings of entrapment experienced by women within society's traditional roles. There is not much difference between Emilia's real life and her soap opera life because women are confined in both environments.

Strengths and Weaknesses: The tape effectively contrasts the reality of housework with the fantasy of romance, as well as the tragedy of both the fantasy and Emilia's daily nonexistence. The soap opera's story of a woman trapped between her past and her future mirrors the sense of daily entrapment experienced by the young housewife. Her past dominates both her present and her future. The film portrays Emilia's wifely and motherly duties and her transition into womanhood.

No insight is offered into the background of the young housewife. At times, the transitions between real and soap opera life are invisible. This is both a strong and a weak point—strong because it suggests there is little difference between the two realities, and weak because some audiences may be confused.

Introducing the Tape: U.S. audiences, accustomed to linear narratives, should be told that two different planes of reality occur in the tape. It could also be helpful to have information on popular culture and the role of the telenovela, particularly in Latina women's culture.

How to Use: I might use the tape in *Gender Studies* courses to discuss the invisibility of women's lives and work and the fantasies that serve to displace anger and action. Others could use it in courses on *Gender and Popular Culture*, the *Politics of Romance*, etc. (Babb)

I will use this film in a *Women in Hispanic Literature* course to contrast the portrayal of women by male and female authors and to examine the extent to which the portrayal of women by male authors tends to extend stereotypes drawn more from the dimension of myth than from life. (Birmingham-Pokorny)

The tape could be used in *Media Studies* regarding the voyeur culture of soap operas. The tape explores the place of soap operas in a working-class woman's life. It suggests that soap operas are neither liberating nor alleviating; rather, they fit unobtrusively into a pattern of isolation and oppression. (Guardado)

Suggested Readings: Anzaldua, Gloria. *Haciendo Caras: Making Face, Making Soul: Creative and Critical Perspectives by Women of Color.* It takes up gender, family, and cultural questions.

Richardson, Laurel, and Taylor Verta. *Feminist Frontiers II: Rethinking Sex, Gender, and Society;* addresses gender socialization.

Richardson, Laurel, and Taylor Verta. *Feminist Frontiers III.*

Moraga, Cherrie. *Race, Class, and Gender.*
Level: High School—University

EL MILAGRO DE LAS TORTILLAS (The Miracle of the Tortillas)

Animation.   In English.   16 min. 1983
Directed by: Daniel Salazar
Produced by: Impossible Artz (2633 W. 36th Ave., Denver, CO 80211; tel: [303] 477-6037; fax: [303] 894-2615)
Distributed by: Daniel Salazar, IMRE
Evaluators: Angelique M. Acevedo, Linda W. Ferguson, Lavina Tilson Gass, Elinor Melville, Johanna Mendelson-Forman, Stephen P. O'Neill, Debbie Reyes, Naomi Smith, Aleta Ulibarri Abelman

Description: This delightful, animated short is a colorful and humorous tale about the contributions of the tortilla to Mexican culture. It parodies the legend of Our Lady of Guadalupe as well as several other traditions crucial to Mexican culture. Using experimental cutout animation techniques, narration, and music, the video recounts the magical and heroic role that tortillas have played in Mexican history. It was made by elementary school children in Denver's predominantly Chicano neighborhood.

Strengths and Weaknesses: This is a creative and vibrant work, both entertaining and educational at the same time. The pictures are charming, the animations creative, and the overall piece well edited. The visuals are accompanied by an upbeat song and by narration by the children that reflects their humor and innocence. One evaluator pointed out that the film's underlying social significance and its parodic style appear to be more significant to young people of Mexican/Chicano background than to Anglo Americans. Yet, the story line and *joie de vivre* so transcend ethnicity as to make the work an excellent introduction to Mexican/Chicano culture. Although the visual imagery is developed from young people's artwork, the piece is effective with diverse age levels. It has been equally well received at film festivals and in schools.

One evaluator felt the tape could be confusing to students because it mixes actual history with fantasy and comical clips. Also, references to Mexican historical figures may require some familiarity with Mexican history and culture. One evaluator felt that pride in Mexican culture is offset by stretches of fiction that take great liberty with history.

Introducing the Tape: It is important to note that the tape presents a Chicano perspective of Mexican culture and history and that the film is intended as entertainment and parody, not history. The tongue-in-cheek comments about Mexican culture need to be discussed and contrasted with the realities of Mexican culture and history. Although the piece can stand alone, educators may wish to enhance its significance or use by attaining some familiarity with Mexican history, the tradition of Our Lady of Guadalupe, and the importance of corn to the society. It should be explained that none of the uses to which the tortilla is put in this film are factual.

How to Use: I used this tape to inspire several students to write a script that was turned into a video media/art tape. The script won a contest sponsored by the Public Education Coalition. The tape could be used as a springboard to teach/demonstrate stop-motion animation and creative writing. My students wrote a script entitled *500 Years of Teen Fashion.* (Abelman)

I have used this tape as part of a unit on *Mexico,* the *Art of Mexico,* and the *History of Mexico* as an introduction to the human aspects of Mexican viewpoints. The humor is typically Mexican, with hilarious tongue-in-cheek segments. (Acevedo)

The film can be adapted to a wide range of curricula. In *High School Social Studies* the film could be shown and students assigned overnight reading about Mexican history. The following day, the film could be shown a second time, with the rest of class time spent in discussion. In a college-level *Film Writing* class the film can be used to help students develop their own scripts. (Ferguson)

The tape is excellent for younger children, especially in the Southwest, where the fun with the tortilla would be appreciated. (Melville)

This tape is appropriate for elementary school classes or possibly as an art piece in an *Anthropology* course. (Mendelson-Forman)

In *Film/Video Production* classes the tape could be used to point out work done by creative elementary students and note their talents. (O'Neill)

Perhaps the video could be used while teaching about *Mexican Culture and History.* The historical events can be discussed further in class after the viewing of the film. (Reyes)

I showed the tape in a workshop for *English as a Second Language* teachers and *Spanish Language* teachers of kindergarten through twelfth grade. It would also be instructive in a *Mexican Culture* course to discuss the domestication of food and the importance of corn to indigenous peoples. It serves as a stimulus for discussion about *Mexican History.* (Smith)

A significant use for the film is to encourage critical thinking and questioning on the part of the intended audience. Children need to understand that the fact that something appears on television or film and/or in print and assumes a documentary or news approach is not a guarantee of accuracy or honesty.

Suggested Readings: Caraway, Caren. *Aztec and Other Mexican Indian Designs.*

Clendinnen, Inga. *Aztecs: An Interpretation.*

Fell, Barry. *America B.C.: Ancient Settlers in the New World.*

Fussell, Betty. *The Story of Corn.*

Kibbe, Pauline. *Guide to Mexican History.*

Litvinoff, Barnet. *1492: The Decline of Medievalism and the Rise of the Modern Age.*

Salazar, Maruca, G. *Food of the Americas, Lesson Plans K-12.*

Sale, Kirkpatrick. *The Conquest of Paradise: Christopher Columbus and the Columbian Legacy.*

Somerlott, Robert. *Death of the Fifth Sun.*

Weatherford, Jack. *Native Roots: How the Indians Enriched America.*

Weatherford, Jack. *Indian Givers: How the Indians of the Americas Transformed the World.*

Wilford, John Noble. *The Mysterious History of Columbus: An Exploration of the Man, the Myth, the Legacy.*

Any brief history of Mexico.

Level: Elementary School—University

Ñ (ENN-YAY)

Experimental.   In English.   8 min.   1982
Directed by: Tony Labat
Distributed by: Electronic Arts Intermix
Evaluators: Jules Benjamin, Enrique R. Rodríguez, Pamela M. Smorkaloff
Description: Exploring cultural loss and the modes by which a dominant culture reworks history in its own image, this narrative pastiche is a sophisticated deconstruction of the myth of America as the promised land and the role of the media in reinforcing that illusion. For video maker Labat, the disappearance of the tilde sign (ñ) in the Anglicized pronunciation of Spanish words is a metaphor for what is "lost or left behind" by acculturation. This fragmented collage of cultural myth and reality includes a young man reciting his version of Columbus's discovery of the New World and a *Marielito* (the term for the Cubans who set sail for the United States from Mariel Bay in 1980) recalling his disorienting journey of uncertainty and optimism.
Strengths and Weaknesses: The tape is well made and visually memorable. The Mariel migration theme from Cuba is portrayed with emotional complexity.

Labat's tapes are extremely experimental and can be obscure and confusing if not contextualized for students.
Introducing the Tape: Viewers should be told that Labat's tapes are satirical, experimental pieces exploring aspects of the experiences of immigrants, mostly Cubans, in the United States. Some background on the reasons for the Cuban migration to the United States would be helpful, as would an introduction to video art.
How to Use: In *Video Production/Cinema Studies* this could be used as an example of experimental video.

The tape would be useful in a class on *Transnationalism* or *Migration* to highlight issues of identity and acculturation.
Level: University

PLENA: CANTO Y TRABAJO (Plena Is Work, Plena is Song)

Documentary.   In English with Spanish Portions Subtitled.   29 min.   1989
Directed by: Pedro Rivera and Susan Zeig
Produced by: Cine Productions
Distributed by: The Cinema Guild
Evaluators: René Arbelado Gonzáles, Elba D. Birmingham-

Pokorny, Rebecca Harclerode, María A. Lazarini, Nancy Levy-Konesky, Gerardo Piña

Description: This film explores in great depth the historical and cultural origins and political significance of the *plena,* a uniquely Puerto Rican musical form of expression in which romance, personal tragedy, social issues, and daily experiences become the target of satirical humor. *Plena* has its roots in the experience of the poor and working-class Puerto Ricans of African ancestry, particularly those in the rural areas. The film carefully recreates the emergence, in the 1920s, of the *plena* in these working-class communities on the island, its resurgence in the Latin barrios of New York, and its formal popularization in 1954 with Moncho Rivera's recorded hit song, "Alo quién nama?" in the United States. The video includes people in the street talking about what *plena* means to them and old footage of *pleneros* in the 1940s.

Strengths and Weaknesses: The film is an authentic, revealing, spontaneous type of documentary. It carefully documents the origins and progressive evolution of this musical form of expression and stresses the tremendous significance of the *plena* as an important vehicle for social and political protest. It provides an excellent view of Puerto Rican culture, its social struggle, and dual identity split between New York and the island. The technical quality, editing, and camera work are excellent.

One evaluator felt that the video is difficult to follow and leaves questions unanswered. It does not give background on *bomba, seis, danza-música,* or *jíbara,* even though they are used as comparison. The tape lacks subtitles for some songs.

Introducing the Tape: Students can become confused if *plena* is not clearly defined before showing the film. The tape would benefit from a brief introduction to the history of Puerto Rico, its relationship to Spain and the United States, and music as part of the cultural/historical process. Some information could be provided to bring the tape up to date.

How to Use: I would use this tape in *Spanish American Culture and Civilization* and in *Spanish Phonetics* to illustrate the way Latin American people use music as a vehicle of social protest, as well as to call attention to some of the major problems affecting Latin American societies today: land reform, unemployment, and socioeconomic inequalities. In addition, this film can be extremely useful in the teaching of different patterns of intonation of the Spanish spoken in Puerto Rico. (Birmingham-Pokorny)

In a *Spanish Language* class I would use this film for a cultural lesson with a focus on *plena's* lyrics, instruments, social implications, history, and the Spanish used. (Harclerode)

As a folklorist and teacher of dances from Puerto Rico, I found this film a better depiction of what *plena* is about than any explanation I could have come up with. It shows the social and cultural aspects of the *plena.* (Lazarini)

In my *Spanish Composition* courses I would make a list of words and idiomatic expressions used in the tape (in Span-

ish, of course) and ask the students to write a composition based on the tape. (Piña)

Suggested Readings: Alegria, Ricardo. *Puerto Rico's Dances—Bomba y Plena.*

Babin, María Theresa. *La cultura de Puerto Rico.*

Instituto de Cultura de P.R. *Música de Puerto Rico.*

Nieves, Cesareo Rosa Nieves. *La historia del baile.*

Level: Junior High School—University

ROOM SERVICE

Experimental. In English. 7 min. 1980
Directed by: Tony Labat
Distributed by: Electronic Arts Intermix
Evaluators: Jules Benjamin, Enrique R. Rodríguez, Pamela M. Smorkaloff

Description: Using confrontational humor and performance, video maker Labat replicates the frustration and anxiety of cultural disorientation in the witty yet pointed *Room Service.* Playing the role of a newly arrived Hispanic immigrant, he is seen in a motel room, rehearsing his only English phrases in preparation for a call to room service. Interrupting this narrative, he also appears in the guise of a stand-up comic who tells a joke about an immigrant bewildered by ordering food in English. Labat's satirical role-playing and manipulation of language convey a broader cultural critique. Through his fragmented, staccato narratives, which often throw the viewer off balance, he parallels the complex and often terrifying process of displacement and transformation that accompanies acculturation.

Strengths and Weaknesses: This is an early creation by a talented video maker. The issues of migration from Cuba and language are creatively presented.

Labat's works, however, are extremely experimental and may be seen as obscure and confusing. The ironic humor is geared to other Cuban Americans. Many U.S. students would lack the understanding of cinematic symbolism necessary to grasp Labat's messages.

Introducing the Tape: Viewers should be told that this is a satirical, experimental work dealing with aspects of the experience of immigrants, mostly Cubans, in the United States. An introduction to issues of Cuban exiles, as well as to experimental video forms and cinematic symbolism, would be helpful.

Level: University

SIN FRONTERAS (Without Borders)

Documentary. In English with Spanish Portions Subtitled. 26 min. 1991
Directed by: José Martínez
Produced by: Deep Dish TV (339 Lafayette St., New York, NY 10012; tel: [212] 473-8933; fax: [212] 420-8223)
Distributed by: Deep Dish TV, IMRE
Evaluators: Robert Alvarez, Angela Carreño, Gary S. Elbow, Raúl Leyba, Joan A. McGinnis, Laura Elisa Pérez
Description: This documentary humanizes the plight of un-

documented Mexican laborers who cross the U.S.-Mexican border and exposes the violence and vitriolic hatred they are subjected to by some Caucasian U.S. citizens. The video centers on the Immigration and Naturalization Service's (INS) Border Patrol in the San Diego-Tijuana area from the perspective of human rights groups and victims of INS violence. The film examines the sociopolitical repercussions of illegal border crossings in the area after 1984, when a border crime-prevention unit was disbanded. After 1984, there is a marked increase in the abuse of power by Border Patrol agents, according to relatives of the illegal immigrants and local Mexican Americans. Border agents kill and maim immigrants with impunity, while there is a code of silence and acceptance of the coverups within the INS. The tape effectively expresses outrage about the abuse by contrasting the views of a number of bigoted white San Diego residents with the first-hand accounts by eyewitnesses of horrendous border experiences. Photos of actual victims are presented. Former INS district commissioner Harold Egell is shown and quoted making racist statements. The film makes several points about migration: (1) the crushing poverty far outweighs the danger of the crossing; (2) Mexicans contribute to economic growth in the United States; and (3) the land to which Mexicans migrate was once theirs. The film ends with Mexican American protests and a call for no borders.

Strengths and Weaknesses: The documentary is effective in bringing into public understanding a view of the Mexican immigrants' motives and contributions and a more critical view of white racist intolerance and violence. It brings to light the plight of Mexicans and others who attempt to cross the border into the United States without proper documentation and documents the little-publicized violent actions on the part of the Border Patrol. It is a strong statement about undue harsh treatment of undocumented immigrants, with realistic vignettes of border crossings, speeches from various rights groups and workers, and perspectives of border residents. The visual depiction of the fence and the new "Berlin Wall" are vivid.

One evaluator felt that the video's presentation is too one-sided. There are no interviews with Border Patrol agents or representatives to present their side of the argument. The presentation is quite impressionistic, with little in the way of background to help the viewer sort out the issues. Some evaluators felt that the tape's editing could have been better; at times the tape jumps from scene to scene, with little continuity except for the broad treatment of injustice.

Introducing the Tape: Students need some background on the problems of illegal border crossing, especially in southern California; a general introduction about the border itself; and background on immigration law and history. Some statistical data on illegal border crossings, captures, and rights abuses would highlight the extent of the problem. The Border Patrol's point of view could be added for balance, pointing out that the patrol faces substantial difficulties in controlling the border.

How to Use: The tape could be used as a perspective on the plight and problems of undocumented migrants to the United States and a critique of the harsh realities that exist on the U.S.-Mexican frontier. (Alvarez)

The film could be used to highlight one side of the issue, the dangers and hardships confronted by those who attempt a border crossing. I would want to have a discussion afterward to examine the other side of the issue, pointing out that the United States has a right to protect its frontiers against illegal immigrants, that Border Patrol agents have a tough job, and that systems to which we contribute or from which we benefit (low wages and unequal distribution of resources in Latin American countries) play a major part in stimulating the illegal migration that causes the problem in the first place. It also would be worthwhile to note that few Mexicans really want to leave home and come to the United States and that most who leave family at home eventually go back. (Elbow)

The video could be used in modules studying *Illegal Immigration, Farmworkers, Border Issues,* etc. Several issues emerge, such as importation of produce from Mexico but not of people, English-only laws, Border Patrol brutality, border vigilantes, etc. (Leyba)

I would provide a geographical and historical background, vocabulary list, study guide, and essay topics. In a *High School Language* class role-playing immigrants vs. *la migra* (the U.S. immigration department) would work well. The essay topics would be written from the perspective of an immigrant and a border guard. (McGinnis)

I would include the tape as a text that raises problematic issues of nation/identity and analyze its particular narrative strategies and politics. (Pérez)

Suggested Readings: Davidson, John. *The Long Road North.* A journalist accompanies an illegal immigrant across the border and on his journey through south Texas.

Martínez, Oscar Jaquez. *Troublesome Border.*

Shorris, Earl. "Borderline Cases: The Violent Passage across the Rio Grande."

There is a sizable body of literature in Chicano and Mexican studies on U.S.-Mexico border relations and culture.

Complementary Films/Videos: *Esperanza* (U.S.A.)

Level: High School—University

EL SUPER (The Super)
Feature.   With Subtitles.   90 min.   1979
Directed by: L. Ichaso, O. Jiménez-Leal
Distributed by: IMRE
Evaluators: Nancy Levy-Konesky, Roger A. Sánchez-Berroa
Description: This is a comic/tragic story of the life of a Cuban exile and his family in New York City, where he works as the superintendent of an apartment building. The super dreams of improving his family's socioeconomic level and hopes someday to return to a free Cuba. He is faced only with disappointment.
Strengths and Weaknesses: This excellent film is a realis-

tic and humorous portrayal of an immigrant and his family trying to cope with a totally different country, weather, lifestyle, and culture. It is well acted and captures many of the idiosyncracies of Cuban culture.

Introducing the Tape: Students should be introduced to modern Cuban history to help them understand the variety of reasons why the U.S. Cubans left Cuba.

How to Use: I have used this film in a *Seminar on Puerto Rico and Cuba* to show the cycle of those who migrate to New York from the Caribbean in hopes of "making it" in the land of opportunity but are faced with racism, language and culture barriers, different values, and a different climate and find only shattered hopes and dreams. (Levy-Konesky)

A segment of the film could be used in class to illustrate language use, variations, and cultural aspects. After preparing a series of questions, I could use the whole film for discussion in *Spanish Language Conversation* classes. (Sanchez-Berroa)

Level: High School—University

LOS SURES (Los Sures)

Documentary. With Subtitles. 58 min. 1983
Directed by: Diego Echeverría
Produced by: Terra Productions (588 Broadway, Suite 804, New York, NY 10012; tel: [212] 226-3170; fax: [212] 226-2561)
Distributed by: The Cinema Guild
Evaluators: Judith M. Collins, Henry Funez, Rebeca Harclerode, Miguel Huarcaya, Chon Noriega, Christopher Ortiz, Deborah Pacini-Hernández, Enrique R. Rodríguez
Description: This is a documentary about life in the Puerto Rican section of Williamsburg, New York, called "Los Sures." Through various vignettes, the tape provides insight into the lives of five people: a petty criminal, a woman involved in the religion Santería, a single mother raising five children, a self-employed carpenter, and a social worker who works in the neighborhood. Their personal stories provide different perspectives on life in the community. The tape addresses the multiple coping and survival strategies employed by the people. It deals with the concerns of drug use, student dropouts, teenage pregnancy, joblessness, and incarceration. It also presents issues of race relations among the Puerto Ricans and Hasidim living in the neighborhood. Another dimension illustrated is how many of the immigrants have brought spiritualism in the tradition of Puerto Rico to their community in the United States.

Strengths and Weaknesses: This beautifully crafted and sensitive film examines the culture of poverty in one of the poorest neighborhoods prior to the AIDS epidemic. It demonstrates good research and choice of subjects and allows the people to tell their stories in their own voices, conveying different personal perspectives on problems faced by the community as a whole. The tape is provocative, as it challenges expectations at the level of form as well as content. The lush cinematography is rarely used to depict a slum, and the testimonials are made without voice-over narration. There is much realistic, strong footage that gives the spectator the impression of being a witness to the events as they occur.

Some evaluators criticized the film's focus on marginalized members of the community and the omission of stable working-class families. A couple of reviewers felt that while there is sympathy for the residents' plights, there is not enough attention to possible solutions, resulting in a dismal view. This pessimism may not be a weak point, but it limits the potential uses of the film. There is no discussion of a larger picture of systematic racism and economic oppression. The pacing is uneven is some areas.

Introducing the Tape: Statistics need to be presented on this Puerto Rican community detailing family, education, and employment. A geographic picture of where the community is located and the demographic patterns that have formed it should be supplied. Instructors should update the discussion by addressing urgent problems such as AIDS and crack use.

How to Use: I would like to use segments of the film but would need to do research at Puerto Rican agencies to better equip myself with current facts and figures. (Collins)

I would use the tape to introduce my high school students to one aspect of the Puerto Rican experience in the United States. In a class on *Multiculturalism* it can elicit a discussion of racism and its results, urban issues and problems, immigration, institutional and chronic unemployment, single-parent housholds, criminality, etc. (Funez)

I think the tape would be useful to show nonurban students a slice of life in a poor Hispanic neighborhood in New York City. (Harclerode)

This video could be useful in a *Sociology/Anthropology* class focusing on the problems of the inner cities and/or the problems of Puerto Ricans in the United States. However, the lack of any suggestion of possible solutions or changes, especially from barrio residents themselves, limits its use. (Pacini-Hernández)

Some of my students reside in this neighborhood. I would ask then to lead the discussion concerning racial and housing issues affecting this community. I would introduce the film and hand out questionnaires for further discussion. (Rodríguez)

Suggested Readings: *Centro,* Spring '90 Puerto Rican Studies Bulletin, Hunter College, resources from Institute of Puerto Rican Policy.

Thomas, P. *Down These Mean Streets* (novel).

The multicultural curriculum for high school social studies from the New York City Board of Education.

An introductory text in Puerto Rican studies.
Level: High School—University

TANTO TIEMPO (So Much Time)

Fiction. In English with Spanish Portions Subtitled. 26 min. 1992
Directed by: Cheryl Quintana Leader

Produced by: Hispanic Film Project (1820 S. Bundy Dr. #4, Los Angeles, CA 90025; tel: [310] 207-8897)
Distributed by: Cheryl Quintana Leader, Hispanic Film Project
Evaluators: Virginia Shen
Description: A young Mexican American woman is raised by her Anglo father, who demands that she assimilate by conforming to his values. When she decides to explore her Latino heritage, she begins to uncover many secrets that were hidden from her and discovers the value of her ancestry.
Strengths and Weaknesses: This is a touching film that would encourage bicultural people in the United States to reevaluate their own identities and appreciate their own cultures of origin. The woman's mental transition, set off by memories and conveyed through flashbacks, works effectively. The narration of Mexican history is dramatic and the impact extremely powerful.
Introducing the Tape: None is needed.
How to Use: When I teach *Chicano Literature,* I would like to use this tape to discuss the diverse attitudes and conflicts of Chicano students regarding their own identities. (Shen)
Complementary Films/Videos: *Café norte y sur (Cafe North and South)* (U.S.A.); *Latino Images* (U.S.A.).
Level: High School—University

EL TEATRO CAMPESINO: VEINTE AÑOS (The Teatro Campesino: First 20 Years)

Documentary.   In English with Spanish Portions Not Subtitled.   30 min.   1985
Produced by: El Teatro Campesino (P.O. Box 1240, San Juan Bautista, CA, 95045; tel: [408] 623-2444; fax: [408] 623-2444)
Distributed by: El Teatro Campesino
Evaluators: René Arbelado González, Alberto J. Carlos, Osvaldo Chinchón, Juan Espadas, Suzanne Oboler, Virginia Shen, Ann Marie Stock
Description: The film is an audiovisual history of the first twenty years of the Teatro Campesino. Luis Valdez, creator of the group, explains the history and development of the theater company and the Chicano movement of the 1960s. Interviews with group members are interwoven with scenes both from the members' participation in the United Farm Workers' strike and from most of the theater company's successful dramatic productions. César Chávez and Luis Valdez are seen conducting work related to the strike. Clips are included from *Honest Sanchos' Shop,* the *Story of Rascuache, The Pastorela,* and *Zoot Suit,* in which Edward James Olmos enacts one of the roles that propelled him to prominence. The excerpts use humor and satire to depict not only the discrimination and anti-Chicano attitudes in the United States but also the Chicano response and struggle to improve the conditions of Mexican American workers, particularly in rural areas. The film describes the itinerant nature of the early guerrilla theater group and its eventual establishment of a

stable, more sedentary, although not less active, theater company in San Juan Bautista.
Strengths and Weaknesses: This tape provides an overview of one of the most important cultural institutions of the Chicano movement, successfully addressing both the history and the aesthetic concerns of the movement. The film shows the importance of Mexican traditions in shaping Mexican American culture and points out the diversity encompassed by the term "American culture." The film portrays the open political attitude of the people who direct the Teatro Campesino and the Teatro's desire to represent groups of people whose voices are never heard in the public arena. The troupe is enormously talented and the film's real theatrical representations of the migrant workers' problems are terrific.

The tape leaves some questions unanswered. The technical quality of some of the archival clips is not high. From the perspective of a Spanish language teacher, the linguistic mixture of English and Spanish does not enable the tape to be used as a model of the standard use of the language.
Introducing the Tape: Background on the United Farm Workers and César Chávez and the Chicano movement of the 1960s and 1970s is necessary. Some more background on Teatro Campesino would be helpful, answering such questions as: How or why did Luis Valdez get the idea of the Teatro Campesino? What was the background of the founding members? How did they survive at the beginning? What is their relationship to the United Farm Workers now? Were any of the members farmworkers? A good introduction would be the essay *Historical Antecedents to Chicano Theater.* In *Language* courses the teacher should introduce the topics of the *pachuco* life and the role of death in Mexican culture.
How to Use: I would use this tape merely to show the evolution of an idea to the creation of a theater. I would try to fill in precisely the details that I think have been left out of the tape, such as Valdez's political and professional commitment and his constant pursuit of his dramatic aspirations both as an actor and director. (Carlos)

I would use this video as an example of forms of organizing for change in the context of the 1960s civil rights struggles. (Oboler)

I would present the film after I give an introduction to El Teatro Campesino and Luis Valdez, particularly focusing on the nature, mission, and emergence of Chicano theater. (Shen)
Suggested Readings: Acuña, Rodolfo. *Occupied America,* pp. 153–86.

Castañeda Shular, Antonia, Tomás Ybarra-Frausto, and Joséph Sommers, eds. *Literatura Chicana,* pp. 44–56.

Feyder, Linda, ed. *Shattering the Myth: Plays by Hispanic Women.*

"Historical Antecedents to Chicano Theater," pp. 1–7; and "Chicano Valdez," pp. 15–16. *Contemporary Chicano Theater,* ed. Roberto J. Garza.

Valdez, Luis. *Zoot Suit and Other Plays.*

Other Chicano poetry.
Level: High School—University

2371 SECOND AVE: AN EAST HARLEM STORY
Documentary. With Subtitles. 13 min. 1986
Directed by: A group of N.Y.C. high school students.
Produced by: Educational Video Center (55 E. 25 Street, New York, NY 10010; tel: [212] 725-3534; fax: [212] 725-6501)
Distributed by: Educational Video Center
Evaluators: Rebeca Harclerode, Nancy Levy-Konesky, Christine List, Suzanne Oboler, Angharad N. Valdivia
Description: This moving documentary about housing conditions in East Harlem, New York, was made by a group of New York City high school students in a documentary workshop. The students take a personal approach, using the deplorable situation in one student's own apartment building, where rats are rampant and there is no hot water. Millie introduces viewers to her family and neighbors, and they demonstrate to the camera their daily battle to live in these conditions. The students then document Millie's efforts to organize her neighbors to sign a petition and get the landlord to act on the problems.
Strengths and Weaknesses: The intimate relationship of the high school students to their subjects makes this an effective and sincere documentary. Although the technical quality is weak, the tape provides a realistic picture of the relentless brutality of daily survival, illiteracy, and poverty faced by these people. The tape's theme is clear and presentation simple. It is an excellent and inspiring example of young people taking action to better their communities and the use of video as a tool for education and activism.

One evaluator felt the tape portrayed the members of the community as victims.
Introducing the Tape: It should be explained that this is a student-made production.
How to Use: The tape could be used to generate a discussion of the urban conditions of Hispanics. Certainly students in New York City or other urban centers would identify issues as being familiar to them. In *Spanish Language* class I would compare and contrast the two largest Hispanic groups in the United States (Puerto Rican and Mexican), discussing their reasons for coming to this country and some of the problems they encounter as minorities in this society. (Harclerode)

I would use this tape to motivate students to make socially conscious documentaries. (List)
Level: Junior High School—University

UNEASY NEIGHBORS
Documentary. In English with Spanish Portions Subtitled. 35 min. 1989
Directed by: Paul Espinosa
Produced by: Paul Espinosa (5200 Campanile Dr., San Diego, CA 92182-5400; tel: [619] 594-5996; fax: [619] 265-6417)

Distributed by: University of California Extension Center
Evaluators: Stephen K. Ainsworth, Richard Stahler-Sholk
Description: This documentary studies the migration of Mexicans and other Latinos into northern San Diego County and the concomitant social/cultural clashes that occur. The tape depicts the conflict between Mexican migrant workers living in a hillside encampment in San Diego County and wealthy Anglo homeowners in the nearby development of Encinitas. It clearly demonstrates the contradiction between the need for cheap labor in the U.S. economy and the inability of that economy to provide housing and basic necessities for persons paid low wages.
Strengths and Weaknesses: The film does an excellent job of showing the human dimension of the migrants' struggle for survival. It highlights the contradiction of a system that demands cheap labor but fails to provide basic necessities, or respect, for the laborers. Interviews with the migrants provide the opinions of the people directly.
Introducing the Tape: More historical context about migrant labor and its contribution to the U.S. economy would be useful. Also, background about immigration laws, including an explanation of the 1986 amnesty, and anti-immigrant legislation, such as California's Proposition 187, would aid understanding.
How to Use: This film could demonstrate the continuing problems that plague the relationship between the United States and its Latin American neighbors. In a real sense, the uneasy relationship that exists between migrants and wealthy San Diego County residents is the same one that characterizes the relationship between the United States and the countries of Latin America. (Ainsworth)

The video would be useful in a course on *U.S.-Latin American Relations* that includes a unit on immigration and economic issues. It could be used to illustrate immigration issues from the perspective of comfortable U.S. homeowners versus Mexican laborers denied decent wages. (Stahler-Sholk)
Suggested Readings: Nathan, Debbie. *Women and Other Aliens: Essays from the U.S.-Mexico Border.*

Sassen, S., et al. "Coming North: Latino and Caribbean Immigration."
Complementary Films/Videos: *Esperanza* (U.S.); *Sin Fronteras (Without Borders)* (U.S.); *Work in Progress* (U.S.).
Level: High School—University

LOS VENDIDOS (The Sellouts)
Fiction. In English. 22 min. 1972
Directed by: José Luis Ruiz
Produced by: El Teatro Campesino (P.O. Box 1240, San Juan Bautista, CA 95045; tel: [408] 623-2444)
Distributed by: El Teatro Campesino
Evaluators: Elba D. Birmingham-Pokorny, Alberto J. Carlos, Suzanne Oboler, Ann Marie Stock
Description: The video opens with a brief overview of the Teatro Campesino (the farmworkers' theater group) and explains its origin and political interests. The focus of the tape is

a performance of their play, *The Sellouts*. The play deals with the fictitious Honest Sancho's Used Mexican Shop, where one can purchase any desired type of Mexican. A secretary from the governor's office, Miss Jiménez (pronounced as if the name were not Hispanic), arrives with the intention of buying a Mexican who will be acceptable to her employers in Sacramento. The store's salesman shows her different Mexican types: the revolutionary, the *pachuco* of the 1950s, and the zoot suiter of the 1940s. Eventually the secretary finds what she is looking for: the new 1972 Mexican American wears a business suit and says what he thinks the system's bosses want him to say. He is obviously a sellout.

Strengths and Weaknesses: The tape effectively points out with humor and poignancy the stereotypes of the Mexican American. It is an excellent portrayal of the Chicano reality in the United States, as well as an insightful analysis of the painful and ever present dilemma faced by those living within or between two cultures. The tape makes excellent use of satire to capture the experience of those Mexican Americans and other Latinos who have fallen victim to U.S. consumerism. It satirizes, above all, the sellouts, the weak-willed Mexicans who collaborate in the establishment's nefarious official enterprises.

The video's preface contains images and explanations that quite adequately summarize the props and intellectual accoutrements used by the Teatro Campesino. The skits are politically motivated and target the participation of Mexican Americans in the Vietnam War and racism. It alludes to the redneck, white supremacist mentality among some U.S high school students and mocks the state government's attempt to use Chicanos in its political games.

One evaluator found the preface's explanations stilted and overly dramatic and felt that some of the acting is overdone yet mentioned that exaggeration is part of the parody. A few shots are out of focus.

Introducing the Tape: Some introduction to the Teatro Campesino group would be useful. Students would benefit from a discussion of stereotypes, as this play relies heavily on their use. The play should also be preceded by explanations about Mexican Americans in California, the social and economic problems encountered by farmworkers in that state during the 1970s, and specific translation of the Spanish words and expressions. Perhaps a glossary could be provided for the Chicano Spanish vocabulary and dialogue crucial for complete comprehension.

How to Use: I would use this tape to introduce students to the prominent Hispanic presence in the United States and to the diversity and richness of their cultures. This film also is extremely helpful in a *Phonetics* course to introduce students to different pronunciations of the Spanish language. (Birmingham-Pokorny)

I would assign reading materials about the way Mexican farmworkers have historically been treated in such places as the San Joaquín Valley and the origin and history of the United Farm Workers Union headed by César Chávez. (Carlos)

This is an excellent introduction to stereotypes and identity construction in U.S. society. It could also be used to conclude a unit on *Media and Ethnic Stereotypes*. Students could be asked to perform their own version of 1990s expectations about ethnic minorities. (Oboler)

I would use this tape to provide students with a visual version of the play *Los Vendidos*. I would first discuss the history of the farmworkers' theater and show the video *El Teatro Campesino* to complement this tape. (Stock)

Suggested Readings: Acuña, Rodolfo. *Occupied America,* chap. 7.

Connor, Walker, ed. *Mexican-Americans in Comparative Perspective.*

Garza, Roberto, ed. *Contemporary Chicano Theater,* contains the text of the play (pp. 15–27).

Tatum, Charles, ed. *Mexican-American Literature.*

Valdéz, Luis. "Los vendidos" in *Zoot Suit and Other Plays.*

Complementary Films/Videos: *El Teatro Campesino: veinte años (The Teatro Campesino: The First Twenty Years)* (U.S.A.); *La pastorela,* another filmed version of a play by Teatro Campesino (distributed by El Teatro Campesino).

Level: High School—University

WORK IN PROGRESS

Experimental.   In English.   14 min.   1990

Directed by: Luis Valdovino

Produced by: University of Colorado (Fine Arts Department, Boulder, CO 80309; tel: [303] 492-5482; fax: [303] 492-4886)

Distributed by: Luis Valdovino, Third World Newsreel, Video Data Bank

Evaluators: Robert Alvarez, Robin Andersen, John Higgins, Raul Leyba, Martha Rees

Description: This is an innovative, abstract, and ironic look at U.S. immigration laws, practices, and contradictions. The video exposes the hypocrisy of the official status of undocumented Mexican workers in the United States. Throughout, it contrasts the dehumanization of workers with their productive contribution to the economy. There is condemnation of the English-only movement, the treatment of farmworkers and their exposure to harmful pesticides, and a biting satire of the American dream when viewed from Latino reality.

Most intriguing is the tape's inspired use of footage from old movies and U.S. government propaganda films, from which alternative meanings are forged. Much is made of the word "alien," both as satire and as condemnation. Footage of flying saucers invading earth are equated with the invasion of illegal aliens. Old (1950s) government civil-defense footage warning of the dangers from nuclear fallout is presented as an "Illegal Aliens Watch" segment, educating the public on how to spot aliens. The director plays with split-screen images that contrast people who are deported with fruit that is imported. Border Patrols' view through night-vision binoculars is presented as a manhunt along the border.

Most jolting is the use of a television segment by Mike Wallace on illegal immigration that celebrates infrared cameras with the "capacity to hunt human beings." This is juxtaposed with testimonials of the brutality suffered by those trying to cross the border.

Strengths and Weaknesses: In general, this is an excellent, creative video. The piece keeps moving, using a variety of techniques to get its ideas across. Strong points are its creative use of old footage, recognizable as popular culture, to forge new meanings through the use of irony. A dehumanizing process is exposed that will undoubtedly challenge North American viewers and their complicity with official policies. Some information on the 1986 immigration law is provided—for example, the amnesty reform that granted legal status to those who came to the United States before 1982.

Evaluators commented that the video's format is disjointed, without much story line, but it eventually conveys its thesis in a powerful way. One evaluator felt that more women should have been included in the tape. In terms of providing knowledge about legal status, the piece is too sketchy to be effective as "information" as such. Also, some of the subtitles are difficult to read.

Introducing the Tape: The tape's visual content is recognizable and effective, and its overall message is revealed accumulatively. However, one evaluator felt that the tape is not clearly introduced and that a preface was necessary. Viewers should be told that the video is an artistic glimpse into the many facets and problems faced along the border and in both countries in general. Instructors could also provide more information on the reasons that immigrants leave their homelands, what immigrants contribute to U.S. society, and U.S. immigration law, including anti-immigrant legislation such as California's Proposition 187.

How to Use: I would use the tape to generate class discussions about historical/political trends along the U.S.-Mexican border. (Alvarez)

The tape would be especially useful in *Communication* courses. Its use of visuals is inventive and effective and is a creative example of "alternative" video. It would be a good catalyst for discussion, as it raises issues without providing all the answers. When all the answers have been provided, students are sometimes intimidated, as you never really know what they think unless they talk! (Andersen)

I would use the tape to study illegal immigration, farmworkers, and border issues. Several issues emerge, such as importation of produce, not people, from Mexico; English-only laws; Border Patrol brutality; border vigilantes, etc. (Leyba)

The tape could be a good basis for discussions about the relation between the United States and Mexico and the role of racism, the world economy (especially in relation to the (NAFTA), and immigration laws in creating the new international division of labor. (Rees)

Suggested Readings: Martínez, Oscar Jaquez. *Troublesome Border.*

Pastor, Robert, and Jorge G. Castañeda. *Limits to Friendship: The United States and Mexico.*
Complementary Films/Videos: *Sin Fronteras* (U.S.A.)
Level: High School—University

YO SOY JOAQUIN (I Am Joaquin)
Experimental. In English. 20 min. 1969
Produced & Directed by: Teatro Campesino (P.O. Box 1240, San Juan Bautista, CA 95045; tel: [408] 623-2444; fax: [408] 623-2444)
Distributed by: Teatro Campesino
Evaluators: Alberto J. Carlos, Osvaldo Chinchón, Suzanne Oboler

Description: This recital and visual representation of Rodolfo Corky González's famous bilingual poem "I am Joaquín" incorporates images of past and present Chicano life from its Aztec and Spanish origins to contemporary existence in the barrios of the U.S. Southwest. Luis Valdez's rich and melodious voice recites most of the González text, which invokes Mexican ancestors: Cortés, Cuauhtémoc, Hidalgo, Juárez, Madero, Villa, and Zapata. Images from Diego Rivera's murals of the Mexican Revolution serve as a backdrop and are interspersed with glimpses of barrio life. The accompanying music underscores the cultural nationalism and pride of the 1960s Chicano movement.

Strengths and Weaknesses: This is an important historical documentary of the Chicano struggle that reflects pride in Chicano and Mexican culture. The multimedia format is excellent for students who may not know much about the poem or the movement behind it. The cinematography and choice of images bring the poem to life.

The tape fails to mention women in the forefront of the movement.

One evaluator found it a confusing conglomeration of facts.

Introducing the Tape: It is important to contextualize the poem with a brief introduction to the Chicano nationalist struggle of the 1960s. Students should also be familiar with Gonzalez's text.

How to Use: After having students read *I am Joaquín,* I would then ask them to do research about the Mexican heroes referred to in the text. Students should study the chronology on pp. 103–18, and become familiar with the book's many pertinent illustrations. (Carlos)

I would give students a copy of the poem and show this video after some discussion about Chicano participation in the struggle for *Civil Rights* in the 1960s. (Oboler)

As women's contributions are not covered in the tape, this video can be shown together with *Chicana,* a film about Mexican and Mexican American women's contributions to Chicano culture.

Suggested Readings: González, Rodolfo. *I Am Joaquín. Yo soy Joaquín, an Epic Poem.*
Complementary Films/Videos: *Chicana* (U.S.A.).
Level: University

URUGUAY

DE REPENTE (Suddenly)

Animation.   No Dialogue.   5 min.   1990
Directed by: Pablo Casa Cuberta
Produced by: CEMA (Yaguaron 2044, Montevideo; tel: [5982] 946-421; fax: [5982] 946-470)
Distributed by: IMRE
Evaluators: John Hays, Jesikah María Ross, Jennifer M. Taylor
Description: This is an experimental short that combines film, video, animation, and claymation to comment on the power of television. In *De repente* a young boy separates himself from his group of friends when he becomes entranced by a television set in a window display. All of a sudden his point of view transforms. A Don Quixote figure rides his horse past a series of images that act as a commentary on the use and role of television in Latin American culture and society.
Strengths and Weaknesses: This is a short, artistic, and innovative tape. It creatively uses the symbol of Don Quixote to set the context of television's power and the battle against this force. Aspects of film/video production within the narrative of the piece visually reinforce the commentary on the power and role of television. Showing time code over the images on the video monitor distances the viewer from what is being viewed. The use of stop motion and freeze frames reveals television's unreality and its ability to manipulate images. The tape also uses untraditional angles and quick cuts, resulting in a frenetic pace and rhythm that work wonderfully with the subject and its treatment.

One evaluator found the tape's message somewhat confusing. Another found some transitions awkward.
Introducing the Tape: As the tape uses the symbol of Don Quixote, it would be helpful for U.S. audiences to know a brief version of the story of Don Quixote and what Don Quixote symbolizes in Spanish and Latin American cultures. An introduction to the urban setting of Montevideo would be useful as well.

Viewers should be told that this piece was created for the meeting of popular video makers held in Montevideo in 1990. It is a commentary on the power of media in society and how video can champion change when put in the hands of everyday people.
How to Use: In *Video Production* classes, the tape can be used as an example of creative uses of the medium.

In a *Latin American Culture* course, the tape could be used to examine the impact of television.
Suggested Readings: Cervantes Saavedra, Miguel de. *Don Quixote.*

McLuhan, Herbert Marshall, and Fiore Quentin. *The Medium Is the Message.*
Level: University

THE EYES OF THE BIRDS

Feature.   With Subtitles.   82 min.   1982
Directed by: Gabriel Auer
Distributed by: First Run/Icarus Films
Evaluators: David William Foster
Description: This is a powerful narrative of a visit to Uruguayan political prisons by members of the French Red Cross. The humanitarian mission becomes a process of discovery as the human rights workers become aware of the abuses and torture behind the façade of a supposedly humane and well-regulated, if stern, authoritarian regime.
Strengths and Weaknesses: This is a strong portrayal of the destruction of human dignity. The film brings out the distinctive characteristics of the political penitentiary regime in Uruguay, in contrast to the more overtly brutal repression in Argentina, Brazil, and Paraguay during the same time period.
Introducing the Tape: The film is self-explanatory and needs no specific introduction. Background on the dictatorships of the Southern Cone countries would put the film into a broader context.
How to Use: I would use the film in two ways. First, I would use it on an explicit level in terms of the representation of the Uruguayan model of political repression and its attempts to recondition public political respect for authoritarianism. I would point out the purported conflicts between the military dictatorship and Uruguay's purported social democratic tradition with a strong component of anarchistic and bohemian values. (Foster)
Suggested Readings: Sosonowski, Saul, ed. *Represión, exilio, y democracia: la cultura a.*
Level: High School—University

GUARDA Y PASA

Documentary.   Without Subtitles.   14 min.   1988
Directed by: Pablo Casacuberta and Matias Bervejillo
Produced by: CEMA (Yaguaron 2044, Montevideo; tel: [5982] 946-421; fax: [5982] 946-470)
Distributed by: IMRE
Evaluators: James W. Cooper, Janet B. Norden, J. Julian Rívera, Aaron Vinck
Description: This film provides a dramatic presentation of the conditions faced by patients in a government facility for the chronically mentally ill. The camera roams freely through the institution, recording the surroundings. The human neglect is shocking. The unsanitary conditions are appalling, and the minimum needs of the patients are not met. Juxtaposed with these images of misery are brief sound bites from several patients and an administrator who laments the low budgets supporting these institutions.
Strengths and Weaknesses: The film is both thought-provoking and moving. Scenes are shocking and powerful. The portrayal of conditions in the institution is effective; particular emphasis is placed on the patients' perspective as human beings with feelings and awareness of their plight. The tape graphically shows conditions that can probably be found in mental institutions in many parts of the world. Using limited dialogue and no narration, it is an effective international

communication tool. The music and visual style, with good pacing, editing, camera work, and composition, draw viewers into the plight and misery of the patients. The introduction and conclusion artfully frame the tape.

Although there are good interviews with residents and staff, the tape could have included more. Technically, there are a few problems: the black-and-white scenes cannot be distinguished, and a few graphics go by quickly. One evaluator felt that the tape lacked clarity in presentation and said that the reasons for such conditions need to be addressed specifically. The ending credits state there are nineteen hundred patients, yet the video doesn't suggest a facility of such size.

Introducing the Tape: The tape needs some sort of introduction to locate it within time, place, and social structure. Students need to be told that the film documents conditions in a mental institution in Uruguay. Some geographical and economic context would be helpful. As the film speaks of a universal human situation, instructors should draw parallels with other examples of these conditions, as well as with conditions in U.S. institutions of the past and urban public institutions of the present.

How to Use: Classes could discuss how societies treat people who have physical and mental deficiencies, and the conditions around the world for these people. Students could talk about what society should do about birth defects and mental illness and who should be responsible for those less fortunate people. (Cooper)

The tape could be used to demonstrate that social policies regarding the treatment of mental patients are influenced by religious, economic, and political factors. (Rívera)

This piece could be used in conjunction with a segment from a documentary called *Health Care: Your Money or Your Life* that shows parallel conditions at King's County Hospital in Brooklyn, New York; with *Casa Primavera,* which focuses on a group home for Hispanic residents in Boston; and with *A Garden of Hope,* which documents a psychiatric hospital in Cuba.

Complementary Films/Videos: *Health Care: Your Money or Your Life* (distributed by Downtown Community Television Center in New York City); *Casa Primavera* (U.S.A.); and *A Garden of Hope* (distributed by IMRE).

Level: University

EL MUERTO (The Dead Man)

Feature. With Subtitles. 103 min. 1975

Directed by: Hector Olivera

Produced by: Fernando Ayala

Distributed by: IMRE

Evaluators: Alberto J. Carlos, Daniel P. Hunt, Daniel C. Scroggins

Description: This is a well-known, feature-film version of the Borges short story. The plot follows a knife-wielding fugitive's rise to power in nineteenth century as the protegé of a frontier smuggler and political opportunist. A wealthy landowner unknowingly hires a young man exiled for having killed another man in a knife fight. The new hacienda employee at first impresses his boss with his wit and ambition. His hard work and valor earn him the esteem of his peers, and soon the upstart tries to displace his aging boss in both his arms business and his bedroom. His remarkable success makes him feel invulnerable, yet one day, to his surprise, his boss informs him that he was only allowed many privileges because he was already considered a dead man. He is then mercilessly gunned down.

Strengths and Weaknesses: This is an excellent rendition of the Borges plot and atmosphere. Students of Argentine literature, in particular readers of Borges and *Martín Fierro,* will benefit from the scenes of nineteenth-century rural River Plate life and will learn about the civil wars in between *Blancos* and *Colorados.* Particularly convincing is the portrayal of the life of gauchos. Many scenes depict how they work and amuse themselves. Drink, song, and women cheer their more-than-dismal lives. The scenes of Tacuarembo will be of particular interest to Borges's readers.

The film tends to confirm our stereotypical ideas about gaucho life with its rather traditional tale of loyalty and betrayal. The language in the film is mostly not suitable for language students because it is overburdened with vocabulary (*flete, mamao, pingo, entuavia*) that is typical of the gauchos and with Spanish spoken by a Brazilian. Only advanced language students would listen to the dialogue rather than read the subtitles. The film is overladen with a peculiarly garish cult of *lo gauchesco* and is a bit long and slow paced for most young U.S. audiences.

Introducing the Tape: The audience will get a great deal more out of the film if the Borges short story is read first and some critical introduction to Borges's themes and motifs is provided. Also, information about turn-of-the-century rural Argentina and would be helpful.

How to Use: In a *Latin American Film* course, I would show this tape as an example of a rather successful adaptation of a Borges short story, pointing out that the film is the work of competent and tremendously creative people such as Fernando Ayala, Oliviera, and a Uruguayan writer, Juan Carlos Onetti. I might assign a paper in which students would be required to compare the Borges story with the film in order to study how far the filmmakers deviate from the bare outline of the story. I would also show the Spanish television production of *El hombre de la esquina rosada,* comparing it to the original *Street Corner Man* story. A comparison of both adaptations might be enlightening. (Carlos)

In a *Literature* course dealing either with the concept of machismo or with gaucho culture, this film would provide good background. (Hunt)

I would have students read Borges's *El muerto* first and would acquaint them with the importance of *lo gauchesco* in Borges's stories by having them read a short portion of José Hernández's *Martín Fierro* and then Borges's *La muerte de Tadeo Isidoro Cruz.* To complete the Borges theme of death among the gauchos, I would ask students to read *El sur.* (Scroggins)

Suggested Readings: Borges, Jorge Luis. *Prose Works. The Aleph and Other Stories, 1933–1969, Together with Commentaries and an Autobiographical Essay.*

Other works by Borges, including *El muerto, Street Corner Man, Rosendo's Tale,* and *The South* (see bibliography for selected citations).

Guiraldes, Ricardo. *Don Segundo Sombra.*

Hernández, José. *Martín Fierro.*

Martínez Estrada, Ezequiel. *Radiografía de la pampa.*

Level: University

LOS MUERTOS (The Dead)

Fiction, With Subtitles. 22:30 min. 1992
Produced & Directed by: Guillermo Casanova (Méndez Núñez 2712, ap. 904, Montevideo; tel: [5982] 775-802)
Distributed by: IMRE
Evaluators: Osvaldo Chinchón, Joan A. McGinnis, Margarita Pont
Description: This film is based on a short story by writer Mario Levrero. The protagonist, Eduardo, lives with an aunt, who rents a room to a mysterious tenant. The aunt objects to the tenant's playing her piano. However, she never tells him to stop and doesn't even seem to know his name, referring to him only as "he." The tenant would seem to represent Eduardo's alter ego. Eduardo himself leads a parasitic life, as he depends entirely on his aunt. One day the tenant commits suicide, and Eduardo's only concern is that he will have to report the death to the police. He feels he is going crazy and that he'll have to make his report before the dead body begins to smell. After spending the night with his girlfriend, he returns home to find his aunt playing the piano. She tells him that "he" has left and that she couldn't stand that "he" had the audacity to play her piano.
Strengths and Weaknesses: The video is a surrealistic adaptation of Levrero's short story and recalls the work of film director Luis Buñuel. The video attempts to echo the sense of mystery, anguish, and fantasy in the original short story, without attempting to explain the layered meanings embedded within the text. One evaluator felt that the sepia tones add to the video's dreamlike quality and that the special effects and dissonant music are effective in creating a disturbing feeling for the spectator. The symbolism is ambiguous, and some reviewers found the tape confusing; however, it would seem the filmmaker's intention is to leave the narrative and images open to multiple interpretations and to produce in the spectator a need for deeper reflection. The film contains some nudity that may not be suitable for all classes.
Introducing the Tape: An introduction to the writer Mario Levrero and the context in which he wrote would be useful. Perhaps some introduction to surrealism and the basic tenets of the surrealist manifesto would provide some understanding of nonrealistic representation in twentieth-century modern art. A short review of Luis Buñuel might provide some

context for the filmmaker's style. Basic Uruguayan history could also be reviewed.
Level: University

SEÑAL DE AJUSTE (Bad Signal)

Fiction. With Subtitles. 15 min. 1984
Directed by: Juan José Ravaioli
Produced by: Estudio Imagem (Av. Agraciada 1641 Esc. 202, Montevideo; tel: [5982] 915-441)
Distributed by: IMRE
Evaluators: Robin Andersen, Carol Becker, Alicia Ramos
Description: Based on the short story "Algo muy extraño" by Silvia Guerrico, this surrealistic story is a chilling commentary on television's influence on people's lives. It opens with a harshly lit interrogation session of a man who is accused of murdering his wife. He relates to unseen interrogators the events that led to his wife's death. The story moves back and forth from the man's testimony to enacted segments of the story. He explains that the television he bought for his wife consumed her every waking moment. Little by little, it destroyed their relationship. She took the television to bed as a substitute for making love. And ultimately it killed her; she buzzed and burned out. The man becomes obviously frustrated by his interrogator's apparent disbelief of his account. The tape ends as he is led away babbling and repeating his story, seemingly obsessed and on the verge of madness.
Strengths and Weaknesses: This story of television's destructive power is told within a social/personal context. The man is not devoid of responsibility for his wife's death. His detached sexist treatment of her undoubtedly led to the void in her life that is filled by the television. Although the tape's pacing is slow by U.S. standards, a level of dramatic tension is achieved throughout. Evaluators had mixed feelings about the theme. One found it silly, another clever. One reviewer felt the acting was unprofessional.
Introducing the Tape: The implication of the couple's lack of communication and the man's sexist treatment of his wife should be discussed in connection with her need for the television set.
How to Use: This tape would be especially useful in a *Television and Mass Media Criticism* course. (Andersen)

I would use the tape in a study of parody and in a critique of television culture. (Becker)

I would use this in a *Spanish Language* or *Literature* class in conjunction with the short story "Algo muy extraño," on which it is based. (Ramos)
Level: High School—University

SIN PEDIR PERMISO

Documentary. Without Subtitles. 33 min. 1989
Directed by: Maida Moubayed and Hilary Sandison
Produced by: Grupo Imagenes (Maldonado 1792, Montevideo 11200, Casilla 6149; tel: [5982] 796-539; fax: [5982] 963-689)

Distributed by: IMRE

Evaluators: Susana Conde, Graciela Michelotti, Catherine Russo, Jennifer M. Taylor

Description: Without asking for their permission, the producer of this documentary used sequences from the speeches of male politicians. This unauthorized filming of patronizing, condescending, male chauvinist statements by members of Congress and delightfully humorous animation make this an interesting, forceful, and entertaining piece. The point is made that the female voice has been silenced for too long in Uruguayan politics, and that women will no longer tolerate this inequity. Through voice-over narration and turn-of-the-century still photos picturing men and women in their traditional roles, the first part of the tape explains that at the beginning of the century Uruguayan women were not considered citizens: they did not have the right to own property, to have custody of their children, or to vote. Although the female vote became a reality in 1932, the following year all Uruguayans lost their rights after a coup. Women fought to reclaim democracy for all, but after democracy was restored, only the men returned to their usual places of power.

The film offers pointed interviews with congresswomen who are allowed to substitute temporarily for men; women dairy workers who have become activists in the women's movement; a worker in a fish-canning plant; and workers in women's cooperatives that promote women's rights and services, such as health care provided by women medical workers.

Strengths and Weaknesses: Serious but not grim, chiding but not scathing, this well-paced film makes its point succinctly, humorously, and powerfully. There is a great opening, listing feminine ideals, with visuals of naked women. The interviews are strong and compelling and motivate discussion. Cartoons provide comic relief and are a good way to express outrage. The ending shot of a woman cleaning the Congress provides great irony.

The Spanish may be a little difficult to follow for beginning-level students.

Introducing the Tape: Background on the history of the region, the cultural heritage of the population, and the changing role of women in would add to the understanding of the film.

How to Use: I could use the tape in a *Spanish Language* class, since the Uruguayan (as well as the Argentine) accent offers a different challenge from the Mexican, Puerto Rican, and Central American accents to which most North American students are accustomed in Spanish language classes. (Conde)

The activities and daily lives of Uruguayan women shown in this film could be contrasted with the role of peasant women in other countries. (Michelotti)

Suggested Readings: Bergmann, Emilie, Janet Greenberg, Gwen Kirkpatrick, Francine Masiello, Francesca Miller, Marta Morello-Frosch, Kathleen Newman, and Mary Louise Pratt. *Women, Culture, and Politics in Latin America.* Seminar on Feminism and Culture in Latin America.

Black, Jan Knippers, ed. *Latin America: Its Problems and Its Promise.*

Castro-Klaren, Sara, Sylvia Molloy, and Beatriz Sarlo. *Women's Writing in Latin America, an Anthology,* particularly part 3: Women, History, and Ideology.

Miller, Francesca. *Latin American Women and the Search for Social Justice.*

Skidmore, Thomas E., and Peter H. Smith. *Modern Latin America.*

Level: University

EL SOL DEL JUEZ (The Judge's Coin)

Fiction. With Subtitles. 10 min. 1983

Directed by: Juan José Ravaioli

Produced by: Estudio Imagem (Av. Agraciada 1641 Esc. 202, Montevideo; tel: [5982] 915-441)

Distributed by: IMRE

Evaluators: Gerard Aching, Robin Andersen, Iris Engstrand, Joan A. McGinnis, Johanna Mendelson-Forman

Description: This is a poetic adaptation of a historical event that led to the largest peasant uprising in Peru. Never mentioning the uprising itself, the tape presents a metaphorical story about coercion and resistance (or lack of it). An entire village is brought to its knees by fear of a powerful judge. He unknowingly drops a coin on the street, but no one dares to pick it up, despite their impoverished conditions. The coin lies there for months, untouched. One evening after drinking a great deal, a man gets the courage to take the coin. When he falls asleep, his wife puts it back. Everyone fears the consequences. Later the judge walks by and picks up the coin himself saying, "Look, someone dropped a coin." The community breathes a sigh of relief, and the drunk man, now sober, is shown enraged.

Strengths and Weaknesses: This tape illustrates the strong hierarchical nature of Spanish colonial society and its endurance into this century. The story line, dramatic effects, closeups, and music are strong points.

No context is given; thus, without an introduction, the video's message may be confusing and could reinforce stereotypes with U.S. audiences. One evaluator found the tape slow moving and the acting weak.

Introducing the Tape: Students need a historical introduction and analysis of the story as a metaphor to better understand the film's message.

How to Use: In *High School Spanish* class I would use a study guide complete with vocabulary, discussion questions, and a "supposition" question: "What would you do if you were starving and saw a coin that you didn't dare touch?" (McGinnis)

The tape could be useful in a *Sociology* course covering class and hierarchy in Latin American history. (Mendelson-Forman)

Suggested Readings: Burkhelder, Mark. *The Audiencia of Lima.*

Level: Junior High School—University

TAHITI (Tahiti)
Experimental.   With Subtitles.   37 min.
Directed by: Pablo Dotta
Produced by: Producciones del Tomate (Joaquin Nuñez 3092, Montevideo; tel: [5982] 797-269; fax: [5982] 953-104/981-256)
Distributed by: IMRE
Evaluators: Jesikah María Ross, Catherine Russo, Jennifer M. Taylor, Aaron Vinck
Description: This video is an artistic portrayal of the modern-day youth of Uruguay from director Pablo Dotta. Through a series of vignettes, the experimental, dreamy film portrays the emptiness and isolation of both the interior and the exterior landscapes of the characters and the setting. We see persons who love, struggle, are bored, and are prisoners of apathy. Scenes of streets from a bus, a man and woman fighting, cows being slaughtered, a man trying to commit suicide, a choir of children singing are all loosely interwoven with the theme of alienation. The force of the narration is magnified by the provocative camera angles. The film contains brief nudity and some violence.
Strengths and Weaknesses: The film contains strong imagery and an evocative soundtrack. The visual composition and editing style are creative. It is a thought-provoking and mysterious piece.

Most evaluators found the tape confusing and could not discern its meaning or value.
Introducing the Tape: An introduction would be extremely helpful to give a context for this film. A brief explanation of what the film deals with would be helpful, as the purpose and meaning are unclear.
Level: University

VENEZUELA

AMAZONAS, EL NEGOCIO DE ESTE MUNDO (The Amazon, The Business of This World)
Documentary.   Without Subtitles.   70 min.   1986
Directed by: Carlos Azpúrua
Produced by: Caralcine (2 Transversal, Qta. El Laurel, Caracas 1071; tel: [582] 752-4564, [582] 285-9056 or [582] 234-2365)
Distributed by: CIMR, IMRE Archive (available for viewing only)
Evaluators: Cliff Welch
Description: This disturbing documentary reveals the complicity of various institutions in the destruction of the Venezuelan Amazon rain forest and its indigenous cultures. It is a powerful film, quite different from typical U.S. documentaries in that it has a clear point of view, explicitly stated at the beginning and end of the film. The documentary is dedicated to "all those who have never been discovered because they have always existed" and blames all viewers who, through their silence, allow the destruction of the Amazon to continue. The

armed forces, foreign companies, anthropologists, sociologists, politicians, and U.S. evangelical missionaries (particularly the New Tribes Missions) are held accountable for contributing to the destruction of the Amazon. The documentary depicts evangelists as viewing the Amerindians as devil worshippers and "black gold," ripe for the picking. Their enterprise is characterized by a materialist scramble for souls, and the knowledge they gather about the communities and the role they play in introducing indigenous people to the modern world are shown to be part of larger colonization and modernization goals. U.S. companies, like General Dynamics and Westinghouse, are revealed to be major investors in the development of mines and processing plants in the Amazon. Amerindians are depicted largely as victims of this process, and their rights to their land and culture are defended. The film covers the years 1979 to 1984; the two primary locations depicted are the National Congress in Caracas and the TamaTama mission on the upper Orinoco. Adopting a cinema-verité style, the film links many interviews without voice-over narration.
Strengths and Weaknesses: A great strength of this film is its Venezuelan focus. As so many Amazon films are about Brazil, it's refreshing to see another national perspective. Unlike many films on the Brazilian Amazon, this work emphasizes the human costs of development over the ecological ones. The tape is clear and accessible, and its lack of narration and the use of dramatic music make it more compelling to watch than many documentaries.

Although the indigenous communities are sympathetically portrayed, the film can be criticized for failing to show the complexities of their relationship with the modern world and the Christians.
Introducing the Tape: The film is self-explanatory and does not need an introduction to be understood. However, it could be mentioned that the filmmaker, Carlos Azpúrua, is a congressman for the MAS (*Movimiento al Socialismo*) party.
How to Use: I would use the tape to discuss the relationship between contemporary Protestant missionaries, the disintegration of indigenous communities, and the development of virgin areas. This link was clearly demonstrated in the film and is one that many college students would find interesting. (Welch)
Level: High School—University

AMERIKA, TERRA INCOGNITA (Amerika, Unknown Land)
Feature.   No Dialogue.   98 min.   1988
Directed by: Diego Rísquez
Produced by: Producciones Guakamaya (Qta Solange Calle Oriente, Country Club, Caracas; tel: [582] 261-7181/8685; fax: [582] 283-9377)
Distributed by: IMRE
Evaluators: Emperatriz Arreaza-Camero, Elinor G. K. Melville, Cynthia L. Stone
Description: *Amérika, terra incognita* is the third in director Rísquez's trilogy of avant-garde cinematic meditations on

Latin American history and the relation between Europeans and indigenous peoples. Familiar images, such as the arrival of European conquistadors in the Americas, are made unfamiliar through inversion. Rather than following the journey of the Europeans westward, we witness the capture and subsequent voyage to Europe of an Amerindian *cacique*. Instead of the romantic portrayal of the scantily clad indigenous woman seduced by the European "discoverer," it is the European princess who falls in love with the young *cacique*. Director Rísquez's penchant for playing with the boundaries between art and reality is aptly realized through a series of parodies of Velázquez paintings and Vivaldi opera. The slow pans over the various New World treasures laid out in the baroque European court invoke both the art of Velázquez and the Flemish still-lifes of which the Spanish Hapsburgs were so fond. The trilogy defies conventional cinema by refusing dialogue and traditional plot techniques.

Director Diego Rísquez has said of this film, "For me, *Amérika, terra incognita* is the end of the work I started in 1979, when I decided to make a trilogy on the history of my country, and at the same time, on that of South America. The first part of the trilogy was *Bólivar, sinfonía tropikal*, which was about independence in 1800. This was followed by *Orinoko, nuevo mundo*, which concerns the mythical and the real history of our great river, from before the conquest of America until the end of the seventeenth century. *Amérika, terra incognita*, the third part, tells the story of a conquistador who returns to Europe with treasures from the New World: gold nuggets, emeralds, tropical fruits, parrots, plants, animals, and . . . a man, an Indian chief. Of course, the European court is filled with wonder at this indigenous, surrounded by music, artists, nuns, and jugglers. The princess falls immediately in love with this man with exotic charms. From this union, the first bastard prince of a European court is born, and he comes to the world covered in gold. I think that after 500 years, it is now up to us to tell our version of the facts. I want to dedicate this work to the great masters of Latin American cinema, Glauber Rocha and Fernando Birri."

Strengths and Weaknesses: This is a visually beautiful film, with good music and acting. It defies traditional expectations of the production of meaning and thus can be seen as either a rewarding cinematic experience or an unmemorable film, depending on the viewer. The film received many national and international awards.

Introducing the Tape: As the film has no dialogue, viewers will need a brief introduction to the historical events. A reading of Shakespeare's *The Tempest* could invite interesting discussion. A general introduction to Diego Rísquez's films would be helpful, as would an introduction to experimental film techniques. It should also be mentioned that the film was originally shot on super-8mm and enlarged to 35mm.

How to Use: I would use this film to show the cultural clash of two different worlds since 1492, how Europeans misrepresented or fictionalized the indigenous cultures, and raise the issue of *mestizaje* in Latin America. (Arreaza-Camero)

An interesting aspect of the film is the way in which it alternates images and sounds from a Western and an Amerindian point of view. In this sense, it could be used in a course that attempts to sensitize students to the ways in which a Eurocentric worldview influences artistic representation. The film can also be approached as a sort of modern-day tribute to, and meditation on, the paintings of Diego Velázquez. In a *Latin American Film* course it can be used as an example of an avant-garde film that has developed a substantial cult following. (Stone)

Suggested Readings: Franco, Jean. "High-Tech Primitivism: The Representation of Tribal Societies in Feature Films." In *Mediating Two Worlds: Cinematic Encounters in the Americas,* ed. John King, Ana M. López, and Manuel Alvarado.

King, John. *Magical Reels: A History of Cinemas in Latin America.*

Miranda, Julio E. "El nuevo cine venezolano."

Shakespeare, William. *The Tempest*

Shohat, Ella, and Robert Stam. "Aesthetics of Resistance." In *Unthinking Eurocentrism: Multiculturalism and the Media.*

Todorov, Tzezvan. *The Conquest of America: The Question of the Other.*

Complementary Films/Videos: *Bólivar, sinfonía tropikal (Bólivar, Tropical Symphony)* (Venezuela); *Orinoko, nuevo mundo (Orinoko, New World)* (Venezuela).

Level: University

BOLIVAR SINFONIA TROPIKAL (Bolivar, Tropical Symphony)

Feature.   No Dialogue.   75 min.   1980

Directed by: Diego Rísquez

Produced by: Producciones Guakamaya (Qta Solange Calle Oriente, Country Club, Caracas; tel: [582] 261-7181/8685; fax: [582] 283-9377)

Distributed by: IMRE

Evaluators: Kendall W. Brown, Robert P. Davis, Donald J. Mabry, Pamela M. Smorkaloff, Cynthia L. Stone

Description: This is the first of Diego Rísquez's trilogy of avant-garde cinematic treatments of historical subjects. Using a painterly style, it features portraits, still-lifes, and scenes shot as tableaux vivants. The film provides an experimental interpretation of the arrival of the Spanish and their domination of the New World as well as the Venezuelan independence movement, focusing on the role of Simón Bolívar. There is no dialogue or narration, simply a musical score and the depiction of events from Bolívar's career. The images play with the myths surrounding Bolívar and the independence fighters, the question of slavery, popular culture, and folklore, among other things. Although seen as heroic in many respects, Bolívar is not treated as a saviour.

Director Diego Rísquez has said: "Venezuela is a country suffering from an identity crisis of great magnitude, mainly because of oil. The petrodollar mentality has deeply affected every aspect of Venezuelan life. Today, 'money' is the most common word. This is why I thought it was important to show a man who was moved by an ideal of freedom. The film attempts to be a synthesis of Venezuelan history. Two actors play the role of Bolívar: one represents a Bolívar known through textbooks, a superhero, an emperor in Napoleon's era; the other is the romantic warrior, the revolutionary, the lover, the man. What I have tried to do is to touch the collective unconsciousness of the people. I was mainly inspired by the Venezuelan iconography at the time of its war of independence. The symbolism may appear obscure to an outsider, but it forms a part of every Venezuelan's background. The painter's brush has been replaced by the movie camera. The film represents the poetic alternative to Venezuelan cinema."

Strengths and Weaknesses: This is an imaginative attempt to deal with the greatest of Venezuelan heroes. The long trek though the varied landscapes of South America is beautifully filmed, with many innovative shots. The lack of dialogue and plot puts the focus on the visual and the emotive. If the viewer surrenders to the flow of images and music, there are many interesting moments. The film received numerous national and international awards.

Evaluators had diverse reactions to the film's experimental and impressionistic nature. One felt the principal themes were not difficult to infer, as they were kept relatively simple, with a strong emphasis on symbolic and dramatic effect. The juxtaposition of historical figures and symbols creates a general sense of confusion and apprehension, appropriate to the anxiety of the period. Other evaluators, however, felt that the film's experimental format would be difficult for viewers unfamiliar with the iconography and historical events depicted, as the film does not provide any historical explanation.

Introducing the Tape: This film needs an introduction to the history of Latin America, particularly the periods of colonization and independence. Some comments regarding Diego Rísquez's films, experimental filmmaking, and super-8mm filmmaking would also be helpful. Viewers should be told that the film includes what may seem to be some historical inaccuracies (which suggest key figures may have been elsewhere in history interacting with different events). It should be pointed out that the director intentionally used this experimental format, in part to make viewers question "history" produced from a Eurocentric point of view. See *Amérika, tierra incógnita* for an introduction to the trilogy by the filmmaker.

How to Use: This film would be a potentially useful addition to any course that focuses on Simón Bolívar's role in history and/or representation in literature and art. It is helpful to know something about the broad outlines of Bolívar's life before seeing the film. It could also be used as an example of contemporary, avant-garde Latin American cinema. (Stone)

Suggested Readings: Franco, Jean. "High-Tech Primitivism: The Representation of Tribal Societies in Feature Films." In *Mediating Two Worlds: Cinematic Encounters in the Americas,* ed. John King, Ana M. López, and Manuel Alvarado.

King, John. *Magical Reels: A History of Cinemas in Latin America.*

Masur, Gerard. *Simón Bolívar.* And other biographies of Bolívar.

Miranda, Julio. "El nuevo cine venezolano."

Shohat, Ella, and Robert Stam. "Aesthetics of Resistance." In *Unthinking Eurocentrism: Multiculturalism and the Media.*

Complementary Films/Videos: *Amérika: tierra incógnita (Amérika: Unknown Land)* (Venezuela); *Orinoko, nuevo mundo* (Venezuela)

Level: University

CRONICAS GINECOLOGICAS (Gynecological Chronicles)

Documentary.   With Subtitles.   60 min.   1992

Directed by: Monica Henríquez

Produced by: Luna Films/Contraluz Films (c/o 7–9 Earlham Street, London WC2 2HA; tel: [441-71] 485-1189; fax: [441-71] 497-0446)

Distributed by: IMRE Archive (available for viewing only), Jane Balfour Films

Evaluators: Emperatriz Arreaza-Camero, Julia Lesage, Laura Elisa Pérez

Description: This is an outstanding, creative documentary that reconstructs the history of middle- and upper-class Venezuelan women's social and political struggles for empowerment from the 1920s through the 1950s. The tape makes extensive use of archival footage, popular cultural materials, and interviews with the prominent Venezuelan women writers and political activists María Teresa Castillo, Mercedes Fermín, and Lucila Palacios.

Strengths and Weaknesses: This is a highly imaginative and effective documentary. It is extremely well shot and edited. The music and footage from the period are skillfully integrated into the piece.

Evaluators noted that the tape focused primarily on upper- and middle-class women's conditions, yet it did put these narratives within the broader political and historical context.

Introducing the Tape: U.S. viewers will need some background on the Gómez dictatorship period and contemporary Venezuelan history (1935–1958). The film presents three parts: (1) the visit of Carlos Gardel in 1935, (2) Gómez's death and afterward, and (3) the first exercise of election and women's vote through a beauty contest in 1944.

How to Use: I would use this tape as an exponent of the Venezuelan political situation in the first half of the twentieth century and also the role of women in the political struggles at that time. It combines different media, including magazines, radio soap operas, cinema, and oral history to portray a historical period. (Arreaza-Camero)

I would use the tape to teach about the potential blend of different elements in a documentary. I would also talk about how film can present history. In a *Women's Studies* class it's useful to point out different national trajectories that shaped women's lives. (Lesage)

The tape could be used in *Literature, History,* and *Culture* courses to supplement written narratives of Venezuelan history (1920–1950s). In *Film* courses it could be shown as a example of a creative documentary. (Pérez)

Suggested Readings: Aguirre, Jesus M., and Marcelino Bisbal. *El nuevo cine venezolano.*

Gaines, J. "Race and Gender in Feminist Film Theory." In *Cultural Critique.*

Lerner, Elisa. *Crónicas ginecológicas.*

López, A. "The Melodrama in Latin America."

Mulvey, L., and C. Penley. *Feminist Film Theory.*

Other books on Venezuelan history, particularly the Gómez dictatorship.

Level: University

CUANDO QUIERO LLORAR, NO LLORO

Feature. Without Subtitles. 90 min. 1972

Directed by: Mauricio Walerstein

Distributed by: IMRE Archive (available for viewing only)

Evaluators: Lavina Tilson Gass, Marlene Gottlieb, John Hays

Description: Based on the novel by Miguel Otero Silva, this film deals with Venezuelan politics in the first half of the twentieth century. It traces the lives of three characters, all named Victorino. Each Victorino came from a different social class and lived during the one of the dictatorships that plagued Venezuela. All three are victims of society.

Strengths and Weaknesses: Evaluators had mixed reactions to the film. One felt it was a creative and unique production, making a powerful social statement. It provides a picture of life in Caracas, contrasting luxury and poverty and showing the danger faced by political protestors.

Others found the film's format confusing. Students need to be familiar with the original novel and/or the history of Venezuela to understand the film. It is best directed to adult viewers, as it contains violence, drugs, political torture, and nudity.

Introducing the Tape: An explanation both before and after viewing would aid those not familiar with Venezuela. Audiences should be given the time frame and be presented with background on the Venezuelan political situation, including the factions and politics in Latin America. If possible, viewers should read the original novel first or be given an introduction explaining the film's technique of intertwining three life stories.

How to Use: College teachers might use the film for a discussion of political and social conditions in Latin America. (Tilson Gass)

I would have my class read Miguel Otero Silva's novel and then view the film. We would compare the film to the novel and comment upon the salient themes. (Gottlieb)

This tape could be used as a supplement for discussion to help students understand modern Venezuela, from Rómulo Gallegos to Peret. (Hays)

Suggested Readings: Otero Silva, Miguel. *Cuando quiero llorar, no lloro.*

Level: University

CUBAGUA (Cubagua)

Feature. With Subtitles. 75 min. 1978

Directed by: Michael New (Apartado Postal #42, La Hechicera, Mérida; tel: [5874] 713-903; fax: [5874] 401-725 or 401-720)

Distributed by: IMRE

Evaluators: Emperatriz Arreaza-Camero, Richard C. Boly, Cynthia L. Stone

Description: Based on the 1931 novel by the Venezuelan writer Enrique Bernardo Núñez (1895–1964), *Cubagua* is a cinematic meditation on Venezuelan history that cuts back and forth between settings and time periods to combine into one narrative framework the stories of three highly charged historical events. The first segment, set in the island of Cubagua in the sixteenth century, shows how the slave trade destroyed most of the indigenous Caribbean population during the colonial period. The second is set in Caracas in the 1930s, when oil exploitation began. And the third, set in the Amazon in the 1970s, portrays the role of multinational companies in undermining Venezuelan political autonomy. These three themes are interwoven through the juxtaposition of successive incarnations of an Italian count, a petrochemical engineer, and a company representative, all played by the same actor, who encounters the same beautiful, courageous woman and radical priest in each of his lives. Finally, the protagonist breaks the cycle of exploitation in his last incarnation as an engineer in the rain forest. The film's underlying message is the need to come to terms with the mistakes of the past in order to overcome injustice in the present.

Strengths and Weaknesses: Evaluators found the cinematography and quality of production excellent and the theme interesting. One reviewer commented that the strengths and weaknesses of the film are similar to those in the novel on which it is based. The creation of a mythical space in which to explore the analogies between widely divergent historical periods is a provocative idea developed in the novel, which anticipates (by over thirty years) the work of acclaimed Latin American writers Carpentier, García Márquez, and Fuentes. However, the realization of this idea is not presented with sufficient complexity to fulfill its potential. For those not well acquainted with Venezuelan history, the film can be somewhat confusing.

Introducing the Tape: The film's structure alternates between three different time periods and settings. This should be clarified to viewers before screening. Historical background for each of the three periods, as well as the Venezuelan-U.S. relationship, should be presented.

How to Use: I would use the tape as an example of *New Latin American Cinema* to discuss issues of national identity and the role of the *mestiza* as an allegory of national liberation. (Arreaza-Camero)

This film could be used in a *Colonial Latin American History* or *Literature* course in conjunction with selected passages from Bartolomé de las Casas's *Historia de las Indias* that tells of the enslavement and death of the indigenous peoples of Cubagua and the surrounding islands. One could also view it along with the novel on which it is based in order to explore issues of cinematic adaptation. For courses focusing on *Venezuelan* and *Latin American History,* the film provides an interesting perspective on issues of colonialism and neocolonialism. In a *Film* course it can be used to examine contemporary filmmaking set in the Latin American colonial period. (Stone)

Suggested Readings: Araujo, Orlando. *La obra literaria en Enrique Bernardo Núñez.*

Arreaza-Camero, Emperatriz. "Cubagua, or the Search for Venezuelan National Identity."

Casas, Bartolomé de las. *Historia de las Indias (1559).*

Núñez, Enrique Bernardo. *Cubagua.*

Shohat, Ella, and Robert Stam, eds. "Formations of Colonialist Discourse." In *Unthinking Eurocentrism: Multiculturalism and the Media,* 55–99.

Stam, Robert. "Rewriting 1492: Cinema and the Columbus Debate," 66–71.

Vilanova, Angel. *Para una lectura crítica de "Cubagua," de Núñez.*

Complementary Films/Videos on the Spanish American Colonial Period (and Brazil): *Bartolomé de las Casas* (Sergio Olhovich 1992, distributed by IMRE); *1492: The Conquest of Paradise* (Ridley Scott 1992); *Yo, la peor de todas (I, the Worst of All)* (María Luisa Bemberg 1990); *Cabeza de Vaca* (Echevarría 1990); *Jericó* (Luis Alberto Lamata 1990); *El Dorado* (Carlos Saura 1988); *Nuevo mundo* (Gabriel Rete 1987); *The Mission* (Roland Jaffe 1986); *La Monja Alférez (The Nun Ensign)* (Emilio Gómez Muriel 1944 and Javier Aguirre 1986); *Orinoko, nuevo mundo* (Diego Rísquez 1984); *Tupac Amarú* (Federico García 1984); *Quilombo* (Carlos Diegues 1984); *Cimarrones* (Ferrando 1982); *La última cena (The Last Supper)* (Tomás Gutierrez Alea 1976); *El santo oficio (The Holy Office)* (Arturo Ripstein 1977); *Aguirre, der Zorn Gottes (Aguirre, the Wrath of God)* (Werner Herzog 1972, distributed by Facets); *Como era gostoso meu francaise (How Tasty Was My Little Frenchman)* (Nelson Pereira dos Santos 1971, distributed by New Yorker Films); *Terra em transe (Land in Anguish)* (Glauber Rocha 1967); *Ganga Zumba* (Carlos Diegues, 1963, distributed by New Yorker Films); *Christopher Columbus* (David MacDonald 1949); *O no coronado* (Baldwin).

Level: University

EL DIABLO DE CUMANA (The Cumaná Devil)
Documentary. With Subtitles. 26 min. 1984
Directed by: John Dickinson
Produced by: Cinematográfica (Apartado Postal 101, San Antonio de los, Aestado Miranda)
Distributed by: Documentary Educational Resources
Evaluators: John Chasteen, Judith Elkin, María Fernández.

Description: Luis del Valle Hurtado (Tarzán), a native of Cumaná, learned to masquerade as a Carnival devil from a man who brought the custom from Trinidad to Venezuela. Tarzán is regarded as the best impersonator of Satan in the town. This film documents his ritualistic transformation for the town's religious festivities. Finally, it shows scenes of Tarzán's street dancing, now a dying art form as "young people are ashamed to dress up."

Strengths and Weaknesses: This film documents a practice that seems in danger of disappearing in Venezuela. Tarzán is a virtuoso performer. His lively rehearsals of the devil's expressions and sounds, as well as his enthusiastic explanations of the process, make this a jewel of performance art. One evaluator, however, found the tape too long. Another felt it was less effective because Tarzán defines himself more as an entertainer than a participant in a religious ritual.

Introducing the Tape: The tape is self-explanatory. However, some discussion of Carnival practices and religious and cultural syncretism could enhance its meaning.

How to Use: This film illustrates the influence and spiritual importance of masquerading practices among various Carnival celebrations in the Caribbean and South America. (Chasteen)

In my courses in *Latin American Art* I would use the tape to illustrate cultural and religious syncretism. I would also use it in my general art classes as an example of a glorious performance. (Fernández)

Suggested Readings: Kinser, Samuel. *Carnival, American Style: Mardi Gras at New Orleans and Mobile.* Discusses issues of masquerading practices and spiritual importance of carnivalization, though mostly in reference to Mardi Gras in New Orleans.

Taussig, Michael. *Shamanism, Colonialism, and the Wild Man.*

Level: High School—University

DISPAREN A MATAR (Shoot To Kill)
Feature. With Subtitles. 90 min. 1991
Directed by: Carlos Azpúrua (2 Transversal, Qta, El Laurel, Caracas 1071; tel: [582] 285-9056 or 752-4564; fax: [582] 234-2365)
Distributed by: Facets, IMRE
Evaluators: Emperatriz Arreaza-Camero, Alberto J. Carlos, John Hess, Laura Elisa Pérez
Description: The suspenseful plot begins with a police raid on a violence-ridden apartment complex in one of the marginalized sectors of Caracas. A mother watches as her son is unjustly murdered by a police captain. The mother, Mercedes, embarks on a crusade to discredit the official version of the crime. Santiago, a young journalist, moved by Mercedes's passion and determination, rediscovers his own integrity by taking on the case, endangering his life, and separating from his family as his investigation reveals the depth of the corruption of power within the country. This film can be read as an allegory of social conditions and the struggle against police repression in Latin American nations.

Strengths and Weaknesses: This fast-action film is full of suspense and realism, with excellent acting, storytelling, and editing. It captures the atmosphere of corruption, violence, privilage, and cynicism amidst the Venezuelan professional middle class in the 1980s. The fast narrative pace avoids a documentary or didactic effect.

While one evaluator mentioned that the film was especially useful in its handling of the complexities of class and gender interests, another felt that the women's roles were in some ways stereotyped and sexist. Evaluators had diverse reactions to the film's ending. One commented that the film was weakened by leaving the situation unresolved. Another felt that the ending reflected the reality of corrupt officials continuing with "business as usual" while the challenges against them remain "unresolved."

Introducing the Tape: Background on the political, economic, and social context of Venezuela since the 1980s could be useful. After the reelection of President Carlos Andrés Pérez and his imposition of International Monetary Fund-inspired economic reforms, a spontaneous popular uprising occurred in all major cities on February 27, 1989. The uprising was met with brutal military repression. Curfews were imposed, civil rights were suspended, and an official figure of three hundred dead was later announced. The film would seem to be a response to this event. Some comparison of contemporary Venezuelan politics to other countries in Latin America such as Brazil or Mexico could be of interest.

How to Use: I would present this tape as a contemporary example of the tradition of politically committed cinema in Latin America. Political research and social denunciation are presented in a creative way. (Arreaza-Camero)

I would use this film as a text that allows us to see the contradictions of modern Latin American states. (Pérez)

Suggested Readings: Armes, Roy. *Third World Filmmaking and the West.*

Burton, Julianne. "The Camera as 'Gun': Two Decades of Film Culture and Resistance in Latin America."

Burton, Julianne. *Cinema and Social Change in Latin America: Conversations with Filmmakers.*

Burton, Julianne. *The New Latin American Cinema: An Annotated Bibliography of Sources in English, Spanish, and Portuguese, 1960–1980.*

Chanan, Michael, ed. *Twenty-five Years of the New Latin American Cinema.*

Cortez, Carlos E., Leon G. Campbell, and Allan Curi. *A Filmic Approach to the Study of Historical Dilemnas.*

Fusco, Coco, ed. *Reviewing Histories: Selections from New Latin American Cinema.*

Pick, Zuzana M., ed. *Latin American Filmmakers and the Third Cinema.*

Pick, Zuzana M., ed. *The New Latin American Cinema: A Continental Project.*

Other Venezuelan and Latin American history books.

Level: High School—University

EL ESCANDALO

Feature. Without Subtitles. 105 min. 1987
Directed by: Carlos Oteyza (Av. Diego Cisneros Colgate ala 2, Los Ruices, Caracas; tel: [582] 283-9377; fax: [582] 239-4786)
Produced by: Antonio Almeida/Helen Bocco
Distributed by: IMRE Archive (available for viewing only)
Evaluators: Robert DiAntonio, Johanna Mendelson-Forman, Stephen Webre
Description: This film is about a real case of administrative corruption in Venezuela's national oil company, Petroleos Nacionales. Portraying the life of an employee, the filmmaker shows how management coopts and corrupts the worker into the scandal-ridden life of the big-oil business. Antonio Campos is a young, ambitious engineer who becomes a national celebrity after appearing in one of the company's television commercials. Promoted to director of sales, he finds himself managing millions of dollars in international transactions but receiving only a public servant's salary. Antonio proves vulnerable when approached by the cynical, high-living Aroldo Benavides, who has already corrupted several members of the sales staff. Benavides works for a foreign oil company and offers money in exchange for privileged information, useful to his clients. Antonio gradually surrenders his scruples, becoming wealthier and more arrogant as he stoops to increasingly serious betrayals of the public trust. Unfortunately for Antonio and his confederates, the company's security chief is suspicious and pushes an investigation. In the end, Antonio escapes prosecution but loses his family, his good name, and his ill-gotten gains.

Strengths and Weaknesses: The film has many of the characteristics of made-for-television, commercial films in the United States. It has high production values, combining good acting, directing, and camera work with a production budget adequate to the project. There are wonderful scenes of Caracas and beaches, and even a location sequence shot in New York City. The story deals in a straightforward fashion with an issue of public concern and provides a tidy ending in which the characters come to some sort of closure, even if the societal problem does not.

Evaluators felt that the story lacked depth and was confusing at times. Antonio Campo's metamorphosis from straight-arrow family man to corrupt bureaucrat, for example, occurs with little obvious inner conflict or strong motivation. Some other aspects of the story line are poorly integrated into the whole.

Introducing the Tape: U.S. viewers would benefit from some background on the current economic and political situation in Venezuela, including information on its state-run oil company and the overarching issue of corruption in public office. Students in Spanish language courses could be briefed on the colloquial use in Venezuela of the word *vaina* instead of the more familiar *cosa* for "thing," as well as on some elementary profanity.

How to Use: I would use this tape in a course on *Venezuelan*

Cinema pointing out the country's dependence on the oil industry. I would explain that while money from oil production has been used for some aspects of economic development in the country, the industry has also been riddled with corruption. I would take note of the relationship between women and men, seniors and juniors in the business, and parents and children as examples of the interrelation between the political and the personal. (Arreaza-Camero)

Instructors could use this film as an opener for an exploration of white-collar crime as a cross-cultural phenomenon, perhaps comparing the plot with the insider-trading scandals on Wall Street and the astounding corruption unearthed in PEMEX, the Mexican equivalent of Venezuela's Petroleos Nacionales. Other possible subjects for class discussion include workplace ethics in state-owned enterprises, as compared to private ones, and the historical role of corruption in Spanish American governments and bureaucracy. (Webre)
Level: University

FEBRERO (February)
Animation.   No Dialogue.   17 min.   1989
Directed by: María Eugenia Martínez
Produced by: University de los Andes (Universidad de los Andes, Mérida; tel: [5874] 401-725; fax: [5874] 401-720)
Distributed by: IMRE Archive (available for viewing only)
Evaluators: Emperatriz Arreaza-Camero, Graciela Michelotti, Lewis A. Tambs
Description: This five-minute animation presents the events of the February 1989 riots in Caracas, Venezuela, accompanied by an ironic narrative. It begins with an image of an empty chair in front of a television and the transmitted sounds of the inauguration of President Carlos Andrés Pérez. A collage of quickly edited, child-like drawings punctuated by still photos and music recreates the highly charged atmosphere of the popular uprising that erupted after Pérez's announcement of International Monetary Fund-inspired reforms. One such reform was an end to government subsidies for food and oil, a move that would undoubtedly result in a dramatic decline in the standard of living. The uprising consisted of massive looting in all of the major cities. Curfews were imposed, civil rights were suspended, and an official figure of three hundred dead was announced after the uprising was repressed. The tape's animated images depict how the military intervention violated civil rights, while political speeches and news commentary continue as the soundtrack. At the tape's end, the television broadcasts Pérez's forecast of a magic year 2000 when the country can look forward to an end to all its problems.
Strengths and Weaknesses: The film makes wonderful use of animation, drawings, still photos, news footage, sounds, and images. Evaluators mentioned no weak points.
Introducing the Tape: The film assumes that viewers are already familiar with the depicted event, so U.S. viewers may

need to be told that the film responds to the events of February 1989 and be given a description of the political and economic landscape of Venezuela's last forty years.
How to Use: Venezuela is one of the primary oil suppliers to the United States and a founding member of OPEC, placing the country among the richest nations in Latin America. Yet, the social inequalities among the population make evident the poor distribution of wealth. This film shows in a creative way how the Venezuelan people reacted to this process of injustice. (Arreaza-Camero)

The film functions as testimony and/or document to another "reality" or version of the event in order to counter the official version. This could be used as a point of departure to discuss events in recent Latin American history and popular uprisings. (Michelotti)

In *Film Production* class the tape can be used as an excellent example of animation as documentary and creative techniques that can be used instead of traditional documentary forms. The use of television as a structuring device in the film can stimulate discussion in a *Media Criticism* class.
Suggested Readings: López, Carmen A. *Crisis fiscal e industrialización en el desarrollo Latinoamericano.*

Silva. Michelena, José A. *Crisis de la democracia.*

Local Publications: *El nacional* (daily newspaper); *SIC* and *Comunicación* (monthly journals).
Level: University

LA GUAJIRA (The Guajira)
Documentary.   With Subtitles.   58 min.   1984
Directed by: Calogero Salvo (40 West 15th St. #6B, New York, NY 10011; tel: [212] 727-8231)
Distributed by: Canyon Cinema, Chip Taylor Communications
Evaluators: Walter R. Adams, Julia Lesage
Description: The Guajiro Indians of Venezuela are a people who have survived the harsh elements of their desert environment and the intervention of outside cultures. Through the centuries, they have learned to interpret the values and laws of those outside cultures to ensure the perpetuation of their race. In this film, the Guajiro Indians' art and ancient ceremonies are intermingled with the economic and sociopolitical realities existing in Latin America today. Themes covered include the drought, *maracaibo,* salt mines, the market, and a religious school in the area that strives to maintain traditions.
Strengths and Weaknesses: This is a personal exploration with lovely, respectful, and intimate images. The tape includes long wordless passages of labor, including images of weaving, pottery making, and marriage preparations, as well as great music.

It is not clear until late in the film where it takes place. Also, at critical points the subtitles are absent.
Introducing the Tape: Viewers should be told that the film is set in Venezuela.

Suggested Readings: Nichols, Bill. *Representing Reality: Issues and Concepts in Documentary.*
Level: High School—University

JERICO (Jericó)

Feature.   With Subtitles.   85 min.   1991
Directed by: Luis Alberto Lamata
Produced by: Thalia Producciones y Foncine (Urb. San Rafael de La Florida, Caracas; tel: [582] 242-6420; fax: [582] 744-480 or [582] 746-491)
Distributed by: IMRE
Evaluators: Emperatriz Arreaza-Camero, Peter Bakewell, Paul J. LaReau, Joan A. McGinnis, Patricia Smith, Pamela M. Smorkaloff, Ann Marie Stock
Description: *Jericó* is the fictional account of Friar Santiago, a Dominican monk who is sent by the Catholic Church at the beginning of the sixteenth century to participate in one of the expeditions to the Amazon. The expedition breaks up, and Santiago is captured by an indigenous Caribe tribe, where he remains for five years. Depicted with ethnographic authority, this is the story of a man who wanted to transform a world and instead found himself transformed by that world. The film is also a metaphor for the priest's spiritual journey. Through his diary notations, viewers witness his mental examinations of the nature of good and evil and the existence of God. The title *Jericó* could be interpreted as referring to the walls of the indigenous culture as well as to the walls of the mind/soul that refuse to fall.
Strengths and Weaknesses: This forceful film achieves a convincing sense of realism by appropriating an ethnographic style of filmmaking more common to documentary films. A number of evaluators felt its treatment of indigenous people was respectful without idealizing the characters. Others felt that the film used a "colonizing" lens, viewing events through European eyes, and maintaining a certain anthropological gaze in presenting this world. Nonetheless, the film is a powerful examination of the moment of "encounter," while it poses questions of a more complex nature. It received a number of national and international awards.

The film contains scenes of violence, cannibalism, and full frontal nudity that may not be suitable for some audiences. For Spanish language classes, the second half of the film contains little Spanish dialogue for listening practice.
Introducing the Tape: Some history of the conquistadors and the expeditions to South America could be useful, including some background on the different nationalities that made up these expeditions. An introduction about the role of the Catholic Church in Latin America could provide some supplementary context. Viewers should be told that the female voice that narrates parts of the film is that of the friar's sister, who is introduced at the film's beginning, as she reads from his diary.
How to Use: I would use this tape as an example of the new Latin American cinema and the rewriting of Latin American history through the indigenous people's perspective. (Arreaza-Camero)

In a high school *Spanish* class I would have my students imagine that they were the first white men to see Latin America. I would ask them to write essays from an explorer's perspective and to contrast their view to that of an Indian seeing a white man for the first time. Spanish vocabulary could be presented before, after, or concurrently with comprehension questions. (McGinnis)

I would use the tape in undergraduate courses in *Development of Latin American Culture* and graduate courses in *Latin American Cultural History* in the sections that explore the role of the church. (Smorkaloff).

It would be useful for introducing some of the many issues of colonization in a course on the *History of Latin America*. The film examines the motivations of those intent upon converting "natives," as well as the implications of the cross-cultural interaction. I might opt to show only a few sequences from the film. (Stock)
Suggested Readings:
Columbus, Christopher. *Personal Narrative of the First Voyage of Columbus to America.* (excerpts)
Franco, Jean. *Plotting Women: Gender and Representation in Mexico*
Lockhart, James, and Stuart B. Schwartz. *Early Latin America: A History of Colonial Spanish America and Brazil,* section 2.
Ricard, Robert. *Spiritual Conquest of Mexico.* Different region, but gives a comparative account of mission methods and aims.
The biblical story of Jericho.
Complementary Films/Videos: Werner Herzog's *Fitzcaraldo* and *Aguirre the Wrath of God* (both distributed by Facets).
Level: High School—University

JUAN FELIX SANCHEZ (Juan Félix Sánchez)

Documentary.   With Subtitles.   27 min.   1982
Directed by: Calogero Salvo
Produced by: Dennis Scheichler and Calogero Salvo (40 W. 15th St. #6B, N.Y.C, NY 10011; tel: [212] 727-8231)
Distributed by: Chip Taylor Communications
Evaluators: Elba D. Birmingham-Pokorny, Jorge J. Rodríguez-Florido, Antônio R. M. Simões
Description: This documentary centers around the life of Juan Félix Sánchez, an eighty-two-year-old popular artist who lives in a remote valley in the Venezuelan Andes near the Colombian border. Juan Félix lives with his wife, Epifania, whose mother taught him how to weave. Juan Félix and Epifania narrate their own lives as they weave a new blanket. After presenting their weaving and way of life, the film turns to the sculptural work of Juan Félix. His motifs derive from Catholicism. Of particular interest is a project where he builds a chapel to the patron of Venezuela, Our Lady of Coromoto. He recreates the Calvary, including the apostles, the Virgin, Christ, Mary Magdalen, the thieves, and the sepulchre.

Strengths and Weaknesses: This work, originally shot on 16mm film, is a portrait of an exceptional artist, focusing on the daily activities of Juan Félix and Epifania. Their humility, simple way of life, and work harmonize with the sublime, extremely beautiful natural landscape of Mérida state. One evaluator commented that some may find Juan Félix and Epifania's lives a source of spiritual inspiration.

The film lacks an appropriate introduction and context for U.S. viewers. There is no link between Sánchez and the rest of cultural life in Venezuela.

Introducing the Tape: The importance of Juan Félix Sánchez among Venezuelan folk artists should be established, along with information about where he sells his work. An introduction to Venezuela and Latin American Catholicism could also be provided for U.S. audiences.

How to Use: I would use this documentary in connection with a course in *Latin American Culture* to show the industriousness, talent, and religious spirit of Latin American popular culture. It can be used in a conversational *Spanish* class to discuss the life and works of Sánchez. (Rodríguez-Florido)

I would use this film to show students the diversity of Venezuela's culture and geography, to introduce them to spoken Spanish, and to help them gain a better understanding and appreciation of Latin America's different cultural/art forms. (Birmingham-Pokorny)

Suggested Readings: Arvelo, Alberto, and Sigfrido Gever. *Juan Felix Sánchez.*

Burton, Julianne. *The Social Documentary in Latin America.*

Rowe, William, and Vivian Schelling. *Memory and Modernity: Popular Culture in Latin America.*

Level: University

LAUGHING ALLIGATOR

Experimental.   With Subtitles.   27 min.   1979
Directed by: Juan Downey
Distributed by: Electronic Arts Intermix
Evaluators: Deirdre Boyle, Brian Goldfarb, John Higgens, Rebecca Torres-Rívera
Description: This is Juan Downey's experimental, personal ethnography of his experiences living eight months with the Yanomami in the Amazon jungle. As a participant-observer, Downey explores and depicts Yanomami myths, legends, and traditions. He discovers that the Yanomami, characterized by anthropologists as cannibalistic, believe that the dead live on in the bodies of those who consume their pulverized bones. We learn of the legend of the tribe's origin, which is comparable to the biblical description of creation. We observe the people manufacturing their own hallucinogens to permit them to communicate with other worlds. The final myth presented deals with the discovery of fire, which gives Downey's film its title.

Strengths and Weaknesses: This tape offers a counter to standard anthropological analyses of a Third World culture by providing Downey's participant-observer commentary on the Yanomami Indians. Downey appropriates and problematizes the conventions of ethnography and anthropology, weaving together images of the village, enactments of myths and customs, and accounts of his own cultural identity. The work is groundbreaking as one of the pioneer uses of video to question the formal distinctions between documentary and fiction, ethnography and testimony. Its pacing and image sequences are interesting, helping to impart a sense of a "different" reality.

Most U.S. audiences will find the tape's experimental format a bit unusual. One reviewer found the narrator's voice and style monotonous. The work is a bit long for classroom viewing and discussion and would be better for a separate screening session.

Introducing the Tape: The tape is self-explanatory; however, it would be useful for U.S. viewers to have a bit more information about indigenous tribes and their living and social conditions. Some information on the history of U.S. video art (and of Juan Downey's earlier work) would also be helpful.

How to Use: I would use this tape to raise questions about how traditional ethnographic films have projected Western fantasies onto indigenous peoples. I would discuss narrative and filmic strategies that Downey uses to draw attention to, and undermine constructions of, colonialist authority. Comparisons could also be drawn to other art videos that engage in critique of ethnography (Trin T. Minh Ha's *Sur Name Viet, Given Name Nam* and *Living Is Round,* and Edin Vélez's *Meta Mayan II,* for example) as well as to works such as the *Spirit of TV* (Brazil) produced by indigenous groups that had previously been the subject of ethnographic films by anthropologists. (Goldfarb)

The tape could be used to start a discussion regarding alternative uses of video to express personal reality, and how the camera can be considered a "weapon" within a certain cultural perspective. (Higgens)

It could be used to demonstrate the diversity of people in Brazil. (Torres-Rívera)

Suggested Readings: Churchill, Ward. *Fantasies of the Master Race: Literature, Cinema, and the Colonization of American Indians.*

Crawford, Ian Peter, and David Turton, eds. *Film as Ethnography.*

Downey, Juan, "Smell of Turpentine." In *Illuminating Video: An Essential Guide to Video Art,* ed. Doug Hall and Sally Jo Fifer.

Fusco, Coco. "Ethnicity, Politics, and Poetics: Latinos and Media Art." In *Illuminating Video: An Essential Guide to Video Art.* ed. Doug Hall and Sally Jo Fifer, 304–16.

Michaels, Eric. *Bad Aboriginal Art: Tradition, Media and Technological Horizons.*

Minh-Ha, Trinh T. *Woman, Native, Other: Writing Postcoloniality and Feminist.*

Morre, Rachael. "Marketing Alterity."

Shohat, Ella. "Imaging Terra Incognita: The Disciplinary Gaze of Empire."

Tobing-Rony, Fatimah. "Those Who Squat, Those Who Sit: The Visualizing of Race in the 1895 Films of Félix-Louis Regnault."

Turner, Terence. "The Social Dynamics of Video Media in an Indigenous Society," 68–76.

Complementary Films/Videos: *O espiritu da TV (Spirit of TV)* (Brazil); Trin T. Minh Ha's *Sur Name Viet, Given Name Nam,* and *Living Is Round;* Edin Vélez's *Meta Mayan II* (Guatemala).

Level: University

MACU, LA MUJER DEL POLICIA (Macu, the Policeman's Wife)

Feature. With Subtitles. 90 min. 1987
Directed by: Solveig Hoogesteijn
Produced by: Macu Films (Qta. Fridmer Av. Humboldt, Urb. San Bernadino, Caracas; tel: [582] 513-381, fax: [582] 525-621 or 746-491)
Distributed by: IMRE, Latina
Evaluators: Charles Berquist, Susana Conde, Julia Lesage, Cynthia L. Stone
Description: This is an extremely well made and compelling film that tells the story of relations between Ismael Ramírez, a middle-aged police captain, and his teenage bride, Macu, in contemporary urban Venezuela. Based on a real-life, highly sensationalized murder case, the film follows the classic structure of a police thriller. Much of the story is narrated through flashbacks. Ismael begins to fancy Macu when she is eight years old. Her mother approves of the relationship, knowing the privileges to be gained from having a member of the police force in the family. When Macu is eleven, the two are married and later have two children. Macu, however, falls in love with Simón, an adolescent her own age. The nineteen-year-old Macu attempts to piece together the fragments of her eight-year marriage. But the final blow comes when she discovers that her husband has killed her lover and "disappeared" two of his friends. The obsessive intensity with which the press, the police, and the neighbors blame Macu for the disappearances only serves to highlight the injustice inherent in a social system that assumes wives are the sexual property of their husbands.
Strengths and Weaknesses: Brilliantly conceived and photographed, this film's suspenseful plot maintains a high level of viewer interest. The acting is strong, and the complex characters resist easy stereotyping. The film embraces the contradictory aspects of life on both a social and an emotional level and deals with the issues of police brutality and child brides. It reveals the intersection of exploitative (and internalized) class and gender roles in this society. It also shows the power of the police and relates it to unbridled machismo, while portraying women's confinement to the home and their limited parameters for individual liberties. The film creates a strong characterization of Chapellin, the

working-class Caracas neighborhood in which it is shot. The film received a number of national and international awards.

Although the flashbacks can lead to some confusion, the complex plot becomes clear by the film's end.

Introducing the Tape: It would be useful for U.S. audiences to know that despite the disclaimer in the initial credits, the film is based on a real-life multiple-murder case that took place in Caracas between 1980 and 1982.

How to Use: I would show the film in *Women Directors Cinema* class and would use the contradictions it portrays to elicit opposing audience reactions, which we would then analyze in relation to the narrative construction of the film. (Lesage)

Since there is a female point of view in the film, it would be useful in any course that explores the role of women in Latin American society, whether the primary focus is on film, literature, culture, history, or sociology. The film is also well suited for courses that seek to challenge "official history" and canonical texts, whether from a feminist, aesthetic, or left-wing political perspective. (Stone)

Suggested Readings: Goldman, Karen S. "A 'Third' Feminism? Solveig Hoogesteijn's *Macu: The Policeman's Wife.*"

King, John. *Magical Reels: A History of Cinemas in Latin America.*

Miranda, Julio E., "El nuevo cine venezolano," 49–60.

Schwartzman, Karen. "A Descriptive Chronology of Films by Women in Venezuela, 1952–1992."

Schwartzman, Karen. "The Seen of the Crime."

Schwartzman, Karen. "Time Is Like a Round Thing: An Interview with Solveig Hoogesteijn." Unpublished (1992).

Trelles Plazaola, Luis. "*Solveig Hoogesteijn,*" *Cine y mujer en América Latina. Directoras de largometrajes de ficción,* 169–92.

Literature on women and gender in contemporary Latin America.

Complementary Films/Videos: Luis Correa. *Ledezma el caso mamera* (1982 Venezuelan documentary based on the same murder case).

Level: University

MANOA

Feature. Without Subtitles. 103 min. 1980
Directed by: Solveig Hoogesteijn
Produced by: Helikon Films/Xanadu Films (Qta. Fridmer Av. Humboldt, Urb. San Bernadino, Caracas; tel: [582] 513-381, fax: [582] 525-621 or 746-491)
Distributed by: IMRE
Evaluators: Robert DiAntonio, Irene Matthews, Patricia Smith
Description: Hoogesteijn's road movie follows the spiritual journey of two young men as they travel through Venezuela in search of identity. Juan and Miguel represent different races, cultures, and social classes. At the outset they share only one thing: music. The young men travel through a country where simply getting out of the supermodern capital is a journey

through time. Dominated by a North American culture that influences their own national identity, they embark on travels that put them in touch with Venezuela's Hispano-Afro-Indian ancestry. As frustrated Latin American youth, they vacillate between modern city life and the traditional life of the countryside. During the journey, Juan and Miguel find their collective history, their personal history, their Manoa.

Strengths and Weaknesses: This is a moving film that portrays the bonding of two young men, one black and one white. There is marvelous characterization of the odd friends with an even odder itinerary. The characters show a certain irresponsibility but also moral growth, despite meetings with unethical and violent people. "The narrative remains linear, yet the attempt to achieve a kind of Brechtian distanciation through various means and the coincidence of the same actors reappearing in different roles serve to keep the spectator always evaluating her or his relation to fact and fiction. In addition, a play is staged within the film, which gives the search for a history or identity a certain complexity and allows for a multiplicity of meaning and discovery." (Schwartzman, "Chronology," 37.)

One evaluator felt that the characters encountered at times were exaggerated or melodramatic and that occasionally the acting was weak. Another felt the tape moved slowly. In general, however, reviewers agreed this was an entertaining film and an interesting view of a very different culture. The spoken Spanish would be difficult for nonnative speakers to understand.

How to Use: The film would be useful to study the culture of Venezuela. (DiAntonio)

I might use it in a *Film* course, comparing it to *Thelma and Louise, Easy Rider* or Wim Wender's *King of the Road.* (Matthews)

The film could be used when discussing New Latin American Cinema; a comparison could be made with New German Cinema. "Hippie culture" or U.S. counterculture of the 1960s and 1970s might be explored within the context of the "road-movie" genre. Also, some research of Brechtian theater would be interesting for university-level students.

Suggested Readings: Schwartzman, Karen. "A Descriptive Chronology of Films by Women in Venezuela, 1952–1992," pp. 33–50

Complementary Films/Videos: *Thelma and Louise; Easy Rider* (both distributed by Facets)

Level: University

EL MAR DEL TIEMPO PERDIDO

Feature.   Without Subtitles.   80 min.   1981
Directed by: Solvieg Hoogesteijn
Produced by: Xanadu Films (Qta. Fridmer Av. Humboldt, Urb. San Bernadino, Caracas; tel: [582] 513-381, fax: [582] 746-491 or [582] 525-621)
Distributors: IMRE
Evaluators: Richard C. Boly, Sandra M. Boschetto-Sandoval

Description: "A feature-length film based on a story by Gabriel García Márquez in which the mysterious appearance of the smell of roses in an arid coastal village attracts many visitors, some out of curiosity, some on pilgrimage, and others to exploit the event, converting the desolate village into a kind of circus." (Schwartzman, "Chronology," p. 35) In surrealist fashion, the film recounts the tale of the dying village by the sea, transformed miraculously through imagination and illusion into a boisterous and prosperous colonial town. When the smell of roses blows in from the ocean, strange things begin to happen. "Progress" is sparked by the arrival of a victrola; the unexpected, unexplained arrival of the Cadillac of Mr. Herbert (a rich businessman from the United States), and finally Mr. Herbert himself. Ultimately, however, the town is condemned to suffer another death, one not evoked in the magical smell of roses, but by the gregarious and unscrupulous *gringo* who "consumes too much air and ends up swallowing the whole town." Mr. Herbert admonishes the people to "face up to the reality." He leaves when there is nothing left to eat, and the people yearn for the return of the smell of roses.

"Hoogesteijn's film is concerned with the structure of time and the relating of the narrative, which is told by a succession of storytellers, serving to blur the boundaries of 'fact and fiction,' a device characteristic of 'magical-realism'." (Schwartzman, "Chronology," p. 35)

Strengths and Weaknesses: The film has excellent visual imagery, good use of color and sound, and fluid editing. It is an excellent filmic representation of one of the Colombian author's literary and magical realist motifs. In addition to several references to *One Hundred Years of Solitude,* there are numerous metafictional references to other stories including *Eréndira, Blacamán el bueno,* and *No One Writes to the Colonel.*

The film seems to be edited to reflect the pace of the town and thus may seem to be slow in places. Also, some Brechtian distanciation devices seem to be employed, making some scenes appear artificial.

Introducing the Tape: An introduction to the work of Gabriel García Márquez, including the reading of one or two works by the author, would provide a good context for the film. Some background would also be useful on Latin American "boom" writers; New Latin American Cinema and New German Cinema; and 1970s Venezuelan history and politics. It should be pointed out that Hoogesteijn was strongly influenced by New German Cinema.

How To Use: I would use this tape in conjunction with reading literary works by García Márquez, as filmic illustration of literary motifs used by the author to portray Latin American history and reality. (Boschetto-Sandoval)

Readings: García Márquez, Gabriel. *No One Writes to the Colonel and Other Short Stories; One Hundred Years of Solitude;* and other works.

Schwartzman, Karen. "A Descriptive Chronology of Films by Women in Venezuela, 1952–1992."

Schwartzman, Karen. "Time is Like A Round Thing: An Interview with Solvieg Hoogesteijn." Unpublished (1992).
Level: University

MAYAMI NUESTRO (Our Beloved Miami)
Documentary. With Subtitles. 34 min. 1981
Directed by: Carlos Oteyza (Av. Diego Cisneros Colgate ala2, Los Ruices, Caracas; tel: [582] 283-9377; fax: [582] 239-4786)
Distributed by: IMRE Archive (available for viewing only)
Evaluator: Allen Poor
Description: This documentary explores the economic impact of Venezuelans in the Miami area during the "boom" years of the 1980s. With their shopping excursions, vacation homes, and principal residences, Venezuelans are responsible for at least twenty thousand jobs in the Miami area.
Strengths and Weaknesses: Shots and interviews with visiting Venezuelans, shopkeepers, and construction workers are animated and varied; however, the interviews with diplomatic and chamber of commerce functionaries are quite long. The soundtrack is good.
Introducing the Tape: Without background to place the tape in context, some of the nuances in its critique of rich expatriate Venezuelans could seem too subtle. The impact of offshore spending and investment by the Venezuelan upper and middle classes on the Venezuelan economy might be brought out explicitly in an introduction or postscript.
How to Use: The film would be useful in discussing the impact of the 1980s oil "boom" on Venezuelan society; as well as looking at New Venezuelan Cinema as a sociological critique.
Level: University

ORIANA (Oriana)
Feature. With Subtitles. 87 min. 1985
Directed by: Fina Torres
Produced by: Pandora Films
Distributed by: IMRE Archive (available for viewing only)
Evaluators: Emperatriz Arreaza-Camero, Joan A. McGinnis
Description: Based on a story by Marvel Moreno, *Oriana* is an exploration of memory, time, and desire initiated when Marie returns to the family hacienda where she spent time as an adolescent. The secret past contained within the house emerges in fragments, little by little, revealing a family story that has been repressed for two generations. The narrative, contained within the vision of Aunt Oriana via the flashbacks of Marie, constructs an intimate portrait of a woman's desire, while at the same time alluding to the larger portrait, as it were, of the country's violent past.
Strengths and Weaknesses: The film is extremely engaging, with beautiful photography, excellent acting, and a great script. One evaluator felt that even the brief nudity was discreet enough that high school students could view the film.
   The numerous flashbacks might be confusing.

Introducing the Tape: It would be useful to have a historical background of Venezuela from 1905 to 1935, in comparison with 1985, the year of the film's production, as well as information about Marvel Moreno, the author of the book upon which the film is based. Viewers could also be told: In 1985, Fina Torres won the Camera d'Or at the Cannes Film Festival with *Oriana,* making her and Margot Benacerraf the only Venezuelans to receive awards at this festival. For such a slow-paced, intimate story, *Oriana* (a French coproduction) was unusually successful in Venezuela. One reason may be that its stylish images and soundtrack were technically equal to those of any European or U.S. production; until then such standards had only been reached in 'foreign' films.
How to Use: I would use this film as an example of contemporary film production in Venezuela made by *Women Filmmakers,* as well as to portray the race, class, and gender relations during the Gómez dictatorship. (Arreaza-Camero)
Suggested Readings: Aguirre, Jesús M., and Marcelino Bisbal. *El nuevo cine venezolano.*
   Gaines, J. "Race and Gender in Feminist Film Theory." In *Cultural Critique.*
   López, A. "The Melodrama in Latin America."
   Mulvey, L., and C. Penley. *Feminist Film Theory.*
   Schwartzman, K., "A Descriptive Chronology of Films by Women in Venezuela, 1952–1992."
   Any books on Venezuelan history (1905–1935).
Level: University

ORINOKO, NUEVO MUNDO (Orinoko, New World)
Feature. No Dialogue. 90 min. 1984
Directed by: Diego Rísquez
Produced by: Producciones Guakamaya (QTA. Solange Calle Oriente, Country Club, Caracas; tel: [582] 261-7181 or 261-8685; fax: [582] 283-9377)
Distributed by: IMRE Archive (available for viewing only)
Evaluators: Emperatriz Arreaza-Camero, John Hess, Marilyn Jímenez, Cynthia L. Stone
Description: With layers of hallucinatory images and no dialogue, *Orinoko* narrates the Spanish and English explorations of the Orinoco River and the quest for El Dorado, first by Columbus and subsequently by Alexander von Humboldt. These explorers encounter and initiate the destruction of indigenous communities. With magnificent photography and a haunting soundtrack, the film captures the first explorers' phantasmagoric experience; it makes it almost possible for the contemporary viewer to understand how men like Sir Walter Raleigh or Antonio Berrio could report having seen mermaids, men with their heads below their shoulders, and rivers of gold.
   The film begins before the first encounter with a stunning sequence of an Amerindian tribe going about their daily activities. Each shot seems meant to distance and disorient the viewers, compelling us to decipher each action (much as the conquistadors may have done). When the European charac-

ters make their appearance on the Orinoco, they are filmed in an equally opaque manner. No word is spoken; it is a silent adventure, except for the strange and ominous sounds of the jungle. Viewers are not encouraged to identify with these strange, rather bizarre, yet colorful individuals. Toward the end of the film, it becomes clear that the entire "Europeans in the Americas" sequence has been filmed from the point of view of a Yanomami shaman in a drug-induced trance.

The Orinoco River is the main character of the film. It recalls the various people who have travelled on its waters. The first part of the film takes place during the time before the conquest of America, seen as an earthly paradise. In this fake anthropological documentary, there is a shaman, Yanomami, who uses a drug called *Yopo* which provokes premonitory visions. He sees Christopher Columbus in 1498, arriving at the delta of the Orinoco. A duel follows between the spiritual fathers of these different cultures: Walter Raleigh and the search for Manoa and El Dorado; Alexander de Humboldt, the German naturalist; and Aime Bomplant and the scientific discovery of the New World. At the same time, the film recounts a mythical journey while going up the river, where characters of Latin American mythology, part gods, part men, part animals, warn us that we are at its source. We see a woman, America, give birth to the river. The film tries to fill a gap of three hundred years in the history of my country, from this discovery until its independence in 1810. (Director Diego Rísquez)

Strengths and Weaknesses: With excellent photography and performances, this film confounds viewers' expectations. The film makes an effective parody, demonstrating the limitations of anthropological films, which traditionally convey cultural practices from an outsider's point of view. Those parts of the film dealing with the indigenous peoples take on the look of ethnographic films and are accompanied by modern synthesized instrumental music. The parts dealing with European explorers are highly stylized tableaux vivants. The Spanish and English are portrayed as fetishists who fervently worship wooden crosses and lifesize statues of Queen Elizabeth. Later, scientific expeditions (the Von Humboldt expedition in the nineteenth century, for example) are shown as equally deluded, with scientific objectivity giving way to dream visions. At times, the film's images are powerful. Other parts seem more forced.

Orinoko would best be shown to an audience which has some familiarity with experimental fiction filmmaking. The film communicates on many levels, but is quite long for an experimental film and demands a great deal of background, interest, and perseverance on the part of the viewer.

Introducing the Tape: A detailed knowledge of the history of this region's conquest and an appreciation of medieval allegorical thought, as well as a description of the tribes and the different explorations through the Orinoco River by various explorers (Spaniards, Germans, French, English) with an explanation of the land's "attraction" to Europeans, are necessary. In addition, information about Amerindian myths

would clarify many of the symbols. A detailed introduction to director Diego Rísquez's work with clips would also be essential. Viewers should be informed that the film is experimental and that Diego Rísquez developed an international cult following for his trilogy. He used minimal resources, worked with friends rather than a professional crew, and shot in super-8mm film which was then enlarged to 35mm.

How to Use: I would use this film to discuss the European representation of the native "other." Indigenous Amazon communities have always been and are still an "exotic" attraction for foreigners. I would also analyze the aesthetic dimension of the film. (Arreaza-Camero)

I would show the first sequence with the Amerindian tribe before the conquest without comment or introduction. Then I would stop the film and ask the students to express how they felt as viewers. I would want to draw out of students the sense of pre-Columbian cultures as whole, inviolate societies, that is, as if the camera were truly neutral and invisible. Some instructors may be more interested in the content, such as the actual customs. The second sequence which portrays the Spanish and English expeditions needs to be preceded by information on the history of the exploration of the region. (Jímenez)

The tape can be used to help students gain a critical perspective on traditional anthropological films. It also provides an interesting, albeit somewhat simplistic, view of important historical figures such as Columbus, Raleigh, and Humboldt. It can be taught as an example of avant-garde cinema in general and of contemporary trends in Latin American film. (Stone)

Suggested Readings: Harris, Wilson. *The Palace of the Peacock.*

King, John. *Magical Reels: A History of Cinemas in Latin America.*

Naipaul, V. *The Loss of Eldorado: A History.* (Indispensable).

Raleigh, Sir Walter. *The Discovery of the Large, Rich, and Beautiful Empire of Guiana.*

Level: University

LA QUEMA DE JUDAS (The Burning of Judas)

Feature.   Without Subtitles.   113 min.   1974
Directed by: Roman Chalbaud (tel/fax: [582] 51-6039)
Distributed by: IMRE
Evaluators: Stephen Webre
Description: *La quema de Judas* is set during Holy Week in 1970s Caracas, Venezuela. Jesús María Carmona is a policeman who is killed during a guerrilla assault on an armored car. A ministry official, outraged by the frequency with which policemen have been dying in the line of duty, decides to mount a publicity campaign focusing on Carmona to generate public sympathy and respect for law enforcement officers. The campaign begins with an effort to humanize the victim. Interviews with Carmona's family and friends reveal him to have been a kindly, caring, and fun-loving person. Un-

fortunately, as plans go forward for a state funeral with full military honors for the fallen hero, evidence also surfaces that he was, in fact, a criminal. This film comprises one of three early seminal works in director Chalbaud's oeuvre (including *The Smoking Fish* and *Sagrado y obsceno*), adapted from his own plays.

Strengths and Weaknesses: This entertaining and thought-provoking film offers a good study of moral ambiguities in modern South American society and is also a good portrayal of urban life. Settings and depictions of cultural behavior and attitudes seem authentic. The acting is strong as are the directing and camera work (which in some places are reminiscent of Alfred Hitchcock's work).

The complex narrative structure with its heavy use of flashbacks may be difficult for some viewers to follow. The film contains brief scenes with nudity and graphic violence.

Introducing the Tape: U.S. audiences will need an introduction to the observances surrounding Holy Week. This religious event is not as central to the film as the title suggests; however, chronological references are made to days in the ecclesiastical calendar, people are seen on the street dressed to participate in processions, and the closing scene requires some understanding of the Good Friday tradition of burning Judas in effigy.

Students of the Spanish language could be briefed on the colloquial use in Venezuela of the word *vaina* instead of the more familiar *cosa* for "thing," as well as on some elementary profanity.

How to Use: Students may be invited to ponder the politics of image, particularly in relation to the power of the mass media in both developed and developing societies. The national press is deliberately encouraged to inflate the murdered Carmona into a hero in order to combat the negative public image of the police. Once this process is set in motion and the sordid truths about the dead man begin to be discovered, the campaign cannot be stopped without producing the opposite effect. Moral complexities to be explored include the warm recollections of Carmona still cherished by his family, friends, and fellow police officers and the captured guerrillas' claim that it is they who are the defenders of the people and the police who are the criminals. (Webre)

Appropriate for courses in *Ethic, Film, and Media.*

Suggested Readings: King, John. *Magical Reels: A History of Cinemas in Latin America.*

Chalbaud's books.

Level: University

RUFINO: "EL ILUMINADO" (Rufino: "The Illuminated")

Documentary.   With Subtitles.   23 min.   1989
Directed by: Andres Agusti
Produced by: Lidia Córdoba (Aptdo. Postal 51443 ZP 1050, Caracas, Sabana Grande; tel: [582] 576-2284; fax: [582] 577-6518)
Distributed by: IMRE

Evaluators: Mary Jo Dudley, Miguel Huarcaya, María A. Lazarini, Janet B. Norden, Deborah Pacini Hernández, José Pérez, Linda Whiteford
Description: Multitudes of people from different parts of Venezuela believe Rufino has been touched by God's hand. They wait in long lines and sleep in the streets to be healed by this popular *curandero* (faith healer). Rufino describes how he acquired his ability to cure and his feelings and philosophy about this gift. He explains that he works with the power of God through a current that emanates from both his hands. Eight years before, during a terrible illness, he experienced a cross touching his chest. The illness disappeared and he received this power, adding a great responsibility to his life. Rufino explains that he was not told when he would be given the power nor does he know when it will be taken away. He just proposes to use it while it lasts for the good of humanity.

Strengths and Weaknesses: This thought-provoking film provides a good description of a sincere form of alternative healing. It takes a serious look at a particular practitioner of a popular medicine that is widely relied upon by millions of Latin Americans. The film's balanced treatment shows Rufino as an ordinary person who watches television, drinks beer, and hunts and is a self-taught philosopher and humanist. The footage of the crowds waiting for the healer and interacting with Rufino is particularly interesting. The film is perfect for classroom use because it introduces the topic and leaves time for discussion.

A few evaluators wanted to see more research and different opinions about Rufino; however, the majority agreed that the way the multitudes followed and believed in Rufino was moving and valuable as an example of a phenomenon. A few reviewers mentioned that the tape was loosely structured.

Introducing the Tape: The instructor could offer analogies to popular healers in this country and discuss the connections between psychological and physical health. One evaluator suggests using this tape in conjunction with medical anthropology. A discussion of Latin American popular culture, syncretic religions, and faith healers would be useful.

How to Use: This tape is relevant for the course I teach on contemporary topics in Latin America. We discuss the role of the *curandero* in native communities. We also discuss concepts such as *mal de susto, mal de viento,* and *mal de agua.* (Dudley)

I would use this to enhance discussions of popular culture/religion/medicine. It also raises issues of why healers such as Rufino are in high demand. (Pacini Hernández)

I teach about alternative medical systems and would use Rufino as an example of faith healing. (Whiteford)

Suggested Readings: Arden House Conference on Medicine and Anthropology. *Man's Image in Medicine and Anthropology.*

Burton, Julianne. *The Social Documentary in Latin America.*

Level: University

SALTO AL ATLANTICO (Jump over the Atlantic)
Documentary. With Subtitles. 30 min. 1990
Directed by: María Eugenia Esparragoza
Produced by: Asoc. Salto en el Atlántico (Edif. San Martín
#12-K, Parque Central, Caracas 1010; tel: [582] 572-1370)
Distributed by: IMRE
Evaluators: Reid Andrews, Emperatriz Arreaza-Camero,
Aline Helg, Lori Madden, Gloria Romero-Downing, Kathleen Ross
Description: This film traces cultural similarities and continuities between a small Afro-Venezuelan settlement in
Barlovento (Estado Miranda, Venezuela) and the Belgian
Congo in Africa, where people were captured as slaves in the
nineteenth century. The tape cuts back and forth between the
two groups as they perform music, dance, prepare food,
make musical instruments, braid women's hair, etc. As people in each community watch the film of the other, they comment on their similarities and differences. This cross-cultural
ethnographic exercise shows that centuries after their migration from Africa, Afro-Venezuelans retain many African
practices and even use some of the same words and names as
the Congolese. The film addresses the accommodation of
African culture to the materials and circumstances found in
the New World and for the first time establishes communications between the two related communities.
Strengths and Weaknesses: This fascinating and innovative ethnographic documentary includes vivid shots of drumming, dancing, and daily life in both places. The film has
many layers: members of each group watch films of the other
community and comment on what they see. These comments/reactions are in turn filmed and brought back to the respective groups. The research, camera work, and editing are
well done.
Introducing the Tape: Instructors might provide background on slavery and the African diaspora communities in
Latin America, including geography and demographics. Because the filmmaker studied in France with the ethnographer
Jean Rouche, some introduction to Rouche's work, the practice of ethnography, and ethnographic filmmaking in general
would be useful. In addition, viewers could be told that a key
to keeping track of the film's locations (Venezuela or Africa)
is to note that the Venezuelans are speaking Spanish and the
Africans are speaking French.
How to Use: I would ask students to comment on, or question, the various cultural continuities documented in the film.
Then, to bring it a little closer to home, I might ask about features of modern U.S. life which could be traced back to
African or European or Asian antecedents and how those features have changed over time in response to twentieth-century urbanization, industrialization, modernization, etc.
(Andrews)

I would use this film in a course on the African presence
and influence in the Americas. Also, it would be useful for
the study of audience response to ethnographic films. (Arreaza-Camero)

I would use the tape to illustrate my section on slavery in
South America and the vital contribution of African culture
in Latin America. (Helg)

This would complement a course syllabus where the
African diaspora in Latin America is included, especially in
light of a new black consciousness that focuses on mutual
ties linking communities in African and American enclaves.
(Madden)

The film could be used as background for the subject of
slavery in nineteenth-century Latin America. (Romero-Downing)

In a *Social Studies* class students could watch the film,
note similarities and differences between the groups, and
discuss their observations. In a *Music* class students could
recreate the rhythm patterns seen in the tape and discuss
similarities and differences in the rhythms used in the
Congo and Venezuela. A discussion of the significance of
drumming within the respective cultures could follow.
(Ross)
Suggested Readings: Acosta-Saignes, Miguel. *Vida de los
esclavos negros en Venezuela.*

Barnes, Sandra T., ed. *Africa's Ogun: Old World and New.*

Brito-Figueroa, F. *Las insurrecciones de los esclavos negros en sociedad colonial Venezolana.*

Burton, Julianne. *The Social Documentary in Latin America.*

Chacon, A. *Curiepe.*

Klein, Herbert S. *African Slavery in Latin America and the
Caribbean.*

Lombardi, John V. *The Decline and Abolition of Negro
Slavery in Venezuela.*

Moreno Fraginals, Manuel, ed. *Africa in Latin America.*

Nichols, Bill. *Representing Reality.*

Picón Salas, M. *Pedro Claver, el santo de los esclavos.*

Pollack-Eltz, Angelina. *Religión africana en Venezuela.*

Troconis de Veracochea. *Documentos para el estudio de
los esclavos negros en Venezuela.*

Wright, Winthrop. *Café con Leche: Race, Class and National Image in Venezuela.*
Level: Junior High School—University

SAN PEDRO DE COCHE: A PLENA SOL
Documentary. Without Subtitles. 27 min. 1989
Directed by: Miguel Angel Ortega, Yolanda Oranaz
Produced by: Div. de Tecnología Educativa (Canicuao La
Hacienda UD4 Sect., Leon de Payara Edf 28, #16–01, Caracas; tel: [582] 562-2836 or 432-8260)
Distributed by: IMRE
Evaluators: Emperatriz Arreaza-Camero, Elba D. Birmingham-Pokorny, Wilma Cordero, Lourdes Fernández
Description: An educational/cultural program made for
state television, this tape documents the life of a fishing village in Venezuela. It shows how the villagers depend economically on sardine fishing or related industries such as carpentry, which service the boats. The tape also presents some

of the environmental issues affecting the livelihood of this community. Through a news format using interviews and the fishermen's storytelling, we learn of their struggle for survival.

Strengths and Weaknesses: The filmmaker beautifully combines legends and folklore to document the daily existence of the people of this small, remote fishing village. The fishermen speak for themselves about their lives. There are excellent shots of the sea and fishing boats. The tape, which was produced with limited resources as an educational video, also functions as a good anthropological document.

Some segments containing the elderly residents' lengthy conversations and monologues may be boring for U.S. audiences. Also, the background music is distracting.

Introducing the Tape: It would be useful to introduce this video with a brief historical explanation of the economic situation in Venezuela over the last forty years.

How to Use: Since this film illustrates the intimate relationship and the dependency between the villagers and the sea, I might ask my students to put themselves in the shoes of the children in the film who were listening to the stories of the elderly people. I would have them write a list of questions they would ask about their work, their lives, and their feelings. Framing questions often provides as many insights as the answer does. (Arreaza-Cordero)

I would use this film to introduce my students to spoken Spanish and to one aspect of Venezuelan culture. (Birmingham-Pokorny).

Suggested Readings: López, Carmen A. *Crisis fiscal e industrialización en el subdesarrollo Latinoamericano.*

Silva Michelena, José Agustín. *Crisis de la democracia.*
Handbook of Latin American Studies.

Level: University

SAN PEDRO Y SUS PARRANDEROS

Documentary.   Without Subtitles.   28 min.   1989
Directed by: Miguel Angel Ortega, Yolanda Oronoz
Produced by: Div. de Technología Educativa (Caricuao La Hacienda UD4 Sect., Leon de Payara, Edf. 28, #16–01; Caracas; tel: [582] 562-2836 or 432-8260)
Distributed by: IMRE
Evaluators: Emperatriz Arreaza-Camero, Elba D. Birmingham-Pokorny, Wilma Cordero, Lourdes Fernández, José Pérez, Jorge J. Rodríguez-Florido
Description: This video is part of an educational series made for state-run television. It uses popular testimonies to describe the origins of the Festival of San Pedro, celebrated on June 29 in various communities on the north-central coast of Venezuela, where most of the Afro-Venezuelan population lives. The video follows the villagers who reenact the legend and the ceremony. The legend tells that during the colonial period a slave's little girl, Rosa, was cured of a mortal illness by her mother's promise to St. Peter. Most of the black slaves, like María Ignacia's husband, worked on the sugar plantations. The devotion to St. Peter grew to be a popular street procession, as well as a religious ceremony with dance. Several weeks before June 29, the devotees sing, dance, and collect alms in preparation for the feast. The festival was made official in 1964. The video portrays the history of religious syncretism from the period when African slaves worked in the sugar cane plantations to the present incorporation of these rituals into Catholicism with processions, blessings, songs, and popular theater.

Strengths and Weaknesses: The tape sheds light on a little-known subject from Venezuela in presenting important aspects of Venezuelan and Afro-Venezuelan culture: religious rituals, music, dance, costumes, and beliefs. Also important is the use of theater in teaching religious rituals and beliefs. The video creatively combines narrative, theater, interviews, and music. Its earnest approach is aided by excellent editing.

Introducing the Tape: Some background on Venezuela's history of slavery, linking past and present, would be useful. A connection should also be made between the devotion featured and other forms of Afro-Venezuelan devotion, pointing out that only a small percentage of the entire country actively celebrates the Festival of San Pedro.

Students would benefit from an explanation of how the concept of *mestizaje* differs from *miscegenation* in Venezuela, as well as an introduction to religious syncretism, popular culture represented in music and theater, and race issues in Venezuela.

How to Use: I would use the tape as an example of how race relations in Latin America are different from those in the United States. For example, in Venezuela the process of *mestizaje* began early in the colonial period. Today it is possible to find popular cultural expressions that incorporate elements from the Spaniards, the Indians, and the African ancestors of the population. (Arreaza-Camero)

I would use this film to introduce students to conversational Spanish and to help them develop a deeper appreciation and understanding of Latin American popular culture. The video provides a good example of the richness of African-based culture in Hispanic America and its contribution to Latin American culture. (Birmingham-Pokorny)

The tape would be useful in my *Afro-Hispanic Culture* class to show a concrete example of Afro-Venezuelan culture. (Rodríguez-Florido)

Suggested Readings: Acosta Saignes, Miguel. *Vida de los esclavos negros en Venezuela.*

Brito Figueroa, Federico. *Las insurrecciones de los esclavos negros en la sociedad colonial Venezolana.*

Cardona, Miguel. *Temas del folklore Venezolano.*

Guss, David M. "The Selling of San Juan: The Performance of History in Afro-Venezuelan Community."

Pollak-Eltz, Angelina. *Cultos Afroamericanos.*

Rout, Leslie N. *The African Experience in Spanish America: 1502 to the Present Day.*

Wright, Winthrop. *Café con Leche: Race, Class and National Image in Venezuela.*

Level: University

SOY UN DELINCUENTE (I Am a Delinquent)
Feature.   With Subtitles.   109 min.   1976
Directed by: Clemente de la Cerda
Distributed by: IMRE Archive (available for viewing only)
Evaluators: Reed Anderson, Lavina Tilson Gass
Description: This testimonial film is based on the autobiography of a marginalized Venezuelan youth, Ramón Antonio Brizuela. It follows his turbulent life as a young thief who becomes immersed in increasingly serious and ultimately violent criminal activity. Incorporating nonactors from the marginal districts of Caracas, the film provides a stark view of the almost total assimilation of young people into a life where criminality is its own culture. At the age of twelve years, Ramón was a byproduct of marginal society, a common criminal doomed to an early death. Upon reaching twenty-one years of age, he was thoroughly convinced, and declared publicly in his book, that criminals had to organize in order to constitute a real power. At twenty-one years of age he was dead, gunned down by the police in the middle of a robbery. The film represents a critical attack on the brutality of police in dealing with young people and the arbitrariness and inconsistency of the justice system. It also condemns society for contributing to social delinquency.

The film contains some nude scenes and sexual activity.
Strengths and Weaknesses: Evaluators had divergent views of this tape. One evaluator described the film as lewd and boring, while another was impressed by the authenticity of the actors, the film's strong message, and the innovative nature of the casting and the film's conception. The authenticity of the dialogue is impressive. However, the local street slang is at times quite obscure and needs subtitles even for some Spanish-speaking audiences.
Complementary Films/Videos: *Rodrigo D: No futuro (Rodrigo D: No Future)* (Colombia); Bunuel's *Los olvidados* (distributed by the IMRE)
Level: University

TERRA NOVA (New Land)
Feature.   With Subtitles.   103 min.   1991
Directed by: Calogero Salvo
Produced by: Cinelife/Producciones Terra Nova (40 W. 15th St. #6B, N.Y.C, NY 10011; tel: [212] 727-8231)
Distributed by: Cologero Salvo
Evaluators: Emperatriz Arreaza-Camero, Robert DiAntonio, José Pérez, Cynthia L. Stone
Description: The experience of Italian immigrants in post-World War II Venezuela is treated in this charming film by focusing on the classic conflict between love for the new country and longing for the old. The difficulties of immigrant life are more successfully negotiated by the wife, a down-to-earth survivor type, than by her husband. A third characterization is presented by the wife's younger brother, a good-hearted playboy portrayed by the Spanish actor Antonio Banderas. A subplot is the friendship between the wife and an aristocratic Venezuelan woman who has been exiled to the countryside by her father for refusing to give up her illegitimate child. By the end of the film, it is the working-class immigrant family that offers a means of escape and liberation for the aristocratic woman.
Strengths and Weaknesses: An excellent film of artistic merit, the film provides a refreshing perspective on the classic theme of European immigrants coming to America. In this film, America means Latin America, rather than the United States. The film portrays the difficulties of immigrant life with touching, compelling stories about human relationships. The alternation between the use of Italian and Spanish effectively conveys the multicultural experience of immigrant communities. One evaluator mentioned that the film is slow for most U.S. audiences and felt that its wonderfully lyrical pace may also be its most serious drawback. Reviewers had diverse reactions to the acting, ranging from "excellent" to "overly melodramatic." While many enjoyed the film, one evaluator felt the plot was weak.
Introducing the Tape: An introduction to this film should include a discusssion of twentieth-century European immigrants in South America and the multiethnic composition of Venezuela. The interplay among the Spanish and indigenous peoples and the new immigrants would also be important.
How to Use: I would use this film to examine cross-cultural effects. The lifestyles of the Italian immigrant farmers and the Venezuelan landowning family, although diametrically opposed economically, can lead to certain alliances. (Arreaza-Camero)

Because of its focus on the immigrant experience, *Terra nova* would integrate well into any course on *Latin American Culture* that touches on this topic. For U.S. students, it provides an interesting point of comparison between immigration to North and South America. The prevailing stereotype of Latin America as an almost exclusively poor and backward region is challenged by a film in which Venezuela is seen as a land of opportunity. The film thus encourages discussion of the booming Venezuelan economy of the postwar years and the particularly strong ethnic mix of contemporary Venezuelan society. (Stone)

Because this is a feature-length film, it may need to be assigned for out-of-class viewing.
Suggested Readings: Gerbani, V. *Mi padre, el immigrante.*
   López, A. "The Melodrama in Latin America."
   Mulvey, L., and C. Penley. "Visual Pleasure and Narrative Cinema." In *Feminist Film Theory.*
   Pribam, D. *Female Spectators.*
Level: High School—University

URIHI: TIERRA YANOMAMI
Documentary.   Without Subtitles.   27 min.   1990
Directed by: Miguel Angel Ortega
Produced by: Division de Tecnologia Educ. (Ministerio de Educación, Caracas; tel: [582] 562-2836; fax: [582] 562-0175)
Distributed by: IMRE

Evaluators: Emperatriz Arreaza-Camero, Elba D. Birmingham-Pokorny, Wilma Cordero, Jorge Rodríguez-Florido, University of Pittsburgh group—María Consuelo Acosta, John Frechione, Shirley A. Kregar, Nichole Parker, Lynn Young, José Zevallos

Description: This documentary presents the history and living conditions of the Yanomami in the Venezuelan Amazon, near the Orinoco River close to Brazil. The video presents the culture's early creation myths and legends from the arrival of the Spanish to the present. The indigenous people testify to their way of life, their aspirations, and their religious beliefs. Daily life is documented: their use of the rain forest as the source of food, housing materials, and healing and the struggle to maintain their autonomy against the "civilization" of the Venezuelan government. The documentary defends this community's demand for autonomy and human rights. Part of the tape is narrated in their language. Of interest is a detailed narration about "Western" man's incursion into Yanomami territory since the eighteenth century. As the film progresses, it becomes apparent that modernity and technology cannot respect the Yanomami's way of life, as they infiltrate these communities through work, education, and medical care. The film addresses the need to enact legislation to protect the Yanomami and their culture.

Strengths and Weaknesses: The video provides an example of an indigenous community's struggle for autonomy. It allows the Yanomami to speak for themselves and is an excellent introduction to their culture. The tape powerfully combines myths and legends, creatively using still photography and archival footage.

The video seems to take a long time to reach its main point. The Spanish is difficult to understand, even for native speakers, and some segments contain only untranslated indigenous language. A few evaluators found the background music inappropriate.

Introducing the Tape: It would be useful to introduce the tape with a brief presentation on Latin American indigenous cultures. It is important to establish context and discuss the geographical region where the Yanomami reside in Venezuela and Brazil.

How to Use: I would use this film to introduce students to the different multiethnic and multicultural groups that form the fabric of Latin American society, as well as to introduce some of the primary problems affecting the cultural and economic survival of native populations. (Birmingham-Pokorny)

The video could be used to help students appreciate other cultures and understand the importance of not superimposing one's own culture on another group of people. I might have my students work in groups to draft a law to protect the Yanomami land and people. (Cordero)

I would use this in my *Latin America Culture* course to show an indigenous point of view and the amalgamation of indigenous cultures with Spanish culture. (Rodríguez-Florido).

Suggested Readings: Acosta Saignes, Miguel. *Estudios de etnología antigua de Venezuela.*

Lizot, Jacques. *Tales of the Yanomami.*

Sanoja Mario, and Iraida Vargas. *Antiguas formaciones y modos de producción Venezolano.*

Serbin, A., and O. González: *Indigenismo y autogestión*

Smole, William J. *Yanomami.*

Level: University

VENEZUELA: FEBRERO "27" (Venezuela: February 27)

Documentary.   With Subtitles.   28 min.   1989

Directed by: Liliane Blaser

Produced by: Co-train (Ave. Las Acacias No. 59, Caracas; tel: [582] 74-1786; fax: [582] 793-2908)

Distributed by: IMRE

Evaluators: Emperatriz Arreaza-Camero, Rosario Espinal, Joan A. McGinnis, Marie Price, Lewis A. Tambs

Description: This film reports the events surrounding the riots that took place in Caracas, Venezuela, on February 27–28, 1989, shortly after the reelection of President Carlos Andrés Pérez when International Monetary Fund-inspired economic reforms were imposed. A popular uprising ensued and was brutally put down by the military. Documentary footage shows scenes from the riots as well as interviews with the victims, their relatives, and scholars. In addition, the video provides some statistical information on poverty in Venezuela. However, context is minimal, as the video was intended specifically for a Venezuelan audience. The director's emphasis on violence in the video is in response to the censorship imposed by the government, which did not allow the public to be informed about the true dimensions of the violence that occurred. In this sense, the work attempts an unofficial reading of this event.

Strengths and Weaknesses: This is a short and well-produced documentary with a strong montage of interviews, documentary coverage, newsreel footage, and music. Its interviews with victims are particularly powerful. The film counters the official story and is one of the few independently produced documents about this event.

This work graphically presents the popular frustration with political promises and the uneven distribution of wealth but does not provide enough context for the event. One evaluator felt that the film was somewhat sensationalistic and focused too much on the violence suffered by the victims rather than broadening the view by following some of the investigations into police misconduct and disappeared people. Another reviewer found the subtitles inadequate.

Introducing the Tape: To fully understand this video, a context is necessary. Viewers need some knowledge of contemporary Venezuelan history; the development of democracy in Venezuela; the economic crisis of the 1980s and 1990s and its social consequences; some history of the two democratic political parties, particularly Acción Democrática; the president's affiliation with the Socialist International and his long-standing popularity; Venezuela's history as an oil-producing nation; and how Pérez helped the nation to incur its massive foreign debt. Director Blaser's dedication to providing community-produced audiovisual works that attempt to grapple with contemporary social issues and events should be discussed. What is the the role of community video? How can community video work to shape and to counter official versions of events?

How to Use: The tape can be used as an illustration for discussions about the debt crisis and its sociopolitical consequences or development policies and their consequences. (Espinal)

It would also be useful to discuss community video and political activisim that uses video. How do these kinds of documents shape our reading of history; contribute to our understanding of contemporary history, etc. A comparison of this video with some "official" coverage of the event (both Venezuelan television, newspaper, and U.S. versions) would be a productive exercise.

Suggested Readings: Ewell, Judith. *Venezuela: A Century of Change.*

Malavé, Héctor. *Formación histórica del antidesarrollo de Venezuela.*

Margolies, Luise. *The Venezuelan Peasant in Country and City.*

Silva Michelena, José A. *Política y bloques de poder: Crisis en el sistema mundial.*

Silva Michelena, José A., ed. *Latin America: Peace, Democratization and Economic Crisis.*

Local Venezuelan Publications: *El nacional; SIC*

Level: University

WANADI (Wanadi)

Animation.   With Subtitles.   15 min.   1981
Directed and Produced by: Armando Arce
Distributed by: IMRE Archive (available for viewing only)
Evaluators: Emperatriz Arreaza-Camero, Joan A. McGinnis, Enrique R. Rodríguez
Description: This is an animated interpretation of a Makiritare vision about the origins of human beings. The Makiritare inhabit the Amazon region on Venezuela's southern border. The birth of Odosha, the spirit of evil, comes to represent the conquest of America by the European colonizer. According to this legend, the only way for people to find their true identity is through reconciliation with the gods.
Strengths and Weaknesses: This creative piece has a short narrative and convincing and imaginative animation.

Some of the animated characters' speech is difficult to understand.
Introducing the Tape: A basic familiarity with the Conquest, indigenous concerns (e.g., cultural politics and representational issues), as well as general information about folklore/mythology, would be helpful. An introduction to the Makiritare culture could be added. Some information about the political aspirations of the New Latin American Cinema

should also be provided, such as the importance of questions of identity.
How to Use: The film could be used for cross-cultural comparison of different creation myths. (McGinnis)
Suggested Readings: Acosta Saignes, Miguel. *Estudios de etnología antigua de Venezuela.*

Civrieux, Marc de. *Watunna: Un ciclo de creación en el Orinoco.*

Jiménez Graziani, Morella. *La esclavitud indígena en Venezuela, siglo XVI.*

Zambrano, Ivan. *Cine venezolano.*

Books on Native American folklore; the Andes
Level: Elementary School—University

YO HABLO A CARACAS (Listen Caracas)

Documentary.   With Subtitles.   19 min.   1978
Directed by: Carlos Azpúrua (2 Transversal, Qta, El Laurel, Caracas 1071; tel: [582] 285-9056 or 752-4564; fax: [582] 234-2365)
Distributed by: The Cinema Guild
Evaluators: Lydia M. Garner
Description: A member of the Yanomami community in Venezuela refuses to accept Western culture and religion, seeing no possibility for acculturation, since Western values, religion, and modes of labor are in conflict with those of the indigenous community. Although some tribes and individuals have accepted acculturation, the spokesman refuses to submit, electing for the community to remain autonomous. He respects the white man's culture, and in return demands respect for indigenous cultures. In addressing the people of Caracas, he reminds them that his community once lived near Caracas but has been pushed toward the peripheries of the country (Amazon state) by expanding urbanization. The spokesman reserves the harshest words for the Christian missionaries, one of whom describes the Amerindians as "savages without law or culture, human beings that have descended to the level of beasts or even lower."
Strengths and Weaknesses: The film portrays well the spokesman's demand for autonomy to preserve his culture. It provides a strong denunciation of the work of the missionaries to convert the people and thereby eradicate the Amerindian religion and culture.
Introducing the Tape: Viewers need introductory information about the location and name of the tribe. They should also be familiar with the history of the Conquest, missionary activities, and the ongoing marginalization of, and resistance by, indigenous communities. A context of contemporary history and politics in Venezuela and familiarity with indigenous organization and struggle in Latin American would be useful.
How to Use: I would use this tape to show the struggle of the indigenous communities in Latin America to preserve their culture and communities. (Garner)
Level: University

Bibliography

This bibliography is organized according to the following subcategories:

ARGENTINA

Abel Martín, Jorge. *Una cierta mirada.* Buenos Aires: Ediciones Corregidor, 1985.

———. *Cine argentino '79.* Buenos Aires: Corregidor, 1979.

———. *Cine argentino '80.* Buenos Aires: Corregidor, 1980.

———. *Cine argentino '81.* Buenos Aires: Corregidor, 1981.

———. *Cine argentino '82.* Buenos Aires: Editorial Legasa, 1982.

———. *Cine argentino '83.* Buenos Aires: Editorial Legasa, 1983.

———.*Cine argentino '84.* Buenos Aires: Editorial Legasa, 1984.

———. *Diccionario de realizadores contemporáneos.* Buenos Aires: Instituto Nacional de Cinematografía, 1987.

———. *Los films de Armando Bo con Isabel Sarli.* Buenos Aires: Corregidor, 1981.

———. *Los films de Leopoldo Torre-Nilsson.* Buenos Aires: Corregidor, 1980.

Aguilar, Gonzalo Moises. *Lautaro Murua.* Buenos Aires: Centro Editor de América Latina, 1993.

Aguinis, Marcos. *La cruz invertida.* Barcelona: Planeta, 1970.

Ambrosi, Alain, and Nancy Thede, eds. *Video the Changing World. See Cinema.*

Andersen, Martin Edwin. *Dossier Secreto: Argentina's Desaparecidos and the Myth of the "Dirty War."* Boulder, Colo.: Westview Press, 1993.

Aufderheide, Patricia. "Awake Argentina." *Film Comment,* April 1986, 51–55.

———. *Cross Cultural Film Guide. See Cinema.*

———. "Latin American Cinema and the Rhetoric of Cultural Nationalism: Controversies at Havana in 1987 and 1989." *Quarterly Review of Film and Video. See Cinema.*

Barnard, Tim, ed. *Argentine Cinema.* Toronto: Nightwood, 1986.

Barney Finn, Oscar. *Luis Saslavsky.* Buenos Aires: Centro Editor de América Latina, 1993.

Beceyro, Raúl. *Ensayos sobre cine argentino.* Santa Fe: Universidad Nacional del Litoral, 1986.

Bergmann, Emilie, et al. *Women, Culture, and Politics in Latin America. Seminar on Feminism. See Latin America.*

Birri, Fernando. *La escuela documental de Santa Fe.* Santa Fe: Documento, 1964.

Bottone, Mireya. *La literatura argentina y el cine.* Santa Fe: Facultad de Filosofía y Letras, Universidad Nacional del Litoral, 1964.

Brenner, Fernando. *Adolfo Aristarain.* Buenos Aires: Centro Editor de América Latina, 1993.

Burgin, Victor, James Donald, and Cora Kaplan, eds. *Formations of Fantasy.* London and New York: Methuen, 1986.

Calistro, Mariano, Oscar Cetrángolo, Claudio España, Andres Insaurralde, and Carlos Landini. *Reportaje al cine argentino: Los pioneros del sonoro*. Buenos Aires: Anesa-Editorial Crea, 1978.

Calvert, Susan. *Argentina: Political Culture and Instability*. Pittsburgh: University of Pittsburgh Press, 1989.

Carlson, Marifran. *Feminismo: The Woman's Movement in Argentina from Its Beginnings to Eva Perón*. Chicago: Academy Chicago Publishers, 1988.

Castro, Donald. "Popular Culture as a Source for the Historian: Why Carlos Gardel?" *Studies in Latin American Popular Culture,* no. 5 (1986): 144–62.

———. "Popular Culture as a Source for the Historian: The Tango in Its Era of Guardia Vieja." *Studies in Latin American Popular Culture,* no. 2 (1983): 70–85.

Castro-Klaren, Sara, Sylvia Molloy, and Beatriz Sarlo, eds. *Women's Writing in Latin America: An Anthology. See Latin America.*

Collier, Simon. *The Life, Music, and Times of Carlos Gardel*. Pittsburgh: University of Pittsburgh Press, 1986.

Comisión Nacional sobre la Desaparicion de Personas. *Nunca Más: The Report of the Argentine National Commission on the Disappeared*. New York: Farrar, Straus Giroux, in association with Index on Censorship, London, 1986.

Couselo, Jorge Miguel. *Leopoldo Torres-Rios: El Cine del sentimiento*. Buenos Aires: Ediciones Corregidor, 1974.

———. *El negro Ferreyra: Un Cine por instinto*. Buenos Aires: Editorial Freeland, 1969.

———. ed. *Historia del cine argentino*. Buenos Aires: Centro Editor de América Latina, 1984.

Couselo, Jorge Miguel, and Leopoldo Torre Nilsson. *Torre Nilsson*. Buenos Aires: Editorial Fraterna, 1985.

Cozarinsky, Edgardo. *Borges in and on Film*. New York: Lumen, 1986.

———. *Borges y el cine*. Buenos Aires: Editorial Sur, 1974.

Crasswaller, Ronald. *Perón and the Enigma of Argentina*. New York: Norton, 1987.

Curubeto, Diego. *Babilonia gaucha*. Buenos Aires: Planeta, 1993.

Di Núbila, Domingo. *Historia del cine argentino*. Buenos Aires: Edición Cruz de Malta, 1959.

Eckstein, Susan, ed. *Power and Popular Protest: Latin America Social Movements. See Latin America.*

Erens, Patricia, ed. *Issues in Feminist Film Criticism. See Cinema.*

Erro, David G. *Resolving the Argentine Paradox*. Boulder: Lynne Rienner Publications, 1993.

España, Claudio. *Luis César Amadori*. Buenos Aires: Centro Editor de América Latina, 1994.

———. *Medio siglo de cine: Argentina sono film*. Buenos Aires: Editorial Abril, 1984.

Farina, Alberto. *Leonardo Favio*. Buenos Aires: Centro Editor de América Latina, 1993.

Ferguson, Russell, et al. *Out There: Marginalization in Contemporary Culture. See Cinema.*

Foster, David William. *Contemporary Argentine Cinema*. Columbia: University of Missouri Press, 1992.

Fraser, Nicholas, and Marysa Navarro. *Eva Peron*. New York: W. W. Norton, 1981.

García Oliveri, Ricardo. *Cine y dependencia: El Cine en la Argentina*. Buenos Aires: Puntosur Editores, 1990.

———. *Notas sobre cine argentino y latinoamericano*. México: Edimedios, 1984.

Getino, Octavio. *Cine, cultura y descolonización. See Cinema.*

———. *Hacia el tercer cine. See Cinema.*

———. *Notas sobre cine argentino y latinoamericano. See Cinema.*

González, Horacio, and Eduardo Rinesi, eds. *Decorados: Apuntes para una historia social del cine argentino*. Buenos Aires: Manuel Suárez, 1993.

Grinberg, Miguel. *Mario Soffici*. Buenos Aires: Centro Editor de América Latina, 1994.

Guest, Lain. *Behind the Disappearances: Argentina's Dirty War against Human Rights and the United Nations*. Philadelphia: University of Pennsylvania Press, 1990.

Guiraldes, Ricardo. *Don Segundo Sombra. See Uruguay.*

Guy, Donna J. *Sex and Danger in Buenos Aires: Prostitution, Family, and Nation in Argentina*. Lincoln: University of Nebraska Press, 1991.

Heath, Stephen. *Questions of Cinema. See Cinema.*

Hodges, D. C. *Argentina 1943–1976: The National Revolution and Resistance*. Albuquerque: University of New Mexico Press, 1976.

Hodges, Donald. *Argentina's "Dirty War": An Intellectual Biography*. Austin: University of Texas Press, 1991.

Hudson, William Henry. *Far Away and Long Ago: A History of My Early Life*. New York: E. P. Dutton, 1918.

Insaurralde, Andrés. *Manuel Romero*. Buenos Aires: Centro Editor de América Latina, 1993.

Inzillo, Carlos. *Queridos Filipipones: Una biofilmo-radiografía afectiva de Pepe Arias*. Buenos Aires: Corregidor, 1991.

King, John. *Magical Reels: A History of Cinemas in Latin America. See Cinema.*

King, John, and Nissa Torrents. *The Garden of Forking Paths: Argentine Cinema*. London: British Film Institute Publication, 1988.

Kuhn, Annette, and Susannah Radstone. *Women in Film: An International Guide. See Cinema.*

Landini, Carlos. *Héctor Olivera*. Buenos Aires: Centro Editor de América Latina, 1993.

———. *Sergio Renán*. Buenos Aires: Centro Editor de América Latina, 1993.

Lavrin, Asunción, ed. *Latin American Women: Historical Perspectives. See Latin America.*

López, Daniel. *Catálogo del nuevo cine argentino, 1987/88*. Buenos Aires: Instituto Nacional de Cinematografía, 1989.

———. *Catálogo del nuevo cine argentino, 1989/91*. Buenos Aires: Instituto Nacional de Cinematografía, 1989.

Lozano, Jaime. *El síndrome del cine nacional.* Buenos Aires: EDI-SICA, 1985.

Lynch, John. *Argentine Dictator: Juan Manuel De Rosas, 1829–1852.* New York: Oxford University Press, 1981.

Magrini, César. *Cine argentino contemporáneo.* Buenos Aires: Revista Cultura, 1985.

Mahieu, José Agustín. *Breve historia del cine nacional, 1896–1974.* Buenos Aires: Alzamor Editores, 1974.

Maranghello, César. *Hugo del Carril.* Buenos Aires: Centro Editor de América Latina, 1993.

Mármol, José. *Amalia: Novela histórica americana,* 9th ed. Buenos Aires: Editorial Sopena, 1965.

Martínez, Tomás Eloy. *La Obra de Ayala y Torre-Nilsson en las estructuras del cine argentino.* Buenos Aires: Ediciones Culturales Argentinas, 1961.

Masiello, Francine. *Between Civilization and Barbarism: Women, Nation, and Literary Culture in Modern Argentina.* Lincoln: University of Nebraska Press, 1992.

Monteagudo, Luciano. *Fernando Solanas.* Buenos Aires: Centro Editor de América Latina, 1993.

Núñez, María. *Juan José Jusid.* Buenos Aires: Centro Editor de América Latina, 1994.

Oms, Marcel. *Leopoldo Torre-Nilsson.* Lyon: SERDOC, 1962.

Oubiña, David. *Manuel Antín.* Buenos Aires: Centro Editor de América Latina, 1994.

Page, Joseph A. *Perón, a Biography.* New York: Random House, 1983.

Paz, Octavio. *Laberinto de la soledad. See Mexico.*

Peña, Fernando. *Leopoldo Torre Nilsson.* Buenos Aires: Centro Editor de América Latina, 1993.

———. *René Mugica.* Buenos Aires: Centro Editor de América Latina, 1994.

Peralta-Ramos, M., and C. H. Waisman. *From Military Rule to Liberal Democracy in Argentina.* Boulder: Westview Press, 1987.

Poggi, Alberto. *Cine argentino en democracia, una historia no oficial: Notas publicadas entre 1984 y 1988 en distintos medios.* Argentina, 1989.

Posadas, Abel. *Carlos Schlieper.* Buenos Aires: Centro Editor América Latina, 1994.

———. *Niní Marshall: Desde un ayer lejano.* Buenos Aires: Ediciones Coluhue, 1993.

Previtali, Giovanni. *Ricardo Guiraldes and Don Segundo Sombra: Life and Works.* New York: Hispanic Institute in the United States, 1963.

Puig, Manuel. *Bajo un manto de estrellas: Pieza en dos actos.* Barcelona: Editorial Seix Barral, 1983.

———. *Betrayed by Rita Hayworth.* New York: Vintage Books, 1981.

———. *Blood of Requited Love,* 1st American ed. New York: Vintage Books, 1984.

———. *Boquitas pintadas.* Barcelona: Seix Barral, 1985.

———. *The Buenos Aires Affair: A Detective Novel.* New York: Vintage Books, 1980.

———. *Buenos Aires, cuando sera el día que me quieras: conversaciones con Manuel Puig.* Buenos Aires: Editorial Vinciguerra, 1992.

———. *La cara del villano: Recuerdo de Tijuana.* Barcelona: Seix Barral, 1985.

———. *Drama Contemporary, Latin America: Plays.* New York: P.A.J. Publications, 1986.

———. *Eternal Curse on the Reader of These Pages.* New York: Random House, 1982.

———. *Heartbreak Tango: A Serial.* New York: Dutton, 1973.

———. *Kiss of the Spider Woman and Two Other Plays.* New York: W. W. Norton, 1994.

———. *Mystery of the Rose Bouquet.* Boston: Faber & Faber, 1988.

———. *Pubis Angelical.* New York: Vintage Books, 1986.

———. *Tropical Night Falling.* New York: W. W. Norton, 1993.

Rapallo, Armando. *Fernando Ayala.* Buenos Aires: Centro Editor de América Latina, 1993.

Rock, David. *Argentina, 1516–1982: From Spanish Colonization to the Falklands War.* Berkeley and Los Angeles: University of California Press, 1985.

———. *Authoritarian Argentina: The Nationalist Movement, Its History, and Its Impact.* Berkeley and Los Angeles: University of California Press, 1993.

Roman, Eduardo. *Literatura/cine argentinos sobre las fronteras.* Buenos Aires: Catálogos, 1991.

Rosado, Miguel Angel. *Daniel Tinayre.* Buenos Aires: Centro Editor de América Latina, 1994.

Rossi, Juan José. *El cine documental etnográfico de Jorge Prelorán.* Buenos Aires: Ediciones Búsqueda, 1987.

Santos, Laura, et al. *Nina Marshall: Artesana de la risa.* Buenos Aires: Ediciones Letra Buena, 1993.

Sarmiento, Domingo Faustino. *Civilización y barbarie; vidas de Quiroga, Aldao i el Chacho.* Buenos Aires: Lajouane, 1889.

———. *Facundo: Civilizacion y barbarie.* Caracas: Biblioteca Ayacucho, 1977.

Scobie, James R. *Argentina: A City and a Nation,* 2d ed. New York: Oxford University Press, 1971.

Sendrós. *Fernando Birri.* Buenos Aires: Centro Editor de América Latina, 1993.

———. *Paraná. Eliseo Subiela.* Buenos Aires: Centro Editor de América Latina, 1993.

Simpson, John, and Jana Bennett. *The Disappeared and the Mothers of the Plaza: The Story of the 11,000 Argentinians Who Vanished.* New York: St. Martin's Press, 1985.

Skidmore, Thomas E., and Peter H. Smith. *Modern Latin America. See Latin America.*

Slatta, Richard W. *Gauchos and the Vanishing Frontier.* Lincoln: University of Nebraska Press, 1992.

Smith, Peter H. *Argentina and the Failure of Democracy.* Madison: University of Wisconsin Press, 1974.

Solanas, Fernando. *Cine, cultura, y descolonización.* Buenos Aires: Siglo Veinte, 1973.

———. *La mirada: Reflexiones sobre cine y cultura: entrevista con Horacio González.* Buenos Aires: Punto Sur, 1989.

Taquini, Graciela. *Jorge Prelorán.* Buenos Aires: Centro Editor de América Latina, 1993.

Taylor, J. M. *Eva Perón: Myths of a Woman.* Chicago: University of Chicago Press, 1979.

Thornton, Lawrence. *Imagining Argentina.* New York: Doubleday, 1987.

Timerman, Jacobo. *Prisoner without a Name, Cell without a Number.* New York: Knopf, distributed by Random House, 1981.

Valenzuela, Luisa. *Como en la guerra.* Buenos Aires: Editorial Sudamericana, c. 1977.

———. *He Who Searches.* Elmwood Park: Dalkey Archive Press, 1988.

———. *Other Weapons.* Hanover, N.H.: Ediciones Del Norte, 1985.

———. *Strange Things Happen Here: Twenty Short Stories and a Novel.* New York: Harcourt Brace Jovanovich, 1979.

Vallejo, Gerardo. *Un camino hacia el cine.* Buenos Aires: El Cid, 1984.

Vila, Pablo. "Tango to Folk: Hegemony Construction and Popular Identities in Argentina." *Studies in Latin American Popular Culture,* no. 10 (1991), 107–40.

Wolf, Sergio. *Cine argentino: La otra historia.* Buenos Aires: Ediciones Letra Buena, 1992.

Wynia, Gary W. *Argentina: Illusions and Realities,* 2d ed. New York: Holmes and Meier, 1992.

BOLIVIA

Albo, Xavier, José M. Barnadas, and Arturo Sist. *La cara campesina de nuestra historia,* 2d ed. La Paz: Unitas, 1985.

Anner, John. "Aymara: With Help from Indian People in the United States, Aymara Indians from Bolivia Recover their Sacred Weavings." *Native Peoples Magazine,* Winter 1994.

———. "Native Peoples: The Arts and Lifeways." *Study Guide,* Winter 1994 (Native Peoples Education Program [tel: 602-252-2236])

Arteaga, Vivian. *La mujer pobre en la crisis económica: las vendedoras ambulantes de La Paz.* La Paz: FLACSO, 1988.

Barrionuevo, Alfonsina. *Los dioses de la lluvia.* Lima: CONCEYTE, 1989.

Barroso, Carmen, and Cristina Bruschini, eds. *Third World Women and the Politics of Feminism. See Latin America.*

Bomberry, Victoria. "Text and Context: Organizing the Return of the Sacred Textiles to the Community of Coroma, Bolivia." *Akwe:kon Journal,* Winter, 1993.

Browman, David L., ed. *Advances in Andean Archaeology.* The Hague and Chicago: Mouton, distributed in the U.S. by Aldine, 1978.

Chungara, Domitilia. *Let Me Speak.* New York: Monthly Review Press, 1978.

Isbell, Billie Jean. *From Unripe to Petrified: The Feminine Symbolic in Andean Gender.* Schema: Ms., 1992.

Klein, Herbert S. *Historia general de Bolivia.* La Paz: Librería, 1988.

Lindert, P. Van. *Bolivia: A Guide to the People, Politics and Culture.* London; New York: Latin American Bureau, distributed in North America by Monthly Review Press, 1994.

Lobo, Susan. "The Fabric of Life." *Cultural Survival Quarterly,* Summer 1991.

Mantilla, Roberto. "Arquitectura Rupestre en Copacabana." *Arte y arqueología,* no. 2 (1972): 61–70. (Instituto de Estudios Bolivianos, Sección Arte)

Moseley, M. *The Incas and Their Ancestors: The Archaelogy of Peru. See Peru.*

Pereira, David H. "Incallacta." *Cultura,* no. 2 (1992): 7–12.

Salomon, Frank, and George L. Urioste. *The Huarochiri Manuscript: A Testament of Ancient and Colonial Andean Religion.* Austin: University of Texas Press, 1990.

Sanjines, Jorge. "The Courage of the People: An Interview with Jorge Sanjines." *Cineaste* 5, no. 2 (Spring 1972): 18–20.

———. "Language and Popular Culture." *Framework: A Film Journal,* no. 10 (Spring 1979): 31–33.

Spalding, Karen. *Huarochiri: An Andean Society under Inca and Spanish Rule.* Stanford: Stanford University Press, 1984.

Susz Kohl, Pedro K. *Filmografía video boliviano básico.* La Paz: Editorial Cinemateca Boliviana, 1991.

Weatherford, Jack. *Indian Givers: How the Indians of the Americas Transformed the World. See Latin America.*

Zuidema, R. T. *Inca Civilization of Cuzco. See Peru.*

BRAZIL

Adler Lomnitz, Larissa. *Networks and Marginality: Life in a Mexican Shantytown. See Mexico.*

Agosta, Diana. "Mo' Better News: A Discussion on Media Education." *See Cinema.*

Albornoz, Suzana. *Na condicao de mulher.* Santa Cruz do Sul: Grupo Acao Mulher, 1985.

Alencar, Francisco, et al. *Historia da sociedade brasileira,* 3d ed. Rio de Janeiro: Aso Livro Técnico S.A., 1989.

Alfaro Moreno, R. *Tarea.* "Democracia y comunicación en la organización popular." *See Cinema.*

Alvarez, Sonia E. *Engendering Democracy in Brazil: Women's Movements in Transition Politics.* Princeton: Princeton University Press, 1990.

Amado, Jorge. *Cacau: Romance.* Rio de Janeiro: Editora Record, 1982.

————. *O cavaleiro da esperanca.* Rio de Janeiro: Editora Record, 1985.

————. *Gabriela, cravo, e canela: Cronica de uma cidade do interior.* Rio de Janeiro: Editora Record, 1986.

————. *A morte e a morte de Quincas Berro Dagua: Romance.* Rio de Janeiro: Editora Record, 1984.

————. *O pais do carnaval: romance.* Rio de Janeiro: Editora Record, 1986.

————. *Os pastores da noite.* Rio de Janeiro: Editora Record, 1984.

————. *Suor: romance.* Rio de Janeiro: Editora Record, 1984.

————. *Tenda dos milagres: romance.* Rio de Janeiro: Editora Record, 1984.

————. *Tereza Batista cansada de guerra: romance.* Rio de Janeiro: Editora Record, 1986.

Ambrosi, Alain, and Nancy Thede, eds. *Video the Changing World. See Cinema.*

Amnesty International. *Torture in the Eighties.* London: Amnesty International Publications, 1984.

Andrade, Oswald de. *Seraphim Ponte Grande.* Austin: Nefertiti Heads Publications, 1979.

————. *Un homem sem profissão: Memórias e confissões.* Rio de Janeiro: Livraria José Olimpio Editor, 1954.

Andrews, George Reid. *Blacks & Whites in São Paulo, Brazil, 1888–1988.* Madison: University of Wisconsin Press, 1991.

"Anthropology and the Politics of Indigenous People's Struggles." *Cambridge Anthropology,* 1979.

Araujo, Denise. *Rocky Mountain Review.* Salt Lake City: Rocky Mountain Modern Language Association, 1992.

Ataide, Vincente. "Introduçao à literatura Brasileira contemporânea." *Estudos brasileiros* 6, no. 11 (June 1981).

Aufderheide, Patricia. *Cross Cultural Film Guide. See Cinema.*

Augusta, Nisia. *Floresta brasileira, 1809–1885. Opusculo humanitario,* Ed. atualizada. Sao Paulo; Brasilia: Cortez Editora; INEP, 1989.

Avila Neto, María Inacia d'. *O autoritarismo e a mulher: O jogo da dominacao macho-femea no Brazil.* Rio de Janeiro: Achiame, 1980.

Bacha, Edmas L., and Herbert S. Klein, ed. *Social Change in Brazil, 1945–85: The Incomplete Transition.* Albuquerque: University of New Mexico Press, c. 1989.

Bad Object Choices, eds. *How Do I Look? Queer Film and Video.* Seattle: Bay Press, 1991.

Banzhaf, Marion, and the ACT UP/New York Women and AIDS Book Group et al. *Women, AIDS, and Activism. See United States.*

Barnes, Sandra T., ed. *Africa's Ogun: Old World and New. See Latin America.*

Barroso, Carmen, and Cristina Bruschini. *Third World Women and the Politics of Feminism. See Latin America.*

Bastide, Roger. *African Civilisations in the New World. See Latin America.*

————. *The African Religions of Brazil: Toward a Sociology of the Interpenetration of Civilizations.* Baltimore: Johns Hopkins University Press, 1978.

Bastide, Roger, and Florestan Fernandes. *Brancos e negros em São Paulo,* 2d ed. Sao Paulo: Editora Companhia Nacional, 1959.

Beezley, William H., and Judith Ewell, eds. *The Human Tradition in Latin America: The Twentieth Century. See Latin America.*

Benton Foundation. *Making Video. See Cinema.*

————. *Using Video. See Cinema.*

Bethell, Leslie, ed. *Colonial Brazil.* Cambridge: Cambridge University Press, 1987.

Biorn Maybury-Lewis, Alan. *The Politics of the Possible: The Brazilian Rural Workers' Trade Union Movement, 1964–1985.* Philadelphia: Temple University Press, 1994.

Bizzotto, Margarida. *Mulher em suas evidencias.* Rio de Janeiro: Editora Catedra, 1987.

Black, Jan Knippers, ed. *Latin America. Its Problems and Its Promise. See Latin America.*

Boxer, Charles Ralph. *The Golden Age of Brazil, 1695–1750; Growing Pains of a Colonial Society.* Berkeley and Los Angeles: University of California Press, 1962.

Branford, Sue, and Bernardo Kucinski. *Brazil: Carnival of the Oppressed, Lula and the Brazilian Workers Party.* London: Latin America Bureau, 1995. (Distributed in North America by Monthly Review Press.)

"Brazil: The Persistence of Inequality." *NACLA Report on the Americas* 28, no. 6 (May/June 1995).

Brooke, James. "Conflicting Pressures Shape the Future of Brazil Indians." *New York Times,* Sunday, February 1990.

Brookfield, Stephen. *Harvard Educational Review.* "Media Power and Literacy." *See Cinema.*

Brumana, Fernando Giobellina. *Spirits from the Margin: Umbanda in Sao Paolo: A Study in Popular Religion and Social Experience.* Uppsala: Academia Uppsaliensis, 1989.

Burmeister, Tereza. *Decada da mulher, 1976–1985: Avaliacao.* Rio de Janeiro: Pontificia Universidade Catolica do Rio de Janeiro, Nucleo de Estudos Sobre a Mulher, 1987.

Burns, E. Bradford. *A History of Brazil,* 2d ed. New York: Columbia University Press, 1980.

Burton, Julianne. *Cinema and Social Change in Latin America: Conversations with Filmmakers. See Cinema.*

————. *Heresies.* "Women Behind the Camera." *See Cinema.*

————. *The Social Documentary in Latin America. See Cinema.*

Caipora Women's Group. *Women in Brazil/Caipora Women's Group.* Edited by Duncan Green. London: Latin America Bureau, 1993.

Cardoso, Gerald. *Negro Slavery in the Sugar Plantations of Veracruz and Pernambuco, 1550–1680: A Comparative Study.* Washington, D.C.: University Press of America, 1983.

Carneiro, Sueli, and Thereza Santos. *Mulher negras: Politica governamental e a mulher*. São Paulo: Conselho Estadual da Condicão Feminina, 1985.

Castaño, Eleonora Ferrieira, and Joao Paulo Castaño. *Making Sense of the Media: A Handbook of Popular Education Techniques*. See Cinema.

"Cem anos de abolição: a liberdade passada a limpo." *Isto É*, no. 59 (20 Abril 1988): 30–45.

"Cem anos depois: a espera da abliçao." *Afinal*, no. 190 (19 Abril 1988): 36–43.

Chandler, Billy Jaynes. *The Bandit King: Lampiao of Brazil*. College Station: Texas A&M University Press, 1978.

The Cineaste Interviews on Art and Politics of the Cinema. See Cinema.

Colasanti, Marina. *Aqui entre nos*. Rio de Janeiro: Rocco, 1988.

Conrad, Robert Edgar. *Children of God's Fire: A Documentary History of Black Slavery in Brazil*. Princeton: Princeton University Press, 1983.

Cooley, Mike. *Architect or Bee?The Human/Technology Relationship*. Edited by Shirley Cooley. Boston: South End Press, 1982.

Costa, Emilia Viotti da. *The Brazilian Empire: Myths and Histories*. Chicago: University of Chicago, 1985.

Cowell, Adrian. *The Decade of Destruction: The Crusade to Save the Amazon Rain Forest*. New York: H. Holt, 1990.

Crawford, Ian Peter, and David Turton, eds. *Film as Ethnography*. See Cinema.

Creusa de Goes Monteiro Negreiros, Teresa. *Emancipacao da mulher: Uma luta*. Rio de Janeiro: Pontificai Universidade Catolica do Rio de Janeiro, Nucleo de Estudos sobre a Mulher, 1988.

Crimp, Douglas, ed. *AIDS: Cultural Criticism/Cultural Activism*. Cambridge: MIT Press, 1988.

Criticos, S., and T. Quinlan. "Community Video: Power and Process." *Visual Sociology*. See Cinema.

Cunha, Euclydes da. *Rebellion in the Backlands*. Chicago: University of Chicago Press, 1944.

Curran, Mark J. "A literatura de cordel antes e agura." *Hispania Magazine* 74, 3 (September 1991).

Curran, Mark J. *A literatura de cordel*. Recife: Imprensa da UFPE, 1973.

D'Ans Hughes, José Oscar Beozzo, et al. *Mulher: Da escravidao a libertacao*. São Paulo: Edicoes Paulinas, 1989.

Davis, Shelton H. *Victims of the Miracle: Development and the Indians of Brazil*. Cambridge: Cambridge University Press, 1977.

Dean, Warren. *Brazil and the Struggle for Rubber: A Study in Environmental History*. New York: Cambridge University Press, 1987.

Degler, Carl N. *Neither Black nor White: Slavery and Race Relations in Brazil and the United States*. Madison: University of Wisconsin Press, 1986.

Diacon, Todd A. *Millenarian Vision, Capitalist Reality: Brazil's Contestado Rebellion, 1912–1916*. Durham: Duke University Press, 1991.

Dimenstein, Gilberto. *Brazil: War on Children*. London: Latin American Bureau, 1991.

———. *Meninas da noite*. São Paulo: Editora Atica, 1992.

Elsworth, Elizabeth, and Maríanne Whatley, eds. *The Ideology of Images in Educational Media: Hidden Curriculums in the Classroom*. See Cinema.

Escher, Adelmo, et al. *Mulheres trabalhadoras rurais: Participacao e luta sindical*. Rio de Janeiro: Departamento Nacional dos Trabalhadores Rurais, CUT, 1991.

Escobar, Arturo, and Sonia E. Alvarez, eds. *The Making of Social Movements in Latin America: Identity, Strategy, and Democracy*. See Latin America.

Fernandes, Florestan. *The Negro in Brazilian Society*. New York: Columbia University Press, 1969.

Ferreira dos Santos, Anizio. *Eu, negro: Discriminacao racial no Brasil, existe?* Sao Paulo: Edicoes Loyola, 1988.

Ferreiro, Emilia. *Les relations temporelles dans le langage de l'enfant*. Geneva: Droz, 1971.

———. *Nuevas perspectivas sobre los procesos de lectura y escritura*. Mexico: Siglo Veintiuno, 1982.

———. *Proceso de alfabetización en proceso*. Buenos Aires: Centro Editor de America Latina, 1986.

Ferreiro, Emilia, and Ana Teberosky. *Literacy before Schooling/Sistemas de escritura en el desarrollo del niño*. Exeter: Heinemann Educational Books, 1982.

Festa, R., and C. E. Lins da Silva. *Movimentos sociais, comunicacao alternativa e popular no Brasil*. São Paulo: Edicoes Paulinas, 1986.

Fine, Michelle. *Framing Dropouts: Notes on the Politics of an Urban Public High School*. See United States.

Fitz, Earl E. *Clarice Lispector*. Boston: Twayne Publishers, 1985.

Fonseca, María Augusta. *Oswald de Andrade: Uma biografia*. São Paulo: Art Editora, 1990.

Fontes, C. *Defining Popular Video: Emerging Strategies in Latin America and the U.S. See Latin America*.

Forman, Shepard. *The Brazilian Peasantry*. New York: Columbia University Press, 1975.

Foucault, Michel. *Discipline and Punish: The Birth of the Prison. See Mexico*.

Fox, Elizabeth, ed. *The Media and Politics in Latin America: The Struggle for Democracy. See Latin America*.

Francisco, Alencar, et al. *Historia da sociedade Brasileira*, 3d ed. Rio de Janeiro: Aoi Livro Técnico, 1985.

Freire, Paolo. *Pedagogy of the Oppressed*. New York: Continuum, 1988, 1970.

Freitas, Decio. *Palmares, a guerra dos escravos*, 5th ed. Porto Alegre-RS: Mercado Aberto, 1984.

Freyre, Gilberto. *Apipucos: Que ha num nome?* Recife: Fundacao Joaquim Nabuco, Editora Massangana, 1983.

———. *Assombrancoes do Recife velho*. Rio de Janeiro: Edicoes Conde, 1955.

———. *O brasileiro entre os outros hispanos*. Rio de Janeiro: Livraria J. Olympio Editora, 1975.

———. *Brazil*. Washington, D.C.: Editorial Division, Dept. of Public Information, Pan American Union, 1963.

————. *Brazil, an Interpretation.* New York: A. A. Knopf, 1945.

————. *Cana e reforma agraria.* Recife: Instituto Joaquim Nabuco de Pesquisas Sociais, 1970.

————. *Como e porque sou e não sou sociologo.* Brasilia: Ed. da Universidade, 1968.

————. *Dona Sinha e o filho padre; seminovela.* Rio de Janeiro: Livraria J. Olympio, 1964.

————. *The Gilberto Freyre reader,* 1st American ed. New York: Knopf, distributed by Random House, 1974.

————. *Guia pratico, historica e sentimental da cidade do Recife,* 4 ed. Rio de Janeiro: José Olympio, 1968.

————. *The Mansions and the Shanties: The Making of Modern Brazil.* Berkeley and Los Angeles: University of California Press, 1986.

————. *The Masters and the Slaves (Casa-grande & senzala): A Study in the Development of Brazilian Civilization,* 2d ed. Berkeley and Los Angeles: University of California Press, 1986.

————. *Modos de homem & modas de mulher.* Rio de Janeiro: Editora Record, 1986.

————. *Mother and Son; A Brazilian Tale,* 1st American ed. New York: Knopf, 1967.

————. *New World in the Tropics; The Culture of Modern Brazil.* New York: Knopf, 1959.

————. *Olinda; 2. guia pratico, historico e sentimental de cidade brasileira,* 3d ed. Rio de Janeiro: Livraria José Olympio, 1960.

————. *Order and Progress: Brazil from Monarchy to Republic.* New York: Knopf, 1970.

————. *Pessoas, coisas, & animais: 1a. serie,* 2d ed. Porto Alegre: Editora Globo, 1981.

————. *Poesía reunida.* Recife: Edicoes Pirata, 1980.

————. *The Portuguese and the Tropics.* Lisbon: Executive Committee for the Commemoration of the Vth Centenary of the Death of Prince Henry the Navigator, 1961.

————. *Portuguese Integration in the Tropics; Notes Concerning a Possible Lusot.* Lisbon, 1961.

————. *Problemas brasileiros de antropologia,* 3d ed. Rio de Janeiro: Livraria J. Olympio Editora, 1962.

————. *A proposito de frades.* Bahia: Publicacoes da Universidade da Bahia, 1959.

————. *Quase politica,* 2d ed. Rio de Janeiro: Livraria J. Olympio Editora, 1966.

————. *O Recife, sim! Recife, não!.* São Paulo: Arquimedes, 1967.

————. *Retalhos de jornais velhos,* 2d ed. Rio de Janeiro: Livraria J. Olympio Editora, 1964.

————. *Sociologia,* 4th ed. Rio de Janeiro,: Livraria J. Olympio Editora, 1967.

————. *Sugestoes em torno do Museu de Antropologia no Instituto Joaquim Nabuco.* Recife: Universidada do Recife, Imprensa Universitaria, 1960.

————. *Um brasileiro em terras portuguesas.* Rio de Janeiro: Livraria J. Olympio Editora, 1953.

————. *Um engenheiro frances no Brasilia.* Rio de Janeiro: Livraria J. Olympio, 1940.

————. *O velho Felix e suas memorias de um cavalcanti, incluindo a 2.* Rio de Janeiro: Livraria J. Olympio Editora, 1959.

————. *Vida social no Brasil nos meados do seculo XIX.* Recife: Instituto Joaquim Nabuco de Pesquisas Sociais, Ministerio da Educacao e Cultura, 1964.

Frota, Monica, ed. " 'Other Visions?' From the Ivory Tower to the Barricade." *Visual Anthropology Review* 7, no. 2 (1991).

Galeano, Eduardo H. *Open Veins of Latin America: Five Centuries of the Pillage of a Continent. See Latin America.*

Garson, Barbara. *All the Livelong Day: The Meaning and Demeaning of Routine Work.* Revised and updated ed. New York: Penguin Books, 1994.

Gennino, Angela, ed. *Amazonia: Voices from the Rainforest (A Resource and Action Guide). See Latin America.*

Giroux, Henry A. "Radical Pedagogy and the Politics of Student Voice." *Interchange. See Cinema.*

Goldfarb, Brian. "Video Activism and Critical Pedagogy: Sexuality at the End of the Rainbow." *Afterimage. See Cinema.*

Gordan, Beverly M. "The Necessity of African American Epistemology for Educational Theory and Practice." *Boston Journal of Education. See United States.*

Green, Duncan. *Faces of Latin America. See Latin America.*

Green, James N. "The Emergence of the Brazilian Gay Liberation Movement, 1977–81 [S.l.]." *Latin American Perspectives,* 1992.

Guillermoprieto, Alma. *Samba.* New York: Knopf, 1990; distributed by Random House.

Gutiérrez, Gustavo. *The Future of Liberation Theology: Essays in Honor of Gustavo Gutiérrez. See Latin America.*

Hahner, June Edith. *Emancipating the Female Sex: The Struggle for Women's Rights in Brazil, 1850–1940.* Durham: Duke University Press, 1990.

————. "Recent Research on Women in Brazil." *Latin American Research Review* 20, no. 3 (1985): 163–79.

————. *Poverty and Politics: The Urban Poor in Brazil, 1870–1920.* Albuquerque: University of New Mexico Press, 1986.

————. *Women in Brazil: Problems and Perspectives.* Albuquerque: Latin American Institute, University of New Mexico, 1984.

Hall, Doug, and Sally Jo Fifer, eds. *Illuminating Video: An Essential Guide to Video Art. See Cinema.*

Hanchard, Michael. *Orpheus and Power: The Movimiento Negro of Rio de Janeiro and Sao Paulo, Brazil, 1945–1988.* Princeton: Princeton University Press, 1994.

Hasenbalg, Carlos Alfredo. *Race and Socioeconomic Inequalities in Brazil.* Rio de Janeiro: IUPERJ, 1983.

————. *Race Relations in Post-Abolition Brazil: The Smooth Preservation of Racial Inequalities.* 1978.

Hecht, Susanna B., and Alexander Cockburn. *The Fate of the*

Forest: Developers, Destroyers, and Defenders of the Amazon, 1st U.S. ed. New York: Harper Perennial, 1990.

Hemming, John. *Red Gold: The Conquest of Brazilian Indians.* Cambridge: Harvard University Press, 1978.

Herbert, Daniel. *Sexuality, Politics, and AIDS in Brazil.* Washington, D.C.: Falmer Press, 1993.

Horowitz, Irving Louis. *Revolution in Brazil: Politics and Society in a Developing Nation.* New York: Dutton, 1964.

Humphrey, John. *Gender and Work in the Third World: Sexual Divisions in Brazilian Industry.* London and New York: Tavistock Publications, 1987.

IBASE (Instituto Brasileiro de Análises Sociais e Econômicas). *A situação do negro no Brasil: Siscriminacao, trabalho, história.* Rio de Janeiro: IBASE, 1986.

———. *Children and Adolescents in Brazil: Lives in Peril.* Rio: IBASE, 1989.

Ireland, Rowan. *Kingdoms Come: Religion and Politics in Brazil.* Pittsburgh: University of Pittsburgh Press, 1991.

Jesus, Carolina María de. *Child of the Dark: The Diary of Carolina María de Jesus.* New York: New American Library, 1962.

Johnson, Randal. *The Film Industry in Brazil: Culture and the State.* Pittsburgh: University of Pittsburgh Press, 1987.

———. "Film, Television and Traditional Folk Culture in Bye Bye Brazil." *Journal of Popular Culture* 118, 1 (1984).

Johnson, Randal, and Robert Stam. *Brazilian Cinema.* Austin: University of Texas Press, 1982.

———. *Cinema Novo X 5 Masters of Contemporary Brazilian Film.* Austin: University of Texas Press, 1984.

Juhasz, Alex. "Wave in the Media Environment: Camcorder Activism in AIDS Education." *Camera Obscura. See United States.*

Karasch, Mary C. *Slave Life in Rio de Janeiro, 1808–1850.* Princeton: Princeton University Press, 1987.

Karunanayake, Nandana. "Community Radio: A Promising Experiment." *Agricultural Information Development Bulletin. See Cinema.*

Keck, Margaret E. *PT: A logica da diferenca: O Partido dos Trabalhadores na construcao da democracia brasileira.* São Paulo: Editora Atica, 1991.

King, Anthony D. *Culture, Globalization, and the World-System: Contemporary Conditions for the Representation of Identity. See Latin America.*

King, John. *Magical Reels: A History of Cinemas in Latin America. See Cinema.*

Kottak, Conrad Phillip. *Prime Time Society: An Anthropological Analysis of Television and Culture, 1990. See Cinema.*

Kowarick, Lucio, ed. *Social Struggles and the City: The Case of São Paulo.* New York: Monthly Review Press, 1994.

Kruger, Barbara, and Phil Maríani, eds. *Remaking History.* Seattle: Bay Press, 1989.

Lage da Gama Lima, Lana, et al. *Mulheres, adulteros e padres: Historica e moral na sociedade brasileira.* Rio de Janeiro: Dois Pontos, 1987.

Landes, Ruth. *The City of Women.* New York: Macmillan, 1947.

Langguth, A. J. *Macumba: White and Black Magic in Brazil.* New York: Harper & Row, 1975.

Lankshear, Colin, and Peter L. Mclaren, eds. *Critical Literacy: Politics, Praxis, and the Postmodern. See Cinema.*

Lauderdale-Graham, Sandra. *House and Street: The Domestic World of Servants and Masters in 19th Century Rio de Janeiro.* Cambridge: Cambridge University Press, 1988.

Leite, Miriam Moreira. *Outra face do feminism.* São Paulo: Editora Atica, 1984.

Lernoux, Penny. *Cry of the People. See Latin America.*

Levine, Robert. *Vale of Tears: Revisiting the Canudos Massacre in Northeastern Brazil, 1893–1897.* Berkeley and Los Angeles: University of California Press, 1992.

Lewin, Linda. *Politics and Parentela in Paraiba: A Case Study of Family-Based Oligarchy in Brazil.* Princeton: Princeton University Press, 1987.

Lisboa Bacha, Edmar, and Herbert S. Klein. *Social Change in Brazil, 1945–1985: The Incomplete Transition.* Albuquerque: University of New Mexico Press, 1989.

Lispector, Clarice. *Hour of the Star and Other Stories.* Manchester: Carcanet Press, 1986.

Lopes, Helena Teodoro, et al. *Negro e cultura no Brasil.* Rio de Janeiro: UNIBRADE, 1987.

Luhr, William, ed. *World Cinema since 1945. See Cinema.*

Luz, Marco Aurelio. *Cultura negra e ideologia do recalque.* Rio de Janeiro: Achiame, 1983.

Machado, Arlindo. "Inside Out and Upside Down: Brazilian Video Groups TVDO and Olhar Electronico." *Independent* 14, no. 1 (January/February 1991): 30–33.

Macrae, Edward John Baptista das Neves. *A construcao da igualdade: Identidade sexual e politica no Brasil da "abertura."* Campinas, SP, Brazil: Editora da Unicamp, 1990.

Martin, Wilson. *The Modernist Idea: A Critical Survey of Brazilian Writing in the Twentieth Century.* New York: New York University Press, 1970.

Mattelart, Michele, and Armand Mattelart. *Carnival of Images: Brazilian Television Fiction.* New York, Westport, and London: Bergin & Garvey, 1990.

Mattoso, Katia de Queiros. *To Be a Slave in Brazil.* New Brunswick: Rutgers University Press, 1986.

Maxado, Franklin. *O que é a literatura de cordel.* Rio de Janeiro: Codecri, 1980.

McGregor, Pedro. *The Moon and Two Mountains: The Myths, Ritual, and Magic of Brazilian Spiritism.* London: Souvenir Press, 1966.

Medeiros da Fonseca, Romy. *A condicao feminina.* São Paulo: Vertice, 1988.

Mejia, A. L. "Um novo conceito de comunicacao: O destinatario e o sujeito." *Proposta,* no. 43 (1989): 57–63. [Rio de Janeiro: Federacao de orgaos para assistencia social e cultural.]

Mendes, Chico, and Tony Gross. *Fight for the Forest: Chico Mendes in His Own Words.* London, New York: Latin American Bureau, distributed in North America by Monthly Review Press, 1989.

Michaels, Eric. *Bad Aboriginal Art: Tradition, Media, and Technological Horizons. See Cinema.*

Miller, Francesca. *Latin American Women and the Search for Social Justice. See Latin America.*

Minh-Ha, Trinh Thi. *Woman, Native, Other: Writing Post-coloniality and Feminism. See Cinema.*

Mintz, Sidney. *Workers in the Cane.* New Haven: Yale University Press, 1960.

Mohanty, Chandra, Ann Russo, and Lourdes Torres, eds. *Third World Women and the Politics of Feminism. See Latin America.*

Moises, Massand. *A literatura brasileira através dos textos.* São Paulo: Editora Cultrix, 1971.

Moody, Roger, ed. *The Indigenous Voice: Visions and Reality. See Latin America.*

Moore, Rachael. "Marketing Alterity." *Visual Anthropology Review. See Cinema.*

Moraes, María Quartim de. *Mulheres em movimento: O balanco da decada da mulher do ponto de vista do feminismo, das religioes, e da politica.* São Paulo: Nobel: Conselho Estadual da Condicao Feminina, 1985.

Moraes, Vinicius de. *Orfeu da conceicão: Tragedia carioca; desenhos de Carlos Scliar,* 2d ed. Rio de Janeiro: Editora Dois Amigos, 1956.

Morgado, Belkis. *A marca do gado: Rotulo da mulher.* Rio de Janeiro: Livraria J. Olympio Editora, 1987.

Moura, Clóvis. *Brasil: As raizes do protesto negro.* São Paulo: Global Editora, 1983.

Mulher negra: Dossie sobre a discriminacao racial. São Paulo: Litarte Fotolitos Ltda., 1986.

Muraro, Rose Marie. *Sexualidade da mulher brasileira: Corpo e classe social no Brasil.* Petropolis: Vozes, 1983.

Murphy, Yolanda, and Robert F. Murphy. *Women of the Forest,* 2d ed. New York: Columbia University Press, 1985.

Mutirao de educacao popular: Mulher trabalhadora rural. São Paulo: Edicoes Rede Mulher, 1988.

Nascimento, Abdias do. *Brazil, Mixture or Massacre? Essays in the Genocide of a Black People.* Dover: Majority Press, 1989.

———. *Dois negros libertários.* Rio de Janeiro: IPEAFRO, 1985.

———. *Sitiado em Lagos: Autodefesa de um negro acossado pelo racismo.* Rio de Janeiro: Editora Nova Fronteira, 1981.

Nash, June C., Helen Safa, and contributors. *Women and Change in Latin America. See Latin America.*

Needell, Jeffrey D. *A Tropical Belle-Epoque: Elite Culture and Society in Turn-of-the-Century Rio de Janeiro.* Cambridge: Cambridge University Press, 1987.

O'Gorman, Frances. *Morro, mulher.* São Paulo: Edicoes Paulinas e FASE Programa NUCLAR, 1984.

Oliveira Costa, Albertina de, and Cristina Bruschini. *Rebeldia e submissao: Estudos sobre condicao feminina.* São Paulo: Vertice: Fundacao Carlos Chagas, 1989.

Osorio, Pepon. *Con to' los hierros: A Retrospective of the Work of Pepon Osario: May 2–August 4, 1991.* New York: Museo del Barrio, 1991.

Pacheco, Eliezer. *Colonizacao e racismo: Relacoes raciais em uma zona de colonizacao europeia.* Rio de Janeiro: Editora Artenova, 1976.

Paim, Paulo. *Dia internacional para a eliminacao da discriminacao racial: Discursos em homenagem ao transcurso do Dia Internacional do Negro.* Brasilia: Centro de Documentacao e Informacao, Coordenacao de Publicacoes, 1988.

Parker, Andrew, ed. *Nationalisms and Sexualities. See Latin America.*

Patai, Daphne. *Brazilian Women Speak: Contemporary Life Stories.* New Brunswick: Rutgers University Press, 1988.

Pereira, Joao Baptista Borges. "Negro e cultura negra no Brasil atual." *Revista de Antropologia,* no. v. 26 (1983): 95–105.

Perlman, Janice E. *The Myth of Marginality: Urban Poverty and Politics in Rio de Janeiro.* Berkeley and Los Angeles: University of California Press, 1976.

Perlman, Janice E. *Portrait of the People: Migrants to Rio de Janeiro.* Cambridge: Migration and Development Study Group, Center for International Studies, Massachussetts Institute of Technology, 1975.

Pines, Jim, and Paul Wileman. *Questions of Third Cinema. See Cinema.*

Pinto, Regina Pahim. "O movimento negro e etnicidade." *Estudos afro-asiáticos,* no. 19 (1990). (Rio de Janeiro.)

Place, Susan, ed. *Tropical Forests: Latin American Nature and Society in Transition. See Latin America.*

Poppino, Rollie. *Brazil: The Land and People,* 2d ed. New York: Oxford University Press, 1973.

Protz, M. *Seeing and Showing Ourselves. See Cinema.*

Puig, Manuel. *Bajo un manto de estrellas: Pieza en dos actos. See Argentina.*

———. *Kiss of the Spider Woman and Two Other Plays. See Argentina.*

Queiros Mattoso, Katia M. de. *To Be a Slave in Brazil, 1550–1888.* New Brunswick: Rutgers University Press, 1986.

Ramos, Arthur. *The Negro in Brazil.* Philadelphia: Porcupine Press, 1980.

Renov, Michael, ed. *Resolutions.* Minneapolis: Minnesota University Press, 1995.

Revkin, Andrew. *The Burning Season: The Murder of Chico Mendes and the Fight for the Amazon Rain Forest.* Boston: Houghton Mifflin, 1990.

Rocha, Glauber Pedro de Andrade. "Glauber Rocha acerca del cine latinoamericano." *America Latina.*

————. "El manifesto del 'cinema novo': 'La estetica del hambre'." *Brasil/Cultura. See Cinema.*

Rojas, Marta. *Tania: Guerrillera heroica.* Buenos Aires: Rafael Cedeno, 1993.

Rubenstein, Anne. "Seeing Through AIDS: Media Activists Join Forces with the NYC Department of Health." *Independent. See United States.*

Ruby, J. "Speaking for, Speaking about, Speaking with, or Speaking alongside: An Anthropological and Documentary Dilemma." *Visual Anthropology Review. See Cinema.*

Russell-Wood, A. J. R. *The Black Man in Slavery and Freedom in Colonial Brazil.* New York: St. Martin's Press, 1982.

Saalfield, Catherine. "Pregnant with Dreams: Julia Barco's Visions from Latin America." *The Independent. See Cinema.*

Sader, Emir. *Without Fear of Being Happy: Lula, the Workers Party, and Brazil.* London and New York: Verso, 1991.

Saffioti, Heleieth Iara Bongiovani. *Mulher brasileira: Opressão e exploracão.* Rio de Janeiro: Achiame, 1984.

Santoro, Luiz Fernando. *A imagem nas mãos: O video popular no Brasil.* São Paulo: Sumas Editorial Lgda, 1986.

Scheper-Hughes, Nancy. *Death without Weeping: The Violence of Everyday Life in Brazil.* Berkeley and Los Angeles: University of California Press, 1992.

Schmink, Maríanne, and Charles H. Wood. *Contested Frontiers in Amazonia.* New York: Columbia University Press, 1992.

Schuler, Margaret, ed. *Freedom from Violence: Women's Strategies from Around the World. See Latin America.*

Schwartz, Stuart B. *Slaves, Peasants, and Rebels: Reconsidering Brazilian Slavery.* Urbana: University of Illinois Press, 1992.

————. *Sugar Plantations in the Formation of Brazilian Society: Bahia, 1550–1835.* Cambridge: Cambridge University Press, 1985.

Schwoch, James, Mimi White, and Susan Reilly. *Media Knowledge: Readings in Popular Culture, Pedagogy, and Critical Citizenship. See Cinema.*

Sector Audiovisual Fase. "Percepcao, relexao, e expressao: Uma discussao metodologica." *Proposta,* no. 43 (1989): 17–21. (Rio de Janeiro: Federacao de orgaos para assistencia social e educacional.)

Sedgwick, Eve Kosofsky. "How to Bring Your Kids Up Gay." *Social Text* 29 (Fall 1991).

Shohat, Ella, and Robert Stam. *Unthinking Eurocentrism: Multiculturalism and the Media. See Cinema.*

Silva, Nelson do Valle. *Relacões raciais no Brasil contemporâneo.* Rio de Janeiro: Rio Fundo ed., 1992.

Simpson, George Eaton. *Black Religions in the New World.* New York: Columbia University Press, 1978.

Skidmore, Thomas E. *Black into White: Race and Nationality in Brazilian Thought.* New York: Oxford University Press, 1974.

————. *Fact and Myth: Discovering a Racial Problem in Brazil.* Notre Dame: University of Notre Dame, Helen Kellogg Institute for International Studies, 1992.

————. *Politics in Brazil, 1930–1964; An Experiment in Democracy.* New York: Oxford University Press, 1967.

Skidmore, Thomas E., and Peter H. Smith. *Modern Latin America. See Latin America.*

Slater, Candace. *Stories on a String: The Brazilian Literatura de Cordel.* Berkeley and Los Angeles: University of California Press, 1982.

————. "Literatura de Cordel and the Mass Media in Today's Brazil." *Studies in Latin American Popular Culture,* no. 7. (Las Cruces: s.n.)

Smith, T. Lynn. *The Process of Rural Development in Latin America. See Latin America.*

Souza, Barbara M. de, et al. *Meu nome e mulher: Temas para debate.* São Paulo: Edicoes Loyola, 1990.

Stam, Robert. *Subversive Pleasures. Bakhtin, Cultural Criticism, and Film. See Cinema.*

Stavenhagen, Rodolfo. *Agrarian Problems and Peasant Movements in Latin America. See Latin America.*

————. *Rural Social Movements in Latin America. See Latin America.*

Stein, Stanley J. *Vassouras, a Brazilian Coffee County, 1850–1900: The Roles of Planter and Slave in a Plantation Society.* Princeton: Princeton University Press, 1985.

Stepan, Alfred C. *The Military in Politics; Changing Patterns in Brazil.* Princeton: Princeton University Press, 1971.

Stolcke, Verena. *Coffee Planters, Workers, and Wives: Class Conflict and Gender Relations on Sao Paulo Plantations, 1850–1980.* New York: St. Martin's Press, 1988.

Terkel, Studs. *Working.* New York: Avon, 1975.

Tocantins, Leandro. *O rio comanda a vida: Uma interpretacao da Amazonia,* 7 ed. Rio de Janeiro: Livraria J. Olympio Editora, 1983.

Todaro, Michael P. *Economic Development in the Third World: An Introduction to Problems and Policies in a Global Perspective. See Latin America.*

Tomaselli, K. "Transferring Video Skills to the Community: The Problem of Power." *Media Development. See Cinema.*

Toplin, Robert Brent. *Freedom and Prejudice: The Legacy of Slavery in the United States and Brazil.* Westport, Conn.: Greenwood Press, 1981.

Treichler, Paula. "Beyond: AIDS, Identity, and Inscriptions of Gender." *Camera Obscura,* no. 28 (1993).

————. "AIDS and HIV Infection in the Third World: A First World Chronicle." *Camera Obscura,* no. 28 (1993).

Turner, Michael. "Brown into Black: Changing Racial Attitudes of Afro-Brazilian University Students." *Fontaine,* 1985, 73–94.

Turner, Terence. "Defiant Images: The Kayapo Appropriation of Video" *Anthropology Today* 8, no. 6 (1992): 5–16.

————. "The Social Dynamics of Video Media in an Indigenous Society." *Visual Anthropology Review* 7, no. 2 (Fall 1991): 68–76.

———. "Visual Media, Cultural Politics, and Anthropological Practice." *Independent* 14, no. 1, January/February 1991, 34–40.

Valdeavellano, P., ed. *El video en la educacion popular. See Cinema.*

Vargas Llosa, Mario. *The War of the End of the World. See Colombia.*

Wagley, Charles. *Amazon Town: A Study of Man in the Tropics.* London and New York: Oxford University Press, 1976.

———. *An Introduction to Brazil.* Revised ed. New York: Columbia University Press, 1971.

———. *Race and Class in Rural Brazil.* Paris: UNESCO, 1963.

Wasco, Janet, and Vincent Mosco. *Democratic Communication in the Information Age. See Cinema.*

Watney, Simon. *Policing Desire: Pornography, AIDS, and the Media. See Cinema.*

Weatherford, Elizabeth. "Native Visions: The Growth of Indigenous Media." *Aperture,* Summer 1990, 58–61.

Weatherford, J. McIver. *Native Roots: How the Indians Enriched America.* New York: Crown, c1991.

Weis, Lois, and Michelle Fine, eds. *Beyond Silenced Voices. See United States.*

Winant, *Racial Conditions: Politics, Theory, Comparison.* University of Maine Press, 1994.

Worcester, Donald Emmet. *Brazil, From Colony to World Power.* New York: Scribner, 1973.

Zak, Monica. *Salven mi selva.* México, D.F: Sitesa, 1989.

CHILE

Agosin, Marjorie. *Scraps of Life: Chilean Arpilleras, Chilean Women, and the Pinochet Dictatorship.* Trenton, N.J.: Red Sea Press, 1987.

Aguero, Felipe. "Chile: South America's Success Story?" *Current History 92,* March 1993, 130–35.

Allende, Isabel. *Eva Luna.* Edited and translated by Margaret Sayers Peden. New York: Knopf, 1988.

———. *The House of the Spirits.* New York: Knopf, 1985.

———. *The Infinite Plan.* New York: Harper Collins Publishers, 1993.

———. *Of Love and Shadows,* 1st American ed. New York: Knopf, 1987.

Aman, Kenneth, and Christina Parker. *Popular Culture in Chile: Resistance and Survival.* Boulder: Westview Press, 1990.

Arriagada, Genaro. *Pinochet: The Politics of Power.* Boston: Unwin Hyman, 1988.

Aub, Max. *La calle de Valverde.* Madrid: Catedra, 1985.

———. *Campo abierto, novela.* México: Tezontle, 1951.

———. *Campo cerrado.* Xalapa, México: Universidad Veracruzana, 1968.

———. *Campo de los almendros.* Madrid: Alfaguara, 1981.

———. *Campo del moro.* México: Mortiz, 1963.

———. *Campo frances,* 2d ed. Madrid: Ediciones Alfaguara, 1982.

———. *Crimenes ejemplares.* Barcelona: Editorial Lumen, 1972.

———. *El desconfiado prodigiosa.* Madrid: Madrid Taurus, 1971.

———. *Discurso de la novela espanola contemporanea.* México: Colegio de México, 1945.

———. *La gallina ciega; diario espanol.* México: J. Mortiz, 1971.

———. *Geografia.* México: Era, 1964.

———. *Guia de narradores de la revolucion mexicana.* México: Fondo de Cultura Economica, 1969.

———. *Los muertos.* México: Joaquin Mortiz, 1971.

———. *Los pies por delante y otros cuentos.* Barcelona: Seix Barral, 1975.

———. *Retrato de un general, visto de medio cuerpo, y vuelto hacia la izquierda.* México: J. Mortiz, 1969.

———. *San Juan: tragedia.* Barcelona: Fundacion Caja de Segorbe, Anthropos, 1992.

———. *Ultimos cuentos de la guerra de Espana.* Caracas: Monte Avila, 1969.

———. *La una y otras narraciones.* Barcelona: Ediciones Picazo, 1972.

———. *La verdadera historia de la muerte de Francisco Franco; y otros cuentos.* México: Libro Mex, 1960.

———. *Vida y obra de Luis Alvarez Petreña.* Barcelona: Seix Barral, 1972.

———. *Las vueltas.* México: J. Mortiz, 1965.

———. *El zopilote, y otros cuentos mexicanos.* Barcelona: E.D.H.A.S.A., 1964.

Aub, Max, ed. *La rosa espanola del siglo XIX.* México: Antigua Libreria Robredo, 1952.

Baver, Arnold J. *Chilean Rural Society from the Spanish Conquest to 1930.* Cambridge: Cambridge University Press, 1975.

Beneria, Lourdes, and Martha Roldan. *The Crossroads of Class and Gender: Industrial Homework, Subcontracting, and Household Dynamics in Mexico City. See Mexico.*

Castaneda, Tarsicio. *Combatting Poverty: Innovative Social Reforms in Chile during the 1980s.* San Francisco: ICS Press, 1992.

Chanan, Michael, ed. *Chilean Cinema.* London: British Film Institute, 1976.

Chavkin, Samuel. *Storm over Chile: The Junta under Siege.* Chicago: Lawrence Hill Books, 1989.

Cheney, Theodore A. Revs. *Writing Creative Nonfiction: How to Use Fiction Techniques. See Cinema.*

Constable, Pamela, and Arturo Valenzuela. *A Nation of Enemies: Chile under Pinochet.* New York: W. W. Norton, 1991.

Dinges, John, and Saul Landau. *Assassination on Embassy Row.* New York: Pantheon Books, 1980.

Dorfman, Ariel. *Death and the Maiden.* New York: Penguin Books, 1992.

———. *Widows.* New York: Pantheon Books, 1983.

Drake, Paul W., and Ivan Jaksic, eds. *The Struggle for Democracy in Chile, 1982–1990.* Lincoln: University of Nebraska Press, 1991.

Falcoff, Mark. *Modern Chile, 1970–1989: A Critical History.* New Brunswick, N.J.: Transaction Publishers, 1989.

Fox, Elizabeth, ed. *The Media and Politics in Latin America. See Latin America.*

García Márquez, Gabriel. *La aventura de Miguel Littín clandestino en Chile. See Colombia.*

———. *Clandestine in Chile: The Adventures of Miguel Littín,* 1st American ed. New York: Henry Holt, 1987.

Garretón, Manuel Antonio. *The Chilean Political Process.* Boston: Unwin Hyman, 1989.

Gumucio Dragón, Alfonso. *El cine de los trabajadores: Manual teórico y práctico a la generación de talleres de cine Super 8,* reviewed by Julianne Burton in Latin American Popular Culture (Vol. 2). *City Publisher* 1983, 256–61.

Guzmán, Patricio. *La batalla de Chile: La lucha de un pueblo sin armas.* Pamplona: Peralta, 1977.

Hassett, John J., and Grinor Rojo. *Chile: Dictatorship and the Struggle for Democracy.* Gaithersburg, Md.: Ediciones Hispamérica, 1988.

Hersh, Seymour. *The Price of Power: Kissinger in the Nixon White House. See United States.*

Heyck, Denis Lynn Daly, and María Victoria González-Widel. *Tradición y cambio: Lecturas sobre la cultura latinoamericana contemporánea.* New York: Random House, 1988.

Hijuelos, Oscar. *The Fourteen Sisters of Emilio Montez O'Brien.* New York: Farrar, Straus, Giroux, 1993.

Hojman, D. E. *Chile: The Political Economy of Development and Democracy in the 1990s.* Pittsburgh: University of Pittsburgh Press, 1993.

Horne, Alistair. *Small Earthquake in Chile: New, Revised and Expanded Edition of the Classic Account of Allende's Chile.* New York: Penguin Books, 1990.

Jara, Joan. *An Unfinished Song: Life of Victor Jara.* New York: Ticknor and Fields, 1984.

Jelin, Elizabeth, ed. *Women and Social Change in Latin America. See Latin America.*

King, John. *Magical Reels: A History of Cinemas in Latin America. See Cinema.*

Ladrón de Guevara, Matilde. *Destierro: diario de una Chilena.* Barcelona: Editorial Fontamara, 1983.

Landau, Saul. *The Dangerous Doctrine: National Security and U.S. Foreign Policy. See United States.*

Lihn, Enrique. *El arte de la palabra.* Barcelona: Pomaire, 1980.

Lloyd, Peter Cutt. *The "Young Towns" of Lima: Aspects of Urbanization in Peru. See Peru.*

Lobo, Susan. *A House of My Own: Social Organization in the Squatter Settlements of Lima, Peru. See Peru.*

Loveman, Brian. *Chile.* New York: Oxford University Press, 1979.

———. *Chile: The Legacy of Hispanic Capitalism,* 2d ed. New York: Oxford University Press, 1988.

MacEoin, Gary. *Chile, under Military Rule.* New York: IDOC/North America, 1974.

Miller, Francesca. *Latin American Women and the Search for Social Justice. See Latin America.*

Nash, June C., Helen Safa, and contributors. *Women and Change in Latin America. See Latin America.*

Parra, Nicanor. *Chistes para desorientar a la poesía.* Madrid: Visor, 1989.

Paz, Octavio. *Laberinto de la soledad. See Mexico.*

Pick, Zuzana. "Chilean Cinema in Exile." *Framework,* no. 34 (1987): 39–57.

Sater, William F. *The Heroic Image in Chile: Arturo Prat, Secular Saint.* Berkeley and Los Angeles: University of California Press, 1973.

Sigmund, Paul. *The Overthrow of Allende and the Politics of Chile. 1964–1976.* Pittsburgh: University of Pittsburgh Press, 1977.

Skidmore, Thomas E., and Peter H. Smith. *Modern Latin America. See Latin America.*

Smith, Brian H. *The Church and Politics in Chile: Challenges to Modern Catholicism.* Princeton, N.J.: Princeton University Press, 1982.

Stallings, Barbara. *Class Conflict and Economic Development in Chile, 1958–1973.* Stanford: Stanford University Press, 1978.

Timerman, Jacobo. *Chile: Death in the South.* New York: Alfred A. Knopf, 1987.

———. *Prisoner without a Name, Cell without a Number.* New York: Knopf, distributed by Random House, 1981.

Vale, Eugene. *The Technique of Screenplay Writing: An Analysis of the Dramatic Structure of Motion Pictures. See Cinema.*

Valenzuela, J. Samuel, and Arturo Valenzuela, eds. *Military Rule in Chile: Dictatorship and Opposition.* Baltimore: Johns Hopkins University Press, 1986.

Valenzuela, Luisa. *Como en la guerra. See Argentina.*

———. *He Who Searches. See Argentina.*

Wilson, Fiona. *Sweaters: Gender, Class, and Workshop-Based Industry in Mexico. See Mexico.*

Winn, Peter. *Weavers of Revolution: The Yarur Workers and Chile's Road to Socialism.* New York: Oxford University Press, 1986.

CINEMA/MEDIA/CULTURAL STUDIES

Andersen, Robin. *Consumer Culture and TV Programming,* Boulder, Colo.: Westview Press, 1995.

Agosta, Diana. "Mo' Better News: A Discussion on Media Education." *Afterimage* 18, no. 4 (November 1990): 5–8.

Alfaro Moreno, R. "Democracia y comunicación en la organización popular." *Tarea* 9–10 (1984): 3–12. (Lima: Centro de Publicaciones Educativas.)

Allen, Robert C. *Channels of Discourse: Television and Contemporary Criticism.* Chapel Hill, N.C.: Methuen & Co. and University of North Carolina Press, 1987.

Ambrosi, Alain, and Nancy Thede, eds. *Video the Changing World.* Montreal and New York: Black Rose Books, 1991.

Armes, Roy. *Third World Film Making and the West.* Berkeley and Los Angeles: University of California Press, 1987.

Aufderheide, Patricia. *Cross Cultural Film Guide.* Washington, D.C.: American University, 1992.

———. "Latin American Cinema and the Rhetoric of Cultural Nationalism: Controversies at Havana in 1987 and 1989." *Quarterly Review of Film and Video* 12, no. 4 (1991): 61–76.

Bachelard, G. *La poétique de l'espace.* Paris: P.U.F., 1957.

Bakhtin, Michail. *A cultura popular na idade média e no renascimento.* São Paulo: Hucitec, 1987.

Baudrillard, Jean. *Simulacres et Simulation.* Paris: Galilée, 1991.

Benton Foundation. *Making Video.* Washington, D.C.: Benton Foundation, 1993.

———. *Using Video.* Washington, D.C.: Benton Foundation, 1990, 1991.

Bergson, Henri. *L'evolution Créatrice.* Paris: Felix Alcan, 1939.

Bordwell, David. *Making Meaning: Inference and Rhetoric in the Interpretation of Cinema.* Cambridge: Harvard University Press, 1989.

Brookfield, Stephen. "Media Power and Literacy." *Harvard Educational Review* 59, 3 (May 1986):297–324.

Burgin, Victor, James Donald, and Cora Kaplan, eds. *Formations of Fantasy.* London: Routledge, 1989.

Burns, E. *Latin American Cinema: Film and History.* Los Angeles: UCLA Latin American Center, University of California, 1975.

Burton, Julianne. "The Camera as Gun: Two Decades of Culture and Resistance in Latin America." *Latin American Perspectives,* Issues 16 5, 1 (1978).

———. *Cinema and Social Change in Latin America: Conversations with Filmmakers.* Austin: University of Texas Press, 1986.

———. "The Hours of the Embers: On the Current Situation of Latin American Cinema." *Film Quarterly* 30, no. 1 (Fall 1976).

———. "Marginal Cinemas and Mainstream Critical Theory." *Screen* 26, nos. 3–4 (1985).

———. *The New Latin American Cinema: An Annotated Bibliography 1960–1980.* New York: Smryna Press, 1983.

———. *The Social Documentary in Latin America.* Pittsburgh: University of Pittsburgh Press, 1990.

———. "Women behind the Camera." *Heresies,* no. 16 (1983).

Calabrese, Omar. *A Idade neo-barroca.* Lisbon: Ed. 70, 1987.

Caldeira, Teresa. *A Presenca do Autor e a Pós-Modernidade na Antropologia.* Novos Estudos Ceprab, 21, julho, 1988.

Calvino, Italo. *Seis Propostas para o Próximo Milenio.* São Paulo: Companhia das Letras, 1990.

Campos, Haroldo de. *A Arte no Horzonte do Provável.* São Paulo: Perspectiva, 1969.

Carson, Diane, and Les Friedman, eds. *Shared Differences: Multicultural Media in the Classroom.* Urbana-Champaign: University of Illinois Press, 1995.

Carson, Diane, Janice Welsch, and Linda Dittman, eds. *Multiple Voices in Feminist Film Criticism.* Minneapolis: University of Minnesota Press, 1994.

Castaño, Eleonora Ferrieira, and Joao Paulo Castaño. *Making Sense of the Media: A Handbook of Popular Education Techniques.* London: Monthly Review Press, 1993.

Chanan, Michael. *Twenty-Five Years of New Latin American Cinema.* London: British Film Institute, 1983.

Cheney, Theodore A. Revs. *Writing Creative Nonfiction: How to Use Fiction Techniques to Make Your Nonfiction More Interesting, Dramatic, and Vivid.* Cincinnati: Writer's Digest Books, 1987.

Churchill, Ward. *Fantasies of the Master Race: Literature, Cinema, and the Colonization of American Indians.* Monroe: Common Courage Press, 1992.

The Cineaste Interviews on Art and Politics of the Cinema. Chicago: Lake View Press, 1983.

Contreras, José Miguel. *Vidapolítica y televisión.* Espasa Mañana, 1990.

Couchot, Edmond. *Images: de l'optique ao numérique: Les arts visuels et l'evolution des technologies.* Paris: Hermés, 1988.

Crawford, Ian Peter, and David Turton, eds. *Film as Ethnography.* Manchester and New York: Manchester University Press, 1992.

Criticos, S., and T. Quinlan. "Community Video: Power and Process." *Visual Sociology* 6, no. 2 (1991): 39–52.

Daney, Serge. *Devant la recrudescence des vols des sacs a main, Cinema, Television, Information.* Paris: Aléas.

———. *La rampe.* Paris: Cahiers Gallimard, 1979.

———. *Le salaire du zapper.* Paris: Ramsay, 1988.

Davis, D., and Simmons, eds. *The New Television: A Public/Private Art.* Cambridge: MIT Press, 1977.

Davis, Douglas. *The Five Myths of Television. Power—or, Why the Medium is Not the Message.* New York: Simon & Schuster, 1993.

Deleuze, Gilles. *Cinema 1: L'image—mouvement.* Paris: Minuit, 1983.

———. *Cinema 2: l'image—temps.* Paris: Minuit, 1985.

———. *Conversacoes.* Rio de Janeiro: Ed. 34, 1994.

———. *Lógica do sentido.* São Paulo: Perspectiva, 1985.

———. *Le Pli. Leibniz et le barroque.* Paris: Minuit, 1987.

Deleuze, Gilles, and F. Guattari. *Mille plateaux: Capitalisme et schizoprénie.* Paris: Minuit, 1980.

Dorine, Mignot, ed. *Het Luminneuze Beeld/The Luminous Image.* Amsterdam: Stedelijk Museum, 1984.

Dorine, Mignot, and Kathy Rae Huffman, eds. *The Arts for Television*. Los Angeles and Amsterdam: Museum of Contemporary Art-Stedelijk Museum, 1897.

Downing, John D. H., ed. *Film and Politics in the Third World*. New York: Praeger, 1987.

Eisenstein, Sergei Mikhailovich. *Film Form*. New York: Harcourt, Brace & World, 1949.

———. *The Film Sense,* Revised ed. New York: Harcourt, Brace & World, 1970.

Elsworth, Elizabeth, and Maríanne Whatley, eds. *The Ideology of Images in Educational Media: Hidden Curriculums in the Classroom*. New York: Teachers College Press, 1990.

Erens, Patricia, ed. *Issues in Feminist Film Criticism*. Bloomington: Indiana University Press, 1990.

Fargier, J. P., ed. *Ou va la vidéo?*. Paris: Etoile, 1896.

Ferguson, Russell, et al. *Out There: Marginalization in Contemporary Culture*. New York and Cambridge: New Museum of Contemporary Art, M.I.T. Press, 1990.

Fiske, John. *Television Culture*. London: Methuen Drama, 1987.

Fiske, John, and John Hartley. *Reading Television*. Metheun & Co., EUA, 1978.

Flichy, P. *Les industries de l'imaginaire: Pour une analyse economique des media*. Paris: PUG-INA, 1980.

Flitterman-Lewis, Sandy. *To Desire Differently. Feminism and the French Cinema*. Urbana: University of Illinois Press, 1990.

Fontes, C. *Defining Popular Video: Emerging Strategies in Latin America and the U.S.* Paper Presented at the Eighteenth São Paulo International Association for Mass Communication Research, 1992.

Fox, Elizabeth, ed. *The Media and Politics in Latin America: The Struggle for Democracy. See Latin America.*

Francastel, P. *Imagem, visao, e imaginacao*. Lisbon: Ed. 70, 1987.

———. *A realidade figurativa*. São Paulo: Perspectiva, 1975.

Fusco, Coco. "The Latin Boom in American Film." *Centro* 2, no. 8 (Spring 1990): 49–56.

———. ed. *Reviewing Histories. Selections from New Latin American Cinema*. Buffalo, N.Y.: Hallwalls, 1987.

Gabriel, T. *Third Cinema in the Third World. The Aesthetics of Liberation*. Ann Arbor: UMI Research Press, 1982.

Gaines, J. "Race and Gender in Feminist Film Theory." *Cultural Critique,* no. 4 (Fall 1986).

García Espinosa, Julio. *For an Imperfect Cinema*. Cuba: 1969.

Getino, Octavio. *A diez años de "Hacia un tercer cine."* México: UNAM, 1984.

———. *Cine, cultura y descolonización*. Buenos Aires: Siglo Veintiuno, 1973.

———. *Cine latinoamericano: Economía y nuevas tecnologías audiovisuales*. Buenos Aires: Editorial Legasa, 1988.

———. *Hacia el tercer cine*. Buenos Aires: 1973.

———. *Notas sobre cine argentino y latinoamericano*. México: Edimedios, 1984.

———. "Cine indigenista: entre la inmovilidad y el cambio." *Plural,* 2a. epoca 15, no. 4 (Enero 1986): 172. (México: Excelsior Compañia Editorial.)

Gibbs, V. "Latin American Film." *Latin American Research Review* 27, 3 (1992).

Giroux, Henry A. "Radical Pedagogy and the Politics of Student Voice." *Interchange* 17, no. 1 (1986): 48–67.

Goldfarb, Brian. "Video Activism and Critical Pedagogy: Sexuality at the End of the Rainbow." *Afterimage* 20, no. 10 (May 1993).

Guevara, Angel, et al. *El nuevo cine latinoamericano en el mundo de hoy: Memorias del IX Festival Internacional del Nuevo Cine Latinoamericano*. México: Universidad Nacional Autónoma de México, 1988.

Gumucio Dragón, Alfonso. *Cine, censura, y exilio en América Latina,* 2d ed. México: STUMAN-CIMCA-FEM, 1984.

Gutiérrez Alea, Tomás. *Dialéctica del espectador*. La Habana: Union de Escritores y Artistas de Cuba, 1982.

Hall, Doug, and Sally Jo Fifer, eds. *Illuminating Video: An Essential Guide to Video Art*. New York: Aperture/Bay Area Video Coalition, 1990.

Himmelstein, Hal. *On the Small Screen: New Approaches in Television and Video Criticism*. Praeger Publishers, 1981.

Kaplan, E. Ann. *Women and Film*. New York and London: Methuen, 1983.

Karunanayake, Nandana. "Community Radio: A Promising Experiment." *Agricultural Information Development Bulletin* 9, no. 4 (1987): 2–4.

King, John. *Magical Reels: A History of Cinemas in Latin America*. New York: Verso, 1990.

King, John, Ana López, and Manuel Alvarado, eds. *Mediating Two Worlds: Cinematic Encounters in the Americas*. London: British Film Institute, 1993.

Kottak, Conrad Phillip. *Prime-Time Society: An Anthropological Analysis of Television and Culture*. Belmont, Calif.: Wadsworth, 1990.

Kraus, R. *The Originality of Avant-Garde and Other Modernist Myths*. Cambridge, Mass.: MIT Press, 1985.

Kuhn, Annette, and Susannah Radstone. *Women in Film. An International Guide*. New York: Fawcett Columbine, 1990.

———. *Women's Pictures*. London: Routledge and Kegan Paul, 1982.

Lankshear, Colin, and Peter L. McLaren, eds. *Critical Literacy: Politics, Praxis, and the Postmodern*. New York: State University of New York Press, 1993.

León Frías, Isaac, compiler. *Los años de conmoción 1967–1973. Entrevistas con realizadores sudamericanos*. México: UNAM, 1974.

Lévy, Pierre. *As Tecnologias da Inteligencia. O futuro do pensamento na era da informática*. Rio de Janeiro: Ed. 34, 1993.

López, A. "An 'Other' History: The New Latin American Cinema." *Radical History Review,* no. 41 (1988).

———— "The Melodrama in Latin America." *Wide Angle* 7, 3 (1986).

Luhr, William, ed. *World Cinema since 1945.* New York: Ungar, 1987.

Lyotard, Jean-Francois. *La condition postmoderne.* Paris: Minuit, 1985.

————. *L'inhumain. Causeries sur le temps.* Paris: Galilée, 1989.

Machado, Arlindo. *A Arte do Video.* São Paulo: Brasiliense, 1988.

————. *A Ilusao Especular.* São Paulo: Brasiliense, 1984.

————. *Máquina e Imaginário.* São Paulo: Edusp, 1993.

Magill, Frank N., ed. *Magill's Survey of Cinema, Foreign Language Films.* Englewood Cliffs, N.J.: Salem Press, 1985.

Mahieu, José Augustín. *Panorama del cine iberoamericano.* Madrid: Ediciones de Cultura Hispánica, 1990.

Martin, J. "Communication from Culture." *Media, Culture, and Society* 10 (1988).

Martínez Torres, Augusto, and Manuel Pérez Estremera. *Nuevo cine latinoamericano.* Barcelona: Editorial Anagrama, 1973.

Mast, Gerald, and Marshall Cohen. *Film Theory and Criticism: Introductory Readings,* 3d ed. New York: Oxford University Press, 1985.

Mattelart, A., and M. Mattelart. *International Image Markets.* London and New York: Comedia Publications Group, in association with M. Boyars, 1984.

McLuhan, Herbert Marshall, and Fiore Quentin. *The Medium Is the Message.* New York: Bantam Books, 1967.

Merleau-Ponty, M. *Fenomenologia da percepcao.* Rio de Janeiro: Freitas Bastos, 1971.

————. *L'oeil et l'esprit.* Paris: Gallimard, 1964.

————. *Le visible et l'invisible.* Paris: Gallimard, 1964.

Michaels, Eric. *Bad Aboriginal Art: Tradition, Media, and Technological Horizons.* Minneapolis: University of Minnesota Press, 1994.

Miller, Randall M., ed. *The Kaleidoscopic Lens. How Hollywood Views Ethnic Groups.* Englewood Cliffs, N.J.: J. S. Ozer, 1980.

Minh-Ha, Trinh Thi. *Woman, Native, Other: Writing Postcoloniality and Feminism.* Bloomington: Indiana University Press, 1989.

Moore, Rachael. "Marketing Alterity." *Visual Anthropology Review* 8, no. 2 (Fall 1992): 16–26.

Mulvey, L., and C. Penley. *Feminist Film Theory.* London: British Film Institute Publishing, 1988.

Munford, L. *Art and Technics.* New York: Columbia, 1952.

Muylaert, R. *Marketing cultural e comunicacao dirigida.* São Paulo: Ed. Globo, 1993.

Nichols, Bill. *Representing Reality: Issues and Concepts in Documentary.* Bloomington: Indiana University Press, 1991.

Novaes, A. *Rede imaginária, democracia, e televisao.* São Paulo: Companhia das Letras, 1991.

Palacios More, René, and Daniel Pires Mateus. *El cine latinoamericano: O por una estética de la ferocidad, la magia y la violencia.* Madrid: Sedmay Ediciones, 1976.

Paper Tiger Television Collective. *The Paper Tiger Television Guide To Media Activism.* New York, 1991.

Parente, A. (org.). *Imagem Máquina: A era das tecnologias do virtual.* Rio de Janeiro: Ed. 34, 1993.

Payant, R. *Vidéo.* Montreal: Artexte, 1986.

Pick, Zuzana. *The New Latin American Cinema: A Continental Project.* Austin: University of Texas Press, 1993.

Pick, Zuzana, ed. *Latin American Film-makers and the Third Cinema.* Ottawa: Carleton University Film Studies Program, 1978.

Pines, Jim, and Paul Wileman. *Questions of Third Cinema.* London: British Film Institute Press, 1989.

Plazaola, Luis. In *Cine y mujeres en America Latina: Directoras de largometrajes de ficción,* ed. Matilda S. Landeta, 211–31. Rio Piedras: Editorial de la Universidad de Puerto Rico, 1991.

Podesta, Patti, ed. *Resolution: A Critique of Video Art.* Los Angeles: Lace, 1986.

Pribam, D. *Female Spectators.* London: Verso, 1988.

Prigogine, I. Stengers. *La nouvelle alliance.* Paris: Gallimard, 1979.

Protz, M. *Seeing and Showing Ourselves.* New Delhi: CENDIT, 1991.

Rich, B. "After the Revolution: The Second Coming of Latin American Cinema." *Village Voice,* February 10, 1989, 23–27.

————. "An/Other View of New Latin American Cinema." *Iris,* 13 (Summer 1991).

————. Bay of Pix: Improper Conduct." *American Film,* July/August 1984.

Rocha, Glauber Pedro de Andrade. "Glauber Rocha acerca del cine latinoamericano." *America Latina,* 1 (1977). [USSR]

————. "El manifesto del 'cinema novo': 'La estetica del hambre'." *Brasil/Cultura* 13, no. 61 (July 1988): 4–5.

Rosenthal, Alan. *The Documentary Conscience: A Casebook in Film Making.* Berkeley and Los Angeles: University of California Press, 1980.

————. ed. *New Challenges for Documentary.* Berkeley and Los Angeles: University of California Press, 1988.

Ruby, J. "Speaking For, Speaking About, Speaking With, or Speaking Alongside: An Anthropological and Documentary Dilemma." *Visual Anthropology Review* 7, no. 2 (Fall 1991): 50–67.

Saalfield, Catherine. "Pregnant with Dreams: Julia Barco's Visions from Latin America." *Independent* 14, no. 10 (December 1991).

Santaella, Lúcia. *Cultural das Midias.* São Paulo: Razao Social, 1992.

Schnitman, Jorge. *Film Industries in Latin America: Dependency and Development*. Norwood: Ablex, 1984.

Schumann, D. A., and W. L. Partridge, eds. *The Human Ecology of Tropical Land Settlement in Latin America*. Boulder, Colo.: Westview Press, 1989.

Schwoch, James, Mimi White, and Susan Reilly. *Media Knowledge: Readings in Popular Culture, Pedagogy, and Critical Citizenship*. New York: State University of New York Press, 1992.

Shohat, Ella, and Robert Stam. *Unthinking Eurocentrism: Multiculturalism and the Media*. London; New York: Routledge, 1994.

Simondon, G. *Du Mode d'existence des objets techniques*. Paris: Aubier, 1958 & 1989.

Sklar, Robert, and Charles Musser, eds. *Resisting Images: Essays on Cinema and History*. Philadelphia: Temple University Press, 1990.

Sodré, Muniz. *A Máquina de Narciso*. Rio de Janeiro: Achiamé, 1984.

Solanas, F., and Octavio Getino. "Hacia un Tercer Cinema." *Hojas de cine* 1–2–3. [México: Filmoteca de la UNAM.]

Stam, Robert. "Rewriting 1492: Cinema and the Columbus Debate." *Cineaste* 19, no. 4 (1992): 66–71.

———. *Subversive Pleasures. Bakhtin, Cultural Criticism, and Film*. Baltimore: Johns Hopkins University Press, 1989.

Subirats, E. *A cultura como espectáculo*. São Paulo: Nobel, 1989.

Thelfilakis, E. *Modernes et aprés. Les immatériaux*. Paris: Autrement, 1985.

Tobing-Rony, Fatimah. "Those Who Squat, Those Who Sit: The Visualizing of Race in the 1895 Films of Félix-Louis Regnault." *Camera Obscura*, 28 (January 1992).

Toledo, Teresa. *Diez años del nuevo cine latinoamericano*. La Habana: Verdoux, S.L., 1990.

Tomaselli, K. "Transferring Video Skills to the Community: The Problem of Power." *Media Development* 36, no 4 (1989): 11–15.

Usabel, Gaiska de. *The High Noon of American Films in Latin America*. *See United States*.

Valdeavellano, P., ed. *El video en la educacion popular*. Lima: IPAL, 1989.

Vale, Eugene. *The Technique of Screenplay Writing; An Analysis of the Dramatic Structure of Motion Pictures*. New York: Grosset and Dunlap, 1972.

Video Rating Guide for Libraries. Santa Barbara: ABC-CLIO (P.O. Box 1911, Santa Barbara, CA 93116-1911).

Virilio, Paul. *L'écran du désert*. Paris: Galileé, 1991.

———. *O espaco crítico*. Rio de Janeiro: Ed. 34, 1993.

———. *Guerre et cinéma 1. Logistique de la perception*. Paris: Galilée, 1984.

———. *La machine de Vision*. Paris: Galilée, 1988.

———. *Vitesse et politique*. Paris: Galilee, 1977.

Wasco, Janet, and Vincent Mosco. *Democratic Communication in the Information Age*. Toronto: Garamond Press, 1992.

Watney, Simon. *Policing Desire: Pornography, AIDS, and the Media*. Minneapolis: University of Minnesota Press, 1989.

White, Hayden V. *Tropics of Discourse: Essays in Cultural Criticism*. Baltimore: Johns Hopkins University Press, 1978.

William Luhr, ed. *World Cinema since 1945*. New York: Ungar, 1987.

COLOMBIA

Bautista Gutiérrez, Gloria. *Realismo magico, cosmos latinoamericano: Teoria y practica*. Santa Fé de Bogotá: Editorial América Latina, 1991.

Becquer, Gustavo Adolfo. *Rimas*. Madrid: Espasa-Calpe, 1991.

Bergquist, Charles, Ricardo Peñaranda and Gonzalo Sánchez, eds. *Violence in Colombia: The Contemporary Crisis in Historical Perspective*. Wilmington: Scholarly Resources, Inc., 1992.

Black, Jan Knippers, ed. *Latin America. Its Problems and Its Promise. See Latin America*.

Borrego Plá, María del Carmen. *Palenques de negros en Cartagena de Indias a fines del siglo XVII*. Seville, 1973.

Braun, Herbert. *The Assassination of Gaitan: Public Life and Urban Violence in Colombia*. Madison: University of Wisconsin Press, 1985.

Buitrago Salazar, Evelio. *Zarpazo the Bandit: Memoirs of an Undercover Agent of the Colombian Army*. Tuscaloosa: University of Alabama Press, 1977.

Burton, Julianne. *Cinema and Social Change in Latin America: Conversations with Filmmakers. See Cinema*.

———. *The Social Documentary in Latin America. See Cinema*.

Bushnell, David. *The Making of Modern Colombia. A Nation in Spite of Itself*. Berkeley and Los Angeles: University of California Press, 1993.

Chagnon, Napoleon A. *Yanomamo, the Fierce People*, 2d ed. New York: Holt, Rinehart & Winston, 1977.

"Culture of Death." *Semana*, no. 408 (February 27-March 6, 1990): 26–33.

Curtin, Philip D. *The Atlantic Slave Trade; A Census. See Latin America*.

Dix, Robert. *The Politics of Colombia*. New York: Praeger, 1987.

Friede, Juan. *Los Andaki, 1538–1947. Historia de la aculturación de una tribu selvática*. México: Fondo de Cultural Económica, 1953.

Galeano, Eduardo H. *Open Veins of Latin America; Five Centuries of the Pillage of a Continent. See Latin America*.

García Márquez, Gabriel. *The Autumn of the Patriarch*. New York: Harper Perennial, 1991.

———. *La aventura de Miguel Littín clandestino en Chile*, 2d ed. Madrid: Ediciones El Pais, 1986.

———. *Chronicle of a Death Foretold*. New York: Knopf, 1983.

————. *Collected Novellas.* New York: Harper Collins, 1990.

————. *Collected Stories.* New York: Harper & Row, 1984.

————. *Cuando era feliz e indocumentado.* Barcelona, Esplugas de Llobregat: Plaza & Janes, 1974.

————. *Entre cachacos.* Barcelona: Bruguera, 1982.

————. *Los funerales de la Mama Grande,* 10th ed. Barcelona: Bruguera, 1986.

————. *The General in His Labyrinth.* New York: Knopf, 1990.

————. *La Hojarasca,* 14 ed. Buenos Aires: Editorial Sudamericana, 1977.

————. *In Evil Hour.* New York: Harper Perennial, 1991.

————. *Innocent Erendira.* New York: Harper & Row, 1978.

————. *Isabel viendo llover en Macondo.* Buenos Aires: Estuario, 1967.

————. *Leaf Storm and Other Stories.* New York: Harper & Row, 1972.

————. *Love in the Time of Cholera.* New York: Knopf, 1988.

————. *No One Writes to the Colonel and Other Stories.* New York: Harper & Row, 1968.

————. *Ojos de perro azul,* 7 ed. Barcelona: Bruguera, 1983.

————. *El olor de la guayaba: conversaciones con Plinio Apuleyo Mendoza,* lst ed. Barcelona: Bruguera, 1982.

————. *One Hundred Years of Solitude.* New York: Harper Perennial, 1991.

————. *El rastro de tu sangre en la nieve; El verano feliz de la señora Forbes.* Bogotá: W. Dampier Editores, 1982.

————. *El secuestro: guión cinematográfico,* 2nd ed. Colombiana. Bogotá: Editorial Oveja Negra, 1984.

————. *La soledad de América Latina; Brindis por la poesía,* 1st ed. Colombiana. Cali: Corporación Editorial Universitaria de Colombia, 1983.

————. *The Story of a Shipwrecked Sailor Who Drifted On a Life Raft for Ten Days.* New York: Knopf, 1986.

————. *Strange Pilgrims.* New York: Knopf, 1993.

————. *Textos costeños,* 1st ed. Colombiana. Bogotá: Editorial Oveja Negra, 1983.

Green, Duncan. *Faces of Latin America. See Latin America.*

Hartley, Jonathan. *Politics of Coalition Rule in Colombia.* New York: Cambridge University Press, 1988.

Henderson, James D. *When Colombia Bled. A History of the Violencia in Tolima.* Tuscaloosa: The University of Alabama Press, 1985.

Herman, D. L., ed. *Democracy in Latin America: Colombia and Venezuela.* New York: Praeger, 1988.

Janvery, Alain de. *The Agrarian Question of Reformism in Latin America. See Latin America.*

Kahn, Douglas, and Diane Neumaier, eds. *Cultures in Contention.* Seattle: Real Comet Press, 1985.

King, John. *Magical Reels: A History of Cinemas in Latin America. See Cinema.*

Kline, Harvey F. *Colombia: Portrait of Unity and Diversity.* Boulder: Westview Press, 1983.

Lernoux, Penny. *Cry of the People. See Latin America.*

Martz, John D. "Colombia at the Crossroads." *Current History* 90 (February 1991): 69–72, 80–81.

Miller, Francesca. *Latin American Women and the Search for Social Justice. See Latin America.*

Molano, Alfredo, and Alejandro Reyes. *Los bombardeos en el Pato.* Bogotá: Centro de Investigación y Educación Popular, 1980.

Murphy, Yolanda, and Robert F. Murphy. *Women of the Forest. See Brazil.*

Nichols, Bill. *Representing Reality: Issues and Concepts in Documentary. See Cinema.*

Oquist, Paul H. *Violence, Conflict and Politics in Colombia.* New York: Academic Press, 1980.

Pacini, Deborah, and Christine Pranouemont, eds. *Coca and Cocaine: Effects on People and Policy in Latin America. See Latin America.*

Parker, Andrew, ed. *Nationalisms and Sexualities. See Latin America.*

Pearce, Jenny. *Colombia: Inside the Labyrinth.* London: Latin America Bureau Limited, 1990.

Pescatello, Anne, ed. *Female and Male in Latin America. See Latin America.*

Price, Richard, ed. *Maroon Societies: Rebel Slave Communities in the Americas. See Latin America.*

Quevedo, Francisco de. *An Anthology of Quevedo's Poetry.* Manchester: Manchester University Press, 1969.

————. *Antología poética.* Madrid: Editorial Castalia, 1989.

————. *Cién poemas.* Esplugas de Llobregat, Barcelona: Plaza & Janes, 1981.

————. *Poems of Love and Strife, Death and Life: A Representative Anthology.* York, England: Spanish Literature Publications Co., 1991.

————. *Poems to Lisi.* Exeter, England: University of Exeter, 1988.

————. *Poesía selecta,* 1st ed. Barcelona: P.P.U., 1989.

————. *Poesía varia.* Madrid: Catedra, 1981.

Reichel-Dolmatoff, Gerardo. *Colombia.* New York: Praeger, 1965.

Salazar, Alonso J., and Ana María Jaramillo. *Medellín: las subculturas del narcotráfico.* Bogotá: CINEP, 1992.

————. *Born to Die in Medellin.* London: Latin American Bureau, 1992.

Schuyler, George W. *Hunger in a Land of Plenty.* Cambridge: Schenkman, 1980.

Vargas Llosa, Mario. *Aunt Julia and the Scriptwriter.* New York: Farrar, Straus, Giroux, 1982.

————. *Los cachorros.* Madrid: Ediciones Cátedra, 1982.

————. *Captain Pantoja and the Special Service.* New York: Harper & Row, 1978.

————. *La ciudad y los perros.* Barcelona: Seix Barral, 1990.

————. *Contra viento y marea, III (1964–1988).* Barcelona: Seix Barral, 1990.

———. *Conversation in the Cathedral.* New York: Harper & Row, 1975.

———. *The Cubs and Other Stories.* New York: Harper & Row, 1979.

———. *Elogio de la madrastra.* Barcelona: Tusquets, 1988.

———. *Entre Sartre y Camus.* Rio Piedras, P.R.: Ediciones Huracán, 1981.

———. *A Fish in the Water: A Memoir.* New York: Farrar, Straus, Giroux, 1994.

———. *The Green House.* New York: Harper & Row, 1968.

———. *La guerra del fin del mundo.* Barcelona: Editorial Seix Barral, 1981.

———. *La historia secreta de una novela.* Barcelona: Tusquets, 1971.

———. *In Praise of the Stepmother.* New York: Farrar, Straus, Giroux, 1990.

———. *Los jefes,* 2d ed. Barcelona: Editorial Bruguera, 1978.

———. *Kathie y el hipopótamo: comedia en dos actos.* Barcelona: Seix Barral, 1983.

———. *Lituma en los Andes.* Barcelona: Planeta, 1993.

———. *Pantaleón y las visitadoras.* Barcelona: Editorial Seix Barral, 1973.

———. *The Perpetual Orgy: Flaubert and Madame Bovary Llosa.* New York: Farrar, Straus, Giroux, 1986.

———. *The Real Life of Alejandro Mayta.* New York: Farrar, Straus, Giroux, 1986.

———. *La señorita de Tacna,* 8 ed. Barcelona: Seix Barral, 1989.

———. *Sobre la vida y la política.* Buenos Aires: Editorial Inter Mundo, 1989.

———. *The Storyteller.* New York: Farrar, Straus, Giroux, 1989.

———. *Three Plays,* 1st American ed. New York: Hill and Wang, 1990.

———. *The Time of the Hero.* New York: Grove Press, 1966.

———. *La utopía arcáica.* Cambridge: Centre of Latin American Studies, University of Cambridge, 1978.

———. *La verdad de las mentiras: ensayo sobre la novela moderna.* Lima: PEISA, 1993.

———. *The War of the End of the World.* New York: Farrar, Straus, Giroux, 1984.

———. *Who Killed Palomino Molero?* New York: Farrar, Straus, Giroux, 1987.

Vera, Hernan. "Arpilleras: An Iconography of Contemporary Childhood." *Children's Literature* 15 (1987).

Wade, Peter. *Blackness and Race Mixture: The Dynamics of Racial in Colombia.* Baltimore: Johns Hopkins University press, 1993.

West, Dennis, and Joan M. West. "Rodrigo D. No Future." *Cineaste* 18, 4.

Williams, Raymond L. *The Colombian Novel, 1844–1987.* Austin: University of Texas Press, 1991.

COSTA RICA

Guevara Berger, Marcos, and Rubén Chacón Castro. *Territorios Indios en Costa Rica: Orígenes, Situación Actual y Perspectivas.* García Hermanos S.A., distributed by Cultural Survival, 1991.

Marranghello, Daniel. *El cine en Costa Rica, 1903–1920.* San José: Ediciones Cultura Cinematográfica, 1988.

———. *Cine y censura en Costa Rica.* San José: Ediciones Cultural Cinematográfica, 1989.

Stock, Ann Marie. "On Location in Costa Rica: Critical Constructions of Latin American Cinema." Ph.D. Diss., University of Minnesota, 1993.

CUBA

Agramonte, Arturo. *Cronología del cine cubano.* La Habana: ICAIC, 1966.

Aguilar, Luis E. *Cuba 1933: Prologue to Revolution.* New York: Norton, 1974.

Aguirre, Mirta. *Ayer de hoy.* La Habana: Unión de Escritores y Artistas de Cuba, Bolsilibros Unión, 1980.

———. *Crónicas de cine.* La Habana: Editorial Letras Cubanas, 1989.

———. *Del encaustro a la sangre, sor Juana Ines de la Cruz.* La Habana: Casa de las Américas, 1975.

———. *Estudios literarios.* La Habana: Editorial Letras Cubanas, 1981.

———. *Un hombre a través de su obra: Miguel de Cervantes Saavedra.* La Habana: Sociedad LYCEUM, 1948.

———. *La obra narrativa de Cervantes.* La Habana: Instituto Cubano del Libro, 1971.

———. *Perfil histórico de las letras Cubanas.* Orlin: (Incomplete at the time of her death).

———. *Un poeta y un continente.* La Habana: Editorial Letras Cubanas, 1982.

Alderete Ramírez, Ada Nilda. *El sonido y el ritmo en la poesía de Nicolás Guillén.* La Banda: Argentina, 1969.

Allende, Isabel. *The House of the Spirits. See Chile.*

Amira, John, and Steven Cornelius. *The Music of Santería: Traditional Rhythms of the Baba Drums.* Crown Point: White Cliffs Media Co., 1992.

Aufderheide, Patricia. *Cross Cultural Film Guide. See Cinema.*

Augier, Angel I. *Nicolás Guillén.* La Habana: Instituto Cubano del Libro, 1971.

Augustín, Marie. *Le Macandal: episode de l'insurrection des noirs a St. Domingue par Tante Marie.* Nouvelle-Orleans: Imprimerie Geo. Muller, 1892.

Azicri, Max. *Cuba Politics, Economics and Society.* London and New York: Pinter Publishers, 1988.

Ballagas, Emilio. *Elegía sin nombre y otros poemas.* Ciudad de la Habana: Letras Cubanas, 1981.

———. *Obra poética de Emilio Ballagas,* Ed. póstuma. Miami: Mnemosyne Publications, 1969.

———. *Obra poética*. La Habana: Editorial Letras Cubanas, 1984.

———. *Orbita de Emilio Ballagas*. La Habana: Unión Nacional Escritores y Artistas de Cuba, 1972.

Barnet, Miguel. *Gallego*. Habana: Editorial Letras Cubanas, 1988.

Bastide, Roger. *African Civilisations in the New World. See Latin America.*

Bejel, Emilio. *Escribir en Cuba: entrevistas con escritores cubanos, 1979–1989.* Rio Piedras: Editorial de la Universidad de Puerto Rico, 1991.

———. "La poesía de Eliseo Diego." *Revista de literatura hispanica* 18–19 (Fall/Spring 1983–84): 43–58. (Maracaibo: Universidad del Zulia, Escuela de Letras.)

Benjamin, Medea. *No Free Lunch, Food and Revolution in Cuba Today.* San Francisco: Institute for food and Development Policy, 1984.

Bilby, Kenneth M. *The Caribbean as a Musical Region.* Washington, D.C.: Latin American Program, Woodrow Wilson International Center for Scholars, 1985.

Black, Jan Knippers, ed. *Latin America: Its Problems and Its Promise. See Latin America.*

Boggs, Vernon. *Salsiology: Afro-Cuban Music and the Evolution of Salsa in New York City.* New York: Greenwood Press, 1992.

Bolívar Aróstegui, Natalia, and Carmen González. *Los orishas en Cuba.* Ciudad de la Habana: Ediciones Unión, 1990.

Bonachea, Ramón L., and Marta San Martín. *The Cuban Insurrection, 1952–59.* New Brunswick: Transaction Books, 1974.

Brenner, Philip et al., eds. *The Cuba Reader.* New York: Grove Press, 1989.

Brouwer, Leo. *La música, lo Cubano y la innovación.* La Habana: Editorial Letras Cubanas, 1982.

Burton, Julianne. *Cinema and Social Change in Latin America: Conversations with Filmmakers. See Cinema.*

———. *Screen.* "Marginal Cinemas and Mainstream Critical Theory." *See Cinema.*

———. "Seeing, Being, Being Seen: Portrait of Teresa, or Contradictions of Sexual Politics in Contemporary Cuba." *The Social Text,* no. 4 (1981).

Cabral, Manuel del. *Antología tres.* Santo Domingo: Editora Universitaria, 1987.

———. *Chinchina busca el tiempo.* Santo Domingo Publicaciones América, 1980.

———. *Cuentos cortos con pantalones largos.* Ciudad Trujillo: Publicaciones América, 1981.

———. *Diez poetas dominicanos: tres poetas con vida y siete desenterrados.* Santo Domingo: Publicaciones América, 1980.

———. *Obra poética completa,* 2d ed. Santo Domingo: Editora Alfa y Omega, 1987.

———. *Poemas de amor y sexo.* Buenos Aires: Ediciones de la Flor, 1974.

Cabrera Infante, Guillermo. *Así en la paz como en la guerra.* Bogotá: Editorial Oveja Negra, 1987.

———. *Exorcismos de estilo.* Barcelona: Seix Barral, 1976.

———. *La Habana para un infante difunto.* Barcelona, Esplugues de Llobregat: Plaza & Janes, 1986.

———. *Holy Smoke.* New York: Harper & Row, 1985.

———. *Infante'st Ed.* New York: Harper & Row, 1984.

———. *Mea Cuba,* 1st ed. Mexicana. México, D.F.: Vuelta, La Reflexión, 1993.

———. *Three Trapped Tigers.* London and Boston: Faber and Faber, 1990.

———. *A Twentieth Century Job.* London and Boston: Faber and Faber, 1991.

———. *Un oficio del siglo 20: G. Cain 1954–1960.* Bogotá: Editorial Oveja Negra, 1987.

———. *Vista del amanecer en el trópico.* Barcelona: Editorial Seix Barral, 1974.

———. *Writes of Passage.* London and Boston: Faber and Faber, 1993.

Cabrera, Lydia. *Anago: vocabulario lucumí: el yoruba que se habla en Cuba,* 2d ed. Miami: Ediciones Universal, 1986.

———. *Los animales en el folklore y la magia de Cuba.* Miami: Ediciones Universal, 1988.

———. *Ayapa; cuentos de Jicotea.* Miami: Ediciones Universal, 1971.

———. *Cuentos negros de Cuba.* Barcelona: Sociedad Estatal V Centenario: ICARIA, 1989.

———. *Koeko iyawo, aprende novicia: pequeño tratado de regla lucumí.* Miami: Ultra Graphics Corporation, 1980.

———. *La lengua sagrada de los Nanigos.* Miami: V. and L. Graphics, 1988.

———. *La regla kimbisa del Santo Cristo del buen viaje,* 2d ed. Miami: Ediciones Universal, 1986.

———. *Reglas de Congo: Palo Monte Mayombe,* 2d ed. Miami: Ediciones Universal, 1986.

———. *Supersticiones y buenos consejos.* Miami: Ediciones Universal, 1987.

———. *Yemaya y Ochun,* 2d ed. New York: CR; Eastchester: Distribucion exclusiva E. Torres, 1980.

Cardenal, Ernesto. *Antología. See Nicaragua.*

———. *Apocalypse, and other poems. See Nicaragua.*

———. *Oración por Marilyn Monroe. See Nicaragua.*

Carpentier, Alejo. *Concierto barroco,* 5th ed. San Juan: Editorial de la Universidad de Puerto Rico, 1994.

———. *Guerra del tiempo, El acoso y otros relatos.* México, D.F.: Siglo Veintiuno Editores, 1983.

———. *Los pasos perdidos: novela.* Mexico: Cia. General de Ediciones, 1959.

———. *El recurso del método: novela,* 8 ed. México: Siglo Veintiuno Editores, 1975.

———. *El reino de este mundo.* Barcelona: Seix Barral, 1986.

———. *El siglo de las luces.* Madrid: Catedra, 1985.

———. *Tientos, diferencias y otros ensayos.* Espluques de Llobregat, Barcelona: Plaza & Janes, 1987.

Carrión, Miguel, de. *La esfinge; novela.* Habana: Comisión nacional Cubana de la UNESCO, 1961.

Casal, Lourdes. *Revolution and Race: Blacks in Contemporary Cuba.* Washington, D.C. : The Wilson Center, Latin American Program, 1979.

Casaus, Víctor. *Silvio, que levante la mano la guitarra.* La Habana: Editorial Letras Cubanas, 1984.

Castro, Fidel. *The World Economic and Social Crisis.* New York: Ediciones Vitral, 1983.

Castro, Fidel, et al. *Women and the Cuban Revolution: Speeches and Documents.* Ed. Elizabeth Stone. New York: Pathfinder Press, 1981.

Castro, Martha de. *Arte cubano colonial, resumen de un curso ofrecido en la Universidad de la Habana, curso de verano, Julio–Agosto de 1944.* La Habana: Universidad de la Habana, 1950.

Center for Cuban Studies. "Emerging Voices of Dissent from Jorge Mas Canosa's CANF Right-Wing Exile Party Line." *Cuba Update,* no. 3–4 (1993).

Cervantes Saavedra, Miguel de. *El casamiento engañoso y coloquio de los perros; novelas.* Madrid: Tipografía de la Revista de Archivos, 1918.

Chacón y Calvo, José María. *Estudios heredianos.* La Habana: Editorial Tropical, 1939.

Chanan, Michael. *The Cuban image: Cinema and Cultural Politics in Cuba.* Bloomington: Indiana University Press, 1985.

Cipriano de Utrera, Fray. *Heredia.* Ciudad Trujillo, Rep. Dominicana: Editorial Franciscana, 1939.

Cortázar, Julio. *Blow-up and Other Stories.* Ed. and translated Paul Blackburn. New York: Pantheon Books, 1985.

———. *La casa tomada.* Buenos Aires: Minotauro, 1969.

Cortez, Enrique. *Secretos del Oriate de la religión yoruba.* New York: Vilaragus Artículos Religiosos Corp and Original Publications, 1980.

Dawes, Neville. *Prolegomena to Caribbean Literature.* Kingston: Institute of Jamaica for the African-Caribbean Institute, 1977.

Desnoes, Edmundo. *Memories of Underdevelopment.* Harmondsworth, Middlesex, England: Penguin Books, 1971.

Díaz, Lomberto. *Heredia, primer romántico hispanoamericano.* Montevideo: Ediciones Géminis, 1973.

Didion, Joan. *Miami.* New York: Simon & Schuster, 1987.

Diego, Eliseo. *Acerca de Eliseo Diego.* Edited by Enrique Seinz. Havana: Editorial Letras Cubana, 1991.

———. *A través de mi espejo.* Havana: Union de Escritores y Artistas de Cuba, 1981.

———. *Los días de tu vida.* Havana: Unión de Escritores y Artistas de Cuba, 1977.

———. *Divertimientos.* Havana: Editorial Arte y Literatura, 1975.

———. *En la calzada de Jesús del Monte.* Havana: Unión de Escritores y Artistas de Cuba, 1981.

———. *En las oscuras manos del olvido.* Havana: Editorial Letras Cubanas, 1979.

———. *Inventario de asombros.* Havana: Editorial Letras Cubanas, 1982.

———. *Muestrario del mundo: o libro de las maravillas de Boloña,* 3d ed. Madrid: Visor, 1978.

———. *Nombrar las cosas.* Havana: UNEAC, 1973.

———. *Poesía.* Ed. Enrique Sainz. Havana: Editorial Letras Cubanas, 1983.

———. *Por los extraños pueblos.* Havana: 1958.

———. *Versiones.* Havana: UNEAC, 1970.

Donoso, José. *El obsceno pájaro de la noche,* 4th ed. Bercelona: Seix Barral, 1974, c1970.

Dorschner, John, and Roberto Fabricio. *The Winds of December.* New York: Coward, McCann & Geoghan, 1979.

Downing, John D. H., ed. *Film & Politics in the Third World. See Cinema.*

Ecún, Obá. *Addimu: Ofrenda a los Orishas.* Miami: Editorial SIBI, 1988.

———. *Ita: Mythology of the Yoruba Religion.* Miami: Obaecun Books, 1989.

Elder B. "Report on Cuba's First Symposium on Politics, Ideology and Law." *Crime and Social Justice* 23 (1985).

Entralgo, Elias José. *La liberación étnica cubana.* Havana, 1953.

"Especial: Eliseo cumple setenta y La Gaceta lo felicita." *Gaceta de Cuba,* July 1990, 10–18. (Havana: Unión de Escritores y Artistas de Cuba.)

Estenger, Rafael. *Heredia; la incomprensión de si mismo.* Havana: Editorial Trópico, 1938.

Evenson, Debra. *Revolution in the Balance: Law and Society in Contemporary Cuba.* Boulder: Westview Press, 1992.

Farber, Samuel. *Revolution and Reaction in Cuba, 1933–1960: A Political Sociology from Machado to Castro.* Middletown, Conn.: Wesleyan University Press, 1976.

Fernández Retamar, Roberto. *El son de vuelo popular.* Havana: Editorial Letras Cubanas, 1979.

Fitzgerald, Frank T. *The Cuban Revolution in Crisis: From Managing Socialism to Managing Survival.* New York: Monthly Review Press, 1994.

———. *Managing Socialism: From Old Cadres to New Professionals in Revolutionary Cuba.* New York: Praeger, 1990.

Fleites, Alex. "Fragmentos de una nueva conversacion en la penumbra." *Gaceta de Cuba,* July 1990, 12–13. (Havana: Union de Escritores y Artistas de Cuba.)

Freyre, Gilberto. *The Masters and the Slaves (Casa-grande & senzala: A Study in the Development of Brazilian Civilization). See Brazil.*

Fuentes, Norberto. *Hemingway in Cuba.* Secaucus: L. Stuart, 1984.

Fuerzas Armadas Revolucionarias, Dirección Política, Sección de Historia. *Historia de Cuba.* Habana: Pueblo y Educación, 1970.

Fusco, Coco, ed. *Reviewing Histories. Selections from New Latin American Cinema. See Cinema.*

Galeano, Eduardo H. *Open Veins of Latin America; Five Centuries of the Pillage of a Continent. See Latin America.*

Gallegos, Rómulo. *Doña Bárbara.* San José: Editorial Alma Máter, 1988.

Garcerán de Vall, Julio. *Heredia y la libertad.* Miami: Ediciones Universal, 1978.

García, Christine. *Dreaming in Cuba.* New York: Ballantine Books, 1993.

García Espinosa, Julio. *For an Imperfect Cinema. See Cinema.*

García-Carranza Baddetti, Araceli. *Bibliografía de Eliseo Diego.* Havana: Biblioteca Nacional José Martí, 1970.

García-Carranza Baddetti, Araceli, et al., eds. *Bibliografía de arte cubano.* Havana: Editorial Pueblo y Educación, 1985.

Geyer, Georgie Anne. *Guerrilla Prince: The Untold Story of Fidel Castro.* Boston: Little Brown and Company, 1991.

Giacoman, Helmy F., comp. *Homenaje a Alejo Carpentier: Variaciones interpretativas en torno a su obra Fernando Alegría [et al.].* New York: Las Americas Publications Co., 1970.

Gilbert, Jorge. *Cuba, from Primitive Accumulation of Capital to Socialism.* Toronto: Two Thirds Editions, 1981.

Gilroy, Paul. *The Black Atlantic: Modernity and Double Consciousness. See Latin America.*

Gómez, Jorge. *Canciones de la nueva trova.* Havana: Editorial Letras Cubanas, 1981.

Gonzáles, Francisco. *Vida de perros.* Lima: Ediciones Fragor, 1977.

González-Wippler, Migene. *The Powers of the Orisha. See Latin America.*

———. *The Santería Experience: Rituals and Spells of Santería. See Latin America.*

———. *Santeria: African Magic in Latin America. See Latin America.*

Green, Duncan. *Faces of Latin America. See Latin America.*

Guerra Ramiro y Sánchez, et al. *Historia de la nación cubana.* Havana: Editorial Nacional de la Nación Cubana, 1952.

Gutiérrez Alea, Tomás. *Casa de las Americas.* "Memorias de 'Memorias'." *See Latin America.*

———. "Enajenación y desenajenación: Eistenstein y Brecht." *Casa de las Américas* 20, no. 115 (July-August 1979): 28–37.

Guevara, Ernesto. *Reminiscences of the Cuban Revolutionaries.* New York: Monthly Review Press, 1974.

Guillén, Nicolás. *Antología clave.* Santiago de Chile: Editorial Nascimento, 1971.

———. *Antología mayor.* Havana: Instituto del Libro, 1969.

———. *Cantos para soldados y sones para turistas,* 4 ed. Tlahuapán, Puebla, Mexico: Premia Editora, 1985.

———. *The Daily Daily.* Berkeley and Los Angeles: University of California Press, 1989.

———. *Las grandes elegías y otros poemas.* Caracas: Biblioteca Anycucho, 1984.

———. *El libro de las décimas.* Havana: Unión de Escritores y Artistas de Cuba, 1980.

———. *El libro de los sones.* La Habana and New York (G.P.O. Box 1913 New York 10116): Editorial Letras Cubanas, Distribuido por Ediciones Vitral, 1982.

———. *Man-Making Words: Selected Poems of Nicolás Guillén.* Havana: Editorial de Arte y Literatura, 1973.

———. *Nueva antología.* Mexico: Editores Mexicanos Unidos, 1979.

———. *Obra poética.* La Habana; and New York (G.P.O. Box 1913, New York, NY 10116): Editorial Letras Cubanas, Distribuido por Ediciones Vitral, 1980.

———. *Páginas vueltas.* Buenos Aires: Grupo Editor de Buenos Aires, 1980.

———. *Patria o muerte!: The Great Zoo and Other Poems.* Habana: Editorial de Arte y Literatura, 1973.

———. *Prosa de prisa, 1929–1972.* Havana: Editorial Arte y Literatura, 1975–1976.

———. *Songoro cosongo y otras poemas: selección del autor.* Madrid: Alianza, 1981.

———. *Summa poética.* Madrid: Catedra, 1976.

Gutiérrez Alea, Tomas. *Dialéctica del espectador. See Cinema.*

Hall, Gwendolyn Midlo. *Social Control in Slave Plantation Societies; A Comparison of St. Domingue and Cuba.* Baltimore: Johns Hopkins University Press, 1971.

Halperin, Maurice. *The Rise and Decline of Fidel Castro; An Essay in Contemporary History.* Berkeley and Los Angeles: University of California Press, 1972.

Harnecker, Marta. *Cuba, dictadura o democracia?.* México: Siglo Veintiuno Editores, 1982.

Hartell, Joanna. "Interview with Director Luis Felipe Bernaza." *Cine Acción,* Winter 1993.

Hays, H. R. *Nicolás Guillén and Afro-Cuban Poetry.* s.l.: s.n., 194.

Heath, Dwight B., ed. *Contemporary Cultures and Societies of Latin America. See Latin America.*

Hemingway, Ernest. *The Old Man and the Sea. See United States.*

Heredia, José María. *José María Heredia.* Toluca, México: Dirección del Patrimonio Cultural y Artistico del Estado de México, 1979.

———. *Niágara y otros textos: poesía y prosa selectas.* Edited by Angel Augier. Caracas: Biblioteca Ayacucho, 1990.

———. *Nota biográfica.* Toluca, Mexico: Dirección del Patrimonio Cultural y Artístico del Estado de México, 1979.

———. *Poesías completas.* Edited by Angel Aparicio Laurencio. Miami: Ediciones Universal, 1970.

Hijuelos, Oscar. *The Mambo Kings Play Songs of Love. See United States.*

Holt-Seeland, Inger. *Women of Cuba,* 1st English ed. Westport, Conn.: L. Hill, 1982.

Horowitz, Irving Louis, ed. *Cuban Communism,* 7th ed. New Brunswick: Transaction Books, 1989.

Huberman, Leo. *Introduction to Socialism.* New York: Monthly Review Press, 1968.

Instituto de Literatura y Lingüística (Academia de Ciencias de Cuba). *Perfil histórico de las letras cubanas: desde los orígenes hasta 1898.* Havana: Editorial Letras Cubanas, 1983.

James, C. L. R. *The Black Jacobins: Toussaint L'Ouverture and the San Domingo Revolution.* New York: Vintage Books, 1973.

Jameson, Robert Francis. *La isla de Cuba en el siglo XIX vista por los extranjeros: en 1820.* Habana: Biblioteca nacional, 1966.

Johnson, Leland J. "U.S. Business Interests in Cuba and the Rise of Castro." *World Politics* 17 (April 1965): 440–59.

Kaplan, E. Ann. *Women and Film. See Cinema.*

King, John. *Magical Reels: A History of Cinemas in Latin America. See Cinema.*

Kling, Merle. "Cuba: A Case Study of a Successful Attempt to Seize Political Power by the Application of Unconventional Warfare." *The Annals of the American Academy of Political and Social Science,* no. 341 (May 1962): 42–52.

Knight, Franklin W. *Slave Society in Cuba During the Nineteenth Century.* Madison: University of Wisconsin Press, 1970.

Kozol, Jonathan. *Children of the Revolution.* New York: Delacorte Press, 1978.

Kuhn, Annette. *Women's Pictures. See Cinema.*

LeRiverend, Julio. *Economic History of Cuba.* Havana: Ensayo Book Institute, 1967.

Lesage, Julia. "Dialectical, Revolutionary, Feminist: One Way or Another (De cierta manera)." *Jump Cut,* 29 (Fall 1979).

———. "Creating History in The Other Francisco." *Jump Cut,* 30 (January 1985).

Lewis, Oscar, Ruth Lewis, and Susan M. Rigdon. *Living the Revolution: An Oral History of Contemporary Cuba.* Urbana: University of Illinois Press, 1978.

Lux, William R. "French Colonization in Cuba, 1791–1809." *The Americas* 29 (July 1972), 57–61.

Magill, Frank N., ed. *Magill's Survey of Cinema, Foreign Language Films. See Cinema.*

Mansour, Monica. *Poesía negra de América, antología.* México: Ediciones Era, 1976.

Manuel, Peter, ed. *Essays on Cuban Music: North American and Cuban Perspectives.* Lanham, Md.: University Press of America, 1991.

Márquez Rodríguez, Alexis. *La obra narrativa de Alejo Carpentier.* Caracas: Ediciones de la Biblioteca, Universidad Central de Venezuela, 1970.

Masiello, Francine. *Between Civilization and Barbarism. Women, Nation, and Literary Culture in Modern Argentina. See Argentina.*

Matas, Julio. "El espacio ideal de la memoria: la poesía de Eliseo Diego." *Imprevue* 1 (1988): 51–76.

McManus, Jane, ed. *From the Palm Tree: Voices of the Cuban Revolution.* Secaucus: L. Stuart, 1983.

Mesa-Lago, Carmelo. *Cuba in the 1970s: Pragmatism and Institutionalization,* Revised ed. Albuquerque: University of New Mexico Press, 1978.

Miller, Francesca. *Latin American Women and the Search for Social Justice. See Latin America.*

Moncega-González, Esther P. *La narrativa de Alejo Carpentier: el concepto del tiempo como tema fundamental: ensayo de interpretación y análisis.* New York: Eliseo Torres, 1975.

Montejo, Esteban. *The Autobiography of a Runaway Slave.* Edited by Miguel Barnet. New York: Meridian Books, 1969.

———. *Biografía de un cimarrón,* 2d ed. Madrid: Ediciones Alfaguara, S.A., 1984.

Moreno Fraginals, Manuel. *Africa in Latin America: Essays on History, Culture, and Socialization. See Latin America.*

———. *The Sugarmill: The Socioeconomic Complex of Sugar in Cuba, 1760–1860.* New York: Monthly Review Press, 1976.

Muller-Bergh, Klaus. *Alejo Carpentier: estudio biográfico-crítico.* Long Island City, NY: Las Américas, 1972.

———. ed. *Asedios a Carpentier; once ensayos críticos sobre el novelista cubano.* Santiago de Chile: Editorial Universitaria, 1972.

Murphy, Joseph M. *Santería: An African Religion in America. See Latin America.*

Museum of Arts and Sciences (Daytona Beach, FL). *Two Centuries of Cuban Art, 1759–1959.* Sarasota; Daytona Beach, FL: John and Mable Ringling Museum of Art; Cuban Foundation Collection of the Museum of Arts and Sciences, 1980.

Myerson, Michael, ed. *Memories of Underdervelopment. The Revolutionary Films of Cuba.* New York: Grossman Publishers, 1973.

Ortiz Fernández, Fernando. *Los negros esclavos.* Havana: Editorial de Ciencias Sociales, 1975.

Ortiz, Fernando. *La africanía de la música folklorica de Cuba,* 2d ed. Havana: Editora Universitaria, 1965.

———. *Los bailes y el teatro de los negros en el folklore de Cuba,* 2d ed. La Habana and New York: Editorial Letras Cubanas, distribuido por Ediciones Vitral, 1981.

Padula, Alfred L., Jr. "Financing Castro's Revolution, 1956–1958." *Revista/Review Interamericana,* no. 8 (Summer 1978): 234–46.

———. "The Ruin of the Cuban Bourgeoisie, 1959–1961." *SECOLAS Annals* 11 (March 1980): 5–21.

Padura, Leonardo. *Lo real maravilloso, creación y realidad.* Havana: Editorial Letras Cubana, 1989.

Palermo, Zulma, and Nora Mazziotti. *Historia y mito en le obra de Alejo Carpentier.* Buenos Aires: F. García Cambeiro, 1972.

Pales Matos, Luis. *Obras (1914–1959)*. Rio Piedras: Editor-ial de la Universidad de Puerto Rico, 1984.

———. *Poesía, 1915–1956*, 4 ed. San Juan: San Juan Edi-torial Universitaria, Universidad de Puerto Rico, 1971.

———. *Poesía completa y prosa selecta*. Caracas: Bib-lioteca Ayacucho, 1978.

———. *Tuntun de pasa y grifería*. San Juan: Instituto de Cultura Puertorriquena: Editorial de la Universidad de Puerto Rico, 1993.

Parejo y Reina, Leopoldo. *Soñar despierto, drama en un acto y en verso*. Madrid: José Rodríguez, 1877.

Pérez, Louis A. *Cuba under the Platt Amendment, 1902–1934*. Pittsburgh: University of Pittsburgh Press, 1986.

Perez, Louis A., Jr. *Cuba: Between Reform and Revolution*. New York: Oxford University Press, 1988.

———. *Intervention, Revolution, and Politics in Cuba, 1913–1921*. Pittsburgh: University of Pittsburgh Press, 1978.

Pérez y Mena, Andrés Isidoro. *Speaking with the Dead: De-velopment of Afro-Latin Religion Among Puerto Ricans in the U.S.: Study into the Interpretation of Civilizations. See United States.*

Pintura española y cubana y litografías y grabados cubanos del siglo XIX: colección del Museo Nacional de la Ha-bana. Madrid: Ministerio de Cultura, 1983.

Portes, Alejandro, and Alex Steick. *City on the Edge: The Transformation of Miami*. Berkeley and Los Angeles: University of California Press, 1993.

———. *Rationality in the Slum: An Essay on Interpretive Sociology*. Austin: Institute of Latin American Studies, University of Texas at Austin, 1973.

Quintero, Aramis. "Las extrañas lindes." *Gaceta de Cuba*, July 1990, 14–15. (Havana: Unión de Escritores y Artistas de Cuba.)

Quirk, Robert E. *Fidel Castro*. New York: W. W. Norton & Company, 1993.

Randall, Margaret. *Cuban Women Now: Interviews with Cuban Women*. Toronto: Women's Press, Dumont Press Graphix, 1974.

Rich, B. Ruby. *American Film*. "Bay of Pix: Improper Con-duct." *See Cinema*.

Rieff, David. *The Exile: Cuba in the Heart of Miami*. Lon-don: Vintage, 1994.

Rigol, Jorge. *Apuntes sobre la pintura y el grabado en Cuba*. Havana: Dirección Nacional de Museos y Monumentos, Consejos Nacional de Cultura, 1971.

Rius. *Cuba For Beginners; An Illustrated Guide for Ameri-cans (and Their Government) to Socialist Cuba*. New York: Pathfinder Press, 1970.

Sarduy, Severo. *De dónde son los cantantes?* Barcelona: Seix Barral, 1980.

Sayles, John. *Los gusanos*. New York: Harper Collins Pub-lishers, 1991.

Sealy, John. *Music in the Caribbean*. London: Hodder and Stoughton, 1983.

Seinz, Enrique. "Eliseo Diego: definición de un poeta." *Re-vista iberoamericana* 56, 152–53 (July-December 1991), 1203–10.

———. "Sitios, cosas, memorias." *Gaceta de Cuba,* July 1990, 18. (Havana: Unión de Escritores y Artistas de Cuba.)

Silvio Rodríguez. Santiago: Editora Granizo, 1985.

Skidmore, Thomas E., and Peter H. Smith. *Modern Latin America. See Latin America.*

Smallwood, Lawrence. "African Cultural Dimensions in Cuba." *Journal of Black Studies* 6 (December 1975): 191–99.

Smith, Wayne S. *The Closest of Enemies: A Personal and Diplomatic Account of U.S.-Cuban Relations since 1957*. New York: W. W. Norton, 1987.

Speratti-Piñero, Emma Susana. *Pasos hallados en el reino de este mundo*. México, D.F.: El Colegio de México, 1981.

Szulc, Tad. *Fidel: A Critical Portrait*. New York: William Morrow and Company, Inc, 1986.

Timerman, Jacobo. *Cuba: A Journey*. New York: Vintage Books, 1992.

Tomas, Hugh. *Cuba: The Pursuit of Freedom*. New York: Harper & Row, 1971.

Una revolución que comienza. Santiago de Cuba: Ed. Ori-ente, 1983.

Venceremos Brigade Educational Commission. *Health Care in Cuba: Only the People Can Perform Miracles*. New York: Venceremos Brigade, 1975.

Vinueza, María Elena. *Presencia arará en la música fol-clórica de Matanzas*. Havana: Casa de las Américas, 1989.

Vitier, Cintio. "Recuento y alabanza de Eliseo Diego." *Gac-eta de Cuba,* July 1990, 10–11. (Havana: Unión de Es-critores y Artistas de Cuba.)

Wald, Karen. *Children of Che: Childcare and Education in Cuba*. Palo Alto: Ramparts Press, 1978.

Welch, Richard E. *Response to Revolution: The United States and the Cuban Revolution, 1959–1961*. Chapel Hill: University of North Carolina Press, 1985.

West, Dennis. "Reconciling Entertainment and Thought. An Interview with Julio García Espinosa." *Cineaste* 16, no. 1–2 (1987–88).

Wood, Dennis B. "The Long Revolution: Class Relations and Political Conflict in Cuba, 1868–1968." *Science and Society* 34 (Spring 1970), 1–41.

Wyden, Peter. *Bay of Pigs: The Untold Story*. New York: Si-mon & Schuster, 1979.

Zulma, Palermo. *Historia y mito en la obra de Alejo Car-pentier*. Buenos Aires: F. García Cambeiro, 1972.

DOMINICAN REPUBLIC

Atkins, C., and Larman Wilson. *The United States and the Trujillo Regime*. Newark: Rutgers University Press, 1972.

Crassweller, Robert. *Trujillo: The Life and Times of a Caribbean Dictator*. New York: Macmillan, 1966.

Diedrich, Bernard. *Trujillo: The Death of the Goat*. Maplewood: Waterfront Press, 1990.

Ferguson, James. *The Dominican Republic: Beyond the Lighthouse*. London; New York: Latin America Bureau (Research and Action), distributed in North America by Monthly Review Press, 1992.

Galíndez, Jesús. *The Era of Trujillo*. Tucson: University of Arizona Press, 1973.

Ornes, German. *Trujillo: The Little Caesar of the Caribbean*. New York: Thomas Nelson and Sons, 1958.

Wiarda, Howard. *Dictatorship and Development: Methods of Control in Trujillo's Dominican Republic*. Gainesvil5le: University of Florida Press, 1968.

ECUADOR

Bourque, Susan Carolyn, and Kay Barbara Warren. *Women of the Andes: Patriarchy and Social Change in Two Peruvian Towns*. See Peru.

Burton, Julianne. *Cinema and Social Change in Latin America: Conversations with Filmmakers*. See Cinema.

Deere, Carmen Diana, ed. *State Policy and Women in Latin America and the Caribbean*. See Latin America.

Galeano, Eduardo H. *Open Veins of Latin America; Five Centuries of the Pillage of a Continent*. See Latin America.

———. *We Say No: Chronicles 1963–1991*. See Latin America.

García Pinto, Magdalena. *Women Writers of Latin America: Intimate Histories*. See Latin America.

Gibbs, V. *Latin American Research Review*. "Latin American Film." See Cinema.

Gutiérrez, Gustavo. *A Theology of Liberation: History, Politics, and Salvation*. See Latin America.

Heath, Dwight B., ed. *Contemporary Cultures and Societies of Latin America*. See Latin America.

Icaza, Jorge. *Huasipungo, The Villagers*. Carbondale: Southern Illinois University Press, 1973.

Kimmerling, J. *Amazon Crude*. Washington, D.C.: Natural Resources Defense Council, 1990.

King, John. *Magical Reels: A History of Cinemas in Latin America*. See Cinema.

López, A. "Setting Up the Stage." *Quarterly Review of Film and Video* 13, 1–3.

Menchú, Rigoberta. *I, Rigoberta Menchú: An Indian Woman in Guatemala*. See Guatemala.

Nash, June C., Helen Safa, and contributors. *Women and Change in Latin America*. See Latin America.

Potter, Jack M., May N. Diaz, and George M. Foster, eds. *Peasant Society: A Reader*. Boston: Little Brown and Company, 1967.

Redclift, M. R. *Agrarian Reform and Peasant Organization on the Ecuadorian Coast*. London: Athlone Press, 1978.

Schumann, D. A. and W. L. Partridge, eds. *The Human Ecology of Tropical Land Settlement in Latin America*. Boulder: Westview Press, 1989.

Sklar, Robert, and Charles Musser, eds. *Resisting Images; Essays on Cinema and History*. See Cinema.

Weismantel, Mary J. *Food, Gender, and Poverty in the Ecuadorian Andes*. Philadelphia: University of Pennsylvania Press, 1988.

Weiss, Wendy. "The Social Organization of Property and Work: A Study of Migrants from the Rural Ecuadorian Sierra." *American Ethnologist*, no. 12 (1985): 468–88.

Whitten, N. *Sacha Runa: Ethnicity and Adaptation of Ecuadorian Jungle Quichua*. Urbana: University of Illinois Press, 1976.

Whitten, Norman E., Jr. *Sicuanga Runa: The Other Side of Development in Amazonian Ecuador*. Urbana: University of Illinois Press, 1985.

EL SALVADOR

Sundaram, Anjali, and George Gelber, eds. *A Decade of War: El Salvador Confronts the Future*. London and New York: Monthly Review Press with the Transnational Institute, the Netherlands, 1991.

GUATEMALA

Alegría, Claribel. *Luisa in Realityland*. Willimantic, Conn.: Curbstone Press, distributed in the U.S. by Talman Co., 1987.

Americas Watch. *Human Rights in Guatemala: No Neutrals Allowed*. New York: Americas Watch, 1982.

Anderson, Marilyn. *Granddaughters of Corn: Portraits of Guatemalan Women*. Willimantic, Conn.: Curbstone Press, 1988.

Anfuso, Joseph, and David Sczepanski. *He Gives—He Takes Away: The True Story of Guatemala's Controversial Former President Efraín Ríos Montt*. Venice, Calif.: Vision House, 1984.

Argüeta, Manlio. *One Day of Life*. New York: Vintage Books, 1983.

Ashabranner, Brent K. *Children of the Maya*. New York: Dodd, Mead, 1986.

Asturias, Miguel Angel. *Leyendas de Guatemala*. Buenos Aires: Editorial Pleamar, 1948.

AVANCSO. *Assistance and Control: Policies toward Internally Displaced Populations in Guatemala*. Washington, D.C.: Center for Immigration Policy and Refugee Assistance, Georgetown University, 1988.

Barry, Tom. *Guatemala: A Country Guide*. Albuquerque: Inter-Hemispheric Education Resource Center, 1989.

———. *Roots of Rebellion: Land and Hunger in Central America*. Boston: South End Press, 1987.

Berryman, Phillip. *Liberation Theology: Essential Facts about the Revolutionary Religious in Latin America and Beyond*. London: Tauris, 1987.

———. *The Religious Roots of Rebellion: Christians in Central American Revolutions.* Maryknoll, NY: Orbis Books, 1984.

Bethell, Leslie, ed. "Guatemala since 1930." In *Cambridge History of Latin America* 8. Cambridge; New York: Cambridge University Press.

———. *The Cambridge History of Latin America* 8. Cambridge: Cambridge University Press, 1984.

Bizarro Ujpan, Ignacio. *Campesino: The Diary of a Guatemala Indian.* Tucson: University of Arizona Press, 1981.

———. *Son of Tecun Uman: A Maya Indian Tells His Life Story.* Tucson: University of Arizona Press, 1981.

Black, George. *Garrison Guatemala.* New York: Monthly Review Press, 1984.

Booth, John A. "Socioeconomic and Political Roots of National Revolts in Central America." *Latin American Research Review* 26, 1 (1991), 33–73.

Cambranes, J. C. *Coffee and Peasants: The Origins of the Modern Plantation Economy in Guatemala, 1853–1897.* Stockholm: Institute of Latin American Studies, 1985.

Carmack, Robert M., ed. *Harvest of Violence. The Maya Indians and the Guatemalan Crisis.* Norman: University of Oklahoma Press, 1988.

Dennis, Philip A., Gary S. Elbow, and Peter L. Healer. "Development under Fire: The Playa Grande Colonization Project in Guatemala." *Human Organization* 47, 1 (1988), 70–76.

Diéguez, María Luz. "La 'polifonía' como imperativo feminista: Desmitificación, subversión, y creación de nuevas." *Dissertation Abstracts International* 50, no. 9 (March 1990): 2918A–2819A.

Farriss, Nancy Marguerite. *Society under Colonial Rule: The Collective Enterprise of Survival.* Princeton: Princeton University Press, 1984.

Fried, Jonathan L., M. E. Gettleman, D. T. Levenson, and N. Peckenham, eds. *Guatemala in Rebellion: Unfinished History.* New York: Grove Press, 1983.

Garrard Burnett, Virginia. "Protestantism in Rural Guatemala, 1872–1954." *Latin American Research Review* 24, 2 (1989), 127–42.

Gleijeses, Piero. *Shattered Hope: The Guatemalan Revolution and the United States 1944–45.* Princeton: Princeton University Press, 1991.

Handy, Jim. *Gift of the Devil: A History of Guatemala.* Boston: South End Press, 1984.

Immerman, Richard H. *The CIA in Guatemala: The Foreign Policy of Intervention.* Austin: University of Texas Press, 1982.

International Work Group for Indigenous Affairs. *Guatemala 1978: The Massacre at Panzos.* Copenhagen: International Work Group for Indigenous Affairs, 1978.

Jonas, Susanne. *The Battle for Guatemala: Rebels, Death Squads, and U.S. Power.* Boulder: Westview Press, 1991.

Jonas, Susanne, Ed McCaughan, and Elizabeth Sutherland

Martínez, eds. *Guatemala: Tyranny on Trial, Testimony of the Permanent People's Tribunal.* San Francisco: Synthesis Publications, 1984.

Kattan-Ibarra, Juan. *Perspectivas culturales de hispanoamérica.* Lincolnwood: National Textbook Company, 1995.

Krauss, Clifford. *Inside Central America: Its People, Politics and History. See Latin America.*

LaFeber, Walter. *Inevitable Revolutions: The United States and Central America. See Latin America.*

Lovell, W. George. "Surviving Conquest: The Maya of Guatemala in Historical Perspective." *Latin American Research Review* 23, 2 (1988), 25–58.

Manz, Beatriz. *Refugees of a Hidden War: The Aftermath of Counterinsurgency in Guatemala.* Albany: State University of New York Press, 1988.

Martínez-Echazabal, Lourdes. "Testimonial Narratives: Translating Culture While Narrowing the Genre Gap Translation." *Perspectives* 6 (1991), 57–65.

Matthiessen, Peter. *At Play in the Fields of the Lord.* New York: Random House, 1965.

Melville, Thomas, and Marjorie Melville. *Guatemala: The Politics of Land Ownership.* New York: Free Press, 1971.

Menchú, Rigoberta. *I, Rigoberta Menchú: An Indian Woman in Guatemala.* Ed. and translated by Elizabeth Debray. London: Verso, 1984.

Montejo, Víctor. *Testimony: Death of a Guatemalan Village.* Willmantic, Conn.: Curbstone Press, 1987.

Oakes, Maud. *The Two Crosses of Todos Santos: Survivals of Mayan Religious Ritual.* Princeton: Princeton University Press, 1951.

Salazar, Claudia. "Rigoberta's Narrative and the New Practice of Oral History." *Women and Language* 13, no. 1: 7–8.

Salvado, Luis Raul. *The Other Refugees: A Study of Nonrecognized Guatemalan Refugees in Chiapas, Mexico.* Washington, D.C.: Center for Immigration Policy and Refugee Assistance, Georgetown University, 1988.

Schlesinger, Stephen C. *Bitter Fruit: The Untold Story of the American Coup in Guatemala,* 2d ed. Garden City, N.J.: Anchor Press, Doubleday, 1983.

Simon, Jean-Marie. *Guatemala: Eternal Spring, Eternal Tyranny.* New York: W. W. Norton, 1987.

Skidmore, Thomas E., and Peter H. Smith. *Modern Latin America. See Latin America.*

Smith, Carol A., and Marilyn Moors. *Guatemalan Indians and the State, 1540 to 1988.* Austin: University of Texas Press, 1990.

Whisnant, David E. "La vida nos ha enseñado: Rigoberta Menchú y la dialéctica de la cultura tradicional." *Ideologies and Literature: Journal of Hispanic and Lusophone Discourse* 4, no. 1 (Spring 1989): 317–43.

Woodward, Ralph Lee. *Central America, a Nation Divided. See Latin America.*

Zan, Julio de, et al. *América conflicto, construcción y desafío.* Santa Fé: Ediciones Sudamericana, 1992.

HAITI

Aristide, Jean-Bertrand. *Aristide: An Autobiography,* Maryknoll, N.Y.: Orbis Books, 1993.

————. *In the Parish of the Poor: Writings from Haiti.* Maryknoll, N.Y.: Orbis Books, 1990.

Bellegarde-Smith, Patrick. *Haiti: The Breached Citadel.* Boulder: Westview Press, 1989.

Chomsky, Noam. *Year 501, The Conquest Continues.* Boston: South End Press, 1993.

Davis, Wade. *The Serpent and the Rainbow.* New York: Simon & Schuster, 1985.

Denning, Melita. *Vodoun Fire: The Living Reality of Mystical Religion.* St. Paul: Llewellyn, 1979.

Desmangles, Leslie Gerald. *The Faces of the Gods: Vodou and Roman Catholicism in Haiti.* Chapel Hill: The University of North Carolina Press, 1992.

Endore, S. Guy. *Babouk.* New York: Monthly Review Press, 1991.

Ferguson, James. *Papa Doc, Baby Doc: Haiti and the Duvaliers.* Oxford and New York: B. Blackwell, 1987.

Frelick, Bill. "Haitians At Sea: Asylum Denied." *NACLA Report on the Americas* 26, no. 1 (July 1992): 34–39.

Greene, Graham. *The Comedian.* New York: Viking Press, 1966.

Healy, David. *Gunboat Diplomacy in the Wilson Era, 1915–1916.* Madison: University of Wisconsin Press, 1976.

Herskovitz, Melville Jean. *Life in a Haitian Valley.* New York: Knopf, 1937.

James, C. L. R. *The Black Jacobins: Toussaint L'Ouverture and the San Domingo Revolution. See Cuba.*

Knight, Franklin W. *The Caribbean.* New York: Oxford University Press, 1990.

Langley, Lester D. *The United States and the Caribbean in the Twentieth Century.* Athens: University of Georgia Press, 1980.

Lawless, Robert. *Haiti's Bad Press: Origins, Development, and Consequences.* Rochester, Vt.: Schenkman Books, 1992.

Lemoine, Maurice. *Sucre amer. English—Bitter sugar: Slaves today in the Caribbean.* Chicago: Banner Press, 1985.

Leyborn, James. *The Haitian People.* New Haven: Yale University Press, 1966.

Metraux, Alfred. *Voodoo in Haiti.* New York: Schocken Books, 1972.

Montague, Ludwell L. *Haiti and the United States, 1714–1938.* New York: Russell and Russell, 1966.

Nicholls, David. *From Dessalines to Duvalier: Race, Color and National Independence in Haiti.* Cambridge and New York: Cambridge University Press, 1979.

Sassen, S., S. Mahler, C. Tactaquin, and M. Jimenez. *NACLA Report on the Americas.* "Coming North: Latino & Caribbean Immigration." *See United States.*

Thoby-Marcellin, Philippe. *Canape Vert.* New York and Toronto: Farrar and Rinehart Inc., 1944.

Trouillot, Michel-Rolph. *Haiti, State Against Nations: The Origins and Legacy of Duvalierism.* New York: Monthly Review Press, 1990.

Weinstein, Brian, and Aaron Segal. *Haiti: Political Failures, Cultural Successes.* New York: Praeger, 1984.

Wilentz, Amy. *The Rainy Season: Haiti since Duvalier.* New York: Monthly Review Press, 1990.

HONDURAS

Alvarado, Elvia. *Gringo, Don't Be Afraid: An Honduran Woman Speaks from the Heart: The Story of Elvia Alvarado.* Edited by Medea Benjamin. San Francisco: Institute for Food and Development Policy (145 9th St., San Francisco, CA 94103), 1987.

CIDCA/Development Study Unit, ed. *Ethnic Groups and the Nation State: The Case of the Atlantic Coast in Nicaragua. See Nicaragua.*

Dennis, Phillip A. "The Costeños and the Revolution in Nicaragua." *See Nicaragua.*

Menchú, Rigoberta. *I, Rigoberta Menchú: An Indian Woman in Guatemala. See Guatemala.*

Nietschman, Bernard. *Between Land and Water: The Subsistence Ecology of the Miskito Indians, Eastern Nicaragua. See Nicaragua.*

————. *Human Ecology. See Nicaragua.*

JAMAICA

Bayer, Marcel. *Jamaica: A Guide to the People, Politics, and Culture.* Ed. and trans. by John Smith. London: Latin American Bureau, 1993.

Smorkaloff, Pamela. *If I Could Write This in Fire: An Anthology of Literature from the Caribbean.* New York: New Press, 1994.

LATIN AMERICA

Acuña, Rodolfo. *Occupied America.* San Francisco: Canfield Press, 1972.

Ambrosi, Alain, and Nancy Thede, eds. *Video the Changing World. See Cinema.*

Aufderheide, Patricia, executive ed. *Latin American Visions.* Philadelphia: Neighborhood Film/Video Project of International House, 1989.

————. "Latin American Cinema and the Rhetoric of Cultural Nationalism: Controversies at Havana in 1987 and 1989." *Quarterly Review of Film and Video. See Cinema.*

Barnes, Sandra T., ed. *Africa's Ogun; Old World and New.* Bloomington: Indiana University Press, 1989.

Bastide, Roger. *African Civilisations in the New World.* New York: Harper & Row, 1971.

Beezley, William H., and Judith Ewell, eds. *The Human Tradition in Latin America: The Twentieth Century*. Wilmington, Del.: Scholarly Resources Inc., 1987.

Bergmann, Emilie, et al. *Women, Culture, and Politics in Latin America. Seminar on Feminism and Culture in Latin America*. Berkeley and Los Angeles: University of California Press, 1990.

Bilby, Kenneth M. *The Caribbean as a Musical Region. See Cuba*.

Black, Jan Knippers, ed. *Latin America. Its Problems and Its Promise*. Boulder, Colo.: Westview Press, 1991.

Broad, Dave and Lori Foster, eds. *The New World Order and the Third World. See United States*.

Burns, E. *Latin American Cinema: Film and History. See Cinema*.

Burton, Julianne. "The Camera as Gun: Two Decades of Culture and Resistance in Latin America." *See Cinema*.

———. *Cinema and Social Change in Latin America: Conversations with Filmmakers. See Cinema*.

———. "The Hours of the Embers: On the Current Situation of Latin American Cinema." *See Cinema*.

———. *The New Latin American Cinema: An Annotated Bibliography 1960–1980. See Cinema*.

———. *The Social Documentary in Latin America. See Cinema*.

———. "Women Behind the Camera." *See Cinema*.

Burton, Julianne, and J. Franco. "Culture and Imperialism." *Latin American Perspectives*, Issue 165, 1 (1978).

Carpentier, Alejo. *Concierto barroco Honduras. See Cuba*.

Casas, Bartolomé de las. *Brevísima Relación de la destrucción de las Indias*. Baltimore: Johns Hopkins University Press, 1994.

———. *Historia de las Indias (1559)*. México: Fondo de Cultural Económica, 1986.

Castañeda, Jorge G. *Utopia Unarmed: The Latin American Left After the Cold War*. New York: Knopf, distributed by Random House, 1993.

Castro-Klaren, Sara, Sylvia Molloy, and Beatriz Sarlo, eds. *Women's Writing in Latin America: An Anthology*. Boulder, Colo.: Westview, 1991.

Chanan, Michael. *Twenty Five Years of New Latin American Cinema. See Cinema*.

Chang-Rodríguez, Eugenio. *Latinoamérica su civilización y su cultura*. New York: Harper Collins Publishers, 1991.

Chilcote, Ronald H., and Joel C. Edelstein, eds. *Latin America: The Struggle with Dependency and Beyond*. Cambridge: Schenkman Publications Co., distributed by Halsted Press, New York, 1974.

Columbus, Christopher. *Personal Narrative of the First Voyage of Columbus to America*. Boston: T. B. Wait and Son, 1827.

Correas de Zapata, Celia. *Short Stories by Latin American Women: The Magic and the Real*. Houston: Arte Publico Press, 1990.

Curtin, Philip D. *The Atlantic Slave Trade; A Census*. Madison: University of Wisconsin Press, 1969.

Deere, Carmen Diana. *Latin American Perspectives. See Peru*.

Deere, Carmen Diana, ed. *State Policy and Women in Latin America and the Caribbean*. Los Angeles: Sage Press.

Eckstein, Susan, ed. *Power and Popular Protest: Latin America Social Movements*. Berkeley and Los Angeles: University of California Press, 1989.

Escobar, Arturo, and Sonia E. Alvarez, eds. *The Making of Social Movements in Latin America: Identity, Strategy and Democracy*. Boulder: Westview Press, 1992.

Faber, Daniel. *Environment under Fire: Imperialism and the Ecological Crisis in Central America*. New York: Monthly Review Press, 1993.

Fell, Barry. *America B.C.: Ancient settlers in the New World*. New York: Pocket Books, 1989.

Feyder, Linda, ed. *Shattering the Myth: Plays by Hispanic Women*. Houston: Arte Publico Press, 1992.

Fisher, Jo. *Out of the Shadows: Women Resistance, and Politics in South America*. London and New York: Latin American Bureau, distributed in North America by Monthly Review Press, 1993.

Fontes, C. *Defining Popular Video: Emerging Strategies in Latin America and the U.S. See Cinema*.

Fox, Elizabeth, ed. *The Media and Politics in Latin America: The Struggle for Democracy*. London and Newbury Park: Sage Publications, 1988.

Fuentes, Carlos. *The Buried Mirror: Reflections on Spain and the New World*. Boston: Houghton Mifflin, 1992.

Fusco, Coco. *Centro. "The Latin Boom in American Film." See Cinema*.

———, ed. *Reviewing Histories. Selections from New Latin American Cinema. See Cinema*.

Galeano, Eduardo H. *Memory of Fire*. New York: Pantheon Books, 1985.

———. *Open Veins of Latin America; Five Centuries of the Pillage of a Continent*. New York: Monthly Review Press, 1973.

———. *We Say No: Chronicles 1963–1991*. New York: Norton, 1992.

García Pinto, Magdalena. *Women Writers of Latin America: Intimate Histories*. Austin: University of Texas Press, 1991.

Gennino, Angela, ed. *Amazonia: Voices from the Rainforest (A Resource and Action Guide)*. Rainforest Action Network, distributed by Cultural Survival, 1990.

George, Susan. *A Fate Worse Than Debt*. New York: Grove Weidenfeld, 1990.

Getino, Octavio. *Cine latinoamericano: economía y nuevas tecnologías audiovisuales. See Cinema*.

Gibbs, V. *Latin American Research Review. "Latin American Film." See Cinema*.

Gilbert, Alan. *The Latin America City*. London and New York: LAB, Monthly Review Press, 1994.

Gilroy, Paul. *The Black Atlantic: Modernity and Double Consciousness.* Cambridge: Harvard University Press, 1993.

González-Wippler, Migene. *Powers of the Orisha: Santería and the Worship of Saints.* New York: Original Publications, 1992.

———. *Santería: African Magic in Latin America,* 2d ed. Bronx: Original Products, 1984.

———. *The Santería Experience: Rituals and Spells of Santería.* Englewoods Cliffs: Prentice Hall, 1982.

Green, Duncan. *Faces of Latin America.* London: Latin American Bureau, 1991.

Green, James N. "Gays and Lesbians: The Closet Door Swings Open." *NACLA Report on the Americas* 26, no. 4 (February 1993): 4–7.

Guevara, Angel, et al. *El nuevo cine latinoamericano en el mundo de hoy: memorias del IX Festival Internacional del. See Cinema.*

Gumucio Dagrón, Alfonso. *Cine, censura y exilio en América Latina. See Cinema.*

Gutiérrez Alea, Tomás. "Memorias de 'Memorias'." *Casa de las Américas* 21, no. 122 (September-October 1980): 67–76.

Gutiérrez, Gustavo. *The Future of Liberation Theology: Essays in Honor of Gustavo Gutiérrez.* Maryknoll, N.Y.: Orbis Books, 1989.

A Theology of Liberation: History, Politics, and Salvation. Maryknoll, N.Y.: Orbis Books, 1988.

Handbook of Latin American Studies. Austin: Austin University of Texas Press, 1990.

Hansen, Edward H. *The Human Condition in Latin America.* New York: Oxford University Press, 1974.

Harss, Luis. *Into the Mainstream; Conversations with Latin-American Writers.* New York: Harper & Row, 1967.

Heath, Dwight B., ed. *Contemporary Cultures and Societies of Latin America,* 2d ed. New York: Random House, 1974.

Hennebelle, Guy, and Alfonso Gumucio Dagrón, eds. *Les cinémas de l'Amérique Latine: Pays par pays, l'histoire, leconomie, les structures.* Paris: L'herminier, 1981.

Herman, D. L., ed. *Democracy in Latin America: Colombia and Venezuela.* Westport, Conn.: Praeger, 1988.

Holt, Marion Peter, and George Woodyard, eds. *Drama Contemporary, Latin America: Plays by Manuel Puig et al.* New York: P. A. J. Publications, 1986.

Janvery, Alain de. *The Agrarian Question of Reformism in Latin America.* Baltimore: Johns Hopkins University Press, 1982.

Jara, Rene, and Nicholas Spadaccini. *Hispanic Issues: 1492–1992: Rediscovering Colonial Writing,* 2d ed. Minneapolis: University of Minnesota Press, 1991.

Jelin, Elizabeth, ed. *Women and Social Change in Latin America.* Geneva and London: United Nations Research Institute for Social Development, Zed books, 1990.

Jesus, Carolina María de. *Child of the Dark; The Diary of Carolina María de Jesus. See Brazil.*

King, Anthony D. *Culture, Globalization and the World-System: Contemporary Conditions for the Representation of Identity.* Binghamton: Dept. of Art and Art History, State University of New York at Binghamton, 1991.

King, John. *Magical Reels: A History of Cinemas in Latin America. See Cinema.*

Klein, Herbert S. *African Slavery in Latin America and the Caribbean.* New York: Oxford University Press, 1986.

Koning, Hans. *Columbus: His Enterprise, Exploding the Myth.* New York: Monthly Review Press, 1991.

———. *The Conquest of America: How the Indian Nations Lost their Continent.* New York: Monthly Review Press, 1993.

Krauss, Clifford. *Inside Central America: Its People, Politics and History.* New York: Summit Books, 1991.

Kuppers, Gaby. *Compañeras: Voices from the Latin American Women's Movement.* London: Latin American Bureau, 1994.

LaFeber, Walter. *Inevitable Revolutions: The United States and Central America,* 2d ed. New York: W. W. Norton and Company, Inc., 1993.

"Latin American Women: The Gendering of Politics and Culture." *NACLA Report on the Americas* 27, no. 1 (July/August 1993).

Lavrin, Asunción, ed. *Latin American Women: Historical Perspectives.* Westport, Conn.: Greenwood Press, 1978.

León Frías, Isaac, compiler. *Los años de conmoción 1967–1973. Entrevistas con realizadores sudamericanos. See Cinema.*

Lernoux, Penny. *Cry of the People.* New York: Doubleday & Co., 1980.

Lockhart, James, and Stuart B. Schwartz. *Early Latin America: A History of Colonial Spanish America and Brazil.* Cambridge and New York: Cambridge University Press, 1983.

López, A. *Radical History Review.* "An 'Other' History: The New Latin American Cinema." *See Cinema.*

———. "The Melodrama in Latin America." *See Cinema.*

López, Carmen A. *Crisis fiscal e industrialización en el desarrollo latinoamericano.* Valencia, Venezuela: Vadell Hermanos, 1988.

Mahieu, José Agustín. *Panorama del cine iberoamericano. See Cinema.*

Martin, David. *Tongues of Fire: The Explosion of Protestantism in Latin America.* Oxford; U.K: B. Blackwell, 1990.

Martínez Torres, Augusto and Manuel Pérez Estremera. *Nuevo cine latinoamericano. See Cinema.*

Mattelart, Armand. *Multinational Corporations and the Control of Culture: The Ideological Apparatuses of Imperialism.* Sussex and Atlantic Highlands: Humanities Press and Harvester Press, 1979.

Miller, Beth Kurti, ed. *Women in Hispanic Literature: Icons and Fallen Idols.* Berkeley and Los Angeles: University of California Press, 1983.

Miller, Francesca. *Latin American Women and the Search for Social Justice.* Hanover, N.H.: University Press of New England, 1991.

Miller, Randall M., ed. *The Kaleidoscopic Lens. How Hollywood Views Ethnic Groups. See Cinema.*

Moctesuma Esparza Productions, Inc. *The Ballad of Gregorio Cortez.* Beverly Hills: Nelson Entertainment, 1988.

Mohanty, Chandra Talpade, Ann Russo, and Lourdes Torres, eds. *Third World Women and the Politics of Feminism.* Bloomington: Indiana University Press, c1991.

Moody, Roger, ed. *The Indigenous Voice: Visions and Reality.* Zed Books, distributed by Cultural Survival, 1988.

Moreno Fraginals, Manuel. *Africa in Latin America: Essays on History, Culture, and Socialization.* New York: Holmes and Meier, 1984.

Murphy, Joseph M. *Santería: An African Religion in America.* Boston: Beacon Press, 1988.

NACLA Report on the Americas. "Brazil: The Persistence of Inequality." *See Brazil.*

Nash, June C., Helen Safa, and contributors. *Women and Change in Latin America.* South Hadley: Bergin & Garvey, 1986.

Nelson, Wilton M. *Protestantism in Central America.* Grand Rapids: W. B. Eerdmans Publishing Co., 1984.

Newman, Mary Louise Pratt. *Women, Culture and Politics, in Latin America. Seminar on Feminism and Culture in Latin America.* Berkeley and Los Angeles: University of California Press, 1990.

Olalquiaga, Celeste. *Megalopolis: Contemporary Cultural Sensibilities.* Minneapolis: University of Minnesota Press, 1992.

Pacini, Deborah, and Christine Pranouemont, eds. *Coca and Cocaine: Effects on People and Policy in Latin America.* Cultural Survival with the Latin American Studies Program, Cornell University, distributed by Cultural Survival, 1986.

Palacios More, René, and Daniel Pires Mateus. *El cine latinoamericano: o por una estética de la ferocidad, la magia y la violencia. See Cinema.*

Parker, Andrew, ed. *Nationalisms & Sexualities.* New York: Routledge, 1992.

Payán, Miguel Juan, and José Luis López. *Manuel Gutiérrez Aragón.* Madrid: Ediciones JC, 1985.

Pescatello, Anne, ed. *Female and Male in Latin America.* Pittsburgh: Pittsburgh University Press, 1970.

Pessar, Patricia R., ed. *When Borders Don't Divide. Labor Migration and Refugee Movements in the Americas. See United States.*

Pick, Zuzana. *The New Latin American Cinema: A Continental Project. See Cinema.*

Pick, Zuzana, ed. *Latin American Filmmakers and the Third Cinema. See Cinema.*

Picon Garfield, Evelyn. *Women's Voices from Latin Amer-*

ica: Interviews with Six Contemporary Authors. Detroit: Wayne State University Press, 1987.

Pines, Jim, and Paul Wileman. *Questions of Third Cinema. See Cinema.*

Place, Susan ed. *Tropical Forests: Latin American Nature and Society in Transition.* Wilmington, Del.: Scholarly Resources, 1993.

Price, Richard, ed. *Maroon Societies: Rebel Slave Communities in the Americas,* 2d ed. Baltimore: Johns Hopkins University Press, 1979.

Randall, Margaret. *Gathering Rage: The Failure of Twentieth Century Revolutions to Develop a Feminist Agenda.* New York: Monthly Review Press, 1992.

Rocha, Glauber Pedro de Andrade. *Brasil/Cultura.* "El manifesto del 'cinema novo': 'La estetica del hambre'." *See Cinema.*

Roddick, Jackie. *The Dance of the Millions: Latin America and the Debt Crisis.* London and New York: Latin America Bureau, distributed by Monthly Review Press, 1988.

Rout, Leslie B. *The African Experience in Spanish America, 1502 to the Present Day.* Cambridge and New York: Cambridge University Press, 1976.

Rowe, William, and Vivian Schelling. *Memory and Modernity: Popular Culture in Latin America.* New York: Verso, 1991.

Saalfield, Catherine. *The Independent.* "Pregnant with Dreams: Julia Barco's Visions from Latin America." *See Cinema.*

Sassen, S., S. Mahler, C. Tactaquin, and M. Jimenez. *NACLA Report on the Americas.* "Coming North: Latino & Caribbean Immigration." *See United States.*

Schnitman, Jorge. *Film Industries in Latin America: Dependency and Development. See Cinema.*

Schuler, Margaret, ed. *Freedom from Violence: Women's Strategies from Around the World.* Washington D.C. and New York: Women, Law and Development, OEF International; Distributed by UNIFEM, 1992.

Schumann, Peter B. *Historia del cine latinoamericano.* Buenos Aires: Editorial Legasa, 1987.

Schuyler, George W. *Hunger in a Land of Plenty. See Colombia.*

Serrano Elías, Jorge. *La participación del cristiano en la vida pública.* Miami: Ed. Unilit, 1990.

Shakif, Jorge Handal, and Carlos M. Vilas. *The Socialist Option in Central America: Two Reassessments.* New York: Monthly Review Press, 1993.

Silva Michelena, José Agustín, ed. *Latin America: Peace, Democratization and Economic Crisis.* United Nations University, 1988.

Simonson, R., and S. Walker, eds. *The Graywolf Annual Five: Multi-Cultural Literacy.* St. Paul, Min.: Graywolf Press, 1988.

Skidmore, Thomas E., and Peter H. Smith. *Modern Latin America,* 3d ed. New York: Oxford University Press, 1992.

Small, Deborah, and Maggie Jaffe. *1492: What Is It Like To Be Discovered?* New York: Monthly Review Press, 1991.

Smith, T. Lynn. *The Process of Rural Development in Latin America.* Gainesville: University of Florida Press, 1967.

Sommer, Doris. *Foundational Fictions: The National Romances of Latin America.* Berkeley and Los Angeles: University of California Press, 1991.

Soto, Hernando de. *The Other Path: The Invisible Revolution in the Third World.* New York: Harper & Row, 1989.

Stam, Robert. "Rewriting 1492: Cinema and the Columbus Debate." *See Cinema.*

Stavenhagen, Rodolfo. *Agrarian Problems and Peasant Movements in Latin America.* Garden City, N.Y.: Doubleday, 1970.

Stern, Theodore. *The Rubber-Ball Games of the Americas. See Mexico.*

Stoll, David. *Is Latin America Turning Protestant?: The Politics of Evangelical Growth.* Berkeley and Los Angeles: University of California Press, 1990.

Taussig, Michael. *The Devil and Commodity Fetishism in South America.* Chapel Hill: University of North Carolina Press, 1980.

———. *Shamanism, Colonialism, and the Wild Man.* Chicago: Chicago University Press, 1987.

Todaro, Michael P. *Economic Development in the Third World: An Introduction to Problems and Policies in a Global Perspective.* London and New York: Longman, 1977.

Toledo, Teresa. *10 años del nuevo cine latinoamericano. See Cinema.*

Usabel, Gaiska de. *The High Noon of American Films in Latin America. See United States.*

Vilas, Carlos M. *Between Earthquakes and Volcanoes: Markets, State and Revolution in Central America.* New York: Monthly Review Press, 1994.

Villarreal, Roberto E., and Norma G. Hernández, eds. *Latinos and Political Coalitions: Political Empowerment for the 1990s. See United States.*

Virgillo, Carmelo, and Naomi Lindstrom, eds. *Women as Myth and Metaphor in Latin American Literature.* Columbia: University of Missouri Press, 1985.

Weatherford, Jack. *Indian Givers: How the Indians of the Americas Transformed the World,* 1st Ballantine Books ed. New York: Fawcett Columbine, 1990.

Weiss, Rachel, and Alan West. *Being America: Essays on Art, Literature and Identity from Latin America.* Fredonia: White Pine Press, 1991.

West, R. C., and J. P Augelli. *Middle America: Its Lands and Peoples,* 3d ed. Englewood Cliffs, N.J.: Prentice Hall, 1989.

Wiarda, Howard J. *American Foreign Policy toward Latin America in the 80s and 90s.* New York: New York University Press, 1992.

Woodward, Ralph Lee. *Central America, a Nation Divided,* 2d ed. New York: Oxford University Press, 1985.

Yudice, George, Jean Franco, and Juan Flores, eds. *On Edge: The Crisis of Contemporary Latin American Culture.* Minneapolis: University of Minnesota Press, 1992.

Zeta Acosta, Oscar. *Revolt of the Cockroach People.* New York: Vintage Press, 1989.

MEXICO

Adams, Richard E. W. *Prehistoric Mesoamerica,* rev. ed. Norman: University of Oklahoma Press, 1991.

Adler Lomnitz, Larissa. *Networks and Marginality: Life in a Mexican Shantytown.* New York: Academic Press, 1977.

Almoina, Helena. *Bibliografía del cine mexicano.* México: Filmoteca de la UNAM, 1985.

Ambrosi, Alain, and Nancy Thede, eds. *Video the Changing World. See Cinema.*

Arrom, Silvia Marina. *The Women of Mexico City, 1790–1857.* Stanford: Stanford University Press, 1985.

Artes de México. "Museo Nacional de Antropología." *Artes de México,* II época, Numero 66/67 (Año XII/1965). (Artes de México.)

Asturias, Miguel Angel. *Leyendas de Guatemala. See Guatemala.*

Aufderheide, Patricia. *Cross Cultural Film Guide. See Cinema.*

Aveni, Anthony F. *Conversing with the Planets: How Science and Myth Invented the Cosmos.* New York: Time Books, 1992.

Ayala Blanco, Jorge. *La aventura del cine mexicano.* México: Ediciones Era, 1968.

———. *La búsqueda del cine mexicano (1968–72)* 1–2. Mexico: Filmoteca de la UNAM, Dirección General de Difusión Cultural, 1974.

Bailey, David C. *Viva Cristo Rey: The Cristero Rebellion and the Church-State Conflict in Mexico.* Austin: University of Texas Press, 1974.

Barrera Vásquez, Alfredo, and Silvia Rendón, translators. *El libro de los libros de Chilám Balám.* México: Fondo de Cultura Económica, 1979, c1948.

Basanez, Miguel. *La lucha por la hegemonía en México, 1968–1980,* 2d ed. México, D.F.: Siglo Veintiuno Editores, 1982.

Beneria, Lourdes, and Martha Roldan. *The Crossroads of Class & Gender: Industrial Homework, Subcontracting, and Household Dynamics in Mexico City.* Chicago: University of Chicago Press, 1987.

Berg, Charles Ramírez. *Cinema of Solitude: A Critical Study of Mexican Film, 1967–1983.* Austin: University of Texas Press, 1992.

Bernal, Ignacio, et al. *Museo Nacional de Antropología de México.* México: Daimon, 1968.

Berzunza Pinto, Ramón. *Guerra social en Yucatán.* Mexico: Costa-Amic, 1965.

Black, Jan Knippers, ed. *Latin America. Its Problems and Its Promise. See Latin America.*

Bordwell, David. *Making Meaning: Inference and Rhetoric in the Interpretation of Cinema. See Cinema.*

Brandes, Stanley H. *Power and Persuasion: Fiestas and Social Control in Rural Mexico.* Philadelphia: University of Pennsylvania Press, 1988.

Brenner, Anita. *The Wind that Swept Mexico; The History of the Mexican Revolution, 1910–1942.* Austin: University of Texas Press, 1971.

Brushwood, John Shibbs. *Mexico In Its Novel; A Nation's Search for Identity.* Austin: University of Texas Press, 1966.

————. *Narrative Innovation and Political Change in Mexico.* New York: P. Lang, 1989.

Burton, Julianne. *Cinema and Social Change in Latin America: Conversations with Filmmakers. See Cinema.*

Camp, Roderic A. *Politics in Mexico.* New York: Oxford University Press, 1993.

Caraway, Caren. *Aztec and Other Mexican Indian Designs.* Owings Mills, Md.: Stemmer House, 1984.

Carmichael, Elizabeth, and Chloe Sayer. *The Skeleton at the Feast: The Day of the Dead in Mexico.* Austin: University of Texas Press, 1992.

Carrillo, Alejandro. *Causas y programa de la revolución mexicana. (Resumen de las dos conferencias sustentadas por el Lic. Alejandro.* México: s.n., 1963.

————. *La industrialización de México; La revolución industrial de México.* México.

Carrillo, Jorge, and Alberto Hernández. *Mujeres fronterizas en la industria maquiladora.* México; Tijuana: Secretaria de Educación Pública; Centro de Estudios Fronterizos del Norte de Mexico, 1985.

Casas, Bartolomé de las. *Brevísima Relación de la destrucción de las Indias. See Latin America.*

Castañeda, Jorge G. *Mexican Meltdown.* Distributed by The New Press (450 W. 41st St., New York, N.Y. 10036).

————. *Utopia Unarmed: The Latin American Left after the Cold War. See Latin America.*

Castellanos, Rosario. *Los convidados de agosto.* México: Ediciones Era, 1964.

Cavanagh, John, et al. *Trading Freedom: How Free Trade Affects Our Lives, Work and Environment.* San Francisco: Institute for Food and Development Policy, 1992.

Chang-Rodríguez, Eugenio. *Latinoamerica su civilización y su cultura. See Latin America.*

Chávez, Leo. *Shadowed Lives: Undocumented Immigrants in American Society. See United States.*

Clendinnen, Inga. *Aztecs: An Interpretation,* 1st pbk. ed. Cambridge and New York: Cambridge University Press, 1993.

Coe, Michael D. *Breaking the Maya Code.* New York: Thames and Hudson, 1992.

————. *The Maya,* 5th ed. London: Thames and Hudson, 1993.

————. *México,* 3d ed. London: Thames and Hudson, 1984.

Coggins, Clemency C., and Orrin C. Shane III. *Cenote of Sacrifice: Maya Tresures from The Sacred Well at Chichen Itza.* Austin: University of Texas Press, 1984.

Cordry, Donald Bush, and Dorothy M. Cordry. *Costumes and Textiles of the Aztec Indians of the Cuetzlan Region, Puebla, Mexico.* Los Angeles: Southwest Museum, 1940.

Correas de Zapata, Celia. *Short Stories by Latin American Women: The Magic and the Real. See Latin America.*

Cortes, Eladio, ed. *Dictionary of Mexican Literature.* Westport, Conn.: Greenwood Press, 1992.

Cypess, S. *La Malinche in Mexican Literature: From History to Myth.* Austin: University of Texas Press, 1991.

Dávalos Orozco, Federico, and Esperanza Vázquez Bernal. *Filmografía general del cine mexicano.* Puebla: Universidad Autónoma de Puebla, 1985.

Demaris, Ovid. *Poso del mundo; Inside the Mexican-American Border, From Tijuana to Matamoros.* Boston: Little Brown and Company, 1970.

Downing, John D. H, ed. *Film & Politics in the Third World. See Cinema.*

Dulles, John W. F. *Yesterday in Mexico: A Chronicle of the Revolution, 1919–1936.* Austin: University of Texas Press, 1961.

Fergusson, Erna. *Fiesta in Mexico.* New York: A. A. Knopf, 1934.

Fernández-Kelly, María Patricia. *For We Are Sold, I and My People: Women and Industry in Mexico's Frontier.* Albany: State University of New York Press, 1983.

Foucault, Michel. *Discipline and Punish: The Birth of the Prison.* New York: Vintage Books, 1979.

Franco, Jean. *Plotting Women: Gender and Representation in Mexico.* New York: Columbia University Press, 1989.

Galindo, Alejandro. *El cine, genocidio espiritual: De 1900 al "crash" de 29.* Mexico: Editorial Nuestro Tiempo, 1971.

————. *El cine mexicano: un personal punto de vista.* México: EDAMEX, 1986.

————. *Una radiografía histórica del cine mexicano.* México: Fondo de Cultura Popular, 1968.

————. *Verdad y mentira del cine mexicano.* México: Editorial Katún, 1981.

————. *Qué es el cine?* México: Editorial Nuestro Tiempo, 1975.

García Garofalo y Mesa, Manuel. *Vida de José María Heredia en México, 1825–1839.* México, D.F.: Ediciones Botas, 1945.

García Márquez, Gabriel. *Chronicle of a Death Foretold. See Colombia.*

García Martínez, Bernardo. *Los pueblos de la sierra: el poder y el espacio entre los indios del norte de Puebla hasta 1700.* México: El Colegio de México, 1987.

García Oliveri, Ricardo. *Lucas Demare.* Buenos Aires: Centro Editor de América Latina, 1994.

————. *Luis Puenzo.* Buenos Aires: Centro Editor de América Latina, 1994.

García Pinto, Magdalena. *Women Writers of Latin America: Intimate Histories. See Latin America.*

García Riera, Emilio. *La guía del cine mexicano de la pantalla grande a la televisión, 1919–1984.* México: Editorial Patria, 1984.

———. *Historia documental del cine mexicano.* Guadalajara: Universidad de Guadalajara, 1992.

Garro, Elena. *Los recuerdos del porvenir,* 2d ed. México: J. Mortiz, 1985.

Geduld, Harry M., and Ronald Gottesman, eds. *Sergei Eisenstein and Upton Sinclair: The Making and Unmaking of "Que Viva Mexico!"* Bloomington: Indiana University Press, 1970.

Getino, Octavio. *A diez años de "Hacia un tercer cine." See Cinema.*

———. *Notas sobre cine argentino y latinoamericano. See Cinema.*

Gil, Carlos B. *Hope and Frustration: Interviews with Leaders of Mexico's Political Opposition.* Wilmington, Del.: Scholarly Resources, Inc., 1992.

Goldston, Iago, ed. *Man's Image in Medicine and Anthropology. See United States.*

Gonzáles, Rodolpho. *I am Joaquin. Yo soy Joaquin; an epic poem. See United States.*

González Boixo, J. C. *Claves narrativas de Juan Rulfo.* México: Universidad de Leon, 1984.

Gossen, Gary H. *Symbol and Meaning Beyond the Closed Community: Essays in Mesoamerican Ideas.* Albany: Institute for Mesoamerican Studies, University of Albany, SUNY 1986.

Green, Duncan. *Faces of Latin America. See Latin America.*

Grinspun, Ricardo, and Maxwell A. Cameron, eds. *The Political Economy of North American Free Trade.* New York: St. Martin's Press, 1993.

Hall, Doug, and Sally Jo Fifer, eds. *Illuminating Video: An Essential Guide to Video Art. See Cinema.*

Hamilton, Nora. *The Limits of State Autonomy: Post-Revolutionary Mexico.* Princeton, N.J.: Princeton University Press, 1982.

Harss, Luis. *Into the Mainstream; Conversations with Latin-American Writers. See Latin America.*

———. *Los nuestros.* Buenos Aires: Editorial Sudamericana, 1975.

Heredia, José María. *Toluca: gobierno del Estado de México.* México: Patrimonio Cultural y Artístico del Estado de México, 1979.

Herrera, Hayden. *Frida, a Biography of Frida Kahlo.* New York: Harper & Row, 1983.

Hurtado Martínez, Raul. *La verdad sobre el volcán "Chichonal": narración verídica sobre la erupción de 1982.* San Cristóbal de las Casas, Chiapas: La Merced, 1984.

Inés de la Cruz, Sister Juana. *The Answer (La repuesta).* New York: Feminist Press at the City University of New York, 1994.

———. *Obras escogidas: respuesta a Sor Philotea de la Cruz, poemas.* México: Editorial "Cultura," 1928.

———. *Poesías completas,* 2d ed. México: Ediciones Botas, 1948.

———. *La segunda Celestina: una comedia perdida de Sor Juana.* Mexico City: Vuelta, 1990.

———. *Selections: A Sor Juana Anthology.* Cambridge: Harvard University Press, 1988.

———. *Sonetos.* México: Ediciones de la Razón, S. A., 1931.

———. *Sonetos y endechas.* México: Partido Revolucionario Institucional, Comisión Nacional Editorial, 1976.

———. *Sor Juana Inés de la Cruz; Poems.* Binghamton, N.Y.: Bilingual Press/Editorial Bilingue, 1985.

———. *Sor Juana; Liras.* México: Ediciones Botas, 1933.

———. *El sueño.* Austin, Tex.: Thorp Springs Press, 1983.

———. *Works.* México: Fondo de Cultura Económica, 1951.

Ingham, John M. *Mary, Michael, and Lucifer: Folk Catholicism in Central Mexico.* Austin: University of Texas Press, 1986.

Jelin, Elizabeth, ed. *Women and Social Change in Latin America. See Latin America.*

Johnston, Edith. *Regional Dances of Mexico.* Skokie, Ill.: National Textbook Co., 1974.

Kibbe, Pauline Rochester. *Guide to Mexican History,* 4 ed. Mexico: Editorial Minutiae Mexicana, 1964.

King, John. *Magical Reels: A History of Cinemas in Latin America. See Cinema.*

Knight, Alan. *The Mexican Revolution* 2. Cambridge: Cambridge University Press, 1986.

Leon-Portilla, Miguel, ed. *The Aztec Image of Self and Society: An Introduction to Nahua Culture.* Salt Lake City: University of Utah Press, 1992.

Lewis, Oscar. *The Children of Sánchez, Autobiography of a Mexican Family.* New York: Random House, 1961.

Leyda, Jay. *Kino.* New York: Colliers, 1973.

Littín, Miguel. *El chacal de Nahueltoro, la tierra prometida,* Textos de Cine #5, Serie Guiones 1. México: UNAM, Dirección General de Difusión Cultural, 1977.

Lockhart, James, and Stuart B. Schwartz. *Early Latin America: A History of Colonial Spanish America and Brazil. See Latin America.*

López Páez, Jorge. *Doña Herlinda y su hijo; y otros hijos.* México: Fondo de Cultura Economica, 1993.

López Portillas, Miguel. *La literatura de los Mayas.* México: Editorial J. Mortiz, 1964.

Lowry, Malcolm. *Under the Volcano.* New York: Harper & Row, 1984.

Luhr, William, ed. *World Cinema since 1945. See Cinema.*

Macías, Ana. *Against All Odds: The Feminist Movement in Mexico to 1940.* Westport, Conn.: Greenwood Press, 1982.

Martínez, Pablo L. *Sobre el libro "Baja California heróica:" contra la defensa de una falsedad histórica.* Mexico City, 1960.

Mattelart, Armand. *Multinational Corps and the Control of*

Culture: The Ideological Apparatuses of Imperialism. See Latin America.

Menchú, Rigoberta. *I, Rigoberta Menchú: An Indian Woman in Guatemala. See Guatemala.*

Merrill, William L. *Rarámuri Souls: Knowledge and Social Process in Northern Mexico.* Washington, D.C.: Smithsonian Institution Press, 1988.

Meyer, Jean. *The Cristero Rebellion: The Mexican People Between Church and State, 1926–1929.* Cambridge: Cambridge University Press, 1976.

Meyer, Michael C., and William L. Sherman. *The Course of Mexican History,* 4th ed. New York: Oxford University Press, 1993.

Michaels, Eric. *Bad Aboriginal Art: Tradition, Media and Technological Horizons. See Cinema.*

Miller, Beth Kurti, ed. *Women in Hispanic Literature: Icons and Fallen Idols. See Latin America.*

Minh-Ha, Trinh Thi. *Woman, Native, Other: Writing Postcoloniality and Feminism. See Cinema.*

Monsivais, Carlos. "Muerte y resurrección del nacionalismo mexicano." *Nexos,* no. 109 (January 1987): 13–22. (México: Ediciones Oceano.)

Mora, Carl J. *Mexican Cinema: Reflections of a Society,* Revised ed. Berkeley and Los Angeles: University of California Press, 1989.

Morley, Sylvanus Griswold, and George W. Brainerd. *The Ancient Maya,* 4th ed. Stanford: Stanford University Press, 1983.

Munguía Cárdenas, Federico. *Antecedentes y datos biográficos de Juan Rulfo.* México: UNED, 1987.

———. "Artes de México." *Museo Nacional de Antropología,* II época, 66–67, Año XII (1965). (México.)

Nelson, Carro. *El cine de luchadores.* México: Filmoteca de la UNAM, 1984.

Núñez Cabeza de Vaca, Alvar. *Los naufragios.* Madrid: Editorial Castalia, 1992.

Nutini, Hugo G. *Todos Santos in Rural Tlaxcala: A Syncretic, Expressive, and Symbolic Analysis of the Cult of the Dead.* Princeton, N.J.: Princeton University Press, 1988.

Olalquiaga, Celeste. *Megalopolis: Contemporary Cultural Sensibilities. See Latin America.*

Oster, Patrick. *The Mexicans: A Personal Portrait of a People.* New York: Harper & Row, 1989.

Pastor, Robert A., and Jorge G. Castañeda. *Limits to Friendship: The United States and Mexico. See United States.*

Paz, Octavio. *Laberinto de la soledad.* Madrid: Catedra, 1993.

Pettit, Florence H., and Robert M. Pettit. *Mexican Folk Toys: Festival Decorations and Ritual Objects.* New York: Hastings House Publishers, 1978.

Picon Garfield, Evelyn. *Women's Voices from Latin America: Interviews with Six Contemporary Authors. See Latin America.*

Plazaola, Luis. *Cine y mujer en América Latina: Directoras de Largometrajes de ficción. See Cinema.*

Poniatowska, Elena. *Hasta no verte Jesús mio.* Madrid; Mexico City: Alianza Editorial; Ediciones Era, 1984.

Price, John A. *Tijuana: Urbanization in a Border Culture.* South Bend, Ind.: University of Notre Dame Press, 1973.

Price, Richard, ed. *Maroon Societies: Rebel Slave Communities in the Americas. See Latin America.*

Puig, Manuel. *Drama Contemporary, Latin America: Plays. See Latin America.*

Raat, William Dirk. *Twentieth-Century Mexico.* Lincoln: University of Nebraska Press, 1986.

Ramos-Escandón, Carmen. *Presencia y transparencia: la mujer en la historia de México.* México, D.F.: Colegio de México, Programa Interdisciplinario de Estudios de la Mujer, 1987.

Reavis, Dick J. *Conversations with Moctezuma: Ancient Shadows Over Modern Life in Mexico.* New York: Morrow, 1990.

Reed, Nelson. *The Caste War of Yucatan.* Stanford: Stanford University Press, 1964.

Revueltas, José. *El luto humano,* 2d ed. México: Ediciones Era, 1981.

Reyes, Aurelio de los. *Cine y sociedad en México, 1896–1930.* México: Universidad Nacional Autónoma de México, Cineteca Nacional, 1983.

———. *Los orígenes del cine en México (1896–1900),* Cuadernos de Cine #21. Mexico City: UNAM, Dirección General de Difusión Cultural, 1973.

Reyes de la Maza, Luis. *El cine sonoro en México.* México: UNAM, Instituto de Investigaciones Estéticas, 1973.

Reyes Nevares, Beatriz. *The Mexican Cinema: Interviews with Thirteen Directors.* Albuquerque: University of New Mexico Press, 1976.

Ricard, Robert. *Spiritual Conquest of Mexico.* Berkeley and Los Angeles: University of California Press, 1966.

Rich, B. Ruby. *Iris.* "An/Other View of New Latin American Cinema." *See Cinema.*

Riding, Alan. *Distant Neighbors: A Portrait of the Mexicans.* New York: Vintage Books, 1989.

Rodríguez O, Jaime E., ed. *The Revolutionary Process in Mexico: Essays on Political and Social Change, 1880–1940.* Los Angeles: UCLA Latin American Center Publications, 1990.

Rodríguez, Richard. *Days of Obligation: An Argument with my Mexican Father.* New York: Viking Press, 1992.

Rojas González, Francisco. *Lola Casanova,* 1a. ed. en Colección Popular. México: Fondo de Cultura Económica, 1984.

———. *La negra Angustias.* México: Fondo de Cultura Economica, 1984.

Rosenthal, Alan. *The Documentary Conscience: A Casebook in Film Making. See Cinema.*

Rosenthal, Alan, ed. *New Challenges for Documentary. See Cinema.*

Roys, Ralph L. *The Book of Chilam Balam of Chumayel.* Norman: University of Oklahoma Press, 1967.

Ruiz, Vicky, and S. Tiano, eds. *Women on the U.S.-Mexico Border: Responses to Change. See United States.*

Rulfo, Juan. *Inframundo: The Mexico de Juan Rulfo.* Hanover, N.H.: Ediciones del Norte, 1983.

———. *Obra completa: El llano en llamas, Pedro Paramo, otros textos.* Caracas: Biblioteca Ayacucho, 1977.

———. *Pedro Paramo.* New York: Grove Press, 1994.

Saalfield, Catherine. *The Independent.* "Pregnant with Dreams: Julia Barco's Visions from Latin America." *See Cinema.*

Sabines, Jaime. *Crónicas del volcán.* Chiapas, Mexico: Tuxtla Gutiérrez, 1988.

Salvado, Luis Raul. *The Other Refugees: A Study of Nonrecognized Guatemalan Refugees in Chiapas, Mexico. See Guatemala.*

Sanders, William T., and Barbara J. Price. *Mesoamerica: The Evolution of a Civilization.* New York: Random House, 1968.

Sanjinés, Jorge. *Teoría y crítica de un cine popular.* México: Siglo Veintiuno, 1979.

Sanjinés, Jorge, et al. *Teoría y práctica de un cine junto al pueblo.* México: Siglo Veintiuno Editores, 1980.

Sayer, Chloe. *Costumes of Mexico.* Austin: University of Texas Press, 1985.

Scarborough, Vernon L., and David R. Wilcox, eds. *The Mesoamerican Ballgame.* Tucson: University of Arizona Press, 1991.

Schele, Linda, and David Freidel. *A Forest of Kings: The Untold Story of the Ancient Maya.* New York: William Morrow and Company, 1990.

Schmidt, Henry C. *The Roots of lo Mexicano: Self and Society in Mexican Thought, 1900–1934.* College Station: Texas A&M University Press, 1978.

Schnitman, Jorge. *Film Industries in Latin America: Dependency and Development. See Cinema.*

Sedillo, Mela. *Mexican and New Mexican Folk Dances,* 2d ed. Albuquerque: University of New Mexico Press, 1945.

Simpson, Lesley Byrd. *Many Mexicos,* 4th ed. Berkeley and Los Angeles: University of California Press, 1966.

Skidmore, Thomas E., and Peter H. Smith. *Modern Latin America. See Latin America.*

Solanas, F., and Octavio Getino. *Hojas de cine.* "Hacia un Tercer Cinema." *See Cinema.*

Sommer, Doris. *Foundational Fictions: The National Romance of Latin America. See Latin America.*

Stephens, John Lloyd. *Incidents of Travel in Yucatan.* London: J. Murray, 1843.

Stern, Theodore. *The Rubber-Ball Games of the Americas,* Monographs of the A.E.S., 17. Seattle: University of Washington Press, 1949.

Stigberg, David K. "Foreign Currents during the '60s and '70s in Mexican Popular Music: Rock and Roll, the Romantic Ballad, and the 'Cumbia'." *Studies in Latin American Popular Culture,* v.4 (1985): 170–84.

Stock, Ann Marie. *On Location in Costa Rica. See Costa Rica.*

Sweezey, William R. "La Pelota Mixteca." *Religión en Mesoamérica,* 1972, 471–78. [México, D.F.: XII Mesa Redonda, Sociedad Mexicana de Antropología.]

Taussig, Michael T. *The Devil and Commodity Fetishism in South America. See Latin America.*

Tedlock, Dennis. *Popol Vuh: The Mayan Book of the Dawn of Life,* 1st Touchstone ed. New York: Simon & Schuster, 1986.

Turner, Victor Witter. *The Ritual Process: Structure and Anti-Structure.* Ithaca, N.Y.: Cornell University Press, 1977.

Vaccarella, Eric Arthur. *John Kenneth Turner and the Mexican Revolution: An American Socialist Critique of Mexico, 1908–1921,* Thesis (M.A.). Austin: University of Texas, 1993.

Valdez, R. Burciaga, Kevin F. McCarthy, and Connie Malcolm Moreno. *An Annotated Bibliography of Sources of Mexican Immigration. See United States.*

Virgillo, Carmelo, and Naomi Lindstrom, eds. *Women as Myth and Metaphor in Latin American Literature. See Latin America.*

Waters, Frank. *Book of the Hopi.* New York: Viking Press, 1963.

Wauchope, Robert. *They Found the Buried Cities.* Chicago: University of Chicago Press, 1965.

Weckmann, Luis. *Herencia medieval de México.* (*The Medieval Heritage of México*). New York: Fordham University Press, 1992.

West, R. C. and J. P. Augelli. *Middle America: Its Lands and Peoples. See Latin America.*

Wilson, Fiona. *Sweaters: Gender, Class and Workshop-Based Industry in Mexico.* New York: St. Martin's Press, 1991.

Wolf, Eric Robert. *Sons of the Shaking Earth.* Chicago: University of Chicago Press, 1959.

Wolfe, Bertram. *Diego Rivera: His Life and Times.* New York: Knopf, 1939.

———. *The Fabulous Life of Diego Rivera.* New York: Stein & Day, 1963.

Womack, John, Jr. *Zapata and the Mexican Revolution.* New York: Alfred A. Knopf, 1969.

Yánez, Augustín. *Al filo del agua,* 18 ed. México: Editorial Porrua, 1984.

Zamora, Martha. *Frida Kahlo: The Brush of Anguish.* San Francisco: Chronicle Books, 1990.

Zazueta, Ochoa, and Jesús Angel. "El Día 2 de Noviembre." *Muerte y muertos,* Septiembre 1974, 103–11. (México.)

NICARAGUA

Ambrosi, Alain, and Nancy Thede, eds. *Video the Changing World. See Cinema.*

Armes, Roy. *Third World Film Making and the West. See Cinema.*

Asturias, Miguel Angel. *Viento fuerte,* 6th ed. Buenos Aires: Editorial Losada, 1972.

Aufderheide, Patricia. *Cross Cultural Film Guide. See Cinema.*

———. "Latin American Cinema and the Rhetoric of Cultural Nationalism: Controversies at Havana in 1987 and 1989." *See Cinema.*

Booth, John A. *The End and the Beginning: The Nicaraguan Revolution.* Boulder: Westview Press, 1982.

Burton, Julianne. *Cinema and Social Change in Latin America: Conversations with Filmmakers. See Cinema.*

Cardenal, Ernesto. *Antología.* Managua: Editorial Nueva Nicaragua-Ediciones Monimbo, 1983.

———. *Apocalypse, and other poems.* Edited by Robert Pring-Mill and Donald D. Walsh. New York: New Directions, 1977.

———. *Oración por Marilyn Monroe.* Managua: Editorial Nueva Nicaragua, 1985.

Chanan, Michael. *Twenty-Five Years of New Latin American Cinema. See Cinema.*

CIDCA/Development Study Unit, ed. *Ethnic Groups and the Nation State: The Case of the Atlantic Coast in Nicaragua.* Stockholm: University of Stockholm, Dept. of Social Anthropology, 1987.

Dennis, Phillip A. "The Costeños and the Revolution in Nicaragua." *Journal of Interamerican Studies and World Affairs* 23, 3 (1981): 271–96.

Galeano, Eduardo H. *Open Veins of Latin America; Five Centuries of the Pillage of a Continent. See Latin America.*

García Márquez, Gabriel. *La aventura de Miguel Littín clandestino en Chile. See Colombia.*

———. *No One Writes to the Colonel and Other Stories. See Colombia.*

———. *One Hundred Years of Solitude. See Colombia.*

Kahn, Douglas, and Diane Neumaier, eds. *Cultures in Contention. See Colombia.*

King, John. *Magical Reels: A History of Cinemas in Latin America. See Cinema.*

Nietschman, Bernard. *Between Land and Water: The Subsistence Ecology of the Miskito Indians, Eastern Nicaragua.* New York: Seminar Press, 1973.

———. "Hunting and Fishing Focus Among the Miskito Indians, Eastern Nicaragua." *Human Ecology,* no. 1 (1972): 41–67.

Ramírez, Sergio. *To Bury Our Fathers: A Novel of Nicaragua.* New York and Columbia, La.: Readers International, U.S. Subscription and Order Dept., 1984.

Rushdie, Salman. *The Jaguar Smile: A Nicaraguan Journey.* New York: Penguin Books, 1988.

Schlesinger, Stephen C. *Bitter Fruit: The Untold Story of the American Coup in Guatemala. See Guatemala.*

Schnitman, Jorge. *Film Industries in Latin America: Dependency and Development. See Cinema.*

Skidmore, Thomas E., and Peter H. Smith. *Modern Latin America. See Latin America.*

Walker, Thomas W. *Nicaragua, the Land of Sandino,* 3d ed. Boulder, Colo.: Westview Press, 1991.

PANAMA

Buckley, Kevin. *Panama: The Whole Story.* New York: Touchstone, 1992.

Cameron, Ian. *The Impossible Dream: The Building of the Panama Canal.* New York: Morrow, 1972.

Crane, Philip M. *Surrender in Panama: The Case Against the Treaty.* Ottawa, Ill.: Green Hill, 1978.

Dinges, John. *Our Man in Panama: How General Noriega Used the United States—and Made Millions in Arms and Drugs.* New York: Random House, 1990.

Greene, Graham. *Getting to Know the General: The Story of an Involvement.* New York: Simon & Schuster, 1984.

Independent Commission of Inquiry on the U.S. Invasion of Panama. *The U.S. Invasion of Panama: The Truth Behind Operation "Just Cause."* Boston: South End Press, 1991.

Kempe, Frederick. *Divorcing the Dictator: America's Bungled Affair with Noriega.* New York: Putnam & Sons, 1990.

Koster, R. M., and Guillermo Sánchez. *In the Time of the Tyrants: Panama, 1968–1990.* New York: W. W. Norton, 1990.

LaFeber, Walter. *Inevitable Revolutions: The United States in Central America,* Expanded ed. New York: W. W. Norton, 1984.

———. *The Panama Canal: The Crisis in Historical Perspective,* Updated ed. New York: Oxford University Press, 1989.

Levine, Isaac Don. *Hands Off the Panama Canal.* Washington, D.C.: Monticello Books, 1976.

MacDonald, Scott B. *Mountain High, White Avalanche: Cocaine and Power in the Andean States and Panama.* New York: Praeger, 1989.

McCullough, David G. *The Path Between the Seas: The Creation of the Panama Canal, 1870–1914.* New York: Simon & Schuster, 1977.

Millett, Richard. "Looking Beyond Noriega." *Foreign Policy,* no. 71 (Summer 1988): 46–63.

Moffett, George D. *The Limits of Victory: The Ratification of the Panama Canal Treaties.* Ithaca, N.Y.: Cornell University Press, 1985.

Ropp, Steve C. *Panamanian Politics: From Guarded Nation to National Guard.* New York and Stanford, Calif.: Praeger, Hoover Institution Press, 1982.

Ryan, Paul B. *The Panama Canal Controversy: U.S. Diplomacy and Defense Interests.* Stanford, Calif.: Hoover Institution Press, 1977.

Weeks, John, and Phil Gunson. *Panama: Made in the USA.* London; New York: Latin American Bureau, distribution in North America by Monthly Review Press, 1991.

PARAGUAY

Lewis, Paul H. *Paraguay under Stroessner.* Chapel Hill: University of North Carolina Press, 1980.

Roa Bastos, Augusto. *Mis reflexiones sobre el guión cine-*

matográfico y el guión de "Hijo de hombre." Asunción: R. P. Ediciones: Fundación cinemateca y Archivo Visual del Paraguay, 1993.

Wiarda, Howard J. *American Foreign Policy toward Latin America in the 80s and 90s. See Latin America.*

PERU

Ambrosi, Alain, and Nancy Thede, eds. *Video the Changing World. See Cinema.*

Americas Watch. *Peru under Fire: Human Rights since the Return to Democracy.* New Haven: Yale University Press, 1992.

Anderson, James. *Sendero Luminoso: A New Revolutionary Model?* London: 1987.

Andreas, Carol. *When Women Rebel: The Rise of Popular Feminism in Peru.* Westport, Conn.: L. Hill, 1985.

Aufderheide, Patricia. *Cross Cultural Film Guide. See Cinema.*

Black, Jan Knippers, ed. *Latin America. Its Problems and Its Promise. See Latin America.*

Blanco, Hugo. *Land or Death; The Peasant Struggle in Peru.* New York: Pathfinder Press, 1972.

Bourque, Susan Carolyn, and Kay Barbara Warren. *Women of the Andes: Patriarchy and Social Change in Two Peruvian Towns.* Ann Arbor: University of Michigan Press, 1981.

Bunster, Ximena, and Elsa M. Chaney. *Sellers and Servants: Working Women in Lima, Peru.* New York: Praeger, 1984.

Burt, Jo-Marie, and Aldo Panfichihi. *Peru: Caught in the Crossfire.* Jefferson City, Mo.: Peru Peace Network, 1992.

Cathelat, Marie-France, and Teresa Burga. *Perfil de la mujer peruana, 1980–1981.* Lima: Investigaciones Sociales Artísticas, Fondo del Libro del Banco Industrial del Perú, 1981.

Chilcote, Ronald H., and Joel C. Edelstein, eds. *Latin America: The Struggle with Dependency and Beyond. See Latin America.*

Collier, David. *Squatter Settlements and the Incorporation of Migrants into Urban Life: The Case of Lima.* Cambridge: Migration and Development Study Group, Center for International Studies, Massachusetts of Technology, 1976.

Deere, Carmen Diana. "Changing Social Relations of Production and Peruvian Peasant Women's Work." *Latin American Perspectives,* 1979.

Degregori, Carlos Ivan. *El surgimiento de Sendero Luminoso: Ayacucho 1969–1979.* Lima: Instituto de Estudios Peruanos, 1990.

Dietz, Henry A., and Richard J. Moore. *Political Participation in a Non-Electoral Setting: The Urban Poor in Lima, Peru.* Athens: Ohio University, Center for International Studies, 1979.

———. *Poverty and Problem-Solving under Military Rule: The Urban Poor in Lima, Peru.* Austin: University of Texas Press, 1980.

"Fatal Attraction: Peru's Shining Path." *NACLA Report on the Americas* 24, no. 4 (December, January 1990/91).

Ferris, H. B. *The Indians of Cuzco and Apurimac.* Millwood, N. J.: Kraus, 1964.

Fisher, John Robert. *Government and Society in Colonial Peru; The Intendant System 1784–1814.* London: Athlone Press, 1970.

Galeano, Eduardo H. *Open Veins of Latin America; Five Centuries of the Pillage of a Continent. See Latin America.*

Green, Duncan. *Faces of Latin America. See Latin America.*

Isbell, Billie Jean. *The Emerging Patterns of Peasants' Responses to Sendero Luminoso.* New York: The Consortium of Colunmbia University, Institute of Latin American & Iberian Studies and New York University Center for Latin American & Caribbean Studies, 1988.

———. *The Text and Contexts of Terror in Peru.* New York: Columbia University-New York University Consortium, 1991.

Jelin, Elizabeth, ed. *Women and Social Change in Latin America. See Latin America.*

Juan, Jorge. *Noticias secretas de America.* Norman: University of Oklahoma Press, 1978.

King, John. *Magical Reels: A History of Cinemas in Latin America. See Cinema.*

Kruijt, Dirk. *Perú, entre Sendero y los militares: seguridad y relaciones, civico-militares, 1950–1990.* Lima, Perú: D. Kruijt, 1991.

Lajo, Manuel. *Food processing in Peru, with particular reference to milk and balanced poultry feeds.* New York: United Nations, 1985.

Levillier, Roberto, ed. *Audiencia de Lima: correspondencia de presidentes y oidores. Documentos del Archivo de Indias.* Madrid: Imprenta de Juan Pueyo, 1922.

Lewis, Marvin A. *From Lima to Leticia: The Peruvian Novels of Mario Vargas Llosa.* Lanham, Md.: University Press of America, 1983.

Lewis, Robert Alden. *Employment, Income, and the Growth of the Barriadas in Lima, Peru.* Ithaca: Cornell University, 1973.

Lloyd, Peter Cutt. *The "Young Towns" of Lima: Aspects of Urbanization in Peru.* Cambridge, U.K., and New York: Cambridge University Press, 1980.

Lobo, Susan. *A House of My Own: Social Organization in the Squatter Settlements of Lima, Peru.* Tucson: University of Arizona Press, 1982.

Mariátegui, José Carlos. *Seven Interpetive Essays on Peruvian Reality.* Austin: University of Texas Press, 1971.

Masterson, Daniel M. *Militarism and Politics in Latin America: Peru from Sánchez Cerro to Sendero Luminoso.* New York: Greenwood Press, 1991.

McClintock, Cynthia, and Abraham Lowenthal, eds. *The Peruvian Experiment Reconsidered.* Princeton, N.J.: Princeton University Press, 1983.

McClintock, Cynthia. "Sendero Luminoso: Peru's Maoist Guerrillas." *Problems of Communism,* September, October 1983.

Meyerson, Julia. *'Tambo: Life in an Andean Village.* Austin: University of Texas Press, 1990.

Moseley, M. *The Incas and Their Ancestors: The Archaelogy of Peru*. New York: Thames and Hudson, 1992.

Oviedo, José. *Mario Vargas Llosa: la invención de una realidad*. Barcelona: Seix Barral, 1982.

Pacini, Deborah, and Christine Pranouemont, eds. *Coca and Cocaine: Effects on People and Policy in Latin America. See Latin America*.

Palmer, David Scott, ed. *The Shining Path of Peru*. New York: St. Martin's Press, 1992.

Poole, Deborah, and Gerardo Renique. *Peru: Time of Fear*. London and New York: Latin American Bureau, Monthly Review Press, 1992.

Portilla Salas, Pedro Hernán. *Apurimac, el perfil de un pueblo olvidado del Perú*. Lima: s.n., 1985.

Quijano, Aníbal. *Dominación y cultura; Lo cholo y el conflicto cultural en el Perú*. Lima: Mosca Azul Editores, 1980.

Reid, Michael. *Peru, Paths to Poverty*. London: Latin American Bureau, 1985.

Skidmore, Thomas E., and Peter H. Smith. *Modern Latin America. See Latin America*.

Soto, Hernando de. *The Other Path: The Invisible Revolution in the Third World. See Latin America*.

Stein, Steve. *Populism in Peru: The Emergence of the Masses and the Politics of Social Control*. Madison: University of Wisconsin Press, 1980.

Stokes, Susan C. "Politics and Latin American's Urban Poor: Reflections from a Lima Shanty Town." *Latin American Research Review* 26, 2 (1991): 75–109.

Tarazona-Sevillano, Gabriela, and John B. Reuter. *Sendero Luminoso and the Threat of Narcoterrorism*. New York: Praeger, 1990.

Valderrama Fernández, Ricardo. *Del tata mallka a la mama pacha: riego, sociedad y ritos en los Andes Peruanos*. Lima: Centro de Estudios y Promoción del Desarrollo, 1988.

Vargas Llosa, Mario. *La ciudad y los perros. See Colombia*.

———. *The Real Life of Alejandro Mayta. See Colombia*.

———. *The Time of the Hero. See Colombia*.

Zuidema, R. T. *Inca Civilization of Cuzco*. Austin: University of Texas Press, 1990.

PUERTO RICO

Alegría, Ricardo. *Música de Puerto Rico. See United States*.

Arrivi, Francisco. *Vejigantes; drama en tres actos*. Rio Piedras, Puerto Rico: Editorial Cultural, 1971.

Babin, María Teresa. *La cultura de Puerto Rico*. San Juan de Puerto Rico: Instituto de Cultura Puertorriqueña, 1970.

Carr, Raymond. *Puerto Rico: A Colonial Experiment*. New York: Vintage Books, 1984.

Mintz, Sidney Wilfred. *Worker in the Cane; A Puerto Rican Life History*. New Haven: Yale University Press, 1960.

Nash, June C., Helen Safa, and contributors. *Women and Change in Latin America. See Latin America*.

Ortiz Cofer, Judith. *The Latin Deli: prose and poetry. See United States*.

———. *The Line of the Sun: a novel. See United States*.

———. *Silent Dancing: A Partial Remembrance of a Puerto Rican Childhood. See United States*.

———. *Terms of Survival: poems. See United States*.

Ostoloza Bey, Margarita. *Política sexual en Puerto Rico*. Rio Piedras: Ediciones Huracán, 1989.

Pérez y Mena, Andrés Isidoro. *Speaking with the Dead: Development of Afro-Latin Religion Among Puerto Ricans in the U.S.: Study into the Interpretation of Civilizations. See United States*.

UNITED STATES

Acuña, Rodolfo. *Occupied America. See Latin America*.

Alegría, Ricardo. "Puerto Rico's Dances—Bomba y Plena." *Música de Puerto Rico* (Instituto de Cultura de Puerto Rico).

Anaya, Rodolfo, and Francisco Lomeli. *Aztlan: Essays on the Chicano Homeland*. Albuquerque: University of New Mexico Press, 1992.

Anzaldua, Gloria. *Borderlands (La frontera: The New Mestiza)*. San Francisco: Aunt Lute, 1987.

———. ed. *Making Face, Making Soul (Haciendo caras: Creative and Critical Perspectives by Women of Color)*. San Francisco: Aunt Lute Foundation Books, 1990.

Arrom, Silvia Marina. *The Women of Mexico City, 1790–1857. See Mexico*.

Banzhaf, Marion, and the ACT UP/New York Women and AIDS Book Group et al. *Women, AIDS, and Activism*. Boston: South End Press, 1990.

Barrera, M. *Ethnic Autonomy*. South Bend, Ind.: University of Notre Dame Press, 1988.

———. *Race and Class in the Southwest: A Theory of Racial Inequality*. South Bend, Ind.: University of Notre Dame Press, 1988.

Bautista Gutiérrez, Gloria. *Realismo mágico, cosmos latinoamericano: teoría y práctica. See Colombia*.

Bergquist, Charles, Ricardo Peñaranda, and Gonzalo Sánchez, eds. *Violence in Colombia: The Contemporary Crisis in Historical Perspective. See Colombia*.

Bhabha, Homi K., ed. *Nation and Narration*. London; New York: Routledge, 1990.

Boggs, Vernon. *Salsiology: Afro-Cuban Music and the Evolution of Salsa in New York City. See Cuba*.

Booth, John A. *The End and the Beginning: The Nicaraguan Revolution. See Nicaragua*.

Broad, Dave, and Lori Foster, eds. *The New World Order and the Third World*. New York: Black Rose Books, 1992.

Bushnell, David. *The Making of Modern Colombia. A Nation in Spite of Itself. See Colombia*.

Calderón de la Barca, Pedro. *La vida es sueño (English: Life is a dream)*. Woodbury, N.Y.: Barron's Educational Series, 1958.

Cantarow, E., ed. *Moving the Mountain: Women Working for Social Change*. New York: Feminist Press, 1980.

Caraway, Caren. *Aztec and Other Mexican Indian Designs. See Mexico*.

Carrera, John Wilshire. *Immigrant Students: Their Legal Right of Access to Public Schools: A Guide for Advocates and Educators*. Boston: Immigrant Student Program, National Coalition of Advocates for Students, 1989.

Castañeda Shular, Antonia, T. Ybarra-Frausto, and J. Sommers, eds. *Literatura chicana*. Englewood Cliffs, N.J.: Prentice-Hall, 1972.

Castilla-Speed, Lillian. *The Chicana Studies Index: Twenty Years of Gender Research. 1971–1991*. Berkeley and Los Angeles: Chicano Studies Library Publications Unit, University of California, 1992.

Castro, Tony. *Chicano Power: The Emergence of Mexican America*. New York: Saturday Review Press, 1974.

Cervantes, Lorna Dee. *Emplumada*. Pittsburgh: University of Pittsburgh Press, 1981.

Chávez, César. "The California Farm Workers' Struggle." *The Black Scholar* 7, 9 (June 1976): 16–19.

Chávez, Leo. *Shadowed Lives: Undocumented Immigrants in American Society*. Fort Worth, Tex.: Harcourt, Brace Jovanovich College Publisher, 1992.

Chomsky, Noam. *Deterring Democracy*. New York: Hill and Wang, 1992.

Cisneros, Sandra. *The House on Mango Street*. New York: Vintage Books, 1991.

———. *My Wicked, Wicked Ways*. Bloomington, Ind.: Third Woman Press, 1987.

———. *Woman Hollering Creek and Other Stories*. New York: Vintage Books, 1992.

Clendinnen, Inga. *Aztecs: An Interpretation. See Mexico*.

Cockcroft, James. *Outlaws in the Promised Land: Mexican Immigrant Workers and America's Future*. New York: Grove Press, 1986.

Connor, Walker, ed. *Mexican-Americans in Comparative Perspective*. Washington, D.C.: Urban Institute Press, 1985.

Conover, Ted. *Coyotes: A Journey Through the Secret World of America's Illegal Aliens*. New York: Vintage Books, 1987.

Cruz, Pablo. *Pablo Cruz and the American Dream: The Experience of an Undocumented Immigrant from Mexico*. Layton, Utah: Peregrine Smith, Inc., 1975.

Davidson, John. *The Long Road North*. Austin: Texas Monthly Press, 1981.

Davis, Marilyn P. *Mexican Voices, American Dreams: An Oral History of Mexican Immigration to the United States*. New York: Henry Holt, 1990.

Fell, Barry. *America B.C.: Ancient settlers in the New World. See Latin America*.

Fernández, Celestino. *The Border Patrol and News Media Coverage of Undocumented Workers*. Tucson: Mexican American Studies and Research Center, University of Arizona, 1981.

Fernández-Kelly, María Patricia. *For We Are Sold, I and My People: Women and Industry in Mexico's Frontier. See Mexico*.

Feyder, Linda, ed. *Shattering the Myth: Plays by Hispanic Women. See Latin America*.

Fine, Michelle. *Framing Dropouts: Notes on the Politics of an Urban Public High School*. Albany: State University of New York Press, 1991.

First, Joan McCarty. *New Voices: Immigrant Students in U.S. Public Schools*. Boston: National Coalition of Advocates for Students (100 Boylston St., Suite 737, Boston, MA 02116), 1988.

Franco, Jean. *Plotting Women: Gender and Representation in Mexico. See Mexico*.

Fussell, Betty Harper. *The Story of Corn*. New York: Knopf, 1992.

Galarza, Ernesto. *Barrio Boy*. South Bend, Ind.: University of Notre Dame Press, 1971.

García, Alma. "The Development of Chicana Feminist Discourse 1970–1980." *Gender and Society* 3, 2 (June 1989): 217–38.

Garza, Roberto J., ed. *Contemporary Chicano Theatre*. South Bend: University of Notre Dame Press, 1976.

Goldstein, Iago, ed. *Man's Image in Medicine and Anthropology*. Arden House Conference on Medicine and Anthropology, 1961. New York: International University Press, 1963.

Gonzáles, Rodolpho. *I am Joaquin. Yo soy Joaquin; an epic poem. With a chronology of people and events in Mexican and Mexican American history*. Toronto and New York: Bantam Books, 1972.

Gordan, Beverly M. "The Necessity of African American Epistemology for Educational Theory and Practice." *Boston Journal of Education* 172, 3 (1990).

Gutiérrez, Ramón A. *When Jesus Came, the Corn Mothers Went Away: Marriage, Sexuality, and Power in New Mexico, 1500–1846*. Stanford: Stanford University Press, 1991.

Guzmán, R. "Reasoned Radicalism: An Alternative to Fear and Institutional Oppression." *El Grito* 2, 4 (1969): 39–45.

Hammerback, J., et al. *A War on Words*. Westport, Conn.: Greenwood Press, 1985.

Heer, David M. *Undocumented Mexicans in the United States*. Cambridge and New York: Cambridge University Press, 1990.

Hemingway, Ernest. *The Old Man and the Sea*. New York: Collectors Reprints, Inc., 1990.

Hersh, Seymour M. *Kissinger: The Price of Power: Henry Kissinger in the Nixon White House*. London: Faber, 1983.

Hijuelos, Oscar. *The Mambo Kings Play Songs of Love*. New York: Farrar, Straus, Giroux, 1989.

Hinojosa, Rolando. *Claros varones de Belken* (Fair Gentlemen of Belken County). Tempe, Ariz.: Bilingual Press, 1986.

————. *Dear Rafe*. Houston: Arte Público Press, 1985.

————. *Klail City*. Houston: Arte Público Press, 1987.

————. *Partners in Crime: A Rafe Buenrostro Mystery*. Houston: Arte Público Press, 1985.

————. *Rites and Witnesses: A Comedy*. Houston: Arte Público Press, 1982.

————. *The Useless Servants*. Houston: Arte Público Press, 1993.

————. *The Valley: A Re-Creation in Narrative Prose of a Portfolio of Etchings*. Ypsilanti: Bilingual Press, 1983.

Hintz, Eugenio. *Historia y filmografía del cine uruguayo. See Uruguay.*

Hundley, Norris, Jr., ed. *The Chicano*. Santa Barbara: Clio Books, 1975.

Icaza, Jorge. *Huasipungo. The Villagers, a Novel. Authorized translation* (from the expanded 1953 version). Carbondale: Southern Illinois University Press, 1964.

Jensen, Joan M., and Darlis A. Miller, eds. *New Mexico Women: Intercultural Perspectives*. Albuquerque: University of New Mexico Press, 1986.

Juhasz, Alex. "Wave in the Media Environment: Camcorder Activism in AIDS Education." *Camera Obscura,* no. 28 (1993).

Keller, Gary D., Rafael J. Magallan, and Alma M. García. *Curriculum Resources in Chicano Studies: Undergraduate and Graduate*. Tempe, Ariz.: Bilingual Review Press, 1989.

Kibbe, Pauline Rochester. *Guide to Mexican History. See Mexico.*

Kinser, Sam. *Carnival, American style: Mardi Gras at New Orleans and Mobile*. Chicago: University of Chicago Press, 1990.

Knouse, S., et al., eds. *Hispanics in the Workforce*. Newbury Park: Sage Publications, 1992.

La pastorela. Houston: Arte Público Press.

Landau, Saul. *The Dangerous Doctrine: National Security and U.S. Foreign Policy*. Boulder, Colo., 1988.

Laviera, Tato. *American*. Houston: Arte Público Press, 1985.

————. *Mainstream Ethics (Etica corriente)*. Houston: Arte Público Press, 1988.

Lewis, Oscar. *The Children of Sánchez, Autobiography of a Mexican Family. See Mexico.*

Litvinoff, Barnet. *Fourteen Ninety Two: The Decline of Medievalism and the Rise of the Modern Age*. New York: Scribner's, Macmillan International, 1991.

Macías, Ana. *Against All Odds: The Feminist Movement in Mexico to 1940. See Mexico.*

Mansour, Mónica. *Poesía negra de América, antología. See Cuba.*

Martínez, Oscar Jaquez. *Troublesome Border*. Tucson: University of Arizona Press, 1988.

Martínez, T. *Voces: Readings from El Grito*. Berkeley and Los Angeles: Quinto Sol Publications, 1971.

Martz, John D. *Current History.* "Colombia at the Crossroads." *See Colombia.*

McWilliams, Carey. *North from Mexico: The Spanish-Speaking People of the United States*. New York: Greenwood Press, 1990.

Meier, Matt S. *Bibliography of Mexican American History*. Westport, Conn.: Greenwood Press, 1984.

Menchú, Rigoberta. *I, Rigoberta Menchú: An Indian Woman in Guatemala. See Guatemala.*

Minh-Ha, Trinh Thi. *Woman, Native, Other: Writing Postcoloniality and Feminism. See Cinema.*

Mohr, Nicholasa. *El Bronx Remembered*. New York: Harper & Row, 1975.

————. *In Nueva York*. Houston: Arte Público Press, 1988.

————. *Nilda*. New York: Harper & Row, 1973.

————. *Rituals of Survival: A Woman's Portfolio*. Houston: Arte Público Press, 1985.

Moraga, Cherrie. "Este puente, mi espalda: voces de mujeres tercermundistas en los Estados Unidos," reviewed by Erica Frouman-Smith. *The Americas Review* 19, no. 1 (Spring 1991): 117–19.

Morales, Alejandro. *The Brick People*. Houston: Arte Público Press, 1988.

————. *Death of an Anglo*. Tempe, Ariz.: Bilingual Press, 1988.

Muñoz, Carlos. *Youth, Identity and Power*. London: Verso, 1989.

Nathan, Debbie. *Women and Other Aliens: Essays from the US-Mexico Border*. El Paso: Cinco Puntos Press, 1991.

National Association for Chicano Studies; Teresa Cordova, chair, et al. *Chicana Voices: Intersections of Class, Race, and Gender*. Austin: Center for Mexican American Studies, 1986.

Noriega, Chon A., ed. *Chicanos and Film: Essays on Chicano Representation and Resistance*. New York: Garland, 1992.

Ortiz Cofer, Judith. *The Latin Deli: prose and poetry*. Athens: University of Georgia Press, 1993.

————. *The Line of the Sun: a novel*. Athens: University of Georgia Press, 1989.

————. *Silent Dancing: A Partial Remembrance of a Puerto Rican Childhood*. Houston: Arte Publico Press, 1990.

————. *Terms of Survival: poems*. Houston: Arte Público Press, 1987.

Paredes, Américo. *With His Pistol in His Hand*. Austin: University of Texas Press, 1958.

Pastor, Robert A., and Jorge G. Castañeda. *Limits to Friendship: The United States and Mexico*. New York: Knopf, 1988.

Pearce, Jenny. *Colombia: Inside the Labyrinth. See Colombia.*

Pérez, Ramón "Tianguis." *Diary of an Undocumented Immigrant*. Houston: Arte Público Press, 1991.

Pérez y Mena, Andrés Isidoro. *Speaking With the Dead: Development of Afro-Latin Religion Among Puerto Ricans in the U.S.: A Study into the Interpretation of Civilizations in the New World*. New York: AMS Press, 1991.

Pessar, Patricia R., ed. *When Borders Don't Divide. Labor*

Migration and Refugee Movements in the Americas. Staten Island, N.Y.: Center for Migration Studies, 1988.

Peters, Cynthia, ed. *Collateral Damage: The "New World Order" at Home and Abroad.* Boston: South End Press, 1992.

Piri, Thomas. *Down These Mean Streets.* New York: Knopf, 1967.

Portes, Alejandro and Alex Steick. *City on the Edge: The Transformation of Miami. See Cuba.*

Prago, Albert. *Strangers in Their Own Land.* New York: Four Winds Press, 1973.

Quiñones, Juan Gómez. *Chicano Politics: Reality and Promise, 1940–1990.* Albuquerque: University of New Mexico Press, 1991.

Rasmussen, Waldo, ed. *The Latin American Arts of the Twentieth Century.* New York: New York Museum of Modern Art Department of Publication, 1993.

Reimers, David M. *Still the Golden Door: The Third World Comes to America.* New York: Columbia University Press, 1985.

Richardson, Laurel, and Verta Taylor. *Feminist Frontiers III.* New York: McGraw-Hill, 1993.

———. eds. *Feminist Frontiers II: Rethinking Sex, Gender, and Society,* 2d ed. New York: Random House, 1989.

Rios, Alberto. *Five Indiscretions.* Riverdale-on-Hudson; New York: The Sheep Meadow Press, distributed by Persea Books, 1985.

Rios, Alberto. *The Iguana Killer: Twelve Stories of the Heart.* Lewiston, ID and New York: Blue Moon and Confluence Press, distributed to the trade by Kampmann, 1984.

———. *Teodoro Luna's Two Kisses: poems.* New York: W. W. Norton, 1990.

Rivera, Edward. *Family Installments: Memories of Growing up Hispanic.* Harmondsworth, Middlesex; New York: Penguin Books, 1983.

Rodríguez, Richard. *Hunger of Memory: The Education of Richard Rodríguez.* Toronto and New York: Bantam Books, 1983.

Rosaldo, Renato, Robert A. Calvert, and Gustav L. Seligmann, eds. *Chicano: The Evolution of a People.* Minneapolis: Winston Press, 1973.

Rose, Margaret. "Traditional and Non-traditional Patterns of Female Activism in the United Farm Workers of America, 1962–1980." *Frontiers* 9, 1 (1990): 26–30.

Rubenstein, Anne. "Seeing Through AIDS: Media Activists Join Forces with the NYC Department of Health." *The Independent* 16, no. 1.

Ruiz, Vicky L. *Cannery Women, Cannery Lives: Mexican Women, Unionization, and the California Food Processing Industry, 1930–1950.* Albuquerque: University of New Mexico Press, 1987.

Ruiz, Vicky, and S. Tiano, eds. *Women on the U.S.-Mexico Border: Responses to Change.* Boston: Allen & Unwin, 1987.

Sale, Kirkpatrick. *The Conquest of Paradise: Christopher Columbus and the Columbian Legacy.* New York: Knopf, 1991.

Sassen, S., et al. "Coming North: Latino & Caribbean Immigration." *NACLA Report on the Americas* 26, 1 (July 1992): 14–33.

Schorr, Alan Edward. *Refugee and Immigrant Resource Directory, 1990–91.* Juneau, Alas: Denali Press, 1990.

Shohat, Ella. "Imaging Terra Incognita: The Disciplinary Gaze of Empire." *Public Culture* 3, 2 (Spring 1991).

Shorris, Earl. "Borderline Cases: The Violent Passage Across the Rio Grande." *Harper's Magazine,* August 1990, 68–78.

Skidmore, Thomas E., and Peter H. Smith. *Modern Latin America. See Latin America.*

Somerlott, Robert. *Death of the Fifth Sun.* New York: Viking, 1987.

Takaki, Ronald, ed. *From Different Shores: Perspectives on Race and Ethnicity in America.* New York: Oxford University Press, 1987.

Tatum, Charles, ed. *Mexican American Literature.* Chicago: Harcourt Brace Jovanovich Publishers, 1990.

Thomas, Piri. *Down These Mean Streets.* New York: Knopf, distributed by Random House, 1981.

Twain, Mark. *The Adventures of Huckleberry Finn.* Edited and with introductions by Brander Matthews and Dixon Wecter. New York: Harper, 1948.

Usabel, Gaiska de. *The High Noon of American Films in Latin America.* Ann Arbor: UMI Research Press, 1982.

Valdez, Luis. *Zoot Suit and Other Plays.* Houston: Arte Público Press, 1992.

Valdez, R. Burciaga, Kevin F. McCarthy, and Connie Malcolm Moreno. *An Annotated Bibliography of Sources of Mexican Immigration.* Santa Monica, Calif.: The Rand Corporation, 1987.

Villarreal, Roberto E., and Norma G. Hernández, eds. *Latinos and Political Coalitions: Political Empowerment for the 1990s.* New York: Greenwood Press, 1991.

Villaseñor, Víctor. *Rain of Gold.* Houston: Arte Público Press, 1991.

Walker, Thomas W. *Nicaragua, the Land of Sandino. See Nicaragua.*

Wallerstein, Immanuel. *The Modern World-System.* London: Academic Press, 1974.

Weatherford, J. McIver. *Native Roots: How the Indians Enriched America.* New York: Crown, 1991.

Weatherford, Jack. *Indian Givers: How the Indians of the Americas Transformed the World. See Latin America.*

Weis, Lois, and Michelle Fine, eds. *Beyond Silenced Voices.* New York: State University of New York Press, 1993.

White, Hayden V. *Tropics of Discourse: Essays in Cultural Criticism. See Cinema.*

Wiarda, Howard J. *American Foreign Policy toward Latin America in the 80s and 90s. See Latin America.*

Wilford, John Noble. *The Mysterious History of Columbus: An Exploration of the Man, the Myth, and the Legacy.* New York: Knopf, 1991.

Woodward, Bob. *The Commanders*. New York: Simon & Schuster, 1991.

Yudice, George, Jean Franco, and Juan Flores, eds. *On Edge: The Crisis of Contemporary Latin American Culture. See Latin America.*

Zeta Acosta, Oscar. *Revolt of the Cockroach People. See Latin America.*

URUGUAY

Bergmann, Emilie, et al. *Women, Culture, and Politics in Latin America. Seminar on Feminism and Culture in Latin America. See Latin America.*

Black, Jan Knippers, ed. *Latin America. Its Problems and Its Promise. See Latin America.*

Borges, Jorge Luis. *The Aleph and Other Stories, 1933–1969.* New York: Bantam Books, 1979.

Castro-Klaren, Sara, Sylvia Molloy, and Beatriz Sarlo, eds. *Women's Writing in Latin America: An Anthology. See Latin America.*

Cervantes Saavedra, Miguel de. *Don Quixote*. London: Bloomsbury Books, 1993.

Guiraldes, Ricardo. *Don Segundo Sombra*. Long Island City: Las Americas, 1972.

Hernández, José. *Martín Fierro*. Buenos Aires: Universidad de Buenos Aires, revista de la Facultad de Filosofía y Letras, 1972.

Hintz, Eugenio. *Historia y filmografía del cine uruguayo*. Montevideo: Ediciones de la Plaza, 1988.

Martínez Estrada, Ezequiel. *Radiografía de la pampa,* 2d ed. Buenos Aires: Losada, 1957.

McLuhan, Herbert Marshall, and Fiore Quentin. *The Medium is the Message. See Cinema.*

Miller, Francesca. *Latin American Women and the Search for Social Justice. See Latin America.*

Pastor Legnani, Margarita, and Rosario Vico de Pena. *Filmografía uruguaya*. Montevideo: Cinemateca Uruguaya, 1973.

Skidmore, Thomas E., and Peter H. Smith. *Modern Latin America. See Latin America.*

Sosnowski, Saul. *Represión, exilio y democracia: la cultura uruguaya*. College Park and Montevideo: University of Maryland and Ediciones de la Banda Oriental, 1987.

Timerman, Jacobo. *Prisoner Without a Name, Cell Without a Number. See Chile.*

VENEZUELA

Acosta Saignes, Miguel. *Estudios de etnología antigua de Venezuela*. Caracas: UCV, Ediciones de la Biblioteca Central, 1961.

————. *Vida de los esclavos negros en Venezuela*. Caracas: EBUC, 1967.

Aguado, Fray Pedro de. *Historia del descubrimiento y de la fundación de la gobernación y provincia de Venezuela*. Caracas: Imprenta Nacional, 1913–15.

Aguirre, Jesús M., and Marcelino Bisbal. *El nuevo cine venezolano*. Caracas: Editorial Ateneo de Caracas, 1980.

Anales para la historia de Venezuela 2: 49–50. (Caracas: Biblioteca de la Academia Nacional de la Historia.)

Anderson, B. *Imagined Communities*. London: Verso, 1987.

Araujo, Orlando. *La obra literaria en Enrique Bernardo Núñez*. Caracas: Monte Avila, 1980.

Armes, Roy. *Third World Film Making and the West. See Cinema.*

Arreaza, E. *Violencia cultural en Venezuela*. Maracaibo: Ediluz, 1982.

Arreaza-Camera, Emperatriz. "Cubagua, or the Search for Venezuelan National Identity." *Iowa Journal of Cultural Studies*, 1993.

Arvelo, Alberto, and Sigfrido Gever. *Juan Felix Sánchez*. Caracas: Fundación La Salle de Ciencias Naturales, 1981.

Barnes, Sandra T., ed. *Africa's Ogun; Old World and New. See Latin America.*

Brito, F. *Historia económica y social de Venezuela* 2. Caracas: UCV, Direc. Cultural., 1966.

Brito-Figueroa, F. *Las insurrecciones de los esclavos negros en sociedad colonial Venezolana*. Caracas: Cantaclaro, 1961.

Burton, Julianne. *Latin American Perspectives*. "The Camera as Gun: Two Decades of Culture and Resistance in Latin America." *See Cinema.*

Cardona, Miguel. *Temas del folklore Venezolano*. Caracas: Ministerio de Educación, 1964.

Carrera, G. *Una nación llamada Venezuela*. Caracas: Monte Avila, 1984.

Carrera, P. *Cronistas e historiadores*. Caracas: EBUC, 1982.

Casas, Bartolomé de las. *Historia de las Indias (1559). See Latin America.*

Chacon, A. *Curiepe*. Caracas: EBUC, 1980.

————. *Contra la dependencia*. Caracas: Síntesis Dosmil, 1973.

Churchill, Ward. *Fantasies of the Master Race: Literature, Cinema and the Colonization of American Indians. See Cinema.*

Cine-ULA. *Cubagua: un filme de Michael New*. Merida: Ediciones del Dpto. de Cine, 1987.

Cinemateca Nacional. *Cronología del cine en Venezuela*. Caracas: Cuadernos de la Cinemateca Nacional, 1989.

Civrieux, Marc de. *Watunna: un ciclo de creación en el Orinoco*. Caracas: Monte Avila Editores, 1992.

Columbus, Christopher. *Personal Narrative of the First Voyage of Columbus to America. See Latin America.*

Coppens, W. *Inventario de películas realizadas en las zonas indígenas de Venezuela*. Caracas: Instituto Autonomo Biblioteca Nacional, 1983.

Crawford, Ian Peter, and David Turton, eds. *Film as Ethnography. See Cinema.*

Ewell, Judith. *Venezuela: A Century of Change.* Stanford: Stanford University Press, 1984.

Franco, Jean. *Plotting Women: Gender and Representation in Mexico. See Mexico.*

Fusco, Coco, ed. *Reviewing Histories. Selections from New Latin American Cinema. See Cinema.*

Gaines, J. *Cultural Critique.* "Race and Gender in Feminist Film Theory." *See Cinema.*

García Márquez, Gabriel. *No One Writes to the Colonel and Other Stories. See Colombia.*

Gerbani, V. *Mi Pàdre, El Immigrante.* Caracas: Editorial Arte, 1970.

Getino, Octavio. *Plural.* "Cine indigenista: entre la inmovilidad y el cambio." *See Cinema.*

Goldman, Karen S. "A 'Third' Feminism? Solveig Hoogesteijn's *Macu: The Policeman's Wife.*" *Iris* 13 (1991): 87–95.

Goldston, Iago, ed. *Man's Image in Medicine and Anthropology. See United States.*

Hall, Doug, and Sally Jo Fifer, eds. *Illuminating Video: An Essential Guide to Video Art. See Cinema.*

Handbook of Latin American Studies. See Latin America.

Harris, Wilson. *Palace of the Peacock.* London: Faber and Faber, 1960.

Herman, D. L., ed. *Democracy in Latin America: Colombia and Venezuela. See Colombia.*

Jiménez Graziani, Morella A. *La esclavitud indígena en Venezuela, siglo XVI.* Caracas: Academia Nacional de la Historia, 1986.

King, John. *Magical Reels: A History of Cinemas in Latin America. See Cinema.*

King, John, Ana López, and Manuel Alvarado, eds. *Mediating Two Worlds: Cinematic Encounters in the Americas. See Cinema.*

Kinser, Sam. *Carnival, American style: Mardi Gras at New Orleans and Mobile. See United States.*

Klein, Herbert S. *African Slavery in Latin America and the Caribbean. See Latin America.*

Lerner, Elisa. *Crónicas ginecológicas.* Caracas: Linea Editores, 1984.

Lizot, Jacques. *Tales of the Yanomami.* Cambridge: Cambridge University Press. Canto Ed., 1991.

Lockhart, James, and Stuart B. Schwartz. *Early Latin America: A History of Colonial Spanish America and Brazil. See Latin America.*

Lombardi. *The Decline and Abolition of Negro Slavery in Venezuela.* Westport, Conn.: Greenwood, 1971.

López, A. *Wide Angle.* "The Melodrama in Latin America." *See Cinema.*

López, Carmen A. *Crisis fiscal e industrialización en el desarrollo latinoamericano. See Latin America.*

Luxner, L. "Building on the Ruins." *Americas* 43, 3 (1991): 39.

Malave, Héctor. *Formación historica del antidesarrollo de Venezuela.* Caracas: Ed. Rocinante, 1975.

Margolies, Luise. *The Venezuelan Peasant in Country and City.* Caracas: EDIVA (Apdo. 3305, Caracas), 1979.

Masur, Gerhard. *Simón Bolívar.* Albuquerque: University of New Mexico Press, 1969.

Michaels, Eric. *Bad Aboriginal Art: Tradition, Media and Technological Horizons. See Cinema.*

Minh-Ha, Trinh Thi. *Woman, Native, Other: Writing Postcoloniality and Feminism. See Cinema.*

Miranda, Julio E. "El nuevo cine venezolano." *Cuadernos Hispanoamericano,* no. 481 (1990): 49–60. (Madrid: Ediciones Culturales Hispánica.)

Moore, Rachael. *Visual Anthropology Review.* "Marketing Alterity." *See Cinema.*

Moreno Fraginals, Manuel. *Africa in Latin America: Essays on History, Culture, and Socialization. See Latin America.*

Mulvey, L., and C. Penley. *Feminist Film Theory. See Cinema.*

Naipaul, V. S. *The Loss of Eldorado: A History.* New York: Vintage Books, 1984.

Nichols, Bill. *Representing Reality: Issues and Concepts in Documentary. See Cinema.*

Núñez, Enrique Bernardo. *Cubagua.* Caracas: Monte Avila Editores, 1987.

Oropeza, J. *Para fijar un rostro: notas sobre la novelistica venezolana actual.* Caracas: Vadell Hermanos, 1984.

Otero Silva, Miguel. *Cuando quiero llorar no lloro.* Caracas: Editorial Tiempo Nuevo, 1970.

Perera, M. "Cuevas y cerros en la tradición oral y ceremonial de los amerindios de Venezuela." *Revista de Indias* 51, 193 (September/December 1991). (Madrid.)

Pick, Zuzana. *The New Latin American Cinema: A Continental Project. See Cinema.*

———. ed. *Latin American Film-makers and the Third Cinema. See Cinema.*

Picón, M. *De la conquista a la independencia.* México: FCE, 1969.

Picón-Salas, Mariano. *Pedro Claver, el santo de los esclavos.* Madrid: Ediciones de la Revista de Occidente, 1969.

Pines, Jim, and Paul Wileman. *Questions of Third Cinema. See Cinema.*

Pollack-Eltz, Angelina. *Religión africana en Venezuela.* Caracas: EBUC.

———. *Cultos afroamericanos.* Caracas: UCAB, 1979.

Pribam, D. *Female Spectators. See Cinema.*

Raleigh, Sir Walter. *The Discovery of the Large, Rich, and Beautiful Empire of Guiana with a relation of the Great and Golden City of Manca.* London: Robert Robinson, 1596.

Ricard, Robert. *Spiritual Conquest of Mexico. See Mexico.*

Rout, Leslie B. *The African Experience in Spanish America, 1502 to the Present Day. See Latin America.*

Rowe, William, and Vivian Schelling. *Memory and Modernity: Popular Culture in Latin America. See Latin America.*

Sanoja, Mario, and Iraida Vargas. *Antiguas formaciones y modos de producción venezolano.* Caracas: Monte Avila, 1978.

Sarmiento, Domingo Faustino. *Civilización y barbarie; vidas de Quiroga, Aldao i el Chacho. See Argentina.*

Schwartzman, Karen. "A Descriptive Chronology of Films by Women in Venezuela." *Journal of Film and Video* 44, no. 3–4 (Fall-Winter 1992–93).

————. "National Cinema in Translation: The Politics of Film Exhibition Culture." *Wide Angle* 16, no. 3 (February 1995): 66–99.

————. "The Seen of the Crime." *Frontiers* 15, no. 1 (1994).

————. *"Time is Like a Round Thing: An Interview with Solveig Hoogesteijn."* Unpublished, 1992.

Serbin, A., and O. González. *Indigenismo y autogestión.* Caracas: Monte Avila, 1980.

Shohat, Ella. *Public Culture.* "Imaging Terra Incognita: The Disciplinary Gaze of Empire." *See United States.*

Shohat, Ella, and Robert Stam. *Unthinking Eurocentrism: Multiculturalism and the Media. See Cinema.*

Silva Michelena, Jose Agustín. *Crisis de la democracia.* Caracas: CENDES-UCV, 1970.

————, eds. *Latin America: Peace, Democratization and Economic Crisis. See Latin America.*

————. *Política y bloques de poder: crisis en el sistema mundial.* México: Siglo Veintiuno Editores, 1976.

Smole, William J. *The Yanoama Indians: A Cultural Geography.* Austin: University of Texas Press, 1976.

Stam, Robert. *Cineaste.* "Rewriting 1492: Cinema and the Columbus Debate." *See Cinema.*

Taussig, Michael. *Shamanism, Colonialism and the Wild Man. See Latin America.*

Tobing-Rony, Fatimah. "Those Who Squat, Those Who Sit: The Visualizing of Race in the 1895 Films of Félix-Louis Regnault." *See Cinema.*

Trelles Plazaola, Luis. "Solveig Hoogesteijn." In *Cine y mujer en America Latina. Directoras de largometrajes de ficción,* 169–92. Rio Piedras: Editorial de la Universidad de Puerto Rico, 1991.

Troconis de Veracochea. *Documentos para el estudio de los esclavos negros en Venezuela.* Caracas: B.A.N.H., 1969.

Turner, Terence. *Visual Anthropology Review.* "The Social Dynamics of Video Media in an Indigenous Society." *See Brazil.*

Wright, Winthrop R. *Café con leche: Race, Class, and National Image in Venezuela.* Austin: University of Texas Press, 1990.

Zambrano, Iván. *Cine Venezolano.* Merida: ULA, 1984.

Subject Index

Ley del monte, la;
Para Onde?;
Pintamos el mundo de colores;
Povo do veneno, o;
Taking Aim;
Tigra, la;
Txai Macedo;
Urihi: Tierra Yanomami;
Video nas aldeias;
Yo hablo a Caracas

Ancient Ruins:
Chichén-Itzá;
Galeano: Memoria, mito, Dios, mensaje;
Mexico: A vuelo de pajaro;
Monte Albán;
Museo Nacional de Antropología;
"Popol Vuh";
Querido diario;
Teotihuacan;
Uxmal

Andean Culture and History:
Así pensamos;
Bolivia desconocida: Lago Titicaca;
Cafe Norte y Sur;
Camino de las almas;
Corage del pueblo, el;
Deuda interna, la;
Gran Poder;
Gregorio;
Hieleros del Chimborazo;
Jallq'a: Identidad y tejido, los;
Llamero y el sal, el;
Marcha por la vida;
Ni leche, ni la Gloria;
No habrá más penas ni olvido;
Puente de Ichu, el;
Tupac Amaru;
Venas de la tierra, las

Anti-Communism:
Ana Mendieta: Fuego de tierra;
Cruz invertida, la;
Dialogo, el;
Elvia: Tierra y libertad;
Hombre de Maisinicu, el;
Krik? Krak!;
Long Road Home, the;
Me dejaron muerto ahi;
Memorias de subdesarollo;
No habrá más penas ni olvido;
Pubis Angélical;
Su nombre, a

Archaelogy: (see Ancient Ruins)

Argentine Politics:
Algunas mujeres;
Allá lejos y hace tiempo;
Cruz invertida, la;
Historia oficial, la;
Madres de la Plaza de Mayo, las;
No habrá más penas ni olvido;
Pubis Angélical;
Voz de los pañuelos, la

Argentine Culture, History, and Politics: (see all in Argentina chapter)

Armed Insurrection: (see Insurgency)

Army:
Alsino y el condor;
Boca del lobo, la;
De donde son los cantantes;
Desaparecidos;
Enamorada;
Entre el diablo y los tigres;
Global Dissent;
Me dejaron muerto ahi;
Panama Deception, the;
Que Hacer?;
Quilombo;
Santiago Atitlan: Canto de un pueblo;
Vida es una sola, la

Artifacts: (see Ancient Ruins)

Artisans: (see Folk Art)

Artists: (see Arts)

Arts:
1492 Revisited;
Amada;
Amerika, tierra incognita;
Ana Mendieta: Fuego de tierra;
Aqui en esta esquina;
Babalu;
Bailar: Journey of a Latin Dance Co., a;
Barrio canta con Johnny Colón, el;
Barroco;
Bella del Alhambra, la;
Bésame mucho;
Bolivar sinfonía tropikal;
Buried Mirror/Conflict of the Gods;
Cafe Norte y Sur;
Canto a la vida;

Espacios de Juan Rulfo;
Foto que recorre el mundo, una;
Frida;
Galeano: Memoria, mito, Dios, mensaje;
Gregorio y el mar;
Heredia;
Ignacio Piñeiro;
João do Pifi;
Machito;
Mirta Aguirre;
My Filmmaking, My Life (M. Landeta);
Oración;
Oswald: um Homem de Profissao;
Poder del jefe, el;
Poesia de Nicolás Guillén, la;
Rebeldes del Sur, los;
Rigoberta Menchu;
Sones Cubanos;
Tupac Amaru;
Veces miro mi vida, a

Black History and Culture: (see Afro-)

Bolivian Culture, History, and Politics: (see all in Bolivia chapter)

Border Issues:
1492 Revisited;
Aca, de este lado, de;
Alma punk;
Corrido, el;
Dialogo, el;
Esperanza;
Iracema;
Krik? Krak!;
Long Road Home, the;
New Tijuana, the;
Sin fronteras;
TLC: Detras de la Mentira;
Troubled Harvest;
Uneasy Neighbors;
Visa para un sueño;
Work in Progress

Brazilian Culture, History and Politics:
Alafin Oyo;
Amazônia: Vozes da floresta;
Antonio das Mortes;
Bairro do Recife a dança da Vida;
Bejo na boca;
Benedita da silva;
Bola na trave;
Bye Bye Brazil;
Cabra marcado para morrer, um;

Clips of Lula's Presidential Campaign;
Construção da escrita;
Cor do sexo, a;
Cordel;
Crisis in Brazil—Part 1;
Espirito da televisão, o;
Favelas;
Forbidden Land, the;
Fundação do Brasil, a;
Garotos do futuro;
Hail Umbanda;
Hay lugar;
João do Pifi;
Juego de la deuda, el;
Light Memories of Rio;
Mentiras & humilhações;
Mulheres da boca;
Mulheres negras;
Mulheres no canavial;
Nascimiento do passo;
Orfeu Negro;
P'Tamuna;
Para Onde?;
Povo do veneno, o;
Quando o Crioulo danca;
Que bon te ver viva;
Quilombo;
Santa Marta;
Seca;
Sexo na classe;
Temporada de caza;
Tierra para Rose;
Varela en Xingu

Bureaucracy:
Chapucerías;
L.E.A.R.;
Más vale tarde que nunca;
Muerte de un burocrata, la;
Plaff!;
Se permuta;
Tecnicas del duelo;
Vecinos;
Yo tambien te haré llorar

Business:
Amazonas, el negocio de este mundo;
Amor, mujeres y flores;
Escandalo, el;
Hands Off Cuba, TV Teach-In I & II;
Isla das flores;
Ni leche, ni la Gloria;
Polvo rojo;
Secuestro;
TLC: Detras de la Mentira;

International Relations: (see International Business, Imperialism)

Invasions: (see Foreign Intervention)

Journalism:

Kidnapping:

Labor Issues:

San Pedro y sus parranderos;
Sangue frio, a;
Santiago Atitlan: Canto de un pueblo;
Seca;
Secreto de Romelia, el;
Sones Cubanos;
Su nombre, a;
Tamboron del Indio Pascual Abaj, el;
Teatro Campesino: Veinte Años, el;
Tenemos sabor, y;
Terra nova;
Tiempo de mujeres;
Tiempo de victoria;
Tierra para Rose;
Tigra, la;
Todos Santos Cuchumatan;
Todos Santos: los sobrevivientes;
Troubled Harvest;
Venas de la tierra, las;
Vida es una sola, la;
Viene naciendo en la caña la fibre;
Winds of Memory;
Work in Progress;
Xente, pois nao, o

Peer Pressure/Social Conformity:
Alma punk;
Bailar: Journey of a Latin Dance Co., a;
Carrousel;
Ciudad y los perros, la;
Danny;
Entre amigos;
Estrellas en la esquina;
Geronima;
Gregorio;
Isla para Miguel, una;
Memorias de subdesarrollo;
Motivos de Luz, los;
Quien lo diría?;
Rodrigo D. (No future);
Semilla escondida, la;
Temporada de caza;
Vendidos, los

Performance: (see Theater)

Peronism:
No habra más penas ni olvido

Petroleum: (see Oil)

Pesticides:
Amor, mujeres y flores;
Troubled Harvest;
Work in Progress

Photography:
Cien niños esperando un tren;
Crisis in Brazil—Part 1;
Foto que recorre el mundo, una;
Iré a Santiago;
Light Memories of Rio;
Meta Mayan II;
Orinoko, nuevo mundo

Plantations:
Alma punk;
Ananeko;
Buried Mirror/The Age of Gold;
Mulheres no canavial;
Todos Santos Cuchumatan;
Ultima cena, la

Poetry:
Amor y dolor;
Buried Mirror/The Age of Gold;
Cantar al sol;
Cartas del Parque;
Cuatro mujeres, cuatro autores;
Donde son los cantantes, de;
Dueno del tiempo;
Hasta la Reina Baila el Danzón;
Heredia;
Latino Images;
Mentiras & Humilhacoes;
Mujer de Nadie, la;
No me olvides;
Oración;
Poesía de Nicolás Guillén, la;
Tamboron del Indio Pascual Abaj, el;
Tango Bar

Police:
Algunas mujeres;
Chile: Sueños prohibidos;
Clandestinos;
Contra corriente;
Crisis in Brazil—Part 1;
Crónica de un Fraude;
Cruz invertida, la;
Cuarteles de invierno;
Desaparecidos;
Dia em que Dorival encarou a guarda, o;
Diario inconcluso;
Disparen a matar;
Garotos do futuro;
Gregorio;
Hasta vencer;
Hay lugar;
Lucha libre;
Macu, la mujer del policía;

Pollution: (see Environment)

Popular Movements/Grassroots Organizations:

Unions: (see Labor Issues)

Urban Life/Urbanization:
2371 Second Ave: An East Harlem Story;
1992;
Abril, el mes más cruel;
Alem de trabalhador, Negro;
Alma punk;
Alô São Paulo;
Amas de casa;
Amor y dolor;
Amor a la vuelta de la esquina;
Arepa Colombiana en Nueva York;
Bairro do Recife a dança da vida;
Barrio canta con Johnny Colón, el;
Bejo na boca;
Benedita;
Bola na trave;
Bye Bye Brazil;
Cafe Norte y Sur;
Chapucerías;
Clandestinos;
Clase de Organo, la;
Conozco a las tres;
Cor do sexo, a;
Crisis in Brazil–Part 1;
Crónicas ginecológicas;
Danny;
Despues del terramoto;
Disparen a matar;
Dolores;
Drugs on the Lower East Side;
Dueno del tiempo;
Escandalo, el;
Espectador, el;
Esperanza;
Esquinas da vida;
Estrellas en la esquina;
Favelas;
Febrero;
Futuro esta en nuestras manos, el;
Garotos do futuro;
Gregorio;
Hasta cierto punto;
Hasta vencer;
Hay lugar;
Hola Hemingway;
Hombre mirando al sur este;
Hora de la Estrella, la;
Improper Conduct;
Infatigable Santiago, la;
Iracema;
Iré a Santiago;
Isla para Miguel, una;
Jau;

Juego de la deuda, el;
Krik? Krak!;
Latino Images;
Light Memories of Rio;
Lucero;
Lucha libre;
Macu, la mujer del policía;
Marley normal;
Masp Movie, the;
Memorias de subdesarrollo;
Mi pecado es quererte;
Mirada de Myriam, la;
Motivos de Luz, los;
Muerte de un burocrata, la;
Mujer transparente;
Mujeres del Planeta;
New Tijuana, the;
Ni leche, ni la Gloria;
Niños deudores;
No les pedimos un viaje a la luna;
Onward Christian Soldiers;
Operación, la;
Orfeu Negro;
Pájaros tirando la escopeta, los;
Pintamos el mundo de colores;
Piropo, el;
Plaff!;
Radio que se ve, la;
Retornado a Chile;
Retrato de Teresa;
Rey del mandolin, el;
Rodrigo D. (No future);
Romance del Palmar, el;
Sangue frio, a;
Santa Marta;
Se permuta;
Seca;
Secuestro;
Sobreviviente de oficio;
Soy un delincuente;
Story of Fausta;
Su Mama que hace?, y;
Super, el;
Tantas vidas, una historia;
Temporada de caza;
Todos Santos: los sobrevivientes;
Vals de la Habana Vieja;
Venezuela: Febrero "27";
Yo no soy una cualquiera;
Yo tambien te haré llorar

Urban Planning:
Abril, el mes más cruel;
Alô São Paulo;
Bairro do Recife a dança da vida;

Women Directors:

Work/Employment: (see Labor Issues)

Writers: (see Literary Adaptation, Literature)

Distributors Index

Adler Video Marketing Inc.
Old Dominion Drive, Suite 360
McLean, VA 22101
Tel: 703-556-8880
Fax: 703-556-9288

American Federation of Arts
41 E. 65th St.
New York, NY 10021
Tel: 212-988-7700

Artcom
70 Twelfth St., 3rd Fl.
San Francisco, CA 94103
Tel: 415-431-7524
Fax: 415-431-7841

The Altschul Group
930 Pitner Ave.
Evanston, IL 60202
Tel: 708-328-6700
Fax: 708-328-6706

Baker & Taylor Books
Mt. Olive Rd.
Commerce, GA 30599
Tel: 800-775-2600

Barr Films
PO Box 7878
12801 Schabarum Ave.
Irwindale, CA 91706-7878
Tel: 818-338-7878
Fax: 818-814-2672

Canyon Cinema
2325 Third St., Suite 338
San Francisco, CA 94107
Tel: 415-626-2255

Carrefour International
5192 St. Denis

Montréal, Québec H2J 2M2 CANADA
Tel: 514-272-2247
Fax: 514-272-1929

CDI
Isa Castro
Rua 13 de Maio, São Paulo BRAZIL
Tel: 5511-288-4694
Fax: 5511-287-2259

Center for Cuban Studies
124 W. 23rd St.
New York, NY 10011
Tel: 212-242-0559
Fax: 212-242-1937

Center for International Media Research
Leonard Henny
Mijndensedijk 74-NL3631
NS Nieuwersluis HOLLAND
Tel: 3129-43-3459
Fax: 3129-43-1877

Centro de Estudios Puertorriquenos
Hunter College
695 Park Ave.
New York, NY 10021
Tel: 212-772-5689

Chip Taylor Communications
15 Spollett Drive
Derry, NH 03038
Tel: 800–876-CHIP
Fax: 603-434-9262

Chirripo
P.O. Box 1065–2050
San Pedro COSTA RICA
Tel: 506-531-1352
Fax: 506–252-307

The Cinema Guild
Gary Crowdus
1697 Broadway, Suite 506
New York, NY 10019
Tel: 212-246-5522
Fax: 212-246-5525

Cinevista
1680 Michigan Ave., Suite 1106
Miami Beach, Fl 33139
Tel: 305-532-3400
Fax: 305-532-0047

Critics Choice Video
P.O. Box 749
Itasca, IL 60143-0749
Tel: 800-367-7765

Current World Events
156 Linden Lane
Mill Valley, CA 94941
Tel: 415-388-2875

Deep Dish TV Network
339 Lafayette St.
New York, NY 10012
Tel: 212-473-8933
Fax: 212-420-8223

Direct Cinema Ltd.
P.O. Box 69589
Los Angeles, CA 90069
Tel: 213-396-4774
Fax: 213-396-3233

Documentary Educational Resources
101 Morse St.
Watertown, MA 02172
Tel: 617-926-0491
Fax: 617-926-9519

Downtown Community TV Center
87 Lafayette St.
New York, NY 10013
Tel: 212-966-4510

Duende Pictures
42 Bond St.
New York, NY
Tel: 212-254-7636

Educational Video Center
Steve Goodman
55 E.25 St.
New York, NY 10010

Tel: 212-725-3534
Fax: 212-725-6501

Electronic Arts Intermix
536 Broadway, 9th Fl.
New York, NY 10012
Tel: 212-966-4605
Fax: 212-941-6118

Embassy Films
1438 North Gower, Box 27
Los Angeles, CA 90028
Tel: 818-972-8686

Esther Duran/Macario Films
357 W. 55th St., #2J
NY, NY 10019
Tel: 212-315-5607

Facets Multimedia Inc.
1517 West Fullerton Ave.
Chicago, IL 60614
Tel: 800-888-0775
Fax: 312-929-5437

Festival Films
6115 Chestnut Terrace
Shorewood, MN 55331
Tel: 612-470-2172

Filmmakers Library Inc.
124 E. 40th St., Suite 901
New York, NY 10016
Tel: 212-808-4980
Fax: 212-808-4983

Films Around the World
342 Madison Ave., Suite 812
New York, NY 10173
Tel: 212-599-9500
Fax: 212-599-6040

Films for the Humanities and Sciences
P.O. Box 2053
Princeton, NJ 08543-2053
Tel: 800–257 5126
Fax: 609-275-3767

Films Incorporated Video
5547 N. Ravenswood Ave.
Chicago, IL 60640-1199
Tel: 800-323-4222 ex43
Fax: 312-878-0416

Films Transit
Jon Rofekamp
402 East Notre Dame
Montréal, Québec H2Y 1C8 CANADA
Tel: 514-844-3358
Fax: 514-844-7298

First Run/Icarus Films
Johnathan Miller
153 Waverly Pl., 6th Fl.
New York, NY 10014
Tel: 212-727-1711
Fax: 212-989-7649

Flower Films
10341 San Pablo Ave.
El Arrito, CA 94530
Tel: 415-386-8920

Foothill Video
P.O. Box 547
Tujunga, CA 91043
Tel: 818-353-8591

Frameline
P.O. Box 14792
San Francisco, CA 94114
Tel: 415-861-5245

Global Exchange
2141 Mission St.
San Francisco, CA 94110
Tel: 415-255-7296

Groupe Intervention Video
5505 Saint-Laurent Bureau 4203
Montréal, Québec H2T 1S6 CANADA
Tel: 514-271-5506
Fax: 514-271-6980

Hen's Tooth Video
1124 S. Solano
Las Cruces, NM 88001
Tel: 219-471-4332
Fax: 219-471-4449

Homevision Films, Inc.
5547 N. Ravenswood Ave.
Chicago, IL 60640-1199
Tel: 800-262-8600

IBASE
Rua Vicente de Souza 29
Rio de Janiero, RJ BRAZIL
Tel: 5521-286-6161
Fax: 5521-286-0541

IMRE—International Media Resource Exchange
124 Washington Pl.
New York, NY 10014
Tel: 212-463-0108
Fax: 212-243-2007

Indiana University Instructional Support Services
Franklin Hall, Room 0001
Bloomington, IN 47405-5901
Tel: 800-552-8620
Fax: 812-855-8404

Ingram Video
1 Ingram Blvd.
Lavergne, TN 37086-1986
Tel: 800-621-1333

Institute Familiar de la Raza
2515 24th St.
San Francisco, CA 94110
Tel: 415-647-4141
Fax: 415-647-0740

Institute for Policy Studies
1601 Connecticut Ave. NW
Washington, DC 20009
Tel: 202-234-9382

International Cinema
200 W. 90th St., Suite 6H
New York, NY 10024
Tel: 212-877-2972
Fax: 212-877-3462

International Film Circuit
Wendy Lydel
419 Park Ave South, 20th Fl.
New York, NY 10016
Tel: 212-779-0660
Fax: 212-779-9129

J&N Distributors
Rene Pabon
776 10th Ave.
New York, NY 10019
Tel: 212-265-1313
Fax: 212-265-1349

Jane Balfour Films
35 Fortress Rd.
London, NW5 1AD ENGLAND
Tel: 44071-267-5392
Fax: 44071-267-4241

Kannis Home Video S.A.
Preciados 113, Higuereta Surco
Lima PERU
Tel: 482901
Fax: 480122

Keith Adis & Associates
8444 Wilshire Blvd.
Beverly Hills, CA 902XX
Tel: 213-653-8867

Kino
333 W. 39th St., Suite 503
New York, NY 10018
Tel: 212-629-6880
Fax: 212-714-0871

Kit Parker Films
1245 10th St.
Monterey, CA 93940
Tel: 408-649-5573
Fax: 408-649-8040

Landmark Films Inc.
3450 Slade Run Dr.
Falls Church, VA 22042
Tel: 800-342-4336; 703-536-9540
Fax: 703-241-2030

Laser Video
1218 Nostrand Ave.
Brooklyn, NY 11225
Tel: 718-467-3141

Latin Nostalgia
Rogelio Agrasanchez
3305 Lazy Lake
Harlingen, TX 8550X
Tel: 210-423-7371
Fax: 210-412-7556

Latina S.A.
Atletas no. 2, Pasillo A-301
Col. Country Club, CP 04220
04220 Mexico, D.F. MEXICO
Tel: 525-689-3850 or 549-3060
Fax: 525-549-1820

Latino Mid-West Video Project
Raul Ferrera-Balauquet
2032 W. Moffat St.
Chicago, IL 60647
Tel: 312-663-1600 Ex. 172

Library Distributors of America
32–65 Palms Centre Dr.
Las Vegas, NV 89103

Live Entertainment
15400 Sherman Way #500
Van Nuys, CA 91406
Tel: 818-908-3030

M & A Editions
Route 5, Box 332
San Antonio, TX 78221
Tel: 525-610-1037
Fax: 525-610-1171

Manley Sales Corp.
Richard DeCroce, Walter Manley
14 E. 60th St., Suite 501
New York, NY 10022
Tel: 212-980-4800
Fax: 212-980-8188

Max Films
5130 Blvd. Saint Laurent, 4 étage
Montréal, Québec H2T 1R8 CANADA
Tel: 514-272-4425

Media Buenos Aires
Malabia 2319, 2 Piso B (1425)
Capital Federal ARGENTINA
Tel: 541–35-18–63
Fax: 541–46-92–62

Meridian Video Corp.
1575 Westwood Blvd., Suite 305
Los Angeles, CA 90024
Tel: 310-231-1350
Fax: 310-231-1359

Mex-American Home Video Corporation
8060 Melrose Ave., Suite 400
Los Angeles, CA 90046
Tel: 213-658-8078

Mexcinema Video Corp.
7231 Santa Monica Blvd.
Hollywood, CA 90026
Tel: 213-874-1114
Fax: 213-874-7182

Million Dollar Video
5900 Wilshire Blvd., Suite 500
Los Angeles, CA 90036
Tel: 213-933-1616
Fax: 213-931-1999

Movies Unlimited
6736 Castor Ave.
Philadelphia, PA 19149
Tel: 215-722-8398
Fax: 215-725-3683

Museum of Modern Art
11 W. 53rd. St.
New York, NY 10019
Tel: 212-708-9530

National Latino Communications Center
3171 Los Feliz Blvd., Suite 200
Los Angeles, CA 90039
Tel: 213-663-8294
Fax: 213-663-5606

New Day Films
121 W. 27th St., Suite 902
New York, NY 10001
Tel: 212-645-8210
Fax: 212-645-8652

New York Film Annex
1618 W. 4th St.
Brooklyn, NY 11223
Tel: 718-382-8868

New Yorker Films
16 W. 61st St.
New York, NY 10023
Tel: 212-247-6110
Fax: 212-307-7855

Pacific Arts Video
50 North La Cienega Blvd., #210
Beverly Hills, CA 90211
Tel: 213-657-2233
Fax: 213-657-0395

PBS Video
1320 Braddock Pl.
Alexandria, VA 22314-1698
Tel: 800-424-7963
Fax: 703-739-8938

Phoenix Films & Video
2349 Chaffee Dr.
St. Louis, MO 63146
Tel: 314-569-0211

PICS
The University of Iowa
270 International Center
Iowa City, IA 52242-1802
Tel: 800–373-PICS

Picture Start
1725 W. Catalpa Ave.
Chicago, IL 60640
Tel: 312-769-2489
Fax: 312-769-4467

Progress Communications Corp.
900 Third Ave.
New York, NY 10022
Tel: 212-418-7650

Publications Exchange
Rafael Betencourt
8306 Mills Dr., Suite 241
Miami, FL 33183
Tel: 305-256-0162

San Francisco Study Center
1095 Market St., #602
San Francisco, CA 94103
Tel: 415-626-1650

Select Media
60 Warren St., 5th Floor
New York, NY 10007
Tel: 212-431-8923

Signals
274 Filmore Ave E.
St. Paul, MN 55107
Tel: 800-669-9696

Southwest Entertainment Inc.
5415 Bandera Rd., Suite 504
San Antonio, TX 78238
Tel: 210-523-2616
Fax: 210-684-6300

Star Video
550 Grand St.
Jersey City, NJ 07302
Tel: 800-251-5432

Swank Motion Pictures
201 South Jefferson Ave.
Saint Louis, MO 63166
Tel: 314-534-6300

Swedish Film Institute Educational Film and Video Project
Box 27126
Stockholm 10252 SWEDEN
Tel: 4608–665-1100
Fax: 611–820

Taller Cine La Red
PO Box 6359
Santa Rosa, Bayaman, PUERTO RICO
Tel: 809-798-0047

Tania Cypriano
37 King St., 6A
New York, NY 10014
Tel: 212-691-5303

Teatro Campesino
P.O. Box 1240
San Juan Bautista, CA 95045
Tel: 408-623-2444

Third World Newsreel
Ada Griffen
335 W. 38th St., 5th Fl.
New York, NY 10018
Tel: 212-947-9277
Fax: 212-594-6917

UCLA Film & TV Archive
302 E. Meluitz/405 Hilgard Ave.
Los Angeles, CA 90024-1323
Tel: 310-206-8013
Fax: 310-206-3129

University of California Extension Center for Media & Independent Learning
2176 Shattuck Ave.
Berkeley, CA 94704
Tel: 510-642-0460
Fax: 510-643-8683

Vid-Dimension
424 South "C" St.
Madera, CA 93638
Tel: 209-661-6040
Fax: 209-661-6060

Video Data Bank
37 South Wabash Ave.
Chicago, IL 60603

Tel: 312-345-3550
Fax: 312-541-8072

The Video Project
5332 College Ave., Suite 101
Oakland, CA 94618
Tel: 510-655-9050

Video Treasures
The Family Room
P.O. Box 4481
Troy, MI 48099
Tel: 800-745-1145

Videographe
Rue Garnier 455
Montréal, Québec H3J 3S7 CANADA
Tel: 514-521-1676
Fax: 514-521-2116

Videoteca del Sur
P.O. Box 20068
New York, NY 10009
Tel: 212-334-5257
Fax: 212-274-9673

Videowaves
Gustavo Vazquez
787 Clayton St., #4
San Francisco, CA 94117
Tel: 415-664-1838

Warner Home Video
4000 Warner Blvd.
Burbank, CA 91522
Tel: 818-954-6000
Fax: 818-954-6540

Women Make Movies Inc.
462 Broadway, 7th Fl.
New York, NY 10013
Tel: 212-925-0606
Fax: 212-925-2052

Title Index

PART I: TITLES IN SPANISH AND PORTUGUESE

PART II: TITLES IN ENGLISH

About the Authors

Karen Ranucci has worked for the past twenty years in the field of independent video/film production. She began working at Downtown Community TV Center (DCTV) in New York, where she taught video production workshops to community groups and assisted DCTV's directors, Jon Alpert and Keiko Tsuno, on three of their PBS productions. In 1978, she traveled with Alpert and Tsuno to Vietnam to make the PBS documentary, "Vietnam: Picking up the Pieces." In 1979, she codirected "El Dialogo," a documentary about the Cuban exile community in the United States and its relationship to Cuba. Together with Jon Alpert, Ranucci worked as a freelance correspondent for the *NBC Nightly News* and *Today Show*. In 1985, she won a National Emmy for Best Investigative Reporting for a series she developed about industrial disease in the Tungston Carbide industry. In 1988, she founded the Latin American Video Archives, a nonprofit organization dedicated to facilitating the distribution of Latin American and U.S. Latino–made film and video. Since then she has become one of the nation's leading experts on Latin American national cinema and community video.

Julie Feldman worked for four years as the associate director of the Latin American Video Archives, where she facilitated the integration of Latin American film and video into courses of various disciplines. Prior to this, she codirected video documentaries in India and the republic of Georgia and worked for two years as the assistant director of the Educational Video Center in New York City. Feldman is currently the director of education at the 52nd Street Project theater company, supervising a mentoring program for inner-city youth. She is completing her doctorate in international education at New York University, where she has taught English as a second language and currently coedits the faculty development newsletter. Feldman also works as an intercultural communications consultant.

DH